ESSEX
COUNTY CRICKET CLUB

THE OFFICIAL HISTORY

ESSEX
COUNTY CRICKET CLUB

THE OFFICIAL HISTORY

David Lemmon and Mike Marshall

HEINEMANN KINGSWOOD

Heinemann Kingswood
Michelin House, 81 Fulham Road, London SW3 6RB

LONDON MELBOURNE AUCKLAND

First published 1987
Reprinted 1988

0 434 98111 7

Typeset by Scarborough Typesetting Services
Printed in Great Britain by
Redwood Burn Ltd, Trowbridge
and bound by Butler & Tanner Ltd, Frome

Contents

List of Illustrations

IMPEX IMPEX IMPEX

SPONSORS OF THIS BOOK

The story of Impex Management began on 1 January 1972 when I took the first steps in pursuit of my belief that many United Kingdom confectionery manufacturers were not realising the full export potential of their products. Since then the Company has grown to become one of the foremost exporters worldwide of such items.

It was from these small beginnings that, together with my wife Anna, we applied our expertise to this specialised venture. Two years later I was joined by John Santer and over the years of consistent growth, colleagues and staff were carefully selected to ensure the creation of a highly committed, professional and vastly experienced team of Export Managers.

It has become a source of much pride and evidence of considerable achievement that over this period the Impex Group has been responsible for confectionery exports valued at well over £50,000,000 and currently has export sales in excess of £10,000,000 per annum. Moreover, the Group is committed to a dramatic planned expansion programme over the next five years.

Especially successful has been *Fisherman's Friend*, the world famous Extra Strong Throat and Chest Lozenge, which is now sold worldwide in 37 countries. Although first formulated 126 years ago, it was not until

1973 that the first package was sold overseas, since when it has become the largest selling lozenge in Europe, South East Asia and Australasia.

Other well known products marketed overseas by the Impex Group include high quality chocolates from Bendicks of Mayfair, Elizabeth Shaw, Fullers and George Payne. Chewits, one of the fastest selling items in this country, is now very successfully sold overseas together with a whole range of children's items and biscuits from Fox's and Burtons.

The excellence of these achievements over the years are very much in line with those of the Essex County Cricket Club, who we are happy to support in a number of areas. To all of us at Impex Management, it is an honour to be associated with the County, and with this very fine publication. Together, we look forward to continued success for many years to come.

Ivan G Gibson
Chairman & Managing Director

Acknowledgements

A comprehensive history of Essex County Cricket Club has been long overdue and the Club is indebted to David Lemmon and Mike Marshall for writing this volume.

They have delved through many documents, including old minute books, score-cards and filed Club manuscripts to unearth hitherto unknown facts. And they have checked and double-checked the legends that make up the history of the Club.

In addition the co-authors have interviewed many former players and administrators in their search for the complete story.

The statistics have been provided by Leslie Newnham, the doyen of Essex cricket statisticians, and many of the photographs for the book have come from Mike Marshall's collection. Others have also provided pictures, and these are also gratefully acknowledged.

The amount of research necessary for a book of this complexity could not be undertaken by anyone without a deep interest in the subject matter and in David Lemmon and Mike Marshall the Club were fortunate in finding authors who have presented the history accurately but with a bright and sensitive hand.

Both authors would particularly like to acknowledge the very great help received from Tom Pearce and Douglas Insole.

David Lemmon has asked that the assistance of the following be acknowledged: Brian Croudy, John Wilcox, P Wynne-Thomas, Essex Records Office, Stephen Green (MCC Library), British Museum (London and Colindale), The late Jim Coldham, Paul Andrews, H J Pack, Charles Steggell, Trevor Bailey, J A Bailey, Donald Scott, Alan Howick, Peter Grant, R G Teague, Brian Goodwin, Keith Gregson, W F Dyson, T F Evans, Ken Porter, M J Dowsett and Cecile Paterson.

Mike Marshall has received considerable assistance from, and would like to acknowledge the following: Peter Roberts, Tony Debenham, C A G (Jack) Russell's son Tim and daughter (Mrs Lilian Seggins), the late Tom Cable and his daughter, Jan Kemp, Leslie Gutteridge, Jack and Maureen Appleby, many retired Essex players, notably Roy Sheffield and his daughter Meg, Sonny Avery, Frank Rist, Frank Vigar and Brian Taylor and the staff at the Essex CCC offices, especially Caroline Fardell and Valerie Moth. And very special thanks go to Mike Marshall's wife Amy who assisted with the project in many ways.

We would also like to thank members of the Committee and staff of the Club who also gave so much of their time to the production of the material for this book.

Finally we must thank Impex Management who have sponsored this history. Details of the company's activities are outlined early in this book. We very much appreciate their involvement with the publication.

Peter Edwards — January 1987
Secretary/General Manager,
Essex County Cricket Club

Most importantly tribute should be paid to Peter Edwards, the Essex CCC Secretary and General Manager, whose brain-child this history was and whose untiring efforts ensured that first, the work would get off the ground and second, reach the publication stage. The number of hours Peter has devoted to this project is incalculable and the Club owes him a debt of gratitude.

Mike Marshall — January 1987

Forewords

There has not been a history written of the Essex County Cricket Club apart from the brief histories so ably produced by Leslie Newnham covering the period 1876 to 1975, and Charles Bray's book *Essex County Cricket* published in 1950.

Now two devoted supporters of the County Club have completed the painstaking work of producing a fuller record of the Club including the most successful years from the 1979 season.

In this latter period the Club has developed into what is probably the most outstanding County side of the last decade, and it is a particular honour for me to be asked to write this foreword, as I have had such wonderful pleasure from the results achieved.

The acknowledgements appear elsewhere; the assistance of many people has been greatly appreciated and the thanks given have been richly deserved.

Tom Pearce

For some years past I have been concerned that the trials and tribulations of the Essex County Cricket Club have not been chronicled in sufficient

Tom Pearce and Douglas Insole go in to bat (1950). (Barratt's Photo Press Ltd)

detail to provide other interested parties with the opportunity of sharing more fully the suffering endured by those closely involved with the Club's fortunes.

This book, even though it has been written at a time of comparative stability in our history, repairs that omission. It also tells something of the pleasure gained and the friendships forged during a hundred years of frustrating but marvellously enthusiastic effort from Essex people who clearly loved the game of cricket and were determined that our County should be a part of it.

It is possible, in 1987, to look back with some satisfaction at the tangible successes of the past decade and at the same time to appreciate the heroic deeds of our forefathers who worked so hard over the past century to keep the Club afloat.

I hope you enjoy the experience.

Doug Insole — March 1987

C R I C K E T.

A MATCH of CRICKET will be played on the Cricket Ground at TIMOTHY DRURY's, the SUN Parrock near Graveſend, on THURSDAY, June the 27th, between the Gentlemen of Weſt-Kent againſt the Gentlemen of Eſſex, for 100 GUINEAS.

Wickets to be pitched at 11 o'clock, and the game played out.

(21 June, 1793, Kentish Gazette)

COUNTY CRICKET CLUB

A PUBLIC MEETING will be held in the SHIRE HALL, CHELMSFORD, on FRIDAY, the 14th day of January, 1876, at Three o'clock, to consider the desirability of FORMING a COUNTY CRICKET CLUB, with a ground at Brentwood.

(Signed) J. W. PERRY WATLINGTON,
JAMES ROUND

(7 January, 1876, Chelmsford Chronicle)

CHAPTER 1

Prologue and Epilogue

Saturday, 7 September 1985, dawned bright and crisp, a combination of that warmth and freshness which only an early September day can bring. It was some compensation for what had been, in the main, a miserable summer.

In the early part of the season, cricketers had spent as much time huddled in pavilions as they had on the field, and county secretaries cursed the rain as they mourned lost days and lost revenue. Towards the end of May, the match at Sheffield between Yorkshire and Essex had been abandoned without a ball being bowled, and nearly three months later, the first Sunday in August had seen the abandonment of all seven John Player Special League matches, six of them without the players leaving the dressing-rooms.

There were, of course, days of fine weather. Only a week after the abandonment of the game at Sheffield, the three Texaco Trophy matches between England and Australia were played in glorious sunshine, and, in spite of the rain, results were achieved in four of the six Cornhill Test matches.

It was important to lovers of the game that this particular Saturday should be fine, for this was the day of the NatWest Bank Trophy Final at

Lord's, one of the highlights of the season. The 60-over knock-out competition had been in existence since 1963, and until 1980 it had been sponsored by Gillette. In 1981, the NatWest Bank became sponsors so that the 1985 Final was the fifth under their sponsorship, the 23rd in all.

Neither Essex nor Nottinghamshire, the contestants, had reached the final of the tournament before, and the fact that there would be a new name on the trophy gave the match a particular interest. More significantly, the two counties had a rivalry of their own. Twelve months earlier, in a thrilling climax to the previous season, Notts had lost at Taunton on the penultimate ball of the season, and their defeat had left Essex as county champions.

Nottinghamshire were eager to compensate for the bitter disappointment of 1984; Essex were fiercely ambitious to capture the one trophy that had so far eluded them.

For Essex, there was unexpected dismay on the morning of the final when it was learned that Neil Foster, the young England fast bowler, was suffering from glandular fever and would be unable to play. Foster had become a vital component of the Essex attack. He had returned from touring India earlier in the year with his reputation much enhanced, but injury and the vagaries of the Test selectors had marred his season. But in August he had found his best form, and he had played a most important part in his county's run of success. Essex would feel his loss deeply.

Ironically, he was replaced by Ian Pont, who had been on the Nottinghamshire staff and had played four matches for the county in 1982 before being discarded. Essex, the county of his birth, had engaged him at the beginning of the 1985 season, and, with that hint of fairy tale which so often attends sport and sportsmen, he now found himself chosen to open the Essex bowling in the most important match of the season in front of a crowd of more than 20 000 people.

Lord's seemed to catch the mood of the day, and was at its bubbling best; the crowd was good humoured and appreciative, the sun burned down and the cricket was to match both the weather and the occasion.

Clive Rice won the toss and asked Essex to bat first. It could not have been an easy decision to make, but what little assistance the wicket was to offer the bowlers was likely only to come in the first half-hour, a time when the seamers also had the benefit of what little cloud the day was to bring.

The evidence of the first few overs justified Rice's decision. The ball moved quite sharply, and Richard Hadlee, from the Pavilion end, was quick and menacing. Gooch edged short of slip in his opening over and the crowd was stilled, tense and excited. Like Hadlee, Cooper began with a maiden, and the first run did not come until the third over. After six overs, Essex had scored six runs.

Gooch looked solid and assured. He had the air of a man contemplating violent assault. A week earlier at The Oval, he had hit a glorious hundred for England against Australia, an innings punctuated by magnificent cover drives and thrilling pulls and hooks. At the end of the first day, it seemed that he had Hutton's record 364 within his sights, but he had gone for 196 on the second morning. England won by an innings. He had not batted since then and now he seemed settled to continue in the vein he had shown in the Test, tempered, if possible, by a greater sense of responsibility, for much was expected of him. In a limited-over final there is no second innings chance of redemption.

In contrast, Brian Hardie exuded a sense of freedom and gaiety. He began to throw the bat at almost every ball in a most exciting manner. When Clive Rice brought himself into the attack as a replacement for Kevin Cooper, Essex were 55 from 19 overs, and Brian Hardie had scored 41.

In the 25th over, Hardie off-drove Andy Pick for two, almost to the Pavilion rails, to reach his fifty. Gooch's half-century came nine overs later. In five limited-over finals at Lord's, he had failed to reach 50 only once, and that was in the Benson and Hedges Cup Final of 1983 when he made 46 against Middlesex.

The hundred came up in the 30th over, and, at lunch, after 38 overs, Essex were 145 for 0. Hardie and Gooch had assured the innings of a firm foundation and had given a thrilling exhibition of batting.

It was vital that the lunch interval should not be allowed to bring a lapse in concentration and so bring down the tempo of the innings. In a match where overs are limited each one is important, and had the Nottinghamshire bowlers been allowed an economical spell after lunch, they could have loosened the grip that Essex had taken on the game with their pre-lunch batting. Realising this, Hardie and Gooch were quickly onto the attack again. The first three overs of the afternoon produced 18 runs.

Hardie reached his century in the 44th over. It had come off 136 deliveries and included 14 fours. It was his first century in the 60-over competition. At the end of the over, Essex were 175 without loss.

Brian Hardie had never batted better than he did at Lord's that day. One of the most reliable of county cricketers, he is a man of humour with a touch of delightful eccentricity. In his batting he is composed and resourceful. In limited-over cricket he adds the dimension of panache. When Rice removed the slips after Hardie and Gooch had blunted Hadlee and Cooper's early endeavours Hardie would slash fiercely to send the ball skimming fast and fine to the third man boundary. Next ball, with purists still shaking their heads, he would produce a cover drive of total glory which sent the ball crashing over the boundary rope. And all the time he batted with infectious glee.

If Graham Gooch was more restrained, he was equal in stature. None doubted that his was the scalp that Nottinghamshire most sought. The capture of Gooch's wicket would have given them an indisputable psychological advantage, for, by the mid-eighties, it had become the most coveted prize among bowlers in county cricket. In all humility, Gooch was aware of this, and he refused to surrender. He concentrated on blunting the attack, and as the Notts' fielding showed signs of wilting, he attacked with his own customary power and authority. He moved down the wicket to hit Pick into 'Q' Stand by the Pavilion for a memorable six, and he smote Saxelby through the covers for a mighty four. He should have been stumped off Hemmings when he was on 70, a difficult leg-side chance, but was finally bowled by a ball from Pick in the 49th over, the ball coming back a little. He had scored 91, and he and Hardie had put on 202, a record for any wicket in the NatWest competition.

As the sun shone, Ken McEwan came down the Pavilion steps at Lord's on the occasion of a great cricket match for the last time. It was an

1. *Brian Hardie.* (Steve Lindsell)

emotional moment, and he was applauded with greatest warmth all the way to the wicket by both spectators and players. Few men who have been so gifted or brought such pleasure into the lives of others have borne it all with such modesty and charm.

In the 51st over, with the score on 203, Brian Hardie was run out by Hemmings' fine throw to the bowler's end from mid-off. This was a crucial point for both sides, for had Essex lost their way now, the splendid work of Gooch and Hardie would have been eroded and Nottinghamshire could have clawed their way back into the game.

Fletcher sent in Pringle to join McEwan and they combined in a stand which determined that the Nottinghamshires' target would be a formidable one. They came together with less than nine overs remaining and they added 77 runs. As Clive Rice commented later: 'They put the match ten runs out of our reach.'

McEwan was badly dropped by Broad at mid-on in the 56th over, but this was the only blemish in a glorious farewell display by the gentlest of men. He was well aided by Derek Pringle who employed the reverse sweep on occasions and displayed confidence and power. Saxelby's last over, the 58th of the innings, brought 17 runs. McEwan cover drove him for six into the Mound Stand. It was a shot of rare genius.

The task that faced Nottinghamshire was a daunting one. No side had ever approached 281 to win a Lord's final when batting second, but if they were dismayed by the score that Essex had made, they certainly did not show it.

Robinson, who had established himself as an England opener of the highest quality during the season, and Broad, desperately unlucky to be out of the England side after performing so nobly against the West Indies, began in workmanlike fashion. Like Gooch and Hardie, they established a solid platform before they attempted to accelerate. Indeed, their pattern of scoring traced the pattern of the Essex openers. After 19 overs, they too were 55 without loss. At tea, after 35 overs, the Nottinghamshire openers had reached 124, and the Essex total began to look less daunting.

Broad was particularly strong on the leg side, and he punched the ball through mid-on with ease of timing. Robinson, as he had shown all year, was particularly forceful square on both sides of the wicket.

At the break, Nottinghamshire required 157 more runs to win at 6.28 an over. As the need to score more quickly, in order to reduce that required rate, became more acute, the difference between the two sides became more apparent. The Essex attack offered few loose deliveries, and the Essex fielding was superior in every way. It was an outstanding piece of fielding that brought about the desired breakthrough.

Robinson played the ball towards the Grand Stand, the longer boundary, and the batsmen ran a brisk, comfortable single. Broad turned for a second run, but Robinson, rightly, did not respond. Broad turned back, seemingly unaware of any danger, only to be beaten by Ian Pont's long, fast and accurate throw to the wicket-keeper. Broad had scored 64, and the total was 143 when the wicket fell.

Rice joined Robinson, but the impetus of the Nottinghamshire innings was evaporating. Only ten runs had been added when Robinson attempted to hit the ever-accurate Turner high to the square-leg boundary. In normal circumstances Robinson would never have contemplated the shot; it failed now as Hardie clutched the ball on the boundary.

Rice scurried while the new batsman, Randall, took time to establish himself. The required run rate moved above seven an over, and continued to climb. Rice, conscious that his side was losing ground in the run chase, sought to break the shackles that were being imposed and clipped Turner to mid-wicket, but Hardie, enjoying a day of glory, took a simple catch.

Nottinghamshire's hopes rested, seemingly, with Richard Hadlee, for here was the one batsman who could hope to score at the furious rate that was now required. He hit a six over long-on with ominous nonchalance and the 200 was posted. At this point though, mention should be made of Ian Pont. He had bowled a fine opening spell for Essex, displaying a lively pace, a commendable accuracy and an admirable temperament for one who had been thrust so unexpectedly into such an important occasion. He had beaten the bat on several occasions in the first four overs, but Fletcher, wisely, had used him in brief spells after that opening burst, unwilling to subject the young and inexperienced player to the assault which was sure to come.

He was brought back at the Nursery end to complete his quota of overs. Hadlee hit him mightily and classically to the long-off boundary, and the crowd thrilled to the shot. Fletcher chatted reassuringly with the young bowler and next ball Pont knocked back Hadlee's leg stump. Nottinghamshire were 214 for 4.

Like Essex, Nottinghamshire had been troubled by injuries, and the promising young batsman Paul Johnson had been robbed of a place in the final through an operation for appendicitis. His place had gone to Duncan Martindale who had batted most impressively in a first-class career which was only a few weeks old. It was Martindale who joined Derek Randall, and he settled to play with a great sense of maturity. There were some fine shots and some brisk running, but the asking rate became greater every over. When the last over was reached Notts were 18 runs short of victory.

Rarely can there have been such a dramatic last over in an important match at Lord's. It was bowled by Derek Pringle who concentrated his attack on leg stump. The field was spread to cut the boundaries, leaving only a gap on the off-side Tavern boundary. The batsman was Derek Randall, who had enjoyed a splendid season, and who, in the opinion of many, should still have been a regular member of the England side. Certainly no man has brought a greater sense of fun to the game.

Pringle's first delivery was on length and on the line of the leg stump. Randall stepped back and hit the ball into the off-side field for two. He repeated the shot next ball but this time he reached the boundary. Two more runs came off the third ball, and the excitement in the ground became intense. Ten runs were needed off three deliveries and Randall was cast in heroic mould.

Pringle's fourth ball, again outside the leg stump, was sent crashing to the Tavern boundary. The fifth produced a shot of breathtaking grandeur. Again stepping outside the leg stump, Randall drove the ball expansively past long-off for four. The fielder, Turner, stood rooted to the spot as the ball sped past him, for, in the evening light, he had not been able to sight it.

So, after more than eight hours of play and 559 runs, Nottinghamshire needed two runs to win off the last ball of the match.

Fletcher regrouped his field, calmed his bowler and determined that all was as he wanted before the last ball was bowled. The off-side gap had been plugged, and men had been brought up in an attempt to thwart sprinted twos.

As Pringle bowled, Randall moved down the wicket. It is possible that, had he stayed in his crease, the ball would have been signalled wide, for again Pringle aimed outside the leg stump, perhaps readjusting as he saw Randall advancing. How can one tell what Pringle and Randall were thinking? One thing is certain – the batsman found himself with the ball pitching on his toes. The fullness of the length distorted his swing and cramped his movement. He was contorted into clipping the ball to mid-wicket, and there Paul Prichard took a comfortable catch. Essex had won one of the finest matches seen at Lord's – by one run.

Randall walked down the wicket and shook hands with Pringle, and then he trudged from the field looking suddenly older and more tired.

The crowds gathered in front of the Pavilion and Peter May named Brian Hardie as 'man-of-the-match'. Keith Fletcher held the NatWest Bank Trophy aloft. The supporters cheered and glasses clinked in celebration.

Three weeks later, at Arundel, Clive Rice spoke of the match: 'They batted better than we did. They bowled better than we did. They fielded better than we did. We were only in the game in the last two balls. If we had won, I would have had to apologise to Fletch for daylight robbery.'

As the euphoria subsided into more thoughtful reflection, one realised that Essex had now joined Kent and Lancashire as the only counties to

2. *It is a unique occasion when Essex change captains, as there have been only six since the war: Tom Pearce, Doug Insole, Trevor Bailey, Brian Taylor, Keith Fletcher and now Graham Gooch.*

Gooch has the great fortune to take over a winning side, as at the end of Fletcher's reign in 1985 Essex were the holders of the NatWest Bank Trophy and the John Player League, but Gooch immediately stepped into the role by winning the County Championship title in 1986.

In Fletcher's period as captain, Essex won the County Championship three times, the John Player Special League on three occasions, the NatWest Bank Trophy and the Benson & Hedges Cup once each. Essex also played in three other Benson & Hedges Cup finals. (Clive Tarling)

National Westminster Bank Trophy 1985

The County winning the Trophy will receive a prize of £17,000, the losing Finalist £8,500, the losing Semi-finalists £4,250 each and the losing Quarter-finalists £2,125 each.

MARYLEBONE CRICKET CLUB

NatWest Bank Trophy Final

20p **ESSEX v. NOTTINGHAMSHIRE** 20p

at Lord's Ground, †Saturday, September 7th, 1985

ESSEX

1 G. A. Gooch	b Pick	91
2 B. R. Hardie	run out	110
3 K. S. McEwan	not out	46
4 D. R. Pringle	not out	29
5 P. J. Prichard		
‡6 K. W. R. Fletcher		
7 A. W. Lilley		
*8 D. E. East		
9 S. Turner		
10 I. L. Pont		
11 J. K. Lever		
B 1, l-b 3, w , n-b ,	...	4
	Total...	280

FALL OF THE WICKETS

1...202 2...203 3... 4... 5... 6... 7... 8... 9... 10...

Bowling Analysis	O.	M.	R.	W.	Wd.	N-b
Hadlee	12	4	48	0	...	...
Cooper	9	3	27	0	...	...
Saxelby	12	0	73	0	...	...
Rice	7	0	38	0	...	...
Pick	8	0	36	1	...	...
Hemmings	12	1	64	0	...	...
	...	...	...	...	...	...

NOTTINGHAMSHIRE

1 B. C. Broad	run out	64
2 R. T. Robinson	c Hardie b Turner	80
‡3 C. E. B. Rice	c Hardie b Turner	12
4 D. W. Randall	c Prichard b Pringle	66
5 R. J. Hadlee	b Pont	22
6 D. J. R. Martindale	not out	20
*7 B. N. French		
8 E. E. Hemmings		
9 R. A. Pick		
10 K. Saxelby		
11 K. E. Cooper		
B , l-b 14 , w , n-b 1,	...	15
	Total...	279

FALL OF THE WICKETS

1...143 2...153 3...173 4...214 5...279 6... 7... 8... 9... 10...

Bowling Analysis	O.	M.	R.	W.	Wd.	N-b
Lever	12	2	53	0	...	...
Pont	12	0	64	1	...	1
Turner	12	1	43	2	...	...
Gooch	12	0	47	0	...	...
Pringle	12	1	68	1	...	...
	...	...	...	...	...	...
	...	...	...	...	...	...

Any alterations to teams will be announced over the public address system

RULES—1 The Match will consist of one innings per side and each innings is limited to 60 overs.
2 No one bowler may bowl more than 12 overs in an innings.
3 Hours of play: 10.30 a.m. to 7.10 p.m. In certain circumstances the Umpires may order extra time.

Luncheon Interval 12.45 p.m.—1.25 p.m. Tea Interval will be 20 minutes and will normally be taken at 4.30 p.m.

‡Captain *Wicket-keeper

Umpires—D. J. Constant & B. J. Meyer Scorers—C. F. Driver, L. Beaumont & E. Solomon

†This match is intended to be completed in one day, but three days have been allocated in case of weather interference

Nottinghamshire won the toss and elected to field

Essex won by 1 run

Total runs scored at end of each over:

First Innings	1	2	3	4	5	6	7	8	9	10	11	12	13	14	15	16	17	18	19	20
	21	22	23	24	25	26	27	28	29	30	31	32	33	34	35	36	37	38	39	40
	41	42	43	44	45	46	47	48	49	50	51	52	53	54	55	56	57	58	59	60
Second Innings	1	2	3	4	5	6	7	8	9	10	11	12	13	14	15	16	17	18	19	20
	21	22	23	24	25	26	27	28	29	30	31	32	33	34	35	36	37	38	39	40
	41	42	43	44	45	46	47	48	49	50	51	52	53	54	55	56	57	58	59	60

3. *The NatWest Bank Trophy Final, Essex v Nottinghamshire, 7 September 1985.*

have won all four major trophies for which the first-class clubs compete. The record became all the more remarkable when one considered that it had been achieved within the space of seven seasons, that Keith Fletcher was the only captain in the history of the game to have led a county to success in all four competitions, and that before these years of triumph stretched an immense period of frustration and disappointment.

The winning of the NatWest Bank Trophy in 1985 was the culmination of the greatest period in the history of Essex county cricket, a period that had begun with the Benson and Hedges Cup triumph of 1979. Players like Fletcher, Gooch, McEwan and Lever had achieved international acclaim. They drove sponsored cars and, rightly, had gained handsome rewards from benefits. In the years before this time of glory, however, there had been men who had never attained such heights, nor received accolades for themselves. They were men who were destined to exert much energy, endeavour, courage and good humour in the cause of Essex cricket, but they were men who were to be denied the ultimate success. Nevertheless, without their efforts, the glories of the 1980s would not have been possible. Without men like Charles Green, Walter Mead, Johnny Douglas and Hubert Ashton, there would have been no Essex County Cricket Club.

It is right that we should honour them, for as Burke said in reflecting upon a more bloody revolution than that which was brought about in Essex cricket, 'People will not look forward to posterity, who never look backward to their ancestors'.

CHAPTER 2

Out of the Mist: The Eighteenth Century

To trace cricket to its origins has been found to be an impossible task, and despite much research, it is still not known when it was first played or how it was introduced. References lead us to the reign of Edward I at the end of the fourteenth century, to Guildford in 1598, to Maidstone in the first part of the seventeenth century and to Aleppo in 1676.

The first mention that we have of a match between two counties is in *The Post Man*, 25 June 1709: 'On Wednesday the 29th instant will be play'd a famous match of Cricket at Dartford Brimpth for £50 by Kent and Surrey.'

As we will find in the following pages, the use of the name of a county is not always a true indication that the players were fully representative of that county. Often, perhaps from a desire to magnify the importance of a match, no distinction is drawn between a club and its county. The Hambledon Club, for example, was often referred to as Hampshire in Bentley's book of scores, and the Hornchurch Club was frequently named as Essex in the eighteenth century. The match at Dartford Brimpth in 1709 could well have been between an eleven of Dartford and an eleven of a Surrey town or village.

That cricket was being played in Essex at this time is probable; that it was being played in the county within the first 35 years of the century is certain. Rowland Bowen puts the first mention of cricket in Essex as 1731, but on 24 September 1726, *Mist's Weekly Journal* published an anonymous letter of complaint. The letter came from Writtle and alluded to a match between Mr Stead's Club and Chingford.

> A Justice of the Peace in the neighbourhood was obsessed with the idea that such games as cricket etc. were only pretences to collect a crowd of disaffected people in order to raise a rebellion; and he therefore went on Saturday, September 10th with a constable, and caused the Proclamation to be read in form to disperse the few well meaning neighbours who were innocently at that play.
>
> The late Lord Chief Justice, Sir John Pratt, had made a rule ordering a Cricket match to be played at Dartford Heath. Was it lawful to play cricket in Kent, but not in Essex?

The mists that shroud the beginnings of the game are best exemplified by the reports of a match at Richmond on Monday, 23 August 1731. *St James's Evening Post* advertised this match as being between ten men of Middlesex and ten men of Essex. The Essex party was to be led by Lord Richmond, 'the Duke who was Cricket', and the Middlesex party by Mr Chambers. The match was left unfinished, and this incensed some of the spectators so that 'The Duke of Richmond and his Cricket players were greatly insulted by the mob at Richmond, some of the men having their shirts tore off their backs: and 'tis said a law suit will commence about the play.'

This report comes from *Fog's Weekly Journal* where the contestants are named as Sussex and Surrey, which is much more accurate, for the two sides had met at Chichester a week earlier, and Lord Richmond is associated with Slindon, in Sussex, rather than with any estate in Essex.

On 6 July 1732, London met Essex and Hertfordshire in Epping Forest for £50 a side, and by 1735, cricket was being played on Woodford Green. Cricket was also being played on Shenfield Common, for, on 26 July 1735, Romford beat Brentwood there by 37 'notches'.

By this time, Brentwood had one player of note, Cook, who had played for London against Surrey a month before the match on Shenfield Common. Cook was not originally in the London side, but Ellis, London's best bowler, 'put out his finger in throwing up the ball before the match', and Cook was drafted in.

At Ilford, on Monday, 1 August 1737, 'Essex' beat London by seven notches, but again we should be wary of the title 'Essex', for there was no known county organisation at that time, and cricket was essentially local in character.

One of the most energetic of cricket centres in Essex in the mid-18th century was Manningtree. The *Ipswich Journal* announced that 'on Monday, August 5th, 11 black velvet jockey caps of 15s. value each to be played for by any 22 gamesters within 24 miles of that place, [Manningtree] each to put in 6s. Wickets pitched at Two.' That was in 1745, and four years later, on 22 August, Manningtree and Brightlingsea played Colchester for 11 guineas. The sides were 'to meet at the Sign of the Fencers in Tenant's Lane, Colchester'.

In 1751, Manningtree met Mistey and Ipswich for 11 guineas, and, in conjunction with Brightlingsea, played the parishes of St Nicholas and St Botolph's, Colchester. On this occasion the ground was 'roped in'. Challenges were common, and the same year Colchester advertised that they would 'play any eleven for 11 black velvet caps; to meet at the Sign of the Pig at Botolph's Gate; a Sixpenny Ordinary provided'. Eleven black caps were also the prize when Manningtree met the Colchester parishes mentioned above.

By the second half of the century, cricket was abounding in all parts of Essex. In 1752, notice was given to all gentlemen cricketers 'that the long depending match is to be played at Lowlayton, between the gentlemen of Hackney, and the gentlemen of Layton and Walthamstow, on Coppy Down, near the Bowling Green, July 29, for £50'.

The amount at stake on a match varied from district to district. In the country it was generally not more than a guinea a man, but in and around London, the stakes were higher. They were also high when the opponents were geographically far apart, and when the promoters were wealthy men, more than £1000 could be at stake.

In the first part of the century matches were expected to be finished in one day which, as there were no single innings matches, meant the fall of between 30 and 40 wickets a day. As the game developed, matches were played out, and if they could not be finished on the second day, they were sometimes completed, with the same personnel, some weeks later.

A cricket match was a matter of personal pride and local honour, and towns vied with each other for the position of dominance within the county. In 1755, two towns, Maldon and Chelmsford, asserted their right to take on all-comers. On 28 June, the *Ipswich Journal* carried the challenge:

> The Gentlemen belonging to the Maldon Club (Essex) challenge any one town in Essex provided every man belongs to that town for six months. To play on Thursday, July 15th, for eleven gold rings value 15s. each: every player to put in 6s. Thomas Brand, King's Head, Maldon.

Six weeks later, on 9 August, the *Ipswich Journal* carried a challenge from another quarter:

> Eleven Cricket Players of the Parish of Chelmsford (Essex) will play with any eleven Cricket Players in any one parish within the county of Essex, for 5s. or 10s.6d. a man. Reply to William Dines, Green Man at Moulsham.

The emphasis on the residential qualification in both challenges is important. It was customary for a side in a hopeless position to concede the match, but, as cricket matches were widely used as a medium for gambling, some form of handicapping was often applied to make sure the sides were of reasonably equal strength. One way of effecting equality was to bar the best man or men from the stronger side; another was to allow the weaker side 'given' men, that is guest players who were not qualified for the team. These 'given' men were usually well known players whose presence in the match gave it an added attraction.

Another method of strengthening the weaker side was to allow them extra men, so producing a match against the odds. The earliest record of this in a double wicket match comes from the *General Evening Post* in 1761:

> Thursday, 3 September, at Woodford-row in Essex, 8 of Dartford with Faulkner, Durling and one other v. 22 of the County of Essex for £50 each side.

The following year there is an example of the attraction of the guest player when a game was announced at Wandsworth between 'Wandsworth with one of Barnet (who is esteemed as good a player as most in England) against Waltham Abbey in Essex'.

Matches were frequently announced and then not reported, but those that were often gave indication of other matches that had been played. The *Gazeteer and London Daily Advertiser* in 1765, for example, reported: 'On Monday, August 5, Walthamstow beat Low Leyton and Leytonstone by 62 runs, to the great mortification of the losers who had beaten all the villages thereabouts.'

Major collapses and sensational finishes are not the monopoly of the 20th century. A match between Epping and Ware, played at Ware in Hertfordshire on the first Monday in September, 1768, for a stake of £50, caused much comment and excitement.

> The Epping side went in twice, and the Ware side once. Night coming on, the match was deferred till the next day, when the Ware eleven had to go in for 95 notches. Their first four men fetched four score, which occasioned the bets to rise to 10 to 1 against Epping; but to the amazement of the spectators, the other six men were all bowled out for 1 notch.

Epping followed their sensational win over Ware by playing Brentwood at the Green Man on Navestock Common.

In the 18th century it was an almost universal practice to play for money, and this custom persisted into the early part of the next century. Whether or not they had any interests in the stakes, players often had bets on their own performances, and the amount of money at stake, which in many cases they could ill afford to lose, occasioned dispute and heartache. The passion for gambling was fashionable and intense, and often, as the *St James's Chronicle* reported on 22 August 1765, the cause for misery:

> Monday last a young fellow, a butcher, being entrusted with about £40 by his mistress to buy cattle in Smithfield Market, instead went into the Artillery Ground and sported away the whole sum in betting upon the Cricket players.

By 1769 cricket was well established in the Chelmsford area. The local side met Stock near the Water-House at the end of May and won by 79 notches. A week later, they won the return game at Stock by two wickets. Their strength had obviously become well known, for, following the return game with Stock, they were to have played 22 of Springfield and Boreham, but their opponents chose to pay forfeit instead.

The name 'Essex' was liberally used. In June 1770, a side so named played Brentford and Richmond on Richmond Green, and in the following year, when Hambledon was reported to have suffered its first defeat, 'eleven picked men of the county of Essex' played the Temple Mill Club for £20 at the Crown, Billericay, and won comfortably by three wickets.

Although local encounters dominated, county matches were not uncommon. In 1770 Harlow were alleged to have played Middlesex, 'with great odds in their favour', and won. More interestingly concerning the same area is a report in the *Norfolk Chronicle* on 4 October 1777:

> In imitation of the late Cricket played at the Oaks, on Wednesday sennight [Wednesday week] was played at Hamstead in Essex a match between eleven old women of that place and an equal number of the parish of Harlow in the same County which was decided in favour of the latter.

Mostly, however, the encounters were between men, proud of their parish. Kelvedon met Witham, and, in 1772, Ingatestone and Stock played each other three times. Ingatestone also played elevens from Brentwood, Navestock, Herongate and Mountnessing, and Middlesex and Essex met at Blackheath for £100 a side. The meeting between Ingatestone and the combined side at Brentwood began at nine in the morning, and two matches were completed in one day.

It was not always money that was the prize offered to the winning side. Fashion was often an incentive. At Colchester, in 1772, a notice appears to inform the cricketers that: 'There will be 11 fashionable hats, at the real value of 10s 6d each, to be played for on Monday, Aug. 23, at Mr. Eisin's, at the Swan. Every man to put in 5s 3d to enter. N.B. – A dinner will be provided.'

The married men and bachelors of Chelmsford were more financially minded, and a few days after this match they met twice in the Brickfield at Chelmsford. The bachelors won both matches and 'a considerable sum', but the practice of playing for fashion continued. In 1776, Billericay met Barstable and Chafford Hundreds at the White Hart, Billericay, for 11 gold laced hats.

The 18th century was essentially an age of challenge and hazard. In its first quarter, it had given birth to the Hell-fire Club, a band of wild young men intent on accomplishing riotous deeds against the odds, and the century never lost its taste for the daring.

On Monday, 7 June 1773, for example: 'the long depending cricket match, Mr. Berrington of Stock against 10 gentlemen of the neighbourhood of Romford, was played at Romford. John Nair, Esq., and Mr. John Taylor, beat Mr. Berrington, who beat the 7 others, and 1 gentleman paid forfeit. There were about 600 notches played.' Within a month of this contest, Hambledon and All England met for 1000 guineas.

However high the stakes, money was, at times, the least important factor to be considered. Games engendered a passionate local support. Often the intensity of this support, and the sense of honour that was at stake, caused a feeling of suspicion and distrust between teams. It was an age of both gentility and violence. The 18th century gave us the novels of Richardson and Smollett, and the poetry of Alexander Pope, but it also occasioned the footpad, the forerunner of today's mugger.

One of the most famous matches in Essex cricket history is one that is alleged to have taken place at Tilbury in 1776. Passions still run high about this game and even today there is heated argument as to whether or not it took place.

The occasion of the story was a letter from Gravesend which was published in the *London Chronicle* on 31 October 1776. The letter was dated two days earlier, and part of it read as follows:

> A terrible affair happened this day at Tilbury Fort. A great match at Cricket being to be played between Kent and Essex, the parties assembled on both sides. When they were met, a man appearing among the former who should not have been there, the Essex men refused playing, on which a battle ensued, and the Kentish men being likely to be worsted, one of them ran into the guard-house, and getting a gun from one of the invalids, fired and killed one of the opposite party. On seeing this, they all began running to the guard-house, and there being but four soldiers there, they took away the guns and fell to it, doing a great deal of mischief. An old invalid was run through the body with a bayonet, and a sergeant who commands at the fort in the absence of the officer, endeavouring with his four men to quell them,

> was shot dead. At last the Essex men took to flight, and running over the drawbridge made their escape. The Kentish men then made off in their boats, and search is making after them.

This account remained unchallenged for nearly two centuries until Leslie Thompson raised doubts as to its authenticity in an article in *Essex Countryside*. Thompson, who later included his article in his privately published book, *Cricketing in Essex*, considered the letter a hoax and challenged the truth of the report on several grounds – the date, the venue and the lack of any further evidence or news as to whether the miscreants escaped completely or were apprehended and charged.

Perhaps it would be best first to clarify a point of vocabulary. At the time that the letter was written, and in the context of the report, the term 'invalid' referred to a soldier or sailor disabled for active service.

Leslie Thompson insists that the date for such an 'important' match is too late in the year, but cricket in October and November was by no means uncommon at that time. The married men and bachelors of Hadleigh met on 14 October 1779; there was a match at Snaregate in October 1780; in Odiham, in October 1782; and at the beginning of November 1783, there were matches at Windsor and Sunninghill. It is not too much to believe then that 11 players labelled 'Kent', but most probably ten of Gravesend and one other, and 11 called 'Essex', but most probably men from the neighbourhood of Tilbury, could have arranged a match in late October.

It is hard to support Mr Thompson's dismissal of Tilbury Fort as a site for a match, for the annals of 18th century cricket would suggest that the game could be played practically anywhere, and was.

The strangest thing about the reported fracas, for Mr Thompson, is that no further news of the event was ever published or recorded, and one would have imagined that an event involving murder of the military would have been pursued further and reported more fully. To balance this view, it must be accepted that law enforcement was somewhat haphazard in the 18th century, as a study of the fascinating novels of Henry Fielding will testify. We have moved into an age when crime is fully documented, but, as Laurie Lee points out in *Cider with Rosie*, this was not even the case in country areas, as little as 60 years ago.

The cause of the dissension at Tilbury was common enough. Before the formation of clubs became general, the necessary qualification for a side was residence within an agreed distance of a parish or township. The inclusion in a side of a player whose qualification was open to doubt could cause disagreement and sometimes the abandonment of the match. As early as 1750 residential qualification is mentioned. When Kent met Surrey at the Artillery Ground the announcement was that:

'Each county have a right to alter what men they please, providing they live in the county they play for.'

In short, all the details reported of the strange affair at Tilbury, in October 1776, could be authentic. We lack only corroborative evidence, and that in itself is not unusual in the early history of the game.

In the years which immediately followed the Tilbury report, contests between Colchester and Mersea Island were among the most publicised cricket events in Essex. Initially Mersea had total dominance although, in 1781, a third match was arranged as a decider between the two sides, but it was not reported. The men of Colchester did not have the best of reputations. A match against Stowmarket in 1777 had ended in disturbance, while in the following year the *Ipswich Journal* carried an announcement from the cricketers of Nayland:

> Nayland, Aug. 6.
>
> In order to deter any honourable party of Cricketers from playing with the Colchester party, we think ourselves in honour bound to inform the public that on Tues., Aug. 4th, we intended to play a Cricket Match with them on Lexden Heath, but the partiality of the fellow they had hired for their umpire was such that though the game was greatly in our favour, we were obliged to decline playing it. The many impositions they were guilty of (and which we for some time submitted to) being too numerous for an advertisement, the particulars may be known by applying to
>
> The Nayland Cricketers

At this time, each side appointed its own umpire, and he had a close association with his side who had a tendency to appeal to him for a verdict. The ethic of accepting the umpire's decision as final was still being learned by both players and spectators.

There were redeeming features about Colchester cricket, for the *Chelmsford Chronicle* of 19 August 1785 told how a brandy merchant had played against three master hairdressers, and how the former 'ran more notches at one innings than all the gentlemen of the puff did in their two'.

By this time, however, the dominant place for cricket in Essex was Hornchurch, a club which occupies the same position in the annals of Essex cricket as Hambledon does in Hampshire. In 1785 they ventured as far afield as Datchet Common, near Windsor, where, on Thursday and Friday, 9 and 10 June, they played Berkshire for 100 guineas. Hornchurch included Davidson and Rimmington as 'given' men, but Berkshire scored 113 and 115 to Hornchurch's 37 and 43. The Berkshire side was a strong one and included G Boult, who hit a fifty in each innings, Beldam, Harris and Yalden.

Yalden was a most agile wicket-keeper who had played for Surrey in their matches against Kent and Hambledon. He was reputed to have once jumped a fence and fallen flat on his back while taking a catch, but he was also accused of 'acts of low cunning, as is not consistent with the character of an Englishman'.

A few days after the defeat at Datchet, it was announced that Hornchurch would meet Middlesex at Hornchurch for 100 guineas, and that they were to play the County of Essex on Stock Common. The use of the name is confusing, for the title, 'County of', was generally applied to a side comprising the leading amateur players of a county who would not be as strong as a club side which would have outside professionals attached to it. We do know, however, that an Essex County Club was in existence by 1790.

It is interesting to note, amid this confusion of names, that a month after the match at Datchet Common, Hornchurch entertained the *Windsor* Club at White Hart Inn, Hornchurch. The Essex-based side were well beaten again. This has all the marks of a return match, and there is every reason to believe that Windsor and Berkshire were one and the same, just as Hornchurch and Essex were often one and the same. The match at Hornchurch created much interest. The stake was £500, and it was confidently expected that the Prince of Wales, Lord Winchilsea and other important figures of the day would attend.

The esteem in which Hornchurch cricket was held can be seen from the exalted company in which they moved. In 1787 they entertained Moulsey Hurst where, in that same year, Lord Winchilsea had set up an establishment that was to play an important part in the development of Surrey cricket. Moulsey Hurst won by six wickets, and their star bowler was Lumpy, who took nine.

Foremost of the opponents of Hambledon, Lumpy, a short, round-shouldered man whose real name was Stevens, was considered the finest bowler of the age. He was quick, and, according to John Nyren, 'Beyond all the men within my recollection Lumpy would bowl the greatest number of length balls in succession.'

Hornchurch were also well beaten in the return match when Moulsey Hurst were aided by five of the White Conduit Club. Hornchurch's two 'given' men, White and Butcher, were the only two to reach double figures in a second innings score of 38, but the most interesting aspect of the match was the dismissal of Mr G Talbot, who was recorded as being out 'P.H.O.'. This description puzzled historians of the game and led to several interpretations, but Buckley is almost certainly correct in invoking the wording of the Laws of 1744: 'If the player goes out of his ground with an intent to run before the ball is delivered, the bowler may *p*ut *h*im *o*ut.'

Whatever was happening in Essex, momentous events had been taking place outside the county, events which were to change the organisation and administration of the game. Thomas Lord, a Yorkshireman, was the son of a Roman Catholic farmer who had been forced to work on the farm he had once owned after his property and land had been confiscated following the 1745 rebellion. The family later moved to Norfolk where Thomas Lord was brought up, and from whence he came to London to find employment. For the game of cricket, Lord's most significant form of employment was when he was taken on at the White Conduit Club as a bowler and general attendant.

Formed in 1782, the White Conduit Club was an offshoot of a West End Club called the 'Je ne sais quoi'. Members of this club frequented White Conduit House and played cricket matches in the adjoining fields near Islington.

In 1786, the members seemed to have tired of playing cricket on the Islington site, for Lord Winchilsea, the great patron of the game, and Honorable Colonel Charles Lennox, later Duke of Richmond, agreed to guarantee Thomas Lord against loss if he would set up a new private ground.

Assured of support, Lord quickly got to work. In May 1787, he opened the first Lord's cricket ground on what is now Dorset Square. The first match on the new ground was heralded in the *Daily Universal Register*, to be known within two years as *The Times*, on 29 May 1787:

> A Grand Match will be played on Thursday, the 31st of May, 1787, in the new Cricket-ground, the New Road, Mary-le-bone, between nine gentlemen of the county of Essex, with two given men, against eight gentlemen of the county of Middlesex, with two gentlemen of Berkshire, and one of Kent, for One Hundred Guineas a side.
>
> The wickets to be pitched at ten o'clock and the match to be played out.
>
> No dogs will be admitted.

Apart from the scores, our knowledge of the match is limited. The two gentlemen of Berkshire in the Middlesex side were G Louch and G Boult, and at least four of the Essex side were from Hornchurch. The Essex player Rimmington had been a 'given' man in the matches against Windsor (Berkshire). How truly representative the Essex side was we do not know, but that men of Essex were present on this auspicious occasion is a testament to the high standing of their cricketers at that time. Indeed the fact that Hornchurch played members of the White Conduit Club later in the same year is further evidence of this standing, for the White Conduit Club was the acorn from which grew the MCC.

At Lord's, 31 May and 1 June 1787

Middlesex, with two of Berkshire and one of Kent

	1st innings		*2nd innings*	
Stanhope, Esq.	run out	3	b Butcher	1
T Lord	b Butcher	1	c Newman	36
J Boorman	b Butcher	23	b Butcher	37
W White	b Butcher	5	run out	12
Z Boult, Esq.	P O Clark	0	b Butcher	18
W Bedster	b Martin	13	P O Clark	14
G Louch, Esq.	b Martin	0	b Butcher	14
G Boult, Esq.	b Butcher	3	b Martin	36
A Boult, Esq.	b Martin	3	b Butcher	0
Slater, Esq.	b Butcher	0	b Martin	23
Oliver	not out	0	not out	1
	byes	7	byes	11
		58		203

Essex, with two given men

	1st innings		*2nd innings*	
Newman, Esq.	c Louch	51	b Boorman	5
Rimmington	run out	28	c G Boult	0
Graham	b Bedster	4	run out	0
Clark	c Louch	13	c Boorman	1
Wyatt, Esq.	b Boorman	5	c Louch	14
Butcher	c Z Boult	3	c Slater	0
Jones	b White	16	c G Boult	1
Davies	b Boorman	1	b Boorman	2
Dent	not out	4	b White	1
Martin	b White	0	not out	4
Barker	b Boorman	2	b Boorman	9
	byes	3	bye	1
		130		38

Middlesex won by 93 runs

The defeat by 93 runs after leading by 72 on the first innings is a pattern that will be all too familiar to followers of Essex in the three decades immediately after the Second World War.

To the north, men of Essex joined with men of Suffolk to combat Nayland, at Nayland, but the home side, who had complained so bitterly about Colchester a few years earlier, won with ease. The social aspects of the game were becoming most important, and another Mr Lord won praise for his conduct of affairs at Nayland.

> Upwards of 2000 persons were within the ground, who conducted themselves with the utmost decorum; the utility of the batten-fence

> was made very evident, as it kept out all improper spectators. The ground, though somewhat rough at present, will be laid out next year like a bowling green. A very good cold collation was spread under a cover recess, for the accommodation of the cricketers and subscribers. The tents were also prepared with refreshments for the spectators. Mr. Lord, the proprietor of the ground, and the adjoining tavern, deserved much praise for the management and order displayed.

There was less generous feeling in the match between Essex and Kent a month later. Perhaps as a legacy from the legend of Tilbury, the game ended in bad feeling. 'The long depending match of cricket, between Essex and Kent, was decided at Swanscombe, when the former gained a complete victory over their adversaries in that noble game, at only 1 innings, and had 44 notches to spare. This so exasperated the gentlemen of Kent, that they would not so much as drink with competitors.' The roots of the great modern rivalry between the two counties certainly stretch far back.

Although they were beaten by Brentwood in 1788, the supremacy of Hornchurch was accepted and once more they threw down the challenge to 'Essex'. The year of their greatest triumph was to be 1789.

On 8 and 9 July, 'Essex', as the side was named, beat MCC by 102 notches, and on 6 and 7 August, the sides met again at Hornchurch. The *Morning Post* recorded this match as Essex v MCC, but three other newspapers spoke of it as Hornchurch v The Marylebone Club, and, as it has all the marks of a return match, there is every reason to suppose that the game at Lord's had been contested by Hornchurch.

As in the first match Hornchurch gained a convincing win. This was, in effect, the first great achievement in Essex cricket history, for, by 1789, MCC had already moved to a position of eminence in the administration of the game, having been responsible for a complete revision of the laws the previous year.

Hornchurch looked set for an innings win in the second match, but they were held up by Louch and Boult. Louch was reported killed at Bourne Paddock a few days after this match when, it was alleged, a ball was struck with such force that it lodged in his body. The report was later denied and Louch was to play for MCC for another eight years.

Captain Lloyd was evidently a substitute and the Mr Clarke who played a significant part in the match was the gentleman who played as a guest for Ingatestone and 'so eminently excels' in the noble game.

This was not to be the last time that Hornchurch would beat the MCC, but it marked a pinnacle of achievement, and in some sense it brought to an end the first phase in the history of Essex cricket.

At Hornchurch, 6 and 7 August 1789

Marylebone Club

	1st innings		*2nd innings*	
Lord Winchilsea	b Martin	3	b Martin	1
Lord Darnley	not out	2	b Boorman	21
Hon. E Bligh	b Martin	0	c Wyatt	1
Anguish, Esq.	run out	0	st Clarke	5
Dehaney, Esq.	c Clements	4	c Barker	9
Louch, Esq.	b Martin	11	b Martin	46
Boult, Esq.	b Boorman	14	c Wyatt	38
Butcher	c Wyatt	1	not out	17
Hunt	b Boorman	2	c Boorman	11
Stanhope	b Martin	2	c Clarke	5
Shackell	run out	13	b Martin	1
		52		155

Hornchurch

	1st innings		*2nd innings*	
R B Wyatt, Esq.	not out	0	st Butcher	6
Denn, Esq.	b Butcher	2	c Louch	8
Mr Clarke	c Capt Lloyd	26	b Butcher	8
Mr Barker	c Hunt	24	c Lloyd	17
Boorman	b Butcher	17		
Clements	b Winchilsea	3		
Gouldstone	c Butcher	0		
Graham	b Butcher	34		
Murray	b Shackell	33	not out	0
Hicks	b Stanhope	5	not out	3
Martin	b Butcher	0		
	byes	23	byes	2
		167		44

Hornchurch won by 6 wickets

CHAPTER 3

Heroes and Pioneers: The Early Nineteenth Century

The first mention of an Essex County Club is to be found in 1790, but the details as to its lifespan and to its achievements are hazy. Neither does its existence clear up the ambiguity as to names. What is certain is that the county did not always come out creditably from its matches as *The Times* noted on 23 August 1791:

> On Saturday last at the game of cricket at Ware, between Hertfordshire and Essex, the greatest shuffling took place that was ever known amongst Gentlemen. The County of Essex would not permit their last man to go in for the last run. Wy –, Esq. by gaining Ing – m, refused it! because it did not suit their INTEREST.

The Times makes a poor show of disguising the names. The players in question are Wyatt and Ingram. Thomas Ingram's first recorded match was in 1788, and he played a few times for Surrey before he became resident in Essex, where he was certainly living by 1791 when his name is found in the Hornchurch side. He was a left-handed batsman as we know from the fact that he played for the Left-Hand against the Right-Hand, at Lord's, in 1790. Haygarth, in *Scores and Biographies*, notes that: 'It is presumed that he also excelled as a wicket-keeper: for in the

Kent v Essex match, played August 29th, 1792, he stumped 3, and caught 5.'

Ingram was certainly a fine bat, for he scored 80 out of Hornchurch's second innings of 208 when they gained another famous victory over MCC, at Lord's, in June 1791. In the return match, at Hornchurch, the side is referred to as 'Essex'. This time, MCC won comfortably, and Haygarth makes the comment:

> Whether the losers were the true Essex Eleven, that is to say, comprised the best men in the county, cannot now be said; the names on their side are all unknown to fame, and none of them ever chosen [except Boorman and Ingram] to play in any of the great matches of the day.

The following year, 1792, men of Essex played on the most famous of ancient cricket grounds, for it was announced: 'A match of cricket will be played on Broad-Halfpenny, on June 17, 11 of the Hambledon Club, against 22 of Herts and Essex. Numerous bets are already laid on this match.'

The outcome was never reported, but the Reverend James Pycroft, in his famous book of recollections, *The Cricket Field*, is rather disparaging of Essex's willingness to join forces with Hertfordshire in an effort to bring down giants, albeit unsuccessfully. He says: 'Essex and Herts, too near not to emulate the fame of Kent and Surrey, were content, like second-rate performers, to have, though playing twenty-two, one benefit between them, in the shape of defeat in one innings from England.'

Pycroft makes no mention of the proposed match at Navestock, in August 1793, when 'the first eleven players in the world' (namely T Walker, H Walker, Beldham, Ring, Small junior, Boxall, Freemantle, Hammond, Wells, Purchase and Harris) took on 50 from Essex and Hertfordshire! Odds of six to four were bet in favour of the All-England team, but the outcome of the match, and indeed whether it was played or not, is unknown.

Pycroft intimates that cricket in Essex, towards the end of the 18th century, was essentially parochial and therefore of a lower standard than some other counties, although he cannot deny the enthusiasm that abounded. He quotes one who was brought up in the county:

> And here we are reminded by two old players, a Kent and an Essex man, that, being schoolboys in 1785, they can respectively testify that, both in Kent and in Essex, cricket appears to them more of a village game than they have ever seen it of late years. 'There was a cricket-bat behind the door, or else up in the bacon rack, in every cottage. We heard little of clubs, except around London; still the game was played by many or by few in every school and village green in Essex and Kent.'

Records give evidence that enthusiasm for the game was strong in the last 15 years of the century. There were matches at Chelmsford, Brentwood, Lexden, Great Totham, Messing, Thaxted, Finchingfield, Writtle, Ingatestone, Maldon, and Coggeshall. Inevitably, the bachelors of Chelmsford maintained their superiority over the married men.

However unsophisticated cricket in Essex may have been compared with other counties, Pycroft has to admit that there were historic achievements. He refers to Hornchurch's victory over MCC in 1791 when the standard in the county 'was sufficiently advanced to win against Marylebone, an occasion memorable, because Lord Frederic Beauclerck there played his first recorded match, making scarce any runs, but bowling four wickets'.

Pycroft is actually mistaken, for Lord Frederic's first recorded match was a few weeks earlier, for MCC against Kent, at Lord's. The fourth son of the fifth Duke of St Alban's, Lord Frederic Beauclerck was only 18 at the time of his debut. He was to develop into one of the greatest cricketers of the age and played a great deal in Essex.

By coincidence, when he made his debut for MCC the side included two 'given' players, Beldham and Fennex, and Fennex was later to become associated with cricket in Essex.

William Fennex's first recorded match was the one between Hambledon and Kent, in 1786, and it is known that he also played for the Mousley Hurst Club. He was a fine field, a fast bowler, and one of the first batsmen to introduce forward play. He was in the Essex side as a 'given' man when they played Kent and Ingram made his three catches and five stumpings in August, 1792. He was also in the Essex (Hornchurch) side which was well beaten in the return match at Langton Park, Hornchurch. The following year, he was a 'given' man for the MCC when they played Essex at Hornchurch.

The confusion caused by conferring the county title on a club side is best exemplified in this year, 1793. Hornchurch and MCC met twice and each won a match. This led to a third match being arranged, at Lord's, where the MCC's opponents were then named as 'Essex' even though the side showed only three changes from the Hornchurch side that had played in the previous matches. Similarly, when 'Essex' were well beaten by Kent at Mr Timothy Drewry's Paddock at the Sign of the Sun, Gravesend, the Essex side consisted of ten Hornchurch players and the 'given' man, Bedster.

It was a few days after this game, at the beginning of July, that the match to which Pycroft refers in *The Cricket Field* took place. At Stoke Down, in Hampshire, 22 of Essex and Hertfordshire scored 47 and 47 against the 115 made by England. The match was for 1000 guineas, but the *Portsmouth Gazette and Weekly Advertiser* called the 'England' team,

'Nine of Hambledon and Two Others'. The return match, a week later, saw the two-counties side fare even worse than they had done in the original encounter, for they were beaten by an innings and 129 runs. One of the outstanding performances in this game was by John Hammond, who stumped six and caught two as his side again claimed the prize money.

The same year, Hammond, who was highly praised by John Nyren, the Hambledon historian, played at Navestock in a game which attracted many celebrities. Mr Newman's side played Mr Leigh's side for 500 guineas, and, as well as the noted Hammond, Fennex, Boorman, John Small junior, Beldham and Harris took part. Another to play in the match was James Stevens. He had been in the Hornchurch side that played MCC, at Lord's, in 1789, and he was to remain in the eleven for nearly 50 years. From 1824 onwards, he was joined by his son John.

A team-mate of Stevens' in the Hornchurch side of 1793 was Richard Francis. His first recorded match was the Surrey v Kent encounter, near Chertsey, in 1773. Francis was a Surrey man, but Nyren tells this story:

> One day I met him in the street of Hambledon, and ran to tell our General that the famous Francis had come to live amongst us; he could scarcely believe me – perhaps for joy.
>
> We enlisted him immediately, for we all knew what he could do, having seen him play on the Surrey side against us. At that time he was a young man, and he remained many years in the club. He was a gamekeeper; a closely made, firm little man, and active.

As he had played for Kent as well as Surrey and Hambledon before he came to Essex, Francis may well have been past his best when he was in the Hornchurch side, but he was still 'a cricketer of much celebrity, both as a batsman and bowler'. His bowling was fast, but it was considered a 'jerk', even so it was allowed as fair by the Hambledon Club, the original law makers.

Although the strength of the county lay to the south, at Hornchurch, cricket continued to thrive in the north. Saffron Walden, who regularly took on Royston, beat Great Sampford and Finchingfield by an innings and 81 runs, on Walden Common, in 1794. The losers were obviously deeply upset and earned a rebuke from the press.

> Stamford and Finchingfield, finding themselves so completely beaten, have refused to play the return match, although Walden gave them the liberty to make the match more equal to take any man out of the Bocking club, or any adjoining parish.
>
> It is to be hoped that Great Stamford and Finchingfield will for the future be cautious who they challenge to play with or against.

There were other occasional mismatches. On 29 July 1800, Ingatestone played Springfield, and: 'It was clearly proved that the gentlemen of Springfield were overmatched. Having admitted Mr. Clark, of Stock, into the Ingatestone eleven, who made 70 runs off his own bat, the game was again won by Ingatestone, at 1 innings and 23 runs to spare.'

In the same year, Colchester were overwhelmed by the Herts Militia, who had the Hon. General Lennox in their side, on Lexden Heath, and the beginning of the 19th century seems to have marked a period of some decline in cricket in the county. Famous players still appeared in matches in Essex. John Nyren played at Chigwell in 1802, and Lord Frederic Beauclerck was a 'given' man for Homerton when they came to Woodford Wells in 1806.

Lord Frederic had entered the church, but his enthusiasm for the game remained undiminished, and he was at Lord's a few months before his death in 1849. He figured prominently in Essex cricket. In 1807, he was a 'given' man for Homerton when they met 'Essex' at Lord's in a 13-a-side match, but a year later, he was on the 'Essex' side in the same fixture.

By 1817 there seems to have been a resurgence of Essex cricket. On 15 August the *Chelmsford Chronicle* wrote: 'We are glad to see the spirit of this noble game reviving in this county.'

The revival seems to have been marked by the performances of Saffron Walden the previous year. They lost narrowly to Cambridge at Parker's Piece, and 'then they retired to the Castle Inn for refreshment'. In the return match, on Walden Common, 'The scores were level when the last Cambridge batsman went in; he struck the ball and ran three.'

Evidence of this resurgence came in a report in *Sporting Magazine* in July of 1816. 'Several well contested matches of cricket were played this month in Essex. The game was played with the new regulation stumps 26 inches, popping crease 4 feet, which seems to be generally adopted. Bats as usual, and laws as before.'

This is an interesting comment, for there are no reports elsewhere to support the assertion that the new regulation stumps had been generally adopted. Stumps had been 24 inches high since 1798 and were to spring up three inches, in two stages, sometime between the years 1821 and 1823, so that the report in *Sporting Magazine* anticipates the generally accepted date of the raising of the height to 26 inches by some two years. It was, of course, a period of immense change in the game, for it was at this time that the controversy over round-arm bowling, instigated by John Willes of Kent, was coming to a head. No-balled at Lord's in 1822, Willes was to ride out of the game in disgust, although his round-arm bowling method was to be legalised within 13 years of his departure.

What effect the changes and revolutions in the game were having on cricket in Essex, or how quickly they came to be adopted, we cannot tell, but that the game was flourishing again is sure. Hornchurch were still to the fore. In August 1824, they beat Navestock by an innings and 97 runs, at Navestock. Hornchurch had Stevens, father and son, in the side, but Navestock had three men barred, one of them being Adlam who was later to appear for Hornchurch.

We should switch our attention now, however, to the north of the county, for it was from Saffron Walden that the first great cricketing hero of Essex was to emerge.

It was apparent that Saffron Walden were growing in strength in the first quarter of the century. They were mostly unsuccessful in their matches with Bury St Edmunds, but the Suffolk side was a powerful one. They inflicted a humiliating defeat on Pattiswick, at Pattiswick, on 28 June 1824, when they bowled out the Essex villagers for 4 and 46. Pattiswick's first innings score was the lowest recorded at the time, and it was to remain a record low score for 31 years until Shillinglee bowled out the Surrey Militia without a run being scored. Pattiswick, who had beaten Bury St Edmunds once in 1822, fared little better in the return match, scoring 35 against the home side's 141 and 146 before conceding the match.

Saffron Walden's strength became clear in 1820. They played Newmarket, who had previously held sway over Bury St Edmunds. Although betting was five to one against the Essex side at the start, they gained a notable victory. In 1826 Saffron Walden beat Bury, and, three years later, they had a massive 208-run win over Royston, on Royston Heath. This match was famous in that in Saffron Walden's first innings of 202, James Adams scored 106 not out. This score must place him among the earliest of Essex centurions, but his feat was to be overshadowed by those of his younger brother Alfred.

Alfred Adams was born in Saffron Walden on 14 November 1814. He was a butcher by trade and became a professional with the town club. His first recorded match was when Saffron Walden beat the Cambridge Town Club by 40 runs, on 2 and 3 September 1835. His contributions to innings of 59 and 172 were 0 and 28. He was on the winning side in the return match at Cambridge a fortnight later, the margin being 82 runs, and, the following year, Saffron Walden's supremacy had increased to 101 runs, Alfred Adams scoring 48 and 30.

On 4 July 1837, Saffron Walden beat Bishop's Stortford by an innings and 1 run, at Bishop's Stortford. Saffron Walden scored 105, of which Alfred Adams made 40. The return match was at Saffron Walden a week later. Alfred Adams opened the home side's innings, and he was last out, allegedly bowled by a full toss, for 279. His innings consisted of four fives, 25 fours, 23 threes, 15 twos, and 60 singles. It was the highest score ever obtained by a batsman at this time, a record of which Essex should be proud.

It was a remarkable achievement on the part of Adams. *Scores and Biographies* tempers the quality of the achievement a little by saying that the score 'was obtained against very inferior bowling and fielding, but of course it must still be considered a wonderful performance'. One would not argue with this except to say that among the opposing bowlers was J G Nash, who certainly won some merit. He was a frequent wicket-taker with his 'slow underhand, with a curious delivery, bringing the ball from behind his back'.

It should also be mentioned that Saffron Walden's innings was one of the very few scores above 400, that it lasted from ten in the morning until seven at night, and that the Bishop's Stortford Club had no innings. Presumably they conceded the match.

At Saffron Walden, Essex, July 11 1837

Saffron Walden

Alfred Adams	b W Nash	279
John Porter	b J G Nash	5
C R Gayton	b J G Nash	4
James Adams	st W Nash	55
W Redhead	b W Cowell	51
H J Smith	b W Cowell	2
Joseph Saward	b J G Nash	9
T Hardwick	b Brooks	22
Josiah Clayden	b W Nash	14
T Howard	not out	1
T Harris	st W Nash	3
	byes	14
	wides	15
		474

It is noted that, in another account, Gayton was run out.

The innings made Adams a hero, at least a local one, and the following year saw him meet Fenner of Cambridge in single combat. Their first single wicket meeting was at Saffron Walden. Fenner faced 51 balls, made 38 hits, and was caught and bowled for 19. In his second innings, he was bowled for 30, having made 91 hits off 117 balls. Adams failed to score in either of his innings, facing 22 and 12 balls, and making 12 and six hits. At Cambridge, six days later, Fenner hit 68 and benefitted from eight wides, while Adams, with the help of two wides, could muster only 18 in his two innings.

These defeats should take nothing away from Alfred Adams, who was a fine hitter. He stood 5′ 7½″ and weighed 10 st 5 lbs, so that he could not be considered a big man. He served Saffron Walden well over the years and brought great credit to the county. The sad thing was that he never played at Lord's, nor was he ever tried in any of the great matches of the day. This is regretted in *Scores and Biographies* where it is suggested that he 'might have excelled against the best bowlers'.

That the focus of Essex cricket had moved from South to North by the middle of the 19th century is indisputable. The great days of Hornchurch were at an end. The Wanstead Park Club played MCC at Lord's in 1837, and Wanstead and Clapton were at headquarters in 1839, but the strength of Essex cricket was to be found primarily on Lord Braybrooke's estate at Audley End where, between 1843 and 1848, several important matches were played.

The Audley End side invariably had the assistance of Ringwood: in 1840, playing for the Cambridge based team St Andrew the Less, against Saffron Walden, he had taken all ten wickets. They also included Fenner and Arnold on occasions. They seem to have been less lucky with the weather than most sides, for several of their matches were unfinished. This was the case with their match against MCC in 1843, and with their matches against Bishop's Stortford, Cambridge Long Vacation Club and Cambridge Town Club the following year. They did, however, beat Haileybury College by 75 runs in 1844, and lost a most exciting encounter with MCC by five runs a few weeks later. They had a tendency to engage in close finishes, beating Bishop's Stortford by one wicket in a return match at Bishop's Stortford in 1844, and gaining a victory over MCC by two wickets the following season.

The majority of the Audley End side were players from The Auberies to whom we should now turn our attention. In 1846, 'Essex' played two matches against Gravesend. The first was at T Adams's Ground, Gravesend, on 27, 28 and 29 July, when Gravesend scored 127 and 177 and 'Essex' made 75 and 144. The Essex side was strengthened by the inclusion of Alfred Mynn and Tom Box, the great wicket-keeper, but they seem to have had little influence on the course of the match, for 'during this match Mr Mynn and Box came into collision, and were both much hurt'. However both played in the return game at Orsett in August along with James Lillywhite. It mattered little. Gravesend won by eight wickets.

It was in this month that the name, The Auberies, first appears in important matches. The Auberies was the estate of Captain Caledon J Alexander, formerly an officer in the Coldstream Guards, a noted racehorse owner, a good, fast round-arm bowler and a great enthusiast for the game. In 1846 he formed his own club and gathered around him many fine players who enjoyed the use of a splendid ground. The club operated until 1850 and engaged in some of the best matches of the day.

It was customary for professionals to be groundsmen at the country houses where owners included cricket for the entertainment of their guests. In 1846, Royston was professional at The Auberies, and the following year, Captain Alexander also engaged Alfred John Diver, although Diver frequently played for the opponents against The Auberies to balance the sides.

Another to play for The Auberies in this year was the great William Lillywhite. The champion of round-arm bowlers, dubbed the 'Nonpareil' bowler and one who shaped wicket history, William Lillywhite played for The Auberies when they were beaten at home by the Cambridge Town Club in August 1847. He was then 55 years old, but he had bowled unchanged in the Gentlemen v Players match a few weeks earlier and returned figures of 11 for 36. His presence in The Auberies side shows how quickly Captain Alexander's side had won esteem.

Diver was followed at The Auberies by John Wisden, who had been born at Brighton on 5 September 1826, so that he was short of his 22nd birthday when Captain Alexander employed him. Nevertheless, he was to make his debut for the Players against the Gentlemen the same year, 1848, and 'The Little Wonder' – he was only 5′ 4″ tall – was destined to become a great all-rounder. In 1850 he was to take all ten wickets for the North against the South at Lord's. Although a Sussex man, he qualified for the North because he and George Parr had become proprietors of a cricket ground in Leamington.

Wisden's year in Essex certainly produced outstanding results. In 1848, the year that F P Fenner opened his new ground at Cambridge, The Auberies were victorious over Norfolk; they also beat Copdock by an innings and 25 runs, Bury and Suffolk by nine wickets and Norfolk again, at Swaffham, when the home side gave up the match even though they were opposed by only nine men and had the assistance of Diver. Later in the same year The Auberies were victorious over Copdock, at Copdock, by eight wickets, and over MCC and I Zingari (a travelling, amateur club). The win over MCC was a close one, by eight runs, but I Zingari were beaten by an innings and 30 runs, and the size of the defeat caused some concern in this club of wandering gentlemen.

Until the advent of the county championship, I Zingari were to hold a place second only to MCC in importance. This was because they provided quality opposition for clubs in the South. At The Auberies, on 22 and 23 August 1848, they were bowled out for 83 and 49, while The Auberies scored 162. This defeat raised the plea that I Zingari should strengthen their bowling in order to be able to cope with sides like The Auberies, but the request was ignored, and Mr William Bolland, the President of the Club, in a long letter which is quoted in Hill and Arrowsmith's *History of I Zingari*, painted instead a lofty picture of the social function that his side was performing in playing against country house sides:

Hear again that happy laugh ringing from yonder group of peasants, in triumph of the downfall of the wicket of some opponent of their lord. It is not the excited laugh of revelry and dissipation issuing from the poverty-stricken frequenters of the beer-house; it is the genuine offspring of esteem and affection begotten in the service of a master who sympathizes with his lowly brethren, softens their trials, and welcomes them to a share in his pleasures and amusements.

It is well to ponder on this piece of rhetoric, for it will remind us that the cricket of the mid-19th century was essentially a gentlemen's game in Essex, and that professionals, like Wisden, however much respected, were servants rather than equals. While Captain Alexander entertained the gentlemen for dinner on the evening of a match, William Caffyn, Wisden's successor at The Auberies, would sit in the park and play a cornet solo for their enjoyment.

Before he left Essex, John Wisden did appear for the county as a 'given' man. Eighteen of Essex, with Wisden, took on the England XI, at Chelmsford. It was a strong England side, including Pilch, Clarke, Parr, Felix, Mynn, William Lillywhite and Box, who stumped five and caught one. The Eighteen of Essex could muster only 58 and 31 while the England XI scored 141 to win by an innings and 52 runs.

As we have mentioned, John Wisden was succeeded at The Auberies by William Caffyn, considered to be one of the best batsmen of his time, and destined, like Wisden, to be a member of George Parr's team to tour North America in 1859, the first England cricket trip overseas. Caffyn was also to be in the first party to tour Australia, in H H Stephenson's team of 1861–62, and he was to spend some time in Australia where he did much to raise the standard of the game.

As well as being an inveterate traveller, William Caffyn was also one of the first to offer his memoirs, and in his *Seventy-One Not Out*, published in 1899, he recalls his year at The Auberies, one of his earliest professional appointments:

My father was much averse to my taking up cricket as a profession, and when I was selected to play for the Players of Surrey v the Gentlemen of Surrey at the Oval, he refused point blank to supply me with any money to get there. I managed to borrow half-a-crown, however, and received 10s. and my expenses for playing in the match, so I felt quite rich when I returned home. In 1849, I was engaged by Captain Alexander of the 'Auberies' in Suffolk to play in all his matches. He was a very keen cricketer, and had a ground in the park at his house. Wisden had been engaged there the previous year, and had, I believe, spoken a good word for me to Captain Alexander. A number of capital matches were played at the Auberies, and very pleasant they were.

The M.C.C. and the Zingari both visited us while I was there; and I thus had to encounter such players as F. W. Lillywhite, W. C. Morse, the Hon. Robert Grimston (who sometimes played with us as well as against us), the Hon. F. Ponsonby, and others.

I never saw Captain Alexander from the time I left the Auberies, at the end of 1849, until I returned from Australia in 1871, when he came up and spoke to me at the Oval.

The country house cricket tradition endured at Hill Hall, the seat of Sir William Bowyer Smith. He was a staunch supporter of the Chelmsford and Essex Club and a prominent cricketer within the county and at Braxted Park, the home of Charles du Cane, later Sir Charles du Cane, Governor of Tasmania from 1868 to 1875.

Charles Du Cane was a hard hitting batsman and an excellent close fielder, but he was most noted for hosting games. The Gentlemen of Essex played the Gentlemen of Suffolk in August 1854 winning by four runs. Only one match was played against the MCC and that was on 9 and 10 August the following year. It seemed not to have been taken too seriously: 'Many members who had *promised* to play for the MCC failed at the last moment, which is not only exceedingly annoying to the manager, but also a disappointment to other members who would have been glad to have attended.'

CHAPTER 4

A Time of Change: The Later Nineteenth Century

The mid-19th century was a period of great social change. Britain reached what has been aptly described as a point of consciousness. A new major generation had come of age in the 1840s, a generation that was confronted by a sense of crisis brought about by the fruits of the Industrial Revolution. They were faced with major radical issues which required decisions, both specific and general. The growth of cities and towns created the first predominantly urban people, and an urban culture which was to see the growth of music halls, parks, museums and libraries. There was legislation on public health and on working hours in factories, and major economic decisions were made on free trade and on the repeal of the corn laws. Fundamentally all this was part of a great issue, the struggle for democracy.

It was one of the greatest creative periods in the history of English literature as the novel, in particular, flourished. These were the years in which Dickens produced *Dombey and Son, David Copperfield* and *Martin Chuzzlewit,* in the last of which he talks of 'green ledgers with red backs, like strong cricket balls beaten flat'. These were the years, too, when Thackeray wrote *Vanity Fair,* Mrs Gaskell provoked public conscience with *Mary Barton,* the Brontës created their haunting romances and Disraeli talked of the two nations.

Yet the most significant social advance came in the closing years of the 1840s, the years of railway mania, when the speed at which a man could travel increased from 12 mph to 50 mph, and he made a more sudden leap than he had ever done before or has done since. This was, in truth, the age of the train, and the face and mind of England were changed in a very short space of time.

No game can stand totally apart from social change and when William Clarke formed his All-England XI in 1846 he was realising the commercial potential that cricket and the age had to offer. Clarke's team played a long programme of matches each summer and travelled all over the country to fulfil their engagements. The fact that the side was able to go to some of the smaller centres brought to the fore several cricketers who might otherwise have remained in obscurity. Clarke was a fine businessman as well as a good cricketer and insisted on a guarantee for every match that his side undertook.

The All-England XI lasted until 1852 when internal dissension led to a split, and Dean and Wisden started the United All-England XI. The break was a bitter one, for the members of the new team stated that they would not play in any match, except county matches, where either side was under the control or management of William Clarke.

Clarke played at Upton Park in Essex on 23 and 24 May 1854, when the England XI, as the team was now styled, beat Twenty-Two of the Upton Park Club, with Brockwell and Stephenson, by seven wickets. Caffyn, George Parr and Julius Caesar were in Clarke's side and one of the umpires in the match was Alfred Mynn. The game was played for the benefit of Goodhew of the Bow Club who later played for Kent.

The 1850s marked the end of the 'Middle Ages' of cricket. Great players like Alfred Mynn and William Lillywhite ended their playing careers, and, on 7 September 1859, George Parr and 11 other professionals set sail from Liverpool for North America where they played five games against sides from Canada and the United States and three exhibition matches. This was the first organised team of England cricketers to venture overseas, and such tours were to become regular features of cricket from then onwards. Two years later, H H Stephenson was to lead the first England party to Australia, although Test matches were still more than a decade away.

Not only was cricket developing internationally, but it was undergoing a period of restructuring domestically. Surrey County Cricket Club was formed in 1845; Kent, later to be reorganised, in 1859; and Hampshire, Middlesex, Lancashire, Worcestershire and Yorkshire followed in the early 1860s, although Hampshire and Yorkshire, like Kent, were also to face later reorganisation.

As these important events took place, cricket in Essex tended to stagnate. In the major matches from 1860 to 1863, so assiduously recorded by the Association of Cricket Statisticians, men of Essex have no place save G Baker, once of Kent, who played a very good innings of 41 in 2½ hours for South Essex against Southgate in 1865. He also played for MCC against Middlesex at Lord's in 1862.

Cricket in Essex tended to remain parochial. A report in the *Brighton Examiner*, July 1858, on the death of a native of the town, hints at a pleasant picture while telling of a sad event. Mr William Beedham was away from Brighton for ten days on 'an excursion for recreation and health, and was at the establishment of Messrs Easter and Ames, at Woodford, in Essex'. On the Monday, a holiday, at mid-day, Mr Beedham went 'among a portion of men who were playing at cricket, and, bowling, knocked down the wicket. The ball was then thrown back to him, which he caught, and while in the act of giving it another jerk suddenly fell back and died instantaneously.'

The rural picture of men in a holiday mood sportingly engaged in Woodford on a Monday in July, is a far cry from George Parr's party returning from America in early November, 1859. Buffeted by the Atlantic Ocean, their situation was 'rather a critical one' with 'jib-boom' broken and 'one poor old sailor had both his legs broken while he and some of the crew were endeavouring to set matters right'. At least Essex can claim that of that first England touring party, three men had a connection with the county, for as we have noted, Wisden, Caffyn and Diver had all been professionals at The Auberies.

The Gentlemen of Essex engaged in several fixtures. They played an unfinished match with the Household Brigade at Lord's, in July 1859, and in the following year, they were beaten by the Gentlemen of Surrey. An 'Essex' side played a return game with the Gentlemen of Surrey, at Chelmsford, later the same season, but rain ruined the match.

On 1 and 2 July 1861, Essex beat the Surrey Club in a 13-a-side match at The Oval. Charles Arnold, also of Cambridge, was in the Essex side as were E B Fane, Charles du Cane and C G Wynch. Wynch played often for the MCC and du Cane appeared at this time in several 'political' matches, Twenty-Two of the Houses of Parliament against I Zingari and The Opposition against The Government, at Lord's, among them.

Less than three weeks after the Essex victory over Surrey, the Gentlemen of Essex lost to the Gentlemen of Cambridge at Chelmsford. In the Essex side on that occasion was James Round; he had played his first match at Lord's a year earlier when he was in the Eton side that drew with Harrow, the first unfinished match that ever took place between these two 'nurseries of gentlemen cricketers'. Round was to play a most important part in the history of Essex cricket.

The Gentlemen of Essex more than held their own against their counterparts from Surrey, Cambridgeshire, Suffolk and Norfolk in the early

1860s, and it was in these matches that men like C E Green and E N Buxton, destined to figure prominently in the development of the game in Essex, first appeared in a side that bore the county name.

In 1864 there were eight leading counties – Cambridgeshire, Hampshire, Kent, Middlesex, Nottinghamshire, Surrey, Sussex and Yorkshire – whose matches were considered as first-class and among whom the county championship was decided. Surrey were considered as champions because they had lost the fewest number of matches, but the championship itself was not officially structured until 1890. With no county club in existence, Essex had no place in first-class cricket, but players like Round, for the Gentlemen of the South and MCC; Green, for Cambridge University, and Charles George Wynch, for the Gentlemen of England, made their first-class debuts in this period. Wynch had lived in India from 1855 to 1858 and, when available, he had appeared for Sussex. But in the 1860s he played for Essex teams; he was an attractive right-handed batsman.

National movements in the game stirred cricketers in Essex into action and, in the winter of 1864–65, a County Club of Essex was formed, securing a 'lease of 21 years for an excellent site for a ground which formed a portion of the old barrack ground'. *Bell's Life* reported the event:

> County of Essex – We understand that the Colchester Club has obtained a lease, for a term of 21 years, of a large and nearly level field in the parish of St Mary, facing Wimpole Lane, and within easy access of the centre of the town, and that it is contemplated to play the County matches there, as well as those of the Club. There are certain funds in hand, and a subscription has been set on foot for the purpose of making the ground.

They soon met with success. In 1866 this County Club beat Surrey Club and Ground at The Oval by ten wickets, the Surrey side being bowled out by William Marten and Frank Silcock for 39 in their first innings. Suffolk were victorious at Bury St Edmunds, but at Lord's, on 23 and 24 July, MCC and Ground were beaten by one wicket in a thrilling finish, Essex having been left to score 150 to win, the highest total of the match.

The return game with Surrey, at Colchester, in August, saw Essex win by an innings and 171 runs. Frank Silcock hit 114 and Surrey were bowled out for 73 and 22. This was a very weak Surrey side, and, arriving two short, they were given two Grimstons, E J and G S, the sons of the Hon. Francis Sylvester, to make up their number. At the end of 1866 though, the Essex Club was dissolved.

Among those who represented the Club were Charles Alfred Absolom, a lively right-handed batsman who was later to play for Cambridge University and Kent and to appear for England against Australia, at

Melbourne, in 1879, scoring 52 in the first innings. He can be considered as one of Essex's first eccentrics, of which there have been many. He was born in Blackheath in 1846 and was an outstanding athlete at Cambridge, where he put the shot, participated in the long jump and was a footballer of merit. 'As a cricketer he always played for his side and never for himself, a philosophy which he carried into other walks of life.' He ended his cricket career in 1879 and went to America, where he spent some ten years travelling around and spending much time with the native Indians. He was killed in Trinidad in 1889 while working as a purser on a ship; a crane loading sugar cane collapsed and crushed him.

The demise of the Essex County Club left a void and reduced Essex again to a cricketing backwater. The United South of England XI made a visit to Southend in August 1865. On 28, 29 and 30 of the month, they met Twenty-Two of Southend, with Alfred Shaw and Frank Silcock. The United South of England side, a strong one, including Pooley, Caesar, John and James Lillywhite, scored 101 and 180 while Southend made 143 and 75 for 12 so that the game was one of those 'cricket abominations, namely, a drawn match, about this time very numerous'.

The following year, the season when the Essex County Club at Colchester was at its height, another outpost shot into prominence when the Players of Essex, with Jupp, took on Twenty-Two of Harlow, at the Harlow Cricket Ground, at the Green Man Inn.

It was alleged that cricket was played in Harlow in the 18th century, and there certainly is evidence of cricket being played there in 1823. But the venture on 28 and 29 September 1866 was the most ambitious undertaken in the area. Sadly, it was not a total success.

Harlow had the services of John Hughes who, for 30 years, was professional for Hertfordshire and a medium-pace bowler of great merit. The Players of Essex were bowled out by Hughes for 48 in their first innings, Frank Silcock scoring 17 not out. As Bunce, for some unexplained reason, was absent, Hughes was able to take only nine wickets. 'The Twenty-Two upon taking their turn at the wicket seemed bent upon following, as regarded a small score, the example of their opponents.' They made 45, Marten taking 14 wickets and Frank Silcock six, one being run out. Eventually, Harlow triumphed by six wickets, scoring 70 for 15 in their second innings.

Frank Silcock was closely associated with Essex although he was born in Sawbridgeworth and played much for Hertfordshire. A stylish and consistent batsman and a brisk round-arm bowler, he made his first-class debut at Lord's in May, 1864, and was given benefits in 1878 and 1893. Having coached at Uppingham, Felsted and Eton, he was re-engaged by Essex at Leyton in 1887 when he was 48 years old. He had strong Essex ties, for he kept the Chequers Inn at Maldon until 1869 and ran a cricket warehouse in Chipping Ongar until his death in 1897.

The unfortunate thing about the match concerns the lack of enthusiasm that it engendered, which is made clear by the report in the *Hertfordshire and Essex Observer*:

> The match, we believe, was got up at considerable expense as a cricketing treat for the inhabitants of the cricketing town of Harlow and its neighbouring not unknown cricket-loving villages. The ground had evidently been got in to as good order as the previous unpropitious weather would permit. A number of capacious and excellent tents had been erected, for the convenience of legitimate visitors around the field, and a quantity of canvas placed at the vacant spots to obstruct the gaze of the illegitimate visitors who might attempt to get sixpen'orth 'on the cheap', from the adjoining fields. Attractive bills had been circulated far and near; advertisements had been for weeks inserted in the newspapers circulating in the district; and the Great Eastern Railway Company had liberally agreed to convey visitors to and fro for one fare. First class professional players had been engaged, and the services of by no means unknown and anything but contemptible local players had been secured. Lastly the weather was the finest and pleasantest we have been favoured with for weeks past, and yet strange to say there were so to speak no visitors to witness the play. There were not more than fifty in the field at any one time on the first day, and not more than 100 on the second. The why and the wherefore we can not tell. It certainly must have been very discouraging to the promoters of the match, we only hope they are not pecuniary losers.

If such apathy was general throughout the county, the reasons for the demise of the County Club at Colchester are obvious, and in the next few years, Essex cricketers had to content themselves with the visits of I Zingari to play the Cricket Company Club at Upton Park and to play the Colchester Garrison and the Shoeburyness Royal Artillery. Incogniti, another travelling club which had come into existence in 1862, also played the Cricket Company, as well as taking on West Essex at Navestock and the Colchester and Essex Club.

Southgate continued their matches with South Essex at Upton Park, which was also the venue for a game between Essex and Norfolk in June, 1868. That encounter was drawn, but Norfolk won the return match at Dereham the following month. The All-England XI played Twenty-Two of Chelmsford, and, over the next two years, the Gentlemen of Essex met the Gentlemen of Norfolk, but, apart from the sorties by I Zingari, the rest was meagre fare.

That there was cricketing talent in the county was undeniable; that it was not being harnessed to the best advantage was equally true. The evidence of talent can be seen in the Essex victory over MCC and Ground at Lord's on 15 and 16 July 1872. Essex had a crushing win by nine wickets, and *Wisden*, in its 10th year, rhapsodised on the match. Its report, however, shows certain historical flaws and confusions in its opening sentence, where Hornchurch and Essex are once again taken as being synonymous. The account of the match itself leaves no doubt as to the strength of the Essex team in 1872:

> The revival of this ancient match at Lord's in 1872 brought up an Eleven from the old County who defeated the Club Eleven in a canter. The County team not only included that very clever head-bowler and hard hitter, Mr. C. Absolom, but Frank Silcock, and three of the 1872 University match bowlers – Mr. C. K. Francis, Mr. Raynor, and Mr. Isherwood; in addition to those cricket experts the County played Mr. J. Round – a few years back one of the very best amateur wicket-keepers that ever asked 'How's that?' – and a very promising batsman in Mr. Herbert; in fact, it is doubtful if a stronger Essex Eleven ever appeared in the cricket field than this one that defeated M.C.C. and G. in 1872. Alfred Shaw did out and out well for the old Club; he scored 87 out of the 230 runs (from the bat) made by M.C.C. in the match, and with his bowling Alfred had 5 of the 11 Essex wickets down. Wootton was so severely hurt, when batting, as to be unable to finish his first innings, to commence his second, or to bowl more than one over; this was a loss to M.C.C., whose Eleven, however, could not have won had this mishap not occurred, for the Essex men were strongest all round and won on their merits. Silcock made 56 runs for Essex, and had 10 M.C.C. wickets – 7 bowled; and it will be seen by the summary that Mr. Raynor, the young Cambridge bowler, when tried, took 3 wickets at a cost of only 4 runs per wicket. The County beat the Club by 9 wickets.

In brief the game went thus: MCC and Ground 131 (Alfred Shaw 58 not out, A Pepys Esq. 39, Frank Silock 6 for 43); and 116) A F Jeffreys 30 not out, Alfred Shaw 39, Frank Silcock 4 for 41, G S Raynor Esq. 3 for 13). Essex 191 (Frank Silcock 56, C A Absolom 28, Alfred Shaw 4 for 62); and 57 for 1 (A W H Herbert 26 not out).

It is worth reflecting on the players who represented Essex in this match. Allen William Henry Herbert was born at Hythe in Kent, in 1852. He made his first-class debut for MCC at the age of 19, and in 1874 he played one first-class game for the county of his birth. The following year, he played once for Middlesex, and the last of his 11 first-class games was for MCC in 1876. He was generally a middle-order right-handed batsman, and he appeared for Wiltshire as well as for Essex in the non-first-class days.

Of the other cricketers that *Wisden* singles out, Absolom and Frank Silcock we have already noted. Absolom, described as an 'eccentric hitter and useful medium-pace right-arm bowler' as well as a brilliant fielder, played four years in the Cambridge University side from 1866 to 1869, and in 57 first-class matches for Kent between 1868 and 1879. As he was born in Blackheath, Essex can only claim a remote hold on him.

Francis Isherwood, a rugby international, was a Hampshire man whose first-class cricket was for Oxford University. Rev. George Sydney Raynor was born in Yorkshire and played for Cambridge University as a fast bowler and lower order batsman. Charles King Francis was a true Essex man, born in Upminster. He was at Rugby School where he gained an enormous reputation as a fast bowler. His first year at Oxford, 1870, promised an equally spectacular career in first-class cricket. He took five second innings wickets to give the University success over the Gentlemen of England, and he had match figures of 7 for 89, including W G Grace in both innings, when Oxford lost to MCC by three wickets.

In the Varsity match of 1870, Francis performed prodigious feats, yet his achievement was so overshadowed by other events as to go unmentioned in Pelham Warner's account of the series of matches, *Oxford and Cambridge at the Wicket*. Francis took 5 for 59 and 7 for 102. Oxford led by 28 on the first innings, but Yardley hit the first century in the history of the matches and Cobden performed the hat-trick when he dismissed the last three Oxford men to give Cambridge victory by two runs. From that point Francis's career seems to have declined, although he did tour North America with Fitzgerald's side in 1872 and played for Middlesex on occasions between 1875 and 1877. In the game for Essex against MCC, he took 1 for 36 and 0 for 13.

Spencer, W E Grimston, R C Davis and Francis Round, the younger brother of James, completed the Essex side that was victorious over MCC.

Unfortunately the match heralded no resurgence in the fortunes of Essex cricket. In the next two years the county had to be content with the visits of I Zingari to the School of Gunnery at Shoeburyness. James Round played for East of England against MCC and W E Grimston played for The Laity against The Clergy, but, with W G Grace in his prime and Gloucestershire and Nottinghamshire vying for the title of county champions, Essex slumbered.

On 21, 22 and 23 June 1875, the United South of England XI came to Chelmsford where they beat 22 of the town by 16 runs. Frank Silcock and Boardman were in the Chelmsford side, who were allowed the assistance of John Hughes, the Hertfordshire bowler, who had taken all nine wickets for Harlow against the Players of Essex in 1866. When he played for the Twenty-Two of Chelmsford Hughes was within one week of his 50th birthday. The honours in the match went to the United South of England's wicket-keeper Harry Phillips. Phillips, Sussex's keeper, was one of the shortest in the game, but at Chelmsford, he caught seven and stumped three, an achievement described in *Scores and Biographies* as 'one of the greatest wicket-keeping feats on record'.

These excursions by the great into Essex were all very pleasant, but, although Cambridgeshire had dropped out, the number of first-class counties had swollen to ten, and still Essex had no county club. Then came the year of 1876.

CHAPTER 5

Essex County Cricket Club: 1876–86

In 1876 Benjamin Disraeli was Prime Minister of Great Britain. He and Gladstone excited the indignation and horror of the British people by informing them of the massacres and atrocities that had taken place in Bulgaria in the Balkans War. In 1876 Alexander Graham Bell invented and exhibited the telephone, Ulysses S Grant was in his last year as President of the United States and John Ruskin was the dictator of artistic taste. In 1876 Alfred Lord Tennyson produced his unsuccessful verse drama, *Harold*, Thomas Hardy published *The Hand of Ethelberta* and Anthony Trollope was still writing his Palliser novels at his home in Waltham Cross. In 1876 Gilbert and Sullivan were at the beginning of their fruitful partnership, General Custer met his death fighting the native Indians close to the Little Big Horn River and Essex County Cricket Club came into existence.

On 7 January, the following notice appeared in the *Chelmsford Chronicle*:

> A Public Meeting will be held at the Shire Hall, Chelmsford on Friday, 14th January, 1876, at three o'clock, to consider the desirability of forming a county cricket club with a ground at Brentwood.
>
> Signed: I. E. Perry Wallington
> James Round

J Round

C E Green

C D Buxton

A P Lucas

H G Owen

C J Kortright

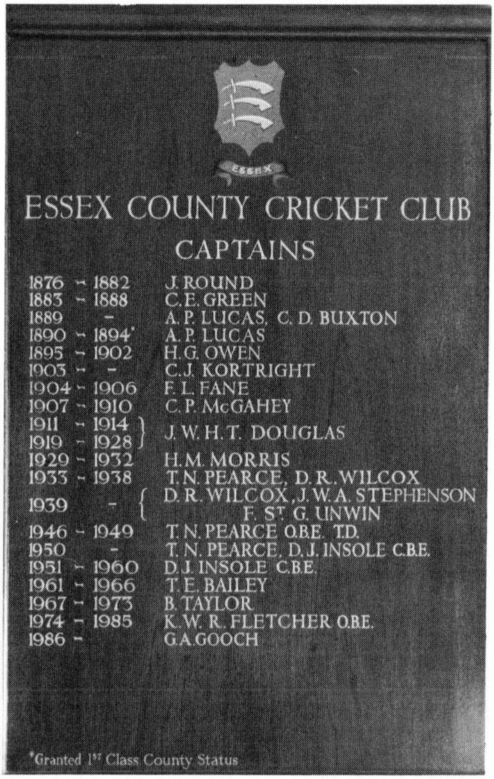

4. *Essex Captains, 1876–1986*

F L Fane

C P McGahey

J W H T Douglas

H M Morris

T N Pearce

D R Wilcox

J W A Stephenson

F St G Unwin

D J Insole

T E Bailey

B Taylor

K W R Fletcher

G A Gooch

The meeting took place with James Round MP in the chair, and the Club was formed with an annual subscription of one guinea. The honorary secretary was Mr J F Lescher of Boyles Court, Brentwood, and it is generally accepted that James Round was chairman of the Club although he also acted as treasurer until the beginning of 1883.

Undoubtedly it was the energy and enthusiasm of James Round which were the dominant factors in bringing the Club into being. His name has already featured in this narrative, but we should now look at him more closely.

He was born in Colchester, on 6 April 1842, and was educated at Eton, playing against Harrow, at Lord's, in 1860. Haygarth describes him as 'a most useful man in the cricket field, though he rather sacrificed his former strong defence for increased hitting. At Eton he was a most effective long-stop; and as a bowler he delivered fast round and slow underhand.'

He went up to Christ Church, Oxford, where he captained the College XI, developed into one of the finest amateur wicket-keepers of the day and was chosen for the Gentlemen against the Players although, surprisingly, he did not receive his blue. In his first Gentlemen and Players game, at Lord's in 1864, he stumped Tarrant and scored five and nine, both not out. He played in both matches in 1867, at Lord's and at The Oval, and in the second match he gave a masterly display, stumping two, catching three, assisting in the run out of three other batsmen and conceding only one bye in an innings of 249. His last game in the series was at Lord's the following year when W G Grace hit his first century for the Gentlemen.

In 1867 Round had played his highest innings, a fierce 142 for Southgate against Oxford University, at Magdalen. This was some revenge for the slight he had received in not being selected for the Varsity match when in residence. The following year he became a barrister and began his political career when he was elected Member of Parliament for East Essex.

In 1878 he became Assistant Private Secretary to Sir Michael Hicks-Beach, the Chief Secretary for Ireland, and he later became MP for Essex, North East Division, and then for Essex, Harwich Division. He represented Essex constituencies in the House of Commons for 38 years. He died at his home at Birch Hall on Christmas Eve, 1916.

A tall, lithe man, he appeared for Essex infrequently, no doubt due to his parliamentary duties, but his contribution to the game was immense. He served on the MCC committee, and he played a decisive part in driving Essex into the top flight of county, and ultimately first-class cricket.

Despite earlier apathy, the response to the decision to establish Essex County Cricket Club was good. The ground at Brentwood was rented from the Countess Tasker at £4 an acre. As the Club was entitled to sub-let, the terms of the agreement were excellent, and by the time that the first Club match was played at Brentwood – Players of Essex v Gentlemen of Essex on 5 and 6 May 1876 – subscriptions amounted to £700. The ground was said to be 'capital', and 'pleasantly situated and well fenced-in'.

The inaugural match at Brentwood was in the nature of a trial, which the Gentlemen won by an innings and five runs. Frank and Joseph Silcock; Marten, who had been professional to the Club formed at Colchester a few years earlier; Handley, destined to play for Twenty-Two Colts of England against MCC in 1878; Andrews, Gregory, Smart, Howell, Button, Goldstone and wicket-keeper Ballard represented the Players, who made 114 and 66. The Gentlemen fielded C H Escott, C R Stevens, A Baker, Capt G B Meares, J Round, W H Bullick, W E Grimston (top scorer with 47), W Howard, T O Nicholas, W H Pemberton-Barnes and C F Reid.

Just over a month later, Essex participated in what is generally believed to be their first county match when they beat Suffolk by eight wickets at Ipswich on 13 and 14 June. There was no report of the match in any of the sporting papers, and we are indebted to Haygarth and his *Scores and Biographies* for the details of the game. Suffolk, who had been resuscitated that year, made 132 and 57. Essex scored 122 and 69 for 2. The Essex heroes were Seth Smart and Marten, who took 5 for 22 and 5 for 19 respectively in the Suffolk second innings. It is only right, however, to name the 11 players who represented Essex on that historic occasion: Escott, Gray, Smart, Howard, Meares, Nicholas, Barnes, Marten, Reid, Ballard and Ridley.

We can only presume that this was Essex's first county match. The scores were discovered in the Suffolk books, and it is, of course, possible that a match could have been played earlier, the details of which have never come to light.

The side which played Hertfordshire at Bishop's Stortford a month later, and who lost by an innings, showed eight changes from the side that had beaten Suffolk. On 12 and 13 July, Suffolk came to Brentwood for the return match, and Essex had the better of a draw. Mr Charles Hay Escott scored the first fifty for the Club, but again there are complaints from historians: 'In the sporting papers no analyses were given, and the scorers seem to have been terribly negligent. A little more care and time devoted to record our national game is greatly to be desired.'

On 18 and 19 July, Hertfordshire came to Brentwood and won by ten wickets. Essex fielded a strong side, with Escott, W E Grimston, Smart, Frank Silcock, Meares and Round, playing his first county game, all present. They were outshone by their old friend and enemy John Hughes, who had match figures of 9 for 105. He was, by then, 51 years old. For

Scores and Biographies, Haygarth obtained details of this match from the Herts scorebook, and there was a lament at the lack of reportage on the game: 'No analyses published, a fact to be regretted, for these *now* second-rate contests may, in a *few years,* become first-rate matches, and their doings ought to be preserved in their entirety. Witness the sudden rise of Gloucestershire.'

It is a salutary reminder of how far up the ladder Essex still had to climb, but the example of Gloucestershire shone brightly. They had been founded in 1871, and in 1876 they were champions for the third time, once shared, in four years. It was the year that W G Grace made 344 for MCC against Kent, the first score of 300 in first-class cricket. He was to follow this with innings of 177 for Gloucestershire against Nottinghamshire and 318 against Yorkshire, inside a week, at Clifton College. He later made 400 not out for the All-England XI against Twenty-Two of Grimsby. Essex, meanwhile, had to be content with scores of 101 and 62 for 5 in the drawn game with Norfolk at Brentwood. Both Rounds played in this match.

On 7 and 8 August Essex lost to MCC at Lord's by five runs. The accounts of this match give varying individual scores, but Haygarth credits James Round with 54 in the second innings. The brunt of the Essex bowling was done by Seth Smart and Frank Silcock, and C H Escott, 44 in the first innings, W E Grimston, Captain Meares and Dr J H Earle also played in the match.

Seth Smart was in his 41st year when the County Club was founded, so that, as a quick bowler, his best years would have been behind him. Born in Saffron Walden, tall and strong, he chose not to seek professional engagements far afield, but remained mostly in his home area and worked as a cabinet maker and upholsterer. It was said that he three times took all ten wickets in an innings in minor matches.

Joseph Herbert Earle was considered a promising batsman although already 32 years old. He was a Brentwood man and practised medicine in the town, having been educated at Harlow College. When MCC came to Brentwood on 24 and 25 August he hit 51 and 46 not out, so playing a most significant part in Essex's eight-wicket victory.

The Club had enjoyed a highly satisfactory first season. The second season, 1877, proved less successful on the playing field.

On 27 and 28 June, Essex ventured to Hitchin to take on Hertfordshire, who were certainly a strong side at the time. The Herts bowling was opened by the evergreen John Hughes and by Valentine Adolphus Titchmarsh, a quick round-arm bowler. Essex made 65 and 75, and Herts won by an innings and 64 runs. In the first innings, Titchmarsh took all 10 wickets for 33 runs, becoming one of the first in a long list of those who were to produce outstanding performances against Essex over the next

100 years. He and Hughes shared the wickets in the second innings and when the return match was played at Brentwood a fortnight later he took 7 for 30 and Herts won by ten wickets.

On a damp wicket at Lord's on 23 and 24 July, MCC won by ten wickets. Only four balls were bowled on the first day, and, in spite of Frank Silcock's 57, Essex were bowled out for 150 in their second innings. They had made only 58 in the first, Rylott finishing the innings with a hat-trick. He and Cloete bowled unchanged throughout the return match at Brentwood less than a month later and MCC won again, this time by 68 runs. The matches with Norfolk brought a six-wicket victory at Brentwood and a draw in the return fixture.

The following season saw defeat at Lord's, when Turner hit 127 for MCC, and a draw at Brentwood. There was a draw at home to Suffolk and defeat in Bury St Edmunds, and there was a draw against Sixteen of South Essex at Brentwood. It was a season without a win in an inter-county match, but it was a season that had its great moments. Escott scored centuries against the Colchester Garrison at Brentwood and against the School of Gunnery at Shoeburyness, but the highlight came in the drawn match with Hertfordshire, at Brentwood, on 16 and 17 July 1878.

Essex made 154 and 311. Hertfordshire scored 128 and 59 for 6. In the Essex second innings, James Turner Welldon hit 136, which, as far as we can tell, was the first century to be scored for Essex County Cricket Club in a match against another county. Welldon, a hard-hitting middle order batsman, played a ferocious innings which lasted 2½ hours. He hit two fives, six fours and 15 threes. It should be remembered that, at this time, to score a six, the batsman had to hit the ball out of the ground.

Welldon was 31 years old at the time, and his first-class career was behind him. He had played four times for Kent between 1867 and 1869, his highest score of 37 coming in his debut match against Hampshire. He also played one first-class game for Cambridge University, against MCC at Fenner's in 1869. Captain of his college, St John's, the same year, he found time to steer the college boat and played for Sixteen of the University against the All-England XI.

Contrary to belief, Welldon was born in Tonbridge and not at Felsted. This fact has been determined by Peter Grant, the astute historian of the Kennington Club, near Ashford, for whom Welldon played. He was the eldest son of James Ind Welldon who, as Headmaster of Tonbridge, did for that school what Arnold had done for Rugby and what Thring did for Uppingham. Paradoxically he abhorred smoking and drinking, although his family connections with the famous brewery firm, Ind Coope, had given him his middle name.

Rev. J I Welldon was a man of evangelical fervour, fired more by a sense of muscular Christianity than by academic study; he imbued strong principles in his children. James Turner was a fine soccer player for London and Wanderers, won the Tonbridge School Fives Championship and was the first captain of Hythe Golf Club, a club destined to have strong links with cricket. He was at Tonbridge School for a record 11 years and excelled at cricket, leading the eleven in his last year, 1866.

On coming down from Cambridge in 1870, he followed the family profession and became a schoolmaster. In 1871 he obtained a post as assistant master at Felsted School, and he was to have a strong influence on the development of cricket there. In this, he was encouraged by his brother-in-law, Rev. D S Ingram, who became Headmaster of Felsted in 1875. Ingram was a keen cricketer, and there were several capable players on the staff of the school. One of the housemasters, A W Rowe, was an Uppingham man, and his sons, Ernest Fentiman and Francis Erskine, later played regularly for Essex.

In 1879 J T Welldon decided upon a change of career and left teaching to study the law. He was admitted as a solicitor in 1882, and joined the Ashford firm of Hallett, Creery, Fuller and Co. This did not dampen his interest in cricket and he played for Incogniti, but to Essex he was lost. Nevertheless, he has a most important place in the history of the Club.

Others to appear in the Essex side at this time were Borrowes, the Earp brothers and Captain Frederick John Fane whose son was to achieve distinction for both Essex and England.

Borrowes, later Lieutenant-Colonel Sir Kildare Dixon Borrowes, played for Essex in 1878 when his regiment was stationed at Colchester. He was a fine wicket-keeper. He had been educated at Cheltenham and he later played for Middlesex, although most of his cricket was played with his regiment in South Africa.

Thomas Earps was a Leicestershire man, educated in Ireland and later a corn merchant in Canning Town. He was a good all-rounder, and captained Barking. The Barking Club had planned to present him with a testimonial in recognition of his services, but he died in Bournemouth in 1881 after a short illness. He was only 26, and his death was a great blow to Essex cricket. His tall, strong brother, William Edward, was a medium-pace bowler and a farmer at Wennington.

Club cricket in the county thrived. Wanstead, Ilford, Southend, Barking and many other areas boasted fine sides. And as the game in the county grew, so cricket was considering ever wider horizons.

The first Test match had been played in 1877, and 1880 saw the first Test in England. From that year, international cricket has grown until its present surfeit. With W G Grace scoring 152 for England against Australia at The Oval, and Blackham, Spofforth, Murdoch and the rest entertaining wherever they went, it was not surprising that the cricket world was not too concerned about the outcome of matches between

Essex, Hertfordshire, Bedfordshire and Suffolk, which was the diet at Brentwood. But importantly, Essex County Cricket Club had negotiated the first phase of its existence. Now a fresh impetus was needed if the County Club was to develop and prosper. That impetus came in the shape of one of the truly great men in Essex cricket history, Charles Ernest Green. His name has already filtered into this story on occasions, a character waiting in the wings. Now he moves centre stage.

Charles Ernest Green was born at Walthamstow on 26 August 1846. He was educated at a private school in Brighton and then went to Uppingham where his feats on the cricket field earned himself, and the school, a great reputation. From Uppingham he went to Cambridge and was in the eleven for all four years of his residence. He captained the side in his last year. Initially a fast opening bowler, he concentrated more and more on his batting, which was free, fierce and joyful.

He was a man who distinguished himself in any sport to which he turned his hand. He was at Cambridge from 1865 to 1868, and, at the Walthamstow Rifle Club Sports in September 1866, he won six events – 100 yards, high jump, long jump, hurdles, throwing the cricket ball and kicking the football. The following year, he won the mile at Cambridge in 5 minutes, 4 seconds, a remarkable time at that period in athletics history. In 1867–68, he won the high jump in the Inter-Varsity Sports.

With no organised club in the county of his birth, he played his first county cricket for Sussex in 1868. The Green family lived for most of each summer in Brighton where his father owned a house, but for the next decade he was a regular member of the Middlesex eleven and one of the most exciting amateurs in the country.

Of his many heroic batting feats, particularly in the great matches of the day, two stand out. The first was at Lord's, in 1870, when he and W G Grace, playing for MCC and Ground against Yorkshire, put on 91 in 70 minutes on a wicket 'so rough as to be quite unfit for a first-class match'. They were confronted by Freeman and Emmett at their most hostile. Green scored 51 and, like Grace, ended his innings covered in bruises from ankle to shoulder. *Wisden* was to quote many years after the event that it was the pluckiest batting ever seen.

The following year Green played an innings of a different nature. In the Gentlemen v Players match at The Oval, the Gentlemen were left to make 144 to win in 1¾ hours. Green went in at the fall of the first wicket, W G Grace and I D Walker having put on 46. Grace was then out at 95 and Hornby went without scoring. When Lubbock and Tylecote were also dismissed it seemed that the match would be drawn, but Green made his last 27 runs in seven hits and the Gentlemen won with three minutes to spare. Green was cheered from the field by a very large crowd.

Fractionally under six feet tall, $13\frac{1}{2}$ stone in weight, elegant in dress and manner, with a twinkle in his eye, Charles Green had the zest of a character from Dickens or, perhaps better, because of his passion for the hunt, from Surtees. For a long time he was Master of the Essex Hunt and broke his collar bone in a fall while hunting in February 1884.

In 1882 he joined Essex and became captain the next year, but it is not just by his achievements on the field that he should be measured. He electrified Essex cricket, thrust it into a new age and took steps to ensure its continuity and survival. He had persuaded H H Stephenson to become coach at Uppingham and raise the cricket there to new heights, and it was from his connection with Uppingham that he was able to induce A P Lucas to come to Essex. He also persuaded C D Buxton to stay with the county, and his general vigour infused a spirit and sense of ambition in the side.

A few months before Charles Green returned to Essex, the county recruited another who was to give noble service, although he came from a very different background to that of Green. This was Henry Pickett. He was average height, stocky and strong, and he bowled quickly; he served Essex well for 16 years.

Pickett was born in Stratford, and at the age of 16, in 1878, he took 80 wickets for Forest Gate Alliance. He moved to the Victoria Club and caused a sensation when he took 7 for 15 against the strong Barking side. His progress was being noted and he was engaged at the Beckton Gas Works where the facilities enabled him to develop and improve. The Beckton Club was very strong at the time and boasted four players who were later to assist the county, Pickett, Regan, Kirkman and Curtis. If you have ambitions to succeed in any game, it is advisable to produce your best performances on the right occasions, in the right places. This is just what Pickett did. The Beckton Club played Brentwood on the County Ground and Pickett took 7 for 1. His bowling so impressed those at the receiving end of this performance that he was included in the County side for the next match. He played in all the remaining matches and ended with 48 wickets. As he also took 110 wickets, at a little over three runs each, for Beckton, he had enjoyed a wonderful start to his professional career.

In 1882 he was engaged by the Liverpool Club, but he still assisted Essex regularly and finished the season with 56 wickets; the veteran Frank Silcock was next with 34. Pickett thrived under Green's leadership. Back at the Beckton Club in 1883, he enjoyed great success for the County. There were 16 wickets in the innings victory over Suffolk at Brentwood and 13 wickets when Hertfordshire were beaten, also by an innings, at Bishop's Stortford. Pickett, Silcock and Kirkman were the three regular professionals and they did nearly all of the bowling. Henry Pickett finished the season with 68 wickets, Frank Silcock had 24 and

5. *Henry Pickett, who took 10–32 against Leicestershire at Leyton in 1895, and yet finished on the losing side. He is one of the only two Essex players to have taken all ten wickets in an innings (if one excludes J C Laker who did the same for England against Australia whilst a Surrey player). Trevor Bailey also took ten wickets, for 90 against Lancashire, at Clacton in 1949.*

Henry Kirkman 17. As well as the victories noted above, Essex beat Herts at Brentwood and Norfolk at Norwich. They lost to MCC and Northants twice, and drew with Norfolk at Brentwood. Green led by example, scoring 235 runs, average 25.50, bettered only by the 237 runs of Dr William Francis. Francis, an Essex man, had previously played first-class cricket for Sussex for two years.

Pickett's feats led to him being engaged by MCC in 1884, although he continued to play for Essex. Essex began this particular season without the help of Green, who was still recovering from his broken collar bone. He did not play in the opening match against Surrey, at The Oval, which saw Essex give a very good account of themselves against one of the strongest sides in the country. Essex made 247 (Silcock 56) and 249 (Mr H G Owen 69, Mr J J Read 66) while Surrey, with Bobby Abel making 98 and Mr Walter Read 91, reached 398 in their first innings; this score owed much to a last wicket stand of 105 between Jones and Barratt. Surrey ultimately won by five wickets. Pickett had 5 for 136 in 72 overs in the first innings. *Cricket* was loud in its praise:

> Mr C E Green, who has worked hard of late years to develop cricket in Essex, is to be warmly congratulated on the excellent show made by the

Eleven of the County, at The Oval, on Thursday last and the two following days (15, 16 and 17 May). Some excellent all-round cricket was displayed, and the batting of the team was throughout much above the average. The play of Mr Owen, in particular, was deserving of the highest credit.

Essex suffered only one other defeat in their remaining seven matches in 1884, losing to Norfolk at Norwich, although they were lucky to escape an innings defeat against Hertfordshire at St Albans. Henry Pickett's number of wickets dropped to 31, and they were more expensive than in previous years, but Frank Silcock, close to 47 years old, took 48 wickets at 15.23 runs each.

It was Silcock who began the next season in splendid form too, in spite of Essex being overwhelmed at The Oval. Walter Read, who always made runs against Essex, hit 148 of Surrey's 238, which was a score big enough to bring an innings victory. Frank Silcock, however, took 6 for 94, finishing his stint in a blaze of glory. 'The veteran Silcock bowled with great success for Essex. His last seventeen overs realised six wickets at a cost of only nine runs.'

The return match with Surrey, on 15 and 16 June 1885, was also lost by an innings, Walter Read hitting 214, but it was a match of great significance, not so much for its result as for its venue – Leyton.

From his first days with the Club, Green had realised that Brentwood was an inadequate centre if Essex was to prosper. It was rural and remote, and however attractive the setting, it had a sense of isolation, and was a considerable distance from the railway station, which was not conducive to attract support. Indeed even in the years immediately following the Second World War, it retained its air of remoteness and travel to it was difficult.

Green was a man of energy, influence and authority. He was to be President of MCC in 1905 and he was active on committees such as those that looked after the Cricketers' Fund and brought about the rationalisation of Test cricket. He was also a power in the business world, being managing director of the Orient Steamship Company (later to amalgamate with P & O Steam Navigation Company). To his qualities of drive and leadership he allied an irritability which erupted if he were ever crossed. Essex cricket was his passion for the latter part of his life, and his dominating personality was agreeable so long as he was not seriously opposed. His generosity was boundless.

It was Green who decided that a move from Brentwood would be in the best interests of the Club, and it was he who motivated and negotiated the move to Leyton. The editor of *Cricket*, C W Alcock, was much attracted

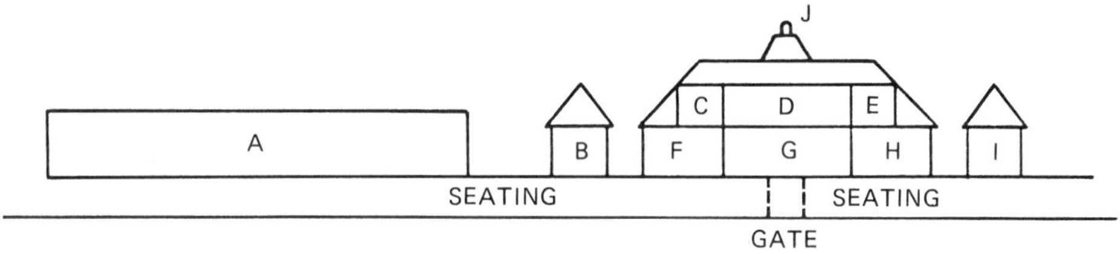

6. *County Ground, Leyton, which was the headquarters of Essex cricket from 1886 to 1934, although the County continued to play there until 1976.*
A. *Members' Stand*
B. *Professionals' Room*
C. *Office*
D. *Committee and Amateurs' Luncheon Room*
E. *Secretary's Office*
F. *Visiting Pros' Changing Room*
G. *Club Room and Bar*
H. *Amateurs' Changing Room*
I. *Printing Score Cards and Gate Money Room*
J. *Bell Tower*

by the venture and was quick to comment on the Essex v Surrey game:

> The fact that the return match between Surrey and Essex was played on the new ground known as the Lyttelton Ground, the joint property, I believe, of Lord Lyttelton and Mr R. Crawley, deserved prominent notice if only for the reason that it is the first important fixture played in that enclosure, leased, I think I am right in stating, by the Insurance Offices. The wicket played well on the first day, and as there is plenty of space outside to make the ground broader – the only improvement needed – there is every reason for its selection in the case of more important fixtures of the Essex Club if suitable arrangements can be made. Situated as it is within an easy railway journey of London, and close to the populous district of Stratford, good cricket should be well supported there. I have, too, every reason to believe that, though as is always the case with a first match, the expenses this week were very heavy, the Essex authorities were quite satisfied with the attendance. Indeed, had the game been fairly even, to judge by the numbers on the first day the venture would have been a decided success financially.

Essex played, and beat, Northamptonshire at Leyton in August, and there were also victories over Norfolk and, more spectacularly, Derbyshire at Derby. This last result was a fine performance, for Derbyshire were then one of the nine first-class counties. The architect of this victory was Mr Francis Augustus Bishop, a fast right-arm bowler with a doubtful, but very successful, action. He was to play for the Gentlemen four years later amid much controversy.

Lancashire beat Essex twice with ease, and the second victory, at Leyton, brought forth from the *Essex Standard* a cry of complaint which, in its turn, was to be severely criticised.

> Essex got well beaten by Lancashire on Monday and Tuesday, and there can be no doubt that the Lancashire eleven made a fine display of cricket. At the same time it must not be overlooked that they were reinforced by no less than seven professionals, who did very nearly all the batting, and the whole of the bowling for them. On the other hand, Essex had only three professionals, who did scarcely anything at all in the way of batting, and only about one third of the bowling. The rage for professional players may be of excellent service in improving the game of cricket; but to outsiders it seems rather a farce to speak of 'county matches' in which counties are represented almost entirely by professionals, *who will play for one county one week and for another the next*. In the match last week between Surrey and Lancashire, six men on each side were professionals. An eastern potentate once expressed his wonderment, in an English ball-room, that the English should take the

trouble to dance for themselves when they could pay persons to dance for them. A foreign observer in England might with more reason wonder why (whilst they are about it), some of our English counties do not pay the *whole of their cricket elevens* to play the 'national game' for them.

This silly, ill-informed article was dismissed with contempt by the national cricket press. It revealed not only an ignorance of the rules of qualification, but also a total insensitivity to the growth and development of the game. As it was featured in a leading Essex paper, it would also suggest that the majority in the county remained unaware of the direction in which cricket in particular, and sport in general, was moving.

Rules of qualification had been drawn up in 1872 and recognised the following June, 1873, in order to put the county championship on a sounder basis. These rules stipulated that, at the beginning of each season, a cricketer must decide to play for the county of his birth or the county of his residence. Initially the residential qualification was three years for professionals and two years for amateurs, but it was later reduced to two years for all classes of player.

Although these rules of qualification were drawn up for the 1873 competition, the county championship was not officially recognised by county secretaries until 1890, by which time a points system had been in operation for three years. It was not until 1894 that the MCC took a hand in the control of the championship. However, competition had been fostered by the sporting press for more than 20 years before this official adoption, and rivalry was intense.

In soccer, the Football Association Challenge Cup had come into existence in the 1871–72 season. For more than a decade the competition concerned the top amateurs of the day, products of the country's leading public schools, but in July 1885, the month before the publication of the article in the *Essex Standard*, professionalism in soccer was finally legalized. Twenty of the first 21 FA Cup Finals were played at The Oval, but after 1892 they moved elsewhere. Geoffrey Green relates: 'The crowds following the Cup were growing every year and the authorities of the Surrey County Cricket Club, fearing for their world famous pitch, quite justly refused permission for it to be used again as a football ground.'

If the crowds following soccer had increased twenty-fold, the same increase had not been witnessed in those watching cricket at Brentwood, and Charles Green acted with wisdom and business sense when he propelled the Club towards Leyton. The move was universally approved, and Alcock, reviewing the season in *Cricket*, 26 November 1885, was warm in praise and anticipation:

Mainly through the personal influence of Mr C. E. Green, Essex has lately made a material advance towards the attainment of a permanent position in the forefront of county cricket. It will be especially gratifying, too, to those who take interest in what I may call the higher development of our national game to learn that there is really every promise of the Essex Club being placed on a solid and substantial foundation.

The removal last year of the headquarters of the Club from Brentwood, where there was comparatively little interest shown in the county's cricket, to the capacious and more convenient ground at Leyton, the property of Lord Lyttelton, proved as most *Cricket* readers are aware, a decided success. The experience of last summer, indeed, showed that in such a populous district as Leyton, within an easy distance of London, there was really an excellent chance for a ground conducted on a proper basis, and cricketers will be glad to learn that the Lyttleton Ground is now in the possession of and under the direct control of the Essex Club.

The liberality of Lord Lyttelton, who has shown great interest in the advancement of Essex cricket, has enabled the Committee to purchase the land on favourable conditions, and the acquisition of a large piece in addition to the area of last year will make the new ground one of the finest in the kingdom. To make it thoroughly suitable for the requirements of a large club a large expenditure is necessary, and it is intended to spend about £3,000 in the erection of a Pavilion with suitable buildings, and in other arrangements for the accommodation of members and visitors.

A *good* club under such management in the East of London should be very popular, and every one will be sure that no pains or expense will be spared to make it as complete as it can be made. Already, I understand, donations amounting to upwards of £1,200 have been received on behalf of the sum requisite for the alterations and improvements to the ground, and those who are interested in the growth of county cricket could render it useful help by sending donations to Mr C. E. Green, Theydon Grove, Epping, or to the Hon. Sec. of the County Club, Mr J. J. Read, High House, Brentwood.

Green showed vision in pressing for the Leyton Ground, for when Essex played there in 1885, the nearest station was nearly a mile away, and there was no tram or bus link with the ground. But this was soon rectified and the London, Tilbury and Southend Railway opened the Midland Road Station, which was only a few minutes' walking distance from the new headquarters. It is amusing to those who know the Leyton Ground today to read in a local report of the time that the move 'gave unwonted loveliness to a district which but a short while since presented an appearance of the abomination of desolation'.

Green was determined to put the Club on a professional, well run basis, and the developments that were taking place demanded that the

Committee found it necessary 'to avail themselves of the assistance of a secretary, who is prepared to give his time to the necessary duties, and they have been fortunate in securing the services of Mr T. Ratliff, and from his large and lengthy experience in the formation and general management of cricket and cricket clubs, very satisfactory results may with confidence be looked forward to.'

Thomas Ratliff was 50 years old and had had experience with both Middlesex and Warwickshire. He was in business in Leadenhall Street, and one of his first duties was to launch the appeal for donations towards the cost of improving the Leyton Ground.

The location cost the Essex Club £12,000, and by February 1886 it was advertised that the amount needed for the improvements on the ground was £3500, of which nearly half had been raised. The *Hertfordshire and Essex Observer* was one of several papers which carried an appeal letter from Green, J J Read, the honorary treasurer, who lived at High House, Brentwood, and from Ratliff.

The letter talked of 'the marked and rapid advance in Cricket made by Essex during the last few seasons, and the increasing interest which is now being taken in the doings of the County Eleven'. This success, the Committee felt, had rendered it necessary for the County Ground to be moved from Brentwood to a 'neighbourhood more accessible to London and the Cricketing World in general'. The Committee had therefore purchased the Leyton Ground and believed that it was likely to be a popular venue. 'To make this Ground, however, thoroughly efficient and suitable in every way for a large Club and County Ground', a sum of about £3500 was needed for the 'erection of a Pavilion and suitable buildings, and general alterations and improvements'.

There was optimism that, if this sum could be raised, Essex would have one of the finest and most attractive grounds in the country. There was no doubt that 'an immense stimulus will be given to our great national game throughout the County, and a great boon conferred upon the public'. Neither was the optimism confined to the ground itself, for the Committee believed that, 'If liberally supported, Essex will shortly take rank as one of the leading counties in the cricketing world.'

The list of subscribers is interesting. Lord Lyttelton headed the list with £200, and Green himself had donated £100, as had E N Buxton. There was £25 each from Read and from 'The Flitterbat Dramatic Club performance at Epping, per S Chisenhale Marsh, Esq.' Harlow's Loftus Arkwright had given 15 guineas, and the list included four Members of Parliament.

The financial problem was to remain with Essex for over 80 years, but in 1886, the immediate outlook was bright, even though, at a lower level, clubs had their own difficulties. For example at the AGM of the Rochford Hundred Club in Southend in January, it was reported that there was a deficit of £14, 'occasioned by the expense incurred in covering in the dining tent'. It was resolved by calling upon each member to subscribe an extra five shillings to meet the cost. Would that all financial crises could be overcome so readily!

It was finance that was the chief concern of a very well attended county AGM at the Great Eastern Hotel on Tuesday, 20 April 1886. Green was ill and unable to attend, and G A Sedgwick, 'prominently identified with the South Essex Club at Upton Park', presided in his stead. Much of what was offered in the report had been covered in the Club's letter of appeal, but the opening statement in relation to the past season, 1885, 'the third season of the County Club under its present administration', is worthy of note:

> From the balance sheet, you will observe that there is a rather heavy deficit, £266-8s-1d, this in a great measure being due to the limited number of members and subscribers to the funds of the Club, and to the small gate-takings at the County Matches at Brentwood. With a view to increase the attendances at, and the interest in, County cricket, your Committee last year decided to play four home matches on the Lyttelton Ground at Leyton, and the results showed a large increase in the attendance, some 4,000 being present during the Surrey match, and about the same number at the Lancashire match, while the remaining two matches were fairly well attended.

Any who had doubted the wisdom of the move from Brentwood to Leyton must have been convinced by this statement, and it was also announced that, of the £3500 that had been necessary for the ground improvements at Leyton, £2900 had already been raised from 'the inhabitants and supporters of Essex'. It was hoped that the remaining £600 would be raised during the coming year.

So the Brentwood Ground was abandoned. It was not to be the scene of a first-class match until July 1922, when Essex met Dublin University there. Indeed its fortunes were inextricably blended with those of Leyton. When the County abandoned Leyton in 1933, Brentwood was allocated a regular festival week. This lasted from 1934 until 1969, when Essex returned again to Leyton. It is unlikely that the Brentwood Ground will ever see first-class cricket again. It is now owned by the Essex County Council Education Committee and is the home of Brentwood Cricket, Hockey and Tennis Clubs.

Brentwood retains an historic, important and affectionate place in Essex cricket history. It is a beautiful tree-lined spot that imposes a sense of tranquility on the viewer, perhaps because the friendly ghosts of Round, Escott, Welldon and the others responsible for the birth of Essex County Cricket Club lurk protectively in the trees.

CHAPTER 6

Towards First-Class: 1886 – 94

There was a buoyancy in the air in the spring of 1886. *Bailey's Magazine* reported: 'Essex especially looks like "training on", and being fairly strong in bowling with Mr Buxton, Pickett, Silcock, and Mr Bishop; they should do even better than last season, when they managed to defeat, amongst others, Norfolk and Derbyshire.'

This sense of ebullience was sustained at the AGM where a most attractive programme of matches was announced, including a game against the Parsees, the first Indian side to visit this country, and a match between Cambridge Past and Present and the Australians, the first first-class game to be played at Leyton. The Leyton Ground was officially opened on Easter Monday, 26 April, with a match between Mr C E Green's XI and H Pickett's XI. Further optimism was expressed with the announcement that 400 members had been elected during the year, which brought the total membership to 660. This is a far cry from the 8000 plus of a century later.

Green did all that he could to encourage support. His team for the opening match included A J Webbe, the Middlesex captain, and the great hitters, C I Thornton and the Australian giant George Bonnor. They fared badly, Pickett and Burton bowling Green's side out for 89.

It was not on this occasion, but a few weeks later, that Green persuaded W G Grace to attend Leyton to afford Essex some prestige. More than 30 years after both Grace and Green were dead, Sir Home Gordon was able to reveal what Green had told him of that visit:

> He had the Old Man to stay with him for the opening match of importance at Leyton, kept him some days afterwards and mounted him on a favourite grey horse. Then followed what I did not choose to publish in that book [*Memorial Biography of W. G. Grace*], though Green had given me full permission to do so. After W G had left, he wrote his host a warm letter of thanks, adding that he would like to receive twenty guineas for the advertisement he had afforded the new ground. Green sent the cheque to his old friend, but told me he felt wrathful at the demand.

It was not to be the last time that Green dipped into his own pocket in the cause of Essex cricket.

Essex began the 1886 season with a creditable performance against Surrey at Leyton. Owen hit a fine fifty, but the County made only 127. Some splendid bowling by F A Bishop, 8 for 39, took Essex to a first innings lead of 38, and there was a scent of victory. Lohmann and Beaumont had other ideas, and Essex were out for 75 in their second innings to lose eventually by four wickets.

In spite of a good showing against the Parsees, a match which was not counted in the Essex averages issued at the end of the season, the return match with Surrey at The Oval produced a poor performance on a damp wicket, Essex being bowled out for 33 and 70 and losing by an innings.

At full strength, and despite C D Buxton scoring 60 and Pickett taking 7 for 61, Essex failed again at Derby. They led by 100 on the first innings, but Derbyshire, following on, scored 212 in their second innings and bowled Essex out for 66 to win by 46 runs. Derbyshire won the return game at Leyton by an innings, and Lancashire also won by an innings at Old Trafford. Frederick Almond's 84 not out against Derbyshire at Leyton proved to be the County's best effort of the season in important matches of which five were won, six lost and one drawn.

Almond, a right-handed batsman, born at Great Bentley in 1855, topped the batting averages, with 218 runs, at 27.25. He had been engaged by the Enfield Club for two seasons, but in 1885 took up a coaching position at Elstree School and remained there for some years.

Essex's main strength was in the bowling of F A Bishop, 60 wickets, and Pickett, who managed one less. There was also the all-round cricket of Cyril Buxton, then in his second year at Cambridge.

C D Buxton was the only Essex representative in the first first-class match played at Leyton, Cambridge University Past and Present versus the Australians, on 23, 24 and 25 August 1886. A G Steel, the Cambridge captain, won the toss and decided to bat. At the end of the first day, the Cambridge side were 311 for 6. Rock, who had opened, was 75 not out, and Buxton, number eight, 38 not out. Rock did not add to his score the next morning, but Buxton went on to make 57 before being bowled by Palmer. Cambridge made 349, and the tourists made 379, George Giffen hitting 119 before falling to Buxton, who had 1 for 32 in 24 four-ball overs.

Buxton was born at Knighton, Woodford, in June 1866. His father was a commanding figure in the Cricket Company at Upton Park and a prominent player for South Essex. Cyril Buxton developed his father's interest with greater talent, enjoying a notable career at Elstree and Harrow schools before taking his place at Trinity College, Cambridge, in the autumn of 1884. He was in the University side for four years, and was captain of the eleven in his last season. Perhaps his form never quite lived up to the exciting promise he showed at the start, but he scored over 1000 runs and took 60 wicket in a first-class career that encompassed only 40 matches. His medium-pace bowling was a later development, but he bowled less after his first three years at university.

He was a fine all-round sportsman, excelling at tennis and rackets, and he served on the Essex Committee and captained the County. Sadly, in May 1892, in a fit of severe depression, he committed suicide. He was only 26 years old, and his tragic death sent a shudder through the world of cricket, but for the moment, that dark event was still five years away.

The Cambridge v Australians match at Leyton was a great success for the County, and when the accounts were issued at the beginning of the 1887 season it was revealed that the takings from that match, £264 12s, had enabled the Club to realise a profit of £53 13s 9d. Actually, £1600 was still outstanding on the Building Fund Account, and there was regret that the appeal which had been made in December 1886 had not been responded to as liberally as had been anticipated.

Green, who chaired the AGM, was proud that the Leyton Ground was as well arranged as any in England, but he urged the need for more members. In addition, he argued that until they played better cricket they could not expect much in the way of gate receipts although, of course, better cricket was only a matter of time. All his life Green was against the importation of cricketers from elsewhere, but recognised that Essex would have to follow the lead of other counties.

Accordingly the County acquired the services of James Burns for 1887, and he played for them until 1896. Burns, a right-handed batsman and occasional slow, left-arm bowler, was born in Liverpool; he had played for Lancashire in non-first-class matches, including one against Essex. He was a good soccer player and represented both West Bromwich and Notts County.

7. John Freeman, who played for Essex for 23 years. He was a middle order right-hand bat, wicket-keeper, occasional right-arm medium-pace bowler, but was never able to emulate the success his brother Tich Freeman achieved with Kent.

Another to make his debut for the County in 1887 was Edward Charles Freeman, the groundsman at Leyton. He is best remembered as the uncle of both John Robert, who was to give the County noble service for 23 years, and 'Tich' Freeman, who played for Essex Club and Ground before joining Kent. His son, Edward John, played 55 times for Essex at the beginning of the century without really establishing himself.

The efforts that Green had made, and was making, on behalf of Essex cricket were recognised by all, and the only note of dissent at the AGM was expressed by Mr Giller, who suggested that the professionals should be paid less and that the railway company should offer a better service.

The improvement that Green looked for on the playing side did not come. There were two creditable victories over Hampshire, but defeats at the hands of Derbyshire (twice), Somerset, Kent and Surrey suggested that Essex were still out of their depth in the top company. However, there were compensations. Bishop took 95 wickets, Bryan 41 and Pickett 40. Cyril Buxton hit 555 runs, including a memorable 79 out of 121 in the first innings against Surrey at The Oval. He batted for two hours and ten minutes, gave a faultless display against a strong attack and played what many considered to be the best innings seen at The Oval during the season. But perhaps the most significant event of the first two seasons at

Leyton was that Alfred Lord Tennyson wrote a poem in honour of the ground, though it was perhaps not one of the great man's most renowned works.

The financial problems persisted. At the beginning of the 1888 season, the Committee reported a deficit of £852 5s 8d, and there was a renewed plea for members. The gate receipts for the 1887 season had totalled £199 10s 7d, some £65 less than had been taken for the single match in which the Australians had featured the year before. Ratliff resigned as secretary and was succeeded by M P Betts.

Morton Peto Betts had been educated at Harrow, but he had failed to make the eleven. He had, however, played for both Middlesex and Kent, although he was better known in club cricket with Bickley Park, Streatham and Incogniti. His greatest fame and accomplishment was as a soccer player. He was one of the seven ex-public school men who established the FA Cup, and it was he, under the pseudonym of A H Chequer (A Harrow Chequer – an Old Harrovian Club), who scored the goal by which Wanderers beat Royal Engineers 1–0 at The Oval in the first Final, 1871/1–172. He later became a noted referee. Like Ratliff, he was to have a short tenure of the Essex secretaryship, his term of office lasting until 1890.

On the field, the County continued to hold its own without threatening the likes of Surrey or Leicestershire. George Littlewood, who had been Pilling's understudy at Lancashire, kept wicket in several matches, having been allowed to play against Surrey in 1887 even though he was not qualified. More interestingly, in the match at Leyton between the Parsees, on their second tour of England, and a Public Schools' side, a young fast bowler named C J Kortright of Tonbridge was on display. He was destined to become a legend in Essex cricket.

Charles Kortright's debut for Essex came in the following season, 1889. He was born at Ingatestone on 9 January 1871, and educated at Brentwood School and Tonbridge School, the latter of which he left with the reputation of being 'a very fast bowler with a high puzzling delivery and often very difficult to play. Ought to develop into a first class bowler.'

He joined the Brentwood Club and was startlingly successful, taking 89 wickets at six runs apiece in 1889 at the age of 18. His feats attracted the attention of the County Club and he was invited to play against Leicestershire at Leyton. The match began on 18 July, and Leics won the toss and batted first. The pitch was a little damp, and the visitors were shot out by Burns and Pickett for 121 in just over two hours. Kortright did not bowl. Lucas and Owen began the Essex innings with a stand of 85, and Hugh Owen went on to carry his bat for 153 out of a total of 295. Kortright, at number nine, did not score. Owen's century was the first made for the new Essex Club in county matches. He batted for just over $4\frac{1}{2}$ hours and,

8. *Charles Kortright, considered by many to be the fastest bowler of all time.*

although offering two chances, gave 'an otherwise irreproachable display of cricket'. Pickett took 7 for 15 and Leicestershire were beaten by an innings. Kortright was allowed two overs at the close and took the wicket of Mr H T Arnall-Thompson. He played in the next match, against Hertfordshire, scored 0 and 11 not out, and took a wicket. Apart from an unsuccessful appearance in the Colts' match at the end of the season, those were his only appearances for Essex in 1889.

Kortright moved to Hythe in Kent to learn the brewery trade. He played a vast amount of club cricket in Kent, resisted overtures from the hop county and, in the years to come, was to serve Essex with fire and passion.

Although Kortright's debut was noted with interest, the major acquisition in 1889 was that of Alfred Perry Lucas. Lucas was considered one of the great stylists of his generation. He was in the Cambridge side for four years and assisted Surrey until 1882. He played spasmodically for Middlesex from 1883 to 1888 when Green, his great friend and mentor, persuaded him to come to Essex, for whom he qualified by residence.

'Bunny' Lucas had been educated at Uppingham, Green's school, where he was coached by H H Stephenson. He was considered an outstanding prospect at school, and he was only 17 when, in 1874, he was picked to play for the Gentlemen of the South against the Players of the North. He hit 48 and 23 against some of the best professional bowling, and his class was never in doubt. He played five times for England, and, in later years, McLaren and Spooner were compared with him in style. *Wisden* said of him:

> A master of both back and forward play, he represented the strictest orthodoxy. No doubt if he had allowed himself a little licence he might have made more runs, but his method served him so well that right into middle age he kept up his form. It may fairly be said of him that no defensive batsman of any generation was more worth looking at. He played the ball so hard and his style was so irreproachable that one could watch him for hours without a moment of weariness.

Lucas was 32 when he made his debut for Essex against MCC at Leyton on 31 May 1889. He played his last match for Essex in 1907 when he was 50. The match against MCC in 1889 saw W G Grace's first appearance at Leyton, and it may well have been this match for which he asked Green payment for attendance, but that can only be conjecture. Lucas and Owen opened the Essex innings and began the match with a partnership of 185 in three hours. Owen was out for 89, but Lucas made 103. 'Everyone will be pleased to see him so appropriately signalise his first appearance for his new county,' wrote the editor of *Cricket*.

Essex, who fielded eight amateurs plus Burns, Littlewood and Cutts, reached 311, and MCC were bowled out for 174 and 116. Cutts, a left-arm fast to medium-pace bowler, was from Nottinghamshire and had been engaged for the season by the Wanstead Club. As he bowled Grace after the great man had scored 71, his debut in important matches was considered very promising. In fact, he was to play little in a season in which Pickett and Bishop were again the leading bowlers.

These two played a significant part in a surprise Essex victory over Surrey at Leyton in August, but well as things may have been progressing on the field, off the field all was far from well.

The annual report, delivered at the beginning of the season, had a sad opening with the announcement of the death of Sir Charles Du Cane, a long-serving vice-president, and a serious conclusion with the news that the Club was running at a great loss in spite of increased takings from football during the winter and the attraction that an American baseball team had provided. Green had given way as captain to Lucas, but as chairman of the Club he was to play a prominent part in steering Essex through the troubles that lay ahead.

On 17 October 1889, a Special General Meeting of the Club was held at the Great Eastern Hotel, Liverpool Street. E N Buxton presided and informed the gathering that the County faced a deficit which it was estimated would be £3851 13s 4d by the end of March the following year. Buxton felt that the problem had to be faced boldly and a remedy had to be found. 'They owed a debt of gratitude to Mr Green for all he had done, but although he had been extremely generous in the past, they could not reasonably expect him to do everything.' The bankers had been pressing, and money had to be raised by the end of the year or the Club would be wound up. An appeal was launched, and it was decided to issue debentures to the value of £5000, which would realise a four per cent interest per annum. The immediate response from the meeting was a total of £500 which included, inevitably, £100 from E N Buxton and £100 from C E Green.

The public reaction was encouraging. Functions were arranged in an attempt to raise money. One of the most notable was at Victoria Hall, Harlow, in February 1890, when Sam Deards, late captain of the Moor Hall Club, arranged an evening of entertainment which included a song composed and sung by himself. It does not read as one of the great literary achievements of the age, but it captures something of the spirit which enabled Essex cricket to survive.

Our late Captain's here, we're glad to see,
A more excellent captain could not be,
Who with such a Big heart there never was seen,
As in our Grand Old Captain C. E. Green.

Sam Deards was one of those magnificent characters whose energy and enthusiasm adorned the nineteenth century. He was an iron worker who took out many patents, including the breeze-block, and he was responsible for moving the Crystal Palace from Hyde Park to Sydenham. He made the first scoreboard at Leyton and was party to one that was constructed at Lord's. His grandson was the one who made the travelling Essex scoreboard of the post-Second World War period.

It was the efforts of people like Sam Deards that helped to save Essex in 1890, but the contributions of other counties should never be forgotten. The annual report which was presented at the AGM of the Club on 2 May 1890, told of the help that had been given and spoke optimistically of the future:

> Your Committee are glad to be able to announce to you that the Tramway is now running between Leyton Station, Lea Bridge and Walthamstow, passing the gates of the Ground, and thus making the latter more accessible to their supporters and intending visitors.
>
> The last six months have been a time of such grave anxiety to all concerned in the welfare of the Club, that it is gratifying to your Committee to be able to announce to you that thanks to the very generous manner in which their appeals have been responded to by Members and the public generally, the estimated deficit of £3,851, which at one time threatened to overwhelm the Club, has now been promised. To this result the Club is very largely indebted to the generous support afforded it by the M.C.C., Surrey, Lancashire and Middlesex County Clubs, as well as the handsome contributions voted it by the Corporation of the City of London and some of the City Companies.

For the first time, it seemed, Essex would start a season without debt, and for the moment the Club was saved. This position had not been reached without traumas. An Extraordinary General Meeting of the Club had been called on 16 January where the attendance was poor. Again E N Buxton presided and stated that the Committee had worked hard to raise the £3850 required for salvation, but that the sum raised stood at £2660. Green assured Buxton that he personally would make this up to £3000. The distressing aspect of the meeting was that 1000 members had failed to respond to the Club's plight, and the scheme for turning Essex County Cricket Club into a limited company had to be dropped. The solution adopted was to double the subscription for one year in order to raise the amount needed.

So Essex entered the 1890 season alive and in better heart. They also embarked upon the strongest list of fixtures yet. As they won only one of their ten matches, it may seem that they were a little too ambitious, but the season had much to commend it, wet as it was, in that it saw the

County fare well in two drawn games with Yorkshire and marked the development of F E Rowe, A S Johnston and Carpenter, and the coming of Walter Mead. It also witnessed a hat-trick by Pickett against Warwickshire when he dismissed Shilton, Pallett and Cresswell with successive balls. Pickett finished the season with 76 wickets.

Francis Rowe, son of a housemaster at Felsted, enjoyed a good year. He had captained the Marlborough XI for two seasons, but failed to get a blue at Cambridge. Arthur Johnston had played for Middlesex and made a rather inauspicious debut for Essex in 1889, but he was to give the middle order batting some substance for a few years. Carpenter and Mead, however, are to be numbered among the great Essex cricketers.

Herbert Carpenter had a fine cricketing pedigree. Born at Cambridge on 12 July 1869, he was the son of one of the very great batsmen of the United All-England and Cambridgeshire sides of the mid-19th century, Robert Carpenter. Herbert copied his father in style, strong, straight and correct in defence and excelling on the back foot in late cutting and forcing the ball off his legs. He first played for Essex in 1888, but initially

9. *Herbert Carpenter.*

made little impression. In 1890 he was engaged as one of the ground bowlers at Leyton, but for the County he bowled little in his infrequent appearances, although he topped the bowling averages with six wickets for 66 runs. His eight innings, once not out, brought him only 80 runs, but within a few years he was to move up the batting order and become an Essex rock, playing as late as 1920 when he was 51. His contact with the County was to continue, for his nephew, Jack O'Connor, moved into the side in 1921.

Walter Mead's association with Essex was brought about when he became professional to Broxbourne Cricket Club. He was born at Clapton, Middlesex, in April, 1868, and took part in a Middlesex Colts match when he was only 16. He was engaged by the Clapton Club, but his move to Broxbourne and to residence in Essex gave him qualification for the East Saxons. He made his debut for Essex in the first match of the 1890 season, against Surrey, at The Oval. F E Rowe was left on 98 not out as

10. *Walter Mead, who still holds the Essex record for the most wickets in a match when he took 17 for 119.*

Essex reached 262. Pickett took 6 for 73 as Surrey were bowled out for 127 and had to follow-on. Mead bowled only two overs in the first innings, but in the second, he sent down 37 and took 5 for 101. Surrey scored 431, and so Essex lost by 136 runs, having led by 135 on the first innings. Mead's first appearance was well received. 'He bowls with judgement, and fielded well, too, in addition.'

He played a big part in Essex's only win of the season which came at Derby in early August. Mead took 6 for 27 in Derbyshire's first innings, and Essex won by 8 wickets. Mead was to finish the season with 33 wickets at 16.15 runs each, a creditable performance, but one that was to fade into insignificance when compared with the years ahead when he became 'The Essex Treasure'.

Whilst other seasons and decades may merge into one, the 1890s have to be considered one year at a time, so tenuous was Essex's hold on existence. In March 1891, *Cricket* reviewed the forthcoming season with optimism:

> The prospects of Essex cricket for this year are, we are glad to learn, very good. All the old members of the team are available, and with Messrs C. D. Buxton, A. P. Lucas, R. C. Gosling, Rowe and Bishop, with Pickett, Burns, Littlewood and Carpenter, the county ought to make a good show. The financial position of the club, too, is more promising than it has hitherto been, and the ground is in splendid condition, having been well looked after by the head groundsman, E. C. Freeman. Mr Borradaile is now secretary in succession to Mr M. P. Betts.
>
> Essex have for some time been bowed down with debt, but thanks to the generosity of the leading county men and the whole-hearted efforts of Mr O. R. Borradaile, the new secretary, the East-end county is likely to take a new lease of life at the Leyton ground.

At the AGM, Green was more guarded. He emphasised that the Club still needed £1500 to put it on a solid financial basis, and he appealed to members to do their best to increase numbers. With A P Lucas unable to play in several matches because of business commitments, Cyril Buxton was to lead the side in what was to be his last season. There were two positive gains in that H M Taberer, the South African who was to captain his country in his one appearance for them in 1903, was to assist the County while he was at Oxford, and Oswell Robert Borradaile had been appointed secretary on 1 October 1890.

Borradaile remains one of the great men in the administration of Essex cricket, and it was to be his energy and enthusiasm, allied to that of C E Green, which was to save the Club from extinction over the next few years. He was a man of strong personality, courteous, kind and popular;

he gave the County stability in administration and endeavour for 31 years.

Born at Westminster in May 1859, he had been educated at Westminster School, but left too soon to win a place in the Eleven. A useful batsman and a medium-pace bowler, he excelled in club cricket and in minor matches for MCC. He played occasionally for the County. He left school to work in the Bank of England and spent nearly 11 years at Lloyd's. He captained Stoics Cricket Club for ten years and was their honorary secretary for 15, but above all he retained, to the end of his life, a passionate belief in Essex cricket.

Whatever the high hopes, the 1891 season did not begin auspiciously, Surrey winning by an innings at The Oval. There was, however, sensation in a Club and Ground match at Leyton at the beginning of June when Walker and Porter, neither of whom was to appear in the full County side, added 189 for the last wicket against Manor Park. News of this could have inspired the Essex team a few days later when they won a remarkable victory over Leicestershire at the Leyton Ground.

Johnston and Carpenter, the latter by now a regular opener, put on 49 for the first wicket, but the next eight wickets went down for only 43 runs, and it was left to Mead and Pickett, in a last wicket stand of 34, to take the home side to 126. Thanks to a bristling 76 from de Trafford, Leicestershire took a first innings lead of 46. Essex were still one run in arrears with one wicket down when the last day began, but they battled to 160, so leaving the visitors needing a mere 115 to win.

Pickett gave Essex early encouragement when he bowled Wheeler, but thereafter the game belonged to Walter Mead. In 19.1 five-ball overs, he took 9 for 23, eight clean bowled, and Essex won by 47 runs. Mead was a hero, and a collection in aid of his wonderful performance brought him £5 10s, a worthy amount.

Mead had been engaged as a bowler at Lord's. His strength was that, even on a perfect wicket, he could turn the ball sharply at his medium pace. He hurried the batsmen in their shots, and although he had a particularly effective leg-break, it was the variety of his bowling that accounted for his success.

This fine victory over Leicestershire was followed by another remarkable win when Hampshire were beaten by an innings at Southampton. Essex were without Buxton, Lucas, Owen and Johnston, but Carpenter gave them a good start with an innings of 65. The outstanding performance, however, came in an eighth wicket stand of 244 between Pickett and Kortright. Kortright, 20 years old, played only two games for Essex during the season and bowled only eight overs, taking two wickets, but his hitting against Hampshire was spectacular. In 1¾ hours, he hit four sixes, a five and 22 fours to reach 158, the highest individual score recorded for

Essex at that time. Henry Pickett made 114 in $1\frac{1}{2}$ hours and Essex were all out for 424, scored at 113 an hour. In all, 543 runs were scored and 15 wickets fell on the opening day. Pickett took nine wickets and Mead eight, and Essex won by an innings and 40 runs inside two days.

It was Mead and Pickett again, with ten and nine wickets respectively, who bowled Essex to a nine-wicket win over Derbyshire, and these three victories roused the attention of the cricket world. 'Long Stop' in *Cricket Gossip* gave the first hint of what those keeping the game alive in the county most wanted to hear: 'I am delighted to see Essex playing up in such gallant style this season. A few more such victories as have just been gained over Leicestershire and Derbyshire will produce a third first-class county in the metropolitan district. Mead and Pickett are doing grand work both as bowlers and batsmen. With careful nursing there is a great future for the East-end county.'

However, success did not continue unabated. Hampshire won the return contest at Leyton by 21 runs in spite of the bowling of Mead and Pickett, and Lancashire, too, survived Mead's 8 for 67 to win by nine wickets at Old Trafford. Warwickshire were beaten in a day and a half, in what was to be the last win of the season.

The matches against Surrey and Leicestershire were ruined by rain, as was the game against Warwickshire at Edgbaston, but not before Lucas had hit 113 and shared a second wicket stand of 168 with Johnston, who made 86. The season ended with defeats at the hands of Lancashire, when Essex were bowled out for 35 in their first innings, and Derbyshire, but these losses could not detract from what had been a year of great promise. Mead's 76 wickets and Pickett's 68 showed where their strength lay.

The euphoria which attended the 1891 season was quickly dispelled. Buxton's tragic suicide heralded a season of gloom which was to end in crisis and despair. But there were some successes on the field, with Charles Kortright leaping to prominence as a fast bowler of distinction. In the opening match at The Oval, he took 3 for 26, his three wickets being captured in the space of four balls. Brockwell was bowled with a yorker on leg stump, which sent the ball spinning back over Kortright's head and breaking in its flight. Essex were beaten, however.

In the return match, at Leyton, F E Rowe hit 129 and he and H M Taberer put on 164 for the seventh wicket, but Essex were still denied victory. Kortright took 36 wickets at an average of 11.80 during the season, and three times took eight in an innings, but wins over Hampshire, Derbyshire and MCC, all at Leyton, were all that came the way of Essex. A P Lucas had taken over from Buxton as captain, but he was not always available, and the County moved to the close of the season with a sense of foreboding as the reality of the financial position became apparent.

C M Tebbutt, another destined to give both work and financial support to the County with unstinting regularity, succeeded Read as honorary treasurer, and in November 1892, an Extraordinary General Meeting was called. Charles Green announced that the Club was overdrawn £1300, and that a further sum in excess of £2000 was needed if the Club was to survive. He felt that the salvation could only come from those at the meeting, for they alone seemed interested in the future of Essex cricket. A proposal was made that the Club should be wound up, but that proposal was not seconded, and Essex County Cricket Club was given a stay of execution until January 1893.

The Special General Meeting reconvened at that time and Borradaile published an open letter in its wake:

> Referring to the recent meeting of the Essex County Cricket Club, you will much oblige by inserting in your valuable paper the following facts in reference to this club. The meeting having decided that it was absolutely necessary to obtain a guarantee fund of at least £3,000, and failing this that steps would be taken to wind up the club, a resolution was passed that unless the above mentioned guarantee was obtained on or before 1st February, 1893, it would be useless to attempt to carry the club on any longer. The sum of £2,237 1s. has been already promised in guarantees and donations (as per 1st herewith), in addition to which the last £500 (conditional on the remainder being raised) has been liberally promised by a gentleman who does not desire his name to appear, and I appeal through you most earnestly to all sportsmen and more particularly to those interested in Essex affairs to assist in finding the additional amount of guarantee required, before the above date. It would indeed be a standing reproof to all sportsmen were the County Club now allowed to disappear when within a measurable distance of the required goal. I shall be pleased to furnish further particulars to any interested in the club.

Two men, above all others, were responsible for saving Essex County Cricket Club at this point of fearful crisis, C E Green and C M Tebbutt. This point was made at the AGM at the Great Eastern Hotel on 4 May where the Committee was able to announce that the necessary sum had been raised. Much help had come from outside the county, but it was the financial support of Green and Tebbut, when the Club was in the greatest difficulties, that had made survival possible. Revenue from football matches played on the Leyton Ground during the winter had been most helpful, but membership, 925 gentlemen and 78 ladies, still stood well short of the 1500 that was needed if the Club was to be economically viable and was to avoid the continuing crises which threatened its existence.

For the time being, however, the County Club was safe, and their continuance had made it possible for Kortright to resist overtures from Kent. He and Mead bowled well in the opening match, at The Oval, but Essex lost by an innings.

Tom Russell had now taken over as the regular wicket-keeper, although he had first played some five years earlier when he was barely 20. In the match against Yorkshire, at Leyton, on 8, 9 and 10 June 1893, Essex gave an outing to a young amateur who had been performing well for Clapton, Charles Percy McGahey. McGahey scored seven and two, but, at the age of 21, he had had his first taste of county cricket; in the years to come no man was to give more of his life to Essex cricket, nor to prove so rich in character.

The man who was stealing the headlines at the time, however, was C J Kortright. Playing for Hythe, where he was still learning the brewery trade, he took five School of Musketry wickets in five balls, and the speed of his bowling was becoming renowned throughout the land. When

11. *Charles McGahey, who had a long association with Essex. After his retirement from the game he became the Club's official scorer.*

Essex went to Sheffield in July, Kortright took eight wickets and Mead 10 for 81 as Yorkshire were beaten by seven wickets in two days. This was a momentous victory and had an important influence on future events. Essex, having made 140, thanks almost entirely to a ninth wicket stand between Kortright, 20, and Mead, 66 not out, bowled out Yorkshire for 41 and 127. Lord Hawke was not playing in the match, but he later remarked that any side that could bowl Yorkshire out for under 50 should be playing in the first-class championship, and his support meant much.

Less than a fortnight later Essex gave another outstanding display which helped to hasten their elevation to first-class status. The Australians had been scheduled to play Cambridge Past and Present at Leyton, but as Cambridge found it impossible to assemble a representative side, Essex took over the fixture. There was some scepticism as to how they would fare in such esteemed company, but they performed admirably. The Australians made 250 and 141, and Essex, in an even batting display, scored 237 and 32 for 1, having been left only half an hour in which to score more than 150. 'The County eleven deserve to be highly congratulated on their excellent show,' said the correspondent of *Cricket*, but if one man deserved congratulations above all others, it was Walter Mead.

In the first innings, Mead took the first nine Australian wickets to fall at a personal cost of 136. He followed this with 8 for 69 in the second innings. It was a magnificent performance by the short, stocky, dark-moustached medium-pacer who always bowled with a twinkle in his eye and took the greatest joy in beating a batsman with his mixture of off-breaks and leg-breaks. A collection on the ground realised £12, and Henry Pickett, who had taken the other three Australian wickets, was given a third of the collection.

The Essex triumphs continued. A weakened Surrey side was routed at Leyton. Essex made only 62 and 170, but Surrey were bowled out for 54 and 76. The honours this time went to Kortright, who took 8 for 29 and 5 for 35. Twelve times he hit the stumps. Kortright was one of the season's great successes. He was described as 'fast, very fast', and at the beginning of the season he had been elected a member of MCC, so that he could be considered for the match against the Australians. More importantly, he was selected for The Gentlemen against the Players at Lord's, the highest honour outside Test cricket. He responded to that selection by taking 7 for 73 and 2 for 67 as the match was drawn. When he bowled Briggs in the first innings he sent a stump reeling back some 17 yards.

Mead's excursions into first-class cricket were equally successful. Playing for MCC against both Universities, he took 26 wickets in three matches and finished second in the national averages. Kortright had eight wickets for MCC against the Australians to add to his nine for the Gentlemen, and he finished 11th with only one amateur, C M Wells, the Cambridge spinner, above him.

The Essex batting had also proved resilient. With, for example, Lucas and Russell adding 165 for the ninth wicket against Hampshire, the County had demonstrated forcibly that they had a side of first-class talent. All that they awaited now was the call to first-class status.

In April 1894, a meeting of the captains of the nine first-class counties resolved to lay the following before the MCC at their annual meeting:

> That the matches played by the following four counties: Derbyshire, Warwickshire, Essex and Leicestershire against the nine counties at present styled first-class, and also against one another and against the MCC, should be regarded as first-class matches, and the records of the players engaged in these matches shall be included in the list of first-class averages.

The resolution was signed by Lord Hawke, W G Grace, J Shuter, S M J Woods, J A Dixon, F Marchant, W L Murdoch, A J Webbe and A N Hornby. It was accepted by the MCC the following week, and from 1894 onwards Essex became a first-class county.

At the AGM of the County, Green announced that MCC had appointed all the Essex County professionals as groundsmen at Lord's, and when he referred to the elevation of Essex to first-class status there was loud cheering and sustained applause. Green, to whom this elevation meant so much and for which he had worked so hard, hoped that 'the sport-loving community of the home county would come to the fore, and by supporting the club, prove that Essex was not to be left behind.'

Doubts still persisted. The membership was still more than 500 short of the number required for economic viability, and the Committee recognised their gratitude to C M Tebbut, who had advanced £2000 so that the debt to the bank and other creditors could be paid.

Essex were not, as yet, participants in the County Championship, but their cricket had now begun in earnest, and on Monday, Tuesday and Wednesday, 14, 15 and 16 May 1894, they engaged in their first ever first-class match, against Leicestershire, at the County Ground, Leyton.

Leicestershire won the toss and batted first. They began badly, and were 37 for 5 before de Trafford found a reliable partner in Chapman and 84 were added. The Leicestershire captain batted 105 minutes for his 70, but after his departure the visitors had little to offer.

In reply, Essex gave a wretched batting performance and were all out in under an hour and a half so that Leicestershire were batting again before the close. Essex had been wrecked by the fast-medium pace of Arthur Pougher, and now it was Pougher, who played once for England against

South Africa in 1891–92, who devastated them with the bat. In two hours and 20 minutes he hit 109, and with Holland, dropped early on, batting 20 minutes longer for his fifty, Essex were left to make 342 to win.

They closed the second day at 162 for 4, a most spirited display, with Owen making a faultless 76 in 1½ hours. The remaining batsmen played pluckily on the final morning, but Pougher was again in fine form, and Essex were beaten by 68 runs.

It was an important event in Essex cricket history and one that we should record fully. As was the custom, amateurs are distinguished from professionals by according them the title of Mr. We have made brief mention of all the Essex players save Henry Hailey, a right-handed batsman from Bow who did not appear for the County until 1891, when he was nearly 40 years old. His first-class career was restricted to two seasons, and he died in Southend in 1932, aged 81.

Whatever encouragement could be gained both from that initial first-class performance and the achievements of the previous season, it could not sustain the County in the coming weeks. Rain saved Essex from defeat by Warwickshire at Leyton, but could not save them at Edgbaston. Tom Richardson, the England fast bowler, took all ten Essex first innings wickets when Surrey won by an innings and 261 runs at The Oval. The only Essex batsman to reach double figures while Richardson was wreaking havoc was Reginald Burrell, who made 31 on his debut.

The only win of the season came at the beginning of July, when a weakened Oxford University side was beaten by nine wickets at Leyton. Mead had 13 wickets in the match, but the hero was Hugh Owen, who hit 109 and 86 not out. Owen's hundred, the first first-class century hit for Essex, was the County's only three-figured score of the season.

There were some individual performances which compensated, in part, for the lack of team success. Maurice Berkley, a slow right-arm bowler, who was the son of the Rector of Navestock, made his debut against Yorkshire at Halifax. He bowled Wainwright with his first delivery and had Mounsey caught with his second. He finished with 6 for 50, but after taking one wicket in the next match, against Hampshire, he only played one more first-class match for Essex and went into the Church.

Other successes were of a less eminent nature. McGahey and Druce, for Leyton against Edmonton, facing a total of 179 with only an hour and 20 minutes left, won the match without losing their wickets. McGahey, as yet, was unable to reproduce such form for the County, and he made only 91 runs in ten innings. Kortright and Owen were the only Essex batsmen to average more than 20 for the season, and the bowling again rested heavily on Mead and Kortright, with Pickett taking only 11 wickets. It was an uncomfortable first season of first-class cricket. Had Essex participated in the County Championship, however, under the

Leyton, 14, 15 and 16 May 1894

Essex v Leicestershire

Leicestershire	1st innings		2nd innings	
†Mr C E de Trafford	c Kortright b Mead	70	run out	8
T H Warren	run out	0	lbw b Burns	21
J Holland	b Kortright	12	b Burns	50
W Tomlin	b Kortright	1	c Mead b Kortright	14
A D Pougher	b Mead	5	(6) not out	109
F Hassall	c and b Mead	0	(7) c Russell b Pickett	13
M Chapman	c Burns b Mead	34	(5) b Burns	15
W Finney	b Mead	0	b Kortright	0
Mr F W Stocks	b Kortright	0	b Kortright	0
*J P Whiteside	not out	4	b Pickett	27
F Randon	b Mead	5	c Hailey b Pickett	0
		0	b 9 lb 1	10
		131		267

	O.	M.	R.	W.	O.	M.	R.	W.
Kortright	18	2	41	3	28	3	90	3
Mead	19.3	6	49	6	39	15	70	—
Pickett	9	1	18	—	23.3	5	44	3
Burns	7	—	23	—	18	5	24	3
Carpenter					9	5	10	—
Owen					1	—	4	—
Lucas					3	—	15	—

Fall of wickets

1–0	2–28	3–30	4–37	5–37	6–121	7–121	8–122	9–124
1–12	2–48	3–77	4–104	5–149	6–170	7–175	8–175	9–265

Essex	1st innings		2nd innings	
H A Carpenter	b Pougher	20	b Pougher	0
J Burns	b Pougher	0	b Randon	36
Mr H Hailey	b Randon	7	(5) c Pougher b Finney	35
†Mr A P Lucas	b Finney	6	b Pougher	7
Mr H G P Owen	b Randon	5	(3) b Pougher	76
*T M Russell	b Pougher	7	lbw b Pougher	26
E C Freeman	b Pougher	0	c Tomlin b Pougher	12
Mr C P McGahey	st Whiteside b Pougher	3	b Pougher	20
Mr C J Kortright	c Holland b Pougher	7	c Chapman b Pougher	25
W Mead	b Randon	1	c Chapman b Pougher	14
H Pickett	not out	0	not out	20
	lb 1	1	b 1 lb 1	2
		57		273

	O.	M.	R.	W.	O.	M.	R.	W.
Pougher	18	7	29	6	40.3	19	60	8
Randon	15.3	6	20	3	36	9	98	1
Finney	2	—	7	1	14	3	55	1
Stocks					7	1	33	—
Hassall					3	—	25	—

Fall of wickets

1–3	2–20	3–34	4–38	5–46	6–46	7–48	8–56	9–57
1–2	2–97	3–119	4–126	5–169	6–185	7–199	8–239	9–242

Umpires – W F Collishaw and H Holmes

Leicestershire won by 68 runs

† Captain * Wicket-keeper

existing regulations, they would have finished above Gloucestershire and Sussex and level with Nottinghamshire.

In October 1894 MCC issued a circular which stated that, at the request of the counties, they would in future regulate the county championship, and that 14 first-class counties, including Essex, would contest it in 1895. The system that the MCC adopted was to award one point for each win and deduct one for each loss. The only stipulation on the competing counties was that each must play a minimum of eight matches home and away. It was this ruling which nearly cost Essex their newly-won status.

When the county secretaries met in December, Essex had been able to arrange matches with only six other counties. It was the 'sportsmanlike attitude of Middlesex and Somersetshire at the meeting of county secretaries which enabled Essex to secure the requisite number of matches to qualify for inclusion in the front rank of counties'.

Once again Essex had been saved. The loan from Tebbutt of £2000 still propped them up financially, but 1097 gentlemen and 112 ladies still left the County short of the 1500 members that they needed if they were to continue. The opening of a new railway station near the Leyton ground gave hope that this number would be attained, but for the present the attention was on Essex's first venture into the county championship.

CHAPTER 7

First Steps in the County Championships: 1895–1903

Pressure of business prevented Lucas from continuing as captain when Essex entered the county championship in 1895, and he was succeeded by Hugh Glendwr Palmer Owen. Owen, a right-handed batsman and occasional medium-pace bowler, had first played for Essex in 1880 when he was 21. He was privately educated before going up to Cambridge where, in spite of doing well for his college, Corpus Christi, he was given little opportunity for the University side and failed to get a blue. Born in Somerset and resident in Derbyshire, for he was a master at Trent College for nine years, he qualified for Essex by means of family home. He played all his county cricket for Essex.

A large, heavy man, Hugh Owen was a steady and reliable batsman, but it was as a captain that he most proved his worth. He was genial, ever smiling and popular, and in some measure, he gave birth to the sense of fun that has permeated Essex cricket for over a century.

His first season as skipper was a marked success, and, after a hesitant start, Essex acquitted themselves well in their first year in the county championship. A pre-season practice match against Sixteen Colts saw Mead take 9 for 24 in the first innings, when the Colts made 54, and Kortright take 12 for 21 in the second, when they made 59. Such form augured well, and both bowlers were to have excellent seasons. Indeed, for Walter Mead, it was a season of unending success. He took 120 wickets for Essex, and, in all first-class matches, captured 179 wickets, a feat which has not been bettered by an Essex bowler in the 91 years since, although Peter Smith took 172 wickets, all for the County, in 1947.

The opening championship match was at Edgbaston on 6, 7 and 8 May. Owen won the toss, and Essex occupied the whole of the first day, scoring 350 for 5. George Higgins, who had made his debut the previous season, hit 118, and Burns hit 114. These were the first centurions of the season, and, of course, Essex's first centurions in the county championship. Owen had earlier begun the day with a fine innings of 64. On the second morning Essex reached 410.

Kortright then took 8 for 94, as Warwickshire were out for 259. They followed on and lost Santall before the close, but on the last day, they reached 344 for 5 and the match was drawn. Nevertheless, Essex had accomplished a great deal in this opening encounter, and there was general pleasure at their good showing:

> Though the Essex and Warwickshire match ended in a draw, the very fine show of the Metropolitan county in its first innings of the season must tell very favourably on the prospects, financial and otherwise, of the over the border team. And everyone will be glad to see them doing well, for they have long struggled against adversity, and it is a fitting award to the labours of the few gentlemen who have fought so hard to keep their county's head above water, that the long score of 410 should give them so good a send off in the season of 1895.

At The Oval, a week later, came a third Essex century when Carpenter hit a magnificent 145 in 270 minutes, but Surrey scored 448, with Bobby Abel making 217, and won by an innings. It is characteristic of the age that the first day's play in this match, which ended with Essex 231, Surrey 37 for 1, could be described as 'batting generally void of interest, though the wicket was very easy, the run getting only averaged about 50 runs an hour. Carpenter's batting overshadowed all the rest.'

A win against MCC at Lord's was a boost to morale, but Middlesex won at Leyton by five wickets. This was followed by another defeat at Leyton when Leicestershire won by 75 runs, yet this match is remembered more in the history of Essex than ever it will be in the annals of the midland county. One turns to *Cricket* for a contemporary account of this match which was played on 3, 4 and 5 June:

> Essex supporters took advantage of the Bank Holiday on Monday to visit Leyton to the number of about 8,000. A. P. Lucas for the first time this season assisted his side and C. E. de Trafford was once more able

> to play. The feature of the day was the remarkable achievement of Pickett, who did for Essex what Richardson last June did against them, taking the whole ten wickets of Leicestershire. They cost him 32 runs only, and though helped by the ground, which was very fast and somewhat fiery, his success was due to grand bowling. He kept a splendid length throughout. A collection made for him on the ground realised nearly £20. The batting of Leicestershire calls for little comment.

Pickett's 10 for 32 remains an Essex record. In 1949 at Clacton, Trevor Bailey took 10 for 90 against Lancashire, but Henry Pickett's analysis remains unapproached. Pickett was 33 at the time and was to play only two more seasons.

It will surprise few who have followed the vagaries of Essex cricket to learn that, although Kortright took 8 for 63 in Leicestershire's second innings, Essex were beaten by 75 runs. McGahey's second innings of 54 was the only batting of note on the Essex side.

Pickett's ten wickets consisted of six bowled (Chapman, Tomlin, Stone, Lorrimer, Woodcock and Whiteside), Holland and Pougher caught behind, and de Trafford and Geeson caught by Kortright and Mead respectively.

Heartening and meritorious as Pickett's performance was, Essex were still without a championship win, and there looked little chance of break ing the duck at the start of the game against Somerset at Leyton on 13 June. Somerset batted first and went off at a tremendous rate. Having lost Hill at 37, they raced to 90 in the first hour.

At 93, Richard Palairet was caught behind off Pickett, but Somerset passed 150 with only four men out. Then Mead and Pickett brought about a collapse, and the visitors were out for 191, the last five wickets falling for nine runs.

Essex opened with Carpenter and F L Fane, an Oxford freshman who had done well at Charterhouse. Frederick Luther Fane's father had played for Essex in the early days at Brentwood, but the son, making his first-class debut in this match against Somerset, was destined to outshine the father. He gave early indication of his ability when he and Carpenter scored 46 in the first 35 minutes of the Essex innings. Fane was eventually second man out when he hit across a straight ball with the score at 75. He had made a most promising 36.

The Essex middle order faded, and they ended the day at 120 for 7. Next morning, Mead played bravely, hit 35 not out, and Essex got to within ten of the Somerset total.

Once again Somerset began well before collapsing. They reached 138 for 4, and were then all out for 177.

In search of 188 to win, Essex began dreadfully. Owen opened with Carpenter and scored only one. Fane played a wretched shot and was out without scoring. Essex were two wickets down for one run. Slowly but surely McGahey and Carpenter gave Essex hope with a solid stand. McGahey's innings ended when he had made 52, and when Higgins went for three, Essex closed the second day on 101 for 4. Carpenter had batted for 80 minutes, and his 42 did not include a single boundary.

He added ten more runs the next day, but his dismissal at 121 again threw Essex into crisis. Burns and Mead joined in a vigorous stand of 44. Mead added a score of 33 to his 35 not out of the first innings and his analyses of 5 for 64 and 5 for 62. Walter Mead's greatest attribute as a cricketer was that he always produced runs and wickets when they were most needed.

But to the dismay of Essex supporters, Mead, Burns for 18, and Russell for 0 were all out with the score at 165. Twenty-three runs were still needed, and just two wickets remaining. Kortright and Bull came together and, in forthright style, took Essex to their first victory in the County Championship. It was 15 June 1895, and whatever has happened since, it is a day that should never be forgotten.

Essex approached the next match at Leyton, against Warwickshire, with confidence, and when Fane and Carpenter began with 80 in 70 minutes the confidence soared higher. Unfortunately, in a wretched batting display, Essex collapsed to 136 all out, and in spite of fine bowling by Mead, Warwickshire took a first innings lead of 34. The Essex second innings was described in the press as a 'complete fiasco'. Five batsmen failed to score, and McGahey, Higgins and Mead scored 92 of the 114 runs made from the bat. Essex were out for 118, but Warwickshire were troubled, inevitably, by Mead and lost seven wickets in scoring the 88 that brought them victory.

When Hampshire came to Leyton on the Thursday the Essex batting showed no improvement. Essex were out for 94, but Mead and Pickett restricted the Hampshire lead to 17. Burns had been left out to accommodate Henry Preece, an amateur who had done well for Bees Cricket Club. Preece hit 49 in Essex's second innings after Carpenter and Owen had begun with a bright stand of 98. Preece was to play only one more game for Essex. A lecturer at King's College, London, he lost his sight when still young.

Kortright and Russell hit lustily, and the last three wickets added 139 runs. Hampshire, needing 286 to win, were bowled out for 178 to give Essex a second championship win. Pickett bowled with remarkable stamina in the second Hants innings to take 6 for 55.

Yorkshire brought Essex down to earth in the next match, but then came the visit to Taunton. The game began on Thursday, 11 July. Somerset batted first and scored a brisk 246. Mead and Kortright each took four wickets. Essex had $2\frac{1}{4}$ hours batting on the first evening. This produced the most exciting play of the day. Owen and Fane were dismissed, but Carpenter hit 135 not out in a score of 224 for 2.

Carpenter's great innings ended when he was run out next morning. His 153 had occupied 155 minutes and he hit a five and 25 fours. McGahey, usually the impetuous one, batted an hour and five minutes longer than Carpenter for his 147, but 'A. P. Lucas played the best cricket of the match, and made no mistake in a great innings of 135, which included a six and 18 fours.' In two hours, Russell, at number nine, hit 99, and Essex reached 692, 'by far their best score and ranked third in a county match'.

Somerset, 38 for 1 at the close of the second day, were bowled out for 129 on the last morning, Kortright taking 7 for 57.

Essex's 692 was made in approximately 425 minutes, and it remains their highest score in first-class cricket.

Lucas, in fact, hit only two first-class centuries for Essex, of which this innings at Taunton was the higher. The Essex innings, not unnaturally, caused a great stir, although one critic suggested that Essex were 'perhaps the last county from which the feat might be expected'.

It was the bowlers who dominated the next match, against Derbyshire at Leyton. Kortright had match figures of 13 for 103 as Essex won by 134 runs. Kortright had, by now, severed his links with the brewery trade and had raised enough capital from his share in the Hythe Brewery to enjoy the life of a gentleman cricketer for the remainder of his career. He also had a particular liking for Derbyshire batsmen and consistently wrought havoc among them over the years.

Hampshire halted Kortright and the Essex run of success with victory at Southampton, where Mead took 8 for 67 and 9 for 52, and still saw his side lose by 171 runs. He then had match figures of 12 for 103 at Leicester, but rain helped the home side to avoid defeat. They were 56 for 8, chasing 164, when the match ended.

Surrey, destined to be champions again, came to Leyton at the beginning of August. A crowd of 6000 packed into the ground on the first day and, at lunch, Bobby Abel and Tom Hayward were in command with Surrey on 129 for 1. In a dynamic spell of bowling in the afternoon, Charles Kortright clean bowled Hayward, Druce, Abel, Lohmann, Walter Read and Street in the space of 15 balls at a personal cost of four runs. He finished with 7 for 72, but Surrey, who had left out Tom Richardson in view of the strong engagements that were crowding upon them, still won by 201 runs.

Rain ruined the game against Middlesex at Lord's, and Essex then travelled to Harrogate to play Yorkshire. The White Rose county had

Essex v Somerset
Taunton, 11, 12 and 13 July 1895

Somerset 246 (Mr R B Porch 85 not out, Mr C J Kortright 4 for 58, W Mead 4 for 100) and 129 (Mr C J Kortright 7 for 57).

Essex		
†Mr H G P Owen	c Gamlin b Woods	37
H A Carpenter	run out	153
Mr F L Fane	b Tyler	12
Mr C P McGahey	b Fowler	147
Mr J F Bawtree	c Fowler b Tyler	47
J Burns	c Woods b Tyler	0
Mr A P Lucas	c L C H Palairet b Tyler	135
Mr C J Kortright	c Woods b R C N Palairet	31
*T M Russell	c sub b Woods	99
W Mead	st R C N Palairet b Tyler	0
H Pickett	not out	1
	b 22 lb 7 w 1	30
		692

	O.	M.	R.	W.
Tyler	60.3	9	215	5
Woods	45	5	171	2
Gamlin	23	6	82	—
L C H Palairet	20	7	50	—
Fowler	25	7	68	1
Porch	4	1	17	—
Evans	3	1	5	—
R C N Palairet	12	1	54	1

Fall of wickets
1–80 2–97 3–257 4–358 5–358 6–442
7–449 8–683 9–691

Essex won by an innings and 317 runs

† Captain * Wicket-keeper

just beaten the formidable Surrey side and were very much in contention for the championship. No one believed that Essex would trouble them in any way, and so it proved to be at the start. Peel and Hirst bowled unchanged and Essex were out for 87, but by the end of the day, they were batting again.

Yorkshire reached 56 for 2, but Mead bowled quite splendidly, and the home side were bowled out for 117. At 25 for 3, Essex were in the greatest peril, but Johnston and Bull, who had seemingly been put in as a night-watchman, hit 62 in 45 minutes. McGahey played an innings of great resolution, sound in defence, but quick to attack. In 65 minutes, he hit 55 and was unbeaten when Hunter stumped Pickett off Peel to end the Essex second innings for 165.

Needing 136 to win, Yorkshire reached 86 for 2, but magnificent bowling, especially by Mead, saw seven wickets fall for 16 runs. Tunnicliffe swung at Mead and was caught on the boundary. Lord Hawke was yorked by Kortright. Wainwright was stumped and Hirst bowled. At 102 for 9, Hunter joined Mounsey. They batted most pluckily, but with the score on 119, Hunter was caught and bowled by Kortright, and Essex had caused something of a sensation in county cricket.

Yorkshire were to finish third in the Championship. Essex, after drawing their last game with Derbyshire, were equal eighth with Somerset. Hampshire, Sussex, Leicestershire, Nottinghamshire and Kent finished below them. It was an eminently satisfactory first season in the Championship and it had seen two records established which have remained to this day.

In reviewing the season, 'Incog', in *Lillywhite's Cricketers' Annual*, said:

> Mead's bowling and Carpenter's batting were among the very best features of the season. In Mr. F. G. Bull Essex found a young player of considerable promise. It was not the season for slow bowlers, but on wickets which help the ball he is sure to be of use, and with more experience ought to develop into a very useful all-round cricketer.

For Essex, Carpenter had scored 976 runs, average 30.50, and his appearances for MCC raised his aggregate to 1087, an outstanding achievement.

Frederick George Bull was indeed an off-break bowler of exceptional promise, and that promise was to be realised in the next four years, although his career was to be all too short. He took only 15 wickets at more than 26 runs each in 1895, so that 'Incog's' prediction showed a deep perception of the game.

Bull was to come to the fore the following season when he took 70 wickets, and Essex rose to fifth place, winning five and losing four of their 12 matches. This was a reduction on the previous season, and no games were played against Middlesex or Somerset, so that Essex qualified for the championship with the minimum number of encounters.

The 1896 season had begun with another display of liberality from Charles Green. He paid for Maurice Read and Bobby Abel to spend three weeks coaching youngsters at Leyton. No football was played on the ground during the winter, and the whole emphasis was now on a successful cricket club.

The beginning of the season did not augur well. In the match against the Australians, Mead took 5 for 68, but the tourists won by seven wickets, and the comments on the Essex performance were not favourable. 'Although the Essex team may prove to be strong somewhat later in the season, its members are at present a little too diffident to be able to do themselves justice.'

The County revived quickly, for in the next match, at Lord's, Kortright and Mead bowled unchanged, and MCC were out for 41. Kortright had 6 for 23, 10 for 57 in a match which Essex won by an innings. But the championship programme did not begin well. Abel, having been dropped by Bull off Kortright when 2, hit 231, to guide Surrey to an innings victory at The Oval. In the Essex side for the first time was Percival Albert Perrin, who was to play 525 matches for the County and to score over 29,000 runs in a career which was to last until 1928, when he was 52 years old.

'Peter' Perrin was born in Hackney and had trials for Middlesex, playing for their 2nd XI. He was an untutored batsman, a natural cricketer who gained experience and knowledge by playing club cricket in Tottenham. He was ever thoughtful about the game, and his astute appreciation of a player's worth was to make him an invaluable Test selector in the years before the Second World War.

Few could have had a more awesome baptism in first-class cricket than Perrin. He was nearly two weeks short of his 20th birthday, and he was confronted by Richardson, Lockwood and Haywood on their own pitch. In a courageous uphill battle, Perrin scored 52. Coincidentally, he was to end his first-class career with a fifty against Oxford University 32 years later. In that first season, Perrin was to score 719 runs for Essex, average 28.76. This placed him second to Owen. He also hit a maiden first-class hundred, 139 against Warwickshire at Edgbaston in a match which Essex won.

More than six feet tall, gaunt, indifferent to what he wore, Perrin became a distinct personality whom spectators watched with interest and delight. He was, as Tom Pearce has remarked, a bluff character, but there was an honesty in his approach to the game which was appealing. His friend, Home Gordon, asserted that Perrin was devoid of self-consciousness, that he said little, listened much and always got his own way because his counsel was the wisest.

He had his own peculiar style and could dominate an attack. He was at his best against fast bowling, was troubled most by slow left-arm spin, but cut productively and prettily against everyone. Essentially a forward player when he began an innings, he scored heavily off the back foot as his stay at the wicket lengthened. It was nothing unusual to see fast bowlers place three or four men on the boundary in an effort to curb his strong driving. He invariably batted at number three and very often had to contend with the opposing attack at its most hostile.

He was a consistent and correct player, and as he scored more than 1000 runs in 18 different seasons, he earned the title of 'the best batsman who never played for England', although his team-mate, 'Bob' Carpenter, could also lay claim to be so labelled. That Perrin never played for England is usually attributed to his slowness in the field. This uncertainty as a fielder has been much overstressed. He was not an active fieldsman, but he was a first-rate catcher in the slips. *Wisden*, in the obituary to Perrin in 1946, drew attention to this fact. 'Heavy on his feet, he could not move quickly to the ball, and this deficiency, though he would hold any catch within his long reach, prevented him from ever appearing in a Test match or for Gentlemen against Players.'

Wisden errs badly here, for Perrin was chosen for the Gentlemen against the Players at The Oval in his first season, 1896, when no fewer than five Essex players were in the match: Perrin, Bull, Kortright, Mead and Carpenter. This was a fine tribute to a county who, only two years earlier, had found it difficult to get fixtures.

The hero of the match was Bull, who took 8 for 94 in the Players' first innings. The Gentlemen were left to make 137 to win but, until the arrival of Perrin, they struggled. Only Grace, who carried his bat for 53, looked to be in form. Perrin hit 32, but when Bull, at number ten, was bowled, the scores were level. Lewis, the last man, who 'as a batsman backs up well', scrambled the necessary single.

Perrin played again for the Gentlemen, at Lord's, in 1906, and was invited to play in 1914 but declined. His fielding was something of a handicap, but he was quick to laugh at himself. When asked once if it were true that he had stopped one of Hobbs's boundaries at The Oval he replied: 'Oh, yes. Mind you, they ran eight.'

He played a decisive innings when Essex beat Yorkshire, the champion county, by four wickets. Fane and Carpenter failed, but Perrin hit a fine fifty. Kortright's furious spell of 5 for 56 in the second innings set up the win.

Against Leicestershire, at Leyton, Perrin hit 52 and 37 not out, but it was Owen and Mead who were the real heroes of this match. Essex were 126 for 5, facing Leicestershire's 141, when Owen scored 82. Then a whirlwind last wicket stand by Mead (41) and Pickett (26 not out) took them to 285. Leicestershire fared better at their second attempt. Russell had been injured and was unable to keep wicket, and with the help of 33 byes, the visitors reached 225. Mead, having taken 5 for 57 in the first innings, took 9 for 75 in the second. The only wicket that evaded him was number eight, Geeson, who was bowled by Pickett. Essex won by seven wickets.

A greater victory than this occurred at Leyton at the beginning of August when the mighty Surrey side was overwhelmed by an innings. The visitors were very unhappy with the Leyton wicket, which crumbled after the first day when Essex had scored 327. In spite of the doubts as to the wicket, *Cricket* pointed out that: 'For all that it was a very great performance on the part of Essex to make over 300 against the Surrey bowling.'

The Essex innings was highlighted by knocks of 76 from Fane, 59 from Owen and a maiden century, 110, by Tom Russell. As a wicket-keeper,

Russell was never perhaps quite in the top flight, but he was extremely good and he had to keep to a most varied attack, the lightning pace of Kortright, the medium quick of Pickett, the movement both ways of Mead and the off-spin of Bull. Sewell, who played in the Essex side with Russell and Kortright on occasions, wrote later: 'I don't think any other wicket-keeper had to stand for so long a period what Russell's hands had to take from Korty.'

Surrey were bowled out for 126, Bull 6 for 51, and in their second innings, Mead and Bull bowled unchanged, taking 5 for 39 and 5 for 38 respectively as the reigning champions were shot out for 82.

Bull was just 20 years old and had been selected for the Gentlemen v Players match, in which he had such a triumph, entirely on merit. In all matches, he took 85 wickets at 16 runs each in 1896, but he was to capture more than 100 wickets in each of the next two seasons. He was an intelligent bowler who kept to impeccable length. He could turn the ball both ways although his stock ball was the off-break. Pelham Warner considered him the best slow bowler in England at the end of the 19th century and included him in his side to America in 1897. The only doubt attending

12. *Frederick Bull. The first of 19 Essex players to become the* Wisden *Cricketer of the Year.*

Bull related to his action. It was a time when the legality of certain actions was questioned. Accusations of throwing were in the air, and not everyone thought Bull's action to be legal.

For the moment, however, all was well at Essex. The opening day of the match against the Australian tourists in 1896 had attracted 12,000 people to Leyton. The *Daily Telegraph* was not altogether happy as to how the crowd was handled. 'Spectators encroached on to the playing area and the game had to be stopped in the afternoon session while the secretary and the police exhorted them to retire to a reasonable distance.'

Such problems must have been welcome after the apathy of earlier years. When the Australians played Cambridge Past and Present at Leyton in 1888 *Wisden* had reported: 'Despite the attractive character of the match, there was not a large gate on the Essex County Ground, people having by this time got rather tired of cricket in rain and mud.'

Success had bred success. In 1897, Essex increased membership by 567 so that at the beginning of the following year, the number stood at 1688, and the 1500 that Green had so long deemed necessary was achieved.

The interest, of course, reflected the form of the team, and the 1897 season began on a note of high optimism. There was initial frustration, however, when, at The Oval, Essex scored 316 and 244 for 8 declared, and Surrey, bowled out for 199 in their first innings, Bull taking 9 for 93, were set a target of 362. They were reduced to 27 for 3, but Abel hit 95, and Surrey saved the game, ending at 269 for 7.

'Bob' Carpenter hit 141 against Warwickshire at Edgbaston, but Essex again had to be content with a moral victory. The next encounter was against Yorkshire, the reigning champions, at Leyton. It was played on a 'bowlers' wicket', but Essex covered themselves in glory as *Cricket* reported:

> What might have happened if the wicket had been perfect has nothing to do with the case, for the match was fairly fought out on its merits, and although it would be going too far to say that the best team won, it was certainly the best team on the day. When Yorkshire won the toss no Essex man, even though he may have remembered that the wicket has, in former years, had a reputation for being fiery on occasions, could have ventured to hope that they would be disposed of for much less than 300 runs. But when Mr Jackson, Tunnicliffe, Brown, Denton, and Peel were out for 26 all the world wondered. Spectators seemed agreed that the wicket was perfect, and yet the Yorkshiremen seemed tied up by the bowling. Even when Moorhouse and Wainwright, the two men in the Yorkshire team who have stopped a rot times out of number, got together and gradually began to raise the score, they never appeared quite comfortable. But they put on 42 during their

partnership, and as Hirst, and Mr Milligan, and Haigh all made runs, the total of the innings was not very bad. Once more the Yorkshire tail had done credit to itself. By this time some of the fire had been taken out of the wicket, and things were a little easier for Essex when they batted, although it was not by any means all plain sailing for them. At the end of the day they were in an excellent position, having put on 145 runs for five wickets, thus being only 9 runs behind with five wickets still to fall. The chief honours fell to Mr Perrin and Russell, who each played a cricketer's innings. With such a good beginning a fair score might have been hoped for, but of the tail only Mr Owen did anything, and the total was but 199 – 45 runs on. In their second innings Yorkshire did very little better than before, but Mr Jackson played distinctly the best innings of the match, and Peel and Mr Milligan distinguished themselves. Essex had to make 132 to win. For the first time during the game Yorkshire now began to get the best of it. They disposed of Carpenter, Mr Perrin, Mr Lucas, and Mr McGahey for 36. Again, at 53, Mr Owen was out, and until Mead and Mr Kortright came together the visitors seemed like winning. But these two men wore down the bowling, until when the time came for stumps to be drawn only 17 runs were required. To the surprise of many cricketers the game was not adjourned until the following day, but was played to a finish, and as Mr Kortright and Mead were well set they kept together until the match was won. Thus Essex gained a memorable and well-deserved victory by 3 wickets.

It was a victory which alerted the attention of the cricketing world. Kortright, 5 for 76 and 3 for 54, and Bull, 4 for 63 and 5 for 95, bore the brunt of the bowling. Bull bowled unchanged in the first innings, while the undefeated stand between Kortright, 33, and Mead 14, was worth 39, mammoth in the context of the match.

The following games, against Sussex and Leicestershire, were both hit by the weather, but Bull inspired comfortable wins over Hampshire and Derbyshire.

The season's half-way mark was the visit to Old Trafford to play Lancashire, who had been runners-up in the championship for the past two seasons. Essex were asked to make 255 to win, but they were all out for 188. The match left a sour taste. In the first place, Mold's action was considered very suspect, and he played a significant part in the Lancashire victory. In the second, Essex suffered from a series of dubious umpiring decisions. In his excellent biography of Kortright, Charles Sale quotes the fast bowler as saying at the time: 'Essex have lost more than they have gained through faulty decisions this season. I only regret that some counties go out of their way to deceive umpires. A preconceived agreement to unanimously appeal without cause often leads to the umpire being confused and giving the batsmen out.' All the troubles in cricket did not begin with the 1970s.

The Essex challenge was revitalised when Warwickshire were beaten by an innings at Leyton. Perrin hit 153 in the Essex innings of 489. The return game against Derbyshire was drawn, and then Essex went to Huddersfield to play the return match with Yorkshire. If the first match at Leyton had been exciting, the second outstripped it in drama in every way. Again we should allow *Cricket* to tell of this astounding match:

> The interest which was taken in this match all over the country was considerable, for in the first meeting between the two teams Essex were victorious after a very close match, and it was certain that both teams would make an extraordinary effort to win in the return. Unfortunately the fast bowlers were dangerous to the batsmen all through the match, and cricket was always played under difficulties. What luck there was went in favour of the visitors. It was a splendidly fought out game. At the first it seemed that very small scores would decide the result, but after each side had completed an innings the bowlers did not have matters all their own way. In the first innings of Essex things went very badly until Mr Turner came in and stopped the rot, which was getting serious; thanks to him and to Mr Fane the total came to 139 instead of about 60 as seemed at one time likely. The Yorkshiremen also began badly and were only saved from collapse by Hirst, who made one more than Mr Turner. Essex had a lead of 5 runs on the first innings, and began so badly that half their wickets were down for 51 and as it was not for a moment to be supposed that the Yorkshiremen would all fail a second time, it seemed certain that the result of the first match would be reversed. But, as in the first innings, Mr Turner and Mr Fane came to the rescue of their side and aided by an amount of good fortune for which the Yorkshiremen (generally such good fieldsmen) had only to thank themselves, they quite altered the appearance of the game. From 51 they brought the score to 172 when Mr Fane was out for a most useful 47. Afterwards Mr Kortright banged the bowling about, while Mr Turner again played very fine cricket, and as Mr Owen also made a good score the total fell just short of 300, and Yorkshire was left with 299 to win, a very formidable task indeed. When they went in on Friday evening they had an hour and a quarter to play. At 2 Brown was bowled by Mr Kortright; Mr Jackson played the next ball onto his foot, whence it rolled into his wicket; at 17 Mr Bull bowled Tunnicliffe, and at 23 Denton was caught at slip off Mr Kortright. Thus with four of the best men out the game seemed practically over, and although Moorhouse and Wainwright kept in the rest of the time, bringing the

> total up to 81, there seemed no earthly chance for Yorkshire on the next day. But the cricket which followed was as remarkable as anything which has been seen this year. The Yorkshiremen, in face of the long odds against them, set their teeth, and although some of them were knocked about by the fast bowling, which was short and bumpy, they played a great game under great difficulties. Moorhouse and Wainwright were not yet parted until the total was 138, but even then the task seemed almost impossible, and as both professionals went at almost the same total it seemed out of the question that their side could still make a fight which should make the Essex men tremble for the result. But Hirst and Milligan treated the bowlers as if they were playing in an unimportant club match. In 40 minutes they increased the score by 85 and when Mr Milligan was bowled by Pickett for a splendid 64 Yorkshire was within measurable distance of winning. And then, sad to say, Hirst was run out, and a wail went up all round the ground. Still the Yorkshiremen did not despair. Lord Hawke played a great innings at a most exciting time, but Haigh did not stay long. When Bairstow, the last man, came in eleven runs were required to win. Lord Hawke made seven of them and Bairstow two, but with only one run required to make a tie Bairstow was lbw. It was a tame conclusion to a wonderful match, a match in which the Yorkshiremen played an uphill game which was worthy of their great reputation. But even when the game seemed to be veering round in favour of Yorkshire the Essex men never lost heart; they played as hard as possible up to the very last. But to lose a match by one run through a run out and lbw! It was trying for the Yorkshiremen.

The report, excited as the writer becomes, fails to give some vital facts. Kortright broke the Yorkshire middle order in the first innings, after Bull had made the initial inroads, and he followed his 4 for 68 with 5 for 123 in the second innings. The 'short and bumpy' fast bowling certainly came from Kortright, and he was barracked by the Huddersfield crowd after he struck Moorhouse with a rising delivery. He was defended in the press where it was claimed that he was fast, but fair.

None would doubt Kortright's sporting spirit, but that he also had the temperament of a great fast bowler is unquestionable. Home Gordon, who admired him greatly, wrote in 1939 that Kortright was the fastest bowler he ever saw and the one 'most willing to hurt the batsmen'. He also added: 'The fact was that not only was Kortright a holy terror as express bowler, but he revelled in being so. He took strong dislikes to certain opponents, and would let fly viciously at them . . . on some occasions he converted the duel between bowler and batsman into one of personal danger to the latter.'

It was not Kortright who eventually brought Essex victory against Yorkshire, but Walter Mead who, used surprisingly sparingly in the match, took the vital wickets of Haigh and Bairstow.

On the last day of the match, a large crowd gathered at Leyton to await news of the result. Charles Green presided, and there were scenes of wild jubilation when the result was announced.

If one man emerges as Essex hero from this great game, it is Arthur Jervois Turner, later Brigadier A J Turner CB, CMG, DSO, Croix de Guerre.

Turner was from a military family. He was born in India where his father was serving as a Major, and it was his father who had incalculated the love of sport. Turner's father was tragically drowned with the rest of the Hong Kong cricket team when, on returning from a match against Shanghai, the ship on which they were travelling was wrecked. In 1897, 'Johnny' Turner played his first season in first-class cricket, although he had previously assisted Bedfordshire. He was 19 years old and a cadet at the Royal Military Academy, Woolwich.

His 111 in the second innings against Yorkshire was the first of 11 centuries he made in 68 matches between 1897 and 1910. C B Fry was not the only one to express the opinion that had he been able to play first-class cricket regularly, Turner would have been a very great batsman indeed. Like Leonard Crawley and Matthew Fosh of later generations, he was one of the great losses to Essex cricket. He was an elegant and accomplished batsman, a good slow bowler and a fine fielder who could also keep wicket. In that first season alone, he headed the batting averages with 590 runs, average 42.14.

Like Frank Milligan, who played so finely for Yorkshire in that famous Huddersfield encounter, Turner served in the South African war. Turner was wounded at Ladysmith; Milligan was a Lieutenant in Colonel Plumer's force and was killed in the attempt to relieve Mafeking in March 1900.

Following the match with Yorkshire, Charlie McGahey hit two centuries in a week. At Hove, Essex reached 475 with McGahey 140 and Kortright 74. Kortright then took five wickets and Sussex were forced to follow-on, but Ranjitsinhji hit 170 in the second innings and saved the game.

At Leyton, McGahey hit 123 and Kortright took 11 wickets as Leicestershire were beaten by an innings, which meant that if Essex were to beat Lancashire in the next match at Leyton, they would be serious contenders for the title.

The previous season, Perrin and McGahey had joined together in their first century partnership, 111 v Leicestershire, at Leicester; now they combined in a partnership of greater importance. After Carpenter had fallen to Mold for four, and Fane to Briggs for 14, they added 129 in just over two hours. Turner, Kortright and Mead made useful contributions, and Essex reached 290.

Frank Sugg batted splendidly for Lancashire and scored 88 not out, but with the wicket deteriorating badly at one end, neither side was anxious to bat last. Bull had destroyed the Lancashire middle-order and was to finish with 7 for 63, but, under the existing laws, Lancashire would be compelled to follow-on if they finished 120 runs in arrears. It was not until 1900 that the margin was increased to 150 and the enforcement of the follow-on became optional. Essex were anxious not to bat last, and Bull attempted to bowl wide to the boundary to give Lancashire the runs that they needed to avoid having to follow-on. Mold, realising what Bull was doing, knocked down his own stumps, and Lancashire were out for 168.

It seemed that this ruse had succeeded when, after Bull had bowled MacLaren, Ward, 68, and Sugg, 81, quickly knocked off the arrears. The ever persistent Bull, who had bowled unchanged in the first innings, sent down 58.1 five-ball overs and was finally rewarded with seven wickets, including those of Ward and Sugg, for 113 runs. Essex needed 130 to win which, on a pitch which was now giving great assistance to the bowlers, was not an easy task.

A crowd estimated at 15,000 watched the final stages, and they paid a record £620 in gate receipts. Essex were aided when Mold was forced to retire from the attack after one over with an injured knee, but there was still the dangerous slow left-arm bowling of 'Boy' Briggs to contend with. He had Fane caught behind for five, but 'Bob' Carpenter played a masterful, watchful innings. Perrin fell to Cuttell, and McGahey to Briggs, who then had Turner lbw.

Russell joined Carpenter, and with Essex three short of their target, he hit Cuttell to the boundary to bring victory by six wickets. The crowd swarmed onto the pitch, and Carpenter, who finished with 57 not out, was carried shoulder-high to the professionals' dressing room. The supporters were in joyful mood, and a collection was made for Carpenter. According to *Wisden*, it realised £43 10s; another report put it at £44 9s 4d! In any case, the batsman did well, but Essex's greatest triumph of the year was essentially a team effort.

The Times was ecstatic: 'Essex have risen from mediocrity to greatness in little more than one season and their success has been almost wholly the work of native talent developed under the guardianship of that splendid Uppingham and Cambridge bat, Mr C. E. Green.'

For the man who had done so much to keep Essex cricket alive, it was a great moment.

Sadly, the time of triumph was not to last long. A week later, Surrey came to Leyton and outplayed Essex to win by 10 wickets. For *The Times* the reversal in Essex's fortunes was too much, and they wrote of them having 'failed dismally'.

Lancashire took the title, Surrey were runners-up, and Essex finished third. There was some disappointment, for they were the only county not to have been beaten twice by another county during the season, but there was hope for the future. The followers of Essex could not have known then that the County would not finish as high again for another 81 years.

The season ended damply with a draw against Hampshire at Leyton. Perrin hit his second century of the season, but the game was for the benefit of Henry Pickett, who was not in the chosen side. Pickett had put on much weight, and his bowling had become less effective. His career with Essex was at an end, but he remains a permanent and important part of the Club's history.

The rain restricted the takings at his benefit match to £150, but the followers of the County were quick to show their affection:

> During the course of his benefit match he was presented with a handsome timepiece, the result of a penny subscription by the schoolboys of Essex, and with a miniature set of stumps, bats and ball in gold and silver, purchased with the proceeds of a halfpenny subscription from the boys of Leyton, West Ham, etc.

Pickett symbolises all that became good in Essex cricket. He was the honest workman, the bread-and-butter cricketer upon whom success is founded. For a time, he became coach at Clifton College, and in 1907, he met the saddest of deaths. He disappeared from his home on 27 September, and his body was found on the beach at Aberavon six days later. Not until the end of December, however, was his fate known, for only then were some articles found on the body identified as his. He was in his 46th year.

Pickett's last season was his worst, his 21 wickets costing more than 30 runs apiece, but even as one star fades, another rises, and 1897 had seen the first appearance of Bill Reeves. In his first match, he scored four and bowled three overs for 12 runs. The next 24 years would see him send down many more overs.

The splendours of 1897 were reflected in the increased membership, the healthier financial position and the general optimism of the Club. The surge in interest brought both benefits and casualties. Leyton was to have more accommodation. There was to be a dining hall for members – but members were no longer allowed to bring friends into the pavilion, and tennis disappeared from the ground.

The optimism seemed well founded when Essex opened the 1898 season with a six-wicket victory over the arch-enemy Surrey. The Leyton wicket and the weather created a situation where either captain would have been glad to lose the toss and put the responsibility on his opponent. In the event, Key won the toss, and Surrey batted first. They were bowled out, mainly by Mead and Kortright, for 188. At the end of the day Essex were 108 for 5. Turner was on 25. Frank Street, who was making his debut, was out next morning at 123, and Kortright, after some characteristically lusty blows, was bowled by Lockwood at 150.

When the ninth Essex wicket went down the score was 200, and Turner had not reached 50. The young soldier now changed his style and attacked the bowling. Mead gave solid support, as always, and the Surrey bowling 'was in a knot'. Lees finally bowled Mead for 34, but the score had reached 289, and 'Johnny' Turner was 101 not out. Kortright and Bull bowled Surrey out for 200 in their second innings, and with McGahey in excellent form, Essex won by six wickets.

Two years later, C B Fry wrote of Turner that he had a fine defence and plenty of strokes, that he was quick on his feet and had a clever way of running out to the pitch of the ball and driving it along the ground.

> Probably his duties will take him abroad for many years of his cricketing life. His performances for Essex have been remarkably good on paper. Moreover, he has played as many match-winning innings as anyone in the last year or two. But beyond that there is in his style and methods so much resource as well as natural ability that if he could continue his career in first-class cricket without interruption, he would probably work his way up to the very top of the tree; become, in fact, one of the three or four best bats in England. In any case, his name is already worthy to be placed along with the very best of soldier cricketers.

The brilliant century in the opening match against Surrey was to be Turner's only hundred in 1898, a season of exciting performances and heroic moments, but one with which the County were only reasonably satisfied as they slipped to fifth in the championship table. They undertook the most ambitious programme in their history to date, playing 20 matches, six more than the previous season. Ten games were won, and six were lost.

Yorkshire, the champions, reversed the form of the previous season and beat Essex twice, as did Gloucestershire, but Lancashire were beaten twice. Against Leicestershire, on 1 August, Essex scored 515. Carpenter hit 133, and Kortright blasted 112, the first of his two first-class hundreds. The fast bowler then took 6 for 41, and Essex won by an innings.

Kortright was also in tremendous form against Hampshire, a spell of 6 for 10 in 20 minutes giving Essex victory with 15 minutes to spare. The most memorable win, however, came at Old Trafford in July when the reigning champions were beaten by six wickets.

'Interesting from start to finish,' said *Wisden*, 'this contest was rendered memorable by the unprecedented achievement – so far as county cricket is concerned – of Essex in their last innings.' Lancashire had seemed to take control of the match on the first day when J T Tyldesley, 85, and Sugg, 104, engaged in a stand of 169 for the third wicket. Bull and Kortright then combined to tumble out the last seven wickets for 48, and Lancashire were restricted to 254. Bull finished with 5 for 88, and Kortright with 4 for 74.

Essex finished the first day on 93 for 4 and appeared in contention, but Mold and Cuttell brought about a collapse on the second morning and the follow-on was only narrowly avoided when a last wicket stand between Mead and Bull took the total to 169.

J T Tyldesley completed his 1000 runs for the season, Hartley and Sugg batted well, and, in spite of another set of failures by the lower order, the home side reached 250. This meant that Essex were set the task of scoring 336 to win, and no side had ever achieved such a target in an inter-county match.

Owen and Carpenter gave their team a good start with a stand of 88, but the basis of a memorable victory came with a third wicket stand of 191 between Perrin and McGahey.

The names of Perrin and McGahey have become inextricably linked in Essex history. They became known as 'The Essex Twins'. It has been generally assumed that this title was conferred upon them because of the number of partnerships in which they were involved, but it was Joe Armour, the Essex scorer, who gave them the name. They were of the same height and build, and Armour had difficulty in distinguishing between them when they were at the wicket together. In fact he asked one of them to wear a scarf round his waist so that he could tell which was which.

Charlie McGahey was the hero of the Old Trafford victory. C B Fry wrote of it in *The Book of Cricket*:

> Mr. McGahey's score was 145, which would have been a splendid achievement under the most favourable circumstances; against the bowling of Briggs, Mold and Cuttell, in the fourth innings of a match, it must be considered one of the great performances of cricket. Mr. McGahey stands well up, and, being tall, has a long reach and a fine command over the ball in playing forward, but he does not use forward play for forcing strokes, being by nature a driver. He defends by playing forward or half-cock, instead of, like Mr. Perrin, making a speciality of back play. He is very clever at pushing a short ball, even if it rises somewhat round to leg, just in front or just behind the umpire. If the ball is a fairly good one he gets two for the stroke, if bad it is a certain

four. His best drive goes between mid-on and the bowler, but he is a strong driver from extra-cover to well outside mid-on. He does not cut much. His game is a curious blend of quietness and aggressiveness. Perhaps he plays best when he is ever so little on the hit.

Fry, intelligent and perceptive, is at his most revealing in this last sentence. McGahey was a natural hitter, initially reckless, and he had to temper his style and his impetuosity with experience. He gained much from the opportunities to practise against professional bowlers at Leyton, which C E Green provided before the start of each season.

In the winter of 1897, McGahey's career had been in doubt, for he was troubled by ill-health, but a trip to Australia cured him. Perrin too was unwell, and there were fears that he was consumptive. He went to book a return passage to Australia on the Orient Line, of which Green was managing director. Some days later, Green returned Perrin's cheque. The trip apparently averted the threat of disease. It is likely that Green paid for McGahey's voyage too, for Charlie was never strong with money. McGahey was assistant secretary of the County for several years, and from 1930 until his death in 1935, he was the scorer. From his early years as captain of Essex, Tom Pearce remembers that McGahey was always short of cash. The second day of an away county game would invariably bring an approach from scorer to captain. 'I'm "Hearts of Oak", skipper. Can you let me have a sub?'

Like Perrin, McGahey was born in Hackney, but he was five years older than his 'twin'. Friends and colleagues in many great partnerships they may have been, but they were very different people. If Perrin was cautious, bluff and even aloof, McGahey was extrovert and expansive. Home Gordon described him as 'a really fine, vigorous bat and a fool only to himself: a good-hearted, light-hearted, excellent fellow'. His generosity was unbounded. For many years, he lived at The Three Blackbirds, a public house in Leyton, which was owned by Bill Golding, chairman of Leyton FC and an Essex committee member. McGahey had a football connection, for he was a fine full-back for Tottenham Hotspur, Arsenal, Clapton Orient and Sheffield United and captained London and Middlesex representative teams.

Pearce recalls that Perrin and McGahey often came to matches together by tram from Leytonstone, and that Charlie McGahey would often complain: 'We've been travelling together for over 30 years, and Peter's never paid the fare yet.'

A fine leg-break bowler who took 330 wickets in his career, McGahey is remembered best, not just for his gloriously entertaining batting, but for his kindness and sense of fun. In essence he was the Mr Micawber of Essex cricket. Charles Bray, who knew him only in his last days when he was scorer, remembers him as one who was the philosopher and friend of the Essex team in the early 30s, ever giving counsel and encouragement. As a young man, he was always getting into scrapes and he had little appreciation of the value of money. Like Mr Micawber, he always believed that something would turn up. Bray recalls:

> You saw little of the great burly figure unless the side had suffered a heavy defeat. Then he would appear in the dressing-room or the railway carriage and in his soft pleasant voice tell stories or recall experiences that made you forget the tragedy of the day. There was always a tomorrow for Charles McGahey. He knew what it was like to be poor in the autumn of his life. It may have been his own fault but never did I know him to be bitter or complaining. He was a most lovable person.

McGahey was to die in January, 1935. He slipped on a greasy pavement on Christmas Day and damaged a finger. Septic poisoning ensued and proved fatal. Perrin was asked to give an appreciation of his friend and colleague in *Wisden*.

> Perrin contended that McGahey was one of the most popular and kind-hearted players ever seen in first-class cricket; certainly he was the most encouraging to any young player. 'I have known him on many occasions go out of his way to give a youngster good advice. Dry humour was an outstanding feature of his attractive characteristics. Having played with him more or less for 25 years I consider McGahey one of the very best cricketers Essex ever had. Really a magnificent cricketer, he was undoubtedly the hardest hitter I ever faced. The opposite batsman had to keep his eyes open, as McGahey used to jump to the ball and drive back very straight. On one occasion he drove the ball back so hard that he broke his partner's arm!
>
> 'I well remember one instance of his quick-thinking wit when I was in at the other end. McGahey was 99, he played the next ball, said ''Come one'', but failed in his stroke and was bowled. As he passed by on his way to the pavilion he said to the bowler: ''Lucky for you I wanted a drink.'' '

Perrin's story captures two aspects of McGahey's character, his wit and his liking for a drink. His glass of Bass was an essential part of Charlie's diet. Certainly Home Gordon told how once at Horsham McGahey said that his tongue was hanging out for a pint of beer and would his friend take over the scoring for a few minutes. Home Gordon obliged, only to find himself scoring for over an hour.

Of all his witticisms, the one that has passed most firmly into cricket folk-lore is his nick-naming of R C Robertson-Glasgow. In a match against Somerset, McGahey was out quickly, and on his return to the pavilion he was asked by a team-mate who had missed his dismissal what had happened. 'Bowled first ball by a bugger I thought died 300 years ago – Robinson Crusoe.' The name stuck, and R C Robertson-Glasgow was 'Crusoe' ever afterwards.

McGahey and Perrin in 1898 became the first Essex batsmen to score 1000 runs for the County in a season. Of the bowlers, Bull and Mead took 100 wickets in all matches, and Kortright, with 88 for Essex, just failed to do the same. Tom Russell, with 40 catches and 28 stumpings, was the leading wicket-keeper in the country.

At this period, Kortright bowled at a furious pace, and he was the central figure in two matches of contrasting styles which followed one upon the other, Essex v Gloucestershire and the Gentlemen v the Players.

At Leyton, on 7, 8 and 9 July 1898, Essex met Gloucestershire for the first time, and a crowd of 7000 swarmed to East London to see W G Grace's first appearance in a county match against Essex. Owen won the toss, but Grace, a week short of his 50th birthday, took 7 for 44 and shot Essex out for 128. The innings was not without incident, however, for Grace tumbled forward to catch and bowl Perrin and claimed a catch which most believed he had taken on the half volley.

Gloucestershire had declined to give Essex a fixture until they had proved themselves, and now they posted a telegram from Bristol in the pavilion which read: 'How cruel of you to bowl the rabbits out.' The Essex team was incensed, and Kortright bowled as fast as he had ever done when Gloucestershire began their innings. Grace scored 126 out of 203 while he was at the wicket, and Gloucestershire reached 231. Kortright took 5 for 41, and, as Altham states in his history of the game, 'was probably as fast as anyone who has ever lived'.

After Owen had gone for 0, Carpenter, 54, and Perrin, 81, rallied Essex. The home side reached 250, but again there was controversy. Lucas, when going well, was adjudged caught behind although the batsman, a man of scrupulous honesty, insisted that the ball had only touched his shirt. The crowd reacted angrily, and there were cries of 'cheat'. Even *Wisden* later remarked: 'It was unfortunate that so fine a game should have been marred by ill-feeling, but it is no secret that the Essex XI were greatly incensed at much that happened after the first day, complaining bitterly of more than one decision.' But if Essex were upset at the Lucas decision, they had more cause for anger to come.

On the second evening, Kortright produced one of the fiercest spells of his career, and Gloucestershire, in search of 148, lost Board and Troup without scoring, both having their stumps knocked over by the Essex pace man. Grace withstood this onslaught, but the breakthrough which Essex most passionately desired seemed to have been made when Mead caught and bowled The Old Man. Grace, however, stood his ground. Mead appealed, and umpire Burton raised his finger. At this Grace roared that it was a bump ball – so that Burton retracted his decision.

Kortright, believing Grace guilty of arrant gamesmanship, subjected the Doctor to a ferocious spell of sustained short pitched bowling which left him bruised and battered, but not out. Gloucestershire finished on 81 for 3, Grace 36.

The next morning the score had reached 96 with Grace on 49 when Kortright, in another fearsome burst, hit the batsman on the pads and appealed for lbw. The umpire, glared at by Grace, gave not out. The next ball appeared to touch Grace's bat on its way through to Russell, but again the umpire shook his head. Kortright thundered in on his 15-yard run and knocked Grace's middle stump out of the ground with his next delivery. In one of those apocryphal stories that are the life-blood of cricket, it is alleged that, as the batsman was leaving, Kortright said: 'Surely you're not going, Doctor, there's still one stump standing.' Grace claimed that he had never been so insulted in his life.

Gloucestershire climbed to 132 for 6 when Wrathall and Jessop came together, and these two took the score to 145 before Wrathall was caught at slip by Carpenter off Mead. Brown scored a single before being bowled by the first ball that he received from Kortright, and Wright was hit on the foot and given out lbw as well as having a toe broken. Two runs needed, and one wicket to fall.

Last man Roberts edged a single off Kortright, survived an over and two appeals from Walter Mead, and Jessop hit Kortright high to the boundary to win the match. Kortright finished with 7 for 57 in the innings, and 12 for 98 in the match.

The ill-feeling from this match persisted for some time. Charles Green, a life-long friend of Grace's as we have noted, said that he and the great man did not speak to each other for a year after this game because Green considered his old friend had been guilty of some sharp practices. They were later reconciled.

The Gentlemen v Players match at Lord's had been put back a week to coincide with Grace's 50th birthday, and over 40,000 people watched the three days' cricket which began on 18 July. 'Kortright bowled at a terrific pace, but with little luck', wrote Warner, and he finished with 1 for 90 and 2 for 83. The Players scored 335 and 263. The Gentlemen made 303 in their first innings, and so had to make 296 on a wearing wicket in order to win.

The atmosphere between Kortright and Grace, in the wake of the Leyton game, had been less than cordial, but now they were thrown together in strange circumstances. Because of a badly bruised hand, Grace had dropped himself down the order, and when he came in the score was 56 for 6. It was soon 77 for 7, and 80 for 9. At this point, Kortright joined his captain, who greeted him warmly and encouragingly. It was just after 5.30 pm when the ninth wicket went down, and the match was scheduled to finish at seven o'clock.

Harry Altham wrote of those closing moments:

> Kortright came in to play the innings of his life. At first the crowd merely awaited the inevitable from over to over, but gradually as the hands of the clock crept towards seven it dawned upon them that even now the Champion and his gallant partner might save the game. Seventy-eight runs had been added, and only four minutes of play were left when Lockwood went on for a final effort. His third ball was on the short side and outside off stump. The fast bowler slashed at it and half hit it, a high, curling hit over Schofield Haigh's head at cover. The latter ran backwards, reached it, and the match was over.

Kortright walked down the wicket. He and Grace linked arms and left the field together. They had been reconciled in their joint efforts to save their side from defeat. To the end of his days, Kortright, always strong in opinion, asserted that Grace was the finest cricketer the world had known, and that no Bradman, nor Hammond, nor anyone else came within a street of him. But how good was Kortright?

He has passed into history with the reputation of being the fastest bowler that ever lived, and he was proud of that reputation and did not dispute it. In the 30s, Tom Pearce heard him say: 'Is this chap Larwood supposed to be fast?' He felt a little aggrieved for a time that he had been forgotten, but when Larwood was on the body-line tour Kortright's name was brought back into prominence. In 1946, Jim Coldham, writer, historian and collector, wrote to him and asked for his opinions in relation to his speed as a bowler compared to others'. Kortright's reply was inevitably non-commital although not unrevealing:

> The question (personal) you ask me is an impossible one for me to answer as I never played my own bowling, and after having been relegated to the long list of have-beens and forgotten for about 30 years I was only dug up by a few ignorant so-called cricket reporters as a means of comparison with the pace of Harold Larwood the Notts and England fast bowler in the Douglas Jardine expedition in Australia, when Australia got some of their own medicine and couldn't stomach it. The best way to compare the pace of any bowler with another is to bat against both of them in my opinion, which in most cases is impossible.

Two years earlier, in *Wisden*, Sir Stanley Jackson had written: 'Kortright was generally regarded as the fastest bowler of his time in this country. Not only was he a very fast bowler, but also a very good one'. The same annual returned to the theme of fast bowling in 1948 when Lindwall and Miller were about to descend upon us, and this time they interviewed Kortright himself. His response was blunt and effective:

> There is no magic in fast bowling; but, on the contrary, much hard work, coupled with intelligent methods, is the key to success. I have little patience with modern bowlers who condemn these 'shirt-front wickets' and ask how can they be expected to get men out when the pitch will not help. There were many such pitches in my playing days, the sort on which if we could bounce the ball high we thought ourselves pretty clever. Yet every county fielded two, sometimes three, genuinely fast bowlers, who were not discouraged by the wickets. A basic principle of cricket which I feel is sometimes overlooked is that the prime object of a bowler is to get batsmen out. For this reason I do not favour the modern craze for such expressions as 'in-swingers', 'out-swingers', all sorts of 'spins' and 'swerves'. Some bowlers seem to concentrate on these dubious achievements so much that they forget to keep a length and to bowl at the stumps.

Kortright practised what he preached. He ran 15 yards to the crease, gathered momentum as he ran and delivered from his full height of six feet. He was very fast and very straight. Between 1895 and 1898, he took 287 wickets for the County, and 206 of them were without any help from the fielders.

At the end of the 1898 season, he was picked to play for the Rest of England against A E Stoddart's team, which had gone to Australia the previous winter, a tour for which many felt that Kortright should have been picked. He was never to come so close again to selection for England, because while Tom Richardson held sway Kortright was playing for a county still struggling to establish themselves. Having reached the peak of his career in 1898 when aged 27, he was never to be quite the same again, for he strained his back in an accident at home and could not play at all in 1899.

If the 1898 season had ended in something of a disappointment in that the County had slipped to fifth, this was not reflected in the interest now being shown in cricket throughout Essex. Green announced a profit of £500 for the season, and Mr Philip Savill had presented the Club with a new, large scoreboard. On the field, Mead, Bull, Carpenter, Perrin and Kortright had appeared in every match, Reeves' 11 wickets had helped him to top the bowling averages and another bowler, a left-arm, Harding Isaac 'Sailor' Young, had taken 19 wickets in his first season. The sadness came a few weeks after the season's close when, on 27 September, C M Tebbut died. His support and generosity had done much to save and foster the Club, and it is good that he lived to see his efforts gain some reward. It was a pity that he could not live to see the beginning of the 1899 season when Essex gained one of their greatest victories. It was against the Australians, at Leyton.

Jack Pollard, the Australian cricket historian, writes of his country's 1899 team as: 'one of the best of all Australian teams, strong in every department. They won the Test series against England, and lost only three of their 35 matches, winning 16 and playing 16 draws.' Their three defeats were at the hands of Surrey, the champions, Kent and Essex. Essex were playing their first game of the season.

The Australians had shown good form in their opening match at Crystal Palace, and, as *Wisden* put it: 'In some respects this was the most sensational match of the whole tour.' The wicket was never easy. It was much affected by a heavy dew, and as the match progressed, runs became increasingly harder to come by.

Owen and Carpenter were never at ease, but they battled well until Hugh Trumble, with his medium-pace off-breaks, began to cause dismay. At lunch, Essex had wilted to only 88 for 5. In the post-lunch period, Tom Russell adopted the principle that the best form of defence was attack and savaged the bowling for a brisk and valuable 22. Lucas played in his usual correct and charming manner, but at the other end wickets continued to fall regularly. When the ninth wicket went down Essex were 144.

Young now joined Lucas and, imitating Russell's earlier example, he hit lustily. In little over 30 minutes, the last pair added 55; Young scored 33 of them before falling to Jones. Lucas was left on 46 not out, Trumble had taken 8 for 79, and Essex had made 199, a highly satisfactory score in the circumstances.

Delighted as they must have been with Trumble's eight wickets, the Australians must have viewed the pitch with some apprehension. They knew Mead of old, and had seen what Trumble had done. The Essex bowler, however, was not to the fore on the first evening. Bull accounted for openers Iredale and Darling, and Young had Clem Hill caught by Fane. The tourists closed at 75 for 3.

On the second morning, no Australian batsman was able to establish himself. Jones and McLeod struck some blows at the last, but Young bowled Trumper for 0, Noble was run out, and Essex led by 55. This was a healthy, though not winning lead. The Australians were renowned for their fighting qualities and few expected them to fare as badly in their second innings as they had done in their first.

Ambitions that Essex may have cherished received a severe setback when Carpenter, Owen and Perrin were out before lunch with only eight scored, but in the afternoon came the turning point of the game when

McGahey and Turner, both enjoying a little luck early on, added 93. They played soundly, but were never afraid to hit. McGahey was bowled for 39, and Turner for 54, the only fifty of the match. The value of their stand was emphasised when the last six wickets fell for only 43 runs. The Australians were left with the last day in which to score 200 to win.

It was generally anticipated that they would win, though not easily. After a few overs by Mead and Young it was realised that if the target was to be reached, the Australians would have to resort to desperate measures. As *Cricket* reported: 'Mead and Young occasionally made the ball do unconscionable things, and very early in the game they established panic.' Iredale was brilliantly caught at third man from a fierce cut. Clem Hill was taken in the slips at the second attempt. Gregory was beaten several times before he was bowled. The Australians were in disarray.

Joe Darling changed tactics by attempting to hit the bowling off its length. Noble, badly missed at slip, played solidly and boldly, but when Darling was out the tourists were 31 for 4. *Cricket* captures the mood of the final stages:

> It was still just possible that the Australians might pull through, for the tail has over and over again shown that it can play an uphill game. But the wickets continued to fall. Jones was sent in earlier than usual to hit, but a fine shooter was too much for him. The rest of the team all played very careful cricket, and were nearly all beaten two or three times before they were out, for Mead and Young were now worked up to such a pitch that they could do nothing wrong. By half-past one the match was over, and Essex had beaten the Australians for the first time. A collection which was made on the ground for the Essex professionals realised £46 15s., including £5 which was telegraphed.

Young finished with seven wickets, and *Wisden* commented: 'Young won the match for Essex on the Saturday morning and at the same time establishing his fame as a bowler. He was practically unplayable, pitching outside the off stump and turning in six or eight inches with his arm.'

Within two months Young was an England player, but he had been beaten by one Test match as Essex's first international. Walter Mead was selected for the second Test, at Lord's, on 15, 16 and 17 June. Australia won by ten wickets, and Mead took 1 for 91. He never played Test cricket again. 'Sailor' Young was brought in for the third and fourth Tests, took 12 wickets for 262 runs and similarly was never picked again.

There were other firsts for Essex in 1899. Fane scored 207 against Leicestershire, at Grace Road, the first double century to be hit for Essex. The County ran up 673, and Fane and Perrin put on 236 for the second wicket. McGahey hit 99, and he and Fane added 189 for the third wicket. Fane and

Perrin finished eighth and ninth in the national averages, with Perrin hitting six centuries.

Kent were beaten twice, and Yorkshire were beaten by nine wickets at Sheffield where Perrin and Turner put on 193 for the third wicket. Buckenham and Walter Turner, younger brother of A J Turner, made their Essex debuts. W M Turner, in particular, impressed but, like his brother, his career was restricted by his army duties although he was to play until 1926.

Mead and Young dominated the bowling, and both passed a one hundred wickets in all cricket. Mead had 146 at 18.04, and Young 139 at 21.79. Bull took fewer wickets, 65, and at a higher cost, 27.18, and although none realised it at the time, his brief first-class career was nearly at its close. The absence of Kortright was sorely felt; Essex slipped to sixth in the table.

The rise of Young had been spectacular. Born in Leyton in 1876, he had joined the Royal Navy and come to prominence in minor cricket, when Green saw him bowl in the nets at the County Ground. So impressed was Green with Young's left-arm medium pace that he bought him out of the Navy in order to play for Essex. Ever after, Harding Young was known as 'Sailor'.

He played well in his few matches in 1898, but his reputation was really founded on that memorable match at Leyton at the beginning of the following season. On the strength of that, and with some consistent bowling in the weeks that followed, he was chosen both for England and the Players. At The Oval he had match figures of 7 for 141 for the Players, and he and Hayward added 135 for the last wicket. Young's 81 was to remain the highest score of his career. Indeed, nothing was ever quite as good for 'Sailor' Young after his first, full, and wonderful season.

He was troubled by rheumatism, and he is perhaps best remembered now as an excellent Test match umpire. Home Gordon believed that Young was over-rated as a bowler and in his chapter on 'Essex Excellencies' in his book, *Background to Cricket*, he makes a valid point:

> There is one case in which my personal judgment was against all the other critics: and that was in my regarding 'Sailor' Young as a somewhat over-rated bowler at the time when he was chosen for England. I had been at Leyton on that memorable morning when he and Walter Mead had so wonderfully defeated the Australians. But it had appeared to me that individually they had been perplexed by the immaculate length and work on the ball effected by the latter, and when they struggled to get away from him, had an impatient crack at his tall colleague and paid the penalty. This was not the general view. I saw

others of his best performances and, excellent though some were, my opinion still remained unchanged. When he became umpire, his remarkable loquacity occasionally worried players, though he was regarded as sound.

It should never be forgotten that bowlers operate in pairs, but equally, nothing should detract from either bowler on that historic day at Leyton.

The rest of the season, as we have noted, did not live up to that exceptional start. Of the 20 matches, six were won and six were lost – and there were some bizarre events. Essex were bowled out for 59 and 64 by Yorkshire at Leyton and lost in two days. In an attempt to try to improve the standard of the wickets, Edward Freeman, the groundsman, consulted Sam Apted at The Oval where the pitches were renowned. Apted advised him to apply a liquid mixture 'three days before the match'.

Surrey were the next visitors to Leyton, and the match proved to be 'the great catastrophe of the Essex season'. The wicket had been over-watered and Essex were bowled out in $1\frac{1}{4}$ hours for 37. Surrey went on to win by nine wickets, but the game was over inside two days and the pitch was completely spoiled. Freeman had applied the mixture on each of the three days, instead of only the third day before the match. He learned his lesson, and thereafter the wickets at Leyton were excellent.

But, whatever the misgivings about the playing record of the last year of the old century, Essex County Cricket Club continued to thrive. There were now nearly 2500 members, the Great Eastern Railway was to run express trains from Liverpool Street to Leyton on match days, and Green was paying for Alfred Shaw and Robert Peel to give three weeks of pre-season coaching. Income exceeded expenditure, the experiment of running a 2nd XI had proved to be a success and was to be continued, and matches with Middlesex were to be resumed. Walter Mead was to have the Essex v Middlesex match at Leyton as his benefit, a fitting tribute to 'the invaluable services which this sterling cricketer has rendered the county in the past ten years'.

In an interview, Perrin was full of optimism. He thought that Lucas's style was the most perfect in the game and that Owen was a cheery, approachable captain who had the full respect of all his men. For Mead, he had only the highest praise, and the return of Kortright would mean that Essex could again be contending for the championship.

The coaching of Shaw and Peel at Leyton aroused much interest. The players treated it most seriously, and large crowds gathered to watch. 'The assemblage behind the nets,' said *Cricket*, 'is severely critical. It consists for the most part of the British working man, who manages to spare an hour or two when duty calls him to superintend the welfare of his county in the cricket field.' Observers were most impressed that

Essex v Australians

Leyton, 11, 12 and 13 May 1899

Essex	1st innings		2nd innings	
†Mr H G Owen	c Darling b Trumble	28	c Iredale b Jones	6
H Carpenter	b McLeod	23	c Kelly b Trumble	2
Mr P A Perrin	lbw b Trumble	5	c Iredale b Jones	0
Mr C P McGahey	b Trumble	12	b McLeod	39
Mr A J Turner	b Trumble	0	b Trumble	54
*T M Russell	b Trumble	22	st Kelly b McLeod	14
Mr A P. Lucas	not out	46	not out	8
Mr F L Fane	b Trumble	0	b Trumble	0
W Mead	c Darling b Trumble	4	b McLeod	8
Mr F G Bull	c Noble b Trumble	11	c and b Trumble	2
H I. Young	b Jones	33	c Jones b McLeod	0
	b 4 lb 11	15	b 8 lb 2 nb 1	11
		199		144

	O.	M.	R.	W.	O.	M.	R.	W.
Jones	12.2	4	27	1	18	3	30	2
McLeod	21	11	45	1	15	6	32	4
Trumble	33	7	79	8	36	16	52	4
Noble	19	8	33	—	10	5	16	—
Laver					4	3	3	—

Australians	1st innings		2nd innings	
F A Iredale	c Carpenter b Bull	4	c Turner b Mead	0
†J Darling	c Russell b Bull	5	b Young	15
C Hill	c Fane b Young	36	c Lucas b Young	4
S E Gregory	c Russell b Young	21	b Young	8
*J J Kelly	b Mead	16	b Young	6
M A Noble	run out	5	b Mead	17
V T Trumper	b Young	0	b Young	3
F Laver	c and b Mead	9	not out	0
C E McLeod	not out	20	b Young	6
H Trumble	b Mead	6	b Mead	0
E Jones	b Young	6	b Young	5
	b 14 lb 2	16	b 4 lb 5	9
		144		73

	O.	M.	R.	W.	O.	M.	R.	W.
Bull	10	2	30	2				
Mead	31	12	56	3	15	6	32	3
Young	27	11	42	4	14.4	6	32	7

Umpires – M Sherwin and W Hearn

Essex won by 126 runs

† Captain * Wicket-keeper

Shaw and Peel had been insisting on fielding practice, 'for fielding has certainly not been the strong point of the Essex team of late years'.

Another remarkable innovation at Leyton was that the groundstaff imported some ducks to reduce the number of worms on the field.

All these preparations seemed to have had the best possible effect, for Essex recorded their first victory over Gloucestershire in the opening match of the season. The western county were without Grace, who had departed to manage and captain the London County side, but this was still an impressive performance. Perrin hit 106 and Carpenter made 67 and 135. Essex declared their second innings closed at 312 for 8 and won by 261 runs. Mead had 7 for 97 and Kortright 10 for 98 in the match. Spirits were high.

It was Carpenter who drew the highest praise from *Cricket*: 'Carpenter, as we have always said, *ought* to be a most successful batsman; he has style and skill, but hitherto he has been very little favoured by fortune. His cricket this year has, however, been excellent in every way.' It was to continue so. He hit four centuries during the season and scored 1468 runs.

The hopes aroused by the victory over Gloucestershire soared when Surrey were beaten by five runs at The Oval. Perrin played a magnificent innings of 96 on a difficult wicket, but the honours ultimately went to the bowlers, especially Mead, who had 12 for 98 in the match.

Surrey needed only 84 to win in their second innings, but Kortright, 5 for 39, and Mead, 5 for 36, bowled them out for 78. Mead ended the match by bowling Lees and Wood with successive deliveries.

Kent won by an innings at Maidstone to reduce the euphoria. At Leyton, Carpenter and McGahey hit centuries against Sussex and added 235 in under three hours for the third wicket, but rain and stubborn defence gave Sussex a draw. Fortunes revived later the same week when McGahey hit 184, his highest score at the time, and Young, with six wickets in the first innings, and Kortright, with seven in the second, ensured an innings win over Leicestershire. Bull's form had been so indifferent that he gave way to Reeves, and his first-class career was virtually at an end.

The win over Leicestershire proved to be Essex's last until Hampshire were beaten in July. There were six defeats against these four victories, and the County slumped to tenth in the table. Catches were tumbled in profusion, but defeats were punctuated with some magnificent individual performances. Mead, inevitably, took 13 for 69 at Eastbourne, but the match was drawn. Carpenter and McGahey again hit sparkling centuries at Derby. Mead took 9 for 40 in the first innings of the draw against Hampshire, which was to be the best bowling performance of his career. He was to take nine in an innings three times, but he never managed all ten. Owen hit the highest score, 134, of a career that was drawing to a close, in the win over Hampshire at Leyton.

Leyton was the scene of a greater batting exploit when Kent were the next visitors. Carpenter hit 59, and Essex were 116 for 2 when McGahey and Perrin came together. Perrin went on to hit 205 before being caught in the deep. He batted for 5¾ hours. McGahey made 142, and together they added 323 in 4¼ hours, by far the highest stand made for Essex at that time.

Carpenter hit his second century of the season against Derbyshire as he and Tom Russell, 139, added 268 for the fourth wicket. And there was still exciting batting to come in the last match, v Middlesex, at Leyton. This was Mead's benefit. Unfortunately the game was ruined by rain and Mead did not get the reward he deserved. But Kortright, going in at number six, hit 131 out of 161 in under two hours to give the game something of a flourish. However, it marked the end of Essex's poorest season since they had entered the championship.

Young had declined. Bull had dropped out of the side. Reeves showed promise, and Kortright, in the last season in which he was at all effective, was the only one to give the incomparable Mead support. In all matches Mead took 131 wickets. Henry Perkins, secretary of MCC from 1876 to 1897, insisted that Mead was the best bowler whom he ever saw walk to the middle at Lord's. Comparisons between generations are not a sensible thing to become involved in, but one would venture to suggest that Essex have never had a better bowler than Walter Mead.

The first year of the century had marked signs of the end of a great era in Essex cricket. A J Turner had been unable to play because he was serving with his regiment in South Africa. F G Bull had played his last. Warner and others insisted that Bull spun the ball more vehemently than any other bowler in the closing years of the 19th century, but by 1900, he had lost the art. He took only five wickets at very high cost and did not play for Essex again. At the beginning of 1901 he resigned as assistant secretary and took up a business appointment in Blackburn. In 1904 he joined East Lancashire, and he later surprised people by turning professional, serving for two years with Perth and then again with East Lancashire and Rishton. On 16 September 1910, he was found drowned at St Anne's-on-Sea in Lancashire. He had last been seen two days earlier when he sent his key to his landlady via a messenger. When his body was found a handkerchief was tied round his neck in which was knotted a stone weighing 7 lbs, and his coat and trouser pockets were lined with stones. It was a tragic and lonely end for one who had served Essex so well for a brief period.

McGahey succeeded Bull as assistant secretary, but the first AGM gave a significant piece of financial information. It was announced that the rate of interest on the mortgage on the ground had been reduced and the ground had been transferred from Mr C E Green and Mr F Green into the names of trustees on behalf of the Club. The number of members had decreased.

So it was in mixed health that the County entered the new season. Freeman had cured the uncertainties of the Leyton wicket, and by 1901, it was one of the most perfect batting pitches in the country. As in the previous season, Essex began with a victory when Sussex were beaten by 171 runs at Leyton. McGahey started one of his finest seasons with innings of 77 not out and 125. The season was to bring him 1838 runs, average 48.36, and a place in MacLaren's side to tour Australia. McGahey never found his form on that tour, but played in the last two Tests without success; he never represented England again.

McGahey set up an Essex record when he hit a century in each innings, 114 and 145 not out, in the drawn match against Gloucestershire at Leyton on 23, 24 and 25 May. He was the first Essex player to hit a century in each innings of a match, and incredibly, later the same week, 'Bob' Carpenter, in his benefit season, equalled the feat with 127 and 104 against Kent. As McGahey was an amateur and Carpenter a professional, both can be said to have established a record.

There was little else for Essex to cheer about. There were usually plenty of runs, but the bowling rested more and more on Mead, for Kortright was a spent force. He had never really survived his season off through injury, nor had he adapted easily when the over was increased to six balls in 1900. In 1901, his 25 wickets for Essex cost more than 40 runs apiece. Young, though he took 70 wickets, was also expensive, and Mead's best support came from Reeves and McGahey, the latter being successful with his leg-breaks.

Tom Russell had begun to give way on occasions behind the stumps to his brother, Alfred Edward, who hit 100, the only century of his career, against Derbyshire in August.

Amid the plethora of runs and the failure to get wickets came a remarkable occasion at Leyton when Yorkshire, although they scored only 104, were victors by an innings and 33 runs!

Essex batted first, and with Hirst taking 7 for 12 and Rhodes 2 for 17, they were bowled out for 30. This remains the lowest score that they have ever made in a county match. In the second innings, Hirst took 5 for 17 and Rhodes 4 for 20, and Essex made 41. Playing his first game for Essex in that match was John William Henry Tyler Douglas. He was a fortnight short of his 19th birthday, and he was bowled by Hirst for 0 in both innings. It was a lowly beginning for one who was to become a dominant force in Essex cricket for a quarter of a century.

Tenth in 1901, 13th in 1902 with only two victories, these were anxious times for Essex, and the spectre of those hard, early days at Leyton began to reappear. But there were bright moments. Perrin, Fane and McGahey still managed to flourish in a wet summer, and Gilbert Tossetti, an amateur from Woodford Wells, hit 132 not out at Old Trafford; but these shafts of light were rare.

Ranjitsinhji and Newham set up a world record seventh wicket partnership of 344 for Sussex at Leyton. Owen could play in only half the matches, and Lucas shared the captaincy with him. Kortright played exclusively as a batsman, his occasional overs of leg-breaks bringing him two wickets for 177 runs.

Owen, now in his 43rd year, stood down as captain. At the AGM in April 1903, Green paid him the warmest of tributes, for he had led Essex into the first-class game, and taught them to play with fun and zest. Had their fielding matched their batting and their bowling at the close of the previous century, he may well have led them to the title. History reveals that he had led them closer than anyone else was to do for the next 75 years. He was presented with a scroll, a gold watch and chain, a gun and a purse of 200 guineas.

Perhaps, as Laura says in *Lark Rise*: 'Nothing ever seemed quite the same again after the old queen died.' Certainly, for Essex cricket, the first golden age was at an end.

CHAPTER 8

The Advent of Johnny Douglas 1903–14

If it is thought that now and then I am apt to emphasize the strength of the Essex bowling, I must mention that we went through a whole season about that time with only one total of over 330 scored off us. I don't think any eleven has done that very often, before or since. And while doing it we were not even in the hunt for the championship! Through a side holding P A Perrin, C P McGahey, 'Bob' Carpenter, A J Turner, F L Fane, H G Owen and sometimes A P Lucas could not be described as other than really strong in batting, our failure to get placed in the annual race used to be ascribed, in a rather monotonous parrot-like fashion, as being due to bad catching. It was really due to other elevens being stronger than ours, the best reason of all, and to the fact that we were not a good batting side when the ball was turning.

In searching for reasons for lack of success, one is always inclined to probe constantly at the weaknesses of one's own side, which makes E H D Sewell's assessment all the more refreshing, particularly as it was made reflectively in 1931.

Sewell was born in India where his father served as an army officer. He returned to England to be educated at Bedford Grammar School and he played for Bedfordshire. He went back to India as a civil servant and made his mark in cricket with some mighty scores. He was the first batsman in India to score three successive hundreds. In 1900 he returned again to England and began a residential qualification for Essex, making his debut as a professional in Owen's last year as captain. He was to be a lively character for three seasons, and he later became a journalist and author, writing several books on cricket and also covering rugby. He always spoke highly of the captaincy of Owen's successor, Charles Kortright, finding him 'a joy to play under'.

The captaincy, of course, had to go to another amateur when Owen stood down. Owen himself was 43; Lucas was two years older and growing increasingly deaf. McGahey was 31, Perrin 26, Fane 27, and Kortright 31. Kortright had been an Essex player since 1889, four years before McGahey first appeared, and it was Kortright who was invited to captain Essex in 1903.

In some ways it was a strange choice. As a bowler, Kortright was almost a spent force. In 1903 he was to bowl only 118.2 overs, a mixture of leg-spin and pace. This did bring him 28 wickets at 14.21 runs each, which placed him at the top of the bowling averages, but no longer did he strike terror into the hearts of batsmen as he had done four or five years earlier. As a batsman, he averaged just over 12 and failed to score a fifty – so the doubt must occur as to whether or not he was any longer worth a place in the side.

That Kortright himself had doubts is certain, for after one year in office, he resigned, the announcement that he was standing down surprising all at the AGM. It should not be imagined that his year of captaincy was without success. In a wet summer, which caused the total abandonment of the matches against Middlesex at Lord's and Hampshire at Leyton, a severe blow to the finances, Essex won seven and lost six of the 20 matches scheduled and climbed to joint eighth in the championship.

The season began badly with Yorkshire outplaying Essex at Leyton and bowling the home side out for 96 and 72. There was little optimism when Essex visited The Oval in their next match, and the game could not begin until 3.00 pm because of the dampness. The first day also came to an early close when, in failing light, Essex reached 161 for 6. They added only another 26 the next morning, and by lunch, with Hayward in control, Surrey were 98 for 3.

In the afternoon, Mead produced a spell of 6 for 2 in 33 balls, and Surrey were out for 107. Sewell, who had already taken 90 off the Surrey bowling for Grace's London County side, hit a brisk 60 when Essex batted again, and with Perrin and McGahey making useful contributions, Kortright declared at 256 for 6.

When Surrey batted again Young reproduced the form of 1899 and took 5 for 25. Mead had 5 for 44, to give him match figures of 12 for 78, and Surrey were out for 76 in under 1½ hours.

A week later the teams played the return match at Leyton. Surrey lost both openers for 4, but Hayes hit finely to lift them to 148 for 4 by lunch. In the afternoon came a collapse similar to the one at The Oval, but this time Claude Buckenham was the architect. He took 8 for 53, and Surrey were out for 169.

A not out 110 by McGahey took Essex to a first innings lead of 88. Eventually, the home side was asked to make 166 to win, and on the last morning there was a splendid finish. Essex slipped to 76 for 6. Edward Russell then joined Buckenham in a stand of 55, and Tremlin stayed with Buckenham until the victory was accomplished. It was the first time that Essex had beaten Surrey twice in a season.

Mead, with 114 wickets at 14.60, dwarfed all other bowlers for the County although Buckenham showed great promise, as did Douglas, and Young displayed glimpses of his old form. Mead was named as one of *Wisden*'s 'Five Cricketers of the Year', and the final sentence of the *Wisden* dedication summed up what most felt: 'Few bowlers, watched from the ring, impress one as so habitually getting spin on the ball.'

He played a vital part in Essex's ten-wicket victory over Leicestershire in the last match of the season at Leyton. This was a magnificent win, for Essex had been put in to bat on a drying wicket.

Fane, McGahey, Douglas and Sewell scored only 26 between them, but The Reverend Frank Hay Gillingham hit his first hundred for Essex, shared a stand of 88 with Perrin and one of 107 with Reeves, who hit 65, and Essex reached a remarkable 308.

Gillingham had made his debut in the opening match of the season, the disastrous game against Yorkshire, and the Leicestershire match was the tenth of his first season. Educated at Dulwich College, a place of learning later to provide Wilcox and Bailey, Gillingham was turned 27 when he first played for Essex, but he was to continue to appear for them until 1928 when he was 53.

He had studied at Durham University, and when he was ordained he was appointed curate at Leyton. This enabled him to qualify for Essex by residence. Tall and powerfully built, he believed in hitting the ball hard in front of the wicket. His maiden hundred was described as showing him 'driving with power and frequently jumping in to meet the ball'.

Rain during the night made Leicestershire's task on the second day a difficult one, and they twice fell to Mead, who took 7 for 50 and 8 for 65. It was to be Mead's last appearance for Essex for two seasons.

Relationships between Committee and professionals had become strained, and a dispute with Carpenter had meant that this fine batsman had not played at all in 1903. Now Mead and the Committee came into conflict as he requested an increase in pay for the winter period. His request could not have come at a worse time, for the Essex finances had again become a grave cause for concern.

Wisden was regretful of Mead's action:

> It is a thousand pities that after the close of the past season he should have become estranged from his county over a question of money. Into the merits of the dispute this is not the place to enter, but one cannot help expressing the opinion that Mead was very ill advised to press for an increase of winter pay at a time when the finances of the county club were in such a bad state. There can be no doubt that by taking the course he did, he alienated a good many of his friends. Some very severe things were said about him when, in November, Essex held a special meeting to devise means for clearing their debts.

The special meeting to which *Wisden* refers is reported in *Bailey's Magazine* for December, 1903:

> A special general meeting of the Essex County Cricket Club was held on November 10th, when that most enthusiastic sportsman, Mr C E Green, told a large number of members that the club had to face a deficit of £1,500, which has to be found by the end of December. There was £300 subscribed in the room, and a committee has been appointed to undertake the collection of funds, but there is still much to be done.
>
> The heavy falling-off of membership is one of the chief causes of the financial crisis, and of course the impossible weather of the past season has had a cruel effect upon the receipts at the gate.

The reporter went on to state that other counties were also experiencing difficulties and had only been saved by the proceeds from the last Australian visit to England.

> There is something rotten in the state of first-class cricket; enormous enthusiasm and pains and troubles are exercised on behalf of these counties, and nothing comes of it all, except drawn games, high averages, both batting and bowling, and high salaries and expenses.
>
> So if there are not so many subscribers to some county cricket clubs as there used to be the fault probably lies with the cricket club, and not with the subscriber, who would probably be eager enough to pay his guinea and get his value for it. At one time the wicket at the Essex County Ground at Leyton was made so absurdly easy that a selfish, scheming batsman could spend whole days at the wicket almost at will, and, after all, the public may be pardoned if they want a little variety in the batting they have to witness.

> The zeal and enthusiasm of Mr C E Green are so great that we feel sure he will pull through this crisis the club of which he himself was the father, but the position looks rather ugly, and we hope that lovers of cricket in Essex will come to the rescue.

That supporters, in the main, follow only success is not a phenomenon of the 1970s and 1980s. The membership, which had reached more than 2500 at the close of the last century, had dwindled to a few hundred. There was a drive to restore it to its former number, and there were donations and smoking concerts in an effort to raise money.

The blight which threatened the County Club threatened others also. Southend Cricket Club had come close to extinction at the end of the 19th century, but it had been revived thanks to the efforts of Mr C F Clark, like Green, an enthusiast. Clark complained at a smoking concert held at Victoria Hotel in March 1903, when, as captain of Southend, he chaired the evening: 'It was always a difficult matter to steer a cricket club through with success. There is not that spirit of enthusiasm shown in cricket as in football. If we could only secure the attendance at cricket matches that football teams secure it would relieve to a very great extent the anxiety that is always attached to the management of a cricket club. The general public do not support a cricket club with any enthusiasm, and this is to be regretted, for cricket is our national game.'

Three months before this, Clark had approached Borradaile with the idea of Essex playing a match at Southend, and the Essex secretary had stated publicly that he was sure the Committee would welcome such a thing, but, for the moment, that was in the future. For the present, Clark was instrumental, as reported later in the *Southend-on-Sea Observer*, in making the Southend Club assist 'the County Executive when the latter were in very low water by contributing the highest sum subscribed by any Club in the county'.

Through the efforts of a few devoted men, and the generosity and kindness of friends, Essex County Cricket Club received a further stay of execution and began the 1904 season under a new captain, Frederick Luther Fane. No captain can ever have succeeded to the position at a more difficult time: the Club had narrowly escaped liquidation and the backbone of their bowling for the past 12 years would not be playing.

Fane had been educated at Charterhouse, narrowly missed getting his blue as a freshman at Oxford, but had appeared against Cambridge in 1897 and 1898. His maiden first-class hundred had been a double one, but his best years were to come after he had become captain of Essex. An attractive, front-footed player, he was most happy when opening the innings. E H D Sewell considered him something of a forgetful captain, and it is likely that he never really relished the job. His first season turned out to be every bit as trying as it had promised to be.

Essex slipped to 14th in the table, the lowest position that they had ever occupied at that time. The first of their three victories came at Leyton at the beginning of June when Buckenham took 8 for 33, his best return in first-class cricket. This was followed by an innings victory at The Oval where Essex made 616 for 5 declared, and McGahey and Carpenter put on 328 for the third wicket. This was to remain a record for any Essex wicket for 33 years. Carpenter hit 199, the highest score of his career, and McGahey made 173. The only other Essex victory was to come at Leicester in the last match of the season.

Gillingham, who headed the batting averages, hit 201 against Middlesex on his first appearance at Lord's. The most sensational happenings, however, came against Derbyshire at Chesterfield. E H D Sewell was playing in this match in which Essex scored 597 in their first innings, Perrin made 343 not out, and Essex lost. Some of Sewell's forthright comments on the match are worth recording:

> A recent history of cricket states that this game was played on a good wicket throughout. That statement is a sheer invention.
>
> When I drew Perrin's attention to it his remark was such that I feel bound to repeat it: 'I wish the writer could have had one of the balls I had in my first over from "Bestie"! It pitched outside my off-stump and passed behind me.' So much for the good wicket! Perrin was speaking of the wicket as it was after about ten minutes' play on the first day, as he went in first wicket down when Carpenter was out for five runs.
>
> Essex batted first, and P. A. Perrin made 343 not out, at the rate of nearly 60 runs per hour for close upon six hours!! In doing this he hit the absolutely unprecedented number of 68 fours, a figure never approached before or since by anybody, not even 'W.G.', who is seldom an 'also ran' where any cricket record is concerned. It is true to say that Chesterfield is one of the smaller county grounds, but those fours would have been fours anywhere. Two fast bowlers, Warren and Bestwick, had four men on the boundary for him, but could not stop the torrent.

In fact, Perrin hit 68 fours, 4 threes, 10 twos and 39 singles. The law still existed until 1910 that a six was only scored when the ball was hit out of the ground, and it is alleged that 14 of Perrin's boundaries would have been sixes four years later. His innings remains the only triple century ever made for Essex.

Derbyshire came within 49 of the Essex total. Their West Indian opening batsman, Charles Ollivierre, hit 229. Essex batted one short in their

13. *Percy Perrin, leaving the field after scoring his record 343 not out against Derbyshire at Chesterfield in 1904. This stands as the highest individual innings by any player for Essex.*

second innings, Gillingham having 'gone in the thigh'. Sewell takes up the story again:

> By this time the never perfect wicket had crumbled.
>
> Nor Derbyshire, nor Yorkshire, Lancashire and Surrey combined, could have got that Essex side, even though one short, out for 97 on a good wicket. But that was what happened. I made over 40 of those runs thanks to the famous Derbyshire pair keeping their unplayables for the batsmen on our side, and Derbyshire had to get 147 to win, with reasonable but not ample time in which to get them.
>
> The interest in this absorbingly interesting game had not by any means yet evaporated. It had happened that in the first innings a man

of colour – C. A. Ollivierre – and, except Ranji and Trumper of deathless renown, no player had better wrists than this coal-black batsman – had made 229. He was soon well on his way to the then rare feat – there were bowlers and captains in those days – of a hundred in both innings of a match. Early on he was joined by the late Bill Storer, a man who believed in England for the English and was not enamoured by importations, especially those of ebon hue. Storer soon dug himself in and proceeded to make tracks for talent money. As 'time' and the inevitable result drew near we had the not unamusing spectacle of one batsman trying to bag the bowling in order to get his second hundred, and the other anxious to secure the strike because of the sovereign now dangling so close that its glitter could almost be seen; while both naturally wanted to win the game. In the end Storer missed talent by two runs and the black his hundred by eight, but Derbyshire got home all right. I have never shared in a better match.

If one can disregard Sewell's rather volatile vocabulary and his concern for racial tensions in the Derbyshire team of the time, there are three things to consider.

First, there was strong opposition to the number of overseas players who were coming into county cricket. Middlesex had Trott and Tarrant from Australia, and Surrey were also to engage an Australian, Marshal. Green, destined to be President of MCC the following year, 1905, was a strong opponent of importations and roundly attacked Surrey in 1907 for their use of Marshal.

Second, the newspapers of the time were of the opinion that Gillingham was not injured, 'gone in the thigh', but had refused to take any further part in the match because the Essex side had celebrated Perrin's innings in too alcoholic a manner. Sewell denies this most emphatically, and as Gillingham, who was to become Chaplain to the King in 1939, was a most compassionate and charming man who spent most of his life working with the poor in the East End of London, it is unlikely that he would have taken so serious an action against the frivolities of other human beings.

And third, it does seem likely that Essex celebrations and inadequacies were more to blame for the second innings collapse than the pitch. If the wicket had crumbled completely, how did Derbyshire manage to score 149 for 1 in less than even time on it?

One wonders what would have happened had Mead been playing, but in 1904, nearly all the bowling was done by Bill Reeves and Claude Buckenham. Reeves took 106 wickets for Essex, but they cost more than 26 runs each, and Buckenham's 66 were also expensive.

This was Reeves's best year as a bowler. He was an honest, medium-pacer, and a furiously hard-hitting batsman. He was one of the very great

Essex stalwarts, an ever-willing workhorse, who never really reached the front rank.

With this dearth of bowling talent, it was sad that Alfred Percy 'Tich' Freeman was allowed to drift away to Kent after playing for Essex Club and Ground sides. His leg-breaks and googlies were to wreak havoc among the counties for more than a decade after the First World War, and he was to make Essex regret that they let him go. Even more sad was the Essex failure to offer a contract to one John Berry Hobbs who, having played for Cambridgeshire, went to Surrey.

Hobbs had played on Parker's Piece against Carpenter and Reeves, and Reeves and Tom Hayward had bowled to him before it was decided that Surrey would offer him a trial. His mentor, Mr Hutt, was anxious that he should join Essex and suggested to the Club that they might engage him, but, as Hobbs wrote in 1933: 'Without giving any reason, Essex declined to let me have even a trial. If there had been a different decision, I might have been playing for Essex for the last thirty years.'

The reason for Essex not pursuing an interest in Jack Hobbs could well have been financial, for the time that he approached them, 1902, was the time when things were just beginning to fall apart.

The continued absence of Mead in 1905 left the bowling as weak as it had been the previous season, particularly as Reeves fell away and took only 44 wickets. In compensation, he improved dramatically as a batsman, scoring 1172 runs, average 30.84. His uninhibited hitting became a feature of Essex cricket. He scored two centuries, both at Leyton, and his career best score of 135 against Lancashire came in two hours.

He also played a whirlwind innings against Yorkshire at Leyton. When Essex scored 521 he and McGahey put on 90 in 50 minutes, and Reeves scored 71 of them. This was the match in which Johnny Douglas made his first great impact. He took five Yorkshire wickets in eight balls, all clean bowled. He bowled Tunnicliffe with a yorker, a slower ball. It was the fifth ball of an over, and the teams went to lunch when the wicket fell. On the resumption he bowled George Hirst with the remaining ball of the over, and with the last three balls of his next over, he bowled Rhodes, Haigh and Myers. It was the first hat-trick to be accomplished by an Essex player in first-class cricket, and years later he was to remember it as a game which gave him the greatest pleasure.

Douglas was essentially a fighter, and contests with Yorkshire always brought the best out of him. They understood the way in which he played cricket, and he was ever striving to make them pay for the indignity of that 'pair' in his first match.

Yorkshire were forced to follow on in the game at Leyton, but they saved the game, ending with three wickets standing. Ernest Smith batted an hour without scoring, and he and Lord Hawke were together at the close. Yorkshire went on to win the championship.

Douglas would have appreciated Smith's effort, for he had stayed 1½ hours at Canterbury for 8 not out and saved the game for Essex against Kent.

As a bowler he showed great potential, his fast-medium pace bringing him 35 first-class wickets that year, but Fane did not always use him to the best advantage. Fane himself had formed a good opening partnership with Carpenter, and McGahey continued to score prolifically. Against Derbyshire, at Leyton, he hit the highest score of his career, 277. Essex won this, and the return match, but the only other victory in the championship was over Middlesex at Lord's when Perrin hit a hundred in each innings, the second against the clock to win the match.

The highlight of the season, however, was the victory over the Australians. This was not one of the best Australian sides, but they lost to no other county but Essex. The County had lost six of their first seven matches so that the victory over the Australians came as a total surprise. It was a personal triumph for both Buckenham and Tremlin, and it meant that the tourists had not beaten Essex since 1896.

In a low scoring match, Essex fell to Laver for 118, but Buckenham and Tremlin gave their side a first innings lead of 18, which solid batting in the second innings helped to bolster. Needing 222 to win, the Australians failed to reach their target by 20 runs, the innings ending in an extraordinary manner. Laver swung at Buckenham and skied the ball to Fane on the boundary behind the wickets where he had posted himself in order to prevent any extras being conceded.

Buckenham had match figures of 12 for 137, and Tremlin had 8 for 135. They finished the season with 90 and 99 wickets respectively.

Bert Tremlin was not the luckiest of cricketers. A right-arm, medium-pace bowler, born in Bristol, he first played for Essex in 1900. It was only the absence of Mead in 1904 and 1905 which gave him anything like a regular place in the side, although he had always performed well whenever he was brought into the team. It was perhaps typical of him that, when he returned his best bowling figures, 9 for 126 against Derbyshire in the match in which McGahey scored 277, he caught the tenth batsman off the bowling of Buckenham.

He was the steadiest and most successful bowler in the side in 1905, but when Mead returned the following year no room could be found for two bowlers so similar in pace and style and Tremlin was selected for only two matches. He still finished with 5 for 104 and, mathematically, topped the bowling averages.

Mead's absence had drained Essex, and support dwindled. *Wisden* suggested that: 'Mead's efforts during the season for the MCC and

PRICE 1d. [Printed on the Ground by PHELP BROTHERS, 450, High Road, Leyton.] 1905.

ESSEX COUNTY CRICKET CLUB, LEYTON.

ESSEX v. AUSTRALIANS,

Thursday, Friday and Saturday, June 22, 23, 24.

PLAY COMMENCES EACH DAY AT 12 O'CLOCK.

STUMPS DRAWN AT 6 THIS DAY. UMPIRES—ATFIELD & ATTEWELL.

ESSEX.	FIRST INNINGS.		SECOND INNINGS.	
1 F. L. FANE	c Cotter b Laver	4	b Noble	16
2 CARPENTER	c Laver b McLeod	24	b Cotter	2
3 C. McGAHEY	b Laver	0	c Darling b Laver	39
4 Rev. F. H. GILLINGHAM	c Hill b Laver	9	c Noble b Laver	21
5 G. TOSETTI	c Newland b Laver	14	b Noble	13
6 P. PERRIN	b Laver	0	c Duff b Laver	0
7 REEVES	c Hopkins b McLeod	11	c Duff b Laver	37
8 J. W. H. T. DOUGLAS	c McLeod b Duff	28	c McLeod b Cotter	22
9 RUSSELL (E.)	c Hill b Laver	8	c Hill b Noble	12
10 TREMLIN	b Duff	6	c sub b Noble	0
11 BUCKENHAM	not out	1	not out	20
Extras	b. 8, l.b. 4, w 1, n.b. ,	13	b 12, l.b 7, w 1, n.b 1,	21
	TOTAL	118	TOTAL	208

FALL OF WICKETS—FIRST INNINGS. SECOND INNINGS.

1	2	3	4	5	6	7	8	9	10	1	2	3	4	5	6	7	8	9	10
4	4	20	54	58	60	69	99	116	118	2	25	25	55	85	106	110	110	175	208

BOWLING ANALYSIS. FIRST INNINGS. SECOND INNINGS.

	Ovs.	Mds.	Rs.	Wks.	Nbs.	Wds.	Ovs.	Mds.	Rs.	Wks.	Nbs.	Wds.
Cotter	10	8	19	0	...	...	11·1	3	35	2	...	...
Laver	25	8	49	6	...	1	37	11	81	4	...	1
McLeod	10	4	20	2	...	...	...	...	...	...	...	...
Duff	5·5	1	17	2	...	...	...	...	...	...	...	...
Noble	...	...	...	...	...	...	26	8	66	4	1	...

AUSTRALIANS.	FIRST INNINGS.		SECOND INNINGS.	
1 R. A. DUFF	c Reeves b Buckenham	29	b Buckenham	8
6 J. DARLING	c Buckenham b Tremlin	1	b Tremlin	15
5 C. HILL	b Buckenham	5	c Gillingham b Buckenham	15
4 M. A. NOBLE	lbw, b Tremlin	1	b Buckenham	42
7 C. E. McLEOD	c and b Tremlin	12	c Buckenham b Tremlin	23
8 S. E. GREGORY	b Buckenham	0	c Carpenter b Tremlin	0
3 A. J. HOPKINS	c Perrin b Buckenham	0	not out	67
2 D. R. A. GEHRS	b Buckenham	0	b Buckenham	2
10 A. COTTER	b Tremlin	38	b Tremlin	4
11 F. LAVER	c Perrin b Buckenham	13	c Fane b Buckenham	18
9 P. M. NEWLAND	not out	0	b Buckenham	4
Extras	b. , lb. 1, w. , n.b. ,	1	b. 5, lb. 4, w. , n.b. ,	9
	TOTAL	100	TOTAL	202

FALL OF WICKETS FIRST INNINGS. SECOND INNINGS.

1	2	3	4	5	6	7	8	9	10	1	2	3	4	5	6	7	8	9	10
12	17	26	42	43	49	49	49	100	100	4	28	56	56	98	118	124	126	157	202

BOWLING ANALYSIS. FIRST INNINGS. SECOND INNINGS.

	Ovs	Mds.	Rs.	Wks.	Nbs.	Wds.	Ovs.	Mds.	Rs.	Wks.	Nbs.	Wds.
Buckenham	11·1	1	45	6	...	...	27·2	4	92	6	...	...
Tremlin	11	1	54	4	...	..	33	10	81	4	...	..
Reeves	...	...	...	...	...	...	8	0	14	0	...	...
Douglas	...	...	...	...	...	...	8	2	6	0	...	...

NEXT COUNTY MATCH at LEYTON— ESSEX v. LANCASHIRE,

Thursday, Friday & Saturday, July 13th, 14th & 15th.

LATEST SCORES FROM OTHER GROUNDS :—

BRIGHTON—Sussex v. Cambridge University.

OVAL—Surrey v Derbyshire.

WORCESTER—Worcestershire v Lancashire.

14. *Essex v Australia, 22–24 June 1905.*

London County hardly suggested that he would under any circumstances have been such an effective bowler as in previous years, but it is likely enough that his absence from county cricket affected his zest for the game.'

Certainly his return brought renewed vigour to Essex, who won nine county matches and climbed to seventh in the Championship. In reviewing the season, *Wisden* was quick to point out the difference that Mead had made to all aspects of Essex cricket:

> In every respect Essex cricket in 1906 showed a most gratifying improvement upon the disastrous experiences of the previous year. Not only did the eleven show far better cricket and meet with a much larger measure of success, but the matches received such public support as to relieve the committee, at any rate for the time, from the financial anxiety that had weighed so heavily upon them. Before the season began the committee frankly stated that unless better support was forthcoming they would at the end of the summer have to call the members of the club together, as they could not undertake the responsibility of carrying on the enterprise at a yearly loss. The fact that no such meeting of the members was found necessary was in itself convincing evidence of an altered state of affairs. The Leyton public heartily rallied round the eleven and the home matches had all their old animation. No doubt the comparative prosperity was due in some degree to the fact that the unhappy difference that had kept Walter Mead out of the team was made up. The famous bowler returned to his place and, though the dry weather was all against him, he showed so much of his skill that close upon a hundred wickets fell to him in county matches. No good purpose would be served by re-opening an unpleasant subject, but one cannot help thinking that with a little tact and diplomacy the whole difficulty might have been got over when it first presented itself. As it was Mead's services were lost to the eleven for two seasons – just at a time when his bowling was most wanted.

In all matches, Mead took 133 wickets at 20.18 runs apiece to emphasise how much he had been missed. But there were other successes. Buckenham had 135 wickets at 24.13 runs each, and Douglas, now beginning to flower as a great all-rounder, took 93 wickets at 23.05.

Douglas also passed 1000 runs as did Perrin, McGahey, Fane and Carpenter, while Walter Turner, able to play almost a full season, hit 924 in impressive style. Perrin's 1883 runs was, at the time, an Essex record although it has since been beaten, of course, by O'Connor and Gooch among others.

Among the nine victories, the most interesting was that at Southend where Leicestershire were beaten by five wickets.

Oswell Borradaile was a regular visitor to Southend Cricket Club functions, and as early as 1902, when a guest speaker at the annual dinner, he had been urged to send a Club and Ground side to play Southend for 'the Highways Committee had arranged to put a covering of red marl on the ground, so that when the heavy roller so much needed was forthcoming they would have a wicket next year good enough to invite the County eleven down to play on it.' The Southend ground at that time, however, was variously described as 'unattractive looking' and a 'wilderness', but efforts were made to improve its appearance, and Essex Club and Ground visited Southend in 1903. For C F Clark, who was to Southend cricket what C E Green was to Essex, this was only the beginning. It was he who raised the sum of £52 13s when Essex were in direst need, and this amount proved to be the largest donated by an Essex club. In addition, Clark nominated 13 new members so that his contribution and energy were well known to the County.

Clark obtained the backing of the local council, and Alderman J T Francis JP, the Southend President, was generous in his support. Keeling was a good groundsman, and he and his wife ran the refreshment pavilion in the park. Borradaile was convinced that Essex's best interests would be served if they could interest a wider public in the activities of the County Club, and he was anxious to try the experiment of playing a home county match away from Leyton. The problem was to find a ground that was good enough for first-class cricket. Southchurch Hall Park was the only ground which could offer the standard of facilities and the wicket required, and the efforts of C F Clark had ensured that if an Essex home game was to be played anywhere else but at Leyton, then it would be played at Southend. In 1906, his ambition was realised.

The magazine, *The Cricketer and Football Player*, carried an article on 9 August 1906, on 'The Rise of Cricket in Southend' in which, telling of the coming cricket week when the county match was to be followed by a game between Southend and the Gentlemen of Essex, it stated that the Southend Club was ambitious and looked forward to future years when it hoped to stage festivals to rival those of Canterbury, Cheltenham and Scarborough.

The game itself was a dramatic one. The first day, the Monday, saw a crowd of just under 4000. The arrangements were exemplary, and the wicket satisfactory, although *Wisden* later described the boundaries at each end of the ground as being too short and the outfield decidedly rough.

Leicestershire won the toss and got off to a flying start, 74 runs coming in the first 45 minutes. They were aided by two straightforward chances being missed at slip, both off Buckenham, who was an eternal sufferer. Borradaile had estimated that 63 simple catches had been put down at Leyton alone by the Essex side in 1905, and Buckenham, a very good soul, told John Clay, the Essex statistician and historian, some years later that he had had 40 slip catches 'put on the floor' in one season.

Douglas broke the stand when he had Whitehead leg before. A E Knight survived two balls before being bowled by a shooter, and when King and Coe quickly followed, Essex had gained the initiative. V F S Crawford played some bold strokes, hitting seven fours in his 37, which took only 20 minutes, and with Wood continuing to play solidly, Leicestershire reached 303. Essex had 80 minutes' batting before the close, during which time they lost Fane to finish on 77 for 1.

Tuesday again brought fine weather and a crowd of just below the 4000 mark. It was a sensational day's cricket. Essex slipped to 130 for 4, but Perrin batted faultlessly for 2½ hours before falling to Odell nine short of his century when the score was 216. There seemed a possibility of a good lead for Essex on the first innings, but Benskin brought the Essex innings to an abrupt conclusion after lunch, dismissing Buckenham, Russell and Mead with successive deliveries to end the innings with a hat-trick and give his side a first innings lead of 23.

The local press insisted that the wicket was a good one, but King had to retire hurt in the first innings after being struck by Mead, and Leicestershire had a torrid time against Douglas in their second innings.

Buckenham and Douglas started the rot by bowling Wood and Whitehard for one run each; within an hour Leicestershire were 54 for 7. Jayes, Benskin and Whiteside hit fiercely, but Leicestershire were out for 107, and Douglas returned what were to be the best figures of his career until he bettered them six years later. He moved the ball appreciably, although seven of his eight victims were bowled.

Essex needed 131 to win, and by the close they had made 54 for the loss of Douglas in 45 minutes' batting.

There were only a few hundred people on the ground on the last day, and a heavy storm shortly before play was due to start prevented any cricket before 2.00 pm. It also ruined the wicket. The Essex task had become exceedingly more difficult than had seemed likely the evening before, but Perrin, McGahey and Walter Turner played with good sense, and the match was won.

The match was a huge success, and it is interesting to note that the *Daily Mirror* realised the implications of the action that the Essex Committee had taken:

> Many of the county families of Essex have never quite forgiven the Essex Cricket Club for making its permanent home in the London suburbs. The Essex committee has broken fresh ground by giving Southend a match. And now Colchester and Chelmsford will be wanting to know when their turns are coming.

Essex v Leicestershire

Southchurch Hall Park, Southend, 13, 14 and 15 August 1906

Leicestershire	1st innings		2nd innings	
C J B Wood	not out	105	b Buckenham	1
Whitehead, H	lbw b Douglas	42	b Douglas	1
Knight, A E	b Douglas	0	b Douglas	16
King, J H	c Russell b Benham	9	b Douglas	11
Coe, S	b Douglas	10	c Carpenter b Douglas	3
†V F S Crawford	c Perrin b Benham	37	b Douglas	9
R T Crawford	b Benham	16	b Douglas	5
Jayes, T	c Fane b Mead	54	b Douglas	15
W W Odell	c Benham b Mead	9	c McGahey b Buckenham	2
Benskin, W E	b Mead	9	not out	23
*Whiteside, J P	c Turner b Reeves	0	b Douglas	10
	b 8, lb 4	12	b 10, lb 1	11
		303		107

	O.	M.	R.	W.	O.	M.	R.	W.
Buckenham	18	—	90	—	13	1	62	2
Douglas	16	4	95	3	13.5	3	33	8
Mead	14	1	68	3	1	—	1	—
Benham	14	3	35	3				
Reeves	2	1	3	1				

Essex	1st innings		2nd innings	
†F L Fane	b R T Crawford	21	b Odell	28
J W H T Douglas	c and b R T Crawford	52	b Odell	19
P A Perrin	lbw b Odell	91	c Whiteside b Odell	29
C P McGahey	c V Crawford b Odell	11	b Jayes	23
W M F Turner	c and b R T Crawford	12	c Whiteside b Odell	15
Carpenter, H	c Wood b Odell	33	not out	7
Reeves, W	c Whitehead b Odell	21	not out	6
Buckenham, C P	b Benskin	3		
Benham, C E	not out	12		
*Russell, A E	c R Crawford b Benskin	0		
Mead, W	c Whiteside b Benskin	0		
	b 18, lb 5, nb 1	24	b 3, nb 1	4
		280	for 5 wickets	131

	O.	M.	R.	W.	O.	M.	R.	W.
Jayes	16	—	49	—	7	—	32	1
R T Crawford	16	2	47	3	8	4	12	—
Odell	28	2	102	4	17.3	—	62	4
Benskin	14.3	2	34	3	4	—	21	—
King	8	1	24	—				

Umpires – F W Marlow and A A White

Essex won by 5 wickets

† Captain * Wicket-keeper

Colchester had eight years to wait; Chelmsford another 19.

An illuminated copy of the scorecard of that first county match at Southend hangs in the Southend CC pavilion today. It is the beautiful work of one who saw the game and commemorated the occasion.

While there was general satisfaction at the all-round improvement of Essex, doubts still remained. *Wisden* reported: 'The strength of the side lay in the batting, the weakness in the uncertain fielding and the want of a first-rate wicket-keeper.'

The boost in success had come at a much needed time, and that the venture at Southend was a profitable one can be seen from the fact that a complete week was given to Southchurch Hall Park for 1907 with matches against Northamptonshire and Surrey.

Before the season began, however, Fane resigned as captain because of his inability to commit himself to play regularly. At the AGM it seemed, once more, that the bad days were over. Green talked of improved cricket, bigger gates and increased membership as he fired his audience with enthusiasm. He pointed to Southend as an example of keenness to other Essex grounds, and he paid tribute to Fane for his efforts on the Club's behalf. He then went on to make a passionate attack upon the importation of overseas players, a speech prompted by Surrey's actions over the Queensland all-rounder, Marshal.

Fane had gone to South Africa with Warner's side in 1905-6. The home team had fielded the same eleven in all five Tests and beaten England 4–1. The South African googly bowlers had dominated the series, and Fane, with 143 in the first innings of the third Test, had been the only English batsman to come out of the series with any credit. Even so, he was not chosen for any of the Tests when South Africa came to England in 1907. He was vice-captain to A O Jones when England went to Australia the following winter and captained his country in the first three Tests when Jones was ill, so being the first Essex cricketer to captain England. He went on another tour to South Africa and, in all, played 14 Tests, scoring 682 runs, average 26.23, but he never played for England in England.

He was succeeded as captain of the County by Charles McGahey. *The Tribune* was revealing on the way in which this appointment was announced: 'The committee made the choice after sounding the other amateurs of the side; and there was warm approval everywhere of the new leader. Mr Green thought that the extra "devil" wanted in Essex cricket could be got out of the side by McGahey, whose seniority and experience thoroughly qualified him for the new post.'

There is none who would have disapproved of Charles McGahey. He was a man of fun and generosity, but whether he was the ideal choice for a captain is doubtful. That the Committee had doubts is apparent from

The Tribune's report. Other amateurs had been sounded, but as McGahey, at 36, was the senior man, it was hard to overlook him although Perrin, in a similar position, was to be overlooked a few years later.

McGahey's first season as leader saw Essex maintain their position in the Championship and win one more match than they had done the previous year. Mead and Buckenham, both a little expensive, dominated as bowlers, and Douglas continued to impress as an all-round cricketer. Gillingham was able to play little, and Carpenter, after one match, dropped out through illness. Young played in ten matches, and, in the twilight of his career, he performed the hat-trick. It came in the second innings of the rain-ruined match with Leicestershire at Leyton. His victims were Knight, lbw, Coe, bowled, and V F S Crawford, caught behind.

It was a year of brave performances, and Essex came very close to beating the champions, Nottinghamshire, at Leyton. In the event, Notts were to go through the season unbeaten. Mead and Reeves bowled unchanged throughout the match, taking 12 for 73 and 8 for 98 respectively. Essex, out for 59, trailed by 41 on the first innings, but through the bowling of these two worthies their final target was only 118. The game was over in two days, and at lunch on the second day, Essex were 94 for 6 in sight of victory. Hallam had bowled unchanged for Nottinghamshire throughout the match and was desperately in need of a rest. The luncheon interval came at just the right time for him. After the break he took the last four Essex wickets, and Nottinghamshire won by seven runs.

Against Sussex at Leyton, Essex trailed by 41 on the first innings, and eventually they had to make 236 to win. Fane played splendidly for 86, but when he was out the score was 169 for 4. Buckenham played steadily, but Albert Relf bowled well, and the ninth wicket went down with Essex five short of victory. Buckenham took a single and last man Mead hit the first ball he received, from Vine, majestically through the covers for four.

Lucas played his last county game against Lancashire at Leyton. He hit 49 and shared a stand of 118 for the seventh wicket with Sam Meston, who hit 130, the only century of his career. Meston was from Loughton, and his brother played for Essex in the 1920s.

Lucas played one more match a few days later, against the touring South Africans, and bagged a 'pair'. He was turned 50, and it was his 98th and last game for Essex. He was a most accomplished player, but alongside his contribution as a batsman must be set his qualities as a man, for he did so much to help shape Essex into a first-class county.

Charles Kortright also played his last game for Essex. It was against Middlesex at Leyton on 24, 25 and 26 June. He did not bowl in the first innings, and he batted at number six, being bowled by Tarrant for 4. As the game petered to a draw he bowled four overs, and at 5.15 pm on

Wednesday 26 June, he had Pelham Warner caught by Buckenham to give him figures of 1 for 20. It was fitting that Warner should be Kortright's 489th, and last, victim in first-class cricket.

Sewell, with that passion for excess that he had, could write in 1931, during the age of Larwood: 'There is nobody now within five or six yards of the pace of C J Kortright.' That may be hyperbole, but Kortright has gone into legend as the fastest bowler of all time, as has the mystery of why he never played for England.

As one star fades, another rises, and the absence of Carpenter had allowed E J Freeman and J R Freeman further opportunities. The following season saw the debut of Charles Albert George Russell. Born near the Leyton ground, the son of Tom Russell, he had played truant from school when a boy in order to watch his father play for the County. He was to become one of the County's greatest batsmen, but his time was in the future, and Essex's problems were immediate.

One of A J Turner's rare appearances inevitably brought a classic century, but indicated only what talent Essex had lost to the army. Gillingham played more, was selected for the Gentlemen and played one memorable innings, against Gloucestershire, at Leyton. He was not out overnight on the first day and hit a hundred before lunch on the second. In four hours, he hit 194, his last 94 coming in 75 minutes. He and McGahey put on 181 in two hours, 20 minutes for the fourth wicket, but McGahey, like Mead and Reeves, began to show signs of decline.

Douglas passed 1000 runs, hit a maiden century and took 83 wickets, but the side won only five matches. Charles Benham promised more than he achieved with his pace bowling, and Buckenham had a disappointing year. The same old spectre reasserted itself. In the November there was yet another special general meeting at which C E Green expounded the seriousness of the financial situation and the necessity of increasing the membership to 2500 if the Club were to survive.

On this occasion the position was made easier because J H Douglas, the father of the promising all-rounder, had taken up the second mortgage on the Leyton ground for £5000. But while this alleviated Essex's financial problems, it put old Douglas in a most powerful position.

The following year, 1909, saw no respite from the pattern of worry as the County ended the season with only two wins and only Derbyshire and Gloucestershire below them in the championship. Perrin and Douglas were the only batsmen to score over 600 runs, and nobody reached 1000. A J Turner hit 117 against Nottinghamshire in the one of the two games in which he played, Perrin scored 101 not out against Lancashire and Fane saved the first of the two drawn games against the Australians with a masterly century. Apart from this there was little of note. McGahey, troubled by injury, and Gillingham had disappointing seasons, and Carpenter returned to play in five matches with only moderate success.

In bowling, Buckenham stood head and shoulders above the rest despite his apparent ill-luck with poor catching and slack fielding. Tall and spare, he was, for five or six years, among the quickest bowlers in England. His reward was to be chosen for Leveson-Gower's side, which went to South Africa in 1909–10. He played in the first four Tests and took 21 wickets, average 28.23.

In all matches in 1909 he took 130 wickets at 20.10, a highly creditable performance which earned him his Test call; he shone through a gloomy Essex season. Morale in the Club was low, and *Wisden* felt that the explanation for the side's bad performances was to be found in 'the depressed condition of the club's affairs, the cricketers having been affected by the prevailing feeling, and as a consequence, not having done full justice to their powers'.

The energy and enthusiasm of Buckenham, a better return from Mead and the resurgence of Tremlin brought renewed hope the following season and a resultant rise to 11th in the table. However, by the end of the first decade of the century, the Essex fielding had become a music hall joke, and there was little cause for either praise or optimism. As a team, Essex were consistently inconsistent.

During 1910 Turner again tantalised, hitting one of the two centuries made for the county; Gillingham made the other, although he played in only five matches. Gillingham's 145 was made against Kent at Leyton when, characteristically, Essex had a splendid 180-run win over the champions. Although they won only five matches, another of their victims, also at Leyton, was Yorkshire, who were beaten by ten wickets.

A positive acquisition was an amateur wicket-keeper of very high quality, Kenneth Lloyd Gibson, later to be knighted. He had shown exceptional promise in the Eton side and was good enough to be selected for the Gentlemen during his three seasons with Essex, but he could never play regularly. His arrival meant restricted appearances for A E Russell, while Tremlin's revival had reduced Reeves's participation to four games. There was a gradual change being brought about in Essex cricket, a movement that was soon to assume the proportions of a revolution.

The financial position was still precarious, and it had not been improved by the wet weather. In the winter of 1910–11 it was decided to seek a one shilling subscription throughout the county in an effort to raise funds. More significantly it was decided that a change of captaincy was necessary in an effort to revitalise the side. McGahey was in agreement and was happy to stand down. At a meeting in February 1911, Kortright was asked to consider taking over as captain again. He had been on the Committee since 1903, but he was now 40 years old. It is perhaps surprising to learn from his excellent biographer, Charles Sale, that he spent a month contemplating the offer before rejecting it. At a further Committee meeting on 29 March, he seconded Lucas's proposal that Johnny Douglas should be offered the captaincy.

To the outside world this came as a great shock. It was taken for granted by most that Perrin would succeed McGahey. Perrin was 35; Douglas was 29. Perrin had been playing for Essex since 1896 and for most of that time had been the side's leading batsman; Douglas had made his unimpressive debut some five years after Perrin's and was still little more than a promising all-rounder. Yet, in offering the captaincy first to Kortright and then to Douglas, the Committee was obviously determined that the job should not go to Perrin.

Sir Home Gordon, in his book, *Background of Cricket*, which is dedicated to Perrin and is hostile to Douglas, wrote of Perrin:

> He ought to have led Essex and would have done it admirably. But old Douglas – who succeeded me on my first chairmanship of the Club Cricket Conference – held the mortgage on the Leyton Ground and intimated that he would foreclose if J.W.H.T. was not made captain.

Certainly the father was desperately ambitious for the son, and even Charles Bray, ever loyal to John Douglas, believes that the old man 'no doubt pulled the strings', but there are other considerations, and the seed of them may lie in remarks by Perrin's champion, Home Gordon: 'Arising from innate shyness there was a trifle of uncouthness in Perrin when he first played in important games, but this soon disappeared, and his dry wit always enabled him to get the better of those who had the temerity to chaff him.'

It is possible that there were those who believed that the 'uncouthness' had not disappeared. There have been cricketers since, some of them with Essex, who have found it hard to escape from the prejudices which the indiscretions of their youth have created; so may it have been with Perrin. That the senior man was upset is undeniable, and he refused to play in the first two fixtures of the 1911 season, but he was not one to hold resentment for long and he quickly returned to play under Douglas.

J W H T Douglas was to lead Essex for 18 years – only W G Grace and Lord Hawke have led a county side for longer, and it is time that we now looked more closely at one who has a most vital place in this history. We must start with the father.

J H Douglas was a successful businessman, controlling a firm which was concerned with the importation of timber from which the caskets for encasing cement were made. He was a sportsman of note, the winner of the Queensbury Amateur Middleweight Championship three times in the 1870s and a club cricketer of note. The family home was in Clapton, Middlesex, and it was here that JWHT was born on 3 September 1882. The boy inherited much from his father, in ability, in temperament and in his unwillingness to admit defeat. Douglas senior inserted in the boy a passion to succeed at sport. He lived his own ambitions through his son, and a link was forged between them that was to last until their deaths.

J H Douglas claimed to have discovered Walter Mead at Clapton Cricket Club and to have introduced him to Essex. It was certainly through his club cricket that he met Hatt, Headmaster of Moulton Grammar School near Spalding, Lincolnshire, and to him that he entrusted JWHT for his formative years. From there, the boy moved to Felsted.

The old man had sworn his son to sport like a young Hannibal, and by the time he arrived at Felsted, JWHT was eminently competent at half-a-dozen sports. On sports day he was to win the $\frac{3}{4}$-mile race, beating future Olympic runners, and a few weeks later he would take the junior fives tournament. He had been taught boxing from an early age, and he twice won the Public Schools' boxing title. He was a soccer player of talent for house and school, and he was most proficient at hockey. All this suggests that Douglas was a natural athlete, but he was not. What he achieved, he achieved through hard work, and for the remainder of his life he believed that others were capable of doing the same.

His participation in other sports continued long after he had begun his cricket career with Essex and Grace's London County side. He played soccer for England against Bohemia, and in 1908, in London, he won the Olympic Games middleweight boxing title when he beat 'Snowy' Baker of Australia in the final of a memorable and close contest. It is his cricket, however, which concerns us.

He captained, with some success, Felsted in his last year, 1901, because the original choice, E W Smith, fell ill. He was not a great academic, for his school life had been largely dedicated to sport. His nickname in senior school was 'Pro', awarded part in admiration, part in envy, and part in criticism that there was something not altogether right in Douglas's ruthless dedication to games. In this sense he anticipated the future.

By the time he left Felsted, the Douglas family had moved to Wanstead where the old man, JH, used his wealth and position to put the Wanstead Club on a firmer footing. He had the wicket entirely relaid with turf from the old Tottenham cricket ground. The operation was supervised by Freeman, the Essex groundsman, and was paid for by JH, who captained the club from 1907 to 1921. JWHT played for them for 28 years.

Old Douglas had championed his son, forwarding his claims at every level, but the boy was far from being a milksop. He was a tough and determined man, who knew his own mind and wanted his own way. He was

15. *JWHT (Johnny Won't Hit Today) Douglas.*

one who demanded a reaction. As his friend Charles Bray wrote: 'You either liked or respected John Douglas or you loathed him.' Most of those in the Essex side would have followed him anywhere.

Beneath his brusque manner and strong sense of discipline was a kindness and consideration for others. He was generous and understanding to the Essex professionals, and helpful to those who got into any troubles, for he looked upon them as part of his household. On away fixtures he would never think of settling down for the evening before checking with the professionals in their hotel that they were happy and comfortable. And although his experience as a captain before he took over at Essex in 1911 was very limited, it was once written:

> He had a splendid conception of a captain's duties, and he was a wonderful all-rounder, with a fighting spirit second only, in my experience, to that of Jardine. Douglas was popular with all the men he led, he was friend to all – he would take an interest in a youngster in the other side just as he would take an interest in a youngster in his own side – and he was brimful of the most sterling qualities.

The writer is not an Essex man, but Herbert Sutcliffe of Yorkshire and England.

If Douglas had a weakness, it came from his own strength. He was hard and fit, and he believed that all were capable of being the same; this gave him a contempt for physical weakness or fatigue. He could bowl for hours without loss of pace, accuracy or enthusiasm, and could never understand why others could not do the same. Often he would become so immersed in his own efforts that he lost track of what was happening elsewhere. As a captain, he relied on endeavour and inspiration rather than imagination and vision. To those who didn't pull their weight, and especially to those he felt were trying to exploit him, he was a merciless tyrant. As a captain, his impact on Essex cricket was immediate.

His reign could not have begun on a better note. He hit 47 and 55 against Yorkshire at Leyton. In the second innings, he and Fane began with a stand of 109, and Essex, having trailed by seven on the first innings, won by 131 runs with Mead and Tremlin to the fore. In the next match, at The Oval, Douglas hit 60 and 34, and he and Fane, who hit a magnificent 217, the highest score of his career, began the match with another century partnership. Essex led by 219 on the first innings, but Tom Hayward played superbly to deny them victory on the last afternoon.

Middlesex were the next visitors to Leyton and reached 498. In spite of Douglas's 80, and an exhilarating 71 out of 89 in 45 minutes by Bill Reeves, Essex had to follow on, but Fane and Douglas put on 81 at the second attempt, and Perrin, playing his first game under Douglas, hit a hundred and shared a stand of 162 with John Freeman, which saved the game. There was a century by Gillingham, in the win over Derbyshire, and then came the first setback, defeat at Eastbourne.

This was a reversion to former days. Thanks to another fine innings by Fane, 162, Essex led by 73 on the first innings, but collapsed on a good wicket in the second and were beaten by 119 runs. Sussex were a moderate side, and the defeat was a bitter disappointment. Unfortunately it was to be repeated.

With Mead taking 13 for 133 and Perrin hitting 101, Worcestershire were overwhelmed. More impressively, Kent, who were to finish second in the championship, were beaten at Tonbridge. Douglas hit 98 and took seven wickets in the match, and Buckenham had 10 for 148. This was championship form, and with lowly Sussex the next visitors to Leyton, morale was high.

All began well. A consistent batting display took the home side to 271. Then Buckenham took 7 for 78, and Essex led by 104 on the first innings. Disaster followed. The brothers Relf bowled unchanged, and Essex were shot out for 89. Essex still had a chance of winning, for Sussex needed 194 to win, but the fielding was deplorable and the visitors won by six wickets. At Tonbridge, the Essex out cricket had been quite magnificent, but against Sussex, it slipped back to its old standard, and hopes of the championship slipped by with it.

There were still some fine wins to come, particularly when Jack Freeman hit 81 and 105 not out against Surrey, and Buckenham had 11 for 161 to give Essex the match by 182 runs, but the County had to be content with sixth place. This was a vast improvement on recent seasons, and generally the morale, which had been so low, had risen appreciably.

The shilling fund had excited a good response, and the matches at Leyton were well supported. Together these factors helped to bring about a far healthier financial position. The success on the field had been founded on good team work. In all matches, Perrin, Douglas and Fane exceeded 1000 runs; the bowling was capable. It is amusing to read now that *Wisden* took Douglas to task for entrusting the new ball to two fast bowlers:

> It is a rather delicate point to touch upon, but one may be forgiven for questioning the wisdom of starting with two fast bowlers, as this always involved having to fall back later upon two men of medium pace. Better results might possibly have been obtained had the attack been more diversified. Without a left-hander at his disposal, Douglas was limited in his resources, but one cannot help thinking that he would have done well at times to open the bowling either with himself or Buckenham and one of the medium-pace bowlers, as a greater

contrast in style and pace would have from the start have pressured the batsmen.

Nothing could detract, however, from the impact that Douglas had made on the Essex team. He had demanded better fielding, and for the most part he had got it. He had concentrated on establishing a team spirit, and he had achieved that too. Only 14 players represented Essex during the season, and of those, Campbell, an amateur, played in four matches, Gillingham and Russell in nine and Reeves in eight. Douglas, Buckenham, Carpenter, Tremlin and Mead played in all 18 county games; McGahey and Gibson missed only one apiece.

Buckenham was chosen for two Test trials, which were arranged to help the selectors in their task of choosing a side to go to Australia; a third match, at Old Trafford, had to be abandoned. Buckenham performed well, but he failed to make the party.

One has referred often in these pages to the contests between The Gentlemen, the amateurs, and the Players, the professionals. They were the height of the social cricket season, and they were treated with the utmost seriousness, both as Test trials and as matches. Selection for such a match was considered the highest honour.

Douglas was selected to play for the Gentlemen, both at The Oval, and at Lord's. The matches followed one upon the other, but the Lord's match was considered the important fixture. He had bowled well throughout the season, batted consistently and played a splendid innings of 176 against Nottinghamshire at Trent Bridge when he and Perrin, who made a hundred in each innings for the third time, added 221 for the second wicket.

At The Oval, Douglas had little success, but at Lord's, he was to register one of his greatest triumphs. Strong teams were assembled and, from the start, the wicket gave the bowlers some assistance. The great S F Barnes threatened to run through the Gentlemen, but Douglas hit 72 in 3¼ hours and thwarted him. The Gentlemen reached 352. *Wisden*, not for the last time, criticised Douglas for being over-cautious, but agreed that his resolution on a doubtful wicket had made his sides' remarkably large total possible.

On the second day, as the Players were bowled out for 201, Douglas produced a magnificent spell of fast-medium-pace bowling to take 5 for 53. He followed this with 22 not out and two wickets in the second innings as the Gentlemen moved to a famous victory. On the strength of this all-round performance, J W H T Douglas was chosen to go to Australia with the MCC side in search of the Ashes.

Fry was to have captained the side originally, but was unable to go, as was Spooner. When Fry dropped out Warner became captain. No one thought to appoint a vice-captain in Warner's place.

The 1911–12 series in Australia proved to be one of the great English triumphs, and it is doubtful if a better England side has ever gone to Australia. Warner played in the opening match, in Adelaide, and then was taken ill. He did not play again on the tour. There were only two other amateurs in the party, Douglas and F R Foster, who had just led Warwickshire to the County Championship. Warner was in the position of being dictator for the tour. He decided to appoint Douglas as captain on the grounds that he had played for the Gentlemen as far back as 1907 and was richer in experience.

In the first Test Douglas is said to have erred in opening the bowling himself instead of giving the ball to S F Barnes. England lost. Thereafter it was a triumph for the Essex captain. England won the next four Tests. Douglas himself was a huge success. His stubborn batting won him the nickname of 'Johnny Won't Hit Today', and he never wore a cap, even in the hottest weather, testing himself against both the elements and his fellow men.

Douglas returned to England a hero, but there was to be something of a disappointment to follow. With Fry and others of the top flight now available, he was not chosen for another Test until the last of the triangular tournament, against Australia at The Oval. It was his first Test in England and the first Test in which he had not been captain. He scored 18 and 24 and did not bowl, but he was cheered all the way to the wicket.

Douglas's problems were not confined to him being ignored by Fry, who was, in fact, the England selector after the first Test. Essex had a dreadful year. In all matches Douglas scored 1411 runs and took 81 wickets, but in a wet summer his side floundered.

16. *A tie clip, presented to England captain J W H T Douglas after the 1911–12 tour to Australia. (From the collection of Mike Marshall.)*

Tremlin could not play through illness; Mead topped the bowling averages, but in a season where conditions were in his favour, it was obvious that his former glories were past; and McGahey's form began to desert him. In the second match of the county season, the 'twins' shared a stand of 312 in three hours for the third wicket. Perrin hit 245 in 5¼ hours, and McGahey made 150. Essex scored 609 for 4 declared having lost Fane in the opening over. They won by an innings, but it proved to be the only win of a season in which they finished one from bottom in the table.

Carpenter lost his place in the side, Fane fell away and Reeves did nothing. Russell's batting was still in embryo, and the one bright light was the form of Jack Freeman, one of the most attractive batsmen in Essex and now often the County's wicket-keeper. Thirty-three players were used during the season, among them Louden and C H Douglas, the captain's younger brother and later to be a famous boxing referee, but nothing could stem the run of failure.

Inevitably, the financial position became wretched. Inevitably, there was a Special General Meeting called in December. Essex County Cricket Club was again under threat, although it was unanimously decided that the Club would continue, but for C E Green, the father of Essex cricket, it was enough. Green was bitterly disillusioned by the trends in county cricket, a game which he had remembered and loved as an essentially amateur game, and he wanted no more of it. He now saw cricket polluted by a brand of professionalism, epitomised by the importation of overseas players, which he found unpalatable. He was heart-broken at the continued lack of support afforded to the County and tired by the continuing struggle for its survival. He resigned as Chairman of the Committee and was to play no further part in the management of the Club. However, he was unanimously elected President and accepted the position. Many of the Committee stood down with him, and a new regime, led by J H Douglas, more commercially minded, more representative of the changing society of the day, took over.

Green's last act was typical of the man who had devoted so much of his life and his wealth to Essex County Cricket. He paid off the Club's debts of £400 so that the new Committee could start 1913 with a clean sheet.

Unfortunately the season was to see no improvement in Essex cricket, two victories over Sussex and only Somerset below them in the table being all that they had to show for the year's work, but at least they stayed solvent.

As an all-rounder, Douglas had what was probably his worst season, and Essex struggled for bowlers. Tremlin, still recovering from illness, was the most effective, but Buckenham had lost his pace and at the end of the season accepted a position in Scotland – although he was to play for

Essex again. Louden, tall and strong, impressed with pace and accuracy, but he could play in only four matches.

Wisden said of Mead that he could not be expected 'to bowl with the same effect as he did years ago', but that no one had yet been found to take his place. His figures, 29 wickets at 26.20 runs each, were still better than those of Tremlin, Douglas or Buckenham. His son, Harold, played in a couple of matches, but he was never to win a regular place.

For Walter Mead, 45 years old, the days with Essex were over. The last of his games for the County came against Kent at Leyton when he bowled only one over, but finished in typically defiant style with 21 not out. The last of his wickets had come at Hove a few days earlier when he had Chaplin caught by Bristowe.

In spite of his two-year breach with Essex, he remained totally committed to them. In 1946 he wrote to Jim Coldham saying: 'I often look back over the years, especially on the personalities of the Essex team of the past in the good days when war did not interfere with getting on with the game. I still take an interest in Essex cricket and watch the county in action although it's so many years since, through AD, I had to give up playing.' Harold died in 1921. He had been badly wounded in the war and never completely recovered, but Walter lived to within two weeks of his 86th birthday. Perhaps, Warner's comment in *The Cricketer* was the most telling: 'He loved cricket with a rare enthusiasm and never for a moment gave in.'

Another whose best days were now clearly behind him was Charles McGahey, and he appeared in only 11 matches. The following season he relinquished his post as assistant secretary, played a few matches late in the summer and was awarded a testimonial.

And while McGahey was passing from the stage, others were moving to the centre. Jack Freeman continued to excite with his batting, and he finished second in the averages to Gillingham, who could play in only nine matches. It was the batting of 'Jack' Russell, however, which raised the highest hopes. He was not included in the opening match of the season, but he played in the remaining 17 games. He established himself as both capable and consistent. Like Freeman, he had benefitted much from the coaching and advice of 'Bob' Carpenter. He was to become one of the most effective batsmen in England and one of the greatest to play for Essex.

His maiden century came in the match against Hampshire at Leyton. He hit 102, and his opening partner, Colin McIver, the Forest School and Oxford University player who kept wicket well for most of the summer, hit 134. They put on 210 for the first wicket, and with Gillingham later hitting 105, Essex reached 507. They bowled Hampshire out for 190, but the south coast county scored 534 for 7 after they had followed on, thus emphasising the paucity of the Essex bowling. In the last match of the season, at Old Trafford, Russell played a faultless innings of 110 and, in doing so, became the only Essex batsman during the season to reach 1000 runs in county matches.

The success of 'Jack' Russell underlined the dynastic characteristics of the Essex Club, for both his father and uncle had played for the County. The Russells were also related to the Freemans, four of whom played for Essex, while a fifth, Jack's brother, 'Tich' played for Kent. On top of this, Bill Reeves had married a Freeman so that the Essex side was very much a family concern.

Despite a mediocre season in England, Douglas was asked to captain the MCC side to tour South Africa. He was not the first choice. Fry, Foster, Warner, Jessop and Fane were all approached at various times in the summer, but Douglas was the only one with the fitness and the time, made possible by the financial backing of his father, to accept. He hit his one and only Test century at Durban and England won the five-match series by four Tests to nil. Had Douglas's career as England's captain ended at that point, with eight wins and one loss in ten Tests, he might well have been considered as one of the greatest of England captains in Test history, but there was a period of darkness ahead.

Once again he returned to England in triumph, and again it seemed that Essex were destined for a bad season.

A fixture list extended to 24 matches opened at Leicester and, although Douglas continued the fine form he had shown in South Africa with match figures of 8 for 139 giving Essex a lead of 19 on the first innings, the home side won by a massive 239 runs. At Hove, the situation was worse as only a brave stand by Douglas and Walter Turner, and some lusty blows from Tremlin, avoided an innings defeat. Louden took 6 for 111 when Yorkshire were the first visitors to Leyton, but the White Rose county still won by an innings. The next match, at Leyton, provided an even greater fiasco.

The pitch was soaked by overnight rain, and it seemed to Douglas that it would prove difficult. He won the toss and asked Middlesex to bat. The sun did not shine, however, and rain on the Sunday – matches now started on a Saturday as they do today – kept the pitch docile. In 3¼ hours, Frank Tarrant and Hon. Rupert Anson put on 235. Anson's 97 was the highest score of his career, as was Tarrant's 250 not out. The Australian shared an unbroken second-wicket partnership of 229 in two hours and five minutes with J W Hearne, who hit 106; Middlesex declared at 464 for 1. Perrin and Douglas made 60s in the second innings, but Essex still lost by an innings. They had been overwhelmed in each of their first four matches of the season.

It says much for Douglas's determination and qualities of inspiration that Essex recovered from that trauma. Rain marred the next game, at

Old Trafford, and Lancashire did not enjoy the best of the conditions, but Essex played remarkably well at the close to fashion a victory. Douglas and Freeman batted rather laboriously at first, and Essex reached 246. Douglas, 6 for 55, and Louden, 4 for 28, bowled out Lancashire for 97, but in spite of some bright batting from Perrin and Russell, only 2¾ hours were left when Douglas declared the Essex second innings closed. The odds seemed very much on a draw, but Douglas, Tremlin and Louden bowled finely and Essex won by 156 runs. Douglas shuffled his trio of pace bowlers well, and the fielding and catching were exemplary. It was a heartening win after the early season disasters.

Derbyshire were beaten at Leyton, Douglas took 12 wickets in the match, and Essex cricket was on the mend. The proof of that rejuvenation came at The Oval.

Essex batted first and began disastrously. Russell was out without scoring and Carpenter managed just one run. Gillingham, Perrin and Fane followed so that five wickets were down for 45. Douglas and captain Walter Turner batted in resolute fashion and put on 84, and Douglas, in 3½ hours of dogged resistance, finished with 74 not out; in so doing he nursed his side to a commendable 264. Douglas, 6 for 60, and Tremlin, 4 for 68, bowled unchanged, and Surrey were out for 132.

Rain caused some disruption, but Perrin and Gillingham put on 171 in two hours. Gillingham scored 121 not out, and Douglas set Surrey most of the last day in which to score 410. They were 22 for 5, 45 for 7, and once again Douglas, 5 for 38, and Tremlin, 5 for 47, bowled unchanged. Surrey were out for 86. It was their only defeat, at The Oval, in their championship-winning year.

Douglas bowled the great Jack Hobbs twice in the match. The Master always considered Douglas one of the finest bowlers he ever faced.

That Gillingham, like the Turners, could not play more first-class cricket was a great loss to Essex and the game. Never a season went by when he did not make some significant contribution in one of his few appearances. Although not at his best against the slower bowlers, he was severe on the pace men, driving into the deep field and through the covers with great power. He was a man of charming individuality, with the deepest compassion for humanity – to know him was to be enriched.

Surrey exacted revenge for their defeat at The Oval with a seven-wicket win at Leyton, but this was followed by Essex's first game at Castle Park, Colchester, on 18, 19 and 20 June. The Southend game was dropped after two seasons, but as the *Daily Mirror* indicated, the precedent had aroused the interest of other areas. Colchester was the next to benefit. The match did not have quite the drama of the game at Southend in 1906, but approximately 2000 watched each day, and Essex, in a most capable

17. The Rev. Canon F H Gillingham. Played for Essex when his ecclesiastical duties permitted, from 1903–28. He was also the BBC commentator in the first ever live broadcast of a cricket match, from Leyton in 1927.

team performance, won by 193 runs. The pitch was excellent, and Essex hit 440 and 183 for 5 declared, while Worcestershire were put out for 216 and 214. W Turner, with 84 in the first innings, and Gillingham, with 83 not out in the second, were the top scorers for the home county, while Pearson, the opener, made 90 and 72 for Worcs. But the real honours of the game went to Geoffrey Davies.

G B Davies, who had obtained a blue at Cambridge, had first played in 1912 and was one of the few players to escape from the ravages of the 1913 season with an enhanced reputation. A slow-medium, off-break bowler and a useful batsman, he took 6 for 51 in the Worcestershire second innings to win the match. He was a player of much promise, but, tragically, he was killed in action at Hulluch in September, 1915, a month before his 23rd birthday. It was probably the greatest loss sustained by Essex cricket during the First World War.

A somewhat checkered course took Essex to the end of July when, in the return match with Leicestershire at Leyton, McIver and Russell established a county record for the first wicket with a partnership of 212, 186 of them coming in two hours before lunch on the first day.

McIver had a good week, following his 90 against Leicestershire with 113 against Hampshire in a match that was drawn. Runs flowed again at Leyton in the beginning of August when Douglas and Freeman, the latter finding himself at number eight, put on 261 in 4½ hours of resolute batting against Lancashire in another drawn match. In the next match, at Derby, Essex won by an innings, and Douglas and Tremlin again bowled unchanged. In the first innings, Tremlin's 4 for 9 in eight overs included a hat-trick. Derbyshire were all out for 31, the lowest score against Essex.

This was to be Essex's last victory until the final match of the season. Carpenter and Russell saved the game at Worcester with an unbeaten second wicket stand of 237. 'Bob' Carpenter hit 126 not out in the last of his 25 first-class centuries. But as this achievement was noted England was already at war, and the last acts of a golden age of cricket were drawing to their close.

At Lord's, in mid-July, the Gentlemen had beaten the Players by 134 runs. Douglas had a marvellous match, taking 9 for 105 and 4 for 67, in what was to be the Gentlemen's last victory over the professionals for 20 years. Douglas enjoyed an outstanding season, completing the 'double' for the first time in his career. For Essex alone, he scored 1151 runs and took 118 wickets. Tremlin took 100 wickets for the only time in his career, and Perrin and Russell both passed 1000 runs.

Douglas was in his 32nd year and had come to full fruition as a great all-rounder. His efforts did much to lift Essex to eighth in the table with nine wins. *Wisden* was lavish in its praise, not only for his leadership, but for his excellent bowling and more aggressive batting, and he was named as one of the 'Five Cricketers of the Year'.

A fortnight after Douglas's triumph for the Gentlemen, Austria declared war on Serbia, and five days after that, Germany demanded that her troops be allowed to march through Belgium to attack France. Crowds clamoured in Whitehall in a thirst for war. None foresaw the carnage and desolation that the next four years would bring.

War was declared on 4 August 1914, but, initially, life and cricket continued as if this were just one of those minor irritations in some far-off place, perhaps like the Boer War or the Crimean War. The Championship continued.

Douglas went down with influenza at Northampton, where Essex were beaten, but he returned for the last game, against Somerset, at Weston-super-Mare. This match was over in two days, ending on 1 September; Davies took 4 for 18, and Somerset were bowled out for 141.

Essex lost their first four wickets cheaply, but Geoffrey Davies came in to hit a sparkling 118 out of 155. It was his second century of the summer and the highest score of his career, which ended with that match. A year later he died in battle.

Somerset missed many chances, and Essex should have trailed on the first innings, but their 235 gave them a 94-run lead. It looked as if the home side was heading for an innings defeat when they lost five men for 25, but they rallied slightly. Buckenham, who had been assisting Forfarshire in Scotland, had returned to play five matches. He had taken 3 for 42 in the first innings and now he finally ended his first-class career with 7 for 37. But for those missed chances, how many wickets might he have taken?

Essex needed 37 to win, and Carpenter and Russell hit off the runs. The Essex side that day was Carpenter, Russell, C P McGahey, P A Perrin, J W H T Douglas, G B Davies, Freeman, C H Douglas, J G Dixon, Buckenham and Tremlin. An era in everybody's lives had come to a close.

CHAPTER 9

The JWHT Years: 1915–29

The First World War is an unbreachable demarcation line in history. At the end of it the world and its people had changed, and in cricket, the amateur spirit which Green had believed to be disappearing was altered considerably.

During the war, Essex, like other counties, attempted to keep the game alive. The ground bowlers were in the services, but the Club played some 30 minor fixtures a season against local clubs and military opposition. At the AGM in 1917, the senior administrators of the County cleared a deficit of nearly £141 out of their own pockets, but this still left a previous deficit of £560, and as the war ended there was the old cry that the Club was desperately in need of more members.

As well as Davies, and ultimately Harold Mead, the war accounted for H D Keigwin, F Street and E C Coleman, but the war years also saw the deaths of two men who had played a most prominent part in the rise of Essex County Cricket Club.

On Christmas Eve 1916, at his home at Birch Hall, James Round died, aged 74. Without his early enthusiasm there would have been no County Club. Three weeks earlier, at his home near Epping, C E Green died aged 70. Perhaps Green died a little saddened at the changes in attitude he had witnessed, and when he was on his death bed, and knew it, he refused to see anyone, even his close friend A P 'Bunny' Lucas. Nothing that has happened since or that can happen in the future will ever detract from Green's contribution to Essex County Cricket Club. He shaped it, loved it and rescued it times without number. If a history of the Club should be dedicated to anybody, it should be dedicated to C E Green, for without him there would have been no history.

Perhaps events immediately after the war would have caused Green even more anguish; cricket administrators have been renowned for some bizarre actions, but the decision to restrict championship matches to two days when the first-class game resumed after the war must rank among the worst rulings ever inflicted upon the game. None enjoyed the experiment, and it was thankfully abandoned after only one season.

For Essex, it was a wretched experience. Lt Col J W H T Douglas returned from the war fit and in form. He and his side were disappointed to find that the home games in which they engaged were dull and monotonous. *Wisden* summed it up most aptly:

> Essex in 1919 found a large public eager to see first-class cricket after a blank of four seasons, but the Leyton ground, as everyone knew would be the case in the event of a fine summer, was not in the least degree suited to two-day matches. In the nineties, when the wickets had not been brought to such a state of perfection, the experiment might have answered very well, but last year it was frankly a failure, match after match having to be left unfinished. Of the nine matches at home in the Championship, six were left drawn, heavy scoring being the sole cause in nearly every instance.

Essex won only two of their championship matches, and only Warwickshire finished below them. The Leyton season began with an innings defeat at the hands of the Australian Imperial Forces, who had another convincing win over Essex at Southend in August. After that, the two victories, over Lancashire and Sussex, came in the first five county matches. It was not just the four years lost to the war that affected Essex, for that had happened to all, but there was a realisation that age had caught up with the nucleus of the side. McGahey was 47, and he played on occasions only when requested to do so in order to help out the side. Fane was 44 and did not play at all. Perrin was 43, but still had a few years batting ahead of him, although in the post-war period he became very stiff. Reeves was 44, and Tremlin, in his last season, was 41. Both men were later to become umpires. Reeves stood at Test level and was a noted character. To him was attributed the remark made to a bowler noted for his zealous appealing: 'There's only one man who appeals more than you do – Dr Barnado.'

Individually, there were some good performances. Russell and Freeman were as impressive as ever, and Russell reached 1000 runs in championship matches alone. Freeman was 35 and Russell 31, so that both men had been robbed of important years by the war.

The bowling was dominated by Douglas and Louden, and in all matches, Douglas completed the 'double' for the second time. He was the same inexhaustible cricketer as ever and showed no signs of fatigue after long days in the field. Only four men in the country sent down more overs, and only two, Rhodes and Hitch, took more wickets.

George Marshall Louden, with 66 wickets, had what was to prove to be his best season for Essex. Coming from Ilford, standing over six feet and with a splendid physique, he bowled very fast with a high action. He could never spare the time to play cricket regularly, but many good judges thought that he should have played for England; he was as quick and as effective as any one in the country. Pelham Warner certainly regretted later that Louden was never included against the Australians in 1921. Sir Home Gordon, during his attack on Douglas, mentioned Douglas's contempt for any physical weakness and fatigue. In support of his argument, he said of Douglas: 'He showed shocking bad judgment. For instance, George Louden was a really excellent fast bowler, who could get away only occasionally from a city office. He assured me he had begun to dread playing for Essex because Johnny would put him on for thirty overs on end until he was dead to the world.'

Louden survived, for he played until 1927 when he was 42, but even Charles Bray suggested that it was wrong to overbowl him for he was not as strong as he looked.

Johnny Douglas never asked anybody to do what he was not prepared to do himself, and he had no favourites. Brother Cecil Herbert had played occasionally before the war, and in 1919 he began to show signs of developing into a good cricketer. For the most part he batted at number seven or eight, and in June, he took the last three Kent wickets at a personal cost of 46 runs. This was to be his career best bowling performance. When the side went up to Old Trafford in July he batted at number five and scored 78. In the next match, he found himself at number seven, and when Essex went to Weston-super-Mare he was down to number ten. He confronted his brother and asked what he thought he was doing; he pointed out that he had hit 78 against Lancashire, and he felt he should be higher than number ten. 'I decide the order,' was all his brother said.

In the Somerset game, C H 'Pickles' Douglas joined his brother when 50 were still needed to save the follow-on. They batted together for two hours and C H got 45. He thought he had proved his point, but when they travelled to Bournemouth for the next match and he asked Johnny what number he would be batting he was told number 10 again.

That was enough for the younger Douglas. He made a rude comment, packed his bags and went home. He played once more, but he decided to concentrate on boxing; he did not play for Essex after 1919.

In the season that C H Douglas departed, Frank Gilligan, whose brothers were to captain Sussex, kept wicket after he had come down from Oxford. He had been in the university side for two years and, with Harold Morris, who did not get a blue while at Cambridge, played some useful innings for the County and was most impressive in the field.

The return to normality in 1920 was a help to Essex. They won nine matches and moved to ninth in the table, but it could not be claimed that they were a good side. *Wisden* commented pointedly: 'The veteran element in the side militated sadly against brilliant work in the field, and the bowling depended to an alarming extent on Douglas who, except on rare occasions from Louden, received no support that was even approximately up to first-class county form.' This was a little hard on Reeves, who enjoyed something of an Indian summer in his penultimate season on the staff and took more than 60 wickets in all matches.

No praise can be too high for Douglas, who again completed the 'double', this time in county matches alone. In energy and enthusiasm he was unquenchable, and he never knew the meaning of defeat. Whether it were a Test match or a game at the Scarborough Festival, he played his cricket hard. Neither should it ever be forgotten that at the time when Leyton was considered a batsman's paradise, that is the ground on which Douglas was doing most of his bowling. Never were his tenacious qualities better exemplified than in the magnificent victory over the champions, Middlesex, at Leyton.

Middlesex, in fact, were to take the title by winning their last nine matches. The defeat at Leyton preceded this run.

A stand of 70 for the sixth wicket between McIver and McGahey roused Essex from the depths, but they still managed only 133. The Middlesex first innings had an air of unreality about it as Warner had to retire on 22 and Douglas leave the field after bowling four overs because both of them had to attend a selection committee meeting at Lord's. Eventually Middlesex took a first innings lead of 79, which, as the wicket was playing with uncharacteristic difficulty, was a formidable one.

Perrin, finding three-day matches tiring on the legs, but seeing the ball as well as ever, hit 50, and Douglas made 36, but Hearne's spin brought him eight wickets, and Essex were out for 196. This left Middlesex to make 118 to win, a task that was not considered anything but straightforward in conditions which now favoured the batsman more than at any other time in the match.

This was the type of situation which Douglas relished. Rubbing the ball on his forearm on his way back to his mark, he bristled with aggression.

He bounded in with long and rhythmical strides, his neat black hair gleaming. He attacked with every ball, and those in his side who could not respond to his fire were left gasping in his wake.

The Douglas break-back was famous. Suspect it the batsman might; to deal with it was another matter. Lee, Haig and Stevens were bowled. Hearne, Hendren and Mann were lbw. Middlesex were 33 for 6, all six to Douglas. Warner battled grimly, but he had scored only one when he put the ball into the hands of forward short-leg, who put down the easiest of chances. The years have hidden the fielder's name, but if you were wedded so passionately to the fate of every ball, as Douglas was, you did not accept such negligence and human weakness without a vehement curse and an angry gesture.

Briefly Douglas took a rest, but Russell had Skeet lbw, and Louden bowled Gunasekera. Middlesex were 67 for 8. Murrell joined Warner in a resolute stand. Douglas returned, and Warner took the bowling of the Essex captain upon himself, but after they had added 35, Murrell was lbw to Russell, and Warner had only Durston left to help him to score the 16 runs needed.

The battle between Warner and Douglas now took on epic proportions. Here were the last vestiges of a golden age, now only dimly perceived. This was Plum Warner's last season. Durston defended doggedly, and Warner took what runs he could make against Douglas. The score mounted, but with Warner on 46 and Middlesex five short of victory, Douglas beat the Middlesex captain with a fast yorker and scattered the stumps.

The Essex side erupted, caught up in their own captain's joy and enthusiasm. He had dismissed the first seven batsmen on the card, without help from the field, at a personal cost of 47 runs. He and Warner left the field with their arms round each other's shoulders.

It was in this year that a week was given to Colchester and a week to Southend. The Colchester ground this time was not Castle Park, as it had been in 1914, but the Garrison ground. It was not a happy debut, Essex losing both matches by an innings, to Hampshire and Gloucestershire.

At Southend, Essex beat Derbyshire, with Louden taking a career best 8 for 36 in the second innings, but in the second match they were well beaten by Yorkshire. This was the occasion when young Herbert Sutcliffe carried his bat through an innings for the first time. He hit 125 out of 307 and remembered the innings some years later:

> I was in a knot most of the time, beaten so completely that I often played at the swinging ball to miss it by inches. In the first three quarters of an hour of 'hard labour' to which I was put that day I began to wonder if I should ever middle a ball. Time and again I played at the

ball only to miss it. Each time J.W.H.T. flung his arms high to protest silently against the foulness of his luck, and finally, at the end of an over about which I had known very little, he came up to me and exploded: 'Why the hell don't you get a bite?'

I got a bite in the next over all right, but it was simply a matter of adding insult to injury, for the ball shot from the edge of my bat to second slip who very kindly put it on to the ground. 'Johnny's' face was a picture. . . .

It was always a great joy to play against Mr Douglas, whose love for the game was as great as could be. He was a fighter second to none, he was a great all-round cricketer, and he was as charming a gentleman as ever donned flannels.

It was during Southend week that Douglas learned that he was to lead the MCC side to Australia the following winter. Once again he had not been first choice, but even if he had known what was ahead, he would have accepted, relishing the challenge.

He was to be accompanied on the tour by a second Essex player, Jack Russell, who had enjoyed a wonderful season. He finished eighth in the national averages, the first Essex player to pass 2000 runs in a season. In fact, he was headed in the first-class averages by two other Essex players, Gillingham, who was fifth, and Hubert Ashton, who was third, but Ashton's runs were made for Cambridge, and his Essex debut was not to come until the following season.

Russell, a splendid on-side player, had consistency as his greatest asset. His highest innings came against Middlesex at Lord's in mid-July when Essex, facing a total of 446, found themselves struggling at 184 for 8. Russell was then joined by Lawrence Eastman, a 23-year-old amateur, who had made his first-class debut in the two previous matches.

Eastman had intended to take up medicine as a profession, but that ambition had been thwarted by the war, in which he won the DCM and MM. His interest in cricket was noted by Douglas and Perrin, and he was invited to play for Essex against Gloucestershire at Bristol in July. The match was ruined by rain. Gloucestershire declared at 175 for 9, and Eastman, tall and medium pace, took 5 for 53, which included a spell of three wickets in four balls. What was not realised at that time was that he was also a good batsman, a clean, straight and elegant hitter. He demonstrated this in the match at Lord's when he scored 91 and helped Russell revive Essex's fortunes in a ninth-wicket stand of 184, a County record at that time. Russell finished with 197.

'Bob' Carpenter played in the last two matches of the season, scoring 8 and 21 against Lancashire at Leyton, and 20 and 0 against Somerset at Weston-super-Mare, where Essex won. He was seven weeks past his

51st birthday, and he had been with Essex for 26 years. His contribution to the County can never be measured solely in terms of runs and wickets, through this was considerable, but must also be considered in terms of the help, coaching and advice he gave to others; this was considerable. He has been called one of the finest professional batsmen never to play for England. He was that, and for Essex he was yet another 'true and faithful servant'.

The experiences of Douglas and Russell in Australia were not happy ones. England were beaten by five Tests to nil, and a most depressing period of English cricket now followed.

Russell failed in the first two Tests in Australia, but hit 135 not out and 59 at Adelaide. He batted in the middle order after the first Test, and his first innings at Adelaide was the highest in the series for England. He missed the fourth Test through injury.

The Australians followed England back to this country and continued to batter the home side into submission. Having lost seven Tests in a row, Douglas was deposed as captain although he retained his place in the side. The selectors wallowed in a bog of indecision and panic. They used 30 players in the series, but although Hobbs was ill and injured, Russell was not called upon until the fourth Test, his first in England, when he hit 101. He followed this with 13 and 102 not out at The Oval. These were the only two matches in which England escaped defeat. It is interesting to note that, according to statisticians, 81 of Russell's 101 at Old Trafford were made on the leg side.

In many ways the Essex season was to mirror the Test series, for the County called upon 39 players in 1921, so that it was hardly likely that any sense of a regular side or stable teamwork was achieved.

The prospects for the year had seemed bright enough. The number of matches was increased, all the old players were available and it was hoped that one or two useful youngsters from the ground staff would make their mark. Reeves, in what was to be his last season, was given the Middlesex match as his benefit.

There were eight amateurs in the Essex side for the opening match of the season at Hove, but the number was reduced to seven for the first home match, against Worcestershire, when Jack O'Connor, a 23-year-old batsman and spin bowler, made his debut. O'Connor made no immediate impression, but he had a good pedigree. He was the nephew of 'Bob' Carpenter and the son of John O'Connor, who had played nine games for Derbyshire in 1900 as well as appearing for Cambridgeshire.

Although they trailed by 155 on the first innings, Essex beat Worcestershire by 132 runs, an amazing win that was due almost entirely to Douglas and Russell. Russell hit 151 and Douglas 123 not out in Essex's second innings of 500 for 5 declared; Douglas had match figures of 14 for 156.

18. *Jack O'Connor, a prolific run scorer. His record of nine centuries in a season, which he achieved in 1934, is held jointly with Doug Insole. O'Connor's run aggregate of 2350 in that year was a record which stood for 50 years, until Graham Gooch overtook it in 1984.*

This was to be one of only five matches won during the season, and the second victory came in the next county match at Leyton. This game was against Derbyshire, and Jack Freeman was the only professional in the Essex side.

The match was played on 25, 26 and 27 May, the eve of the first Test, and was a personal triumph for the Essex and England captain. Derbyshire were bowled out for 114. Douglas took 9 for 47, the best bowling performance of his career. In reply, Essex slipped to 37 for 5, but Douglas stayed to the end of the day when the score was 138 for 7.

McIver went early next morning, but Douglas was joined by Steriker Norman Hare who was appearing in the first of the three matches that were to constitute his first-class career. Hare had been captain of Chigwell School in the last year of the war and played club cricket for Ilford.

He had attracted attention when he hit 104 not out for Ilford against Wanstead at Valentine's Park in 1920, a match played for the benefit of A E Russell, the Ilford groundsman. Douglas and Jack Russell both played in that game.

Hare scored 98 against Derbyshire, and he and Douglas added 251 for the ninth wicket before the Ilford batsman was caught at mid-off. The stand remains a Club record.

Douglas declared. In 5¼ hours, he had hit 210 not out with 28 fours. It was to remain the highest score of his career.

Like Douglas and Russell, Freeman and Perrin reached 1000 runs. Like Douglas, Russell and Freeman both hit the highest scores of their careers, and both came against Northamptonshire. At Northampton, on 11 June, Russell and Freeman put on 189 runs for the second wicket. Russell hit 108 and Freeman batted seven hours to reach 286. A fortnight later, Russell hit 273 in the return game at Leyton. The runs came in 4½ hours, and Russell was finally stumped when he played too soon at a very slow delivery.

Russell scored 2236 runs in the season and was second to Philip Mead in the national averages, yet to Douglas must go the highest praise for saving Essex from total humiliation, for only Warwickshire and Glamorgan finished below them in the championship. Douglas had the cares of losing the England captaincy upon his shoulders as well as worries over his sister's illness, but in the five matches that Essex won, his contribution was 562 runs in four completed innings and 53 wickets at 9.76 each. They are statistics which are a measure of the man's worth. For the fourth season in succession, discounting the war years, he completed the 'double' in all matches.

The support he received in bowling was negligible. Louden took 43 wickets but played in only seven matches, and J G Dixon's 72 wickets were very expensive. Joseph Dixon was a Felsted product, a fast-medium bowler and a capable batsman. Business claimed him, and he was able to play for only one more season.

Dixon scored a century against Hampshire in Colchester week which, in spite of two defeats, was a success, as was the week at Southend where the Australians, who played and beat Essex twice by an innings, were the second visitors. The first were Somerset, who won on a wearing wicket.

Robertson-Glasgow was in that Somerset side, and he always remembered Southend with much affection, for the game against Essex was only his second for his county:

> I have a weakness for Southend, and in later years, when reporting cricket for the *Morning Post*, I never failed to impress on my employers the importance and brilliance of its Cricket Festival. In August, the

homely smell of mankind in the streets was set off by the abundance of whelks, cockles, and stick-jaw rock. Rides were to be had on the miniature railway to the end of the pier and in mechanical boats on the lake below the Palace Hotel. Nowhere else have I found such invigorating air; and morning brought no sense of lassitude or remorse to the nocturnal reveller.

The cricket ground was adorned at one end by a lake, on which prophetic ducks floated, and quacked as nervous batsmen made their way to the crease. Festooned around were private tents, whose occupants said and drank what they liked. One of them belonged to the Mayor, another to the Yachting Club. In both of these the hospitality was warm, and from the latter marine telescopes were sometimes directed on to the cricket.

Paul Andrews, now retired and living in Sussex, saw his first cricket in that Southend week of 1921 and recalls: 'Quite near to where the pavilion now stands in Southchurch Park, there was a large pond which seemed to act as a magnet or aiming point for the big hitters, and nearby there was a cage of peacocks and peahens. Very pretty birds no doubt; but they always seemed to delight in shrieking out an ear piercing cry just as the bowlers ran up to the crease.'

The pond could hardly be described as ornamental today, and shortly after Robertson-Glasgow first played at Southchurch Hall Park, as it then was, the wicket was relaid and the old, small pavilion was replaced by the one which stands now sited in front of the pond.

The success of the festivals at Colchester and Southend was to have a significant influence on events within the coming months.

The feature of Southend week had been an innings of 90 by Hubert Ashton against the Australians, and this season was to see the beginning of the association of the Ashton brothers, Hubert and Claude, with the Club. Both men were fine cricketers, and neither was able to play as much county cricket as Essex would have wished. Both captained Cambridge, as did the third brother, Gilbert, who played for Worcestershire.

Colchester week witnessed the last appearance on the cricket field in a county match of Charles McGahey. He was five months past his 49th birthday and sadly made 0 and 6 against Hampshire, but there were still some 15 years left for him to give joy to all those with whom he came in contact.

Also to make his last appearance for Essex, against Kent at Leyton in 1921, was Trayton Grinter, who appeared eight times for the County after his debut in 1909. In June 1921, *The Cricketer* carried an interesting item:

Mr T. G. Grinter, as the result of a wound in his left arm, has practically lost the power of this limb. Nevertheless, he is still a batsman of exceptional merit, and despite his unfortunate handicap, is a prolific scorer in London club cricket. It is understood that Essex have invited him to play again in several matches this season, when he can get away from the claims of business. Mr Grinter now skippers Wanstead, but used to play for South Woodford. In 1913 he scored six successive hundreds in club cricket, and only failed to get seven by 3 runs.

Grinter had been wounded in the war, and in fact he batted virtually one-handed in the post-war period. He later played for Frinton and, ignoring his disability, he also turned his attention to golf, becoming a seven-handicap player. More important to Essex than his cricket was the contribution he was to make to the Club in other ways. He had joined the wine merchants Cockburn as an office boy on Mafeking Day, 1900, and by 1933, he was chairman. In his senior position in the firm he was able to engage Tom Pearce and make it possible for him to have the time to captain Essex in the 1930s.

There were important changes in Essex cricket as the season drew to its close. Oswell Borradaile, for 31 years the Club secretary, was forced to resign through ill-health. During his long period of office the fortunes of the side had fluctuated dramatically, although financial problems had remained constant. Determined and quietly efficient, Borradaile had negotiated the most difficult times with courtesy and energy. He was a most popular man, and the vital factor in his enthusiasm for the job he did so well was his passion for Essex cricket. Like Peter Edwards in another era, he was totally committed to the Club. He lived and breathed Essex cricket. He had played for the County, and he had supported their interests all his life. To Green he had been a most able lieutenant, and the followers of Essex cricket were quick to respond to the announcement of his retirement with a generous testimonial. Borradaile was elected a life-member of the Club, and he continued to maintain a devoted interest in Essex and the game until his death in 1935.

Borradaile's successor was N R E Wilkinson, who operated from Bishopsgate close to the offices of Douglas's timber importing business. Shortly before he retired Borradaile had instigated a system at Leyton whereby players, umpires and public were informed of the number of balls bowled during the over, and score-cards were issued which recorded the chief hits made by a batsman during a longer than usual innings. But Leyton was to become more noteworthy when it was revealed at the end of the season that the County was to sell the ground to the Army Sports Control Board. For Essex, the deal was beneficial, for they would be rid of the millstone of the £10,000 mortgage which had weighed heavily upon them since 1886, while at the same time being allowed to continue to play cricket on the ground.

Leyton had never brought the prosperity which had been anticipated, but few could have foreseen the rapid social changes which would alter that part of London and, for some, would rob it of its Essex flavour and association.

The surrender of Leyton did not bring an immediate glut of cricket to other grounds. Southend and Colchester retained their weeks, but the only other ground in Essex to be granted a first-class match was Brentwood, the original county ground in the days before the Club was first-class. Forty-six years after the formation of the Club, on 5, 6 and 7 July 1922, the first first-class game was played at Brentwood when Essex drew with Dublin University. J G Dixon took 7 for 61, which was the best return of his career, and this a month after he hit 173 against Worcestershire at Leyton, the highest score made for Essex during the year; but this was Dixon's last season with the County.

The season showed an improvement in victories, seven, a reduction in losses, four, and a rise in position, to eighth, all of which was encouraging without being dramatic. The same problems persisted. Douglas narrowly failed to complete the 'double', but still dominated the bowling. Dixon was expensive, Louden was most effective but played little, and Eastman showed promise. The batting was better than the bowling, and there were two interesting maiden centuries for the County.

On 31 May, at Northampton, Russell, 172, and Perrin, 114, put on 207 in 2¼ hours for the second wicket. Essex finished the day on 423 for 6, and the following morning, Jack O'Connor, with a six and 13 fours, reached the first of his 71 centuries for Essex.

At the beginning of August, against Middlesex at Leyton, Claude Ashton hit 110 not out in 75 minutes. In a 40-minute partnership with Louden for the last wicket, with the follow-on threatening, he scored 91 while his partner made three. He was still short of his 21st birthday, and there was a glorious lack of inhibition in Claude Ashton's cricket.

The same could be said for his most talented older brother Hubert, but after three matches for the County in 1922 he went to India with the Burmah Oil Company and was not seen in county cricket again until 1927.

If one man could be said to have glowed for the County in 1922, however, it was Charles Albert George Russell, known for many years as A C Russell, and most commonly referred to as Jack. He topped the Essex averages with over 2000 runs, hit a century in each innings against Surrey at The Oval, scored a stunning 162 for the Players at Lord's and finished as the leading run-scorer in the country. He was named as one of *Wisden*'s 'Five Cricketers of the Year' and was in Mann's side to go to South Africa.

He did not play in the first Test, which was the only match on the tour which England lost, but his scores thereafter were 39 and 8; 34; 8 and 96;

19. *Jack Russell, the first England batsman to score two centuries in a match, which he achieved in the Test match against South Africa at Durban in 1923.* (Central Press)

and 140 and 111. At Durban, he became the first English batsman to hit a century in each innings of a Test match, and his last wicket stand of 92 with A E R Gilligan remains an English record against South Africa.

Russell was never to play Test cricket again. In ten matches for his country, he hit 910 runs, average 56.87, and scored five centuries. It is a record that compares favourably with even the very greatest like Jack Hobbs. Russell's problem was that, outside Essex, he was never a fashionable player. The accolade to him in *Wisden* of 1923, when he was chosen as one of the 'Five Cricketers of the Year' ends on a strangely critical note:

> Judged by results since the war he is an exceptional player and yet his batting lacks the quality that fascinates. One cannot imagine people jumping into taxi-cabs and rushing off to Lord's or The Oval because they had seen on the tape that he was not out at lunch-time. A master of on-side play, he is rather too utilitarian to rank among the great ones. He has a fine off-drive at his command, but he is very sparing in the use of it. Still he must not be blamed for playing the game that pays him best.

Douglas was always intolerant of him, believing that he had immense talent which was not being completely realised because of laziness and what Douglas considered to be riotous living. This was somewhat harsh, but certainly Russell was not as keen on pre-match practice as the skipper felt he should be.

Russell had risen from a sick bed to complete the second of his centuries in Durban, and illness was to trouble him at the start of the 1923 season. He was not able to find any form until late, and his run-scoring dropped away considerably.

Essex began wretchedly and did not win a county match until they beat Somerset in Colchester week in mid-June. Cambridge University were also beaten at Colchester, but there were only five wins elsewhere, and four of them came in August when Claude Ashton, Gilligan and Henry Franklin, the Oxford all-rounder, were available.

In all cricket, Douglas again did the 'double' and he produced some fine batting performances, but he could never hope to compensate for Russell's loss of form. In bowling, he again carried the attack virtually single-handed. Louden and Eastman were expensive, as was the slow left-arm bowler Hipkin, who appeared in the side for the first time. Philip Morris, a leg-break bowler from Bancrofts, was rarely available.

Perrin, at 47, and Freeman, at 39, soldiered on as reliable as ever, and both reached 1000 runs. The brightest feature of the year, however, was the batting of Jack O'Connor, who made 1000 runs in a season for the first time. It was not simply the runs that he made which excited, but the manner of their making.

Against Hampshire at Leyton in August, Essex needed 181 on a doubtful wicket. Freeman, H M Morris and Russell all went cheaply, and the best support that came to O'Connor was from Perrin, who made 16. Hitting gloriously all round the wicket, O'Connor batted with a natural elegance and freedom. At tea Essex were 16 short of victory, and O'Connor was on 99. He reached his century with a carefully chosen single and then won the match with two resounding fours in one over from Newman. His 111 out of a total of 183 came in ten minutes under three hours and contained 18 fours. O'Connor's innings invariably contained a large proportion of boundaries. The three-wicket win over Hampshire was one of the delights of the season at Leyton.

O'Connor also possessed great fighting qualities. At Cheltenham, with Parker running riot, Essex were 75 for 5, but Douglas joined O'Connor, and in 3½ hours, they added 206. Douglas hit 147 not out and O'Connor 128. Their stand has been equalled but never beaten as a sixth-wicket record for the County.

Essex went on to gain an amazing victory in this match. Claude Ashton took 7 for 51 with his medium pace, the best bowling performance of his career, when Gloucestershire batted again, and Essex were left to make

115 to win. They scored 118 for 4, and Fred Nicholas, later to become wicket-keeper for Sir Julian Cahn's team, hit 71 of them.

The most interesting venture of the season came in early June when Essex, fielding a weak side, entertained West Indies, not yet of Test status, and lost by three wickets. The interest in the match was that it was the first occasion on which Essex had allocated a game to Valentine's Park, Ilford.

Ilford was a rapidly developing area. In the early 1920s there was much private building in the town, and many of the farms that had existed on the northern outskirts vanished as new roads and estates were constructed. In May 1923, the Ilford Club opened a new pavilion which was to remain in existence until 1962, when it was replaced by the present building on the same site.

The match at Ilford anticipated a decision taken at a Special General Meeting held at the end of the year, when it was decided to reconstruct the Committee on a basis of district representation with a view to stimulating interest in the Club throughout the county. It was a bold move towards decentralisation and, in 1924, Ilford, like Southend and Colchester, had its cricket week.

In spreading the Club wider into Essex, the new Committee hoped for a membership of 3000, but they were to be bitterly disappointed. Bad weather, coupled with the side winning only two matches, failed to generate any enthusiasm. Douglas's batting showed some signs of decline and he was to appear for the Gentlemen for the last time and also to take 100 wickets in a season for the last time.

Perrin, Gillingham and Ashton fell away, and for the only time between 1923 and 1939, Jack O'Connor failed to make 1000 runs. Thirty-three players appeared for Essex. Among them were Cutmore and Nichols, who were to play an important part in the Club's fortunes in the next decade. Another was Harold Palmer, a brisk leg-break bowler, who had a significant role in the victory at Eastbourne where Freeman hit a century. Eastman hit a fierce maiden hundred against Surrey at Southend, but the only real success of the season was Hipkin.

Augustus Bernard Hipkin was a discovery of Douglas's. He was a slow left-arm bowler who flighted the ball cleverly and spun it considerably. He took 112 wickets in 1924, did the hat-trick against Lancashire at Blackpool and topped the bowling averages. Sir Home Gordon insisted that Douglas ruined Hipkin by bullying him. Others believed Hipkin was his own worst enemy and did not possess the temperament or stability needed to be a top-flight spinner, despite his natural talent.

There is no doubt that Hipkin was a natural sportsman, a professional footballer as well as a cricketer, but he appeared diffident. Douglas took much from him, more than he would from others, in an effort to help him realise his potential, but eventually Hipkin showed a lack of resource. Tom Pearce remarked that Hipkin was always first to the score-book to see how many runs he had conceded; and a slow bowler who is worried about keeping down runs more than he is about taking wickets has not the attitude needed for success. That 1924 season was to remain Hipkin's best, but, for Essex, it was the worst for 30 years. The black days loomed again. There was an appeal for £1000, and it was stated that unless a good response was forthcoming, the Club would be wound up. To their credit, the people of Essex gave generously, and for a year at least county cricket was saved.

It was given further resuscitation when Essex improved in performance the following season. They opened with five wins in six matches, and while this form could not be sustained, they won four more matches and rose to seventh in the table, their highest position for 15 years.

Russell rediscovered his old form and came close to 2000 runs, and Hipkin's batting showed signs of developing to match his bowling and excellent catching. Perrin and Freeman appeared indestructible while Louden bowled wonderfully well in his limited appearances. Yet the real strength in the side lay in the youth that had now asserted itself, for alongside O'Connor, Cutmore, as an opening batsman, and Nichols, destined to be one of the game's great all-rounders, established themselves in the side.

O'Connor's leg-breaks were utilised well enough to give him 42 championship wickets, including a hat-trick at Worcester where he bowled M K and H K Foster with two deliveries and caught and bowled Gilbert Ashton with the third.

On 20, 22 and 23 June, Chelmsford staged its initial first-class match when Oxford University were the visitors to what is now the County Ground. Eastman hit 93, but to Jack Freeman went the honour of scoring the first century on the ground, 139. The match was drawn, but an important step had been taken. There had been no match at Ilford that year but it was apparent from the successes at Colchester, Southend and now Chelmsford that, by playing in different parts of the county, the Essex Club had increased its membership and was stimulating the interest it needed for its survival.

Amid this increasing optimism there was one note of foreboding: Douglas's form showed a marked decline. What was most noticeable was his loss of both speed and stamina in his bowling. He had been recalled to lead England in one Test against South Africa in 1924 and had gone to Australia as vice-captain in 1924–25. There, at the age of 42, he had played his last Test, although his primary function on the tour was to help the younger players.

As his accuracy then waned in the 1925 season there were muted criticisms, but happily the rise in the County's fortunes tended to distract from the captain's loss of form. Typically, he refused to admit that there was anything wrong with him. He loathed any sign of weakness, and he saw admitting to pain as just this, but the truth was that for much of the season he experienced considerable discomfort. The problem was diagnosed in the winter; he was operated on for appendicitis.

His recovery took longer than was expected, and he could not take his place in the Essex side until 21 July, when Glamorgan were beaten at Leyton. He did not bowl, and in the remainder of the season he was to send down only 87 overs and take five wickets. Never again was he to bowl with the pace and the swerve that had confounded the best in the world, not least the great Jack Hobbs.

Even without him, Essex maintained a record very similar to that of the previous season, for Douglas's absence was compensated for, in part, by the splendid all-round cricket of Nichols, who took 110 championship wickets, and of O'Connor, who narrowly missed the 'double' with 1402 runs and 93 wickets in all matches.

Russell and Freeman continued to score prolifically, and there was a remarkable maiden century for Fred Nicholas. In fact it proved to be his only hundred in the first-class game. He hit 140 in two hours, 40 minutes against Surrey at Leyton, but Essex had to follow on, and in spite of his 52 in 50 minutes in the second innings, they lost by an innings.

Southend and Colchester continued with their festivals, and they were now joined by Chelmsford, where the first county match to be played, on 16, 17 and 18 June, resulted in the first tie in Essex history, although the outcome was not determined until appeal to MCC.

Essex were led by Perrin who, at the age of 50, captained the County in Douglas's absence. *The Cricketer* was to draw some comment on the Chelmsford wicket in that during the two matches against Somerset and Oxford University, 190 extras were recorded, 106 of them being byes.

Certainly the bowlers always received help from the wicket, and MacBryan, who batted nearly three hours in scoring 80 out of 142, was the only batsman to show the necessary technique and application to meet the situation. Essex were well aided by extras in their attempt to match the Somerset first innings of 208, but they still fell 30 short. Where Somerset had relied mainly on spin, Essex trusted pace, and Nichols and Eastman bowled unchanged to rout the visitors for 107 in their second innings. Nevertheless, the task of making 138 on a wicket which was now giving the bowlers considerable help was not an easy one.

Freeman and Cutmore gave their side a solid start, but time and Bridges, the medium-pace off-cutter who was enjoying the conditions, threatened to halt the Essex bid for victory. With barely a minute to go Perrin and Eastman were together; the scores were level and eight wickets had been lost. Eastman, in attempting the winning hit, lashed at Bridges and was caught by Earle. The last man, Ridley, raced from the pavilion to join his captain with still half a minute to go, but the umpires, Chester and Stone, removed the bails. John Daniell sportingly asked that the game should continue, but Perrin bowed to the umpire's decision and left the field. The umpires then ruled that Somerset should be deemed to have won on the first innings. Essex questioned this decision and referred the matter to MCC who, after much deliberation, declared that the match was a tie and the points should be shared.

Perhaps the real hero of this match was Sir George Rowley, whose five matches for Essex were all in 1926 and whose invaluable 23 in the first innings was the highest score of his career.

A glance at the scorecard of the tie at Chelmsford reveals that 15 of those who played were amateurs, although it must be admitted that they were not all of first-class standard. No fewer than 19 amateurs appeared for Essex in 1927, and although they saved the County money, they hardly helped in establishing a settled side or in encouraging the development of promising young professionals.

Leyton still remained a worry, and there was concern as to whether the County would be able to continue to use what was its headquarters. Nevertheless, it retained the bulk of the fixtures. There were changes in the administration. Old Douglas became president, and G H Thompson took over as secretary. Eastman relinquished his post as assistant secretary, and from 1927 until the outbreak of the Second World War played as a professional.

Whatever the uncertainties as to its future as a cricket ground, Leyton continued to make history. On 14, 16 and 17 May 1927, Essex beat the New Zealand tourists at the County Ground, but the match was made memorable in that for the first time in the history of the game, as an exploratory venture, commentary on the game was broadcast. The commentary was, of course, of a limited nature, but it was appropriate that the first commentator should be Canon Frank Hay Gillingham. He was renowned as a fine preacher and the wittiest of after-dinner speakers. When some of his parishioners once questioned his taking time off to play cricket he replied that whereas other vicars took six weeks holiday at a time, he took his in three-day pieces. Would that he could have found more leisure time for Essex.

Gillingham, like Perrin and Freeman, who played in only one match and was succeeded behind the stumps for most of the season by George Eastman, younger brother of Lawrence, was nearing the end of his playing career. Indeed, another era of Essex cricket was slowly drawing to its close.

Douglas returned to full fitness, but his bowling had lost its fire, and although he scored 1000 runs, his batting had changed in character.

Essex v Somerset

Chelmsford 16, 17 and 18 June 1926

Somerset	1st innings		2nd innings	
†J Daniell	b Nichols	21	b Nichols	2
Young, A	c and b Russell	12	b Nichols	15
M D Lyon	lbw b Russell	15	b Eastman	11
J C W MacBryan	c Perrin b Russell	80	b Eastman	12
J C White	c Ridley b O'Connor	18	c and b Eastman	0
P R Johnson	c O'Connor b Morris	24	b Nichols	0
C C Case	run out	4	not out	23
G F Earle	c Morris b Nichols	4	b Nichols	15
Hunt, G E	run out	0	b Eastman	9
*M L Hill	b Nichols	9	b Eastman	0
J J Bridges	not out	1	c Nicholas b Eastman	17
	b 12, lb 4, w 1, nb 3	20	b 1, lb 1, nb 1	3
		208		107

	O.	M.	R.	W.	O.	M.	R.	W.
Nichols	21.5	3	48	3	15	2	45	4
Eastman	26	9	50	—	15	4	59	6
Rowley	8	—	26	—				
Russell	30	15	39	2				
O'Connor	8	1	19	1				
Morris	3	1	6	1				

Essex	1st innings		2nd innings	
Freeman, J R	b Earle	43	c Hunt b Bridges	37
Cutmore, J A	c Hill b White	13	lbw b White	26
O'Connor, J	c White b Hunt	10	c and b White	13
Russell, C A G	c Lyon b White	10	b Hunt	4
Nichols, M S	c Johnson b Earle	0	b Bridges	23
*F W H Nicholas	c Daniell b White	9	b Bridges	13
†P A Perrin	not out	19	not out	15
H M Morris	b Hunt	12	b Hunt	0
G V N Ridley	c White b Hunt	4		
L C Eastman	st Hill b White	0	c Earle b Bridges	0
Sir G W Rowley	c Johnson b White	23	b Bridges	0
	b 30, lb 5	35	b 1, lb 5	6
		178	for 9 wickets	137

	O.	M.	R.	W.	O.	M.	R.	W.
Bridges	15	6	24	—	16	4	33	5
Earle	7	2	10	2	3	1	13	—
White	44	21	57	5	22	5	49	2
Hunt	30	15	42	3	17	6	36	2
Young	6	2	10	—				

Umpires – J Stone and F Chester

Match tied

† Captain   * Wicket-keeper

He had earned the reputation of being a dour defensive batsman, but he had, in fact, been capable of some bold and aggressive batting; his scoring rate was considerably faster than most who play today. But where once there had been defence of character, however, there now seemed simply defence of obsession; scoring shots vanished. His final century in first-class cricket came in the Scarborough Festival in September, for MCC v Yorkshire.

He took 27 wickets for the County in 1927, but his was a minor support role to Nichols and Eastman. Nichols again had more than 100 wickets, and his left-handed batting seemed to improve with every match.

Russell and O'Connor each hit 1000 runs, and Jim Cutmore hit the only double century of his career, 238 not out against Gloucestershire at Bristol. Hubert Ashton, on leave from India, played some entertaining knocks, but the greatest excitement was provided by Leonard Crawley who hit 176 not out against Sussex at Leyton.

L G Crawley was a sportsman of outstanding talent. He represented Great Britain four times in the Walker Cup, was a fine racquets player and a good shot. He was a splendid batsman at Cambridge, and he appeared for Worcestershire during his first year at university. Lord Harris objected to this on the grounds that he was not qualified for the County, he was born in Suffolk and he was able to play for Essex through residence. His first century for Essex was an astounding affair.

Gilligan set Essex to make 276 in 3½ hours. Cutmore took 50 minutes to get eight of the first 42 runs, but O'Connor helped Crawley to add 87 in an hour. Russell stayed until the score reached 163, and Hubert Ashton then joined Crawley in a glorious display of driving which brought the last 114 runs in an hour and gave Essex victory with 25 minutes to spare. Crawley twice hit Tate on to the roof of the pavilion, and his 176 also included 18 fours. Like Gillingham and A J Turner, Leonard Crawley was to frustrate the followers of Essex in that he was so rarely able to play. Tom Pearce estimates that he was the greatest loss to the Club during his time, for Crawley played only 56 matches in 11 seasons. In the 30s, Essex needed one batsman of class to enable them to reach the highest level, and Crawley could have provided the last piece of the jigsaw puzzle.

In the return match with Sussex, at Hove, the last game of the season, Louden made his last appearance for the Club, taking 1 for 78 and 4 for 32 to help set up a ten-wicket victory. That win should have been relished for the following season, 1928, was to see only two victories and must be counted as the saddest year in the history of a great Club.

There were a few high points only – Crawley, 222 against Glamorgan at Swansea, 2000 runs by Russell and O'Connor, 1000 runs for Cutmore, centuries for the amateurs Waugh and the talented Bray. It was the first time that two Essex batsmen had reached 2000 runs in the same season, but the run-getting of Russell and O'Connor put into sharper focus the paucity of the bowling: few wickets at very high cost.

There were excuses. Nichols and Eastman were injured and missed several matches, but there were also panic selections. Thirty-eight players were called upon, and 26 of them bowled. Often the players used were amateurs who had no right to be in a county side, and this had a disheartening effect upon the professionals.

Perrin played his last three games for the County. He captained the side against Oxford University at Colchester and scored 51, which was one less than his age. The season also saw the last of Gillingham, who was 52, and the faithful Freeman. It also saw the last of J W H T Douglas.

Few had expected Essex to have a good season, but most had believed that they would maintain the middle of the table position of the last two seasons. None had anticipated the disasters of 1928. 'In the field,' says Bray of Douglas, 'he had become difficult with a tendency to blame others.' He bowled less and less. He was 46 years old, and the engine was wearing out.

At the end of July, at Leyton, he took 5 for 65 against Glamorgan on a rain-affected pitch. It was the 113th time, and also the last, that he took five wickets in an innings. He scored 848 runs in the season, but they were harder to come by.

The Essex fielding had slipped back to its disastrous level of yesteryear, and Douglas, whose prowess had been earned by dedication and hard work, and not nimble fielding, was now becoming a liability. As he called councils of war to discuss the fielding, he must have been aware of his fading powers. He still encouraged others and was anxious for their success, but as the season progressed there were rumours of political manoeuverings on the Committee and talk of new leadership.

On 25, 27 and 28 August 1928, Douglas led Essex against Leicestershire at Leyton. He hit 32 in 1¾ hours before being lbw to Astill. It was his last innings for Essex.

He had been the virtual dictator of Essex cricket for 18 years. He always did what he considered right, even at the cost of temporary discomfort or annoyance. Sometimes, but not often, he was wrong, but he was never a man for compromise or half-measures. In whatever he did, he had the full support of his father, and one should set down indelibly that had it not been for these two, the existence of the Essex Club might have been short. J W H T Douglas had his faults, but his devotion to Essex was unwavering, and while he was there it was certain that he and his father would make sure that the Club remained alive. He gave of his time, his money and his spirit for Essex cricket.

At the end of the 1928 season, the Committee suggested to Douglas that he should resign as captain. They felt a change of captaincy was desirable, and they intended that H M Morris should succeed him.

20. *Johnny Douglas coaching AG ('Tiny') Waterman, who last played for the County before the 1939–45 war, but who was to play a major role in the administration of the Club for many years as treasurer, and later chairman. As treasurer, he supervised the finances of the Club during the 1960s, a period when money was extremely short.*

Douglas refused. His main objection was that he did not feel Morris should succeed him, for he was not a good enough cricketer and his commitment to the County, in Douglas's view, was lacking. Events were to prove Douglas right, although that would not have pleased him.

Douglas fought the Committee with the same tenacity that he had fought all his battles on the field. It was a sad business, dreadfully managed. The man had given his life to Essex. He had carried them on his broad shoulders for 18 years. His personal achievements had brought honour to the Club. His was a service and record that demanded respect, and that respect was not forthcoming.

Possibly he had been so long in charge that the Committee had no sense of the tact that was now needed to deal with the situation that had arisen. The conflict became a bitter one, and the cricket world was disturbed and shocked by the sight of open wounds. The Committee sent a deputation to Douglas at his office in Bishopsgate. Sadly, the deputation was headed by a solicitor for whom Douglas had a particular dislike. He refused to see them.

On 3 December the Committee met for an hour and a half, and at the close of the meeting, the secretary, G H Thompson, read a statement:

> Mr H M Morris has been asked to captain the Essex County Cricket Club for next season and he has accepted the post. It is very much hoped that the valuable services of Mr J W H T Douglas will be available as a playing member of the team.

Two days later Douglas stated that he had no intention of retiring from first-class cricket, and *The Times* linked his name with Middlesex, for whom he had a birth qualification. There were faults on both sides. It was a sad time.

On Christmas Eve 1928, Essex County Cricket Club issued another statement which was printed in the newspapers of 27 December:

> It is with reluctance that my committee have decided to give publicity to the circumstances under which a change in the captaincy of the Essex County Cricket Club was made. In view, however, of the accounts appearing in the Press recently and in justice to the members of the club and the cricket public in general, they feel it is incumbent upon them to make the following statement:
>
> The committee of the club has been aware for some considerable time that there was a feeling in the county that a change in the captaincy was desirable. When this became very evident at the close of last season, three members of the committee, including myself, called upon Mr Douglas at his office in September and explained to him the situation and asked him whether, in the circumstances, he would resign. He informed us that he would consider this but added that if the committee thought that they would like a change, they should certainly make it.
>
> Mr Douglas attended a meeting of the committee on November 5, when the question of the captaincy was discussed. At this meeting it was decided to refer the matter to the cricket sub-committee for further consideration and report. This sub-committee, of which Mr Douglas is

a member, met on November 12, but Mr Douglas regretted his inability to be present. This meeting, after very fully considering the whole question, decided to recommend that such a change was desirable. The general committee met on December 3 when the recommendation of the cricket sub-committee was fully considered and adopted. Due notice of the meeting was sent to Mr Douglas, but he regretted he was once again unable to attend. Minutes were sent to Mr Douglas very soon after each meeting.

The meetings were not secret, as has been suggested in some quarters, but were properly constituted meetings of the committee held in the board room of the club's honorary solicitors where for years past business has been transacted in the winter months.

I hope it will, therefore, be clear that the appointment of Mr Morris as the new captain was not made without very full and earnest consideration by the committee, nor without Mr Douglas being made fully aware of the fact.

Mr Douglas states there has been disloyalty towards him by certain members of the team. This fact the committee were fully aware of, and it weighed with them in coming to their decision.

Nobody is more fully aware of the wonderful services Mr Douglas has rendered to the game of cricket than the committee, or more grateful to him for his services, and it was with deep regret and only after anxious consideration that it was decided to make the change. Mr Douglas has been asked to play as often as possible for the team and to become a member of the selection committee, and it is the earnest wish of the committee that he will do both.

(Signed) C. Stewart Richardson
Chairman, Essex County Cricket Club,
December 24, 1928.

Douglas did not join the selection committee, nor did he ever again play for Essex.

In 1929, in an effort towards reconciliation, he was made a life member of the Club, but nothing in his life affected Johnny Douglas as deeply as the break with his beloved county.

In March 1929, he went to Malta with Incogniti, and he played ten first-class matches, most of them for MCC, in the months that followed. In 1930, he played only four games.

The winter of 1930 was a miserable one with fog blanketing much of Europe and bringing death with it. At the beginning of December, Douglas and his father sailed to Finland to order the timber which would be delivered the following summer when the Finnish ports were no longer icebound.

They returned on a Finnish ship, *Oberon*, which was commanded by Erik Hjelt. The ship was due to arrive in Hull on Christmas Eve. The *Oberon*'s sister ship, *Arcturus*, was commanded by Erik Hjelt's brother Ossi. The two ships were due to pass each other at the entrance to the Kattegat late on 19 December. The two brothers cabled each other and hoped to pass close enough to see each other and exchange Christmas greetings.

In dense fog the two ships passed too close, and suddenly the *Arcturus* loomed large and collided with her sister ship on the starboard side. The *Oberon* was stove in from midships to stern. She sank inside four minutes. Forty-two people went down with her, including 18 of the 22 passengers.

The first-class passengers were gathered in the saloon at the time of the collision. Old Douglas was seen standing at the top of the stairs leading to the smoke-room as John was trying to find life-boat accommodation. He beckoned to the old man to come, but he gestured that he had to fetch something and went below. John Douglas went after his father,and neither man was ever seen again.

There were dedications and tributes, and the writer and journalist Alan Gibson recalls that one of the sharpest images from his childhood is of flags flying at half-mast at Leyton.

Gillingham gave the address at the memorial service. He said that Douglas had not been a natural games player, but that many men who were far more gifted than he lacked the concentration and application that he had possessed. 'I said when he was living,' Gillingham stated, 'and I say again now that he is dead, that if I had my back to the wall and was in trouble, I would rather have John Douglas alongside me than any other man.'

His end with Essex was not a happy one, but more than half a century has passed since the sea claimed him off the coast of Denmark, and now he is remembered and revered. The debt that Essex cricket owes to him can never be repaid, for the enthusiasm, courage and determination with which he faced crisis and difficulty made certain that what was to happen nearly 50 years after his death was possible.

CHAPTER 10

The Thirties: 1929–39

With the departure of J W H T Douglas from the Essex scene, which he had dominated for so long and to which he had contributed so much, a new era began for the Club. The first year of office of the new captain, H M Morris, in 1929, also saw the first appearance of T N Pearce, who was destined to play such a sterling part in the Club's fortunes.

During the 30s the Club's financial position, which at the best of times barely broke even, reached acute proportions on more than one occasion, notably in 1929 and again in 1932. In each case the storm was weathered, although it was touch and go. A major event was the decision taken in 1933 to abandon Leyton – the home and headquarters of Essex cricket since 1886. This bold step, described in detail at a later stage in this book, was a necessary one, taken in order to attract more support.

Essex in the 30s generally had a side full of character, capable of beating anyone, as they showed most emphatically when they destroyed Yorkshire at Huddersfield in 1935, winning by the resounding margin of an innings and 204 runs. This was in sharp contrast to the situation in the 20s, when the Essex bowling resources were very limited. By the late 30s, with bowlers of the calibre of Farnes, Nichols, Read, Stephenson and the Smith cousins, Essex were considered to be one of the strongest bowling sides in the country. By this time also Essex had become a team to be reckoned with; they were no longer the 'poor relations' of their neighbours Middlesex, Surrey and Kent. Between 1933 and 1939 they finished in fourth position in the county championship twice, in sixth position twice and were never lower than ninth.

Under the new captaincy of H M Morris, Essex advanced from 16th position to 12th in the county championship in the 1929 season, after a very bad start which saw the County lose their first four matches, although one of these was a friendly game. Six matches were won and nine lost, which certainly showed some improvement over the 1928 results of two wins and 13 defeats, although it has to be said that the Essex successes were achieved against counties that finished the season in the bottom five positions in the county championship table.

The most successful batsman in 1929 was O'Connor, who scored 2288 runs at an average of 44.86 with nine centuries, whilst Nichols became the first Essex professional to complete the 'double' of 1000 runs and 100 wickets in a season. In fact the only Essex player to achieve this feat previously was John Douglas, who performed it five times in his career. Hipkin showed considerable improvement and was not far short of a similar achievement, scoring 850 runs and taking 95 wickets. H T O Smith, an amateur fast bowler from the Midland Bank, who made his debut in 1929, achieved a memorable performance in the match against Middlesex at Lord's, dismissing F T Mann, D Russell and R W V Robins in four balls. All three batsmen were clean bowled and the ball that dismissed Robins broke the middle stump in two. Other players who made their debut in 1929 included future captain T N Pearce, leg-break bowler Peter Smith, J R Sheffield, who was to be the Essex wicket-keeper for the next few years and T H Wade, who was to take over from Sheffield as wicket-keeper in 1938.

Wade started his career as an off-break bowler, taking 4 for 11 (all clean bowled) against Nottinghamshire at Colchester and 5 for 64 against Somerset at Chelmsford. Roy Sheffield and Tommy Wade shared a tenth wicket partnership of 110 against Warwickshire at Chelmsford. Sheffield played his early cricket in the Wanstead League and was recommended to the County by Bill Golding, the chairman of Leyton Football Club, who was a member of the Essex Committee. He was an adventurous character who spent his winters in foreign countries. During one such visit to South America, he planned to travel the whole length of the River Paraguay, from Porto Esperanza to Buenos Aires, by canoe. This proving to be impracticable he spent most of his time as a cow-puncher in the wild country of Descalvados. Sheffield eventually became inadvertently involved in the war being waged between Paraguay and Bolivia and was arrested in Asuncion on suspicion of being a Bolivian spy. Fortunately he

21. *Roy Sheffield stumps John Langridge of Sussex, at Leyton in 1933. The fielders are Morris Nichols at slip, and Leonard Crawley in the trilby hat, at mid-on.* (Central News)

was released, thanks to the intervention of a British businessman. Sheffield later wrote an interesting book entitled *Bolivian Spy?* in which he describes his experiences in South America on that visit. He emigrated to New Zealand in 1938, playing for Wellington in the season of 1938–39. An outdoor man, he became a guide in the Southern New Zealand Alps, a physical education teacher at Wellington College and was later employed by the New Zealand Government as a Physical Education Officer and Maori Welfare Officer. He is still, at the age of 80, actively engaged in his favourite sport, canoeing.

Another newcomer (although admittedly he played in one match in 1928) was future joint captain Denys Wilcox, who was then a schoolboy at Dulwich College. Playing for Essex against Middlesex at Lord's in 1929, Wilcox went in to bat when Essex had lost four wickets for 25. Batting with great assurance he rescued the innings from disaster, scoring 71 out of 120.

He subsequently went up to Cambridge, gaining blues in 1931, 1932 and 1933, captaining the side in 1933. In the 1932 university match he scored a magnificent 157. H M Morris was unable to play in the last five matches and the side was captained by Charles Bray and Frank Gilligan on these occasions.

1929 saw a serious financial situation when it was reported by the honorary treasurer that the Club had an overdraft of £460 and liabilities of about £3000 to the end of the season. A further £200 was needed to carry on until the end of August. A special appeal was launched, in an endeavour to raise £1500 and, in the interim, members of the Committee guaranteed personal loans totalling £160. The response to the special appeal by the end of August amounted to £270 which, together with that estimated to come from other sources was totally inadequate to meet the Club's obligations to the end of the year. Once again there was a very real danger that the Club might cease to exist. A special sub-committee was formed to deal with membership subscriptions, fees for ground-letting and any other relevant matters. This sub-committee recommended increased subscriptions, increased ground-letting fees, reduction of staff, general economies, a drive for new members and other measures. A Special General Meeting was called to approve these proposals, the members being told in detail the state of the Club's finances and how they had been trying to balance accounts with a pre-war subscription and a post-war expenditure. The proposed measures were approved and by the following year the position had eased somewhat.

Items of financial interest in the 1929 season included an early mention of advertising, the middle space on the back of the scorecard being offered to Ind Coope at £5 for the season. There was also an experimental 6d (2½p) gate admission charge after 4 pm and a car park levy of 1s 6d (7½p) per day for members (later rescinded).

In Harold Morris's second year as captain (1930) the County enjoyed its most successful season since 1911, finishing in sixth position in the championship. Morris's appearances were somewhat limited; he was unable to play in 11 matches owing to business commitments. During these absences the side was captained by either Charles Bray or Henry Franklin. Seven victories were recorded, as against five defeats. Sixteen matches were, however, left drawn, although in several of these unfinished games there were close struggles for first-innings points, Essex being successful against Gloucestershire by 12 runs, Yorkshire by 14 runs and Middlesex by six; but yielding points to Hampshire by seven runs. Despite a brave innings of 77 by Jimmy Cutmore out of a second-innings total of 111, Essex succumbed to Lancashire at Blackpool, a victory that gave Lancs the championship. The two teams were entertained with champagne by the Lancs President, the Essex players all toasting the winners and Jimmy Cutmore singing one of his tenor songs.

Four batsmen – O'Connor, Russell, Cutmore and Pope – scored 1000 runs for the County. Cutmore was an attractive opening bat who originally intended qualifying for Glamorgan. Essex, however, heard of his success in Club cricket and signed him on. He was known as an excellent vocalist with a fine tenor voice, appearing regularly in several London theatres. Dudley Pope, formerly with Gloucestershire, made his debut in the County Championship, after completing the necessary two-year qualifying period. He soon developed into a sound opening partner for Cutmore. O'Connor again headed the Essex batting averages, scoring 1477 runs in championship matches at an average of 43.44. He scored a century on five occasions, including two hundreds in the match against Gloucestershire at Bristol. Nichols bowled well, taking 108 championship wickets at 19.50 apiece and just missed the 'double', scoring 914 runs in all matches. He returned the excellent figures of 5 for 40 against the Australians at Leyton, which saw the visitors dismissed for 156, although Essex were unable to capitalise on this. Nichols was chosen for England in the fourth Test against Australia at Old Trafford, taking 2 for 33 and scoring 7 not out in a rain-affected match.

In his final season for Essex, Jack Russell returned to his best form, scoring 1335 runs, including four centuries. 1930 also witnessed the debut of Kenneth Farnes from Gidea Park, a bowler whose potential had been spotted by Percy Perrin when he was playing for the Gidea Park Club against Essex Club and Ground, which was captained that day by Perrin. A tall, really fast bowler, standing over six feet five inches and weighing 15½ stone, he had a beautiful action, moving the ball both ways. He took a comparatively short run, bringing the ball down from a great height. This had the effect of lifting the ball sharply off the pitch, which made him very difficult to time. In his second match for Essex, against Kent at Southend, Farnes took 5 for 36 in 17 overs in Kent's first innings. Coming on as first change he very quickly had Aidan Crawley caught behind by Roy Sheffield. Shortly afterwards Frank Woolley edged a ball to second slip where Jack Russell, despite his 43 years, took a brilliant catch to dismiss the batsman for nought. The wickets of Ames, Knott and Freeman then followed. Farnes went up to Pembroke College, Cambridge in 1930 and was to win a blue as a freshman in the following year, followed by further blues in 1932 and 1933 and eventual selection for England in 1934 and later. He played in a Test trial in 1932 and was seriously considered for the tour of Australia in 1932–33 which became the 'body-line' tour.

In 1930 it was agreed to appoint a permanent secretary to the Club. Mr B K Castor was chosen from the applicants and accepted the position.

It was also agreed to appoint Charles McGahey as official scorer at £2 for each home match and £3 10s 0d for each away match. In this year the Committee, rather belatedly, decided to send the cordial thanks of the Essex County Cricket Club to J W H T Douglas for his past valuable services. At the same time the Committee elected Douglas and Perrin as life members. The Club agreed to take on the lease of the Leyton ground for seven years from 1930 at an annual rental of £500. It is interesting to note that in that year it was decided to install electric light in the pavilion at Leyton in view of the cost of renting gas lamps.

1931 was a very poor summer, with many matches being ruined or interrupted by rain. Essex suffered a very bad start to the season, losing their first four matches, three of them by an innings. The remainder of the season was more satisfactory and the County eventually finished in tenth position in the championship, with the same number of wins as in 1930 (seven) but losing 11 matches as compared with five in 1930. O'Connor was again the leading batsman, scoring 1434 runs in championship matches (average 35.85), with five centuries. Charles Bray batted well, scoring 921 runs in all matches (average 32.89) including three centuries, of which one was a fine innings of 129 against the New Zealanders at Southend. Another of Bray's centuries (122) was scored at Chelmsford, against Glamorgan, on the day his son was born. He and Eastman put on 134 for the fourth wicket, Essex winning the match by nine wickets. O'Connor took four wickets for four runs in 13 balls on the last morning. Tom Pearce revealed excellent form in the six matches in which he played and registered his maiden century (152) against Lancashire at Clacton. Nichols again just missed the 'double', taking 97 wickets and making 872 runs. The match against Lancashire at Clacton constituted the first County match to be played at the Vista Road Ground, Clacton, which was added to the list of festival grounds then consisting of Chelmsford, Colchester and Southend. In this match Kenneth Farnes took six Lancashire second innings wickets for 57, Essex soundly defeating Lancashire by an innings and 64 runs. Although appearing in 22 matches, Harold Morris had to miss eight games owing to business calls, the deputy captains again being Charles Bray and Henry Franklin.

In 1931 much time was spent by the Committee in considering the possibility of moving the Club's headquarters from Leyton to a site in the Ilford-Seven Kings area. Sites were inspected at Becontree, Barkingside, Chadwell Heath and Goodmayes. The project was, however, abandoned as it was reported that the cost of establishing a new ground in a similar district was prohibitive. It was considered that the only possible course was to purchase the Leyton ground as the headquarters of Essex cricket. The option to purchase the Leyton ground was extended for three years and it was decided to appeal for funds, the press being notified accordingly.

22. *Tom Pearce, who played a major role in the affairs of the Club. He played from 1929 to 1949, and then continued as an administrator. Here he is pictured with Charles Bray (left), an occasional captain of Essex between journalistic duties, and a former historian of the Club.* (Manchester Guardian & Evening News)

The Committee recorded deep concern and sympathy on its first meeting since the deaths of Mr J H Douglas, a past president and serving member of the Committee and of Mr J W H T Douglas, a former England and Essex captain, who had both lost their lives at sea in December 1930.

Poor results at Colchester led to the Committee issuing a statement to the press, regretting that it could not allot County matches to Colchester in 1932. It was stated that any resumption of county cricket there must be on the basis of the guaranteeing of the actual cost of any matches allotted, plus the cost of the corresponding away matches.

The year 1931 saw a return to financial troubles with the announcement of a serious financial loss on the season. This was to have severe repercussions in the following year.

P A Perrin, who had served as a Test selector in 1926, was again appointed to the selection committee in 1931, serving on the Committee from then until 1939 and being chairman in 1939.

23. *Tom Pearce playing for the Gentlemen against the Players, at Lord's in 1936.* (Sport & General)

The new season proved to be very disappointing on all counts. The weather was bad, several players suffered injuries and no less than six captains acted as substitute for Harold Morris, who only managed to play in two matches. The deputy captains performed their duties creditably but a regular captain was essential for the well-being of the team. The doubts which John Douglas had expressed concerning the ability of Morris to play regularly were now confirmed. The team was young and inexperienced and needed a captain who could take the helm for the whole season. Without such a person the County's prospects were severely limited.

After a moderately good start, which saw three victories in the early part of the season, the County only won one of the remaining 18 matches, of which ten were lost. Not surprisingly, Essex dropped from 10th to 14th position in the championship. Of the injuries suffered during the season the most serious was that sustained by O'Connor, who, when batting in the Test trial at Manchester, had his finger split by a ball from Larwood. This injury kept him out of the game for over a month and was doubly unfortunate in that prior to this mishap he was in top form, having scored 906 runs in 14 innings, including three centuries, by the middle of June.

He did not quite regain this form after his return to the side. But for this injury he might well have gone to Australia on the body-line tour the following winter.

Nichols bowled heroically, sending down nearly 1000 overs in all matches and performing the 'double' for the second time, scoring 1430 runs at 31.77 and taking 115 wickets for 24.92 runs apiece. L G Crawley was able to play in eight matches and performed most successfully, scoring 744 runs, including two centuries, at an average of nearly 50. One of his centuries, against Warwickshire at Chelmsford, when he scored 155 in three hours, was described by *Wisden* as 'a magnificent display of well-timed driving'. He hit one six, one five and 23 fours in this innings, Essex winning the match by 220 runs. Crawley's second century – 138 in the rain-interrupted game against Derbyshire – was also described by *Wisden* as 'a glorious exhibition of off-driving'. Crawley hit 18 fours in a first-wicket partnership of 191 with Pope. *Wisden*, again, recorded that he 'drove splendidly' in his innings of 86 against Leicestershire at Chelmsford, helping Essex to a seven-wickets victory. Leonard Crawley was an engaging character, with a keen sense of fun, who could well have achieved high honours in the cricketing world had he been able to devote more time to the game. Tom Pearce has described how, in 1936, when Leonard Crawley was captaining Essex against Glamorgan at Pontypridd, he arrived at Paddington in his flannels, with his night requirements in a brown paper parcel. Crawley scored a magnificent 118 in the Essex first innings, including five sixes (two of which sent the ball clean out of the ground) and nine fours. Unfortunately, this innings left him so stiff that he was unable to take any further part in the match.

Although Eastman bowled steadily and Farnes was able to assist the County after the end of the university season, the attack was generally very ineffective. As if the injuries and absences were not enough, Essex found themselves on the receiving end of a brilliant partnership by Holmes and Sutcliffe in the match against Yorkshire at Leyton. The pair put on 555 for the first wicket, which established a new record, beating the 554 scored 34 years before by another Yorkshire pair, J T Brown and J Tunnicliffe. This performance, however, was not without drama as, after the score-board had registered the record figure of 555, Sutcliffe threw away his wicket and the two batsmen posed for photographs in front of the score-board. Then, to the astonishment of all, the score-board was altered to read 554! However, after investigation, it was discovered that a no-ball signalled by one of the umpires had not been recorded.

The Yorkshire team was presented with large numbers of '555' cigarettes (the Yorkshire score being a most advantageous one for the manufacturers of this brand of cigarette). The Essex players felt that the firm in question might have considered the poor fielding side in this hand-out. However,

24. *Herbert Sutcliffe and Percy Holmes achieved a record 555 opening stand for Yorkshire against Essex, at Leyton in 1932. Yorks declared when the score was achieved, but later it was discovered that the score-board was wrong, and the official scorers claimed that the total was only 554.*

The Essex captain on the day, Charles Bray, readily agreed to an extra run being found to enable the record to stand, although the matter has been controversial ever since. The score-board here is not correct as it should have recorded that Sutcliffe (313) was out at 555.

the Yorkshire team very kindly shared these cigarettes with the Essex team. Charles Bray, who captained Essex on this historic occasion was, 46 years later, requested by the editor of *The Cricketer* to write an account of what took place. In his account, published in the October 1978 issue, Bray recounts how he was approached by the Essex scorer – the former Essex player Charlie McGahey – who reported that he and the Yorkshire scorer both agreed that the total should be 554 and not 555, and that they had been asked to find an extra run, in order that the record should be beaten and not equalled. Bray agreed to the request to find a run, adding that Holmes and Sutcliffe had batted magnificently and more than deserved the record. Bray states in this account that, by so doing, he agreed to the finding of a run which was never made and admits that he was wrong. The strange thing about this episode is that the record was accepted by the cricket authorities as a fact and was never queried or investigated in any way.

The poor results of 1931, coupled with the depressing situation in 1932, saw another financial crisis which culminated in a statement being given to the press, giving the situation as it stood then and asking the press to open a 'shilling fund' on behalf of the Club and to make it clear that, unless a satisfactory response was forthcoming, the continuance of the Club would be impossible. An appeals committee was set up with a target figure of £2000. This time the response was encouraging, with many national and local newspapers operating 'shilling funds', donations of over £500 being received and other satisfactory fund-raising results being reported. This positive response enabled the Club to keep its head above water. In view of the situation the ground purchase project was abandoned and it was decided that, at the termination of the existing lease, or earlier if possible, the headquarters of the Club be removed from Leyton.

At the end of the 1932 season H M Morris resigned the captaincy after leading the side for four years. Considerable discussion took place as to a possible successor. P A Perrin expressed the opinion that it would not be advisable for him to undertake the captaincy, he having retired from first-class cricket in 1928. It was originally decided to appoint the club secretary, B K Castor, as captain, provided no objections were lodged by other counties as to his qualifications. This proposal was later dropped, owing to the attitude of certain counties. Several other amateurs were considered, and the Committee eventually reported that T N Pearce had agreed to act as captain for May and June and that D R Wilcox would do so for the remainder of the season. Tom Pearce was at that time employed in business by T G Grinter, a keen Club cricketer and Essex supporter, who as described earlier had played for the County between 1909 and 1921.

A cordial letter of thanks was sent to Mr Grinter by the Committee for releasing Pearce. Tom Pearce was by now an established batsman and also a first-class captain. He was also a rugby footballer of note and was later to become well-known as an International referee.

Denys Wilcox had come down from Cambridge and assumed the headmastership of the school in Westcliff founded in 1904 by his father. This school – Alleyn Court Preparatory School – was noted for producing many fine cricketers, the most famous of whom, Trevor Bailey, was a pupil at the school at this particular time. The founder, Theodore R Wilcox, gave both his family and his school a love of cricket. The young pupils at the school were always taken to watch Essex play during the local festival weeks and by so doing were enabled to improve their own knowledge of the game.

The arrangement finally made was for Pearce to lead the side until mid-July and for Wilcox to take over for the remainder of the season. This system worked very well and meant that, for the first time since John Douglas's tenure, the Club had a regular playing captain. An immediate improvement was seen and the County finished the 1933 season in fourth place in the championship, the highest position since 1897. In fact, for a fortnight in June they were lying in second position in the table and were serious contenders for the title. Thirteen matches were won (more than ever before) – seven under the captaincy of Tom Pearce and six under Denys Wilcox. The side's performances, both individual and collective, showed marked improvement under two popular and able captains, both of whom were no mean performers with the bat. The fielding was vastly improved, the batting more forceful and the County boasted a powerful attack, particularly when Kenneth Farnes was available later in the season.

O'Connor, as usual, was the outstanding batsman, scoring over 2000 runs in all matches, with six centuries to his name. Five other batsmen – Cutmore, Nichols, Eastman, Pope and Taylor – all scored over 1000 runs. Never before had six Essex batsmen topped 1000 runs in a season. Other centurions were Laurie Eastman and Stan Nichols (three each), Jimmy Cutmore (two) and Reg Taylor and Leonard Crawley one each. Taylor, a right-hand forcing batsman from Southend, had joined Essex in 1931. He was to play some useful innings for the County and was also a left-arm slow bowler of chinamen and googlies. The bowling was very strong, Nichols taking 120 wickets at 21.55, again accomplishing the 'double' with 1460 runs and 145 wickets in all matches. Peter Smith demonstrated that his leg-break skills had improved tremendously; he took 100 wickets for the first time and Kenneth Farnes, who appeared in the last ten matches, took 67 championship wickets for 16.07, he and Nichols constituting a formidable opening pair of bowlers. Farnes' best performance was 7 for 21 against Surrey at Southend when he and Nichols bowled their opponents out for 57 in their second innings. Farnes also took 13 for 98 in the match against Somerset at Taunton. A curiosity of the match against Sussex at Leyton was that in the Essex score of 561 for 9 declared, no batsman scored 100 and there were no partnerships of 100.

The Committee recorded a very warm vote of thanks and appreciation to T N Pearce and D R Wilcox for the admirable results obtained during the 1933 season and to the team for its loyal and happy support given to these captains.

In 1933 the Club moved to new offices at 6 Duke Street, Chelmsford at an annual rent of £65, inclusive of rates etc. A profit of only £100 was shown for the year 1933, despite the successful playing year. Gate money increased but subscriptions dropped by £390. The following statement was consequently given to the press:

> As a result of the year ended September 30th 1933, the Essex County Cricket Club will show a profit of about £100. Despite the successful playing season membership has dropped by £390. The result, however, is considered satisfactory after the heavy losses suffered in 1931 and 1932.

At the end of the 1933 season the decision to leave Leyton was taken by the Club Committee. Essex relinquished their lease of the Leyton ground, which was purchased by the Metropolitan Police. Chelmsford became the County headquarters and the policy of taking Essex cricket round the County was implemented. Weeks had been held at Southend since 1906, Colchester since 1914, Chelmsford since 1925 and Clacton since 1931. To these were added Brentwood and Westcliff, with Chelmsford being allocated two weeks. Ilford was included in the following year. The Colchester week was moved to Castle Park, which last staged first-class cricket in 1914. These arrangements also saw a return to the original County Ground at Brentwood after 49 years and an abandonment of the subsequent County Ground at Leyton – again after 49 years. Although this policy meant that Essex cricket was being taken to an increasing number of centres in the County, it had the disadvantage of lacking a home base with attendant practice facilities and meant that, in effect, the team was playing 'away' matches all the season. Thus there came into being the so-called 'Essex Circus', all the necessary equipment being moved from Club ground to Club ground, which involved much detailed planning. This arrangement, whilst doubtless causing much hard work for the administration, worked very well, attracting increased support and introducing a feeling of personal participation amongst the spectators, who were made to feel part of the act.

Essex did not sustain the position of the previous year, finishing eighth in the championship in 1934. Although possessing the most formidable pace attack in the country, Essex were rarely able to field their best side. Test trials, Test matches, injuries etc. caused the difficulty and it was not until after the middle of July that the County was at full strength. From the middle of July onwards Essex were unbeaten. Jack O'Connor had his best-ever season, scoring 2350 runs in all matches with an average of 55.95 and nine centuries to his name; he had a top score of 248 against Surrey at Brentwood. He was unfortunate not to be picked for England, despite his sterling performances. Cutmore, Pope and Nichols batted well, each scoring over 1000 runs and Tom Pearce enjoyed a successful season, scoring 815 runs in 17 championship matches, his highest score being 111 against Worcestershire at Chelmsford. A welcome return was made by Claude Ashton, who played in six championship matches, scoring 416 runs including 118 against Surrey at Brentwood, and finishing at the head of the Essex batting averages. Denys Wilcox made some useful contributions, not the least being his 109 against Yorkshire at Southend, which match Essex won by an innings and 46 runs. This was the first win by Essex against Yorkshire since 1911. In this game the former Cambridge University wicket-keeper Adam Powell shared in a stand of 113 for the ninth wicket with Peter Smith, scored in 90 minutes. Powell allowed no byes in the Yorks match total of 395. A very good wicket-keeper who played for Essex in the mid-30s, he was regarded by some as the best wicket-keeper in the country. He was also a competent batsman. Powell captained Suffolk in post-war years and led them to the senior counties championship.

So far as the bowling was concerned, the outstanding performer was Kenneth Farnes, who in 13 innings took 37 championship wickets for an average of 16.40.

An extraordinary week's cricket was seen at Brentwood. In the first match Essex lost to Kent by an innings and 192 runs, Kent amassing the huge total of 803 for 4 wickets declared, Ashdown scoring 332, Ames 202 not out and Woolley 172. In the following match against Surrey, Essex were as completely masters of the scene as Kent had been in the previous game, defeating Surrey by exactly the same margin – an innings and 192 runs. A new Essex fast bowler burst upon the scene in the shape of H D Read, an amateur who had previously had a trial with Surrey and whose father had played for Essex early in the century. Brought in to augment the fast attack in the absence of Farnes and Nichols – both playing in the Test trial at Manchester, Read met with astonishing success, commencing by removing Jack Hobbs' cap with his first ball and bowling him with his sixth ball and taking seven Surrey wickets for 35 runs in 9.1 overs. Read took a very long run and worked up a tremendous pace with devastating effect. Surrey, who came to Brentwood expecting to make a large score, following the huge Kent total in the previous game, were bundled out for 115 and Essex piled up the large total of 570 for 8 declared, O'Connor making 248 (the highest score of his career) and Claude Ashton 118. Surrey were dismissed for 263 in their second innings, leaving Essex victorious in two days. A story was put around after the Kent match to the effect that Frank Woolley (who had scored 172 in this game) met Jack Hobbs at Liverpool Street Station. Hobbs, who was on his way to Brentwood to play for Surrey against Essex, was supposedly told by Woolley to go and help himself to a nice easy 'ton' as the conditions at Brentwood were all in favour of the batsman. Nichols had a poor season with the ball, not having recovered from the effects of the previous winter's tour to India. H D Read finished the season with 57 wickets at an average of 21.64 and the fast attack was given good support by Lawrence Eastman and Peter Smith. Eastman had a remarkable spell in the match against Somerset at Weston-super-Mare, dismissing R A Ingle, G M Bennett, Wellard and Hazell for no runs in 13 balls. Two closely contested matches, in both of which Jimmy Cutmore played a leading part, were seen in the games against Kent at Gravesend and against Leicestershire at Chelmsford. In the former, Essex required 166 to win and had lost eight wickets for 89 when Peter Smith joined Cutmore. These two put on 78 together, to give Essex a win by two wickets, Cutmore scoring 97 not out. Against Leicestershire, Essex, needing 84 to win, were successful by two wickets, Cutmore making the winning hit off the second ball of the last possible over. The side was again jointly captained by Tom Pearce and Denys Wilcox with conspicuous success. Kenneth Farnes was chosen for two Test matches against the visiting Australians.

In view of the fact that the former Essex and England cricketer Charles McGahey had fallen on hard times, the Committee voted to pay him £1 per week during the winter months. Furthermore, the chairman of the Committee arranged interviews with the press with the suggestion that a national testimonial to Charles McGahey be instituted in recognition of his services to cricket. These interviews subsequently showed that the general wish was expressed that the testimonial would be successful. Overall a small profit was recorded for the 1934 season.

The 1934 season ended with the tragic death of Dudley Pope in a car accident at Writtle, when his car was in collision with a lorry. Pope, during his five seasons with Essex, had made his mark as a very sound opening batsman and was excellent in a crisis. He was a very good fielder, who could throw direct to the wicket-keeper's hands from all parts of the ground. He was a partner (with Peter Smith) in the successful Chelmsford sports shop, Pope & Smith. Dudley Pope was a most popular man, whose loss was deeply felt by the Club. He was only 25 years of age. A new opening batsman had therefore to be found and various experiments were made in the 1935 season to this end. Tom Pearce and Denys Wilcox again jointly led the side but the latter was only able to play in five matches after taking over from Tom Pearce. Wilcox was taken ill with appendicitis which necessitated an operation. Essex got off to a terrible start in 1935, suffering five successive defeats. Matters then improved, Essex eventually registering 11 wins to 12 defeats. But the County was severely handicapped by the lack of an opening partner for Cutmore, and the need to revert to a succession of deputy captains during the incapacity of Denys Wilcox. In addition, Kenneth Farnes was out of action for the season with a knee injury. Essex finished in ninth position in the championship table. O'Connor again scored the most runs for the County – 1603 in all matches, – but his average dropped considerably. Tom Pearce had a very successful season, reaching 1000 runs for the first time (1018 in all matches) and scoring two centuries. The second of these – 105 against Lancashire at Chelmsford – was an heroic effort as it was made in the knowledge that his wife was being operated on for appendicitis in the hospital overlooking the ground. Essex, at this time, were a most attractive and unpredictable team, capable of beating the best teams and losing unaccountably to the weakest. That season of 1935 saw them defeat the South Africans, the 1934 champions Lancashire and the 1935 champions Yorkshire. The match against the South Africans at Southend was a personal triumph for the army bowler J W A Stephenson, a mercurial cricketer, brought in for H D Read who was being rested before the fifth Test.

Stephenson took three of the first four South African wickets to fall, at a cost of 11 runs, finishing with 7 for 66. South Africa were dismissed for 250, Essex, with a score of 302, gaining a 52 runs lead on first innings. Thanks to good bowling by Nichols (4 for 35) and Stephenson again (3 for 44), Essex were left with 172 to win, which they achieved with the loss of only three wickets, Cutmore following his first innings score of 72 with 59 not out and Nichols contributing a hard-hit 70. Stephenson, a most dedicated cricketer and gifted all-rounder, was unlucky not to have been picked for England. There was never a dull moment when he was on the field. He was full of boundless enthusiasm and provided much entertainment for the spectators. He bowled fast-medium with a full follow-through, moving the ball both ways, and was a hard-hitting, free-scoring batsman. A brilliant fielder, he was liable to cut off leg-glides made from his own bowling. Known as 'Steve' to his colleagues, he was a regular army soldier who served in India before returning to England, where he was, fortunately for Essex, stationed at Colchester. As Tom Pearce said: 'It is most difficult to write of his cricket because I have never met anybody quite like him. It was nothing to see him running down to third man after he had bowled a batsman out and return to his position via extra cover.'

The Lancashire match at Chelmsford resulted in an easy victory for Essex by ten wickets. Pearce's century in this match has already been described and was the cornerstone of the Essex success. Fine bowling by Nichols (4 for 14), Eastman (3 for 4) and Evans (2 for 10) saw Lancashire routed in their second innings for 83. The match against Yorkshire at Huddersfield provided the sensation of the season. Yorkshire, who had not lost a match since August 1934, were dismissed for 31 – their lowest total for 26 years. At one stage their score stood at 9 for 6. The damage was done through magnificent pace bowling by H D ('Hopper') Read and Stan Nichols, Read taking 6 for 11 in 6 overs and Nichols 4 for 17 in 6.4 overs. Essex got off to a bad start, losing five wickets for 65, but a magnificent partnership by Nichols and the Oxford blue B H Belle, who put 174 for the sixth wicket, enabled Essex to reach a total of 334, Nichols scoring 146 and Belle 63. Yorkshire therefore commenced their second innings 303 runs in arrears. They were very soon in trouble again, being unable to cope with the devastating pace and accuracy of the Essex fast bowlers and were all out for 99 by lunchtime on the second day, Nichols taking 7 for 37 and Read 3 for 51. Nichols' performance was the greatest of his career, with match bowling figures of 11 for 54 and a score of 146, which was 16 runs more than Yorkshire were able to total in two innings. At the end of the match the Yorkshire crowd gave the Essex team a standing ovation. Herbert Sutcliffe was heard to comment, when caught behind by Sheffield off Nichols: 'At least I was good enough to touch it.' The story is told of a Yorkshire committee man who arrived a little late at the Huddersfield ground on the first day of this match and enquired of the man at the gate as to the state of the game. '30 for 9' replied the gate-man with a dead-pan expression. 'Excellent,' said the committee man, 'and how many has Bowes got?' Back came the reply: 'He's only just gone in!'

Nichols took his 100th wicket of the season in this match and again achieved the 'double', scoring 1249 runs and taking 157 wickets in all matches. His all-round consistency earned him selection for four Tests against South Africa. In the South African first innings in the Trent Bridge Test, Nichols took 6 for 35. 'Hopper' Read was picked for the fifth Test against South Africa at The Oval and was also chosen to tour Australia the following winter. Read was a really fast bowler, although erratic, who enjoyed a short but brilliant career, turning in some magnificent performances and achieving highest honours, in a period of only two years, before quietly disappearing from the scene. 'Hopper' Read, who was not well-known for his batting, scored 15 noughts during the 1935 season, of which eight were in successive innings.

Stan Nichols had the honour of being chosen by *Wisden* as one of their 'Five Cricketers of the Year' for 1935. In addition to receiving the talent money then awarded to the professionals for good bowling and batting performances, which in Stan Nichols' case amounted to £28, the Committee voted Nichols an ex-gratia grant of £10 for his outstanding performance in the Yorkshire match at Huddersfield. Nichols was the first player in the country to reach 1000 runs and 100 wickets in 1935, a feat which he was also to accomplish in the following four seasons. When it is considered that he was 35 years old when this sequence commenced, and a fast bowler at that, his performances are all the more commendable. Coming from farming stock, he had a fine physique and could bowl for long spells without losing any of his accuracy. He was not even considered as a bowler by the village team for which he played in his early cricketing days and was taken on the Essex ground staff as a batsman.

YORKSHIRE v. ESSEX

Fartown Ground, Huddersfield, July 31, Aug. 1 and 2, 1935.

YORKSHIRE.	First Innings.		Second Innings.	
1 Sutcliffe	c Sheffield b Nichols	4	c Eastman b Nichols	1
2 Barber	c Wilcox b Read	1	b Nichols	18
3 A. B. Sellers	c Wilcox b Read	2	lbw b Nichols	2
4 Leyland	b Read	0	b Read	2
5 P. A. Gibb	c Rist b Read	0	lbw (N) b Nichols	11
6 Turner	c Sheffield b Read	4	b Nichols	14
7 Hutton	b Nichols	0	lbw b Nichols	0
8 Wood	c Read b Nichols	13	b Nichols	24
9 Fisher	b Read	0	c Rist b Read	2
10 Verity	not out	0	c Smith (P.) b Read	6
11 Bowes	c Rist b Nichols	4	not out	19
	b 1 lb 1 w nb 1	3	b lb w nb	1
	Total ..	31	Total ..	99

Fall of the Wickets.

1	2	3	4	5	6	7	8	9	1	2	3	4	5	6	7	8	9
2	6	6	7	9	9	27	27	27	..	..	..	..	..	..	..	..	..

Bowling Analysis.	First Innings. O	M	R	W	WDS	NB	Second Innings. O	M	R	W	WDS	NB
Nichols	6·4	2	17	4	..	..	15	3	37	7	..	..
H. D. Read	6	1	11	6	..	1	11·4	2	51	3	..	..
Eastman	..	..	..	..	..	..	3	0	10	0	..	..
....	..	..	..	..	..	..	..	..	..	..	..	..
....	..	..	..	..	..	..	..	..	..	..	..	..
....	..	..	..	..	..	..	..	..	..	..	..	..

ESSEX.	First Innings.		Second Innings.	
1 Sheffield	b Verity	5	....	..
2 Rist	c Gibb b Verity	35	....	..
3 D. R. Wilcox	c Wood b Turner	2	....	..
4 Cutmore	c Wood b Fisher	2	....	.
5 O'Connor	b Fisher	0	....	..
6 Nichols	c Hutton b Bowes	146	....	..
7 B. H. Belle	c Verity b Leyland	63	....	..
8 Eastman	c Gibb b Bowes	28	....	..
9 Smith, P.	b Bowes	5	....	..
10 Smith, R.	not out	16	....	..
11 H. D. Read	st. Wood b Verity	0	....	..
	b 24 lb 13 w nb	37	b lb w nb	..
	Total ..	334	Total ..	..

Fall of the Wickets.

1	2	3	4	5	6	7	8	9	1	2	3	4	5	6	7	8	9
24	30	39	39	65	239	282	..	334	..	..	..	..	..	..	..	..	..

Bowling Analysis.	First Innings. O	M	R	W	WDS	NB	Second Innings. O	M	R	W	WDS	NB
Bowes	37	8	77	3	..	..	..	..	..	..	..	..
Turner	16	2	41	1	..	..	..	..	..	..	..	..
Verity	24·2	4	79	3	..	..	..	..	..	..	..	..
Fisher	25	5	62	2	..	..	..	..	..	..	..	..
Leyland	5	1	30	1	..	..	..	..	..	..	..	..

N signifies lbw. New Rule.

Umpires—F. Chester and Walden.

Play starts at 11.30 first day – until 7 p.m. Second day 11.0 to 7 p.m.
Third day 11 to 4 or 4.30 p.m. Lunch 1.30 to 2.10 p.m. each day.
Tea interval at 4.30 p.m.

25. *Yorkshire v Essex, 31 July – 2 August, 1935.*

However, Percy Perrin spotted his bowling potential when watching him in the nets and thus began the process of making him into a fast bowler. Nichols said afterwards that, as he was ambidextrous, he wished he had started bowling fast left-arm instead of fast right-arm, as the left-arm bowler begins with a natural advantage, since the majority of batsmen are right-handed. The body action break of a left-arm bowler is a leg-break to a right-handed batsman and is a far more difficult break to play, as the ball is running away from the batsman.

Early in 1935 the County received the sad news of the death of Charles McGahey. The chairman expressed the sorrow of the Club in losing such a lovable character. It was decided that the monies already subscribed to Mr McGahey's testimonial fund should be returned to the donors. A letter from Mr McGahey's brother was read by the chairman, expressing appreciation of the help accorded to Charles McGahey by the Committee.

At the first meeting of the newly-formed Council of the Essex County Cricket Club the chairman, C Stewart Richardson, stated that the Council now consisted of gentlemen who not only knew every part of Essex but were also known throughout their own districts. He felt that this should do much to further interest in the County Cricket Club. Despite the good season the Club lost £650. A campaign for new members was introduced.

Again captained by Tom Pearce and Denys Wilcox under the joint arrangement, which continued to prove an admirable one, Essex finished the 1936 season in ninth position with eight wins and eight losses. This was somewhat disappointing as the side possessed the potential for better things. Once again Essex continued to be unpredictable, registering a notable victory by 47 runs against the eventual runners-up, Middlesex, at Lord's (Stan Nichols and J W A Stephenson sharing 14 wickets between them) and administering a sound seven-wickets defeat to the Indian touring team at Brentwood (Cutmore and Peter Smith scoring centuries and Peter and Ray Smith taking 12 of the 19 wickets falling to the bowlers). Yet they contrived to lose the match against Derbyshire at Chelmsford, which they had dominated for the first two days, when, needing 102 for victory and having reached 51 for the loss of three wickets, they then managed to lose their remaining seven wickets for 31 runs, losing the game by 20 runs.

Once more, Jack O'Connor scored most runs (1343 in all matches) but this time he was closely followed by Stan Nichols, who aggregated 1315 runs in all matches. Nichols also took 114 wickets, thus registering his fifth 'double'. Both joint captains batted well, Denys Wilcox heading the Essex batting averages with 596 runs at 42.57 (633 runs in all matches) and Tom Pearce scoring 874 runs at 34.96 (1066 runs in all matches).

Tom reached his 1000 runs in the Gentlemen v Players fixture at Lord's, for which he had been selected for the first time. At the beginning of this match Tom's aggregate for the season stood at 980 runs and this was the last possible chance he had of reaching 1000 runs. A score of one in the Gentlemen's first innings was not promising, but a brilliant 85 in their second innings saw him well past his target and his success was loudly applauded all round the ground. This was the match in which Kenneth Farnes, in the Players' second innings, clean bowled Gimblett, Hammond and Hardstaff, in each case sending the stump catapulting head high before it dropped at the feet of the wicket-keeper, Levett, who was standing more than a dozen yards back. Also, in this same Gentlemen v Players match J W A Stephenson enjoyed an inspired spell of bowling, taking nine Players' wickets for 46 in their first innings.

'Hopper' Read's meteoric career in first-class cricket came to an abrupt end when he found himself unable to spare the time to continue playing. He played in only 54 first-class matches, of which 32 were for Essex. He decided to give up first-class cricket in order to pursue his chosen professional career as a chartered accountant. He played some club cricket thereafter, for the Butterflies and the Gentlemen of Essex and also, occasionally, for MCC. The return of Farnes after his absence in the previous season through injury was therefore very welcome. He took 61 wickets in 11 county championship matches and was chosen to tour Australia in the 1936–37 winter. Farnes surprised everyone in the match against Somerset at Taunton by scoring 97 not out in a last-wicket partnership of 149 with Tom Wade. The Essex bowling throughout the season was good, with Stephenson, Laurie Eastman, and the cousins Peter and Ray Smith all making worthy contributions – but the batting was somewhat uncertain. A sad note was struck with the departure of Jimmy Cutmore, who was not re-engaged for the 1937 season. After his excellent century against the Indians his form completely deserted him and he only managed to score 208 runs in eight championship matches.

A bowler's life was a hard one in the days when Essex played practically all their home matches at Leyton, which regularly provided a batsman's wicket. After leaving Leyton in 1933 it was noticeable that Stan Nichols achieved even greater bowling success and produced even more consistent figures than in the Leyton days, even though he was in his mid-30s at the time of the change.

H S Ashton (father of Hubert and Claude) was elected president of the Club, to succeed Brigadier General Sir R B Colvin. An example of the amounts received by professionals from benefits in those days was seen in the final figure for Stan Nichols' benefit in 1936, which amounted to £1177 6s 5d.

26. *Hubert Ashton. After his playing days he served the Club as chairman from 1946–51, and later as president from 1949–70. He was knighted in 1959.*

During the 1936–37 MCC tour of Australia, Tom Wade kept wicket in two matches for the MCC when both L E G Ames and G Duckworth were injured. Wade was visiting Australia at the time and was awarded an MCC touring cap for these appearances. He and Roy Sheffield travelled out to Australia with the MCC team on the *SS Orion*. Wade stayed with the team and was a very useful additional player. Sheffield went on to New Zealand, where he took on a position as chief guide in Tongariro National Park. When the MCC team moved to New Zealand Kenneth Farnes went by train to stay at Château Tongariro and, in a party of six, guided by Roy Sheffield, climbed Mount Ruapehu, 9200 feet above sea level.

Essex, again under the joint leadership of Tom Pearce and Denys Wilcox, finished the 1937 season in sixth position in the championship – an advance of three places in the table. Thirteen matches were won and 11 lost, six of these wins being obtained during the month of August. Even so, 11 defeats seemed to underline the team's inconsistency and it was felt that they had the ability for greater things. Tom Pearce and Denys Wilcox both enjoyed successful seasons with the bat, Wilcox finishing first and Pearce second in the County averages.

Wilcox scored 1390 runs in all matches, including four centuries, and Pearce 939 runs in all matches, with one century. Two of Denys Wilcox's hundreds (129 and 104) were scored in the same match – against Kent at Westcliff. This was the first time that two centuries in a match had been scored by an Essex batsman since 1930. Wilcox came very close to repeating this feat, against Nottinghamshire at Southend, when he scored 90 in the first innings and 99 in the second.

Jack O'Connor again scored the most runs – 1364 in championship matches, but his average dropped to 28.41. Stan Nichols again enjoyed a successful season and with 1247 runs and 148 wickets in all matches registered his sixth 'double'. He was the first in the country to perform this feat in 1937 as indeed he had been in each of the two previous seasons. A V Sonny Avery, who had joined the staff in 1935, made a great advance. Appearing in 22 county championship matches he scored 909 runs, including a maiden century (109) against Nottinghamshire at Nottingham. Hailing from New Beckton, Avery was a natural batsman who learned his early cricket in the back streets of Leyton. He started his career with Essex as an office-boy at the age of 15½ and, as the office was situated above the pavilion, he had a perfect view of the playing area, of which he took full advantage, watching the great players in action. This, he says, was the finest coaching he could have had. No mean footballer, he was signed on by Tom Cable, manager of Leyton Football Club, and played for Leyton against Dulwich Hamlet in the 1936–37 F A Amateur Cup Final.

Peter Smith showed a tremendous improvement, taking 155 wickets in all matches with his leg-spinners, at an average of 19.60 and being invited to tour India with Lionel Tennyson's team. Essex were handicapped later in the season through injuries to Stephenson and Farnes. Stephenson damaged an achilles tendon in July which put him out of cricket for the rest of the season. Farnes, who had bowled very well for the Gentlemen at Lord's, taking 5 for 65 in the players' first innings, then suffered a strain which kept him out of the third Test match against New Zealand.

It is interesting to note the subscription rates for members at this time. The 1937 rates were as follows:

	£	s	d
Full Privilege (men)	1	11	6
Full Privilege (ladies)	1	1	0

	£	s	d
Life	50		
Ordinary (men)	1	1	0
Ordinary (ladies)		15	0
Boys and girls		10	6
Club	1	1	0

Hubert Ashton was appointed deputy-chairman of the Committee. Due to loss of form by Roy Sheffield, Tom Wade took over as wicket-keeper and Sheffield was not re-engaged. The Committee agreed to recommend Sheffield for consideration for appointment to the first-class umpire's list. No objection was raised by the Committee to Tom Wade taking up all-in wrestling, so long as this did not interfere with his services to the Club!

Captained again jointly by Tom Pearce and Denys Wilcox, Essex in 1938 had an extraordinary season even by their standards. Once again they had a deplorable start, losing eight of their first nine championship matches, the other being drawn, and it was not until the end of June that they recorded their first victory. From then on Essex carried all before them, winning nine out of their last 12 games, drawing two (both with leads on the first innings) and losing one. The County occupied sixteenth place in the championship table until the end of June. Thereafter they moved steadily upwards to finish in sixth position.

At times the County was in brilliant form, with forceful batting, deadly bowling and first-class fielding in evidence, so much so that it is difficult to understand why they experienced such a disastrous start to the season. Stan Nichols enjoyed his finest season, taking 171 wickets at 19.92 each and scoring 1452 runs, average 35.41 in all matches, again performing the 'double' and again being the first player in the country to do so. He was selected for the Gentlemen v Players match at Lord's.

In the match against the Australians at Southend the Essex pace attack dismissed the visitors for 145 and 153, Farnes taking 4 for 43 in their first innings and Nichols 6 for 25 in the Australians' second innings. Essex were, however, bowled out even more cheaply, scoring 114 and 87, the damage being done by the spin bowlers Fleetwood-Smith and Ward. The second day's attendance at this match was 12,500, which was an Essex record, and the total gate for the two days was £20,500. The Australians considered the Essex attack to be the best county attack in the country. Nichols turned in a magnificent performance at Gloucester when Essex defeated Gloucestershire by an innings and 65 runs, scoring 159 out of the Essex total of 553 and taking 9 for 37 and 6 for 128. At one stage in the Gloucestershire first innings Nichols had taken 5 for 6 in five overs. He dismissed Hammond for four in the first innings and two in the second.

27. *Morris (Stan) Nichols, a superb all-rounder, and the main architect of the famous win against Yorkshire at Huddersfield in 1935.*

Kenneth Farnes had a magnificent season and was right back to his top form, taking 56 championship wickets at 14.89 each and 107 wickets at 18.84 apiece, in all matches. He was selected for four Test matches against the Australians, in which he took a total of 13 wickets, and also for the Gentlemen against the Players, at Lord's. In this match Farnes returned the excellent figures of 8 for 43 in the Players' first innings, clean bowling five of his victims. This performance was considered by many to be the best fast bowling seen in this fixture since Arthur Fielder took all ten Gentlemen wickets in 1906. Other fine returns by Farnes were 15 for 113 against Glamorgan at Clacton and 14 for 119 against Worcestershire at Worcester. Farnes was chosen as one of *Wisden*'s 'Five Cricketers of the Year' for 1938 and was also invited to join the touring party to South Africa in the coming winter. He played in all five Tests, including the famous 'timeless Test' at Durban, which lasted for ten days and was still undecided when the touring party had to commence their rail journey to Cape Town to join their ship. When play was finally abandoned England's score stood at 654 for 5, which was 42 runs short of victory. A total of 1981 runs were scored in this match – the highest in

Test match history. Farnes' figures on this perfect batting wicket did not do him justice.

Jack O'Connor again scored more runs than any Essex batsman, totalling 1839 in all matches, including six centuries. He returned to his best form, not only increasing his aggregate but improving his average. Tom Pearce headed the Essex batting averages with 948 runs in all matches to his credit, including two centuries. He batted forcefully and consistently and could always be relied upon in a crisis. Sonny Avery continued to progress but he had the misfortune to break a finger, which put him out of action for six weeks. Even so, he scored 831 runs, with two centuries to his name. One of these was against Nottinghamshire at Trent Bridge, which Essex won by 11 runs after being put out for 58 and seeing Notts gain a first-innings lead of 184. Avery was top scorer in both the Essex innings with scores of 21 and 136.

Reginald Taylor reached 1098 championship runs with a top score of 193. Peter Smith enjoyed a fine season, securing a total of 144 wickets at a cost of 24.36. He also performed well with the bat, scoring 846 runs in all matches, including two centuries. He was chosen for the Gentlemen v Players match at Lord's, taking 4 for 140 and 5 for 68 against the Gentlemen. Stephenson's appearances were limited but he was picked to play for the Gentlemen against the Players at Lord's.

Laurie Eastman and Ray Smith bowled steadily whilst Tommy Wade again kept wicket consistently. Against Kent at Colchester he conceded only two byes in an aggregate score of 742. He allowed no byes until 626 runs had been scored. Another world record was established against Essex in the match with Kent at Colchester, when Arthur Fagg scored two double centuries in the match (244 and 202 not out), the first time such a feat had been performed. However, it should be noted that Essex were without Farnes, Nichols, J W A Stephenson and Peter Smith – all were playing in the Gentlemen v Players match at Lord's.

During the winter of 1938 the County received the very disappointing news that Tom Pearce would be unable to captain the side in 1939, owing to business commitments. After much deliberation the Committee decided to appoint three joint-captains – J W A Stephenson, F St G Unwin and Denys Wilcox. The latter, of course, had been joint-captain with Tom Pearce since 1932. Frederick Unwin first played for Essex in 1932, as did his brother Ernest. Both were in the Haileybury XI; Ernest played rugger for England. John Stephenson had made his mark in 1935 and continued to provide enjoyment for the spectators in his own inimitable fashion. He was later to have a distinguished war record, being extremely popular with his men. After retiring from first-class cricket he took up golf, playing in a style described in *Wisden* as peculiarly his own, giving equal enjoyment to himself and his friends, putting

28. *The Gentlemen of Essex v the Players of Essex, 1938. From left to right, back row: W Mead (umpire), J W A Stephenson, R M Taylor, Dr N Vere-Hodge, J N Dennis, K Farnes, T P B Smith, R Smith, F H Vigar, T H Wade, W (Bill) Reeves (umpire). Seated: N G Wykes, H J Palmer, H W F Franklin, T N Pearce, J O'Connor, D R Wilcox, M S Nichols, L C Eastman. In front: A R Lord, H B Daer, A V Avery, A B Lavers, S J Cray.* (Fred Spalding & Sons Ltd)

one-handed back-hand from any part of the green and holing, if not a proportion that would have satisfied a champion, at least as many as more orthodox players in his own class.

Essex in 1939 enjoyed their most successful season since 1897, finishing fourth in the championship, with 12 wins to their credit, as against ten losses.

The highlight of these victories was that against Yorkshire at Sheffield, which Essex won by an innings and four runs. It is true that Yorkshire were without Hutton and Wood, who were playing in the third Test against West Indies, but Essex were also similarly handicapped by the absence of Nichols, also playing in the same match.

Nichols again had a wonderful season at the age of 39. He was the outstanding player in the team and the best all-rounder in the country. Once again he performed the 'double' with figures of 1387 runs (average 35.56) and 121 wickets (average 18.87) in all matches and once again he was the first player in the country to achieve this. Nichols turned in many fine all-round performances during the season. Amongst these were his 146 against Sussex at Hove, coupled with a total of eight Sussex wickets for 98; 6 for 18 and 5 for 26 (the latter five wickets all being clean bowled) against Derbyshire at Southend; and a total of 80 runs and 9 for 64, against Northamptonshire at Clacton.

Jack O'Connor again scored more runs than any other Essex batsman – 1716 runs at 37.30, with four centuries. This was the 15th consecutive season in which he had scored 1000 runs and his value to the side was immense. Known as 'The Laughing Cavalier', Jack O'Connor had a keen sense of humour, always wore his cap at a jaunty angle and was a first-rate team man. He scored a century against all the other first-class counties and also against both universities.

Although Eastman's bowling fell away he had a good season with the bat, totalling 1027 runs at 26.33. Against Surrey at Colchester he had the misfortune to be run out on 99. Eastman was also dealt a piece of misfortune in his benefit match against Middlesex at Southend, when, suffering from water on the knee, he was forced to bat last. Essex lost the match by five runs but would probably have won had Eastman not been so handicapped. The irony of this was that Eastman had once commented that he had batted in every position except No. 11 and it was, therefore, a cruel blow that he should have filled this gap under such circumstances.

Avery had a very good season, scoring 1335 runs at an average of 41.71, with two centuries, the first of which (121) was against Middlesex at Lord's in a 225 partnership with Jack O'Connor, who scored 128.

Wilcox and Taylor's batting fell away but Taylor secured 46 championship wickets with his slow left-arm spinners. Peter Smith just missed 100 wickets, taking 95 at 20.69 apiece, whilst cousin Ray Smith took 79 wickets at practically the same cost (20.68).

John Stephenson bowled well, securing 57 championship wickets at 23.22 and also scoring 641 runs. Both he and Kenneth Farnes were again selected for the Gentlemen v Players match at Lord's, Stephenson taking six wickets and Farnes five. These two bowlers dominated the proceedings in the four Gentlemen v Players matches between 1936 and 1939; they accounted for 45 wickets between them out of a total of 61 that fell.

Tommy Wade, besides keeping wicket to his usual high standard, scored 736 runs at an average of nearly 20. Frank Vigar, a tall, Somerset-born all-rounder, who had joined Essex in the previous year, scored his maiden century against Gloucestershire at Chalkwell Park, Westcliff. Vigar recalls that he was sent in as night-watchman, to save the valuable wicket of Jack O'Connor and, after having been dropped by Wally Hammond at slip, he went on the next day to score 121, saving Essex from following on. Jack O'Connor, he remembers, was out first ball. This was the match in which Hammond scored 207 in Gloucestershire's first innings, including 4 sixes, one of which cleared the main road, landing on the roof of a house. Kenneth Farnes could not play until August, but he took 33 championship wickets at 18.57 runs each, with 3 for 90 and 5 for 30 against Nottinghamshire at Clacton, including a hat-trick (his first) and in the second match of the Clacton Festival, against Northamptonshire, he took 2 for 79 and 6 for 47. This was the last game of the year and thus ended the County's best season for 42 years, in which they were challenging for honours for most of the summer. The County suffered two narrow defeats at the hands of Middlesex, by five runs and two wickets respectively, which, had the results gone the other way, could have seen Essex nearer the top of the table. This brought to an end an era, as the 1939–45 war was about to break out. Essex, at this time, were stronger than for many years and it is quite possible that, but for the war, they could have won their first championship in the early 40s. Stan Nichols and Peter Smith were both chosen for the MCC team to visit India in the winter of 1939–40 which, of course, was cancelled owing to the war.

Mr A J Spelling resigned as honorary treasurer after 15 years service, despite the efforts of the Committee to persuade him otherwise. The Committee agreed that all members of HM forces in uniform be admitted to all County matches in 1939 at an entrance fee of 6d and to the West Indies match at 1s.

CHAPTER 11

War Stops Play: 1939–45

In 1939 the secretary, B K Castor, announced that he had been ordered to report for duty at Aldershot on 15 November. The Committee agreed to make up any difference between Mr Castor's army pay and the figure of £400 per annum. This decision was to stand for the duration of the war. A J Spelling agreed to carry on as treasurer during the absence of Tom Pearce on active service.

A wartime emergency committee was established in 1940, with H Ashton as chairman, to look after the Club's interests during the war years. A J Spelling, who was already acting as treasurer, was appointed to this as acting secretary. With the outbreak of hostilities, County Cricket was abandoned for the duration of the war. The Essex Committee agreed to play one-day matches against local clubs on the various County grounds and to pay the professionals £1 per match, in addition to out-of-pocket expenses. Six fixtures were arranged in 1940 for an Essex XI against Ilford and District, Chelmsford and District, Chigwell School, Forest School, Bancrofts School and Brentwood School, all being won by the County team, for whom members of the regular side played when on leave. In the match against Forest School, Bill Reeves, the former Essex all-rounder and Test umpire, then aged 64, made a successful appearance for the Essex XI, taking several wickets.

A number of Essex players took part in matches regularly organised by two clubs – the British Empire XI and London Counties. Amongst those who played in 1940 were Jack O'Connor and Laurie Eastman for London Counties and W G Spencer, Ray Smith and Kenneth Farnes for the British Empire XI.

The wartime emergency committee met regularly and on one occasion (16 April 1940) it was recorded that Messrs F R Foster and W J Golding were both prevented from attending, owing to 'enemy action'. Beyond the cricket field Essex players and Committee men were to play distinguished roles during the war. Reginald Taylor, who had joined the RAF, was awarded the DFC as a Pilot Officer in 1940, and the Committee sent him a letter of congratulation. They also wrote to 2nd Lieutenant T P B Smith, congratulating him on receiving a commission. The Committee sent a letter of congratulation to Hubert Ashton on his appointment as Sheriff for the County of Essex.

During 1941 the County suffered two tragic losses with the deaths of Kenneth Farnes and L C Eastman. Farnes joined the RAF in 1940 and was sent to Canada for training, returning to the UK to become a night-flying pilot. He was killed on the night of 20 October when the plane he was piloting crashed. He was 30 years of age. Lawrence Eastman died in hospital on 17 April. He had been injured as a result of a bombing raid whilst serving as an ARP warden. The Committee were represented at the funeral and endeavoured to arrange a match against London Counties for the benefit of Eastman's widow, but owing to difficulties of ground and organisation the idea had to be dropped. Eastman, who was 43, had played for Essex from 1920 until 1939.

The Committee continued the policy of fostering enthusiasm amongst schoolboys, arranging coaching classes at Chelmsford, which proved very popular. It was also arranged for Club and Ground sides to play matches against Chigwell, Forest and Brentwood Schools.

A match between Middlesex and Essex against Kent and Surrey was played at Lord's in August, but unfortunately was curtailed by rain. Middlesex and Essex batted first, scoring 412 for 6 declared, Surrey and Kent reaching 65 for 3 before the weather intervened. Essex were represented by Sonny Avery (96), Stan Nichols (3 for 35), Harry Crabtree and Ray Smith. A collection amounting to £251 4s 6d was handed over to King George's War Fund for Sailors. It was estimated that more than 15,000 watched the first day's play.

Two other matches were played in aid of wartime funds. The first was at Chelmsford where the British Empire XI met Chelmsford and District, whom they defeated by five wickets. Sonny Avery, Tom Pearce,

29. *Kenneth Farnes. His death during the war years was a severe blow to Essex and English cricket. He was a part of the formidable Essex attack before the war, which also consisted of J W A Stephenson, M S Nichols and R Smith. It was one of the main factors in taking Essex to fourth place in the championship in 1939.* (Central Press)

Stan Nichols and Bill Dines played for Chelmsford and District, whilst Harry Crabtree and Ray Smith appeared for the British Empire XI. The match produced a donation of £450 for the Red Cross. The second game was played at Southend between an Army XI and an RAF XI but was unfortunately abandoned owing to rain. Essex players who took part were Jasper King and Peter Smith for the Army and Claude Ashton and Reg Taylor for the RAF. The match was played in aid of the Southend Spitfire fund, to which a useful contribution was made.

Essex continued to be well represented in the London Counties and British Empire XI games, with Jack O'Connor, for the former club, and Sonny Avery, Harry Crabtree and Ray Smith for the latter, again being well to the fore. The Club showed a profit of £355 6s 4d for 1941. This was largely due to the staunch support given by about 600 members of the Club, who continued to pay their subscriptions.

In 1942 another tragic loss was reported, with the death of Squadron Leader Claude Ashton in a flying disaster which also took the life of another County cricketer, R de W K Winlaw. Claude Ashton's career with Essex spanned 20 years. He was an outstanding games player, gaining blues at Cambridge for cricket, association football and hockey and captaining the university cricket team in 1923. In addition to gaining 13 amateur international football caps he earned a full international cap for England against Ireland in 1925, captaining England in this match. He returned to the County in 1934, after a five-year business absence, enjoying a wonderful season, including participation in the Club's fifth wicket record of 287 with Jack O'Connor. He also played a full and successful season in 1936. He was in the running for the captaincy of the England side to Australia in 1936–37, G O Allen being the eventual choice.

It was also reported, with great regret, that the secretary, Lieutenant Colonel B K Castor, was officially posted 'missing' when Singapore fell into Japanese hands.

Easter coaching classes continued at Chelmsford, and Club and Ground teams again arranged to play matches against the schools. Another 'four counties' match was staged at Lord's in 1942, between Essex and Middlesex and Surrey and Kent, on 3 and 4 August. Surrey and Kent, batting first, scored 193, Stan Nichols taking 4 for 47 and Trevor Bailey making a very successful debut, dismissing three batsmen in his first over and finishing with 4 for 36. Essex and Middlesex replied with 281, Stan Nichols contributing 51 and Kent declared their second innings at 277 for 6. At the close, Essex and Middlesex had scored 186 for 4 – just four runs short of victory. A crowd of over 22,000 saw the first day's play. £417 18s 3d was handed over to King George's War Fund for Sailors.

Several other matches were played for war charities, including that between an Essex XI, captained by Ray Smith, and the British Empire XI, at Chelmsford, which raised £148 17s 5d for King George's War Fund for Sailors and a game between Lieutenant P Smith's Army XI and Major A B Sellers' AA Command Team at Chelmsford; this realised £350.

Thanks to the continued loyalty of many members the Club made a working profit of £292 for 1942.

The Essex Committee again pursued the policy of encouraging youth during 1943. Coaching classes were arranged at Chelmsford under Jack O'Connor and matches arranged against schools.

The Club unfortunately suffered a great loss through the death of H S Ashton; he had been president of the Club for eight years. News which stirred mixed emotions was that of the secretary, B K Castor. It was reported that he was alive but a prisoner in Japanese hands. Meanwhile Lieutenant Colonel J W A Stephenson, a former captain of the Club, was awarded the DSO in Tunisia.

The usual wartime match between Middlesex and Essex and Kent and Surrey was again staged at Lord's, Harry Crabtree, Stan Nichols and Trevor Bailey representing Essex. Kent and Surrey ran out easy winners and the proceeds, as usual, went to King George's War Fund for Sailors.

T E Bailey played in several other representative matches at Lord's, including that between an England XI and a West Indies XI. He also played for the British Empire XI when on leave from the Royal Marines.

The Committee congratulated the Chairman, Lieutenant Colonel Hubert Ashton, upon his appointment as High Sheriff of Essex.

Continued generosity on the part of members saw the Club finishing the year 1943 with a profit of £335.

Coaching classes for juniors were held in 1944, as before, under the supervision of Jack O'Connor. He was paid £6 for a week's coaching. Several games were arranged with Essex schools. The Committee voted £25 to the Essex Army Cadets for the purchase of a perpetual trophy, to be competed for annually in a knock-out cricket competition by their various units.

The annual match between Middlesex and Essex and Surrey and Kent was played at Lord's and resulted in a draw. Essex were represented by Sonny Avery, Harry Crabtree, Trevor Bailey and Ray Smith.

A new wartime Essex team was formed, called Essex County Services, which was officially recognised by the Committee. This team played several matches in 1944, including one against New Zealand at Chelmsford, which Essex County Services won by five wickets. Enthusiasm on the part of members brought another profitable year for the County, 1944 showing a profit of £350.

In 1945 the popular coaching classes at Chelmsford, under the supervision of Jack O'Connor, were arranged and the usual matches against Essex schools were again played.

Essex players have often featured on cigarette cards, in early days, and 'trade' cards in later days. Here is a sample, of (top): C J Kortright (1901), F L Fane (1907), J W H T Douglas (1928); (middle) L G Crawley (1931), H D Read (1936), T E Bailey (1948); and Keith Fletcher (1983).

(From the Mike Marshall collection)

Ray East is congratulated by two Essex stalwarts, Stuart Turner and Keith Fletcher. Ray's left-arm spin accounted for 1010 wickets between 1965 and 1984 with an average of 25.54

All-Sport/Adrian Murrell

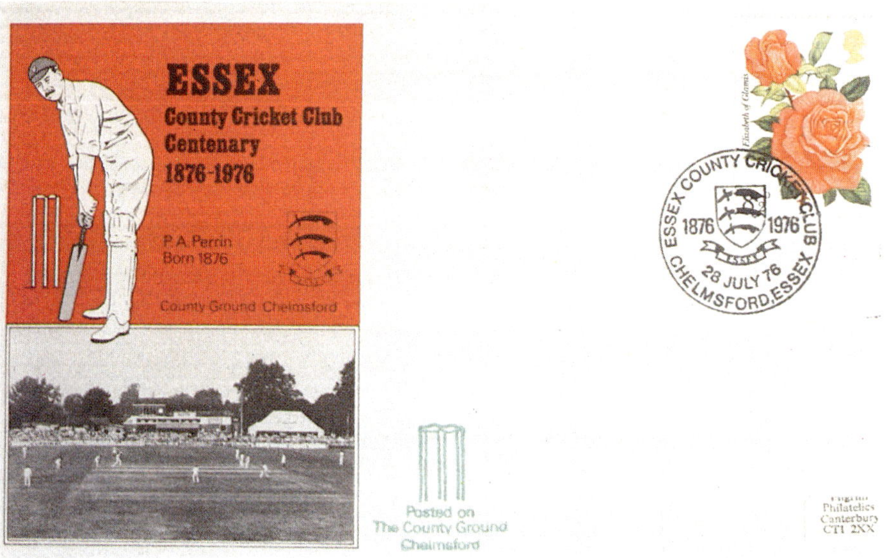

A first day cover printed to commemorate the Club's centenary in 1976.

Clive Tarling

John Lever and injured Keith Fletcher sit on the covers before the delayed start of the 1985 Benson & Hedges Cup Final against Leicestershire.

All-Sport/Adrian Murrell

David East shows why he is grateful for sponsorship of his laundry bill. In 1985 he set a new county record with eight catches behind the stumps against Somerset, which also equalled the world record for first class cricket.

All-Sport/Adrian Murrell

David Acfield, one of the many ex-Cambridge University players who have graced the Essex side this century. Between 1966 and 1986 he took 855 wickets at an average of 27.49.

All-Sport/Mike Powell

Allan Border and Graham Gooch in tandem at Hove, 1986.

All-Sport/Adrian Murrell

It was announced with much pleasure that Lieutenant Colonel B K Castor had returned safely to this country, after his experiences in the Far East.

The wartime emergency committee continued to direct the Club but Mr A J Spelling's acting secretaryship terminated with the cessation of hostilities in August 1945. Wing Commander L L Bray was appointed temporary secretary for the remainder of 1945 and it was decided that he and Lieutenant Colonel Castor should be joint-secretaries for the 1946 season.

The Committee decided to give every support to the 'Intensive Weeks Coaching Scheme' being organised by H P Crabtree, who had become very much involved in cricket coaching in state schools and was responsible for organising a group coaching scheme which proved most successful.

The British Empire XI, for whom a number of Essex cricketers had regularly played and which had been captained by Ray Smith, was wound up in 1945, having played 238 matches, winning 150, drawing 52 and losing 36 and contributing a great deal of money to the Red Cross.

The Club's financial position remained satisfactory, the accounts showing a surplus of about £300 in 1945. The only Essex ground to suffer from enemy action during the war was Chelmsford, where the pavilion was damaged. Additionally a letter was received from Denys Wilcox with reference to the future career of T E Bailey. The acting secretary was instructed to see Mr Wilcox on this matter, it being understood that the Club would be prepared to support a proposal which would enable him to play for Essex.

CHAPTER 12

Fresh Beginnings: 1946–50

Essex approached the first post-war championship season of 1946 in the knowledge that many of their strong 1939 first-team squad would not be seen in Essex colours again. Kenneth Farnes, Claude Ashton and Lawrence Eastman were all casualties of the war, Stan Nichols and Jack O'Connor, now aged 45 and 48 respectively, were too old, and such gifted amateurs as Leonard Crawley and John Stephenson were, for various reasons, no longer available. Consequently, Essex faced a period of re-building, having to include a number of young and untried players.

Luckily, Tom Pearce was available and willing to lead the side again, this time as a full-time captain, and Essex were indeed fortunate to be able to call on his high qualities, both as a batsman and as a leader. In the circumstances, Essex did well to finish in eighth position in the championship table, with eight wins, and nine defeats.

C Stewart Richardson was elected as first post-war president of the Club and Hubert Ashton and W J Golding chairman and vice-chairman respectively of the first post-war Committee. A J Spelling was appointed honorary treasurer. B K Castor was appointed sole secretary but he subsequently accepted an offer as secretary to the Surrey County Cricket Club. An advertisement was placed in the press inviting applicants to the position, as a result of which R F T Paterson was appointed to the post. Despite the regular profits made by the Club during the war years, increased costs led the Committee to launch an immediate appeal for financial support.

Sonny Avery carried on in 1946 where he left off in 1939, enjoying a good season with 1210 runs to his credit, including three centuries, one of which was a double century. Tom Pearce batted well throughout the season, totalling 1332 runs with five centuries, whilst a new batsman, T C 'Dickie' Dodds, who had done well in army cricket during the war, had his first season for the County, playing as an amateur. A hard-hitting batsman, who was very likely to hit the first ball of an innings for six, he scored 1050 runs, including two centuries. One of these (103) was in a record-breaking first-wicket partnership of 270 with Sonny Avery (who scored 210) against Surrey at The Oval. Essex scored 597 in this match, defeating Surrey by an innings and 179 runs, Tom Pearce scoring 116 not out and bowling honours going to Peter Smith, who took 11 for 119 in the match. Dickie Dodds recalls how Alf Gover's frustration grew as the Essex opening partnership total mounted. 'How,' he growled at Dodds 'would you like to spend your life bowling on this wicket?' 'Well,' replied Dodds, 'Surrey managed to get out on it.' On returning to the pavilion Dickie Dodds was told by captain Tom Pearce to go and get himself a decent cap, which was Tom's way of telling Dickie that he had been awarded his County cap. Sonny Avery scored his 210 out of 365, hitting 20 boundaries and being particularly strong on the leg side.

Another newcomer to the side was T E Bailey, who showed exceptional promise, although those who knew him as a phenomenal schoolboy cricketer at his preparatory school, Alleyn Court, and at Dulwich College, were not surprised. In the limited number of matches in which he played, he scored 412 runs and took 37 wickets, just missing a maiden century when he made 97 not out against Worcestershire at Worcester.

Schoolmasters Harry Crabtree and Denys Wilcox made very useful batting contributions, scoring, respectively, 793 runs (average 49.56) and 484 runs (average 40.33), Crabtree scoring three centuries and Wilcox one. Harry Crabtree was a jovial Yorkshireman who taught in Essex and became Physical Education Organiser for the County Council. His mass coaching method was taken up by MCC and subsequently adopted world wide. He travelled quite extensively to demonstrate the method, which was aimed at instilling the basic techniques of batting and bowling into large groups of enthusiasts. He was subsequently appointed MCC Coaching Adviser for Youth. Crabtree first played for the County in 1931, but the majority of his playing time with Essex was in the immediate post-war years. A very sound and attractive opening batsman, he played many fine innings for the County.

Reginald Taylor, after a distinguished war record with the RAF and now playing as an amateur, had a good season, registering 919 runs and sharing in another Essex record-breaking partnership, namely, 263 for the eighth wicket against Warwickshire at Southend, in company with Denys Wilcox. Taylor scored 142 and Wilcox 134, the partnership turning an impending follow-on into an innings victory.

Other pre-war stalwarts who made useful scores were Peter Smith (834 runs), Ray Smith (729 runs) and Frank Vigar (753 runs); another amateur, the newly-appointed secretary, R F T Paterson, contributed 680 runs.

The brunt of the bowling fell on the willing shoulders of Peter and Ray Smith. Both had excellent seasons, Peter, with his leg-breaks and googlies, securing 120 wickets at 19.49 apiece, and Ray 116 wickets, with alternate medium-pacers and off-breaks, at a cost of 25.49 each. Frank Vigar's leg-breaks brought him 51 wickets.

In addition to the County's overwhelming defeat of Surrey at The Oval, Essex recorded a notable victory over Lancashire, who finished third in the table, at Old Trafford. After a disastrous start, losing 5 wickets for 66, Essex, thanks to a magnificent 140 by Tom Pearce, scored 349, dismissing Lancashire for 270, Bailey taking 4 for 75. Essex declared their second innings closed, leaving Lancashire 299 to get. The last Lancashire wicket fell at 283 and Essex were the victors by 15 runs, Peter Smith taking 7 for 75.

A very close finish was seen in the County's match against the Indian touring team at Southend. Scoring 301 and dismissing India for 138, Ray Smith taking 6 for 56, Essex declared their second innings closed at 201 for 3, Harry Crabtree scoring a sound 118. India were left to score 367, which they succeeded in doing by one wicket, their winning runs coming in the last over of the match. Peter Smith was chosen for the third Test against India and was also selected for the MCC Touring Team to visit Australia in the winter of 1946–47.

Reginald Taylor retired at the end of the 1946 season, emigrating to South Africa, where he joined the famous Wanderers Club at Newlands, eventually becoming captain.

Essex dropped three places in the 1947 championship table, finishing in 11th place, with six wins and nine defeats. The bowling lacked pace and variety and depended almost entirely upon Peter and Ray Smith, who between them took 297 wickets. The only other bowlers to achieve any success were T E Bailey, who took 25 championship wickets at 36.28 each, and Frank Vigar, whose 64 wickets cost 43.48 runs apiece. Peter Smith bowled 1606 overs – more than any other bowler in the country, and Ray Smith 1557 overs – more than any other bowler except Peter. Both Smiths accomplished the 'double', Peter scoring 1065 runs, average 23.66 and taking 172 wickets (more than any Essex bowler had taken before) at 27.13, and Ray 1386 runs at 28.87 and 125 wickets at 37.26.

Tom Pearce, who again led the side, had another good season. He scored 1597 runs at 45.62 with two centuries. Dickie Dodds, now a professional, in his second season with the County, scored 2147 runs with only one century. Frank Vigar reached 1735 runs with five centuries and Stan Cray 1339 with three centuries. Trevor Bailey, up at Cambridge, appeared in the Varsity match, scoring 60 not out in the Cambridge second innings. Also playing in this match for Cambridge was D J Insole, who scored 38 and 44. Bailey and Insole, both future Essex captains, appeared for Essex after the university term and both registered their maiden centuries for the County, Bailey 205 against Sussex at Eastbourne, and Insole 109 not out, against Lancashire at Clacton.

Essex were involved in a tied match, against Northamptonshire at Ilford. Essex, set 240 to win in five hours, reached 229 when the ninth wicket fell. The last man, Tommy Wade, hit a boundary, which was followed by six singles, before Wade was bowled by C B Clarke.

Another close finish was seen in the match against Worcestershire at Worcester, the County defeating Worcs by one wicket after being 111

30. *Doug Insole and Trevor Bailey, who were at Cambridge together. Their performances for Essex in the late 1940s and during the 1950s provided the backbone of the team.* (J B Hood)

behind on the first innings, Wade hitting two boundaries in the last minute of the extra half hour. In this match Tom Pearce scored 137 not out and 96. The eventual champions, Middlesex, suffered a heavy defeat at the hands of Essex, losing by ten wickets at Colchester. Peter Smith was outstandingly successful in this match, scoring 62 and taking 16 wickets for 215.

Another Essex batting record was set in the game against Derbyshire at Chesterfield, which Essex won by five wickets. Derbyshire scored 223 and Essex were 199 for 9 when Peter Smith joined Frank Vigar. These two put on 218 for the last wicket, Peter Smith scoring 163, the highest score ever made by a number 11 batsman, and Vigar 114 not out. This score was, of course, a tenth-wicket record for Essex, and at that time was the fifth highest total in first-class cricket for this wicket. Frank Vigar was a useful all-rounder who first played for Essex in 1938. A solid batsman and useful leg-break bowler, he was also a good close fielder. He remembers that the score stood at 33 for 3 when he went in, and that the seventh wicket fell at 104 and the ninth at 199. Initially Vigar tried to keep Peter Smith away from the bowling but then, seeing how well Smith was batting, he gave him as much of the strike as possible and recalls that the Derbyshire attack contained three England bowlers in Copson, Pope and Gladwin. This makes this last-wicket partnership even more remarkable and turned what appeared to be a possible defeat into a resounding victory. In the Essex second innings it was again Frank Vigar who laid the foundation, scoring 40 not out in a total of 114 for 5. Vigar therefore scored 154 runs in this match, without being dismissed.

Peter Smith's Benefit, to which the Committee contributed £25, realised £3000.

At the beginning of the 1948 season an approach was made to the chairman by T E Bailey, with a view to him joining the Club in some capacity which would enable him to devote his full time to playing first-class cricket after coming down from Cambridge. An ad hoc committee, consisting of the chairman, Hubert Ashton, and certain other Committee members, had a meeting with Trevor Bailey, when the whole matter was discussed in detail. As a result, a proposal was made to Bailey, subject to approval by the Council. This entailed Bailey assuming the position of assistant secretary and provided for mutual co-operation between the secretary, R F T Paterson, and Bailey. A special council meeting was held, at which the ad hoc committee's report and proposals were fully considered. It was pointed out by the ad hoc committee that it must be realised that in present circumstances fewer and fewer amateurs could afford to play throughout a season without some assistance either directly or indirectly. This was evident from the number of counties which already had an amateur as a paid secretary/captain. The ad hoc committee also felt that the Council should consider carefully before losing the opportunity of the full-time services of a man with Bailey's potential abilities on the cricket field, and in time with guidance off the field also. After further lengthy discussions it was decided to offer T E Bailey a three-year agreement as from 1 October 1948 on the lines drawn up by the ad hoc committee. These were submitted to, and accepted by, T E Bailey.

Essex had a disappointing season in 1948, finishing in 13th position in the championship table with five wins and eight losses. The main problem was again the bowling, with the burden once more resting on Peter and Ray Smith, who took 92 wickets and 104 wickets respectively, although even Peter was not so successful as usual. However, a promising fast bowler from Romford – Kenneth Preston – made his debut for the County, taking 42 championship wickets at 28.83 each. Tom Pearce again captained the side and again headed the County batting averages, scoring 1826 runs at an average of 49.35, including four centuries, and Sonny Avery, Dickie Dodds and Dick Horsfall all had successful seasons,

31. *Peter Smith*

32. *Ray Smith*

The Essex cousins, who played a major part in the Essex attack after the last war. Peter played for England and toured Australia in 1946–47. Ray Smith didn't achieve the same honour, but must be one of the best players never to have played for England.

scoring 1890, 1876 and 1407 runs respectively. Dick Horsfall, a Yorkshireman who had been discovered playing services cricket in the Middle East towards the end of the war, and who had played for Todmorden in the Lancashire League, had joined Essex in the previous year. An attractive and hard-hitting batsman, he was unfortunately prone to back trouble.

Avery made six centuries, including a top score of 214 not out against Worcestershire at Clacton, a match which Essex won by six wickets. In this game Horsfall scored 122 and Ken Preston took 6 for 85, including a spell of three wickets for four runs in six balls. The match against Leicestershire at Westcliff witnessed a magnificent recovery by Essex, inspired by Tom Pearce, which was the highlight of this drawn game. Facing a Leicestershire total of 421, Essex had lost five wickets for 71 when Tom Pearce was joined by Frank Rist. The wicket was beginning to take spin and it looked a certainty that Essex would have to follow on. However these two put on 118 for the sixth wicket before Rist was out for 34. Bill Morris then assisted Pearce in a stand of 81, Morris eventually departing for 39. Ray Smith contributed 15 and a century stand of 108 for the ninth wicket between Pearce and Peter Smith saw the Essex total reach 397, Peter Smith making 32. Amid great excitement Essex passed the Leicestershire total, eventually declaring at 425 for 9, leaving Pearce not out with a score of 211, the highest of his career. Pearce's innings was magnificent. Lasting five hours and 20 minutes, he was complete master of the situation and did not give a chance. Frank Rist, who, as described, assisted Tom Pearce in a sixth-wicket stand of 118 in this match, first played for Essex in 1934. A most loyal servant to the County, he filled in as a stop-gap on many occasions, as opening batsman and emergency wicket-keeper. It was in this latter capacity that he played in 13 matches in 1948 in the absence of Tom Wade through illness. Rist took part in an unbroken last-wicket stand of 72 with Ken Preston against Leicestershire at Loughborough, scoring 56 not out. Had either batsman got out Essex would have been beaten by an innings. He also played a fine innings of 35 against Yorkshire at Huddersfield in the famous Essex victory of 1935, opening the innings and checking a threatened collapse.

The 1948 season witnessed another world record with Essex on the receiving end. This occurred when Bradman's all-conquering Australians visited Southend in May, having won their first five matches, four of them by an innings. The Australians batted first and quickly got into their stride, Sidney Barnes and Bill Brown scoring 145 in 95 minutes for the first wicket. Don Bradman then joined Brown and these two took the score to 202 for 1 at lunch; they were not parted until the score had reached 364. At tea the scoreboard read 493 for 4 and the visitors were finally all out just before the close for 721, which is the record score for a single day's cricket. Bradman scored a masterly 187 by brilliant stroke

33. *Those attending Southchurch Park in May 1948 will never forget the first day's play in the Essex v Australia match when the tourists scored 721 runs. The century makers were Bradman, Brown, Loxton and Saggers. Essex were the only team, including the England Test team, to bowl the Australians out in a single day during their tour. This picture is taken on the second day when Essex made their reply, and shows the captain Tom Pearce, and Donald Bradman.* (J S Townsend)

play, hitting 32 fours and one five. Brown scored 153 with 17 fours, Loxton 120 including 14 fours and a six and Saggers 104 not out, with nine fours. The second wicket partnership of 219 by Bradman and Brown lasted only 90 minutes and the sixth wicket total of 166 by Loxton and Saggers just 65 minutes. The Essex attack was completely annihilated.

Essex could not cope with the skills of Keith Miller and Ernie Toshack in their first innings or Ian Johnson in their second and were dismissed for 83 and 187, the spectators being treated to the melancholy sight of the Essex opening batsmen going out to bat twice before lunch on the second day. However, as Tom Pearce remarked, Essex did at least succeed in bowling out the Australians in one day, becoming the only English county in 1948 to do so!

The attendance of 32,000 and receipts of £3482 were both ground records and the crowd was treated to a masterly display by one of the finest Australian teams ever to tour this country.

An encouraging increase in membership was seen in 1948, the total reaching 4542 members. This showed an advance of 1555 over the 1946 figure.

Tom Pearce was re-elected captain for the 1949 season, which Essex began in the knowledge that their promising young fast bowler, Kenneth Preston, had broken his leg playing football and would be out of first-class cricket for the season. This was a bitter blow as Preston was regarded as a 'white hope' at a time when England had no fast bowlers. Additionally, another promising young player, Dick Horsfall, sustained a back injury which prevented him from playing until late in the season.

However, Essex improved their championship position, finishing equal ninth, with seven wins and nine losses. Trevor Bailey had an outstanding season, commencing by bowling Nigel Howard with his first ball of the season in the match between Essex and MCC, achieving the 'double' with 1380 runs at 35.38 and 130 wickets at 24.20 each, being selected for all four Test matches against the New Zealanders and being chosen by *Wisden* as one of their 'Five Cricketers of the Year'. Furthermore, he was selected for the Gentlemen against the Players at Lord's and took all ten wickets in Lancashire's first innings for 90, at Clacton, being only the second Essex bowler to accomplish this feat, the other being H Pickett, who took 10 for 32 against Leicestershire at Leyton, in 1895. Trevor Bailey recalls that it was not until some time after the interval, when he took his seventh wicket, that it occurred to him, or anybody else, that there was a vague chance of him finishing up with ten. Trevor added that Tom Pearce helped greatly by allowing him to continue at one end for the remainder of the innings and also, after he had claimed nine, Trevor comments that it would be fair to say that everybody, apart from the batsmen, was more concerned in him capturing the last wicket than anything else.

ESSEX v AUSTRALIANS

3 d. AT SOUTHCHURCH PARK, SOUTHEND-ON-SEA. 3 d.

Sat, Mon, Tues, MAY 15, 17, 18, 1948.

* Captain † W-Kpr HOURS OF PLAY :-First 2 Days, 11.30-6.30. 3rd. 11-5.

INTERVALS LUNCH :- 1.30-2.15 TEA 4.15-4.30 or according to state of game

UMPIRES Ashdown & Hendren SCORERS Marshall & Ferguson TOSS WON BY :- Australians

ESSEX		1st Innings		2nd Innings	
1	DODDS T C	c Ring b Miller	0	b Toshack	16
2	CRAY S J	b Miller	5	b Johnson	15
3	AVERY A V	b Johnston	10	c Brown b Johnson	3
4	VIGAR F H	c Saggers b Miller	0	c Miller b Toshack	0
5	HORSFALL R	b Toshack	11	b Johnson	8
*6	T N PEARCE	c Hamence b Toshack	8	c & b Johnson	71
7	T E BAILEY	absent hurt		absent hurt	
8	SMITH R	c Barnes b Toshack	25	c Ring b Johnson	0
9	SMITH P	b Toshack	3	lbw b Barnes	54
†10	RIST F	c Barnes b Toshack	8	b Johnson	1
11	PRICE E	not out	4	not out	4
	Extras	b- 2 lb- 6 nb- 1 w-	9	b- 6 lb- 3nb- 6 w-	15
		TOTAL	83	TOTAL	187

FALL OF WICKETS

1st Innings										2nd Innings									
1	2	3	4	5	6	7	8	9	10	1	2	3	4	5	6	7	8	9	10
0	13	13	19	30	47	63	74	83	......	24	32	35	36	46	46	177	183	187	......

BOWLING ANALYSIS	O	M	R	W	Wd	Nb		O	M	R	W	Wd	Nb
Miller	8	3	14	3				2	1	4	0		
Johnston	7	1	10	1				10	4	26	0		
Ring	11	4	19	0		1		7	3	16	0		1
Toshack	10·5	2	31	5				17	2	50	2		4
							Loxton	12	3	28	0		1
2nd Innings Barnes	9·4	5	11	1			Johnson	21	6	37	6		

AUSTRALIANS		1st Innings		2nd Innings
1	W A BROWN	c Horsfall b Bailey	153	
2	S G BARNES	hit wkt b Smith, R	79	
*3	D G BRADMAN	b Smith, P	187	
4	K R MILLER	b Bailey	0	
5	R HAMENCE	c Smith, P b Smith, R	46	
6	S LOXTON	c Rist b Vigar	120	
7	D RING	c Vigar b Smith, P	1	
8	I JOHNSON	st Rist b Smith, P	9	
†9	R SAGGERS	not out	104	
10	W A JOHNSTON	b Vigar	9	
11	E TOSHACK	c Vigar b Smith, P	4	
	Extras	b- 7 lb- nb- 2 w-	9	b- lb- nb- w-
		TOTAL	721	TOTAL

FALL OF WICKETS

1st Innings										2nd Innings									
1	2	3	4	5	6	7	8	9	10	1	2	3	4	5	6	7	8	9	10
145	364	364	452	499	664	686	692	716	721										

BOWLING ANALYSIS	O	M	R	W	Wd	Nb	O	M	R	W	Wd	Nb
Bailey	21	1	128	2								
Smith, R	37	2	169	2		1						
Smith, P	37	0	193	4								
Price	20	0	156	0								
Vigar	13	1	66	2								

AUSTRALIANS WON by an Innings & 551 Runs

34. *Essex v Australia, 15–18 May, 1948. Note final run-count is incorrect: the Australians won by an innings and 451 (not 551) runs.*

Bailey's Test match performances included 6 for 118 in the first Test, 93 in the second, and 72 not out and 6 for 84 in the third.

After leading Cambridge University to their first victory over Oxford for 13 years, Douglas Insole rendered stalwart service to Essex, scoring 850 championship runs at an average of 65.38 and heading the Essex batting averages. He scored three centuries, including a fine innings of 219 not out in the drawn match against Yorkshire at Colchester, when he and Tom Pearce, who made 65, put on 151 for the fifth wicket.

Pearce, Vigar and Dodds all scored 1000 runs, but Avery just missed this, having again suffered an injury. A young amateur from Upminster, Stanley Eve, enjoyed a very useful first season, scoring 717 runs and making 120 against Warwickshire at Brentwood, which match Essex won by an innings and one run, Peter and Ray Smith taking 18 wickets between them for 181 runs. The Smiths, as usual, did most of the bowling, Ray taking 100 wickets for the fourth year running, although Peter's total of 82 was much lower than usual. An amateur medium-pace bowler from Aveley, G R Pullinger, helped fill the void caused by Preston's absence, taking 38 wickets at 35.07 each. Essex bowlers toiled at Fenner's when Cambridge University scored 441 for 1 declared, J G Dewes (204 not out) and G H G Doggart (219 not out) sharing a second-wicket partnership of 429 – an English record – and at Southend, against the New Zealanders, when opening batsman Bert Sutcliffe scored 243 and 100 not out against the County. Southend had two cricket weeks in 1949. One of these was originally arranged to take place at Chelmsford, but was transferred to Southend because of the unfit state of the wicket.

In 1949 it was decided to institute one Executive Committee consisting of 30 members, instead of two bodies as formerly – the Council and Executive Committee. The death of the Club's president, C Stewart Richardson, was announced with great regret by the Committee, who expressed much appreciation of his work for the Club. Hubert Ashton was elected to take over the office.

The Committee congratulated Tom Pearce on his election to the Test selection committee. Congratulations were also given by the Committee to F S Foster, on his election as chairman of the Essex County Council and to H Ashton on becoming vice-chairman of that body. Another encouraging increase in the total of members was seen in 1949, the number advancing to 4790.

At the end of the 1949 season the decision was taken to appoint Douglas Insole as captain in succession to Tom Pearce, who was then in his 45th year and was occupied in selectorial duties. Insole was a natural choice. Gaining a blue at Cambridge as a freshman in 1947, Insole won further blues in the next two years, being captain in 1949. He was a forceful and consistent batsman who had already played many fine innings for Essex and was a first-class captain. Like his contemporary, Trevor Bailey, he was an accomplished association footballer, a sport at which he also captained Cambridge. The President had ascertained that Douglas Insole's employers were willing to release him 'business permitting', but that it was understood they would allow him to play fairly regularly. In order to give Insole the benefit of Pearce's experience it was decided to appoint him joint-captain with Pearce for 1950 before taking over as sole captain the following year.

1950 proved to be the worst season in the County's history. They finished bottom of the championship with only four victories to their name, being beaten 12 times. They started off well enough, beating Glamorgan and Surrey in May, but thereafter their form deserted them and they lost ten of their last 24 championship matches, winning only two. The County suffered a number of injuries, not the least being a strained muscle incurred by Trevor Bailey, which restricted his bowling.

The 1949 stand-in, George Pullinger, was available for two matches only and Preston was still not completely recovered from his injury. Consequently, there was a repetition of the situation where the brunt of the bowling was borne by the Smith cousins, Peter taking 127 wickets at 27.14 each and Ray securing 102 wickets at 34.77 each. Ray performed the 'double' again, scoring 1149 runs at an average of 23.40, being the only player in the country to achieve this in 1950. Peter bowled 1405 overs and Ray 1267. Despite the overall disappointment, Doug Insole had a successful season with 1985 runs to his credit at an average of 34.82 with four centuries. He was selected for the third Test against West Indies at Trent Bridge.

In addition to Insole and Ray Smith, Dodds, Vigar and Avery scored 1000 runs. A schoolmaster from Ilford, Harold Faragher, played some useful innings, scoring 248 runs in five matches including 69 and 85 not out in the drawn game against Kent at Maidstone. He was later to be very much involved with the successful indoor cricket school at Ilford, as also was W B Morris, who retired at the end of the 1950 season. All-rounder Bill Morris had played regularly for the County since the war.

Because his duties as a selector were taking up more of his time, Tom Pearce relinquished the position of joint-captain, Doug Insole taking over. Tom Pearce's first appearance for Essex was in 1929 against Sussex at Leyton. In this match he took 0 for 122 in 24 overs, being incorrectly described in *Wisden* as 'T. E. Pearce' (no doubt at Tom's request!). The following year his bowling analysis showed an improvement – 0 for 12 in two overs – and in consequence he was correctly initialled by *Wisden* in their next edition. By 1931 the County had discovered that he was a batsman and not a bowler and he finished top of the Essex batting averages with a highest score of 152. Tom Pearce was a free-scoring batsman, with a slightly unorthodox style. He was possessed of an imperturbable temperament and was ideally suited to take up the reins of captaincy, which he did in 1933, at first jointly with Denys Wilcox and later as sole captain in 1946, taking over a side shorn of its pre-war star players and short of bowling strength. In 1947, for example, a large share of the bowling burden was borne by the cousins Peter and Ray Smith. As Doug Insole so aptly puts it, the only tactical ploys available to Tom were to switch Peter and Ray from one end to the other or to instruct Ray to don his cap and revert from off-breaks to seam.

Always completely unruffled and good-natured, Tom Pearce had the ability to bring out the best in his side. He was largely responsible for rebuilding Essex cricket after the war, his experience and temperament, added to his reliable batting, being invaluable. A popular character, he continued to serve Essex after his retirement from the captaincy, as chairman and president, and has given the Club devoted service for well over half a century. He managed the MCC tour of India, Pakistan and Ceylon in 1961–62 and was well known for his untiring work as honorary team manager for the Scarborough Festival. Tom was awarded the OBE in 1979 for his services to sport.

The match at the beginning of the season, against Surrey at The Oval, resulted in a win for Essex by 17 runs. Again, this match was dominated by the spin bowling of the Smiths, Peter taking 13 for 113 and Ray 6 for 142, in the match. Another example of the load which the Smith cousins bore on their willing shoulders was in the match against Kent at Maidstone. Kent scored 532 in 152 overs, of which Peter bowled 65, taking 4 for 190, and Ray 59, taking 6 for 202. Essex used only two other bowlers in this match. Romford was added to the list of Essex festival grounds, the first match played there being against Hampshire in May. The drawn game against Warwickshire at Ilford, in which Gardner scored 113 and 101 not out for Warwickshire, and Doug Insole 106 for Essex, was the first Essex match to be televised. The Club received a fee of £75 from the BBC for this transmission. The last match of the season was against Nottinghamshire at Trent Bridge and was a needle match to decide which of the two counties would finish at the bottom of the County Championship. The match was marred by rain and the team's destiny was therefore decided on first innings points, which unfortunately went to Nottinghamshire. This was despite a fine innings of 141 by Sonny Avery, and it saw Essex relegated to bottom position. Sonny Avery remembers that, as the Essex team were getting changed after the match, they saw a large wooden spoon swinging outside the windows of their dressing-room (which was immediately below that of the home side). This spoon had evidently been specially made for the occasion by C B Harris, the Nottinghamshire batsman, who was a great leg-puller.

Trevor Bailey was picked to accompany the MCC touring team to Australia in the winter of 1950–51 and many thought Doug Insole unfortunate not to have been similarly chosen.

The Committee congratulated the president, Hubert Ashton, on being returned as Member of Parliament for Chelmsford during the 1950 election. A presentation was made to T E Bailey by the president, of one of the balls used by him in taking all ten wickets in Lancashire's first innings at Clacton, in August 1949. The ball was mounted on a plinth, to which was attached a plate, suitably inscribed.

During 1950 the Committee received, and accepted with great regret, the resignation of Mr A J Spelling as treasurer. Mr H G Clark, who had already taken on the position of acting honorary secretary in the absence of the secretary, Mr R F T Paterson, who was in hospital, was appointed temporary treasurer.

A provisional balance sheet for 1950 presented to the Committee showed a loss of £2530 18s 10d on the year's working. Essex, having finished bottom of the county championship in 1950, for the first time in their history, and having shown a considerable financial loss on the season, the Committee met to examine the situation, which was causing considerable disquiet amongst both players and supporters. The Committee unanimously confirmed their confidence in the captain, D J Insole, and decided that a standing sub-committee should be set up to give him more help and advice during the actual cricket season.

This sub-committee immediately arranged a meeting with the professionals and listened to their most sincerely expressed views as to the team's lack of success during the past summer. It was generally agreed that there were matters that required closer attention than in the past. Follow-up meetings were held with the professionals at which various problems were discussed and corrected. As a result of this it was decided to issue a considered statement to the press, signed by the president. The wording of this statement caused considerable discussions on all sides before being finally agreed. The statement, which was dated 21 November 1950, was sent to all the major provincial newspapers in Essex and drew attention to the fact that the Club's financial position was such that expenses were likely to increase and income possibly to decrease. It was for this reason that the Club had reluctantly been compelled not to renew the contracts of certain professionals. The position of Tom Wade, who had given such loyal and splendid service since 1929, and the events which led up to his resignation, were fully explained. The president stated that it was greatly regretted that recent reports in the press, which had been somewhat incomplete, should have caused anxiety in the minds of those concerned, and disquiet in the minds of members throughout the county. The statement made it very clear that Douglas Insole, to whom the captaincy for 1951 was being offered, had the complete confidence of the Committee. Subsequent events were to show that this confidence was not misplaced.

CHAPTER 13

The Douglas Insole Years: 1951–60

The 1951 season began with the re-election of Hubert Ashton as president and Chairman, although he accepted the latter office with reservations about continuing in 1952. Tom Pearce was elected vice-chairman and Douglas Insole's appointment as captain confirmed. The secretary, Robert Paterson, tendered his resignation to the Committee, which was accepted. Although 97 applications for the vacant post of secretary were received in answer to the press advertisement, Mr H G Clark was asked if he would carry on for one more year, in view of no new appointment having been made; this he agreed to do. He was, in fact, to remain secretary for the next four years. Clark was also appointed treasurer.

The year saw a big improvement in the County's fortunes. From bottom place in the championship table they moved up nine places, finishing in eighth position, winning six matches and losing only two. Essex remained unbeaten until late July, when they lost to Gloucestershire at Bristol, and, in fact, remained unbeaten longer than any other county. Their only other defeat was by Yorkshire at Bradford. Two of the County's notable victories were against the 1951 champions, Warwickshire, by seven wickets at Clacton, and against Surrey, the 1950 joint-champions, by 48 runs at The Oval.

35. *Doug Insole, besides being a prolific run scorer, was a fine fielder. He considered this aspect of the game to be of paramount importance, and in his ten years of captaincy, raised Essex fielding standards to a new peak. Here, in 1958 he demonstrated his slip fielding abilities by catching Ken Barrington of Surrey.* (Central Press)

Tommy Wade had retired at the end of the 1950 season, having done yeoman service for the County. Wade was a very large man for a wicket-keeper and was noted for a series of finger exercises that he carried out before each ball was delivered. Some opposing batsmen suspected that Wade was signalling in code to the bowler, but in fact he was pushing each finger into the reinforcement provided inside his gloves. Peter Smith occasionally bowled without a run-up in order to catch his wicket-keeper unawares, but it did not become a habit because Tom Wade was a more than useful wrestler whose brother was widely regarded as the best in England. Tom Wade was also well-known for his high-pitched appeal and as a humorist with a penchant for practical jokes. As Brian Taylor was doing national service, Essex now had to look outside the County for a wicket-keeper, signing Paul Gibb of Cambridge University, Yorkshire and England, who, apart from his excellent wicket-keeping, was a very

36. *Jack Bailey* (Central Press)

37. *Paul Gibb* (Barratt's Photo Press Ltd)

Two players who played briefly for Essex, but with great distinction.

reliable batsman. A slight, bespectacled figure, Gibb had played for Yorkshire from 1935 to 1946, appearing in eight Tests for England, and was a decided asset to the team. He was the first university blue to turn professional. He had scored a century in his first county match for Yorks – 157 not out – in 1935 against Nottinghamshire, for whom Larwood and Voce were the opening bowlers. He followed this by scoring 93 and 106 in his first Test match, against South Africa in 1938. Although he did not score a century on his first appearance for Essex, he soon scored 99 against Kent and, in another match, made 107 against his old county, Yorkshire, at Brentwood, which doubtless afforded him considerable pleasure. During the war Gibb served with the RAF, piloting Sunderland flying boats. He had an enormous appetite with a special liking for ice cream, his slender figure never being troubled by the vast quantities of food that he consumed. He travelled around in a small van, which contained much of his belongings and in which he quite often slept. After retiring from County cricket he became a first-class umpire.

The batting in 1951 was much more consistent, with six batsmen scoring 1000 runs, namely, Insole, Avery, Horsfall, Ray Smith, Paul Gibb and Dodds. Gibb made an impressive debut, scoring 1330 runs including four centuries. Ray Smith and Trevor Bailey both just missed the 'double', Ray scoring 1294 runs and taking 95 wickets, in all matches, and Bailey scoring 1095 runs and taking 91 wickets, in all matches. Bailey again took a wicket with his first ball of the season, when he dismissed J D Robertson in the match between Essex and MCC.

Doug Insole had another good season, scoring 2032 runs at an average of 42.33, finishing top of the Essex batting averages, whilst Bailey finished at the head of the bowling averages. Peter Smith, Ken Preston and Bill Greensmith took 80, 70 and 46 championship wickets respectively.

Trevor Bailey was chosen for the first and fourth Tests against South Africa, scoring 95 in the fourth and participating in a last-wicket partnership of 60 with M J Hilton, of which Bailey's share was 48.

Doug Insole was picked for the Gentlemen v Players match at Lord's, scoring 50 and 44 not out. Undoubtedly the most exciting match of the season was that against the South Africans at Ilford. South Africa declared their first innings closed at 312 for 9, which total Essex passed, declaring at 319 for 7, Dickie Dodds scoring 138 and Doug Insole 60. The South Africans scored 286 for 5 in their second innings, again declaring and leaving Essex to score 280 to win in 2¼ hours. Ray Smith, having been sent in early in the order, immediately attacked the bowling, reaching 50 in 40 minutes and 100 in 70 minutes, which was the fastest hundred of the season. He was finally out for 147, scored in 94 minutes out of a total of 204. Smith hit 26 fours and, with Dick Horsfall, put on 182 in 83 minutes. Essex, however, finished on 255 for 5, still 25 runs short of their objective. They had, however, given the South Africans quite a fright and their captain, Eric Rowan, was understood to have commented that he would never make a declaration again.

A high-scoring match took place at Clacton, when Essex met Nottinghamshire. Winning the toss, Nottinghamshire batted first, scoring 576 for 9 declared. Reg Simpson, who was dropped before he had scored, made 212 and Nottinghamshire declared at 1.15 pm on the second day. Essex lost Dodds without a run on the board but at close of play had reached 293 for 2, Avery having made 70. The third wicket put on 155 before Paul Gibb was out for 118. Horsfall followed, for 123, the score then standing at 328 for 4. A partnership of 117 between Doug Insole and Trevor Bailey took the score to 445 for 5, when Bailey was out for 48. Insole departed at 489 for 6, having scored a hard-hit 88, and then Ray Smith and Frank Vigar took the score past the Nottinghamshire total giving Essex first innings points, Ray Smith being finally stumped for 82.

In the match against Kent at Blackheath, Gibb and Horsfall put on 343 for the third-wicket, which was a new Essex record. Gibb scored 141 and

Horsfall 206. The Committee later presented these two batsmen with a scorecard printed on silk, to commemorate this record.

At the end of the season Peter Smith announced his retirement after a highly successful career that began in 1929. He had an elegant high wrist-spinner's action and his leg-spinners, together with a fairly transparent and much chuckled-about googly, took nearly 1700 wickets. Extremely accurate, he could make the ball dip in flight and was capable of bowling out the opposition on good wickets. He was no mean batsman, scoring eight first-class centuries, including the memorable 163 coming in at number 11, against Derbyshire in 1947. In 1933 Peter Smith suffered a cruel experience when he received a telegram informing him that he had been selected to play for England against the West Indies at The Oval and instructing him to report for play. On arrival at The Oval he found that the telegram was a hoax. Smith, however, made up for this 13 years later when he was chosen for The Oval Test against India. He was also selected for the 1946–47 tour of Australia and New Zealand, playing in two Tests against Australia and one against New Zealand. He took nine wickets in an innings against New South Wales – the only time this had been accomplished by an Englishman on an official tour. He also took nine wickets in an innings on three occasions. Peter was a great figure in Essex cricket and was very popular in the cricket world.

During the winter of 1951–52 Trevor Bailey gained an FA Amateur Cup winner's medal, playing for Walthamstow Avenue, who beat Leyton in the Final.

As he had intimated in the previous year, Hubert Ashton resigned from the office of chairman in 1952, Tom Pearce being elected in his stead. A vote of thanks was proposed to Hubert Ashton, for all he had done during the many years in which he had held office. Hubert Ashton was re-elected president of the Club, which office he was to hold until 1970. Tom Pearce was to hold the chairmanship for the next 21 years.

A proposal to form a supporters' club for the purpose of promoting a weekly football pool was defeated in Committee, the amendment, which was carried, moving that the Essex County Cricket Club should not rely on football pools for its finances.

The County dropped to tenth place, jointly with Warwickshire, in 1952, winning eight matches and losing four – two more wins and two more losses than in 1951. They also tied one match, against Lancashire at Brentwood.

The batting was consistent, with seven players scoring 1000 runs in all matches. The bowling, however, was not as strong as in the previous year, although Ray Smith performed heroically. Two Essex players – Trevor Bailey and Ray Smith – performed the 'double', Bailey scoring 1513 runs, average 36.90 and taking 103 wickets at 29.09 runs each, and

Smith 1045 runs, average 24.30, and 136 wickets at 28.87 each. These two were the only players in the country to perform this feat. Sonny Avery headed the batting averages for the County, with 1441 runs in all matches at an average of 41.17, the other four compilers of 1000 runs being Doug Insole (1816), Dickie Dodds (1801), Dick Horsfall (1560) and Paul Gibb (1519). The opening pairing of Dodds and Avery was most successful, usually getting the innings away to a good start with a fast scoring rate. Dodds, in particular, scored his runs very quickly, averaging more than 40 runs an hour throughout the season, and being generally regarded as the fastest-scoring opening batsman in the country. During his career he scored approximately two-thirds of the runs made whilst he was at the wicket. He was selected for the MCC team against the South African tourists in 1947, but although he scored 80 and 25 in this match he was not considered further, neither was he ever considered for a Gentlemen v Players match.

Essex set out to provide attractive cricket and all their batsmen played attacking innings. The *News Chronicle* newspaper instituted a 'Brighter Cricket Table', which was based on runs per 100 balls received, the winners to be awarded a silver salver. Essex won this trophy in its first year by heading the table with 50.44 runs. Surrey were second with 49.96. Sonny Avery and Paul Gibb set up a new second-wicket record for Essex with a partnership of 294, Avery scoring 224, the highest score of his career, and Gibb 132 (v Northamptonshire).

The match against Lancashire at Brentwood produced an exciting finish, ending in a tie – the third since the County became first-class. Lancashire's declaration set Essex 232 to win in two hours and 20 minutes. The 100 was reached in 50 minutes and 150 in 80 minutes. The last over began with Essex needing nine runs to win with the last pair at the wicket. Bailey drove the first ball for six then hit a two, but in trying for the winning run he was caught at mid-off, leaving the match tied. Another close finish was seen at Westcliff in the match against Glamorgan. Needing only 86 to win, Essex had reached 77 for 3 when they lost six wickets while only four runs were added. At the fall of the ninth wicket, Frank Vigar was joined by Charles Kenny, who scrambled a leg bye, leaving Vigar to face Don Shepherd, with four needed to win. Vigar played his first ball down the leg-side for four runs, leaving Essex the victors by one wicket. Frank Vigar remembers his annoyance on reading in the papers the following day that 'he had snicked a lucky four through the slips'.

The fixture with the Indian touring team also provided an exciting finish. Essex dismissed the tourists for 195, Ray Smith taking 6 for 36. The County then scored 410, Doug Insole hitting 116 and Trevor Bailey 67. The Indians followed this with 368 for 6 declared, leaving Essex to score 154 in 78 minutes. Essex went for the runs, finishing on 144 for nine wickets – ten runs short of victory. Trevor Bailey and Doug Insole represented the Gentlemen against the Players at Lord's, scoring 41 and 64 respectively in both innings of the match, which resulted in a win for the Players by two runs. The attractive cricket played by Essex resulted in an increase in membership, the total topping 5000 for the first time.

It was reported that Ray Smith had received a three-year offer to play league cricket for Accrington Cricket Club. The Committee decided to offer Smith a three-year contract with a testimonial in the third year and that the County should have an option of a further three years if required.

Sadly 1953 began with the news of the death, in February, of Denys Wilcox, a former joint-captain of the County, at the early age of 42. Denys Wilcox was a stylish batsman with a very correct method and was an outstanding fielder. He rendered sterling service to the County, both as joint-captain in the 1930s and as a very useful and attractive middle order batsman, both in pre- and post-war years. His schoolmastering duties meant that he was only able to play for Essex in the school holidays. Had he been able to devote more time to first-class cricket he could well have played for England. Wilcox was held in high esteem and was deeply respected and admired. He was to be sadly missed.

Trevor Bailey was elected vice-captain, holding this position until being appointed captain on Douglas Insole's retirement. Essex dropped two places in the 1953 championship, finishing in 12th place, with six wins and seven losses. The County got off to a very bad start and did not win a match until the end of June and it was only by dint of winning five matches in the last month of the season that they finished as high as they did. Once more, the batting was powerful and attractive to watch. The average scoring rate was high and the County won the *News Chronicle* Brighter Cricket Trophy for the second year running. Dick Horsfall had a very successful season, scoring 1731 runs at an average of 37.63, including five centuries. His hundred in the match against Warwickshire at Clacton in 85 minutes was the fastest championship hundred of the season. Insole, Avery, Gibb and Dodds also scored 1000 runs, as did Bailey (in all matches). Twelve centuries were scored in county championship matches, including a maiden century – 138 not out – by Bill Greensmith. Against Sussex at Ilford Dickie Dodds hit the first ball of the Essex innings, bowled by Ian Thomson (who, incidentally, played for the Ilford Club before joining Sussex) for six on to the pavilion roof.

The bowling was once again limited in depth and much again fell on the shoulders of Ray Smith, who took 100 wickets for the seventh time in his career. He was helped, however, by Ken Preston who, bowling off a shorter run, took 91 wickets. Help was also forthcoming from J A Bailey, a fast-medium amateur from Buckhurt Hill. Bailey, future Oxford University captain and MCC secretary, although playing in only four matches, headed the County and national bowling averages with

25 wickets at 13.04. In his County debut, against Nottinghamshire at Southend, he took 7 for 32 in the Nottinghamshire second innings, his last four wickets falling for the addition of only one run. Trevor Bailey's appearances for the County were limited, owing to absences on Test and other representative match duty. However, he gave an excellent all-round performance in the County's defeat of Somerset by an innings and 70 runs, scoring 68 not out and taking 10 for 77 in the match.

Essex made a great recovery in the match against Gloucestershire at Clacton. Trailing by 133 on the first innings, Essex were set 309 to win in the fourth innings on a wearing pitch. Essex made light of the task, scoring 311 for 2, Horsfall and Dodds hitting the last 67 runs in 30 minutes. In the following match at Clacton, against Warwickshire, Essex completed their programme with a win by two wickets, thanks to a fine 107 by Dick Horsfall and good bowling by Jack Bailey, who took 7 for 91 in the match.

The floods in February saw the pitch at Southchurch Park, Southend, submerged by sea-water to a depth of four feet. In the match against the Australians at Southend, the Australians, winning the toss, scored 477 for 7 declared, J de Courcy striking Bill Greensmith for 6, 6, 6, 4 and 6 in one over. When Essex went in the pitch crumbled and the Australian spinners bowled the County out for 129 and 136.

Trevor Bailey, picked for all five Tests against Australia, displayed his all-round talents to the full. His innings of 71 at Lord's in the second Test, in the epic partnership of 163 with Willie Watson, saved the series for England. In the last hour's play on the fourth day England lost three wickets for 12 runs. Denis Compton went for 33 on the last day, leaving England on 73 for 4, when Bailey, the last recognised batsman, came in with five hours left for play. He and Willie Watson defied the Australian bowling throughout the long afternoon. Watson was eventually out for 109, scored in $5\frac{3}{4}$ hours, whilst Bailey's innings came to an end after $4\frac{1}{4}$ hours. Had Australia won this match they would have retained the Ashes. As it was, England went on to win the Ashes with a victory in the final Test, at The Oval by eight wickets. Here again, Bailey played a vital part, taking England's score to 306 (31 ahead of Australia) through various partnerships with the tail-enders, the Essex player scoring 64. At one stage England's score stood at 210 for 6. Trevor Bailey and Doug Insole were both chosen to represent the Gentlemen against the Players at Lord's.

Membership for 1953 reached the record total of 5029. It was felt by the Committee that if the total reached 6000 it might be necessary to limit the membership and to institute a waiting list.

The same year, 1953, brought with it the death of a well-loved character, Canon F H Gillingham. As popular on the cricket field as he was in the pulpit, he held the attention and admiration of the spectators and congregation alike. A forceful and attractive batsman, who played many fine innings for Essex, he was mourned by the cricketing fraternity and by his flock. G D Martineau in his excellent book *They Made Cricket* has described how, after the memorial service to Gillingham, 'The wife of a well-known cricketer, describing it, was led by her enthusiasm into a *lapsus linguae* of curious aptness: "It was a wonderful service," she declared, "and we had that lovely chapter out of the Book of Wisden." Nobody would have relished this more than Canon Gillingham.'

Essex finished the 1954 season in 15th position in the county championship – a further fall of two places – only winning on three occasions and being defeated 11 times. It was a bad summer – one of the wettest for many years – and the adverse weather seriously affected the state of the counties' finances. Essex, in particular, suffered a considerable financial loss.

The team seemed ill-equipped to deal with the conditions brought about by the slow, wet pitches. Only two batsmen finished the season with an average of over 30 and only two bowlers with an average of below 25. For once, the batting lacked stability and, apart from Doug Insole, who scored 1841 runs in all matches, heading the County's averages, only Trevor Bailey and Dickie Dodds scored 1000 runs. Dick Horsfall had a poor season by his previous standards and Sonny Avery and Paul Gibb were absent for a considerable while owing to injuries.

Trevor Bailey performed the 'double' for the third time, scoring 1344 runs and taking 101 wickets, in all matches. A specially registered Yorkshireman, Gordon Barker, scored a maiden century (107 not out) against the Canadian tourists at Clacton. Brian Taylor played some useful innings and kept wicket well in the absence of Paul Gibb. Trevor Bailey appeared in three Tests against Pakistan and was selected to tour Australia in the winter of 1954–55.

Doug Insole, in the match against Northamptonshire at Romford, came close to registering a century in each innings. In the first innings he scored a magnificent 156 not out and in the second innings he declared the Essex innings closed when his own score stood at 92 not out. The County's victory over Middlesex at Chelmsford in mid-July, which was their first since late May, was a comprehensive innings win. All the batsmen played well and the bowling honours were shared between Trevor Bailey, Jack Bailey, Ray Smith and Doug Insole, the latter taking 4 for 24 with his medium-pacers in the Middlesex first innings. A good win was registered against Derbyshire at Chesterfield in a match curtailed by rain and water on the pitch brought up by the heavy roller. Following two Derbyshire declarations Essex were left to score 131 in 95 minutes, a target they achieved for the loss of four wickets. Avery made 33 in each Essex innings.

The match against Somerset at Southend witnessed some fine bowling by the two Baileys, Jack taking 5 for 9 in the Somerset first innings and Trevor 6 for 42 in their second. The 1954 season represented the diamond jubilee of the Club's admittance to first-class status. Harold Dalton, who had acted most efficiently as masseur to the Essex team since 1950 was honoured by MCC, who chose him to travel to Australia as official physiotherapist to the English team, the first time such an appointment had been made. A memorial to Kenneth Farnes, the Cambridge University, Essex and England fast bowler who was killed whilst serving with the RAF during the war, in the shape of a score-board, was erected at Gidea Park ground, Romford. The memorial was dedicated in June 1954 by the Bishop of Chelmsford. Those who attended the ceremony included G O Allen, Hubert Ashton, Colonel R S Rait Kerr and the Mayor of Romford.

Mr H G Clark advised the Committee that he was unable to carry on as honorary treasurer and honorary secretary. Grateful thanks were expressed by the Committee to Mr Clark for all the work he had put in to assist the Club during the past few years. Trevor Bailey was appointed secretary in his place. Alfred Spelling once again stepped into the breach, being appointed treasurer as from 1 October 1954. The Club registered a loss of £3139 for the 1954 season.

Arrangements were made for the BBC to broadcast part of the Essex matches against Gloucestershire at Westcliff in June and against Kent at Clacton in August, 1955. It was decided to move the Club offices to 60 London Road, Chelmsford, during 1955.

Essex moved up one position in the county championship table in 1955, finishing in 14th position. Six matches were won (twice as many as in 1954) but 15 games were lost, which was four more than in 1954. Doug Insole enjoyed the finest season of his career, scoring 2427 runs – more than anyone else in the country – with nine centuries. Two of these were scored in the match against Kent at Gillingham and two off the Yorkshire bowlers – 142 at Bradford and 119 at Southend. He also scored a fine 129 against the South Africans at Colchester, which included a six and 15 fours. He was the first batsman in the country to reach both 1000 runs and 2000 runs and was selected for the fourth Test against South Africa at Leeds. He captained the Gentlemen against the Players at Lord's and was chosen by *Wisden* as one of their 'Five Cricketers of the Year'. Many at the time thought it strange that Doug Insole should have received such scant Test recognition, being dropped after one game, in the second innings of which he played a defiant innings of 47, more than any other in that innings except Peter May.

Sonny Avery, who retired at the end of the 1954 season, joined the staff originally as a left-arm spin bowler. He developed into a very useful

38. *Gordon Barker, a Yorkshireman, made a century on his debut for Essex and scored a total of 21,895 runs for the County.* (Sport & General)

opening batsman, strong on the on-side and a good cutter. In his opening partnerships with Dickie Dodds, Sonny Avery provided the steadying influence, with Dodds producing the fireworks. He played some very fine innings for Essex, scoring 25 centuries (including four double centuries) and taking part, with Dodds, in two opening stands of over 200 for the first wicket. On three occasions he carried his bat through completed innings: 84 not out against Derbyshire in 1939, 83 not out against Gloucestershire in 1946 and 92 not out against Nottinghamshire in 1954.

The advance of Gordon Barker was most satisfying. In his first season of the county championship he scored 1494 runs at an average of 27.66. He scored his runs quickly, proved a useful opening partner for Dickie Dodds and was awarded his county cap. He was first spotted by Douglas Insole and Trevor Bailey, playing in an army cricket match at Richmond, Yorkshire, where he was serving as a private. He was invited to play against Canada and went on to become a permanent member of the 1st XI. Known as 'The Great Bark' he was an attractive batsman, specialising in the cut and the hook and was to open the Essex innings for the next 16 years.

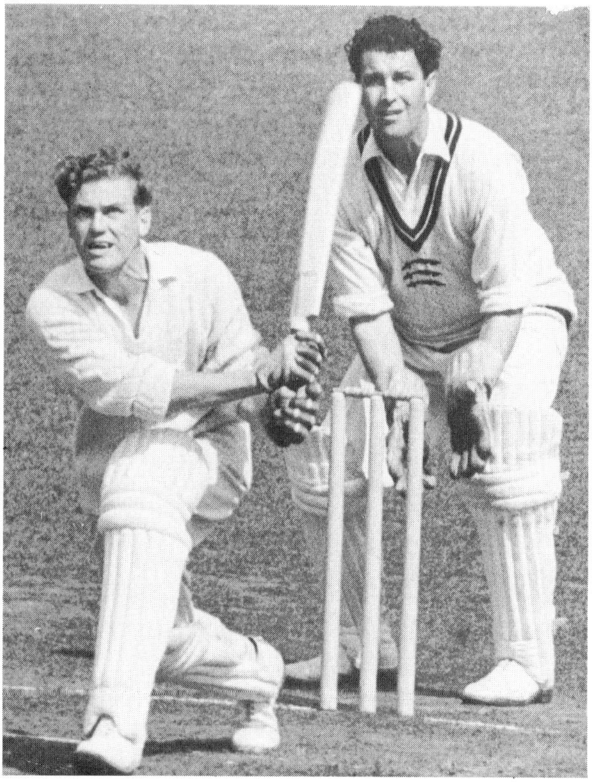

39. *Ken Preston. During his career with Essex from 1948–64 he took 1155 wickets. He was also the first secretary of the Essex Supporters' Club (see p 438).* (Sport & General)

He became an expert at finding the shortest and fastest routes to the various county grounds and delighted in asking stragglers where they had been.

Trevor Bailey, Paul Gibb and Dickie Dodds all scored 1000 runs and Ray Smith won the award for the fastest hundred of the season, scoring 101 not out, against Northamptonshire at Wellingborough, in 73 minutes. Apart from his fastest hundred Ray Smith did not have a good season with the bat, but, as always, he bowled steadily, although his tally of wickets (79) was less than usual. Ken Preston bowled much more accurately than in previous seasons and developed a useful leg-cutter. He took 94 wickets at 24.97 each. Bill Greensmith showed a marked improvement, scoring 698 runs at 23.26 and securing 84 wickets with his leg-breaks and googlies, at 26.42 each. Trevor Bailey bowled well for the County in between his absences on Test duty, taking 63 championship

40. *L C S (Jerry) Jerman. 'Jerry' Jerman played only three matches for Essex in 1950 and 1951 but has made a vast contribution to the Club as Chairman of the Essex Development Association. Formed in 1978, the Development Association and its allied bodies the Essex CCC Promotions Company and the Supporters' Association have passed over to the Club an average of £40,000 per annum in recent years. (See pages 438–39.)*

wickets at an average of 20.85. An amateur from Ilford, Roy Ralph, had a promising season, scoring 329 runs and taking 36 wickets. Although he was 33 years of age at the time of his first-class debut, few, watching his spritely performances, would have judged him to be this age. His first two wickets for Essex were those of Everton Weekes and Frank Worrell. A big hitter, who regarded the ball as an object to be hit as hard as possible, he could produce a big outswinger that sometimes brought a cry of 'ripe bananas' from his slip-fielders. After leaving Essex in 1961 he played professional cricket for Longton in the North Staffordshire League and thereafter club cricket for Ilford. The Essex bowling, however, suffered from the lack of a top-class spinner.

Paul Gibb kept wicket well, although the effects of his injuries in previous seasons were still making themselves felt. Brian Taylor proved to be a very capable deputy behind the stumps and scored 508 useful runs. Trevor Bailey had a good match against Kent at Clacton, scoring 152 not out and taking 7 for 105 in the match, whilst in the Nottinghamshire fixture at Southend he scored 54 and 114 not out and took 5 for 68 in the Nottinghamshire first innings. In this match Bailey and Insole both scored 114 not out and shared in a partnership of 239 for the fourth wicket, scored in three hours. Both their centuries were scored before lunch. Bailey and Insole also both scored centuries against the South Africans at Colchester, Insole making 129 and Bailey 107, in a partnership of 184.

The question of a supporters' club and football pool was again discussed by the Committee, it having been reported by the secretary that, apart from Yorkshire, Surrey, Middlesex and Lancashire, Essex was the only county without a supporters' club and football pool. It was agreed that a supporters' club be formed, for the purpose of running a football pool, under the guidance of a sub-committee and to employ Ken Preston as organiser. A loss of approximately £3000 was reported for the year 1955.

Douglas Insole appeared in the 1955–56 FA Amateur Cup Final, playing for Corinthian Casuals against Bishop Auckland.

The year 1956 opened with a progress report on the newly-created Essex CCC Supporters' Association, which was taking a long time to gather momentum. There was a real danger that the project might end up as a loss-maker and it was therefore agreed by the Committee that top priority should be given to improving the situation. Later reports indicated that the tide had turned and that the number of members was increasing.

In another wet summer Essex improved their position in the championship, finishing in 11th place; this was three better than in 1955. Six matches were won and ten lost. The side showed improved form and, but for injuries and weather interruptions, could well have finished several places higher. Essex were again handicapped through not having a left-arm spinner and an off-spinner capable of exploiting the turning wickets caused by the wet weather. The absence of Trevor Bailey and Douglas Insole on Test and representative match duty naturally weakened the side.

Insole had another outstanding season, scoring 1988 runs in all matches at an average of 41.41, including four centuries. He was again the first batsman to reach 1000 runs. Insole was chosen for the third Test against the Australians at Leeds but was once again dropped after one appearance. However he was chosen to tour South Africa during the 1956–57 winter and had the honour of being appointed vice-captain to Peter May. Insole and Bailey were also chosen for the Gentlemen v the Players in the 150th anniversary match at Lord's.

Trevor Bailey also enjoyed a successful season, heading the County batting and bowling averages and scoring 1186 runs and taking 78 wickets in all matches. He scored three centuries, including a fine 141 not out at his home town, Westcliff, against Hampshire. He was selected for the first four Tests against Australia, standing down from the fifth Test through not being fit. Bailey was also chosen to tour South Africa in the coming winter.

The outstanding improvement of Brian Taylor was a feature of the season. Not only did he keep wicket extremely well, dismissing 75 victims, but he scored 1259 runs in all matches, with an average of 26.22, including a maiden century against Glamorgan at Cardiff. He was awarded his county cap and was chosen by the Cricket Writers' Club as the 'Best Young Player of the Year'. A successful season culminated in his selection to tour South Africa with Peter May's MCC team. With the selection of Douglas Insole and Trevor Bailey to join this tour as well, Essex, for the first time in its history, supplied three members of an overseas touring team.

In addition to Insole and Taylor, Gordon Barker and Dickie Dodds scored 1000 runs and on several occasions their opening partnerships gave the County an excellent start. Several young players made some useful contributions, including Leslie Savill, who scored his maiden century against Somerset at Brentwood; Michael Bear, who just missed his, scoring 98 against Kent at Clacton; Geoffrey Smith, who scored nearly 500 runs, and an all-rounder from East Ham, Barry Knight – a future England player – who scored an impressive 84 against Hampshire at Westcliff. Knight had joined the staff in the previous year, being signed on by Trevor Bailey straight from school. Trevor said that this was one of the very few occasions when he was absolutely convinced that a boy would become a first-class cricketer.

41. *Barry Knight, who with Trevor Bailey was one of the greatest post-war all-rounders.*

Ken Preston's bowling continued to improve, just missing 100 wickets with 96 at 23.19 each. Jack Bailey played regularly after coming down from Oxford University and took 45 wickets for the county at 21.00 apiece. Ray Smith, in what was to be his last season, secured 51 championship wickets and Roy Ralph took 43.

Bill Greensmith enjoyed a successful all-round season, scoring 544 runs and taking 80 wickets. Greensmith, a leg-spinner and useful bat, joined Essex in 1947. He turned in some good performances, one of his best being against Leicestershire in 1952 when, batting at number ten he scored 79, following this by capturing six Leicestershire second innings wickets for 44, of which the first five wickets were taken in 31 balls without a run being scored off him. This performance enabled Essex to win by 107 runs. In the match against the Australians at Southend, Dodds showed that he was no respecter of persons when he hit the opening attack of Lindwall and Miller to all parts of the field, scoring a most attractive 58 out of the first 70 runs on the board. The rest of the side were out cheaply, not being able to cope with the blustery conditions which ripped the Australian flag from its mast and repeatedly blew the bails off the stumps. The bails were eventually dispensed with by the umpires.

An outstanding victory was achieved against Yorkshire at Southend when Essex, after being 85 behind on the first innings, won by five wickets. The former Oxford captain, Charles Williams, played a big part in this match, scoring 48 and 60. This was the first Essex victory over Yorkshire since the Second World War.

At the end of the season it was announced that Ray Smith, in his 42nd year, was retiring. He first played for the county in 1934 and during his career scored 12,041 runs and took 1150 wickets. He reached 1000 runs and 100 wickets three times and won the award for the fastest hundred in 1948 and 1951. For season after season Ray carried the weight of the Essex bowling, opening with his fast-medium seamers and then switching to off-breaks when the shine was off the ball. A more loyal servant it would be difficult to name. He was acknowledged to be one of the very best 'shiners' of the ball, and his in-swinger sometimes moved so prodigiously that he was obliged to go round the wicket to have any prospects of getting an lbw decision or to hit the stumps. Smith was a hard-hitting batsman, very partial to off-spinners, hitting them with the tide to all parts of the on-side field and not infrequently right out of the ground. He invariably appeared to be on target for the fastest century of the season. Ray Smith's unswerving attitude towards the Club was typified by his remark: 'I would give a month's salary if we could beat Yorkshire.'

The Supporters' Association made further progress through the year and were ready to operate the football pool during the winter. The

Association sent a cheque for £200 to the Club towards the cost of the new chairs for the members' enclosure.

The president, Hubert Ashton, suggested early in 1957 that a dinner and presentation be held to welcome home Douglas Insole, Trevor Bailey and Brian Taylor, from South Africa. This was agreed and the dinner arranged to take place at the House of Commons on 13 April 1957.

The Committee reported that the BBC would be broadcasting part of the Essex v West Indies match at Ilford and part of the Essex v Middlesex match at Leyton.

The chairman also reported on the good work of the Supporters' Association, who would be handing over a cheque for £2000 to the Club at the start of the new season. The decision to allow the Supporters' Association to come into being turned out to be a very wise one, since substantial monetary contributions were to be made to the County Club year after year by this organisation.

The following year, 1957, turned out to be the County's best for 18 years. With 11 wins, the highest number since 1939, and six defeats, the County moved up six places in the county championship to finish fifth. Gates and membership increased and the return to Leyton for the first time since 1933 proved a great success, exceeding all expectations. Leyton took the place of Chelmsford, where attendances had been poor. Douglas Insole, in his seventh year as captain, again had a very good season, scoring 1725 runs in all matches, including four centuries. He was chosen for the first Test against West Indies but was again cast aside after one match, and this despite having a most successful tour of South Africa and finishing top of the Test match batting averages.

Vice-captain Trevor Bailey headed the County batting and bowling averages for the second year running and performed his fourth 'double', scoring 1322 runs at 38.88 and taking 104 wickets at 17.02 runs each. His bowling in the first six weeks of the season was almost unplayable. He was chosen for four of the five Tests against West Indies. Gordon Barker and Dickie Dodds were again successful as the County's opening pair, both scoring 1000 runs. They gave the County several good starts to the innings and scored 159 runs before lunch against Kent at Clacton. Brian Taylor had another good season, scoring 1311 runs and dismissing 83 victims. Leslie Savill, Bill Greensmith and Roy Ralph all made useful contributions with the bat, as did Michael Bear, who scored a maiden century against Gloucestershire at Romford. Bear's fielding was outstanding.

The County's bowling was much better and more accurate than in previous years. Ken Preston had a successful season, taking 140 wickets, more than ever before, at 20.35 runs each. Roy Ralph's bowling showed tremendous improvement and, exceeding all expectations, he took 102 wickets at an average of 22.00. Bill Greensmith and Jack Bailey also

42. *Gordon Barker and Dickie Dodds, regular partners for many years, opening the Essex innings at Brentwood, 1957.*

bowled well, taking 63 and 61 wickets respectively, whilst Trevor Bailey took 70 championship wickets. He bowled very well against the West Indians at Ilford, taking 6 for 37 and 3 for 69. Essex lost this match by four wickets after leading on the first innings by 82 runs. Despite being 139 behind on the first innings, Essex defeated Middlesex at Leyton in Dodds' benefit match. Dickie Dodds, typically, scored 48 out of the second innings opening partnership of 70. His partner, Gordon Barker, went on to score 117 and with Preston taking five Middlesex second innings wickets for 42 Essex were victorious by 74 runs. Dodds donated the proceeds of this benefit to the Moral Rearmament Movement, for which organisation he worked tirelessly. Dodds was one of the great cricketing entertainers, who in full cry was a great sight, but he often got out just when he had got in. He was a compulsive hooker and 20 years before the helmet became standard gear, Dickie fitted the hard lining of a riding helmet into his cap because he was being hit on the head so frequently. Fred Trueman expressed considerable surprise in his own particular fashion one day at Bradford when a short pitched ball bounced merrily down to the fine leg boundary via the Dodds cap.

Trevor Bailey had a marvellous match against Hampshire at Romford, scoring 59 and 71 not out and taking 6 for 32 and 8 for 49 to leave Essex victorious by 46 runs. He was on the field for all but 1½ hours of the match. And all this despite suffering from a cracked knuckle bone in his right hand. More good bowling was seen in the match against Leicestershire at Brentwood, which Essex won by 181 runs, Trevor Bailey taking 6 for 28 and Preston 4 for 16 in the Leicestershire second innings, and at Colchester, where Essex defeated Somerset by eight wickets when Roy Ralph took 6 for 33 and 4 for 53. The County enjoyed an excellent win over Surrey, the champion county, at Clacton. Although Essex were 133 behind on first innings, they bowled Surrey out for 119 in their second innings, leaving Essex 253 to get in four hours; this they did with 20 minutes to spare, Doug Insole scoring 115 and being ably assisted by Michael Bear and Leslie Savill, who scored 41 and 32 respectively. Insole was chosen for the Gentlemen against The Players at Lord's, scoring 21 and 79 not out.

The team's fielding showed a marked improvement and benefited considerably from the fielding practice which was held each morning before play began.

But for the new points arrangement, Essex would have finished the season in fourth place in the championship table, one place above Derbyshire, who obtained 14 more bonus points than Essex.

In view of the successful season the Committee decided to reward the players by increasing their win money and revising their salaries.

Nevertheless, Essex dropped one place in the championship table in 1958. They finished sixth, with nine wins and seven losses. The County's batting lacked stability, but the bowling was most satisfactory. Douglas Insole's tally of 1220 runs (average 30.50) was not as good as usual but he suffered an injury when batting against Somerset at Ilford being struck in the eye and having to retire hurt. Doubtless it took him some time to recovery fully from this mishap. Trevor Bailey's batting was not so successful as it was in 1957 either. He scored 904 runs at the considerably lower average of 22.60. The opening pair, Gordon Barker and Dickie Dodds, again scored 1000 runs each and Michael Bear's results showed an improvement over 1957, with 913 runs in all matches, and he was awarded his county cap. Michael Bear was a left-handed batsman who hailed from Brentwood and who joined Essex in 1954. A brilliant fielder, his picking-up and throwing-in became a by-word throughout the country. His batting was correct and contained some classical strokes. He was a great humorist with a gift for mimicry and was a most popular member of the side. Roy Ralph, in his first season as a professional, scored 571 runs and took 78 wickets in all matches.

Brian Taylor's wicket-keeping was as impeccable as ever, with 64 catches and 11 stumpings to his credit, but his batting fell away, with only

582 runs scored, at the low average of 14.92. Charles Williams played some useful innings later in the summer.

The bowling was strengthened by the introduction of not one, but two, off-spinners, Patrick Phelan, from Chingford, and an old Chigwellian, Alan Hurd, a Cambridge blue who bowled very well in the 1958 university match with analyses of 19 overs, 10 maidens, 35 runs, 4 wickets, in the Oxford first innings, and 15.3 overs, 9 maidens, 17 runs, 3 wickets, in their second. Hurd joined Essex after the end of the university term and in the six matches in which he played took 34 championship wickets at the fine average of 13.64, finishing at the head of the County bowling averages.

Trevor Bailey had an excellent season with the ball, taking 102 championship wickets for 16.19 runs each, whilst Ken Preston again did well, missing 100 wickets by one for an average of 23.67. Phelan bowled well in his first season, taking 50 wickets at 26.72 each, but Bill Greensmith had a disappointing summer and lost his place in the team. Jack Bailey, who had torn a cartilage in the University match, could only play in three matches, but played a big part in the victory over Somerset at Taunton, taking 6 for 49 in the Somerset second innings. The success of the Essex bowlers was even more commendable, taking into account the fact that the summer was one of the worst on record and the attack was not ideally suited to the wet wickets which were in evidence all too often.

The Colchester week was ruined, despite switching the second match to the Garrison ground, with both matches being abandoned, and only 1½ days' play was possible during the whole of the Southend week. The County was involved in more 'no decision' matches than any other county except Yorkshire. Three of these abandoned matches were against Nottinghamshire, Warwickshire and Leicestershire, against all of whom Essex must have stood a very good chance of increasing their points tally. In these circumstances the side did very well to finish in sixth position.

A capital innings of 157 by Gordon Barker paved the way for an Essex victory over Nottinghamshire at Trent Bridge by an innings and 112 runs, Roy Ralph taking 5 for 41 in the Nottinghamshire s first innings and Trevor Bailey 5 for 33 in the second. Three declarations in the Sussex match at Hove brought an exciting finish, Essex winning by 85 runs with three minutes to spare, Doug Insole scoring 108 and 51 in this match. The County was at the top of its form throughout the Leyton week, winning both matches comfortably. The champions, Surrey, were comprehensively beaten by an innings and 33 runs, being dismissed for 79 and 74, Ralph taking 6 for 28 in the first innings and Trevor Bailey 7 for 19 in the second. Essex lost six wickets for 60 runs, but their innings was bolstered up by contributions from Bear (32), Greensmith (60) and Ralph (39). The second Leyton match was against Northamptonshire, which Essex won by 72 runs. Williams (69), Bear (70) and Dodds (42) were the top scorers for Essex and Phelan, with 5 for 22, was mainly responsible for the dismissal of Northamptonshire for 118 in their second innings. Alan Hurd bowled very well in the Kent match at Clacton, which Essex won by 71 runs, taking 10 for 77 in the match. The team's fielding was good, indeed brilliant at times, with Michael Bear, as usual, to the fore, saving, in his captain's opinion, ten runs per innings.

The rain-drenched summer of 1958 had its effect financially and, once more, the Club found itself with a large overdraft, although this was expected to be of a temporary nature. It was in circumstances such as these that the financial help given by the Supporters' Association was invaluable.

Although winning 11 matches and losing only seven, Essex dropped to ninth place in the 1959 county championship. The side got off to a wonderful start, winning their first five championship games, but there followed a very bad patch, lasting from mid-June until late July, when they did not win a single match and were beaten five times.

Trevor Bailey performed his fifth 'double', in fact it was a 'double' of 2000 runs and 100 wickets, his figures in all matches being 2011 runs at an average of 46.76 and 100 wickets at 24.69 each. He also scored six centuries, more than in any other season. Douglas Insole had another very good season, making 2045 runs in all matches with an average of 45.44 and five centuries. Barry Knight made a tremendous advance in 1959, just missing the 'double' by five runs, scoring 995 runs at 27.63 and taking 101 wickets at 23.56 each. He was awarded his county cap and scored his maiden century – against Worcestershire at Leyton. He took 20 wickets in the Westcliff week and finished at the head of the County bowling averages. Leslie Savill had a very good season, being promoted to open the innings and making a success of his new job. He scored 1000 runs for the first time, finishing on 1197 runs with an average of 32.35. Gordon Barker again scored 1000 runs, 1432 at 28.07, and Brian Taylor re-captured his batting form with 1837 runs, average 30.61. He also took 60 catches and made 12 stumpings. Michael Bear scored 896 runs at 22.40 and a South African, Joseph Milner, discovered by Insole and Bailey during the 1956–57 tour, scored 792 runs at an average of 27.00, including a maiden century.

Roy Ralph again bowled well, securing 90 wickets in all matches at 23.57 each, but Ken Preston was injured for part of the season and his tally of wickets consequently dropped to 60. Essex brought in the services, under special registration, of the West Indian Test player Dr C B Clarke, who took 36 wickets with his leg-breaks. In the drawn match against the Indians Barry Knight, batting at number eight, scored 89 and Roy Ralph took 5 for 33.

The County was involved in several close finishes during the season. The match against Sussex at Brentwood was won by 21 runs, Bill Greensmith taking 6 for 40 in the Sussex first innings and Trevor Bailey 6 for 34 in the second. At Ilford, in the match against Northamptonshire, fortunes swayed from side to side. Essex declared at 336 for 7, Savill scoring 107 and Bailey 119. Thanks to excellent bowling by Paddy Phelan, 5 for 17, Northamptonshire were bowled out for 193. Essex collapsed in their second innings, being dismissed for 127, leaving Northamptonshire to score 271 in four hours to win. When the last over began Northamptonshire were 268 for 7, but they lost their last three wickets without adding to the score, leaving Essex victorious by two runs. The game against Gloucestershire at Leyton resulted in a tie. Essex scored 364 for 6 declared, Insole 177 not out and Taylor 74, Gloucestershire making 329. Essex declared at 176 for 8 (Insole 90) which left Gloucestershire 212 to score in 170 minutes; they just failed in their task by one run, leaving the match tied. A sound victory was recorded at Lord's over Middlesex by an innings and 22 runs, thanks to a fine innings by Brian Taylor, who scored 135 including 22 fours and 2 sixes. Roy Ralph took 9 for 80 in the match. Against Nottinghamshire at Romford, Douglas Insole scored 180 and Roy Ralph took 12 for 104 in the match, which was won by Essex by an innings and 132 runs. Joseph Milner's maiden century (135) was scored against Leicestershire at Leicester, Essex winning by six wickets. Gordon Barker scored 157 not out in this match. Trevor Bailey and Alan Hurd were selected for the Gentlemen against the Players at Lord's. Unfortunately, Dickie Dodds suffered a complete loss of form during the 1959 season and was not re-engaged at the end of the season.

Douglas Insole was appointed a Test selector for 1959 and the side was well captained by vice-captain Trevor Bailey during Insole's absences on selectorial duties. Bailey's performance in scoring 2000 runs and taking 100 wickets represented the first occasion upon which such a feat had been performed by an Essex player, and only the 20th time such a feat had been recorded in all first-class cricket. The side maintained its good fielding record, with Michael Bear's excellent work being the subject of favourable comment everywhere.

Essex improved upon their 1959 position by moving up three places in the 1960 county championship, finishing sixth. They won nine matches and lost only three – fewer than any other county. Their record against the top four teams in the Championship – Yorkshire, Lancashire, Middlesex and Sussex – was outstanding. A victory against the champions, Yorkshire, at Headingley by 57 runs and a win against the runners-up, Lancashire, at Southend by nine wickets, constituted two of the County's most meritorious results. In all matches against the above four sides Essex allowed the opposition only four points between them. But for the intervention of bad weather Essex might have won a further two matches against this opposition.

Trevor Bailey again had a wonderful season, achieving the 'double' for the sixth time, scoring 1639 runs at an average of 39.02 and taking 117 wickets at a cost of 20.25 each in all matches.

Douglas Insole's duties as a Test selector meant that he played in fewer matches for the County but he still made over 1000 runs – 1269 in all matches, with three centuries to his name. Gordon Barker had a very good season, scoring 1741 runs in all matches at an average of 36.27, hitting two centuries. An outstanding advance was made by Geoffrey Smith, who moved rapidly from the doldrums of the previous season, was promoted to open the innings and scored 1367 runs in all matches, average 27.34 and was awarded his county cap. Geoff Smith, a right-handed batsman from Braintree, possessed some attractive shots and was also an occasional off-spinner. He had taken to wearing spectacles and this undoubtedly contributed towards his improved form.

By contrast, Leslie Savill, who had done so well in 1959, completely lost his form, scoring only 372 runs. Brian Taylor's wicket-keeping was not up to its usual high standard, so much so that his deputy, John Taylor, took his place behind the stumps in several matches. Brian Taylor, however, was in very good form with the bat and this kept him in the side. Brian scored 1358 runs in all matches, at an average of 27.16, playing some very useful and match-winning innings. Neither Joe Milner nor Michael Bear maintained their previous standards, but Roy Ralph continued to demonstrate his usefulness as an all-rounder, scoring 728 runs and taking 56 wickets. He had the knack of getting runs when they were most required; he also scored his runs very quickly. During the season he hit 27 sixes which, for a man of 40, was most commendable.

Barry Knight continued his development as a useful all-rounder, scoring 686 runs and obtaining 88 wickets. But for missing several matches through injury he could well have accomplished the 'double'. The side's batting was, on the whole, not quite up to its usual standard. The bowling, however, was greatly improved.

The attack was well balanced and able to take advantage of all conditions. Ken Preston bowled well, taking 73 wickets and the spinners, Bill Greensmith, Paddy Phelan, C B Clarke and Alan Hurd all played very useful parts. Alan Hurd had a successful season with Cambridge University, and secured 26 wickets in his appearances for Essex. He was chosen for the Gentlemen against the Players at Lord's. The defeat of Yorkshire at Headingley saw another of Trevor Bailey's outstanding all-round performances. In the Essex first innings Bailey scored 60 not out in a total of 180, thereupon bowling Yorkshire out for 86, with a personal tally of 7 for 40. He made 46 of the Essex second innings total of 280 and

43. *Brian Taylor, keeping wicket against Middlesex at Lord's, June 1963.* (Sport & General)

then proceeded to take 5 Yorkshire second innings wickets for 61. The County's win over Lancashire by nine wickets, at Southend, witnessed a stand of 58 for the ninth wicket between Bailey and Preston, Bailey eventually scoring 88 not out. The bowling honours were shared mainly between Preston, 7 for 70 in the match, and Alan Hurd, 8 for 89 in the match.

Against the South Africans at Ilford Douglas Insole scored a century and Bailey took 7 for 81 and 2 for 19, but the South Africans still won by six wickets. The County registered a very good win against Kent at Gravesend. Kent scored 332, in reply to which Essex could not manage more than 251. Kent declared their second innings closed at 191 for 7, which left Essex 273 to get in three hours. This total Essex succeeded in attaining in the last over of extra time, thanks to an aggressive 82 by Brian Taylor and an unbeaten seventh wicket partnership of 100 by Barry Knight and Bill Greensmith. The Westcliff week provided another bonanza for Barry Knight.

Against Glamorgan he took 13 for 143 in the match, Essex winning by 209 runs. Knight also made 27 and 44 in the match. The second game was against Middlesex, rain spoiling what looked like an interesting finish. Knight took 4 for 42 in the Middlesex first innings and had taken 1 for 17 in the second innings before rain stopped play. Essex had the better of drawn games against Yorkshire at Colchester, in which Preston and Ralph both bowled well, and against Sussex, again at Colchester, in which Bailey made 39 and 13 and took 4 for 38 and 1 for 22. Both these matches were curtailed by rain. In the match against Leicestershire at Hinckley, which Essex won by an innings and 27 runs, Essex took the last six Leicestershire first innings wickets for no runs and the last six second innings wickets for 27 runs. Preston took 8 for 59 and Phelan 9 for 101, in the match.

The team's record on home grounds, in terms of wins and losses, was much inferior to that on grounds outside Essex. Three home matches were won and three lost, compared with six wins and no losses, on away grounds. Team spirit was excellent, the side being described by their captain in the following terms: 'I am quite sure that there is no more likeable and presentable group of professionals than ours in the country.'

The bad weather experienced in 1960 had its effect on the gate receipts, which were down by approximately £2000. The Club sustained a substantial loss, but their burden was once more alleviated by the continued financial assistance provided by the Supporters' Assocation. After the end of the 1960 season Douglas Insole announced his resignation from the captaincy, his duties as a selector taking up more of his time. This news was received with much regret by the Club, as it had been hoped he would continue for several more years. He had captained the side since 1950 and had led the team from the front, setting a high example as an astute captain, a forceful batsman and a brilliant fielder. Under his guidance the side moved from the bottom of the county championship into the respectability of the top half of the table. Essex became one of the finest fielding sides in the country, thanks to Insole's insistence upon regular fielding practice each morning before play began. He also placed a great deal of emphasis on playing attractive cricket. His success in this was measured by the team winning, on two occasions, the *News Chronicle* 'Brighter Cricket Table'. An enterprising captain, he was always ready to accept, or to issue, a challenge. An example of this was seen in the match against Gloucestershire at Leyton in 1959, which produced an exciting finish because of Insole's generous declaration, which left Gloucestershire 212 to score in 170 minutes on a Leyton batting wicket. The match ended in a tie and the Gloucestershire captain was heard to comment, when the match was reaching it's climax: 'I don't mind who wins this match – it is cricket as it should be played.'

A popular figure, Doug Insole has a ready wit with a gift for repartee. He is also a very fast driver and there are certain former Essex players who are of the opinion that he missed his true vocation of a Grand Prix racing driver. Following his retirement Douglas Insole has given much service to Essex and to cricket in general, as Test selector, chairman of the TCCB from 1975 to 1978 and MCC committee member. He was awarded the CBE for his services to the game. He is currently chairman of Essex CCC.

CHAPTER 14

Essex under Trevor Bailey: 1961–66

The 1961 season opened with the confirmation of Douglas Insole's resignation from the captaincy owing to business commitments and his duties as a selector. Douglas Insole stated that he hoped, however, to be able to play in some matches. The chairman paid tribute to Insole, saying that he had been a tower of strength in every way for the past ten years. The natural successor to the captaincy was Insole's deputy – Trevor Bailey – who had captained the side with success during Insole's absences on selector's duties, and he was unanimously elected to take over.

The resignation of Mr A J Spelling from the office of honorary treasurer for reasons of health was also announced. The chairman sent a suitable letter of appreciation to Mr Spelling for his invaluable services since 1919. The acting treasurer warned, at the beginning of the season, that it would be necessary to reduce expenditure by approximately £5000 to endeavour to put the Club in a sound financial position.

At the AGM in March the president, Sir Hubert Ashton, received the congratulations of all present on his appointment as president of MCC. At this meeting the President presented to Douglas Insole a canteen of cutlery as a tribute to his captaincy of Essex over the past ten seasons.

44. *Trevor Bailey had a reputation of being a dour batsman, but such performances were generally reserved for his Test match appearances, when he often came to the wicket at a time of crisis. For Essex he played many attractive innings, including a century before lunch against Nottinghamshire at Southend in 1955. Here, he gets a ball past Peter Parfitt of Middlesex in his last appearance at Lord's in August, 1967. The wicket-keeper is John Murray.* (Sport & General)

Mr A B Quick was elected to fill the office of honorary treasurer. Arnold Quick was a cavalier club cricketer from Clacton who made several appearances for the Essex first team, but who also had an interesting spell as captain of the 2nd XI. He was a big hitter and a good cover fieldsman with a hard, but extremely erratic, throw-in. He was often distinguishable in the field by a sweater that covered his knees. He once lent his Rolls-Royce to a group of young professionals so that they could visit the cinema one evening during an 'away' fixture. When they pulled in to a garage for petrol on the way home the proprietor called the police, thinking that the car might be stolen, and explanations were called for.

During the winter of 1960–61 the MCC touring team in New Zealand was, at one stage, so beset by injuries that it became difficult to field 11 players. Michael Bear, who was coaching in Christchurch at this time, was called upon to assist. He played for MCC against New Zealand Colts, scoring 26, and was 12th man against Canterbury.

In 1961, Trevor Bailey's first season as captain, Essex again finished in sixth position in the county championship, with ten wins (one more than 1960) and eight defeats.

Bailey enjoyed another fine season, performing the 'double' for the seventh time and for the third year in succession, with 1240 runs at an average of 27.55, and 133 wickets at 21.01 runs each to his credit. He was again selected to play in the Gentlemen v Players match at Lord's.

The Essex batting was steady and usually reliable. Gordon Barker and Geoffrey Smith made a good opening pair, both scoring well over 1000 runs – Barker 1740 runs, average 34.11, and Smith 1908 runs, average 32.89. Barry Knight was not far off completing the 'double', scoring 1148 runs at 25.51 and securing 89 wickets at 23.95 each. Douglas Insole only played in eight matches but made some very useful scores. His consistent batting was missed throughout the season. Joseph Milner also batted well, scoring 1387 runs at an average of 28.89. The rest of the batting, however, was rather brittle. Leslie Savill and Michael Bear had disappointing seasons and Brian Taylor's batting went right off, although his wicket-keeping greatly improved.

Apart from Bailey and Knight the most successful bowler was Ken Preston, with 88 wickets at 27.36 runs each. The leg which Ken Preston broke when playing football failed to mend properly and, as a result, he completely re-modelled his bowling method while playing for the 2nd XI, and returned to the first team as a bowler of medium-pace seamers, whose repertoire included a very effective leg-cutter. As such he became one of the County's most successful bowlers. Of the spinners, Bill Greensmith secured 64 wickets at 26.15 and Robin Hobbs 23 at 28.65. Barry Knight once again found the Chalkwell Park wicket at Westcliff to his liking, taking 16 wickets during the Westcliff week. He was chosen for the twelve against Australia in the first Test at Edgbaston but was finally left out of the team. He was selected for the MCC team to tour India and Pakistan during the winter of 1961–62. In the drawn match against Derbyshire at Chelmsford Geoff Smith made 148, the highest score of his career, hitting five sixes and 18 fours, and sharing a partnership of 181 with Trevor Bailey for the fourth wicket. A good win for Essex was recorded at Burton-on-Trent against Derbyshire, the County being victorious by 181 runs after trailing by 60 on the first innings. Knight scored 120, reaching his century in 85 minutes. Bailey took 5 for 27 in Derbyshire's first innings and Preston, with 4 for 28 and Greensmith, 4 for 18, were responsible for Derbyshire's second innings dismissal for 137.

The Westcliff week brought two good wins, the first against Nottinghamshire by 120 runs, Milner scoring 117 and Knight 91, Bailey and Knight taking 13 wickets between them, and the second, against Somerset, by 106 runs. In this game Essex batted first and were all out for 177, Geoff Smith making 75 and Knight 34. When Somerset went in they were bowled out for 48 in less than 16 overs, Knight and Bailey bowling unchanged. Knight took 6 for 23 and Bailey 3 for 25. Geoff Smith scored 72 in the Essex second innings, thus making 75 and 72 in one day. In the victory over Kent at Colchester by 166 runs, Gordon Barker scored 181 not out and Douglas Insole, making one of his welcome appearances, made 51 and 73 not out. The County also registered a fine win over the champion county, Hampshire, by eight wickets, Bailey taking 11 for 107 in the match. The County's total membership reached 4814, the second highest in the Club's history.

All in all, the 1961 season was a satisfactory one and the side played attractive cricket. The bowling was better balanced than previously and the fielding was good. The captain said of Ken Preston that he could not have asked for a better or more unselfish senior professional. Preston was highly respected throughout the cricketing circuit for his ability and for his approach to the game. He was a determined cricketer with a likeable personality. He did sterling work in connection with the Essex Supporters' Association, but for whose contributions the County would have been in real trouble.

The Club's chairman, Tom Pearce, was appointed manager of the MCC team to tour India and Pakistan during the winter of 1961–62. Owing to the poor support at the Chelmsford cricket week it was decided not to hold a Chelmsford week in 1962. The Club's financial situation remained acute and at a Special General Meeting held at the end of the year it was agreed to increase members' subscriptions.

The County's ranks were considerably reduced in 1962 through the termination of contracts for Savill and Ralph and the retirement of Milner and John Taylor. However, a most eminent recruit was found in the person of J C Laker, the former Surrey and England off-spinner, who had been playing for Norton in the North Staffordshire League. Laker had intimated, early in the year, that he would like to play in some matches for Essex, as an amateur, during the coming season if required. The Committee agreed to apply for his special registration.

Jim Laker played in 12 matches for the County, the attack being immensely strengthened by his presence and becoming one of the best in the country. Laker had a most successful season, taking 51 wickets at an average of 18.86, heading the County bowling averages and being awarded his County cap. Essex dropped to ninth position in the county championship, winning eight matches and suffering six defeats.

Trevor Bailey and Barry Knight had outstanding seasons, both achieving 1000 runs and 100 wickets, Bailey performing this feat for the eighth time. Bailey's figures were 1460 runs, average 35.60 and 125 wickets at 20.59 runs each. Knight scored 1689 runs at an average of 34.46 and took 100 wickets at 24.05 apiece. Knight was picked for the fourth and fifth Tests against Pakistan at Trent Bridge and The Oval respectively, taking 4 for 38 in the Pakistan first innings at Trent Bridge. He was also chosen for the MCC tour of Australia in the coming winter. Bailey was picked for the Gentlemen against the Players at Lord's, taking 6 for 58 in the first innings. These two apart, the Essex batting during the 1962 season was not up to previous standards, in fact it was the poorest batting side since the war.

Whereas, in previous years, Essex had regularly been one of the fastest scoring sides, they were one of the slowest in 1962. Geoff Smith was kept out of the side for six weeks through injury and although he scored over 1000 runs after his return, his form was not as good as before. Michael Bear took over the opener's position in Smith's absence and enjoyed his best season, scoring 1612 runs, average 29.85 with two centuries. Gordon Barker scored over 1000 runs but he also was disappointing. Brian Taylor broke the Essex record for the number of wicket-keeping dismissals in a season, with 79 catches and ten stumpings. However, apart from a match-winning century against Gloucestershire, his batting was below par. Bill Greensmith had a useful season, making 764 runs and securing 77 wickets. Ken Preston bowled well, with 80 wickets to his credit and Paddy Phelan took 38 wickets with his off-breaks.

When Essex defeated the touring Pakistan team by nine wickets at Leyton, they became the first county to have beaten all the major touring countries. In the Pakistan first innings Bailey took 5 for 47 and Knight 4 for 66.

Amongst Jim Laker's fine performances with the ball were his 7 for 61 in the victory over Leicestershire by eight wickets at Hinckley; 5 for 46 against Somerset at Brentwood; 13 for 159 in the drawn match with Kent at Dover; 6 for 52 in the drawn game with Warwickshire at Colchester and 6 for 49 in the win over Sussex by 72 runs at Worthing. Other notable victories included that over Kent at Romford by one wicket, the winning hit being made by the Essex number ten, Paddy Phelan, off the fourth ball of the last over of extra time; the win over Lancashire at Liverpool by 28 runs, Bailey scoring 97 and Greensmith taking 7 for 59; the defeat of Middlesex by ten wickets at Brentwood in which Knight scored 165 and took 6 for 50; the five-wicket win over Gloucestershire at Clacton, where Essex, needing 298 to win in 4¼ hours, achieved this target with ten minutes to spare, thanks to a fine century by Brian Taylor, who hit 3 sixes and 15 fours; the defeat of Lancashire by nine wickets at Leyton, Ken Preston taking 12 for 85, and finally the excellent win over Warwickshire at Birmingham by 86 runs. In this latter match, Essex were bowled out for 85 in their first innings, Warwickshire then making 278 for 9 declared, Essex consequently being 193 behind. The County then ran up 414 before declaring with five wickets down, Bailey scoring 95 and Knight 88, thereafter dismissing their opponents for 135, Bailey taking 5 for 22 and Phelan 3 for 44. Thus Essex won by 86 runs. Knight, in his innings of 88, scored all but four runs from boundaries, hitting 21 fours.

A curiosity of the 1962 season was that Barry Stead, who had been given a trial by Essex, was credited with a match for Essex against Oxford University, at Oxford, being shown in the score-card as 'did not bat', but, in fact, he was not at the ground as he was playing for Nottinghamshire 2nd XI on the same day.

On the topic of scoring, the mobile Essex score-board, which was to become a familiar sight on all Essex home grounds, made its first appearance at about this time.

Despite total contributions of £8588 by the Supporters' Association during 1962–63, the treasurer reported a debit balance of £1911, to which the bad weather in 1962 had doubtless contributed. 'The Club's aim must be to build up a substantial reserve,' the treasurer said, 'particularly as it was anticipated that the Supporters' Association's donations were expected to decline'.

Mr H P Crabtree reported that a cricket coaching course had been run for teachers during the winter of 1962–63. In addition ten centres had been opened and over 300 boys had received one hour's coaching per week during the winter. The chairman thanked Mr Crabtree for the excellent work he was doing in organising coaching for the youth of the county.

Essex finished the 1963 county championship in 12th place – three lower than in 1962. Only six wins were recorded as against four defeats, leaving the large number of 18 games drawn. Bad weather was responsible for some of these matches being left drawn, but not all. Apart from Barry Knight and Jim Laker, the bowling generally lacked penetration. Knight had an excellent season, performing the 'double' for the second successive year, with 1578 runs at an average of 28.69 and 140 wickets at 21.72 each, to his credit. On nine occasions he took five or more wickets in an innings, his three best performances being 8 for 70 against Gloucestershire at Gloucester, 8 for 69 against Nottinghamshire at Trent Bridge and 7 for 68 against Middlesex at Southend. Despite this form he was not selected for any of the Test matches against West Indies but was chosen for the MCC tour to India in the following winter.

Jim Laker appeared in ten matches and again turned in some useful performances, such as his 10 for 106 in the innings victory over Northamptonshire at Romford, in which match Bailey scored 96 and Keith Fletcher 94; 4 for 59 against Leicestershire at Ilford; 7 for 89 against Leicestershire at Leicester, and 7 for 97 in the match, against Yorkshire at Clacton. He again finished top of the Essex bowling averages, with 43 wickets at 19.25 each.

Trevor Bailey batted well throughout the season, scoring 1568 runs at 37.33. His bowling, however, fell away and for the first time for several years he failed to reach 100 wickets, taking 79 at the much higher than usual average of 29.12. Preston also took fewer wickets (58) at a higher cost and Phelan, Hobbs and Edmeades all proved expensive. Greensmith's form deserted him completely and he retired at the end of the season.

The batting was generally reliable, although some players did not realise their full potential. Michael Bear had a good season, scoring 1170 runs at an average of 30.00, but unfortunately broke his leg, which caused him to miss the last six matches. Gordon Barker and Geoffrey Smith again scored over 1000 runs, but in Smith's case the totals and batting averages were considerably lower than his 1962 figures. Brian Taylor again kept wicket well and just missed 1000 runs, scoring 995 runs at 24.26.

The most promising batsman in 1963 was Keith Fletcher who, in his first full season, scored 1310 runs at an average of 26.20. Keith Fletcher was a natural cricketer who hailed from the Cambridgeshire village of Caldecote, where he was something of a boy prodigy, playing for the Royston Club when he was only 13. His headmaster, who was a cricket addict, contacted Trevor Bailey, with the result that Fletcher was given a game against Colchester and East Essex and was signed on by Essex at the age of 16. He made his debut for the 1st XI in 1962 at the age of 17 and very quickly demonstrated his natural ability. His performance in 1963, when he reached 1000 runs by the end of July, underlined his potential. A most attractive batsman, it was soon apparent that he was destined for high honours, which subsequent events were amply to prove. In the rain-affected match against West Indies at Southend, Essex were all out for 56, Fletcher making 29, and had reached 92 for four wickets in their second innings before rain stopped play. Fletcher was then 34 not out. Bailey and Fletcher shared a 100 partnership against Derbyshire at Romford, Bailey scoring 72 and Fletcher 74, Essex winning the match by 80 runs.

A close finish took place at Ilford in the game against Hampshire, which Essex just won by two wickets, despite leading by 180 on the first innings. Knight scored 124 and took four Hampshire first innings wickets for 39. A good win was recorded over Gloucestershire at Leyton. Batting first, Essex had lost eight wickets for 67 when Brian Edmeades was joined by Paddy Phelan. These two put on 93 for the ninth wicket, Phelan making 63 and Edmeades 44. Despite this Essex were 37 behind on the first innings, but further good innings by Bailey (80) and Fletcher (47) and good bowling by Edmeades (4 for 23) saw Essex winners by 68 runs. A magnificent all-round performance by Knight was largely responsible for the Essex 57-run victory over Nottinghamshire at Trent Bridge. Knight scored 58 and 101 not out and took eight Nottinghamshire first-innings wickets for 69. The 1963 season brought the inauguration of the first limited-overs sponsored competition – the Gillette Cup. Essex did not progress far in the competition, being defeated by Lancashire at Old Trafford. At one stage Lancashire were 97 for 6 but, aided by Essex fielding lapses, no less than six chances being put down, Lancashire reached 213. In reply Essex could only manage 132. The year also saw a momentous change in the game, namely the abolition of the amateur status. All players became 'cricketers', receiving negotiated payments or expenses.

It was around this period, when Essex were regularly finishing in the bottom half of the championship table, that it would have been possible for the Club to have turned out a better football team than a cricket team. From the 1st XI the following regular or occasional players were on the staff: Geoff Hurst (West Ham and England); Eddie Presland (West Ham); Gordon Barker (Southend United); Terry Kent (Millwall); Doug Insole (Pegasus and Corinthian Casuals); Trevor Bailey (Walthamstow Avenue); Brian Taylor (Brentford); Paddy Phelan (local amateur), whilst regular players for the 2nd XI and Club and Ground included Cliff Holton (Arsenal); Dave Sexton (West Ham) and Alan Sealey (West Ham). Additionally, Bobby Moore (West Ham and England) played in testimonial matches.

Sir Frank Foster, having held the office of vice-chairman for ten years, announced his resignation early in 1964. It was proposed, seconded and passed unanimously, that Mr D J Insole be elected vice-chairman. It was agreed that Sir Frank Foster and Mr H G Clark be elected honorary life members in view of their great services to the Club.

Frank Foster was a kindly, genial man with much experience as an administrator, whose enthusiasm for cricket was unbounded and whose involvement with the County Club was a great asset. Horace Clark gave an immense amount of his time for the Club's benefit and was a very efficient and extremely popular secretary. He had a dry and infectious sense of humour and made many friends throughout the game.

Mr H P Crabtree reported that the Essex Schools Cricket Association had enjoyed a successful season, as a result of which a number of extremely promising boys had emerged.

Undoubtedly the highlight of the 1964 season was the six-wickets' defeat of the Australians at Southend. Essex batted first and, thanks to a fine partnership of 184 by Gordon Barker, who made 123, and Keith Fletcher, who scored 125, backed up by an unbroken partnership of 83 for the seventh wicket by John Wilcox and Brian Edmeades, who scored 46 not out and 53 not out respectively, reached 425 for 6. John Wilcox was the son of former Essex captain Denys Wilcox, who was later to follow in the footsteps of his grandfather and father by taking over the headmastership of Alleyn Court School.

Essex declared and then dismissed the visitors for 218, Paddy Phelan taking 5 for 94. Bailey enforced the follow-on – the first time this had happened to an Australian team against an English county for many years. Australia fared better in their second innings but still could only muster 313, Phelan taking 5 for 154, leaving Essex to score 107 to win, which they did for the loss of four wickets. This was the first Essex win against an Australian side since 1905 and went a long way towards making up for the trouncing administered by Don Bradman's team in 1948.

Essex finished tenth in the County Championship in 1964, winning seven and losing 11 matches. Early in the season they appeared to be well placed to finish near the top, but they flattered to deceive and in true Essex fashion then embarked upon one of the most disastrous playing spells ever known to the County, losing six out of their next seven games and only being saved by rain in the other.

A spirited recovery in August improved matters, Essex winning four matches out of six. The attack was not penetrating enough, the majority of the bowlers being less effective and more expensive than usual. Jim Laker played in only eight matches and was unable to reproduce his old form, taking only 17 wickets at 33.94 runs each. Colin Hilton, a fast-medium bowler from Lancashire, who was specially registered for the 1964 season, took 58 wickets, but at the high cost of 34.46 runs each. Worst of all, he gave away no less than 232 no-balls during the season, being unable to cope with the new front-foot law which had been introduced at the beginning of the season. Robin Hobbs took 81 wickets with his leg-breaks and was chosen to tour South Africa in the coming winter with MCC. One of the last of the regular leg-spinners in the country, Robin Hobbs joined Essex in 1961. A brilliant fielder, he also made some useful scores batting at number nine, eventually appearing in seven Test matches for England. Paddy Phelan secured 66 wickets and was awarded his County cap.

The Essex batting was generally consistent, although Gordon Barker began the season in disappointing fashion. However, he found his true form later in the season, producing some really first-class innings.

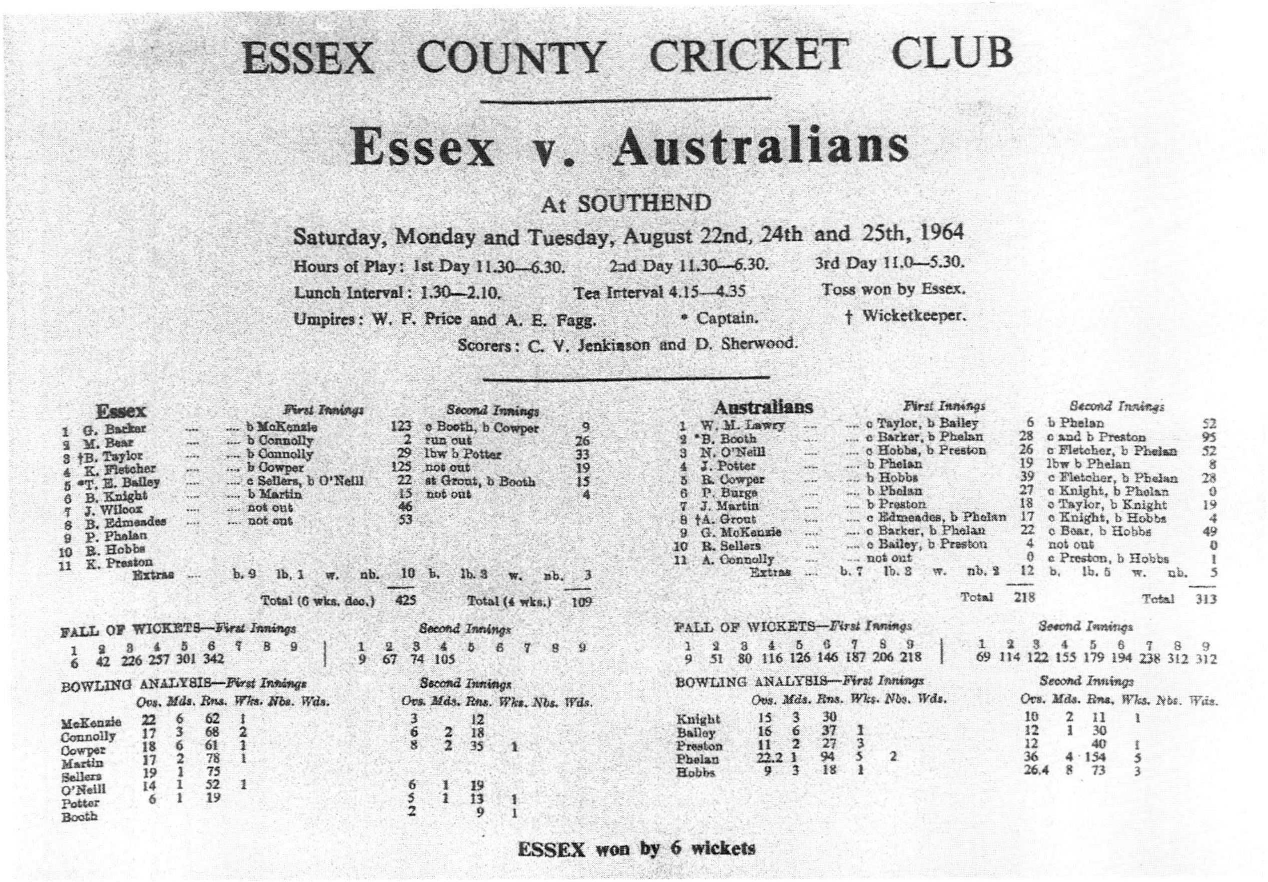

ESSEX COUNTY CRICKET CLUB

Essex v. Australians

At SOUTHEND

Saturday, Monday and Tuesday, August 22nd, 24th and 25th, 1964

Hours of Play: 1st Day 11.30—6.30. 2nd Day 11.30—6.30. 3rd Day 11.0—5.30.

Lunch Interval: 1.30—2.10. Tea Interval 4.15—4.35 Toss won by Essex.

Umpires: W. F. Price and A. E. Fagg. * Captain. † Wicketkeeper.

Scorers: C. V. Jenkinson and D. Sherwood.

	Essex	First Innings		Second Innings	
1	G. Barker	b McKenzie	123	c Booth, b Cowper	9
2	M. Bear	b Connolly	2	run out	26
3	†B. Taylor	b Connolly	29	lbw b Potter	33
4	K. Fletcher	b Cowper	125	not out	19
5	*T. E. Bailey	c Sellers, b O'Neill	22	st Grout, b Booth	15
6	B. Knight	b Martin	15	not out	4
7	J. Wilcox	not out	46		
8	B. Edmeades	not out	53		
9	P. Phelan				
10	B. Hobbs				
11	K. Preston				
	Extras	b. 9 lb. 1 w. nb.	10	b. lb. 3 w. nb.	3
		Total (6 wks. dec.)	425	Total (4 wks.)	109

FALL OF WICKETS—*First Innings*

1	2	3	4	5	6	7	8	9
6	42	226	257	301	342			

Second Innings

1	2	3	4	5	6	7	8	9
9	67	74	105					

BOWLING ANALYSIS—*First Innings* / *Second Innings*

	Ovs.	Mds.	Rns.	Wks.	Nbs.	Wds.	Ovs.	Mds.	Rns.	Wks.	Nbs.	Wds.
McKenzie	22	6	62	1			3		12			
Connolly	17	3	68	2			6	2	18			
Cowper	18	6	61	1			8	2	35	1		
Martin	17	2	78	1								
Sellers	19	1	75									
O'Neill	14	1	52	1			6	1	19			
Potter	6	1	19				5	1	13	1		
Booth							2		9	1		

	Australians	First Innings		Second Innings	
1	W. M. Lawry	c Taylor, b Bailey	6	b Phelan	52
2	*B. Booth	c Barker, b Phelan	28	c and b Preston	95
3	N. O'Neill	c Hobbs, b Preston	26	c Fletcher, b Phelan	52
4	J. Potter	b Phelan	19	lbw b Phelan	8
5	R. Cowper	b Hobbs	39	c Fletcher, b Phelan	28
6	P. Burge	b Phelan	27	c Knight, b Phelan	0
7	J. Martin	b Preston	18	c Taylor, b Knight	19
8	†A. Grout	c Edmeades, b Phelan	17	c Knight, b Hobbs	4
9	G. McKenzie	c Barker, b Phelan	22	c Bear, b Hobbs	49
10	R. Sellers	c Bailey, b Preston	4	not out	0
11	A. Connolly	not out	0	c Preston, b Hobbs	1
	Extras	b. 7 lb. 3 w. nb. 2	12	b. lb. 5 w. nb.	5
		Total	218	Total	313

FALL OF WICKETS—*First Innings*

1	2	3	4	5	6	7	8	9
9	51	80	116	126	146	187	206	218

Second Innings

1	2	3	4	5	6	7	8	9
69	114	122	155	179	194	238	312	312

BOWLING ANALYSIS—*First Innings* / *Second Innings*

	Ovs.	Mds.	Rns.	Wks.	Nbs.	Wds.	Ovs.	Mds.	Rns.	Wks.	Nbs.	Wds.
Knight	15	3	30				10	2	11	1		
Bailey	16	6	37	1			12	1	30			
Preston	11	2	27	3			12		40	1		
Phelan	22.2	1	94	5	2		36	4	154	5		
Hobbs	9	3	18	1			26.4	8	73	3		

ESSEX won by 6 wickets

45. *Essex v Australia, 22–25 August, 1964.*

In particular, his 121 not out in the Essex second innings against Derbyshire at Derby, which contained 14 fours, earned very high praise. Michael Bear batted well, particularly when others were out of form, scoring 1567 runs at an average of 29.56. He and Barker continued to form a useful opening partnership. Brian Taylor's wicket-keeping was as good as ever and he also enjoyed a successful season with the bat, making 1225 runs at an average of 27.22. Brian Taylor first played for Essex in 1949, when he was 16. A sound and competent wicket-keeper, who appealed in stentorian tones, he was a forceful and unpredictable bat who was christened early in his career as 'Tonker', because of his considerable ability as a hard hitter. He once forced Jackson of Derbyshire to bowl the first over of the innings to him with four men posted on the leg-side boundary. He was to become captain of the County and to hold this appointment with considerable success. He was also to establish a record for the most consecutive county championship appearances for Essex.

Keith Fletcher continued to improve, scoring 1616 runs, average 31.07, more than 300 runs better than his 1963 total. He hit his maiden century, 103 not out, against Lancashire at Manchester. Brian Edmeades also registered his maiden century (135) in this match and enjoyed his best season so far. A sound batsman, a useful medium-pace seamer and an excellent outfielder, he was a great favourite with the Essex crowds and was to serve Essex well in the coming years. He was known to his team-mates as 'Chanson', which nickname evidently originated through his choice of a juke box record – *Chanson d'Amour* – when in a café with other Essex players.

Barry Knight again performed the 'double', with 1209 runs, average 23.25, and 100 wickets at a cost of 27.04 each. These figures, however, were considerably lower than his brilliant 1963 returns. Trevor Bailey again batted well, scoring 1106 runs, average 33.51, also capturing 70 wickets at 23.78 apiece.

In the rain-affected match against Hampshire at Southampton, Essex won by five wickets, after three declarations had been made. Essex were required to make 201 in 138 minutes, a rate of 85 runs an hour. This they succeeded in doing with eight minutes to spare. Robin Hobbs scored 19 off four successive deliveries from Shackleton – 6, 6, 4, 3. Essex, in fact, became adept at winning matches against the clock, three more of their victories being achieved in this fashion. Against Gloucestershire at Bristol they were asked to make 181 in 150 minutes, which they accomplished for the loss of four wickets, with ten minutes to spare (Bear 81 not out, Knight 59). Set to score 185 in 140 minutes to defeat Glamorgan at Clacton, Essex reached this target with 27 minutes to spare, winning by five wickets. Fletcher and Taylor hit five sixes between them. A Middlesex declaration saw Essex set to make 252 in 200 minutes at Lord's, reaching this target for the loss of four wickets with seven minutes remaining, Taylor scoring 55, Knight 69 and Fletcher 75 not out.

Essex met Cambridgeshire in the first round of the Gillette Cup, winning by 31 runs. In the second round, against Glamorgan at Neath, a close finish was seen. Glamorgan made 208 for 9 and with four overs left, Essex needed 15 runs to win. Wickets were thrown away however, and Essex could only muster seven of the required number.

Barry Knight won the Carling single-wicket competition, beating Colin Milburn in the final at Lord's.

The Australian share of the match against the County at Southend (£1343) was easily the highest amount earned by an Australian touring side against Essex since the war. The Committee decided to present silk scorecards of the Australian match to the players and to certain hosts at Southend. The Club membership totalled 4383, with 995 new members having been enrolled during the year. The Committee, after a long discussion on the advisability of purchasing the Chelmsford ground, decided to proceed.

Despite increases in both the numbers of members and the amounts of gate money coming in, the large overdraft reported at the beginning of 1965 caused concern to be voiced by the Committee over the present and future financial position of the Club. The Committee were of the opinion that this overdraft should be liquidated as soon as possible.

Mr H P Crabtree expressed his worry at the number of young cricketers in the 16- to 18-year-old age range who were being lost to the game. It was decided to run a competition in the Brentwood and Romford areas, to which the County Club offered to give every support. Six teams would compete on a league basis, with a play-off between the two leading teams being staged at Chelmsford.

Mr A B Quick announced his resignation from the position of honorary treasurer. Mr A G Waterman was elected to fill this office. 'Tiny' Waterman played for Essex in 1937–38, enjoying a successful season in 1938 when he scored 103 against Somerset at Bath, finishing the season with an average of 38.85 and being awarded his County cap. He was to hold the office of treasurer until 1977, becoming chairman of the Club in 1978. A very able administrator, he served as chairman of the finance committee of the TCCB and also on the MCC committee.

In the wet summer of 1965 Essex languished at the foot of the championship table for most of the summer, managing to pull themselves clear by defeating Glamorgan in the last match of the season and finishing in 15th place, with four wins and seven losses. Seventeen matches were left drawn, many of these games being spoiled by the weather.

The Essex batting was not dependable and players appeared to lack confidence. So far as the bowling was concerned, the County missed the services of Preston and Laker, both of whom had retired and, apart from Knight, Bailey and Hobbs, the rest of the bowling was unimpressive and expensive. Barry Knight enjoyed a very good season, achieving the 'double' for the third time, with 1172 runs at 22.98 and 125 wickets at 18.90 runs each. He was, in fact, the only cricketer in the country to complete the feat.

Trevor Bailey also had a successful season, just missing what would have been his ninth 'double' by three wickets, scoring 1026 runs at 25.65 and taking 97 wickets at 19.76 each. Gordon Barker was in first-rate form in the early part of the season, but then missed a few matches due to illness and injury and, although he played some very useful innings on his return, appeared to have lost a little of his confidence. His tally of 1289 runs at 29.29 was, however, very satisfactory. Keith Fletcher enjoyed another good season, making 1486 runs at 29.13. Brian Taylor and Geoffrey Smith just missed 1000 runs, with totals of 929 and 969 respectively. Michael Bear had a disappointing season, scoring only 772 runs, half his total for 1964.

Barry Knight and Trevor Bailey bowled most reliably and successfully, finishing first and second in the Essex bowling averages. In third place was Robin Hobbs, who took 75 wickets at 23.36 each.

Essex defeated the champions, Worcestershire, at Brentwood by 48 runs, Bailey scoring 74 and John Wilcox 87 in the Essex first innings and Knight 53 not out in the second. The spinners were mainly responsible for Worcestershire's downfall, Robin Hobbs taking 5 for 46 in their first innings and Paddy Phelan 7 for 80 in the second. The match against Yorkshire at Bradford was one which Essex should have won. The home side were bowled out for 75, Knight taking 5 for 41 and Bailey 5 for 27. Essex then made 274, Keith Fletcher contributing 81 and Geoffrey Smith 50. Needing 199 to avoid an innings defeat, Yorkshire were 183 for 9, but the last pair, Chadwick and Waring, defended stubbornly for almost half an hour and saved the game for Yorkshire. Knight took 5 for 49 in the Yorkshire second innings. In the game against Derbyshire, at Derby, which Essex won by 85 runs, Geoffrey Smith had one of his rare bowls, being successful to the tune of 5 for 39. Brian Edmeades took 7 for 43 in the Derbyshire second innings. Essex defeated Middlesex comprehensively, at Leyton, dismissing the home side for 134, Knight taking 6 for 30. Essex totalled 362, then put Middlesex out for 238, Paddy Phelan returning 6 for 72, and Essex won by nine wickets. The final match of the season, against Glamorgan at Llanelly, was won by Essex by five wickets and this victory took the County off the bottom rung of the championship. Robin Hobbs bowled extremely well in this game, taking 12 for 94 in the match, while Fletcher played a fine innings of 72.

Essex were knocked out of the Gillette Cup in a first round tie with Derbyshire at Brentwood, the visitors winning by 95 runs.

Many discussions were held by the Committee at this time with regard to the purchase of the Chelmsford ground and it was announced that the Warwickshire County Cricket Supporters' Association had very kindly agreed to lend the Club £15,000 interest-free towards the purchase of this ground. This generous offer from the Warwickshire Supporters' Association originated at a dinner given by the Worcestershire County Cricket Club to celebrate their winning the county championship in 1965. The dinner was attended by Trevor Bailey, who met several Warwickshire friends there. They heard from Bailey that Essex had the opportunity of purchasing the freehold of the Chelmsford ground but were unable to take advantage of the opportunity because of the financial situation, whereupon an assurance was given that the Warwickshire Supporters' Association would supply an interest-free loan to enable Essex to achieve this object. Trevor later stated, that this was easily his most important contribution to the Club. It was decided also to launch an appeal fund for ground purchase and erection of the pavilion.

Towards the end of the 1965 season it was felt that it was essential for the Club to have a full-time secretary and that it was placing too much of a burden on Trevor Bailey's shoulders for him to undertake the joint tasks of captain and secretary. Bailey was therefore offered the position of full-time secretary at an increased salary. After consideration he decided not to accept the offer, feeling that he could be of considerable use as a playing member during the next season, which would be a vital one for the Club. He did not wish to leave the playing scene with the County languishing in their present unhappy position. Trevor Bailey was thanked for his understanding and co-operation and it was decided to advertise for a full-time secretary. As a result, Major C A Brown was appointed to this post, to commence his duties on 1 January 1966.

The latter half of 1965 witnessed a steady deterioration in the Club's financial situation, largely due to the adverse weather conditions which persisted for most of the summer. The Club's bankers agreed to increased overdraft facilities against the Club's securities being charged to the bank as collateral. The treasurer stressed the need for the strictest economy as a first step to bringing the accounts into balance. It was agreed to reduce the playing staff as soon as possible by five, possibly six players.

The youth training scheme continued to flourish in 1965 and was extended to Chelmsford, Colchester, Southend and Brentwood. A shield was presented by Trevor Bailey and the competition would be known in future as the Essex Youth Competition for the Trevor Bailey Shield.

Barry Knight was presented with a clock and a cheque for 100 guineas by the Committee for his performance in 1965 in being the only first-class cricketer to perform the 'double'.

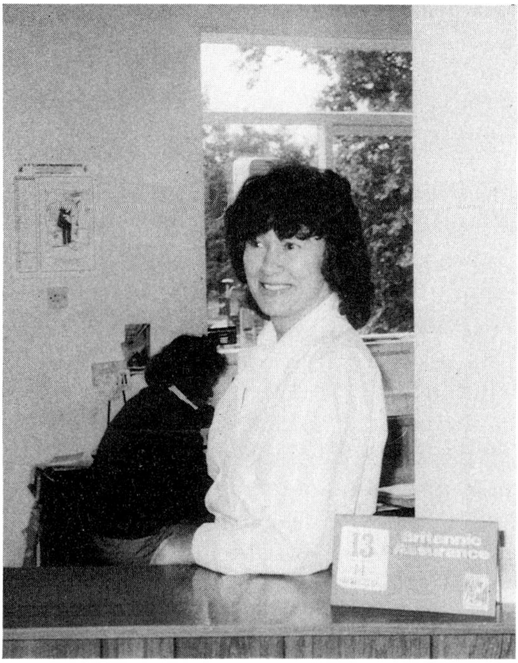

46. *Jeanette Carman joined the Club's staff in 1966 as secretary to the then Club secretary, Major Brown, MBE. She was the only staff member in the office, and for several periods in the 'bad old days' was the Club's sole administrative employee.*

Now assistant secretary (membership), Jeanette's 9000 membership records are computerised and she is one of seven office staff who run the Club's administration.

1966 proved to be a very poor season for the County. They finished in 16th place in the county championship, one worse than 1965, winning four matches and losing ten. The need for economy and the consequent reduction in the playing staff affected the results. Bailey suffered from a leg strain for most of the season, very often playing when he should have been resting and this, of course, led to a decline in his form. The year was another wet one and rain affected the gates accordingly. The first match of the Colchester Festival, against Derbyshire, had to be transferred to the Garrison Ground, as Castle Park was unplayable.

Handicapped by his leg strain, Bailey's all-round figures suffered. He finished the season with 627 runs at 22.39 and 45 wickets at 22.84 runs each. Barry Knight's form also fell away, his figures for the season reading 776 runs at an average of 19.89 and 83 wickets at 21.16 runs each. He was picked for the second Test match against West Indies at Lord's.

The County batting was again unreliable, the only really outstanding batsman being Michael Bear, who enjoyed his best season, with 1833 runs at an average of 32.15. Keith Fletcher did not have quite such a good season as 1965, but scored 1558 runs at 28.32, including a delightful century against the West Indians team at Southend, which included two sixes and 15 fours. Gordon Barker totalled 1301 runs at 26.02 and Brian

Taylor improved his batting figures to 1264 runs at 22.98. Barry Knight ran into a bad patch in mid-season, scoring only 151 runs in nineteen innings. He began and finished the season well, however.

The outstanding bowler of the season was Brian Edmeades. Forced by injuries and depleted playing staff to undertake far more bowling than usual, he responded to the challenge by taking 106 wickets in 725 overs, at the very respectable average of 18.59. On 11 occasions he took four or more wickets in an innings. He also made some useful runs. Robin Hobbs also bowled his leg-spinners well, taking 88 wickets in all matches at 25.77 each. Two new bowlers made useful contributions – Tony Jorden, fast-medium, and David Acfield, off-spinner. Both these players were destined to gain their blues at Cambridge, Jorden eventually to become captain of the University XI, and both were to gain international recognition in other sports, Jorden as an England rugby full-back and Acfield as an England and Olympic fencer. An outstanding debut was made by the young all-rounder from Barbados – Keith Boyce – who was then serving his qualifying period. In the match against Cambridge University, Boyce took 9 for 61 and 4 for 47, his pace proving too much for the University batsmen. Keith Boyce was seen by Trevor Bailey during the Rothman Cavaliers tour of the West Indies in 1964–65. Boyce was included in the Bajaan team in their second match against the touring Cavaliers, proceeding to impress Trevor Bailey with his fast bowling, his tremendous hitting power and his outstanding fielding. As a result, Trevor earmarked him as a future Essex player. An exciting and unpredictable all-rounder, he was destined to provide much entertainment and to achieve very considerable success during the coming years. A natural one-day player, he was capable of changing the entire course of such a match, in a couple of overs. In this same match David Acfield took 6 for 69 against his County, in the Essex first innings.

History was made at Ilford in the game against Somerset. This was the first County match to include Sunday play and proved to be financially successful, some 6000 spectators attending. Nearly £500 was paid by spectators for scorecards, stand seats and collections, it not being permissible at that time to make an admission charge on a Sunday. The match had a close finish, Essex being set 290 to win. With the score at 284 for 7 Robin Hobbs needed to hit the last ball of the match for six to win. He only managed two, leaving the game drawn. In a low scoring match at Romford, Essex defeated Nottinghamshire by 56 runs, Knight taking 4 for 27 in the Nottinghamshire first innings and Edmeades 4 for 20 in the second. Another close finish was seen at Dartford when Essex beat Kent by four runs. Needing only 87 to win, Kent were put out by Edmeades and Bailey who took 4 for 29 and 3 for 25 respectively. Edmeades had also taken 5 for 55 in

Kent's first innings. Robin Hobbs bowled exceptionally well in the drawn game against Glamorgan, taking 13 for 164 in the match.

Essex recorded their first win against a championship side in the Gillette cup, when they beat Derbyshire at Chesterfield. Derbyshire totalled 199, Knight taking 3 for 33, Jorden 3 for 41 and Edmeades 3 for 32. Essex had reached 191 for 5 without difficulty, Bear having made a useful 71, but then contrived to lose three wickets for the addition of only three runs, before finally winning by two wickets with two overs remaining. This was the extent of the Essex success in this competition however, as they were comprehensively beaten by Worcestershire in the third round, at Worcester, by 82 runs, only Knight (52) and Taylor (31) making respectable scores for Essex.

47. *Robin Hobbs, a leg break bowler who played seven Test matches for England and retired from Essex after the 1975 season. He later joined Glamorgan as captain.* (Central Press)

One ironic benefit of an otherwise poor season was that the reduction in playing staff meant that the younger players were able to develop their talents more fully; they knew their places were secure providing they kept fit.

The Committee decided to agree to the playing of County matches on Sundays and to accept the Sunday home fixtures arranged for 1967. The financial position continued to give rise to anxiety during the 1966 season, despite the sale of the Club's investments. By the end of the season the situation had reached alarming proportions and was exacerbated through a resolution passed by the Supporters' Association: 'that no further monies be paid to the County Club and that all future requests for money from the County shall be for a specific purpose and shall be considered by this Committee before any action is taken'. This came as a bombshell to the County, virtually cutting off their regular income from this source. The Supporters' Association were left in no doubt as to the results which would be obtained if this resolution were to be put into effect, but despite this decided to go ahead with its implementation. The County Club thereupon disassociated themselves from the Supporters' Association and sought Counsel's opinion, which was that all monies held by the Supporters' Association were held in trust for the benefit of the County Cricket Club and that the Association should hand over the monies held to the County Club immediately. The Supporters' Association thereupon requested a meeting with the County Club, the upshot of which was that reconciliation terms were drawn up by the County and ultimately accepted by the Supporters' Association with a few minor alterations. Fresh proposals for the administration of the Association were accepted and it was agreed that a press release be made, stating that the differences between the County Club and the Supporters' Association had been resolved.

Towards the end of 1966 a sub-committee was formed to study the question of the captaincy of the 1st XI for 1967 and to make their recommendation to the Executive Committee. After giving consideration to several names, the sub-committee decided, in January 1967, to recommend that Brian Taylor be asked to captain the 1st XI for the coming season. This was ratified by the Executive Committee and Brian Taylor was invited to assume this appointment. Grateful thanks were expressed to Trevor Bailey for his outstanding services to Essex and England and it was agreed to grant him a testimonial in 1968.

The outstanding Essex player for two decades, Trevor Bailey was a phenomenal schoolboy cricketer whose rich promise was amply fulfilled at every subsequent level. One of Essex's finest all-rounders, if not the finest, his value to the Essex side was immense, not only as a cricketer but as a tactician and captain. He first played for Essex in 1946, against

Derbyshire at Ilford, opening both the bowling and the batting, then went up to Cambridge, where he gained his blue. He appeared in 61 Tests, achieving the rare feat of scoring 2000 runs and taking 100 wickets in these matches. His all-round performances for Essex are legion; most are described in this book. Suffice it to say he virtually re-wrote the Essex statistics, becoming one of the most outstanding players in Essex history.

A dedicated cricketer with a deep knowledge of the game, his attitude was best summed up by the title of his book, *Playing to Win*. Brian Taylor described Bailey as fascinating to keep wicket to – an intelligent bowler with a wonderful rhythm who was always making the ball do something and who, when bowling all out, was practically as fast as Tyson, Trueman and Statham.

After retiring from first-class cricket, Trevor Bailey became a regular member of the BBC radio commentary team, where his knowledge of the game and his experience at Test and county levels have enabled him to provide listeners with factual and reasoned descriptions of the matches being broadcast.

A small working party, comprising 'Tiny' Waterman the honorary treasurer, Douglas Insole the vice-chairman and Charles Day, a member of the Committee, was set up and given substantial delegated powers, with a view to reducing expenditure to a level well below that of estimated income. It was recognised in advance that the required economies would include a drastic pruning of the playing staff, which was in fact reduced to 13, the majority of whom were young players. In fact, total expenditure in the following season was reduced to less than £33,000 – a reduction of some 15 per cent as compared with the previous season.

An unwanted 'casualty' of this reduction in staff was Barry Knight, who decided to leave the Club following the appointment, as captain, of Brian Taylor. Knight eventually joined Leicestershire, for which county he became eligible to play in mid-1968, following objections by Essex to his immediate registration. Knight, a 'local' product, had developed into a very good all-round cricketer. He was a whippy pace bowler who could be lethal when helped by the pitch. He was a superb player of slow bowling, even if his technique against pace left something to be desired. He toured, and made many appearances for England before emigrating to Australia, where he continued to play high quality grade cricket and where he now manages a successful cricket school.

One of those who remained was Frank Rist, who had been for some years in charge of Essex young players following his retirement from the first-class game. The Club could not afford a coach, and in any event there was no junior staff to look after, but there was a limited amount of 2nd XI cricket to organise, and there was talent to be spotted, so Frank Rist agreed to work for next to nothing, and continued to do so for a

48. *Frank Rist. Although he made only 65 appearances for Essex, he played a significant part in the development and coaching of young players in the post-war years.*
(Feature Press Photo Agency)

number of seasons. A professional footballer with Charlton and Colchester and subsequently manager of West Ham's junior side, Frank Rist was immensely popular in both games, and many young Essex players who subsequently made the grade and, indeed, many of those who did not, remain indebted to him for the start he gave them. For some years now he has been a director of a highly successful business in the sale of sports goods.

At this time consideration was being given to developing the Chelmsford ground, recently purchased for the sum of £15,000. One or two friends of the Club were invited to assist. Barry East, chairman of Town & City Properties, an Essex member and a very keen sports enthusiast, offered outstandingly generous help which continued for some years. Not only did he guarantee and pay the interest on the Club's overdraft, but he made arrangements for the design and construction of the new pavilion on very advantageous terms – and all without any public recognition. Together with the Warwickshire Supporters' Association, he helped the Club through a very awkward financial situation brought about by a succession of annual deficits. At the same time it would be right to acknowledge the support of Barclays Bank, which provided an overdraft facility which was above and beyond the normal call of duty.

CHAPTER 15

Tonker: 1967–73

By 1960 cricket in England was at a low ebb. A dullness had seized the game in spite of the efforts of counties like Essex to provide brighter cricket, and serious financial problems had to be overcome if the game was to survive. The state of affairs motivated a decade of radical reform which was to revitalise the game while leaving its fabric and institutions intact.

With the distinction between amateur and professional player in first-class cricket being abolished in 1963 Trevor Bailey was, in fact, the last amateur captain of Essex. The same year saw the introduction of the first limited-over competition, a 60-over knock-out tournament initially sponsored by Gillette. Two years later, the Imperial Cricket Conference became the International Cricket Conference, and in 1967, the Cricketers' Association was formed.

In 1969 the John Player League, the Sunday afternoon 40-over competition, came into being, and in 1972 the Benson and Hedges Cup was inaugurated. Where, for more than a century, there had been only one trophy to win in the first-class game, counties now had four competitions in which to participate each summer. For Essex, as for many others, the changes came just in time. But for the boost provided by sponsorship, the Club may well have faced extinction in 1965 and 1966, when the balance sheet recorded substantial losses.

In 1966, the festivals at Leyton, Westcliff, Colchester, Clacton, Ilford and Brentwood had all run at a loss; only Southend and Romford had shown an income greater than expenditure. When Brian Taylor took over as captain the Club was said to be almost 'dead and buried'. In truth, the crisis had been going on for 80 years and this was simply the climax.

As mentioned earlier, the 1966 season had seen one interesting innovation which was later to prove financially rewarding, namely Essex became the first County to introduce Sunday play in a championship match. Ilford was the venue, and the weather on Sunday 15 May was fine. John Woodcock recorded the event in *The Times*:

> If the first objective of first-class cricket on Sundays is to make it more accessible to the public, the experiment got away to a notable start at Ilford yesterday. For the second day of their match with Somerset, Essex had one of their largest home crowds for years. The cricket itself was less auspicious.
>
> It was a pleasant family scene, mother being there with the best of them to see whether it was all worth while. The ground, set in a park, was a congenial place for the outing, and the afternoon was warm and sunny.

However successful this one day in the sun at Ilford had been, the fact remained that on an estimated income of between £31,000 and £32,000 a year, Essex were spending £39,000. That was way above even Mr Micawber's recipe for misery. To add to the financial woes that surrounded the Club was the fact that Barry Knight, the leading all-rounder in the country, had stated that he would not play for Essex again.

On 26 May 1967, Knight was refused special registration for Leicestershire since Essex had made it plain that they required his services. Knight reiterated his intention of playing for Leicestershire and had to serve the 12-month period of qualification. He gained special permission to play in a championship match for Leicestershire on 15 May 1968, one day ahead of the end of his registration period. He emigrated to Australia in 1969.

Trevor Bailey had believed that Knight should succeed him as captain and knew that the all-rounder would leave if Taylor were made captain and he was asked to play under him. Bailey felt, with some justification, that Essex could not afford to lose one who was, in fact, their best player. Tom Pearce, with that wisdom and geniality which has been one of the Club's greatest assets, comments: 'If a cricketer will only play if he's captain, then he's not the man to be captain.' Perhaps Knight, older and wiser now, would feel today that he was wrong. Bailey, an unquenchable, unashamed enthusiast for Essex cricket, has never hidden his

49. *Brian Taylor, appointed to succeed Trevor Bailey in 1966, was Essex's first professional captain. He took over a side of mainly young players which was to form the nucleus of the successful team of the late 1970s and the 1980s.*

admiration for the work that Taylor did in his years as captain of the County and now applauds the foresight of the Committee.

Few captains can ever have taken office in more difficult circumstances than Brian Taylor. He was 35 years old, a hard-hitting left-handed batsman and a wicket-keeper, who had, perhaps, never quite realised his early promise. An *Evening News* colt, he had first played for Essex in 1949 and had gained a regular place in the side, as a batsman, in 1954. In 1956, as noted earlier, he was voted 'Best Young Cricketer of the Year' and the following winter, he went to South Africa with the MCC side as understudy to Godfrey Evans. But Murray, Parks and Knott were to be Evans's successors, and Taylor was never to play Test cricket. Few would have considered him to be one of the game's great tacticians, yet those closest to the Club recognised in him qualities which were to prove invaluable to Essex cricket in the years that followed his appointment as captain, years that were to help shape the success that has attended the County since 1979.

There was no immediate revival in Taylor's first year of captaincy. Indeed it was a most difficult time. Only three championship matches were won, and Essex finished 15th. In the Gillette Cup, they were easily beaten by Kent in their first game. Morale was not high, but, as *Wisden* pointed out: 'It had, however, to be remembered that the County were engaged in an almost constant battle against adversity.'

As well as the dispute with Knight, Essex were weakened by the mid-season departure of Rodney Cass, who had just hit a maiden first-class century and had relieved Taylor of the wicket-keeping duties for much of the season. The season also saw the end of Trevor Bailey's distinguished career, and it was marked by a testimonial that was granted to him in his last year. Another who was to play his last game for Essex in 1967 was John Wilcox.

Never to make the mark on the field that his most accomplished father had done, John Wilcox was, nevertheless, a greater contributor to Essex cricket than can be measured by his 596 runs. He is the present head-master of Alleyn Court School, Westcliff-on-Sea, which, importantly for the future of Essex cricket, in January 1950, hosted the first three-day training course for coaches to be held in England.

The course was inspired by Essex County Cricket Club and the Central Society of Physical Recreation, and it received wide coverage from the press, Movietone Cinema News and BBC radio, so revolutionary was it in concept. Many giants of the game were present – Harry Altham, G O Allen, Alf Gover, Billy Griffith, Patsy Hendren – and the course did much to emphasise another area in which Essex were pioneers and which was to play a vital part in the development of the County Club.

Five years after this momentous event at Alleyn Court School, the Ilford Indoor Cricket School in Beehive Lane, near Gant's Hill, was opened. Trevor Bailey was the link between the two ventures, for he was a founder member of the Ilford School and is still actively concerned, but the prime motivator in the project was Harold Faragher, who has coached there for many years. Faragher could well have had a successful first-class career but for his teaching commitments.

The Ilford School has never been a major financial success, but the service it has done for Essex cricket at all levels is considerable. It has helped the County Club to stretch its tentacles down into clubs and schools and tap their resources. The debt that Essex County Cricket Club owes to the Ilford School is undeniable, not simply in terms of the number of players like Gooch, Lilley, Gladwin, David East, Lever and others who have graduated to the County side, but in terms of the facilities and guidance, through the coaching of Bill Morris, that were offered to the County Club before the school at Chelmsford was developed.

The first fruits were seen in Taylor's first year as captain, 1967, when John Lever made his debut. He 'created a favourable impression and deserved better figures' in a year which was easy for no one. *Wisden* reserved judgment, and was apprehensive of Taylor's leadership:

> Taylor did not satisfy everybody with his handling of the side, and certainly more than one of his declarations proved difficult to understand; but he probably profited from experience during his first season as captain.

It was a year of containment and regrouping, of taking stock of the situation and discovering where and how the County could rebuild. Taylor's first year as leader coincided with the return of county cricket to the Chelmsford ground in New Writtle Street, and it was here that the Club decided to make its base. The ground was purchased and a pavilion was erected, the first in a series of building projects in the past 20 years which has transformed the County Ground.

On the playing side 1967 also brought changes. Keith Boyce made his first appearance in the county championship and David Acfield impressed with his off-spin when he was available after the end of term at Cambridge.

Keith David Boyce was a natural cricketer whom Trevor Bailey had discovered before he had made any mark in West Indian cricket. A lively fast bowler, an electrifying batsman and a thrilling fielder, he became an instant favourite at Essex and came close to completing the 'double' in his first season. Perhaps more than anyone in 1967, he gave the first hint of the revitalisation of Essex cricket, but, in spite of a sensational victory over the champions, Yorkshire, at Scarborough in August when Essex won by nine runs after being bowled out for 87 in their first innings, the revival was still a little way off.

In 1968, Essex won five matches and rose by one place in the championship. The retirement of Mike Bear through injury was compensated for by the re-engagement of Stuart Turner, and the arrival of Lee Irvine, the first overseas player to be signed by Essex under the new immediate registration ruling.

Counties responded rather sluggishly to this ruling, and, arguably, only Nottinghamshire and Lancashire were fully awake to its wider implications and benefits. Essex were, of course, governed by financial restrictions, and they chose to register a little known batsman from Natal rather than an expensive established Test player.

Lee Irvine proved to be an excellent acquisition, although he was to play only two seasons with the County. A trim figure, he was a gloriously free left-handed batsman and a fine fielder who was also a capable wicket-keeper. Like Boyce, he provided a spark that Essex needed, and although he did not hit a century in his first season, he scored 1439 runs, average 32.70, and hit more sixes, 26, than any other batsman in English cricket.

There was always excitement when he was at the crease, and Essex cricket was beginning to reassert its brighter character.

This was never more apparent than in the victory over Glamorgan at the beginning of Ilford week. Essex were 185 for 7 when Robin Hobbs joined Stuart Turner. They flogged the visiting attack mercilessly, and in two hours, added 192. It was Turner's first retort to those who had believed that he wasn't good enough. Like Hobbs, he hit a maiden first-class hundred, and Hobbs went on to take seven wickets as Essex won by an innings. It was characteristic of Essex that, of their five victories, two should be against two of the top three counties, champions Yorkshire and Glamorgan.

The vitality of the side was reflected in the fielding, which was as good as any in the country, and there was a gathering urgency throughout the county. Fletcher rediscovered his best form and regained his place in the Test side, but there were still threats and problems. The standard of wickets in the county was generally low and that at Southchurch Park, Southend, was condemned.

The Club fell at the first hurdle in the Gillette Cup once again, and, as *Wisden* pointed out: 'Limited financial and playing resources again told against the County and once more injuries imposed an additional heavy handicap. Indeed, there were times when little more than a bare team was available.' The Club lost £500, and, seemingly, the financial problem would not go away.

The 'economies' sub-committee began to apply ruthless measures. Jack Insole, Douglas's father, instigated a system of redemption of Green Shield stamps, and there was a surge of other fund-raising activities. The staff was cut back and 2nd XI cricket was reduced, although 1969 was to see the first appearance in this side of G A Gooch, not yet in the Ilford first team; he neither batted nor bowled in his first match.

For Doug Insole, the one who proved to be the leader in the financial recovery was Alfred George 'Tiny' Waterman, who had played for the County as a medium-pace bowler and hard-hitting batsman in 1937 and 1938. A businessman of great experience, Waterman was uncompromising in his attitude to the financial situation. 'He was completely firm,' says Insole. 'He insisted that there was no deviation from our planned economies and that we must not exceed the budget. He was unrelenting, and in a few years, we had built up a reserve.'

The immediate and stringent economy was that Brian Taylor was to operate with a staff of just 12, including himself. This was one of the bravest and most severe measures inflicted upon a county club, yet it is from this time, 1969, that the Essex recovery and ultimate rise to glory should be dated.

It would be well to name first the 'magnificent twelve'. They were Brian Taylor, Brian Edmeades, Lee Irvine, Robin Hobbs and Ray East, all of whom played in each one of the 26 matches, Keith Fletcher, Keith Boyce, Gordon Barker, Brian Ward, Stuart Turner, John Lever and David Acfield. Michael Boyers, one match, and Howard Sherman, three matches, filled in during the course of the season. When it is considered that this was the first season in which the players were also asked to compete in the Sunday League and that Essex rose to sixth in the championship with eight wins, the immensity of the achievements of these 12 players can be seen.

The initial impetus for the Essex revival came from successes in the John Player League. It is no secret that the players regarded this Sunday venture with some scepticism at first, but, as Stuart Turner said later: 'We won a couple of matches, and we suddenly thought that we could do well in this league, and it became important to us because crowds of people turned up to watch.'

It was Turner who played an important part in Essex's first victory in the League, at Chelmsford, on Sunday, 27 April 1969. The opponents were Nottinghamshire, and against Sobers, Forbes, Taylor and Halfyard, Essex slumped to 67 for 6. In 15 overs, Turner and Edmeades then added 92. Turner hit three sixes and three fours in a violent assault on the bowling. Edmeades hit 45, and Turner 48, and Essex reached 185 for 9 in their 40 overs. Little could people have realised then that Turner had embarked on a Sunday league record which was to make him the first player to take 300 wickets and score 3000 runs in the competition. Neither could they have known that when John Lever bowled White he had begun the haul which was to make him the first player to reach 300 wickets in the league.

Essex won the match by 37 runs, but the keynote to their victory was neither batting nor bowling, but breathtaking fielding. Sobers, Hassan and Murray were all run out by direct throws from Irvine, Fletcher and Turner respectively. This was exhilarating stuff, and Essex were to set a pattern in the field which became the envy of others.

A week later, Essex overwhelmed the one-day specialists Lancashire, at Chelmsford. Brian Ward, a most reliable opening batsman, hit the first Essex fifty in the competition, and he was quickly followed by Irvine and Boyce.

Derbyshire were beaten in a 16-over slog at Derby, and it was not until the fourth match, against Worcestershire, at Harlow, that Essex tasted defeat on a Sunday, and then by only one run. Worcestershire struggled painfully against Ray East, who took 5 for 18, but they were revived by Rodney Cass, who was to do well against his old county in the next few years, and scored 151 for 9 in 39 overs. After Ward had gone cheaply, Brian Taylor and Gordon Barker appeared to have put Essex in a winning position, but the last nine wickets fell for 99 and the game ended when Ray East and John Lever, who had come together with 6 needed for victory, attempted to draw level off the last ball only for East to be run out – the shape of things to come.

Essex shrugged off this defeat and 8000 packed into Valentine's Park on 15 June to see them beat Middlesex. Yorkshire, Leicestershire and Kent were beaten, but a narrow defeat at Somerset halted the challenge, and Essex had to be satisfied with third place at the end of the season, one win separating them from top of the table Lancashire.

In the Gillette Cup, they did better than ever before. Comfortable wins over Wiltshire and Warwickshire were followed by defeat at the hands of Nottinghamshire in the quarter-final by two wickets with two balls to spare.

The championship season had started indifferently, but at Ilford all went well. There was a terrible débâcle at Brentwood on 21 and 22 May when Essex (v Kent), caught on a drying wicket, were bowled out for 34 in their second innings. Norman Graham took 8 for 20. Essex, having led by 50 on the first innings, Acfield and East thriving, lost by nine wickets. The second match of the week, against Worcestershire, was drawn, and this was the last first-class match to be played on the old county ground.

Defeat at Bristol was followed by a win at Cambridge, but Essex arrived at Valentine's Park in mid-June without a win in the Championship. There seemed no sign that their luck would change when Hampshire, leading by four in the first innings, reduced Essex to 86 for 5 in the second. Then came Keith Boyce. He reached a maiden century in three hours, hit 21 fours and finished with 147 not out. He and Lever added 97 for the ninth wicket, of which Lever scored 17. Ray East and Robin Hobbs bowled Hants out for 170, and Essex won by 124 runs.

For ten years, the sight of Keith Boyce batting, bowling or fielding for Essex was one of the glories of the game. He was supple and electric. He would coil into a ball and explode as he unwound. The crowds thrilled to his physical movement because his every gesture suggested urgency and an imperative need to win the game. Although he was to claim a regular place in the Barbados side and, belatedly, to be given the Test place he richly deserved, he never ceased to be an Essex man, and his commitment to the County to his last, and beyond his last, match was total.

In the second half of the Ilford week, Essex led Nottinghamshire by five in the first innings, but a strained muscle deprived Essex of Boyce's services as a bowler in the Nottinghamshire second innings, and the home side were left the formidable task of scoring 302 to win. At 173 for 5, the task looked hopeless, but Boyce helped Irvine in a stand of 79, which meant that 50 were needed from the last 13 overs. Only 11 of them were needed as Irvine took the game by the throat and, although unwell, hit 82 not out. The last of his 12 boundaries was the winning hit.

On 1 September, he hit his only century for Essex, 109 against Glamorgan at Swansea. This was the most thrilling game of the season. Irvine's century came in $3\frac{1}{4}$ hours and included 17 fours. With Taylor, who made 70, he took Essex to a first innings lead of 95. Tony Lewis's declaration left Essex two hours in which to score 190, a challenge which was not likely to be refused. Essex went boldly for the runs and maintained the necessary scoring rate. Fletcher, Taylor and Boyce fell while 8 runs were scored, but Hobbs and Barker still kept up the race. With two overs remaining, 16 were needed. The last over began with seven wanted for victory. Roger Davis's first three balls were each played for singles, but Barker was beaten by the fourth and stumped. Essex needed three to win off the last ball with their last pair, East and Lever, together. Lever slashed at Davis, and the ball sped to third man, where Wheatley picked up and threw as Lever turned for the second run, which would have tied the match. The batsman was beaten by yards, and Glamorgan had won by one run. It was the nearest that they had come to defeat in the whole of the season, and three days later they were crowned as champions.

A fortnight after this game, in a draw at Dover, Irvine played his last game for Essex, scoring 32 and 18 not out. He was contracted to play a third season, but, in any case, was likely to have been in the South African party that was due to tour England. That tour never took place, and Irvine did not return. Like Boyce, Francis, McEwan and Phillip, he came to Essex as something of an unknown and left them as a Test player. His time with the County was brief, but he had helped to kindle a spark that was to glow into a fire in the coming years.

In 1969, as in his first season, Irvine scored 1000 runs in championship matches, a feat that was also accomplished by Brian Edmeades, but the achievements of 1969 were essentially those of a team effort. *Wisden* classed it as a vintage season, and in every sense it was. Although nothing had been won, there was joy in the county, and for the first time since the end of the Second World War, there was a profit registered. It totalled £4000, and it marked the beginning of a new era in which every season has seen the County's finances healthy and stable. From 1969 onwards, the emergency meetings that had plagued Green and Douglas in the previous 80 years were to become a misty memory.

With the interest-free loan of £15,000 from the Warwickshire County Cricket Supporters' Association, Essex began work on the new pavilion at Chelmsford, which dates from 1970. It was, indeed, the dawning of a new age in Essex cricket.

The very crisis which had reduced the Essex staff to 12 players had, in fact, given the Club its strength. A small group had been brought together in adversity, and the reduction in their numbers had helped to

50. *Allan Border* (Clive Tarling)

51. *Bruce Francis* (Evening Echo)

Two Australians who played briefly for Essex.

52. *Keith Boyce*

53. *Norbert Phillip*

Two West Indians whose stay with the County was considerably longer.

54. *Lee Irvine* (Sport & General)

55. *Ken McEwan*

56. *Joe Milner* (Sport & General)

Essex has had three South African players in recent years. Joe Milner spent five years with the County from 1957, and Lee Irvine two years, 1968–69. Ken McEwan's stay was much longer, and during his career of 12 years he amassed 18,088 runs.

forge a unity and a spirit which was not bettered anywhere in the country. Equally as important for the future was that the responsibility and work heaped upon young players helped them to develop their talents to the full.

John Lever's Test career was to begin in December 1976, but he has never hidden the debt he feels he owes to those first years on the staff when he was forced to bowl, think and learn day after day. He was able to practise and hone his art, and test and perfect it in the hardest possible school.

What debt, too, do the mature players of the 1980s and the Club as a whole owe to Brian Taylor? 'Tonker', as he became known, had no illusions about the task that confronted him when he took over the captaincy. There have been better cricketers than Brian Taylor, better tactical and more knowledgeable captains, but few have accomplished as much in county cricket. His reaction to the plight of the County when he took over as captain was: 'There is now only one direction Essex can go – up!'

He was entrusted with a group of talented, promising, but mostly untried and untested young men, and he taught them to be professional cricketers. He insisted on standards of dress, tie and blazer, and he insisted on standards of fitness. He had played professional football, still referees, and has always exuded health and radiance. No theorist, nor great tactician, he believed that whatever Essex's limitations and inexperiences in batting and bowling, they would bow to none in the field. He instigated a course of pre-season physical training which frogmarched professional cricket onto a level comparable with other sports. It was rigorous, even austere, and at first other counties found it amusing, but soon some were moved to imitate it. Professional cricket still lags behind many other professional sports in terms of the fitness of its players, but that physical training is seen in any way as an important part of the game is due, in part at least, to Brian Taylor.

Under Taylor, Essex became the most exciting fielding side in the country. 'We run like mad,' said 'Tonker', but what they also did, under his guidance, was work for and help each other. If somebody was struggling in any department of the game, then others were encouraged to help him, and it was this sense of loyalty which took Essex through one of the most difficult periods in the Club's history.

The unity of the side, the loyalty to each other and the physical fitness were perhaps best combined in the running between the wickets. This became one of the most exciting features of Essex cricket in the 1970s. To see Boyce, Turner, Lever or Fletcher sprinting between the wickets, stealing threes where others would have settled long since for twos, was a wonderful sight. It seemed to epitomise the whole character of Essex cricket, the desire to entertain and hopefully to win in the process of so doing, but winning, making that final transition from glorious crowd-pleasers to title-holders and cup-winners, was to prove the last and most difficult hurdle.

Irvine failed to return in 1970 so that Essex were without an overseas player, but Graham Saville rejoined the County as a batsman wiser and technically sounder for his years with Norfolk and the Minor Counties. Another to reappear in 1970 was Eddie Presland.

A fine club cricketer, but better known as a professional footballer with West Ham United and Crystal Palace, Presland was one of those whose cricket was squeezed out because of the increasing length and demands of the soccer season. One of Doug Insole's fiercest contentions, and he himself is a soccer man, is that the excesses of professional football have robbed first-class cricket of some fine players, for it is no longer possible, as it was with Compton, Watson and Milton, to follow both professions. Essex engaged Geoff Hurst for a time and offered terms to Bobby Moore, but football swallowed them up.

The 1970 season began well enough. At Taunton, in May, Essex were 67 for 6, but Stuart Turner hit 121 out of 163 in three hours, the highest score of his career, and Somerset were fortunate to draw in the end.

Turner's century, one of 25 hit in first-class cricket in May 1970, prompted Ted Dexter in the *Sunday Mirror* to focus his attention on Turner and Essex. Turner explained how he had learned to play back, and Gordon Barker told how the senior players had tried to encourage Turner to get closer to the stumps when he bowled to improve his line. This was symptomatic of the help and enthusiasm that was generating from the County, and Dexter saw Essex as 'an up and coming cricket force East of London'. Dexter explained:

> Major Brown, the secretary-cum-major-domo of Essex, who is quite likely to be seen putting on the covers, marshalling the cars, doing the books and cajoling the team all in the space of one hour, is confident of another good year.
>
> 'We are off to a good start,' he said. 'The present formula of fixtures is working out well for us.'
>
> 'Though it is hard keeping up with all the innovations, far be it from me to complain if they continue to bring the lively cricket we have had so far.'

Essex was exuding a sense of energy, and although the lively start was not quite maintained, the season again proved highly satisfactory. Fletcher, Taylor, Saville, Edmeades and Barker all passed 1000 runs, and John Lever, sent in as night-watchman against Glamorgan at Cardiff, hit 91. Glamorgan were to finish second in the championship. Harold Faragher once said of Lever that had he applied himself to his batting, he could have been another Trevor Bailey. This is probably true, for Lever has always been a very useful batsman coming in late in an innings and he was to make a fifty on his Test debut, but arguably he has given so much to Essex with his tireless bowling and consistently fine fielding that there was little time left for batting.

Essex slipped to 12th in the championship, but the drop was not as serious as it might first seem, for rain robbed the side of two victories which would have left them in the same position as the previous season.

True to character, Essex gained a remarkable victory over the champions, Kent, at Tunbridge Wells. Lever and Boyce, who bowled rather too many no-balls during the season, began the match in sensational fashion, sending back Johnson, Woolmer and Nicholls with only five scored. Asif Iqbal, Colin Cowdrey and Leary revived, Kent who reached 250. Essex passed this score with only two wickets down. Taylor began at a blistering rate and hit 66 of an opening stand of 98 with Edmeades. Edmeades, who had established himself as a most consistent and effective opening batsman, went on to make 80, and he shared a second wicket stand, also of 98, with Saville.

Taylor declared with a lead of 72, but Colin Cowdrey hit a fine century and John Shepherd hit some lusty blows to put Kent back in contention. Cowdrey's declaration left Essex two hours in which to score 206.

Taylor and Edmeades gave Essex a sound start, but the impetus to the innings came from Fletcher, who hit two sixes and five fours as he raced to 75 in 88 minutes. He fell to Dye, but Presland and Hobbs scored the last 27 runs required and took Essex to victory off the second ball of the last over.

Kent gained their revenge ten days later in the second match of the only first-class cricket week allocated to Harlow. In the first match, Saville and Taylor scored centuries in the innings win over Cambridge University, but in the second it was Mike Denness's 167 not out which paved the way for Kent's innings victory.

Hobbs, with 90 wickets, was top of the Essex bowling averages, and in an outstanding fielding side, his work often shone. Boyce did not enjoy a good season with the bat, but he took 87 wickets and was a threat to the best of batsmen. Turner, winning a regular place in the side for the first time, bowled his brisk medium pace consistently and finished with 65 championship wickets. Acfield, who won a Gold Medal for fencing at the Commonwealth Games in Edinburgh, also grew in confidence and ability during the season, and with Ray East and John Lever performing well, a balanced and most effective attack, backed by excellent fielding, was shaping.

The John Player League saw Essex begin poorly, but recover to finish in fourth place. There was a sense of optimism, a feeling that the side was growing and developing, that honours were close at hand. Five players, Acfield, Lever, Saville, Turner and Ward, were capped during the season, perhaps representing the increasing maturity.

In August, Essex entertained the touring Jamaican side in a first-class match at Leyton. The County fielded a rather motley team, Sadiq Mohammad, Gloucestershire and Pakistan, making his solitary appearance for Essex, but it did mark the debut of Keith Pont, who was 17 years old and another product of Essex schools.

Pont's county championship debut was to come in August the following year, a year which was to be a most gratifying one for the County. It also was to mark the retirement, after 21 years as president of the County Club, of Sir Hubert Ashton, who had served Essex so faithfully. He was succeeded by Tom Pearce.

The second overseas player to be engaged on immediate registration joined the staff at the beginning of the 1971 season. Little was known of Bruce Francis, but he soon showed that he was an enterprising batsman in the best Essex tradition and he quickly became a favourite.

He began the season in the middle order of the batting, but he prospered more when being promoted to opening, where his aggressive style contrasted sharply with the more patient and often dour Brian Ward. Edmeades missed the first part of the season with an eye injury, but he returned to partner Francis, and they offered a thrustful beginning to an innings.

The season started most encouragingly with four wins in the first seven matches, but this form was not maintained, and Essex finished tenth in the table. In the first match of the season, against Surrey at The Oval, Turner took 4 for 54 in the second innings and bowled Storey, and had Long and Jackman caught behind to perform the hat-trick, a feat that went almost unnoticed and was certainly unrecorded in the *Essex Handbook*.

In the first home match, against Glamorgan at Chelmsford, Keith Fletcher hit 164 not out while at Hove, Francis scored 94 and 121 not out, but the main focus of attention was on the John Player League and the Gillette Cup.

The first seven matches of the John Player League were won, and Essex stood firmly at the top of the table. At The Oval, Keith Boyce hit a magnificent 98 off 54 balls in 50 minutes. The West Indian hit seven sixes and 11 fours, and he and Gordon Barker put on 128 for the fifth wicket. Barker finished on 71 not out, and Surrey were beaten by 22 runs. Barker followed this with 87 not out against Nottinghamshire at Chelmsford, but the honour of the first century to be hit by an Essex batsman in the John Player League went to Brian Taylor.

At Buxton, on 23 May, the match was restricted to 30 overs, but Taylor gave a disciplined display of clean, controlled hitting to reach 100 off

81 balls in 95 minutes. Bruce Francis equalled the feat in the next match when Lancashire were beaten at Old Trafford.

When Northamptonshire came to Ilford the match was all over in two hours, 13 minutes. Boyce took 4 for 10 in eight overs, and the visitors were out for 45, the lowest score recorded in the competition at that time. Essex won by ten wickets.

The first set-back did not come until Dexter inspired a Sussex win at Harlow on 4 July, and this was the first of three defeats in a row, as Somerset won narrowly at Westcliff and Worcestershire won comfortably at Worcester. The slide was halted with wins at Bristol and Bradford. Then came two more set-backs at a most critical time, at the hands of Hampshire and Leicestershire.

This left Essex with two matches to play, both of which had to be won if they were to stay in contention for the title. The first game was at Purfleet, and Kent were beaten somewhat fortuitously.

The pitch was helpful to seam bowlers, and Essex struggled against Graham, Dye, Julien and Shepherd so that they were 72 for 4 after 28 overs. A violent stand of 61 in seven overs between Taylor and Boyce lifted spirits, but four wickets fell for two runs so that the final score of 149 for 9 looked anything but convincing. Kent found runs equally difficult, although they began solidly with an opening stand of 28. Acfield dismissed Denness and Ealham, Boyce had the robust Nicholls caught and Turner bowled Shepherd. With Kent on 46 for 4 in 16.5 overs, the rain arrived and Essex won with a faster scoring rate.

This brought Warwickshire to Chelmsford for the last match of the season, and a consistent batting display gave Essex a comfortable victory.

Essex had now completed their fixtures with 44 points and a run rate of 4.519. Lancashire, the reigning champions, were four points behind with a superior run rate and one match to play, and Worcestershire were also four points behind with a game to play. Lancashire were favourites to retain the title, but their final match was to be played a fortnight after Essex's victory over Warwickshire.

By chance, Worcestershire also met Warwickshire in their final match. A record crowd of 10,000 attended the game at Worcester and saw the home side bowl out Warwickshire for 126 in 37 overs. To win the match was a simple task, but to beat Essex, Worcestershire had to reach their target in 17.5 overs. They lost Stimpson and Yardley for ten, but Headley played a sparkling knock, and the crucial stand was when he and Ormrod hit 55 off 30 balls. Both were dismissed, as were Holder and Wilcock, but Griffith and Wilkinson scrambled the last four runs to give Worcestershire victory in 17.3 overs.

The next week, Lancashire lost to Glamorgan in front of 30,000 people at Old Trafford, and Worcestershire were John Player League champions, having beaten Essex by .003 on run rate. It was the closest Essex had ever come to winning a title, and the frustration was very hard to bear.

That frustration had brought out strong emotions in the Gillette Cup. The first round saw Bedfordshire well beaten at Chelmsford when Brian Ward and Bruce Francis began the match with a stand of 149 in 35 overs. Ward made 101, and Francis 87. Glamorgan were the victims in the second round, Bruce Francis again prominent with an innings of 72.

In the quarter-final, at Chelmsford, Lancashire, the holders, were the visitors. It was a match of great passion.

The crowd was estimated at 8000 although there was a general feeling that many more had found their way into the ground, for, until this time, no game since the war had roused greater interest. Bond won the toss and elected to bat first on a good wicket in excellent weather. He could not have expected what was to follow. Wood was bowled by Boyce, and Pilling was caught behind off the same bowler. Lancashire were 2 for 2. Clive Lloyd joined David Lloyd in a slow stand which set about to repair the innings. With the score on 16, the batsmen were involved in a terrible mix-up which left both at one end of the wicket. To this day, the Essex players insist that Clive Lloyd was the batsman who should have been out, but it was David Lloyd who went to the pavilion.

Clive Lloyd was the only batsman to show any control of the Essex attack. Sullivan was bowled by Boyce for ten, and Engineer was bowled by Lever for nought. Jack Bond fell to East for three, and Lancashire, 59 for 6, were in deep trouble. Simmons and Hughes gave Lloyd the assistance that he had lacked in the earlier part of his innings, and stands of 91 and 23 changed the nature of the match. Clive Lloyd reached his century with a six over square-leg before being caught and bowled by Turner. His 109 had been made out of 171 scored while he was at the wicket. Hughes and Shuttleworth played some extravagant shots, and Lancashire finished on 203 for 9 from their 60 overs.

It was not a massive target for Essex to chase, but they were still lacking in experience compared to their opponents, who had dominated the one-day game in the late 60s and early 70s. Essex could not have begun worse. Inside eight overs, they lost Ward, Francis and Taylor with only 17 scored. Much depended on Fletcher, who finished second to Boycott in the national averages in 1971, and he promised much as he saw off the opening threat of Lever and Shuttleworth, but he was spectacularly caught by Engineer off Hughes, and Essex, 34 for 4, looked beaten.

Boyce was always enterprising, and he now found a steady and reliable partner in Saville. They added 51 before Saville was run out, the pressure mounting to increase the scoring rate. At 112, Boyce tried a drive at Shuttleworth and was caught behind. This brought Turner and Hobbs together in a last ditch stand.

In 13 courageous overs, they added 74, and the Essex crowd scented a great victory, but Peter Lever and Ken Shuttleworth returned, and for Essex, the worst possible thing happened – both batsmen were out at the same total, 186. This left Ray East, John Lever and David Acfield three overs in which to score 18 runs.

It was a task that was beyond them, and Lancashire squeezed to victory by 12 runs when Hughes had Ray East caught by David Lloyd off the second ball of the 60th over.

So 1971 was a year of frustration, but it was also a year when, for the first time, Essex had challenged strongly in all competitions. The season also marked the last in first-class cricket of Gordon Barker. It was fitting that, in his last season, he should finish first in the national averages for the John Player League with 449 runs, average 56.12. He was 40 years old and had played for Essex for 17 years, appearing in 444 matches and scoring well over 20,000 runs. He was the mainstay of the Essex batting for several years, a particularly fine hooker and cutter. There are some outside the county who would suggest that he was too easily satisfied, but this was far from the truth. He was one of the great talkers on the game, constantly self-critical and self-analytical. He was unfortunate in that he played most of his career at a time when Essex were struggling. He would have adorned any championship side.

Barker became coach at Felsted where he has been a great success, but he is often to be seen at Chelmsford, a Yorkshireman whose first love is Essex.

The form of 1971 did not appear to have lasted into the following season. The new Benson and Hedges Cup competition saw Essex lose all four matches in the zonal round, and there was no victory in the county championship until the beginning of June, when Somerset were beaten at Colchester. This was the last match to be played at the Garrison Ground.

Somerset won the toss and batted, but John Lever's 5 for 42 saw them declare at 239 for 9. In spite of losing Saville with a badly damaged finger, Essex took a first innings lead of 11, and Turner then returned what were at the time his best figures in first-class cricket, 5 for 39, and Somerset were out for 116. Fletcher's 70 not out took Essex to their first championship win of the season. There were always worries about the Castle Park ground after the flooding experiences of the early 1960s, but the Garrison Ground had failed to provide the crowds that had been anticipated, and the next Colchester venue was a reversion to Castle Park.

There were reasons for Essex's lack of early season form, notably the absence of Francis with the Australian touring side and the inexperience of Pont, who was brought in to replace him, but there were other factors. Brian Ward's form declined, and following a bad thumb injury at the beginning of 1973, he left the Club and emigrated to Argentina where his wife had been born. He was to reappear in England in the ICC Trophy in 1979, batting rather dourly for his adopted country. Brian Taylor also showed a major loss of form, particularly with the bat and, to some degree, behind the stumps.

For 'Tonker', 1972 marked the beginning of the end. When Essex went to Maidstone to play Kent on 8, 10 and 11 July, he was out of the side through injury, and Keith Fletcher led Essex for the first time. It was the first championship match Taylor had missed since he had come into the side on 17 May 1961, for the game against Middlesex at Lord's. During that time he made 301 consecutive appearances in county championship matches, a record for Essex. His deputy in the match at Maidstone in which Fletcher hit a century was the Brentwood wicket-keeper Richard Baker. It was to be his sole appearance in the county championship.

That Taylor was aware that his career was drawing to a close was obvious from his report for the season in which he spoke of his own position as being one that was being considered, 'for the time is now coming when we should find a replacement to be ready to take over when the time is right'.

To be balanced against the decline of Taylor and Ward, and the moderate bowling form of Hobbs and East, was the continued excellence of Fletcher, the steadiness of Edmeades, the solidity of Saville and the continued development of John Lever. Boyce, too, enjoyed a magnificent season and came close to the 'double', while Ray East showed much improvement as a batsman, hitting 89 not out against Worcestershire at Leyton, on 9 August.

Essex had begun well in this match with Saville scoring 92 and the second wicket not falling until the score was 124. Holder then brought about a collapse which saw eight wickets fall for 62 runs, but East and Lever, 21, added 89 for the last wicket.

A fortnight later, Essex gained what was undoubtedly their best Championship win of the season and one of the most remarkable by any county. Yorkshire were the visitors to Chelmsford, and Taylor put them in when he won the toss. Boycott, missed early on, scored 121, and Yorkshire declared at 285 for 6. Essex stumbled in reply, but Boyce and Pont, in a ferocious assault on the bowling, put on 121 in 69 minutes. Taylor and Turner added 51, and Essex declared three runs in arrears.

Boycott survived a confident appeal in the first over of the Yorkshire second innings and went on to make 86 before declaring at 239 for 5 and leaving Essex 168 minutes in which to score 243 runs. It was not the most generous of declarations, and, in the heat of battle, remarks had been passed between the two sides which tended to raise the temperature of the match.

The Essex challenge began hesitantly. Edmeades, Saville and Ward were out with only 37 scored, and the first 50 took 77 valuable minutes. At this point Keith Fletcher took over, playing what one of his team-mates described as 'the greatest innings it has ever been my privilege to watch'. To the anger of Essex supporters, Fletcher played in only one Test in 1972, when his form and quality were far superior to that of some who had played in several matches. His innings against Yorkshire on Tuesday 22 August gave positive indication that here was a very great batsman who should have held a permanent place in the England side. When the last 20 overs began Essex still needed 154 to win, but Fletcher had embarked on a partnership with Boyce which realised 114. Boyce made 46, and when he was caught, driving mightily at Nicholson, Essex needed 92 in 9.4 overs.

Fletcher's next partner was Keith Pont, who relished such a situation. He hit a six and five fours, and he and Fletcher scored 95 runs in 34 minutes, 7.2 overs. Pont finished with 38, Fletcher with 139 not out which included four sixes and 12 fours.

Essex won at Swansea in their next championship match. It was their sixth win, and lifted them to fifth place, the highest position that they had held since 1957.

The John Player League record mirrored the championship form, for only three victories in the first eight matches blunted the Essex challenge, but a strong finish, which saw seven wins in the last eight matches, took them to third place in the table and to prize money. The penultimate match, at Worcester, was won when Boyce finished the match with a six, but the ground work was done by Brian Ward, who made his highest score in the competition, bowled Gifford for 99.

Yet for all this promise and entertainment there was still nothing to show in the way of trophies, and there was a creeping belief that joyful as Essex cricket might be, it was never going to win anything. Critics pointed to the Gillette Cup competition to support their argument.

Essex drew a bye in the first round, and in the second, on what was described as an 'under-prepared' pitch in Chalkwell Park, Westcliff, they bowled out Middlesex for 41, the lowest score recorded by a first-class county in the tournament. Boyce, 5 for 22, and Lever, 5 for 8, bowled unchanged, the innings lasting 19.4 overs. Boyce was named 'man of the match', for he caught Parfitt at slip, but, in fact, the ball had bounced out of Turner's hands. Essex won by eight wickets.

The quarter-final match, against Kent, at Leyton, aroused tremendous enthusiasm. The weather was mostly fine, and there was a large crowd. For Essex, there was a bitter disappointment before the start when Keith Fletcher was forced to withdraw from the side through illness. He was replaced by Ken Wallace.

Wallace, a club cricketer of outstanding quality, was never quite able to win himself a place on the Essex staff although he captained the 2nd XI for several seasons and always batted well in his limited first-class games which came in the Taylor era. He was, and still is, a prolific scorer for Leigh-on-Sea Cricket Club, who share the Chalkwell Park ground with Westcliff.

Kent won the toss, and Denness decided to bat. He could not have been pleased with his decision when Kent laboured. Johnson and Luckhurst put on 24 for the first wicket, but five wickets then fell as 22 runs were scored, and the Essex seamers were rampant. The only resistance came from Asif Iqbal, and he found a solid partner in Woolmer so that 36 were added. The stand was broken by Ray East who had Woolmer lbw for 15. Asif fell to Turner, rather luckily, the ball going down the leg side bounding back off Taylor's pads onto the wicket while the batsman was out of his crease. The scorecard reads 'Asif, stumped Taylor, bowled Turner 52'. It was an innings that gave Kent some hope, but, as they were all out for 137 in 52 overs, very little.

The crowd settled back to applaud an Essex win. This seemed certain when Edmeades and Wallace, playing with the greatest good sense, began with a stand of 55 in 25 overs. Essex were strolling to victory. John Shepherd changed the character of the game when he came into the attack and took the wickets of Edmeades, Wallace, Ward and Boyce for no runs in five overs. Suddenly, Essex were 69 for 5, and there was no real recovery. Taylor hit 15, Turner 16, and East and Lever put on 19 for the last wicket, but Essex lost by ten runs.

To lose a 60-over match after bowling out the opposition for 137 was a shattering experience, and the defeat emphasised the doubt that, while Essex were rich in talent, their temperament was very suspect. Once enough people began to say this, the players themselves began to believe it might be true.

In retrospect, one wonders now if the Essex side of that time was quite good enough to win anything. They met Middlesex at Chalkwell Park in mid-July. Fletcher hit his second century in successive innings, and eventually Middlesex had to make 216 to win. They reached 108 for 1, thanks to Russell and Radley, but Turner took 3 for 0 in 11 balls and gave Brearley a dreadful time. Acfield replaced him and took 4 for 22 with some beautifully controlled off-spin, and Middlesex were fortunate to avoid defeat.

Brearley was full of praise for the Essex side after the match. He commented on the improvement in Turner as a bowler and on the balance of the attack. He added: 'If there was a bit more strength at number five, they would be a formidable side.'

The County Committee was aware of this and negotiations were already in progress to make additions to the staff. Changes were afoot.

'Topper' Brown resigned as secretary after sterling service and was succeeded by Ronnie Cox, who had recently retired from the army with the rank of captain.

Taylor had hinted, not only at his own retirement and the need to find a replacement, but also at Essex's desire to strengthen the batting, and before the start of the 1973 season, which was to be Brian Taylor's last, three new names were added to the register of players: Brian Hardie, from Scotland, Bob Cooke, from Cheshire, and Neil Smith from Yorkshire.

Cooke was 29, and he was by far the most experienced of the trio. He had played for Cheshire, for the Minor Counties and for Lancashire 2nd XI. He had also played as a professional for two league sides. A highly successful businessman dealing in sports equipment, he cherished a desire to play first-class cricket, and Essex provided him with the opportunity.

Brian Hardie had played for Stenhousemuir in the East of Scotland League, and, like his father and elder brother, had represented Scotland. He was 23, and he had scored two centuries in a match for Scotland against MCC. The game was not recognised as first-class, but the performance had been noted. He was said to have solid defensive qualities, but in pre-season practice both he and Cooke displayed tremendous powers of hitting. What was unsuspected at the time was Hardie's outstanding quality as a fielder at short-leg.

Neil Smith had been considered as successor to Jimmy Binks as Yorkshire's wicket-keeper and had played in seven championship matches before surrendering the spot to David Bairstow. There are still those in Yorkshire who think that this was a mistake, for Smith was one of the most capable wicket-keepers in the game for several seasons.

Bob Cooke was the first to win a place in the County side, but 1973 was to be a season of change rather than of achievement. Brian Taylor had become a Test selector and missed eight matches. Fletcher saved England from defeat against New Zealand at Lord's with an innings of 178, described as the finest knock of the season, and topped the Test averages against West Indies. He could play in only ten championship matches, and Boyce, with the West Indian side, could play in only six. Ward, as we have noted, disappeared from the scene, and Saville, having sustained a hand injury, played in only five games and met with little success. Bruce Francis returned for his second and last season and, after a poor start, was the only batsman to reach 1000 runs for Essex. Unfortunately he announced his retirement at the end of the season, preferring to concentrate on a business career, and, at the last, one felt his talent was never fully realised.

At Ilford, Bob Cooke hit the first of the two centuries he was to hit for Essex. It was made against Sussex at the beginning of June and was a mixture of careful defence and violent hitting. His 139 took 5½ hours and contained four sixes and 17 fours, a proportion of boundaries reminiscent of Jack O'Connor. At Edgbaston, a month later, Keith Pont hit his maiden century, but Essex posed no threat to the leaders in either the championship or the Sunday league.

The best performances were saved for the Gillette Cup and the Benson and Hedges Cup, but, inevitably, both competitions ended in disappointment. The zonal round of the Benson and Hedges Cup had Essex pitted against Middlesex, Surrey, Sussex and Kent, and the game against Surrey, at Chelmsford, saw Gooch in the Essex side for the first time. He was to play in the other two one-day competitions and was to make his first-class debut against Northamptonshire at Westcliff, on 18, 19 and 20 July. Gooch scored 18, caught Bedi in the second innings, and Essex won a good victory over a side who were leading the county championship at the time.

The Gillette Cup matched Essex against Gloucestershire in the quarter-final at Chelmsford. Taylor won the toss and asked the visitors to bat. They made 236, and Essex, in spite of the bravest of ninth wicket stands between Turner and East, were never quite in with a chance. It was the Benson and Hedges competition which provided the real agony.

A win over Sussex and a ten-wicket victory over Middlesex at Harlow were enough to put Essex in the quarter-finals. Brian Edmeades had a fine all-round match against Middlesex, and he followed this with an even better performance against Leicestershire, favourites for the Cup, at Ilford. He took the first five wickets for 22 runs, and the visitors were restricted to 177 in their 55 overs. Edmeades and Cooke both scored fifties as Essex paced their innings well to win by six wickets. This took them to Canterbury for the semi-final.

Denness won the toss and decided to bat, but Essex made a heartening start when Turner had Johnson caught behind in the second over. Luckhurst and Denness brought Kent back into the game with a stand of 66, but East and Turner gnawed away at the Kent batting, and the home side slipped to 91 for 5. Ealham now played a thrilling innings of 48 in an hour before being brilliantly caught on the off-side boundary by Cooke off Lever's bowling. Kent ended on 169 for 9. Essex had bowled well and fielded well, and a sensible batting performance must surely give them victory.

Edmeades left at 28, but, at tea, after 25 overs, Essex were 60 for 1, Francis and Fletcher in command, and happy. In the interval, Kent supporters were asking their Essex counterparts what it felt like to be in a final for the first time. They were not able to answer. Woolmer dismissed both Francis and Fletcher. Cooke and Pont were run out. Shepherd took two wickets in an over. Essex, succumbing to the pressure of excellent fielding and accurate bowling, crumbled to 123 all out, 11 of their 55 overs unused.

On 29, 30 and 31 August, at Chelmsford, Brian Taylor played his 539th and last match for Essex. It was against Nottinghamshire, and he led his side to a nine-wicket victory. He took five catches and made a stumping in the match and passed Herbert Strudwick's record of 964 catches in championship matches. He was as fit, as smart and as enthusiastic at the end of his career as he had been at the beginning.

The ultimate success was denied to Brian Taylor. He would dearly loved to have won something for Essex, but perhaps his victories could not be counted in medals and trophies. He taught strength, fitness and discipline. He provided the ingredients for Essex to become a side that was to command the respect of all. Above everything, he inculcated a sense of loyalty to club, colleague and self. Some may have disagreed with Brian Taylor, none ever disobeyed him. The first sign of unrest or dissent at a debatable decision, on or off the field, was quelled with that stentorian, military voice: 'All right, lads, leave this to me.' And they did.

He took over Essex when morale was at its lowest. He left them on the threshold of honours with the crowds pouring through the turnstiles. He alone was not responsible for this. He was supported by men like Pearce and Insole and a good administration, active and visionary, but to him fell the responsibility of leading the troops in battle, and he was ever the first over the parapet.

His final report as a captain showed a remarkable self-awareness and an acute observation of what he had bequeathed and what was still to be done:

> It has been said that as a captain I was too predictable in my outlook and in my judgment of players. But if one recalls our position in 1967 the only way to build on a sound footing was to do it by a basic plan, one that you believe in and have the courage to carry out. The players grew in stature and from this sound foundation are now in a position to be more flexible in predictability. To use a phrase that is coming into vocabulary, they have flair.
>
> The one problem as I see it with the future of the side is in its character. This has repeatedly let us down in the past and has been the cause of Essex never having won a major competition. I think it is true to say that when the final reckoning comes we appear to falter. This criticism could be levelled at me in so far as I have said I am not one to experiment, nor to take more than a calculated risk. But I felt the time was not right for me to do so and I leave them to do this during the coming years.

The foundation had been provided; now it was for someone else to raise the spire that would touch the clouds.

CHAPTER 16

Fletch's Early Years: 1973–78

As well as Taylor and Ward, Graham Saville ended his playing career at the end of the 1973 season, but he was to maintain the strongest links with the Club, initially serving as assistant secretary, (cricket) and later moving to an important position with the National Cricket Association, but remaining at Chelmsford. Essex have always seen the importance of close contact with schools and clubs, and it has been the work of committee members like Mike Chapman, Reg Hilliard and John Jarvis to foster the youth programme. The Essex Schools' Cricket Association, founded upon the untiring and unpaid efforts of men like John Crew, Haydn Davies, George Talbot, Peter Green, 'Sam' Coster and Lawrie Weston, has proved to be one of the strongest in the country, and Tom Pearce applauds them for the work that they have done in bringing to the County Club players like Gooch, Pont, Foster, Lilley and Gladwin. Gooch first won a regular place in the Essex side in 1974 as did Brian Hardie, Neil Smith and Ken McEwan.

Bruce Francis's decision to leave cricket again left Essex with the option of signing an overseas cricketer on immediate registration, and this time they chose to sign a batsman whose first-class experience was limited to ten matches and 439 runs for Eastern Province and an Invitation XI in

South Africa. He had never hit a first-class century, and he had only twice reached fifty.

Ken McEwan had been educated at Queen's College, Queenstown, where Tony Greig was first a pupil and then a coach. It was Greig who encouraged him to come to England and join the Sussex ground staff. McEwan played for Sussex 2nd XI for two seasons, but there was no prospect of Sussex signing him as they already had their full quota of overseas players. It was not the young McEwan's first disappointment, for, as an outstanding schoolboy cricketer and captain of the South African Schools' side, he had been due to go to Australia in 1971, but the tour had been cancelled, and official international competition was debarred for him just as his career began.

Taylor had seen McEwan in a game and had been impressed. The young South African also interested Northamptonshire, who seemed to be scouring the world for players, and he appeared for their 2nd XI. Essex invited McEwan to play in a friendly match against Scotland in Perth in July, 1973. He did well, was surprised at being asked, but thought little more about Essex until being told that he was to meet Brian Taylor at Victoria Station. He met Taylor who introduced him to Doug Insole and over lunch McEwan became an Essex player.

To offer a three-year contract to an unknown and untested player showed the judgment and vision of those responsible for running Essex cricket. They had assessed the man and the cricketer and knew him to be one that the Club needed.

The signing of McEwan was not without its critics, neither was the appointment of Fletcher as captain in succession to Taylor. In the minds of the administration, there was never any question as to who should follow Taylor. Fletcher was the vice-captain and the possessor of a shrewd cricketing brain. He had been advisor to Taylor, and other players would comment wryly: 'You could always tell when "Tonker" wasn't doing what Fletch believed he should be doing because Fletch would push his cap further and further back on his head.'

Keith Fletcher was 30 when he took over as captain, and he was the veteran of 33 Test matches. He had been in the Essex side since 1962, and he had scored nearly 20,000 runs. His Test debut, at Headingley in 1968, epitomised much that he had suffered. He was brought into the England side, missed two difficult chances at slip and was out for nought. The Yorkshire crowd believe Sharpe, their own man, should have been chosen and gave Fletcher a miserable time. Essentially a private man, he could never provide the press or the media with the ostentation which is their diet, and they allowed his reticence as a man to blind them to his greatness as a player. He was to remain scarred by that early treatment, but he was later to open eyes.

Fletcher had grown up with most of the players he was now asked to lead, and he was confronted with the problem of stamping his own personal authority on a group of lively personalities. His position was not made easier by the fact that in his first season as captain he was able to play in only seven championship matches because of Test duties, and he averaged only 18.76. With Boyce missing most of the season through injury and Lever below form, Essex experienced a wretched time. Hobbs led the side capably in Fletcher's absence, but it was not an easy period for anyone. It was Hobbs's benefit year, and the double pressure of benefit and surrogate leadership did not help his form. Twelfth in the championship, 15th in the John Player League and no progress in the Gillette Cup or the Benson and Hedges Cup caused bitter disappointment among supporters, and it seemed to the casual observer that the spirit and application were lacking in the side, for the fielding fell away to a marked degree.

Yet the discerning eye could perceive that the ingredients for a highly successful side were being gathered together. Brian Hardie became a regular opening batsman and passed 1000 runs. In this, his first full season, his batting was still in embryo. It was characterised by a forward lunge and lacked the variety and personality it was to acquire over the next few years. His maiden century, against Middlesex, at Ilford, took five hours, and he earned a reputation for being slow and dour, descriptions which, in later years, were to prove totally unjustified.

McEwan, shy and ever nervous, charmed on many occasions and was instantly popular. His humility led him to believe that he was in the shadow of Bruce Francis, and that Essex supporters would find him wanting in comparison to the Australian. He could not have had an unhappier start. In the opening match of the season, at Trent Bridge, he was given out lbw first ball although he, and his team-mates, believed that he hit the ball firmly with the bat. His first home appearance was in the Benson and Hedges Cup match against Sussex, at Chelmsford. He scored 54 and felt much better. By the end of the season, he had scored more than 1000 first-class runs and, like Hardie, been awarded his county cap.

The third batsman to create a good impression in 1974 and give hope for the future was Graham Alan Gooch. Born in Leytonstone in July 1953, he had played his first county championship match the previous season, but he did not come into the side in 1974 until the beginning of June when, with Fletcher absent, he played against Gloucestershire at Bristol and managed a pair. In the following weeks, however, he gave the first indication of that brooding power. Generally unsmiling at the crease, even in success, but serious rather than surly, Gooch smouldered through most of the season like a volcano whose eruption one day was inevitable. In 11 John Player League matches, his highest score was 31 not out and he usually batted low in the order, but in the first-class game, usually at number five, he slowly began to assert himself.

At Old Trafford, he hit 94, with 2 sixes and 13 fours, an innings which drew no remark from *Wisden*, but which was the first positive indication of the greatness that was to come. It was in this match that poor Graham Saville, forced into action because injuries and Test calls had reduced Essex to ten players, was rewarded with a broken hand.

Gooch's maiden fifty, against Lancashire, had come in the third week of June, and he did not hit another until the third week of August, when he scored 71 in the drawn game with Glamorgan at Swansea. The heroes of this match, however, were Stuart Turner and David Acfield.

The Essex spinners, Hobbs, East and Acfield, bowled out Glamorgan for 188, but, in reply, Essex lost both openers for four, and, in spite of fine knocks from McEwan and Gooch, they were 202 for 9 when Acfield joined Turner. The all-rounder was on 31 when Acfield came in and his initial response was 'to hit hard and enjoy it' while he could. It became apparent that Acfield was in defiant mood, and he has always been a better batsman than his record or his number 11 tag would suggest. They stayed together for 133 minutes, 42 overs, and in that time added 122 for the last wicket. Acfield was finally lbw to Nash for 31. Turner finished on 118 not out.

It was Turner's only century in what was an outstanding season. In all matches, he hit 963 runs and took 73 wickets. He won the Wetherell Award as the country's leading all-rounder so emulating Keith Boyce, the only other Essex player to win this award. He came close to selection for the England party to tour Australia, but, as one selector put it, 'He needed to turn a few of his 80s into hundreds.'

The performance at Swansea, and in the last three matches of the season when Essex gained two of their four championship victories, gave a truer indication of the side's capabilities than the matches earlier in the year. From Swansea, Essex returned to Chelmsford to entertain Leicestershire, and the visitors made 313 for 4 declared after winning the toss. There was only an hour and three quarters play possible on the Monday, and Essex avoided the follow-on when Hobbs and Acfield were together for the last wicket.

At lunch time on the last day, Illingworth declared, setting Essex a target of 242. Hardie and Edmeades went for 16, but both McEwan and Cooke suggested challenge without permanence. At 156 for 6, Essex looked doomed. It was now that Gooch took over and with powerful driving reached his maiden first-class hundred in under two hours. He totally dominated the innings and hit three sixes and eight fours in his 114 not out, which brought victory off the last ball of the penultimate over.

In the next match, with Hardie hitting 133, Cooke 100, McEwan 94 and Boyce taking 11 wickets, Essex beat Warwickshire by an innings, but the season ended with a rain-sodden dismal draw against the champions Worcestershire, Essex being dismissed for 84.

The gleams of hope in the victories over Leicestershire and Warwickshire were small comfort to a disgruntled band of followers who feared a reversion to the low standards of the middle 1960s. The main target for criticism, inevitably, was Fletcher, the captain who had been absent for most of the season and whose form had been the worst he had shown throughout his career. There were the cries that captaincy had affected him and that he could not give time to the County because he was so much with England. To add to this domestic anxiety, Fletcher had to contend with the fast, furious and unexpected attack of Lillee and Thomson when he went with the England side to Australia in the winter of 1974–75. One draws attention to these facts, for in the euphoria of the years that followed, it is often forgotten what resources and strength of character the man called upon to achieve what he did.

In the first place, although he was never as flamboyant as Brian Taylor, Keith Fletcher was a firm disciplinarian. His was a quiet authority that was founded upon a complete understanding of the game and the respect and loyalty that he had earned from his players because of his own ability. He was calm in adversity, strong and unwavering in decision, and he had the priceless quality of patience. Those closest to the events were well aware of Fletcher's strengths, and in 1975, a wider public began to sense them.

Defeat at Bournemouth in the opening championship match gave no indication of what was to come, but the drawn game with Leicestershire at Chelmsford did. On a wicket that was giving assistance to the spinners, Keith Boyce hit 113 out of a fourth wicket partnership of 122 with Fletcher in 20 overs, 63 minutes. Boyce's century came in 58 minutes, the fastest championship hundred for 38 years, and contained eight sixes and seven fours. He followed this with bowling which reduced Leicestershire to pulp and gave him match figures of 12 for 73.

Ironically, Boyce's hundred was not the fastest of the season, for in the Bank Holiday game against the Australians at Chelmsford, Robin Hobbs reached his hundred in 44 minutes which, at the time, was the fifth fastest ever recorded in first-class cricket, but it must be admitted that the game was played in a carnival atmosphere. Hobbs also reached 1000 wickets in first-class cricket, a feat never likely to be performed again by an English leg-spinner, in the victory over Worcestershire, at Worcester, which followed the Leicestershire game. It was to be Hobbs' last season with Essex, although he was later to return, surprisingly, with Glamorgan.

Ever cheerful and friendly, with piercing, vulnerable blue eyes, Robin Hobbs was an anachronism. He was a leg-break bowler in an age when such bowling had become all but extinct in county cricket. He was rarely used as a bowler in the one-day game towards the close of his career in spite of a hat-trick against Middlesex at Lord's in 1968 in the Gillette Cup, but his brilliant fielding earned him a place in the side. He became saddened that the crowds seemed only to see brighter cricket in terms of sixes and fours, missing the subtleties and joys which were his art, but those who followed Essex cricket in Hobbs' time remember him with affection and gratitude for the last sight of what had been one of the game's great delights.

Bob Cooke also left Essex in 1975, unable to command a regular place as Hardie, Gooch and McEwan prospered. Perhaps, for Cooke, the chance of first-class cricket came a little too late.

Gooch began the season in consistently brilliant form. He hit 100 against Kent at a bitterly cold Castle Park, Colchester, where Essex won by 33 runs, and followed with 85 against Lancashire and 90 against Nottinghamshire on his home ground at Ilford. There was a knock of 82 at Cambridge, and the first half of the season had brought him over 700 runs in belligerent, emphatic style, a county cap and a premature place in an ailing England side.

Few will forget the agony of Gooch's Test debut at Edgbaston, caught behind in both innings without scoring. He played at Lord's, missed a catch and was discarded for three years. His experiences at international level had a most adverse effect upon him, and he struggled painfully in the second half of the season, groping for confidence.

The second half of the season did not match the first for Essex as a whole, six of the seven championship victories coming before the end of the first week in July. The last win was obtained at Leyton on 13, 14 and 15 August, when, after a brisk 73 from Brian Edmeades, McEwan and Pont reached their first centuries of the season and shared a fourth wicket stand of 200. Pont hit three sixes and 17 fours in his 110 off the Glamorgan bowlers and then found himself dropped for the next match, against the Australians, which was to become something of an occupational hazard for him in his career.

McEwan had begun the season indifferently, but ended in good form, reaching 1000 runs in championship matches, as did Hardie and Edmeades, and recalling Tom Pearce's words after McEwan's first first-class innings in England, at the Scarborough Festival in 1973: 'His bat sounded sweeter than anyone else's in the match.' McEwan had failed to reach 20, but Pearce has always been a fine judge of a player.

The late season form of McEwan, the consistent and splendid bowling of John Lever, who formed a threatening new ball partnership with

Boyce, and the reliability of Hardie could not hide what came to be known as Essex's August blues, so much so that, even in the heady days to come, older supporters would look glum amid early season optimism and say: 'Wait until August.' This caution was founded on experience, particularly of the John Player League in 1975.

Somerset won the opening fixture, at Chelmsford, by six wickets. Essex then won eight matches in succession. The decision, after early experiments, to promote Turner to open the innings met with success, and the second setback of the season was not experienced until Worcestershire won at Chelmsford on 20 July. This was a cruel defeat.

Turner and Hardie got Essex off to a brisk start, and Gooch then joined Turner in a stand of 106. Turner went on to make 87, which was to remain his highest score in the league, and Essex finished their 40 overs on 207 for 4.

Worcestershire appeared to be heading for a big defeat when, at 57 for 5 in the 17th over, rain stopped play. On the resumption, their target was reduced to 176 in 34 overs. They lost two more quick wickets, but Cass, who saved his best for his old county, hit furiously, and Worcestershire got home with one wicket and four balls to spare.

Undaunted, Essex, still at the top of the table, won at Cheltenham, lost at Leicester and won at The Oval. Now they were confronted by their greatest rivals, Hampshire, at Chelmsford. With 44 on the board, McEwan brilliantly ran out Gordon Greenidge with a throw from the boundary, but Hampshire were always in control, and a huge crowd were left bitterly disappointed. Defeats by Kent and Yorkshire in the last two games meant that Essex, with the title seemingly theirs for much of the season, finished in fourth place. Keith Pont's 14 sixes in the league in the season, bettered only by Jameson and Viv Richards, was little consolation.

Doug Insole's report at the AGM expressed the feelings of many:

> It is doubtful whether any other County side affords better entertainment value at the present time. Athleticism in the field; panache and staggering inconsistency with the bat; and a variety in attack, together with our general approach to the game, constitute a formidable array of assets which require only competitive success to turn them into gold.

The Essex chairman could have reiterated his case a year later, for the centenary season mirrored 1975. The team again reached the quarter-finals of the Benson and Hedges Cup, but after batting well lost their nerve in the field and went down to Surrey in the last over. Six of the seven championship wins came before 9 July, and August was as traumatic as ever.

The crisis point of the season came in the Gillette Cup at Hitchin on 14 July. Staffordshire had been beaten in the first round, and Essex found themselves confronted by another minor county, Hertfordshire, in the second.

On a pitch which always assisted the spinners, Hertfordshire were bowled out for 153 in 55.3 overs, East taking four wickets. The wicket deteriorated badly in the early afternoon, but after Edmeades had gone for nought McEwan and Hardie put on 70, and McEwan's rich stroke play suggested nothing but an emphatic Essex victory. It was the advent of the spinners, Johns, the Oxford blue, and Doshi, later of India, which turned the course of the match for, by the time they had finished their quota of overs, Essex were 109 for 9 and the game as good as over.

The defeat by Hertfordshire had a demoralising effect upon the side, and once again the temperament of some was called into question. Where coolness and application had been needed, there had been a frenetic approach, and there was a gnawing suggestion that when the pressure was greatest and the prize the richest Essex lacked the character and control necessary for success.

The effect of the defeat at Hitchin could be clearly seen in the John Player League. Six of the first eight matches were won, and Essex were strolling to the title, but following the failure against Hertfordshire, there were immediate losses to Hampshire and Gloucestershire and only four wins in the second half of the competition.

When the last Sunday of the season arrived Somerset and Sussex led the table with 40 points. Essex, Kent and Leicestershire were each on 36. On 5 September, Glamorgan beat Somerset by one run; Sussex lost to Warwickshire by eight wickets; Leics beat Surrey at The Oval; Kent, scoring 278 for 5 in 40 overs, overwhelmed Gloucestershire at Maidstone, and Essex beat Yorkshire by 12 runs at Leyton. This left five teams level on 40 points.

Under the existing rules, places were decided on the number of away wins, and Essex and Kent, with five victories on opponents' grounds, took the first two places. As they were tied on away wins, the winner of the John Player League was decided on run rate. Kent, boosted by their 6.95 an over in the final game, finished with a run rate of 4.98. Essex, who had scored at 3.85 in their last match to bring their rate down, ended with 4.56 an over. Kent were the winners.

Again Essex could bemoan that they had been the victims of cruellest of mathematical calculations, but, in truth, their failure was self-inflicted, and those in the Club were aware of it.

There were other worrying aspects. Boyce missed many matches with a knee injury, and Brian Hardie could not find the form of previous seasons, scoring only 372 runs in championship matches. He held his place in the side only because of the limited staff and because of his magnificent fielding at short leg, 'boot hill', where he had no superior in the country. As Brian Edmeades announced his retirement to take up an appointment in Scotland, it left Essex with an opening batsman problem.

Edmeades had served Essex faithfully for 16 seasons. He had taken more than 100 wickets with his medium-pace bowling in 1966, but the latter part of his career had seen his efforts concentrated mainly on batting, and his reliability as an opener, eager to play his shots, had become an integral part of Essex cricket. Although born in Matlock, he was by speech and inclination essentially an East Londoner, and for 'Chans' there was no immediate replacement. Neither McEvoy, nor Herbert had established himself, and Fosh, of whom so much was hoped, was to prove not to have the appetite for the game.

To balance Hardie's loss of form and Edmeades' imminent departure, McEwan continued to blossom into one of the most exciting stroke players in the world, and Gooch had rediscovered his confidence to win a place in England's one-day side. Fletcher, too, had a splendid season for Essex to end all fears that captaincy had affected his batting form.

The departure of Hobbs had allowed David Acfield more chances, and this intelligent off-spinner had responded with consistently effective bowling. The absence of Boyce had thrown more work onto Turner and Lever, and they had tackled everything with their usual zest, taking 78 and 62 wickets respectively in championship matches alone.

The tall, fair Lever, rhythmical in movement, had begun to excite the attention of the Test selectors. Fast-medium, left-arm with a smooth and easy action, he was not only penetrative, but because of correctness of his technique and his unrelenting professional application, he was also a bowler of immense stamina. Rightly, he was chosen as a member of the party to tour India and Sri Lanka, and he was also to play in the Centenary Test in Melbourne. He proved himself a bowler of international quality, and the England side has always been the better for his presence.

The continued frustration on the field was not reflected in the continuing development of the Chelmsford ground where, in 1977, the splendid indoor school was opened. For those who have come only recently to Essex cricket, it must be difficult to imagine what the Chelmsford ground was like before the imaginative additions and reconstructions of the past few years. The score-board, the Pearce Stand, the Riverside Restaurant, the Executive Suite, the hospitality boxes are all recent additions. There was a time when the ground was notorious for toilet facilities of bucket and tent. The press used to be accommodated in a tent which, seemingly, always faced the wind, and the ground was among the most uncomfortable in the country.

Today the County Ground stands as an ever-improving monument to the achievements of the Club and the foresight and good husbandry of an energetic committee and administration. In 1987, a visiting chairman could point to the Chelmsford ground and cite it as a model as to what can be achieved at a non-Test match venue.

In 1977, however, more urgent problems presented themselves on the playing field. The loss of Edmeades had been covered by the signing of Mike Denness. At 36, the former England captain was approaching the veteran stage, but he had served in many hard campaigns and, like Fletcher, he had his scars. He brought calm, consistency, stability and good sense in plenty to Essex cricket, but he also brought a dimension that had been lacking, the experience of one who had played in title-winning sides. Remarkably, after such a distinguished career with Kent and England, he hit the highest score of his career in his first season with Essex, 195 against Leicestershire, at Leicester, in June.

Denness quickly settled into the side, opening the innings with Hardie, but the first championship win did not come until Ilford week, at the end of May, when Nottinghamshire were beaten by six wickets. The match was a triumph for Ray East, who took 4 for 71 and 8 for 30. His second innings figures were the best of his career and the best recorded by any bowler in 1977.

East's comic antics on the field, acting often like a stringless puppet out of control, were, on his own admission, his way of relieving tension and coping with the pressures of a situation. He became immensely popular for his foolery and his quips to the crowd, suggesting, when fielding on the boundary, that the spectators would have to stop the next ball that came that way for he was dizzy from the number of times that his captain had moved him, but his buffoonery tended to obscure for some his quality as a bowler. To watch from behind the arm and observe that exquisite loop of his left-handed spin bowling was an aesthetic pleasure. He performed the hat-trick in a Test trial, but his feat went unrewarded, and always Underwood, Gifford and, latterly, Edmonds barred his way. He turned the ball appreciably, yet perhaps never quite quickly enough, and kept an immaculate length.

He was well advised by Bill Morris at Ilford and enjoyed a fine season in 1977, taking 73 wickets in first-class cricket. His memorable week was at Leyton in August. In the first match, when only three-quarters of an hour was possible on the first two days, he took eight Derbyshire wickets for 57; and in the second match, he bowled Essex to victory over Glamorgan with 8 for 90 and 4 for 23.

This was the last county match to be played at Leyton, and one could not leave the old county ground without some feeling of regret. It played a significant, sometimes worrying part in Essex history, but it had been

57. *Brentwood was the first home of Essex County Cricket Club after its formation in 1876. The Club played all its matches there until 1885, when it moved its headquarters to Leyton. Brentwood remained a festival ground until 1969.* (Southend Standard)

58. *Southchurch Park, Southend. The first match was played at Southend in 1906, and it is now a regular part of the Essex Festival scene with a home week every July, when a large number of marquees is erected for the use of companies and clubs. The Mayor of Southend is a regular visitor to the Festival, and entertains guests each day in the civic marquee.*

the dream of Charles Green and the scene of many famous encounters. In breaking with Leyton, Essex finally ceased to be a metropolitan county, for Ilford is the last tenuous link with London.

Following the victory over Glamorgan, Essex won two more championship matches, against Somerset and Northamptonshire, and finished sixth in the table as they had done the previous season.

Lever was absent on international duty on many occasions, but the greatest loss was felt when, after his serious knee operation, Keith Boyce was forced to retire. He began the season well enough, but in spite of his 4 for 48 against Nottinghamshire at Ilford and his usual threat and accuracy, it was apparent that he was struggling. He took 4 for 90 and 1 for 19 against the Australians at Chelmsford, bowling McCosker in the second innings. That proved to be his last wicket in first-class cricket.

When, during the John Player League game at Southend, it was announced that he would not play again, it created one of the most moving occasions one can ever remember witnessing on a cricket field. Although Boyce was born and brought up in the West Indies, he was essentially an Essex cricketer and looked upon himself as such. After each defeat he would sit with head in hands, ready to assume total responsibility for whatever had gone wrong. Although he became a Test all-rounder of quality, he never took on the temperament of a 'star', and his total commitment to Essex remained. When told that he would not be able to play again he asked Essex to keep his registration in case he got better. In every way, he epitomised all that was good in Essex cricket at this time, attacking bowling, zestful fielding and batting with panache, the ingredients of great entertainment.

Even though Hardie was injured and had a poor season, Gooch often frittered his talent away impetuously, and neither Pont nor Smith could score runs consistently. Boyce's batting was not missed. In part this was due to the form of Denness and Fletcher, but it was mainly due to the lavish success of Ken McEwan. Here was a batsman of extraordinary flair, languid in movement, explosive in power, who created a murmur of excited anticipation every time he went to the crease. He was eighth in the national averages, followed Taylor, Boyce and Fletcher as one of *Wisden*'s 'Five Cricketers of the Year' and hit four consecutive first-class centuries.

The sequence started when McEwan hit the first double century of his career, 218, against Sussex, at Chelmsford. On the Sunday, he hit 104 against Warwickshire in a John Player League game, and followed this with 102 and 116 against the same county in a championship match at Edgbaston. From there Essex travelled to Southend where McEwan hit 106 not out against Gloucestershire. This marvellous run came to an end in sensational fashion in the second innings of the match against Gloucestershire when McEwan was the second victim in a Procter hat-trick, Hardie being the first and Gooch the third.

If Boyce's batting was not missed, his bowling was, and much responsibility fell on Turner and, to a lesser extent, Pont. Turner responded with his usual endeavour and claimed 77 first-class wickets. He was also the leading wicket-taker, with 22 wickets, in the John Player League, but this was a bitter-sweet year for him, for this was to be the most heartbreaking Sunday season of all.

Essex started with five victories, including the total destruction of Somerset who, with Boyce's last notable performance, 5 for 19, were bowled out for 58. Defeat had seemed probable at Ilford when Acfield joined Lever for the last over against Lancashire with seven still needed for victory. Simmons was the bowler, and Acfield was unable to score from the first two deliveries, but the third went for four byes, and Acfield scrambled a single off the fourth. Lever pushed the fifth delivery through the covers for two and Essex had won by one wicket with one ball to spare.

The following Sunday, Leicestershire won easily at Grace Road in what proved to be a vital match, and the Sunday after, when Boyce's name was down on the Essex team-sheet for the last time, the match at Gloucester was abandoned without a ball being bowled.

There was another abandonment, at Castle Park, Colchester, in August, when Hampshire were the visitors. Play did not start until 5.20 pm, but after 15 balls the rain returned and the match was washed out. On the same day, Leicestershire lost to Northamptonshire by one run so that Essex stood four points clear at the top of the table with only two matches to play.

Essex's penultimate game was at Scarborough. Essex batted first and lost Gooch at 12, but Fosh and McEwan took the score past 100 in the 20th over. They fell to Cooper in quick succession, and it was the medium-pace bowler's economic spell that stifled Essex as they tried to accelerate. Essex's final score of 178 for 7 was something of a disappointment. Yet they frustrated Yorkshire's attempts to match the required scoring rate, and the 100 was not reached until the 28th over by which time Hampshire, Leadbeater, Lumb and Love were out. It seemed certain that Essex would win, but in the closing overs, Bairstow launched a savage attack. Turner, who had bowled with the greatest accuracy, was hit for 17 in one over, and Yorkshire won with three balls to spare.

Leicestershire, meanwhile, beat Warwickshire, and on the last day of the season beat Glamorgan. Essex beat Worcestershire at Chelmsford, but Leicestershire took the title. They had 13 wins and three losses for 52 points to Essex's 12 wins, two losses and two abandoned matches for 52 points. Under the existing rules, Leicestershire took the title on more wins. A total of 52 points would have won the title for Essex in nearly every other season that the John Player League had been in existence.

'Tiny.' Waterman, the chairman, could only reiterate Insole's remarks of the previous seasons. The story had become monotonously familiar: 'Enterprising cricket, unstinting effort, superb fielding, outstanding individual performances, promising young players – nothing to show for it all. Nothing that is, if the winning of a competition – any competition – is the over-riding consideration in the support of a side which, year in, year out, provides entertainment unsurpassed by any other county.'

The urgent need to find a replacement for Boyce had led the County to apply for the special registration of Richard Hadlee for the second half of the 1977 season. The application was refused on the grounds that the TCCB would only sanction Hadlee's registration if he were offered a three-year contract. According to Doug Insole, Hadlee declined to commit himself to a long-term contract, although he was later to sign for Nottinghamshire, and Essex offered terms to Norbert Phillip.

It is generally accepted that Phillip made the first tentative approaches to Essex himself. He had played for Windward Islands and Combined Islands since 1970, but as a fast bowler and hard-hitting batsman, he had not found it possible to break into the West Indies side, which was rich in quick bowlers. He was anxious to further his career in England, but, like his overseas predecessors at Essex, he arrived as a completely unknown quantity.

He was a stiffer cricketer than Boyce and certainly not as liquid a mover in the field, but he was a hostile bowler and quicker than Boyce had been over his last three seasons when he had been struggling against injury. As a batsman, he was never to hit the consistent power of his predecessor, but he produced one innings in his first season, 134, a maiden century of awesome belligerence, which brought a memorable victory at Gloucester.

Phillip's arrival gave Lever the necessary support and released Turner to revert to first change, which was always his favoured position. Able now to hunt as one of a pair, Lever thrived, took 106 wickets at 15.18 in the season – the first Essex bowler to reach this mark for 12 years – was named as one of *Wisden*'s 'Five Cricketers' and was the 'Players' Player of the Year', a coveted award among professionals.

Hot on Lever's heels was Ray East with 92 wickets, and with Phillip, Turner and Acfield all bowling with success, Essex had the most balanced and varied attack in the country – two pace men, one left-arm; one medium-pace; an off-break bowler and a slow left-arm bowler.

Incomprehensibly, Lever could not find a place in the England side, but Gooch was recalled and hit 91 not out against New Zealand at The Oval. He earned his recall with some spectacular batting at the end of

59. *John Lever* (Clive Tarling)

May and beginning of June. He hit 108 at Ilford as Kent were beaten by an innings, and later the same week, he scored 129 against Northamptonshire, who were also beaten by an innings. Lever took 13 wickets in this match.

Gooch hit 13 fours, but he tended to be overshadowed by McEwan who hit a six and 26 fours in an innings of 186 which lasted for four hours. Together they put on 321 for the second wicket, and, in doing so, established a County record.

The successes at Ilford were followed by the win at Gloucester. A double century by Mike Procter took the home side to 350 for 6, but Essex countered with an even batting display which left them at 305 for 3. Eventually, Procter asked Essex to make 313 in 200 minutes, and a draw looked inevitable when the last 20 overs began with the score at 185 for 4. It was now that Phillip played his amazing innings. He hit seven sixes and 12 fours and reached his hundred in 112 minutes. From the last seven overs, the target was 58, and Phillip continued to hit massively. He was finally caught and bowled by Procter with three balls of the match remaining, but by then only two runs were needed, and Lever scored them off the next ball to give Essex a famous victory by two wickets.

Success followed success, until the beginning of August! Thereafter Essex recorded only two wins in the seven matches. The five drawn games proved decisive. Essex had chased Kent every week of the season in the race for the Championship, but they had faltered at the last, and, in spite of only one defeat, at The Oval, in May, they finished second to Kent, 19 points in arrears. It was the highest position that they had ever attained in cricket's oldest competition.

The last match of the season, at Trent Bridge, witnessed the debut of Alan Lilley. A rain-marred match came to its climax with Essex being asked to make 222 in $2\frac{1}{2}$ hours. Gooch hit 97 out of an opening partnership of 159, and Lilley scored 43 of the last 63 runs needed as Essex won by nine wickets with 5.1 overs to spare. Alan Lilley finished on 100, which included four sixes and nine fours.

Whatever delights the County had in achieving the highest championship position in its history were diluted by the annual frustration in one-day competitions. There had been no progress in the Benson and Hedges Cup, and, for the first time for four years, there was no serious challenge in the Sunday League, but Essex survived longer in the Gillette Cup than they had ever done before, yet their run was to end in the bitterest of disappointments.

Denness took the individual honours in a comfortable win over Surrey at Colchester. The quarter-final game at Leicester was reduced to a ten-over slog, but Lever's 4 for 27 off five overs gave him the 'Man-of-the-Match' award. He won the game for Essex when he removed John Steele's leg stump with the last ball of the game as the batsman attempted to hit what would have been the winning boundary. For the semi-final, Essex travelled to Taunton to play Somerset.

No game in the season excited as much interest. It seemed that both sides had reached their peak, and both were in search of their first honour. The ground was bulging, and the atmosphere tense. Rose won the toss and, after some deliberation, decided to bat.

In the second over, Slocombe was lbw to Phillip, but Viv Richards announced his arrival by clouting the second ball he received to the mid-wicket boundary. In the next over, however, he was twice beaten by Phillip, and on 22, he was dropped at first slip off Lever. In Lever's next over, Rose was also put down at slip. These two missed chances were not typical of the Essex fielding which was generally of the highest standard, but they underlined again what Insole, Pearce, Waterman and others had recognised as the temperamental deficiency of the side, the inability to cope with the demands of 'the big occasion'.

Turner bowled a succession of maidens to Rose, who was intent on defence, while Richards hit freely at the other end. Pont dismissed Rose with the score on 86, but Richards hit Pont out of the attack. Turner, so economical in his first spell, was also plundered by Richards, and the West Indian hit East over extra cover for six.

It was Gooch who ended Richards's spree, having him brilliantly caught on the mid-wicket boundary by Denness. Richards had scored 116 out of 187 while he was at the wicket. In the closing overs, Essex lost their way, and runs came at just under eight an over for Somerset to reach a formidable 287 for 6.

Essex needed a sound start, but Denness was caught off Dredge for three, and Gooch and McEwan had to repair and attack. Gooch had an escape, but the two maintained the necessary run rate until, at 70, McEwan swung injudiciously at Burgess and was bowled.

Fletcher began uncertainly, troubled by Botham, but he survived, and in the last over before tea, he and Gooch took 17 off Marks. This brought the score to 119 from 25 overs, which was satisfactory although not cause for over-optimism.

At 127, Gooch, having made 61, was caught behind off Garner, and in the crucial period that followed, Hardie and Fletcher were restrained by the Somerset attack.

Hardie was run out by Slocombe in the 42nd over when 122 were still needed for victory. Pont hit Richards for six, and Fletcher now began to pierce the field so that runs came at more than 6 an over. Botham thwarted Essex when he ran out Pont from third man and bowled Fletcher in the next over. Phillip was also run out in the mad skelter for runs, and Turner slashed Botham for two grotesque and incredible boundaries before missing a straight ball. The last over arrived with Essex on 276 for 8.

Neil Smith pushed the first ball of the over for a single. Ray East lunged at the second, and the ball skidded to the third man boundary for four. At this time, the circles which oblige a captain to place four fielders within them were not in operation, and Rose had posted all his men, bar the wicket-keeper, around the boundary. In an attempt to beat this ring, East swung and was bowled.

One is inclined to suggest that all the temperamental inadequacies lay with Essex at this time, but Somerset proved otherwise. Dredge's fourth delivery was the totally unexpected, and unforgivable, no-ball. Lever pushed it for a single, and Somerset, in a state of corporate panic, conceded two overthrows. This left Essex with four runs to make off the last three balls of the match.

Smith swung violently at the fourth ball and made no contact. The fifth he nudged for a single. Lever, who had bowled tirelessly for his County throughout the season, was now in the position where they asked him to win the game as a batsman. He swung the last ball of the match to fine-leg where Rose failed to gather cleanly. With Lever's speed between the wickets, two runs were guaranteed, but the third and winning run was a grave doubt. Smith pelted for the line, but as he dived in a flurry of dust he was beaten by Rose's throw, though only by inches.

Essex, 287 all out, had been beaten on losing more wickets with the scores level. There was ecstasy in the press and among neutrals that this was the match of the season. The climax was like the ending to a story in *Boys' Own Paper*, but 16 August, 1978, and the weeks that followed once again left Essex as the bridesmaid rather than the bride. Nevertheless, the season had provided self-knowledge rather than self-doubt, and there was a new resolve in the Club. The years of frustration were nearly at an end.

CHAPTER 17

Success at Last: 1978–85

What is so often obscured by the emphasis on records and performances in cricket is that the 17 counties who provide the first-class game in England are, in fact, clubs. In whatever sphere it operates, a club depends upon the efficiency of its administration and organisation for its success. The members elect a committee to carry out their wishes. The committee employ officials to see that policy is implemented. The success that was to attend Essex in 1979, and in the years following, did not come by chance. It was the product of good management both on and off the field. It was the reward, not simply for years of endeavour, but also the reflection of an organisation which had been carefully constructed.

In 1978 it was decided that Ronnie Cox would concentrate on the commercial aspects of the Club, the selling of advertising on the ground and the leasing of hospitality boxes, and that a secretary/general manager would be appointed to conduct the day-to-day running of affairs. From 350 applicants, the man chosen for this new and important post was Peter Edwards ACIS.

Edwards had much to commend him. He was a company secretary in the John Laing Group, the large and successful construction company, and he was a passionate supporter of Essex County Cricket Club. He was

60. *Keith Fletcher* (Chris Cole)

a man of intelligence and vision with a proven record of successful business administration at the highest level. As an Essex member of long standing, he was able to recognise failings from the spectator's point of view; and as a professional man, he realised where and how improvements could be made. With a staff of nine he was to make Essex the envy of other counties, the leaders in a new style of cricket business organisation. The work that is done on behalf of the Club is not seen as a chore. There are no set hours, and for Edwards there has been no holiday for two years at a stretch, but an essential unity between playing staff, administration and members is preserved.

The senior officials of the Club, Tom Pearce, 'Tiny' Waterman and Doug Insole, insisted that, having been appointed, Peter Edwards should be allowed to administer the affairs of the Club within the broad guidelines of policies laid down by the Executive Committee.

61. *Peter Edwards*

Each member of the Committee has a particular talent from which the Club benefits, expertise that ranges from banking and tax knowledge to land culture and to close contact with the National Cricket Association, club and schools cricket. The day-to-day running of the Club is left to Edwards just as the selection of the side is left to the captain. Advice and help can be sought and is given freely, but those trusted with responsibility are allowed to shoulder it unhampered.

Peter Edwards took up his position on 1 January 1979, turning his back on an industry where he could soon have hoped to earn more than he would ever earn as a county secretary. In the next few years, however, the business of cricket was to grow larger and larger, and the Essex turnover was to approach £1 million a year. The budget is drawn up meticulously at the beginning of each year and relevant items are fed through the various sub-committees, although the festival committees, so long a part of Essex cricket, were disbanded as the business side of Essex cricket was streamlined. This was an inevitability, for the central and professional control of affairs is essential in an organisation which now derives only 11 per cent of its total income from gate receipts.

The Club had a long history of friendly co-operation between the Committee, players and staff and Edwards was anxious to do everything in his power to extend this relationship. His first physical act was a symbolic one. He changed the decor in the dressing-room to blue. They had been painted green, and he felt that nobody would win anything with green changing-rooms.

A more significant factor at the commencement of the 1979 season was that for the first time for more than a decade Essex had adequate reserve strength with the staff being increased to 17 players. Pringle, now at Cambridge, had made his debut the previous season, although in a quieter manner than Lilley, and McEvoy, Sainsbury and Herbert were all capable performers. Gooch and Lever had been with Brearley's side in Australia, and both had matured into international cricketers of the highest quality. Gooch had retained his awesome power while throwing off his impetuosity, while all the qualities which had made Lever an outstanding county cricketer, eagerness, application, stamina, wisdom and variety, were now enriched by the flavour of Test match competition which sent him back to Essex with even greater resolve and understanding.

Gooch's maturation had been aided by Fletcher's decision that he should open the innings. This move allowed Gooch more time to build an innings and, in essence, put Essex on the attack from the start. It also allowed Hardie to give the middle order substance and solidity and, when needed, aggression and panache.

Hardie endured two lean years with the bat, but no player could have approached the game with more determination. He came to terms with his technical limitations and fashioned his style within those limits. The result was a batsman for all occasions, anxious always to get onto the front foot, but with the ability to temper his game to the needs of the side. When, later, he was to revert to opening, he was a more accomplished and varied batsman. As he became a rock of Essex cricket, not least for his contribution in the field, Hardie's personality developed. Always a man of wit and humour, within the spirit of success, he also took on a happy eccentricity which marked him as a cricketer of fun, yet never detracted from his growing knowledge of and commitment to the game.

Whatever technical and tactical maturity had been achieved by Essex as a side by the end of the 1970s, the debate as to their temperament continued, and many doubted that they could harness their application, dedication, discipline and attitude into a self-belief that would not waver in moments of pressure and tension. In any initial achievement, a psychological barrier has to be broken.

The 1979 season began chilly and unwelcoming. There was victory in a John Player League game at Edgbaston, but the Sunday matches were not to be the focal point of the Essex year. Appropriately, the opening championship match was against Kent, the reigning champions and seemingly an Essex 'bogey' side. The game was played at Chelmsford at the beginning of May. It began with James Callaghan as Prime Minister and ended with Margaret Thatcher in Downing Street. Play on the first day was limited to 49 overs, and on the second, when Essex threatened to falter at 129 for 5, Turner hit 102 in 110 minutes with five sixes and nine fours. Pont and Phillip afforded exciting support, and Essex reached 305 for 7. In spite of a century from Rowe, Kent trailed by 55 runs, and Essex took six points to the visitors' five.

In retrospect, it is possible to read too much into this performance, but the Essex recovery and the minor success in the match were a strengthener to confidence, an assertion that the County could survive against, and indeed match, the toughest of opposition. For the time being, however, the emphasis was to be on the zonal matches in the Benson and Hedges Cup, where Essex were placed with Northamptonshire, the Combined Universities, Surrey and Sussex.

Fletcher had decided that Alan Lilley would play in the one-day matches, opening the innings with Gooch, and that Denness would be used only in championship games. In the first match, at Northampton, Gooch and Lilley put on 67 for the first wicket, and a fine knock from Fletcher took Essex to 230 for 5 in their 55 overs. Cook and Larkins responded with an opening stand of 85, and it was David Acfield who broke the partnership, having both batsmen caught by Gooch. Acfield's contribution in the one-day game has been greatly undervalued. Accurate and intelligent with his off-spin, he has never been anything but economical and has often been a destructive force. Yardley and Lamb threatened, but Essex won by three runs.

At The Oval, the position was reversed. In spite of Lever's 4 for 29 and Fletcher's 72, Surrey were the victors by seven runs.

The match against Combined Universities at Chelmsford was seen as a certain victory for Essex, but the manner and size of the win was exhilarating. Gooch and Lilley began with what was then a competition record stand of 223. Both batsmen hit gloriously aggressive centuries, and Essex's 350 for 3 and win by 214 runs were Benson and Hedges records. Four days later, Gooch and Lilley continued where they had ended against the Universities, and, chasing a target of 189, Essex beat Sussex by seven wickets with nearly 15 overs to spare and were in the quarter-finals of the Benson and Hedges Cup.

This was, in itself, nothing new, but the success in the Benson and Hedges Cup had been attended by good form in the championship, and the combination of the two had excited morale and raised expectations. A rain-ruined draw at Lord's was followed by a maximum-point innings victory over Derbyshire at Chesterfield. Gooch and Fletcher both hit centuries in this match, and the captain's 140 was his first three-figure innings for Essex for two years.

For Fletcher, this was an important innings, and it anticipated a season which was to see him score more than 1000 championship runs as well as vital contributions in the one-day matches. It was believed then that his Test career was at an end, and, like all else in this great player's career, his international record, seven Test hundreds and an average of more than 40, was ignored by many who mistook quietness and reticence for weakness and ineffectiveness. Ultimately, all were to come to see that he was the possessor of one of the shrewdest brains the game has known, that on the field he was a skillful leader of men, that his judgment of a wicket or a player or of a situation was extremely sound and that he controlled his team with discipline which was at variance with his rather self-effacing personality. He set down no rules, but those under his leadership knew exactly what was expected of them, and they had the utmost respect for him both as a man and as a player. Those who served under him followed him unquestioningly, yet he listened to opinion and explained his actions.

Fletcher's 140 not out against Derbyshire was augmented by destructive bowling by the pace trio, Lever, Phillip and Turner, and by some excellent close catching. Sixteen catches were taken, and when Derbyshire, having been bowled out for 63 in their first innings, defied Essex with a stolid opening partnership in the second, Hardie took a remarkable catch at short-leg to dismiss Wright; the gate was open.

It was, however, the week at Ilford which first gave the hint of championship form. There was play only on the last day in the match with Glamorgan which meant the game was a single-innings one for 12 points. The visitors took 75 overs in which to make 184 for 7, even though they had a liberal helping of leg-breaks from Fletcher and Hardie. Essex had 33 overs in which to make the runs. Denness left at 44, but Gooch and McEwan hit the remaining 141 runs in 82 minutes to bring victory with 5.3 overs remaining. Gooch hit two sixes and 12 fours in his 93 and McEwan two sixes and eight fours in his 67. Over the next few years there was no lovelier sight in cricket than Gooch and McEwan in partnership, and one remains eternally grateful for the privilege of watching these two destroy opposing attacks with an alliance of power and beauty.

The second match in Ilford week saw Hardie reach his first hundred of the season, and Lever take 7 for 27 in the first innings when Lancashire were bowled out for 84. Acfield took 4 for 11 when the Red Rose county followed on, and Essex won by an innings.

Essex lost the services of Gooch after this match, for he was in England's team for the World Cup. Lever had not been selected, and this proved to be a grave mistake on the part of the England selectors although to Essex it proved the greatest boon. He bowled Essex to victory on the last afternoon against Leicestershire at Chelmsford, taking 13 for 117 in the match, after Denness, 122, and Neil Smith, 90 not out, had brought maximum batting points from a seemingly lost cause.

At Edgbaston, Lever took 13 for 87 and McEwan hit a magnificent 208 not out in under four hours with five sixes and 22 fours. Essex again won by an innings. It was the fifth win in succession. At the end of May, they had led the championship by ten points, and that lead was being increased match by match, but attention had again swung to the Benson and Hedges Cup.

The quarter-final against Warwickshire brought a packed house in the sun to Chelmsford, but there was a nervous start for the home side. Although McEvoy deputised for Gooch in the championship matches, Lilley, with considerable success, opened in the one-day games. His experience was still very limited, and the jungle telegraph of the first-class game is quick to broadcast recognised vulnerabilities. Lilley was deemed to be weak outside the off-stump, and bowlers attacked him there. Twice he played tentatively at Ferreira before touching him to Amiss at slip. Essex were 2 for 1 in the second over. McEwan and Gooch now engaged in a partnership which was likely to decide the outcome of the match.

Willis bowled at his fastest and best. He conceded only one run in his first six overs, and of his allocation of 11, five were to be maidens. After 10 of their 55 overs, Essex were 19 for 1.

Gooch and McEwan played with sense and dignity, knowing that the rest of the Warwickshire attack would not maintain the threat that Willis posed. Once the initial assault had been countered, Gooch and McEwan moved on to the attack. In 1½ hours 100 was reached, but McEwan was well caught and bowled soon after reaching his fifty.

Fletcher scurried and dabbed for 43 in a stand of 90. Hardie went quickly, but Pont hit 22 in five overs. The stage now, however, was dominated by Gooch, who ravaged the visiting attack. Three overs from Ferreira brought 45 runs. Five from Willis cost 31. With eight men posted on the boundary, Essex scored 97 runs from the last ten overs of the innings. Gooch, in expansive form, was out to the second ball of the last over for 138, which included a six into the car-park and 19 fours, hit with immense power through the ring of boundary fielders.

Chasing a target of 272, Warwickshire began comfortably, but the advent of Turner brought the breakthrough. Amiss attempted to turn a ball down the leg side and Neil Smith took a fine catch. Two runs later, in a frenzy of indecision, Whitehouse was run out at the bowler's end. The elegant Kallicharran was immediately off the mark, but flashed at Turner to be caught behind. At tea, Warwickshire were 36 for 3, and the match

62. *One-day cricket requires greater score-board space than that of the average club score-board. As a result, Essex created their now famous mobile score-board. The first was made in 1962 from an old moving van adapted by J P Hensman Ltd (now Laidlaws of Brentwood). It was damaged by fire in 1971 and replaced by the articulated vehicle shown above, which was converted by L & A Pinch of Hornchurch.*

virtually settled. Eventually, the visitors made 227, and Essex had qualified to meet Yorkshire in the semi-final.

It is generally accepted in all sports that one is more upset to lose a semi-final than any other round of a knock-out competition, so near and yet so far, so that the tension at this stage of a tournament is at its greatest. The 1979 semi-final of the Benson and Hedges Cup had an added sharpness because, as Pat Gibson of the *Daily Express* remarked, it was a 'contest in which Yorkshire, who have almost forgotten what it's like to win a major title, tormented Essex, who have never found out'.

Fletcher won the toss and asked Yorkshire to bat first in front of another crowded Chelmsford on a day that was warm and sunny. The visitors were without Boycott, but it was more the form of Lever and Phillip and the hint of early moisture that influenced Fletcher in his decision. There was no immediate reward, and the first ten overs produced 41 runs. Turner and Pont applied restraint, but when Pont erred in direction he was hit for 22 in two overs, which included a massive six over long-off by Hampshire. At 107, in 29 overs, Hampshire attempted another giant hit off East, but Turner took a splendid running catch on the long-on boundary.

If the first round of the match had gone emphatically to Yorkshire, the second went most definitely to Essex. In their last 26 overs, Yorkshire lost eight wickets while adding only 66 runs. Sharp, gripped by nerves, was

63. *The electronic score-board at Chelmsford, erected in 1981, was donated to the Club by the contracting company George Wimpey, to commemorate its Centenary in Essex. The score-board, shown here during the final stage of construction, can accommodate the requirements of one-day cricket, and requires only two operators.* (Clive Tarling)

lbw to Phillip. Athey, ill at ease, grotesquely chopped on to East so that, at lunch, Yorkshire were 114 for 3.

In the early afternoon, Love swung Pont to square-leg and was caught by McEwan, and Phillip, who was now bowling with considerable pace, yorked Lumb in the 46th over. The opener had scored 74 and while he remained there was always hope for the visitors. Bairstow was run out by Pont's under-arm throw as he tried to inject some life into his team-mates, and Lever accounted for both Stevenson and Carrick. Sidebottom fell to Turner, and from the last over of the innings, Old managed only a single.

A target of 174 was well within the capabilities of Essex, although the County was notoriously bad at chasing. Two handsome off-side shots by Gooch in the opening over gave a confidence which soon evaporated when Lilley fended outside the off stump to Stevenson's first ball and was caught behind. McEwan began rather feverishly, appeared to settle, but, at 42, he was also caught behind. Fletcher's brief flurry was ended by a spectacular catch in the gully by Sidebottom, the fielder needing to leave the field for repairs, and Gooch's innings of sense and aggression finished when he was caught high on the leg side by Bairstow.

Gooch made 49, and Essex were 99 for 4. A pattern had emerged wherein every time Essex seemed about to take a grip on the game they had lost a vital wicket. Hardie had given the batting a look of solidity without ever losing the opportunity to score, but at 112, he gave Bairstow his fourth catch of the innings, and the game was much in Yorkshire's favour.

Phillip and Pont curbed their natural inclinations to swing the bat, and edged Essex closer to their target, but at 139, Phillip could contain himself no longer and hit Carrick high to mid-off.

Turner now joined Pont, and brisk running, sound defence and the eager eye for the loose ball brought Essex to the brink of victory. Desperately needing a breakthrough, Hampshire, the Yorkshire captain, brought back Old to finish his quota, but Pont and Turner stood firm.

For 26 overs, in conjunction with Hardie, Phillip and finally Turner, Pont played outstandingly, and when he was caught in the 54th over Essex were only five short of victory. Pont's 36, his bowling and fielding won him the Gold Award and underlined the Essex dependence on the bread-and-butter players, the belief that there are no stars and that a total team commitment with each man shouldering responsibility is the formula for success.

The dismissal of Pont gave Yorkshire an outside chance of victory, particularly if the Essex nerve failed, but Turner hit a single and Neil Smith drove the first ball he received through the covers for four; Essex were in their first final.

For Smith, it must have been a most satisfying moment. Rejected by Yorkshire, he had struck the blow which had beaten them. His initial form with Essex was inconsistent, but in 1979, he was the best wicket-keeper in England on day-to-day performance, and his powers of hitting, rather stiff-armed, were considerable. Troubled by weight problems and fitness, he was to have a comparatively short career with Essex, but his prowess behind the stumps in one golden summer marked him as a keeper of high quality whose potential was never consistently realised.

Whatever the excitement at reaching the Final of the Benson and Hedges Cup, attention was also firmly focussed on the championship. A stumble at Bath, where the side was fortunate to escape defeat, was followed by Derbyshire's visit to Chelmsford. The visitors were soon in grave trouble at 53 for 6, but Swarbrook, Tunnicliffe and Walters hit fifties, and Derbyshire made 258. When Lilley was caught for nought, and Essex finished the day on 8 for 1, there were hints that the quality performances which had taken the County to the top of the Championship were nearing their close. On the second morning, however, McEwan and Denness put on 131 in 25 overs for the third wicket. McEwan's knock lasted for 47 overs and he scored 185 out of 239. His innings included three sixes and 29 fours, and Essex finished on 435 for 9. Lever and Phillip bowled Essex to victory by mid-afternoon on the Friday.

In the meantime, Kent, in second place, drew with Middlesex, and the meeting between the two top sides, at Tunbridge Wells, was ruined by rain. Essex entered Southend week at the beginning of July with a championship lead of 67 points. John Lever, who could have served England so well, had taken 53 wickets in the month of June. His constant endeavour, consistent force as a strike bowler, total dedication and commitment, and appetite for bowling have made Lever one of the most important players in the history of Essex cricket, and it is fitting that his worth has been recognised by his fellow professionals who have twice voted him the Reg Hayter Trophy.

Southend week began with a ten-wicket victory over Sussex. Denness, 136, and Gooch, 86, put on 170 for the first wicket, and the seam attack shared all the Sussex wickets, yet in the second half of the week, it was the spinners who brought Essex victory.

The match was against Nottinghamshire, who were among those challenging Essex at the top of the table, and Essex were weakened by the absence of Gooch and Lever, both in the England party for the Edgbaston Test. Initially the game went in favour of Nottinghamshire . Essex lost their last seven first innings wickets for 81, were out for 240 by tea time, and Nottinghamshire finished the day on 100 for 2, Rice in dominant mood. East and Acfield bowled well on the second day to restrict the visitors' lead to 60, but Essex lost four wickets before the arrears were cleared, and they faced their first championship defeat of the season.

Fletcher batted with his customary grit on a wicket which was wearing, but when he chopped a catch to gully Essex were 113 for 6 and likely to be beaten before lunch on the final day. Phillip and Turner elected to attack the bowling, and Turner took 14 in one over from Bore, the main spin threat. Phillip reached 40 before Bore dismissed him, and when Smith and East followed in quick succession the game was still in favour of Nottinghamshire. Acfield, with determined defence, then joined the belligerent Turner in a last wicket stand of 42, another of the resolute performances which was to be the margin between victory and defeat.

Nottinghamshire needed 170 to win, and after 30 minutes they were confronted by the spinners, East and Acfield. Harris was lbw to East at 40, but the crucial point came when Fletcher decided that his bowlers should operate at different ends. Acfield immediately took two wickets, and they went to tea at 108 for 4. In 12.2 overs after tea, the last six wickets fell for 15 runs to give Essex victory by 46 runs. The true value of the Turner–Acfield stand was now apparent. What was equally apparent was the all-round strength of the Essex side. Lever and the seam bowlers had dominated in June, but the spin bowling had proved lethal enough to bring a remarkable victory when it was most needed, and Essex sat high on top of the championship table. This created a happy frame of mind in which to approach the Benson and Hedges Final, the most important match in the Club's history.

Whatever the future holds for Essex cricket, nothing will ever detract from the events of 21 July 1979. In effect, that day separates the past from the present and future. Lord's was lapped in sunshine, and the crowd was happy and expectant. Surrey, the only side to have beaten Essex on their way to the Final, were handicapped by the absence of Clarke, and Essex had decided to include the experienced Denness in place of Lilley. It was a move that had not been unexpected.

Roger Knight won the toss and asked Essex to bat. Denness was to say later that in all his career, with Kent and as captain of England, he had never experienced a reception like the roar which greeted him and Gooch when they appeared on the pavilion steps and began their walk to the wicket.

Denness himself could never have begun better, and flowing shots from the two openers brought 21 runs in the first three overs. Knight brought himself into the attack to attempt to slow the scoring, but Gooch, who had driven Jackman square and flicked Wilson off his toes to the boundary, hit the Surrey captain through mid-wicket for four.

The score was 48 and the innings was not 11 overs old when Denness drove a little lazily at Wilson and was caught at cover by Smith. It had been a sumptuous opening, but it was a mere appetiser for what was to come. McEwan, with the nervous start that suggested human frailty and gave his batting an added appeal, settled after a couple of unwise flourishes at Wilson, and for a time, he and Gooch were quiet against Knight and Intikhab Alam. It was Gooch who decided upon a change of tempo and moving down the wicket, he hit Knight high to the nursery end sight-screen for six. The initiative now passed to Essex, and McEwan attacked Pocock with a savage beauty. His fifty came off 68 balls, and at lunch, after 37 overs, Essex were 166 for 1.

Only six runs were added in the afternoon session before McEwan sliced a ball from Wilson to Richards behind the stumps. Off 99 balls, he had scored 72, which included ten fours. The second wicket stand had realised 124, a record for the Benson and Hedges Cup Final. Moreover, the crowd had witnessed unforgettable batting of the very highest quality, 'a thing of beauty' that was to be 'a joy for ever'.

64. *Stuart Turner (left) and Mike Denness. Mike Denness played for Essex for four years from 1977, following a successful period as captain of Kent. It was not a new experience for him to hold up the Benson & Hedges Cup, but it certainly was for Stuart Turner, who had been striving for many years to help win Essex's first trophy.* (Ilford Recorder)

To sustain the brilliance and momentum of the Gooch and McEwan stand was a most difficult task, yet the innings that followed must rank as one of the most magnificent miniatures ever seen at Lord's. From the start, Keith Fletcher was on the attack. An initiative had been won which he was unwilling to relinquish. From 30 balls, he hit 34 runs in little over half an hour as he and Gooch put on 67 at nearly seven an over. He was bowled when he overbalanced in trying to drive Knight to the off, but he had proved, as so often before and since, a man for the occasion.

Gooch continued with that brooding, powerful majesty that was to bring him the first century in a Benson and Hedges final. The range of shots and the seemingly effortless might were astonishing. Wilson moved in from a run that started almost at the pavilion steps and Gooch flicked the ball off his toes into the Mound Stand. A repeat of the shot lifted the ball on to the roof of the same stand.

Hardie was out when going for a big hit, and Gooch's great innings came to an end in the 53rd over when he swung inelegantly at Wilson and was bowled. There were three sixes and 11 fours in his 120. It was the first of a run of successes in Lord's finals which Gooch was to maintain over the next six years.

Pont struck some heavy blows, and Essex finished on 290 for 6, the highest score a side had made in a Benson and Hedges final.

Much of the Surrey strength rested on Alan Butcher, who had been in splendid form, but with the score on 21, Lever produced an astounding delivery which came back sharply at the left-handed Butcher, took the inside edge and gave Neil Smith a catch. Lynch began fretfully, and he impatiently drove at Ray East, who had come on as first change at the nursery end, and was well caught at deep mid-off by McEwan.

Knight and Howarth engaged in a stand which, although effective, contrasted in style with the Gooch–McEwan stand. After 30 overs, Surrey were ahead of Essex at the same stage, but at the cost of one more wicket, and in 18 overs, Knight and Howarth added 91. Pont had come in for some rough treatment, but it was he who broke the stand. Knight drove hard at a ball just short of a length and the ball flew high and wide down the leg side for Smith to take a spectacular leaping catch.

David Smith kept the pace of the innings going with some brave shots, and when Fletcher brought back Lever, Howarth hooked high to Denness, who missed the catch. It was the hook which was Howarth's downfall, however, for he swung across the line at Pont and sent the ball soaring into the air. Fletcher, close in on the leg side, took a towering catch, and Surrey were 205 for 5 in the 42nd over.

The ambitious Smith was bowled by Phillip, who also claimed Intikhab, caught at long-on. Jackman was beaten in the flight and bowled by East,

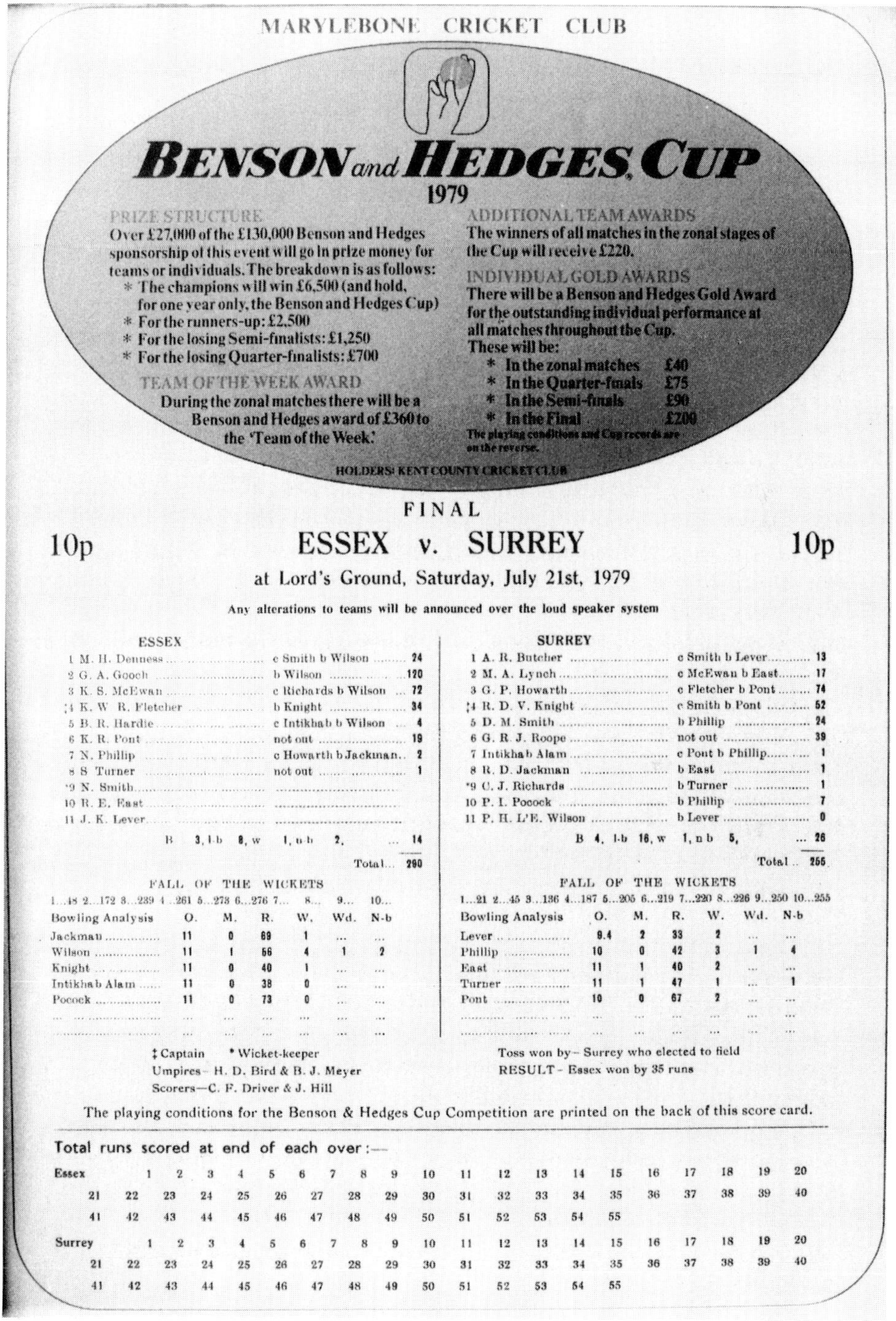

MARYLEBONE CRICKET CLUB

BENSON and HEDGES CUP

1979

PRIZE STRUCTURE

Over £27,000 of the £130,000 Benson and Hedges sponsorship of this event will go in prize money for teams or individuals. The breakdown is as follows:

* The champions will win £6,500 (and hold, for one year only, the Benson and Hedges Cup)
* For the runners-up: £2,500
* For the losing Semi-finalists: £1,250
* For the losing Quarter-finalists: £700

TEAM OF THE WEEK AWARD

During the zonal matches there will be a Benson and Hedges award of £360 to the 'Team of the Week.'

ADDITIONAL TEAM AWARDS

The winners of all matches in the zonal stages of the Cup will receive £220.

INDIVIDUAL GOLD AWARDS

There will be a Benson and Hedges Gold Award for the outstanding individual performance at all matches throughout the Cup. These will be:

* In the zonal matches £40
* In the Quarter-finals £75
* In the Semi-finals £90
* In the Final £200

The playing conditions and Cup records are on the reverse.

HOLDERS: KENT COUNTY CRICKET CLUB

FINAL

10p **ESSEX v. SURREY** 10p

at Lord's Ground, Saturday, July 21st, 1979

Any alterations to teams will be announced over the loud speaker system

ESSEX

1 M. H. Denness	c Smith b Wilson	24
2 G. A. Gooch	b Wilson	120
3 K. S. McEwan	c Richards b Wilson	72
‡4 K. W. R. Fletcher	b Knight	34
5 B. R. Hardie	c Intikhab b Wilson	4
6 K. R. Pont	not out	19
7 N. Phillip	c Howarth b Jackman	2
8 S. Turner	not out	1
*9 N. Smith		
10 R. E. East		
11 J. K. Lever		
	B 3, l-b 8, w 1, n-b 2,	14
	Total	290

FALL OF THE WICKETS

1...48 2...172 3...239 4...261 5...273 6...276 7... 8... 9... 10...

Bowling Analysis	O.	M.	R.	W.	Wd.	N-b
Jackman	11	0	69	1	...	...
Wilson	11	1	56	4	1	2
Knight	11	0	40	1	...	...
Intikhab Alam	11	0	38	0	...	...
Pocock	11	0	73	0	...	...

SURREY

1 A. R. Butcher	c Smith b Lever	13
2 M. A. Lynch	c McEwan b East	17
3 G. P. Howarth	c Fletcher b Pont	74
‡4 R. D. V. Knight	c Smith b Pont	52
5 D. M. Smith	b Phillip	24
6 G. R. J. Roope	not out	39
7 Intikhab Alam	c Pont b Phillip	1
8 R. D. Jackman	b East	1
*9 C. J. Richards	b Turner	1
10 P. I. Pocock	b Phillip	7
11 P. H. L'E. Wilson	b Lever	0
	B 4, l-b 16, w 1, n b 5,	26
	Total	255

FALL OF THE WICKETS

1...21 2...45 3...136 4...187 5...205 6...219 7...220 8...226 9...250 10...255

Bowling Analysis	O.	M.	R.	W.	Wd.	N-b
Lever	9.4	2	33	2	...	...
Phillip	10	0	42	3	1	4
East	11	1	40	2	...	...
Turner	11	1	47	1	...	1
Pont	10	0	67	2	...	...

‡ Captain * Wicket-keeper

Umpires – H. D. Bird & B. J. Meyer

Scorers—C. F. Driver & J. Hill

Toss won by – Surrey who elected to field

RESULT – Essex won by 35 runs

The playing conditions for the Benson & Hedges Cup Competition are printed on the back of this score card.

Total runs scored at end of each over:—

Essex																			
1	2	3	4	5	6	7	8	9	10	11	12	13	14	15	16	17	18	19	20
21	22	23	24	25	26	27	28	29	30	31	32	33	34	35	36	37	38	39	40
41	42	43	44	45	46	47	48	49	50	51	52	53	54	55					

Surrey																			
1	2	3	4	5	6	7	8	9	10	11	12	13	14	15	16	17	18	19	20
21	22	23	24	25	26	27	28	29	30	31	32	33	34	35	36	37	38	39	40
41	42	43	44	45	46	47	48	49	50	51	52	53	54	55					

65. *Benson & Hedges Cup Final, Essex v Surrey, 21 July 1979.*

and Turner, having bowled a vital maiden to Roope, beat Richards's forward shot and bowled him.

Roope hit one splendid six into the Mound Stand, but with 5 overs remaining, Surrey needed 44 to win. Phillip splattered Pocock's stumps, and when Lever beat Wilson's forward push and bowled him, Essex had won by 35 runs, so taking their first major trophy in the 103 years of the Club history. Psychologically, Essex had run their first sub-four-minute-mile.

The excitement that the triumph caused lasted well into the following week when Hampshire were beaten by an innings at Bournemouth, the game ending at lunch on the third day. Lever's wonderful form continued, and his 7 for 40 was largely responsible for Hampshire being bowled out for 128 in their first innings. Essex did not find batting easy, and they lost seven wickets for 208, but Hardie produced an undefeated century of great character, and the last three Essex wickets added 172 runs, East scoring 48, and Acfield again defiant in a last wicket stand of 40.

In May 1974, Hardie had come to public notice when he scored four in two hours, 22 minutes against Hampshire at Chelmsford. A decade later, journalists were still referring to him as the 'dour' Scot, yet this is the most inaccurate of descriptions, for he is a player of individual style, flexible and firm.

Hampshire batted again 252 runs in arrears, but an opening partnership of 117 between Greenidge and Rice gave them hope. However, the introduction of the spinners changed the face of the game. Hampshire lost ten wickets for 102, Acfield took 5 for 61 and East 4 for 48. Essex were now 69 points clear at the top of the Championship with just over a month of the season remaining.

Colchester week began with a match of bewildering eccentricity. An over-watered pitch produced a first day when Gloucestershire made 92 and 66 for 1 and Essex made 170. Eventually, Essex won by four wickets in two days. A first innings recovery from 37 for 6 was brought about by some violent hitting from 'Nobby' Phillip, and David Acfield's 6 for 56 was decisive in the second innings.

In spite of Keith Fletcher's career-best bowling performance of 5 for 41, Essex lost their first county match of the season when Middlesex won by ten wickets in the second half of Colchester week. Ominously, the defeat came on the first three days of August, and as it was followed by an innings defeat at Worcester; there were apprehensions that the August malaise would strike again.

In reality, the Championship was as good as settled. Essex needed 20 points from five games while Worcestershire, their nearest challengers, needed the maximum 80 points from 4 games. On 18, 20 and 21 August, Essex travelled to Northampton while Worcestershire went to Derby.

66. *At last! Essex's first Championship was clinched on 21 August 1979 when Northamptonshire were beaten by seven wickets at Northampton. Brian Hardie hit the winning run in partnership with Keith Pont.* (Fotosports)

67. *The Northampton scoreboard shows the Championship winning score.* (E T Brace)

Essex were soon in good spirits in their match when they reduced Northants to 83 for 5. However, Peter Willey, who had come in at 9 for 3, hit a bravely defiant hundred, 131 out of an innings total of 224. He was lbw to Turner, who took 5 for 70. Essex began well enough, with McEwan and Fletcher scoring freely, but they later floundered against Sarfraz, lost their last seven wickets for 56 and were out for 199.

Northamptonshire threatened to establish a big lead when they passed a hundred for the loss of two wickets in their second innings, but their last seven wickets fell for 97, and Essex needed 229 to win. Stuart Turner finished with 5 for 56, and for the only time in his career achieved the distinction of taking ten wickets in a match.

Essex had five hours in which to score the runs they needed for victory. Denness and Hardie, the two Scotsmen, gave them an admirable start with a stand of 113. The failure of either Lilley or McEvoy to establish himself as an opener in Gooch's absences on international duty had caused Fletcher to call again on Hardie as an opener, and he responded with his usual application.

After Denness had chopped a Williams off-break onto his stumps, McEwan began urgently and hit a massive six over mid-wicket, but he was lbw at 132, and Fletcher joined Hardie in an important stand. By the time that the last 20 overs were called, Essex were only 30 short of victory.

68. *When Essex eventually won the Championship after 103 years, the endeavour was universally acknowledged across the country, and the media were quick to react to the success of a very popular team. This cartoon by David Langdon links Essex's success with the then sponsor of the County Championship, Schweppes.*

At 210, Fletcher edged to slip, but he had made a significant contribution to this decisive match.

Hardie reached his century, and with 9.3 overs remaining, he made the winning hit off Yardley's bowling. Half an hour later, it was learned that Worcestershire had failed to beat Derbyshire and Essex were County Champions.

Fletcher remarked later that, although the win in the Benson and Hedges Cup had been most pleasing, it was the County Championship which was most coveted. This, above all, was the trophy that cricketers wanted to win, and Cinderella had at last arrived at the ball.

Peter Edwards had travelled to Northampton with champagne in the boot of his car in preparation for championship celebrations, and there was a joyous reception for Essex when they entertained Surrey at Chelmsford in the next match. Batting floundered somewhat, but Surrey,

69. *After 103 barren years, it was little wonder that Essex took great pride in winning its first trophies in 1979. Pictured with the Benson & Hedges Cup and the Lord's Taverners Trophy for the County Championship is the Club's teddy mascot created by Mrs G Cook of Brentwood.* (Stanland)

needing only 115 to win, were bowled out for 99 on the last afternoon. The seam attack of Lever, Phillip and Turner had once again proved devastating.

There was another victory over Northamptonshire and losses in the last two games, against Leicestershire and Yorkshire, but the final margin of Essex's championship win was an astonishing 77 points. Lever reached 100 wickets for the season, and the cricket world was genuinely pleased for Essex. In an ecstatic editorial, the *Daily Telegraph* gave unstinted praise to Fletcher and commented that the side had played with the joy that had always marked their cricket:

> With high spirits and good temper, with friendliness and chivalry, with an abundance of horseplay, strokeplay and jokes, without resentment, tantrums or moods, without decisions questioned or selves put first, without undue solemnity, with all the life-enhancing qualities which give pleasure to friend and foe alike. A team full of character and characters, in fact, which has proved that you can enjoy cricket and win as well.

The problem that confronted Essex after 1979 was that where once success had been hoped for, it was now expected. In former times, the 1980 season with an appearance in a Lord's final would have been considered triumphant, but now it was a disappointment.

The first shadow on the season appeared in the first home championship match, against Somerset at Ilford. The visitors were bowled out for 222 on the Saturday, and Essex, with Gooch and Fletcher in command, reached 63 for 2. By the Monday, a mystery virus had decimated the Essex ranks. Gooch, McEwan, Phillip, Denness and Pont were confined to bed while Turner and Hardie were both unwell. The home county could muster only 118 and took the field a second time with only three fit bowlers and four substitutes. Rose set Essex to make 402 on the last day, but a marvellous rearguard action between the unfit Hardie, 95, and Fletcher, 99, forced a draw by adding 193 for the third wicket.

With Phillip and McEwan still unwell, Neil Foster was summoned from his school, Philip Morant in Colchester, to make his first-class debut in the second game of Ilford week, against Kent. He dismissed Woolmer and Tavare in successive overs, finished with 3 for 51, and, thanks to a Gooch century, Essex gained their first championship win. They also won their next match, against Surrey at Chelmsford, but there were only two more victories in the championship in the rest of the summer, and the County finished eighth.

The John Player League brought even less joy, victories in the last four matches lifting the side from bottom to fourteenth in the table.

In the Benson and Hedges Cup, Essex strode to their second final in successive years. They suffered one defeat in the zonal matches when Gloucestershire won at Bristol, but Surrey were swept aside in the quarter-final, and in the semi-final, which rain spread into three days, Worcestershire were beaten by eight wickets. Essex needed 237 to win, a difficult task, but Gooch, who had hit the first double century of his career in the opening first-class match at Cambridge, and Denness began with a stand of 136, and McEwan hit 65 not out in quick time to bring victory with four overs to spare.

The final at Lord's brought Northamptonshire as challengers to the cup holders. In spite of Allan Lamb's 72, Northamptonshire were bowled out for 209, and Essex seemed well on the way to victory with an opening stand of 52 between Gooch and Denness. Fletcher had relied on an all-seam attack, not using Ray East who was in the side which was the same eleven that had won the cup the previous year, but it was the advent of Willey and Williams, the off-spinners, which first prised the game from Essex's grasp.

Denness played rather loosely at Willey and was bowled, and McEwan and Gooch, having taken their side to 112, fell to injudicious and unnecessary shots. Fletcher, usually so capable against spin bowling, struggled painfully, and the run rate required became more demanding as wickets fell. From 112 for 1, Essex slipped to 160 for 6. With only four overs left, 47 were still required.

Lord's had been saturated on the Saturday so that the game lost something of its character in being postponed until the Monday, but that could not detract from the excitement of the closing stages. Griffiths, brought back in place of Williams, who had conceded only 19 runs in seven overs, was hit for 30 in two overs as Turner, briefly, and Phillip launched an attack. The last over began with Essex needing ten to draw level and so win the match on losing fewer wickets.

Unfortunately, Phillip, who more than any other batsman had shown the ability to plunder the Northamptonshire attack, was at the non-striker's end. Smith swung wildly at Sarfraz instead of attempting to give Phillip the strike and was bowled second ball. East nudged a single, but Phillip could not quite snatch victory from the last three balls, and Northamptonshire won by six runs.

The general feeling was that Essex had thrown away a match which they had been winning for most of its course. Nine days later, Essex were to surrender their interest in the Gillette Cup in an even more profligate manner.

A splendid win at Leicester, where McEwan hit a fine 119, gave the County a quarter-final tie against Surrey at Chelmsford. From the start, Essex looked in control as Gooch sent back the dangerous Butcher, Lever had Knight lbw, and only Clinton and Smith, with some solid resistance, made a final score of 195 for 7 possible.

This appeared to be a total well within the reach of Essex, but when Denness, McEwan, Gooch and Fletcher were tumbled out for 35 Surrey looked set for a most decisive victory. Hardie produced his characteristic blend of conservatism in defence and anarchy in attack and with Pont took the score to 100. Turner's stay was brief, but Hardie found an exciting partner in Norbert Phillip.

With resolute and sensible cricket, these two steered Essex towards a position of hope. In the 54th over, Phillip launched a violent attack on Sylvester Clarke, taking 15 runs off his fellow West Indian, and with Hardie collecting two from the last ball, Essex were 184 for 6. Twelve runs from four overs with four wickets in hand and two batsmen, Hardie, 70, and Phillip, 40, in command suggested a comfortable win, but after Phillip had taken a single off Jackman, Hardie played his first rash shot and was caught at mid-wicket. At 191, Phillip was insanely run out, and when Smith was bowled by Clarke Essex were four short of victory with only one wicket remaining.

As the last over was reached with the scores level, Essex still seemed likely to win, but on the fifth ball of the over, in going for the deciding run, Ray East was run out, and Surrey won the match having lost fewer wickets.

Essex's one claim to a trophy in 1980 was the *Daily Mirror* award for winning the floodlit match, the first in England, against the West Indies at Chelsea Football Ground. Sixes abounded, but it cannot be claimed that this was serious cricket.

Mike Denness stood down from first-class cricket at the end of the season and for a time led the 2nd XI and assisted in the Essex County Cricket Club Development Association which 'Jerry' Jerman, who has given so unsparingly of his time for the County, had founded in 1978.

Denness's contribution to Essex cricket was invaluable. In the twilight of his career, he gave his second county the calm experience of winning on the important occasion. It was a gift whose benefits can only be truly assessed by those who were closest to him and played with him.

The 1980 season was also to be the last full season for Neil Smith, for his form fell away at the start of 1981 and he lost his place to David East, a young man of bubble and bounce who had just graduated from the University of East Anglia where he read Biological Sciences. David East had played for the UEA and spent some time with Northamptonshire, but their apparent lack of interest in offering him a career in cricket caused him to write to his first love, Essex, for whom he had played youth cricket. He was engaged and made his first-class debut against Warwickshire at Edgbaston on 4, 6 and 7 July 1981. Essex won by eight wickets. David East was sent in as

70. *Occasionally, Essex have played in strange surroundings. Here, in 1980, they are playing the West Indies in a day-and-night match at Chelsea Football Club's Stamford Bridge ground in front of 11,000 spectators.* (Thomson & Robinson)

71. *Essex take to the field to play Gibraltar in the shadow of the Rock, 1973. Essex players, from left to right are John Lever, Bob Cooke, Keith Boyce, Robin Hobbs, Stuart Turner, Keith Fletcher, Neil Smith, Ray East and Brian Taylor.*

night-watchman and scored six, but Fletcher hit 123 not out. The young wicket-keeper had his first dismissal when he caught Thomas off Lever in the second innings. Essex were asked to make 283 to win in 125 minutes plus 20 overs. Hardie hit 111 not out, Fletcher hit 52, and the final assault on the bowling came from 'Nobby' Phillip who lashed 66 off 25 balls to take Essex to victory with six overs to spare.

This was only the second championship win of the season, the first having come against Middlesex in Ilford week when, with McEwan injured and Gooch on Test duty, Lilley took his opportunity and scored a lively 90 on his home pitch.

The win at Edgbaston, however, marked a change in the fortunes of Essex, and four out of the next five championship matches were won. Hardie reverted to opener, but with Gooch on international duty much of the time and Denness retired, the other opening spot caused some problems. McEvoy failed to establish himself, and he was later to move to Worcestershire. Chris Gladwin, a left-hander, which the County very much needed, opened against Lancashire at Southend, shared a stand of 128 with Hardie and hit 53. Bob Leiper was also given an outing and there was more experience for Pringle, who was as yet, however, not quite up to the standard of the evergreen Turner, who had a good all-round season.

Gooch, Hardie, McEwan and Fletcher, who reached 30,000 runs in his first-class career, enjoyed excellent seasons with the bat and all reached 1000 runs. Lever equalled the best bowling performance of his career when he took 8 for 49 at Headingley, and he finished with 80 first-class wickets in the season, but the outstanding performances came from David Acfield.

At Canterbury, Essex made 310, with McEwan hitting 102, and Kent were bowled out for 166. The seam bowlers sent down only 15 overs as Acfield and Ray East took over after the first 45 minutes. Acfield finished with 8 for 55, the best return of his career, and Ray East had 2 for 68. In the second innings, the positions were reversed. Kent, set to score 267, were bowled out for 126. East had 7 for 49, and Acfield 3 for 58.

When the teams met in the return match at Chelmsford less than a fortnight later, Essex won by an innings. Fletcher played a knock of outstanding quality, 165 not out, and Ray East had match figures of 12 for 123.

The spin combination of Ray East and David Acfield was as good as any in the country. Acfield finished the season with 76 first-class wickets at 22.61 runs each. Here surely is one of the most underrated of bowlers in the modern game. With the emphasis on seam in the one-day matches and with fewer and fewer spinners operating in the first-class game, Acfield's opportunities became more limited than they would have been 20 or 30 years earlier, yet he developed his ability with intelligent application and gentle humour.

Essex climbed to fifth in the Championship, but their main interest was in the John Player League and in the NatWest Bank Trophy. An early exit from the Benson and Hedges Cup was allied to an uncertain start in the John Player League with three wins, two losses and an abandonment in the first six matches.

The second defeat came at Ilford on 21 June, but the next three Sunday games saw Leicestershire, Warwickshire and Lancashire beaten with conviction. At Chelmsford, on 26 July, Gooch and Hardie each scored centuries and began with a partnership of 180. Essex won by 73 runs, and victory over Derbyshire in the next match took them clear to the top.

On 16 August, they went to Southampton, batted indifferently, lost control in the field and went down with an over to spare. Warwickshire were now challenging strongly, but at Milton Keynes, 'Nobby' Phillip hit 83 off 74 balls, a decisive innings on a slow wicket which helped greatly towards a 19-run win.

At Castle Park, Glamorgan were beaten with ease so that it was possible for Essex to clinch the title in the last match at Chelmsford, against Middlesex. The sun shone and the gates were closed before the start. Essex started well when Barlow fell to Lever for one, but Radley and Gatting batted steadily to improve the Middlesex position. It was the arrival of Butcher who scored 88 that lifted the run-rate. Nevertheless, Essex must well have been pleased to have restricted Middlesex to 190 in 38 overs.

The Essex reply began most uneasily. Hardie was out in the first over and Gooch in the ninth.

But McEwan was in splendid form from the start, and Fletcher gave him just the support that was needed. In 19 overs they added 106 before Fletcher was caught off Selvey. McEwan continued in majestic vein, but Phillip and Lilley went quickly, so that suddenly Essex needed 42 off the last 6 overs.

Turner gave McEwan as much of the strike as possible, and in the 36th over, the South African reached his century with two enormous sixes, one into the pavilion and one onto Riverside Stand, to move from 97 to 109. In the next over, however, he mis-hit Emburey and was caught. The last over began with Essex needing three to win and the experienced and well-set Turner at the non-striker's end. Ray East gave Edmonds a simple return catch second ball, but Pringle pushed forward at the third delivery and hit the fourth, hard off the edge, to the vacant area at third man for four. Unfortunately, Warwickshire also won so that the destiny of the John Player League remained open until the last match.

Essex journeyed to The Oval and batted first. After a short delay for rain the umpires decreed a 39-over match, and Essex soon lost Gooch. Thereafter runs were accumulated steadily until Phillip and Turner launched a frenzied attack for what they believed were the last overs, adding 51.

Turner was run out going for an impossible extra run, and the players left the field at 4.10. They returned immediately to play one more over, for as the game had been decreed 39 overs-a-side, 39 had to be bowled. It was an enormous bonus to Essex, for Norbert Phillip plundered 19 runs off this 'extra' over that was bowled by Roger Knight. Twice Phillip hit the ball on to the roof of the Surrey pavilion. He ended with 80 not out, and Essex on 203.

Surrey were never really in touch. Ray East bowled a beautiful spell, having Knight stumped by David East and conceding only 21 runs. Essex won by 21 runs, and Warwickshire were beaten at Taunton. At last, Essex had won the John Player League.

In the space of three seasons, they had won three of the four major trophies, and only the 60-over knock-out competition, now sponsored by the National Westminister Bank, eluded them. Their experiences in this tournament were even more horrendous than they had been the year before.

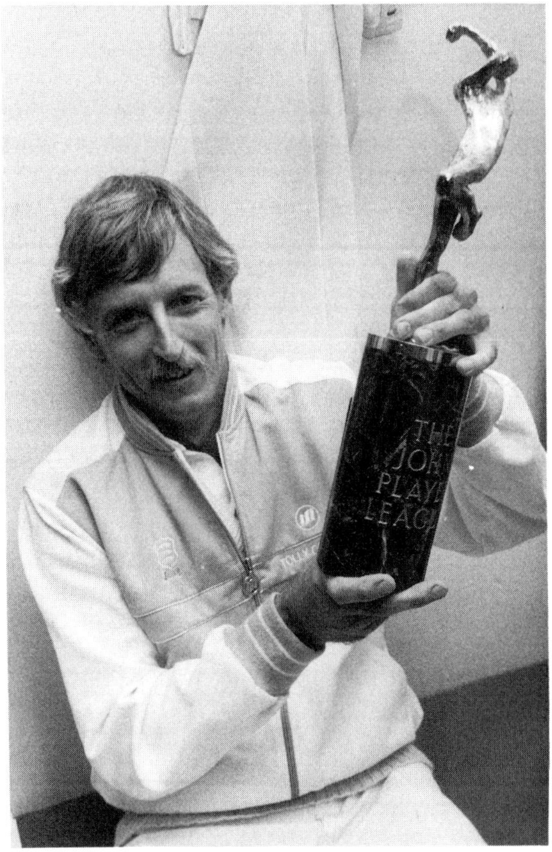

72. *Stuart Turner's record in the John Player League was second to none. He was the only player to score more than 3000 runs and take 300 wickets.*
(Clive Tarling)

The first round went well. Essex had to travel to Hitchin where they had been traumatically beaten five years earlier, but this time a Gooch century in an opening stand of 184 with Hardie set up victory over Hertfordshire by 191 runs. The second round took the County in Bristol to dismal weather, which spread the match over three days. Ray East led Essex in the absence of the injured Fletcher, and he decided to bat first when he won the toss.

Gooch and Lilley played well, but Childs and Graveney usually had the better of the batsmen, and it was the last three Essex wickets, which produced 55, which gave the innings any substance and took the total to 207. This proved more than adequate. Broad was immediately caught behind off Lever, and keeper East held breathtaking catches to account for Zaheer and Hignell. Zaheer fell when David East dived to his right, and Hignell went next ball when the young wicket-keeper dived to his left to hold a snick wide on the leg-side. He later caught Bainbridge and was named 'Man-of-the-Match' as Gloucestershire were shot out for 85.

The quarter-final took Essex to Hove for a most difficult tie against Sussex who were challenging for the championship and one of the strongest sides in the country. Fletcher was back to lead his side and elected to bat when he won the toss. Gooch and Hardie began with 63 in 18 overs, and in glorious weather, Essex looked set for a big total. However, the introduction of Imran and le Roux altered the balance of the game. Imran accounted for Gooch, Hardie and Fletcher. McEwan, playing with restraint, and Lilley appeared to rebuild the innings, but Phillip and Ray East both went first ball, and Essex slipped to 174 for 9. David East and John Lever ran for everything and another 21 were added without loss by the close of the innings.

David East took a sprawling catch down the leg-side to dismiss Barclay in Lever's opening over. Mendis and Parker took the score to 44 before Mendis skied a ball to the wicket-keeper.

Imran attacked Ray East and provided the necessary strokes to lift the Sussex innings, but, in a tense situation, Fletcher had complete control and dictated the pace of the game, frustrating batsmen into rash shots. Turner, told by members of the Sussex crowd that he was 'too old', retorted by dismissing Imran and Gould in the same over. Le Roux was run out by David East's throw, and Lever bowled Arnold and Waller in the 56th over to give Essex victory by 25 runs.

It seemed that the semi-final tie at Derby would be easy in comparison, but damp weather took the game into two days and the Essex batting faltered on a grassy wicket. Phillip and David East came together at 98 for 8 and added 46, but Essex were all out for 149 on the last ball of the 60th over.

Derbyshire enjoyed better batting conditions, but the tenacity of the Essex out-cricket and the relentless accuracy of the Essex seamers made the home side's task most difficult. A splendid 59 by Kim Barnett gave Derbyshire the edge, but when the eighth wicket fell at 133 the game was poised slightly in favour of Essex.

The last over arrived with Derbyshire needing ten to level the scores. Five runs came from Phillip's first four deliveries, and then the West Indian dropped a ball woefully short and Newman pulled it to the square-leg boundary. Fletcher readjusted his field for the last ball which was well pitched up on off stump. Newman could only push forward just out of Fletcher's grasp at silly mid-off. Phillip, following through, picked the ball up and turned. Hardie had taken up a position at the bowler's end and a gentle throw to him would have seen Newman run out by yards, but in the excitement of the moment, Phillip hurled wildly and wide, and Newman went through for the single. For the third time in four years Essex had been knocked-out of the 60-over competition by having lost more wickets in a match where the scores were level.

By now, however, the cricket world had come to recognise the quality of Essex cricket and of its leadership, and Keith Fletcher was named as captain of the England party to tour India and Sri Lanka in 1981–82.

He was to be jettisoned by the England selectors after that tour, and he was not treated well after a difficult time when the slowness of the series and the brooding negotiations which surrounded the South African Breweries' contracting of an 'England' side to play in the Republic tended to dominate all else. Fletcher was the third Essex player to captain England, following in the wake of Fane and Douglas. It was a just and fitting honour for the 'gnome'.

One has always felt that the nickname should have been applied for his wisdom and perspicacity rather than his appearance when wearing a pair of 'winkle-picker' shoes in his youth, for there has been no man of keener understanding of the game. For the years of success that followed 1979, he must take the major credit, not least because in the 'glory' days, he never forgot the fundamentals about men and cricket that he had learned during the time when life at Essex was hard and less successful.

Having lost the captaincy of England on the grounds that he could not be sure to earn a place in the Test side as a batsman, Fletcher proceeded to hit 120 against Middlesex at Lord's in the opening match of the 1982 championship campaign, 64 against Sussex in the next and 122 against Surrey at Chelmsford in the third game. In conjunction with this, at Hove, in a Benson and Hedges Cup zonal match, he hit 101 not out, and he and Gooch, who scored a record 198 not out, put on 268 for the third wicket in 3¼ hours of gloriously attacking cricket. Gooch, whose innings was the highest made in a one-day competition in England, hit five sixes and 22 fours while Fletcher hit seven fours. Essex won by 114 runs, but they failed to maintain form in any of the four competitions, and, ironically it was Sussex who reached the semi-finals of the Benson and Hedges Cup.

Although Gooch and Lever were available for the whole season as they had been banned from international cricket because of their involvement with the tour to South Africa, Essex finished seventh in the championship and fifth in the John Player League. The NatWest Trophy saw the County succumb to Yorkshire at Headingley in circumstances bordering on farce.

The match began at 10.00 am in a heavy, thundery atmosphere, and when Yorkshire won the toss they won the match. Essex were 51 for 9, before 50 not out from Turner in a last wicket stand of 81 with Ray East, 33, took them to 132. Yorks batted in improved conditions, although the match ended in rain with puddles of water all over the field, and won by nine wickets.

The run-getting of Gooch, McEwan, Fletcher and Hardie remained consistent, and Lever, and, in particular, Phillip had good seasons, but,

73. *Play was delayed in the Essex v Somerset John Player League match at Chelmsford in 1982, but amazingly, the Fire Brigade and many others managed to clear the ground of water in time for a ten-over match, which Essex won by one run.*

over all, Essex disappointed. They were hit by injuries to Acfield and Lilley, and especially to the most promising Foster who, just as he was establishing himself as a quick bowler of great merit, suffered a recurrence of a back injury. He did not play after the match against Lancashire at Liverpool in mid-June and underwent an operation in which a metal plate was inserted in his back to help the fusion of wasted vertebrae. When one considers the traumatic effect that such an injury must have had on a young man of 20 at the beginning of his first-class career, his later achievements are all the more remarkable.

David East continued to prosper behind the stumps and was awarded his county cap as was Derek Pringle who, in his last year at Cambridge, had been selected for the England side and was the only Essex player in the party to go to Australia. Well as he had done at Cambridge, Pringle was yet to prove himself in the county game, but he had shown himself an eager learner and had adapted well to the wit and satire of the Essex dressing-room.

74. *Derek Pringle solved the problem of uncomfortable boots by cutting a hole in the toe to enable his big toe to protrude. The solution was tested in Australia, but did not prove quite so practical in the cold and wet English conditions!* (Anglia Press)

Pringle returned from Australia a tougher competitor regularly available for Essex, and Foster, having made an amazing recovery from his injury and operation, was back in the side by the end of May. Foster was to win his first Test cap during the course of the season, and he was to be awarded his county cap for some hostile fast bowling, fine fielding and hard hitting.

The 1983 season opened with promise. Gooch and Hardie put on 263 for the first Essex wicket against Cambridge University. Gooch hit 174 and Hardie 129. John Lever took 7 for 63, and when Essex batted again there were whirlwind knocks from McEwan and Pringle.

This proved to be a false dawn, however. The first county match, against Middlesex at Lord's, was ruined by rain. McEwan and Fletcher hit

75. *Surrey 14 all out. The first day of the Essex v Surrey match at Chelmsford in May 1983 was washed out. On the second day, Essex spent all but an hour scoring 287 (Keith Fletcher 110), leaving Surrey with just 60 minutes to bat. They were bowled out for 14 in 14 overs with Norbert Phillip* (right) *taking 6 for 4 and Neil Foster 4 for 10. It was the lowest first-class score for 76 years.* (Clive Tarling)

centuries at Cardiff, but again rain interfered and the match was drawn. The first ball of the championship season at Chelmsford accounted for Gooch, bowled by Dilley, and in spite of Keith Pont's first century for five years, Kent won a match in which the weather caused the forfeiture of innings. McEwan's 151 at Leicester could not prevent another defeat, and with Hampshire, Leicestershire and Middlesex leading the table, Essex floundered in the bottom half without a win.

May ended more hopefully, however. The Bank Holiday weekend is traditionally wet, and May 1983 was no exception. There was no play on 28 May, when Essex were due to start the match against Surrey at Chelmsford, and on the Monday, Roger Knight asked Essex to bat when he won the toss. Turner and Foster came into the Essex side in place of Lever and Pringle who were injured, and, with Fletcher hitting a fine 110, the home team reached a commendable 287.

Surrey began their first innings with 67 minutes' play remaining. With the first ball of the third over Foster had Butcher caught at the wicket. Two overs later, Foster bowled Needham for nought. Knight was lbw to Phillip in the next over to make the score 8 for 4. In the 12th over, the score was 8 for 8, but Clarke swung at Foster and hit the only boundary of the innings. Monkhouse edged a two and was lbw to Phillip, and with Foster having already bowled Clarke, Surrey were out for 14 in 14.3 overs, the lowest score ever made against Essex. Phillip had figures of 7.3 overs, 4 maidens, 6 wickets for 4 runs and Foster achieved 7 overs, 3 maidens, 4 wickets for 10 runs.

When Phillip and Foster each took a wicket early in Surrey's second innings it looked as though the disintegration of the visitors' batting would continue, but Knight played solidly for 101, and Clinton gave him good support to draw the match.

Apart from establishing an incredible bowling record for the County, the drawn game with Surrey proved to be the turning point of the season for Essex. The first championship victory of the season came in the next match, against Somerset at Taunton. At 123 for 1 in their first innings, Essex seemed certain to score heavily, but Dredge gnawed away at the middle order, and they were out for 262. Somerset declared 12 runs in arrears, Acfield taking 4 for 106. Essex went for quick runs and set Somerset to make 255 in 3½ hours. They began stubbornly, but David Acfield took 5 for 1 in 13 balls, finished with 6 for 34, and Essex won by 141 runs.

Nottinghamshire were swept aside in the next match. Hassan hit a century, but Essex won by eight wickets. This was the only championship win of the season at Chelmsford that Essex recorded, a fact which makes nonsense of later accusations of 'doctored' wickets.

McEwan hit a majestic century at Tunbridge Wells, but Johnson, acting captain of Kent, decided on batting practice and the match was drawn.

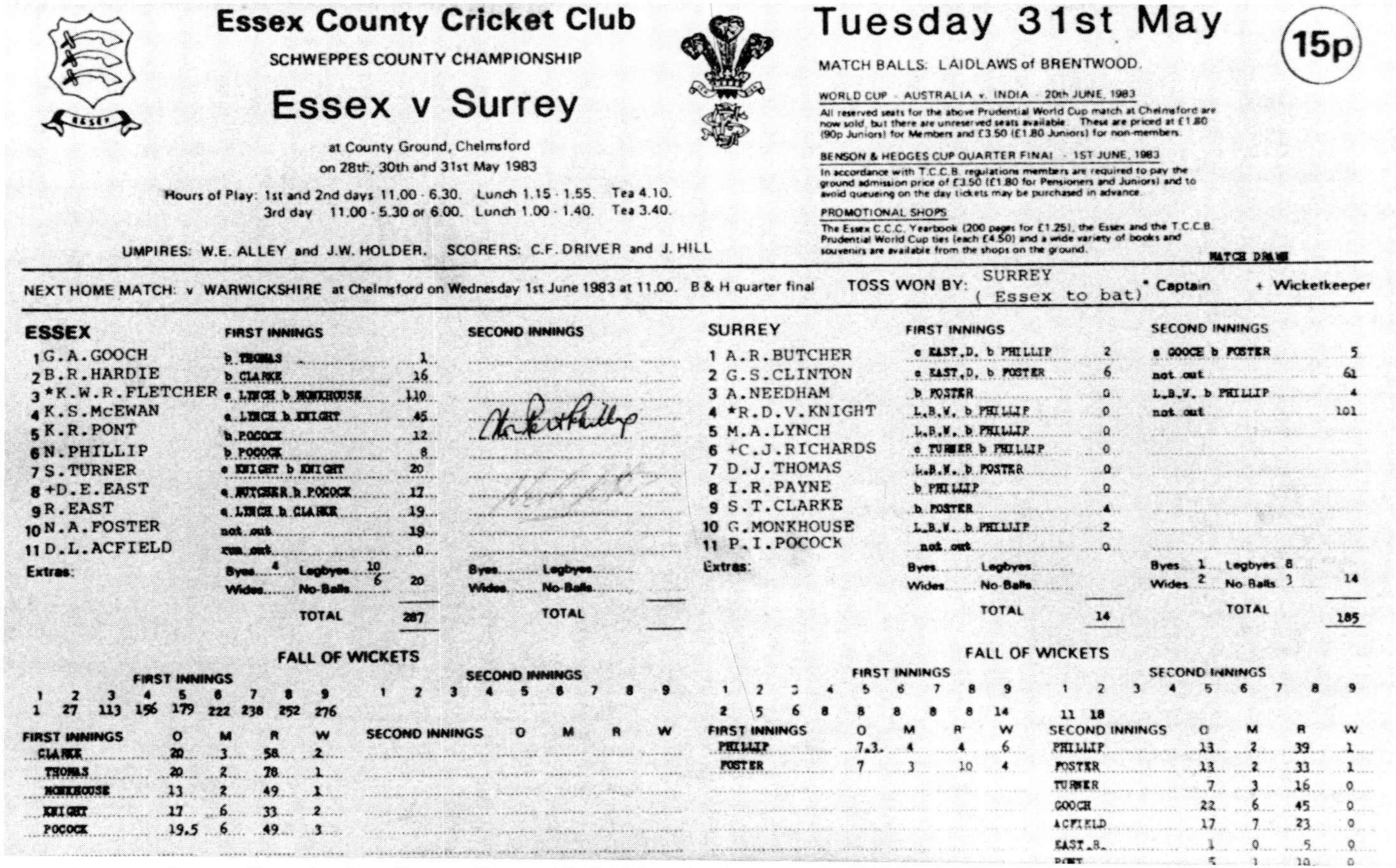

Essex County Cricket Club

SCHWEPPES COUNTY CHAMPIONSHIP

Essex v Surrey

at County Ground, Chelmsford
on 28th, 30th and 31st May 1983

Hours of Play: 1st and 2nd days 11.00 - 6.30. Lunch 1.15 - 1.55. Tea 4.10.
3rd day 11.00 - 5.30 or 6.00. Lunch 1.00 - 1.40. Tea 3.40.

UMPIRES: W.E. ALLEY and J.W. HOLDER. SCORERS: C.F. DRIVER and J. HILL

Tuesday 31st May

15p

MATCH BALLS: LAIDLAWS of BRENTWOOD.

WORLD CUP - AUSTRALIA v. INDIA - 20th JUNE, 1983

All reserved seats for the above Prudential World Cup match at Chelmsford are now sold, but there are unreserved seats available. These are priced at £1.80 (90p Juniors) for Members and £3.50 (£1.80 Juniors) for non-members.

BENSON & HEDGES CUP QUARTER FINAL - 1ST JUNE, 1983

In accordance with T.C.C.B. regulations members are required to pay the ground admission price of £3.50 (£1.80 for Pensioners and Juniors) and to avoid queueing on the day tickets may be purchased in advance.

PROMOTIONAL SHOPS

The Essex C.C.C. Yearbook (200 pages for £1.25), the Essex and the T.C.C.B. Prudential World Cup ties (each £4.50) and a wide variety of books and souvenirs are available from the shops on the ground.

MATCH DRAWN

NEXT HOME MATCH: v WARWICKSHIRE at Chelmsford on Wednesday 1st June 1983 at 11.00. B & H quarter final TOSS WON BY: SURREY (Essex to bat) * Captain + Wicketkeeper

ESSEX	FIRST INNINGS		SECOND INNINGS	
1 G.A.GOOCH	b THOMAS	1		
2 B.R.HARDIE	b CLARKE	16		
3 *K.W.R.FLETCHER	c LYNCH b MONKHOUSE	110		
4 K.S.McEWAN	c LYNCH b KNIGHT	45		
5 K.R.PONT	b POCOCK	12		
6 N.PHILLIP	b POCOCK	8		
7 S.TURNER	c KNIGHT b KNIGHT	20		
8 +D.E.EAST	c BUTCHER b POCOCK	17		
9 R.EAST	c LYNCH b CLARKE	19		
10 N.A.FOSTER	not out	19		
11 D.L.ACFIELD	run out	0		
Extras:	Byes 4 Legbyes 10 Wides No-Balls 6	20	Byes Legbyes Wides No-Balls	
	TOTAL	287	TOTAL	

SURREY	FIRST INNINGS		SECOND INNINGS	
1 A.R.BUTCHER	c EAST.D. b PHILLIP	2	c GOOCH b FOSTER	5
2 G.S.CLINTON	c EAST.D. b FOSTER	6	not out	61
3 A.NEEDHAM	b FOSTER	0	L.B.W. b PHILLIP	4
4 *R.D.V.KNIGHT	L.B.W. b PHILLIP	0	not out	101
5 M.A.LYNCH	L.B.W. b PHILLIP	0		
6 +C.J.RICHARDS	c TURNER b PHILLIP	0		
7 D.J.THOMAS	L.B.W. b FOSTER	0		
8 I.R.PAYNE	b PHILLIP	0		
9 S.T.CLARKE	b FOSTER	4		
10 G.MONKHOUSE	L.B.W. b PHILLIP	2		
11 P.I.POCOCK	not out	0		
Extras:	Byes Legbyes Wides No-Balls		Byes 1 Legbyes 8 Wides 2 No Balls 3	14
	TOTAL	14	TOTAL	185

FALL OF WICKETS (Essex)

	1	2	3	4	5	6	7	8	9
FIRST INNINGS	1	27	113	156	179	222	238	252	276
SECOND INNINGS									

FIRST INNINGS	O	M	R	W
CLARKE	20	3	58	2
THOMAS	20	2	78	1
MONKHOUSE	13	2	49	1
KNIGHT	17	6	33	2
POCOCK	19.5	6	49	3

SECOND INNINGS	O	M	R	W

FALL OF WICKETS (Surrey)

	1	2	3	4	5	6	7	8	9
FIRST INNINGS	2	5	6	8	8	8	8	8	14
SECOND INNINGS	11	18							

FIRST INNINGS	O	M	R	W
PHILLIP	7.3	4	4	6
FOSTER	7	3	10	4

SECOND INNINGS	O	M	R	W
PHILLIP	13	2	39	1
FOSTER	13	2	33	1
TURNER	7	3	16	0
GOOCH	22	6	45	0
ACFIELD	17	7	23	0
EAST.R.	1	0	5	0
PONT	5	1	10	0

76. *Schweppes County Championship, Essex v Surrey, 28–31 May, 1983.*

An innings victory inside two days at Derby was followed by two equally convincing wins during Ilford week. McEwan became the first batsman in the country to reach 1000 runs and Lever and Foster took 16 and 15 wickets respectively.

Another convincing win, against Nottinghamshire at Trent Bridge, where McEwan, Lilley and Gooch produced some ferocious batting in the second innings, seemingly reduced the Championship to a contest between Essex and Middlesex.

As Essex were beating Nottinghamshire, Middlesex were losing to Warwickshire at Edgbaston in sensational circumstances, being bowled out for 78 and 74. Warwicks were next due to play Essex, but this match was at Nuneaton. Aided by some uncharacteristic, bad fielding by Essex, Warwicks reached 379 for 9 by close of play on Saturday evening, Dennis Amiss, the master craftsman, scoring 111. Essex began well enough, Gooch and Hardie putting on 53 in ten overs. Collapse followed. In 27 overs, seven wickets fell for 49 runs. Gifford took 5 for 1 in 11 balls, and Essex followed-on 269 runs in arrears. Gooch and Hardie went early in the second innings, and Ferreira and Gifford nibbled away at the middle order so that the score was 210 when Foster joined Phillip in a last wicket stand of 91, which took the game into the last day but could not save Essex from defeat. This win put Warwicks within two points of Essex, who trailed Middlesex by ten points.

Also challenging strongly were Hampshire, who were Essex's first opponents in Southend week. Put in to bat on a steamy day with the estuary tide coming in, Essex batted in profligate fashion and succumbed to Marshall and Tremlett for 202. The home side were without Lever, who was undergoing minor surgery, but Turner and Pringle, in splendid medium-pace combination, bowled out Hampshire for 136. The second day belonged entirely to Essex, with McEwan and Pringle completing centuries of different character. It was Derek Pringle's first hundred in the Championship. Fletcher declared and asked Hampshire to make 407 to win.

Turner had Greenidge lbw early on the last day, and Essex seemed set for a comfortable win. It was not to be. Chris Smith scored 163, Nicholas 72, and Hampshire won with 11 balls to spare. It was the first time since the end of the Second World War that a side had scored more than 400 in the second innings of a championship match to win, and it echoed Essex's performance 85 years earlier when they had become the first side to score more than 300 in the second innings to win a championship match.

In the Hampshire second innings, Ray East bowled 40.1 overs and took 3 for 161, reaching 1000 wickets in first-class cricket.

The second match of Southend week only just lasted into the third day, and with McEwan and Pont scoring contrasting centuries, Essex won by an innings to resuscitate their fading challenge for the championship, but we should now temporarily leave the three-day game to document one of those traumatic periods which have punctuated the history of the Club at regular intervals.

Essex had won their first three zonal matches in the Benson and Hedges Cup, and a second wicket stand of 150 between Gooch and Fletcher and good all-round cricket from Gold Award winner Pringle were the main factors in a convincing quarter-final win over Warwickshire. The semi-final took Essex to Canterbury where, in sultry conditions, Kent were bowled out for 128, and Essex, with Hardie making 58 not out, won by nine wickets. The Essex out-cricket in this game was outstanding. Ray East broke a threatening second wicket stand when he ran out Woolmer from square-leg, and Turner, who took the Gold Award, stifled the opposition into submission by taking 2 for 15 in his 11 overs.

Kent were also Essex's opponents in the second round of the NatWest Bank Trophy, which was played three days before the Benson and Hedges Final. With rain and cloud in all the surrounding areas, Chelmsford remained an oasis of fine weather, and Chris Cowdrey chose to bat when he won the toss. There was no early penetration from the Essex attack, which was without the sick Lever, but searching bowling by Turner and Phillip put Essex on top; Kent slipped to 75 for 3. Kent's captain, Tavare, and Cowdrey revived Kent with a stand of 70 in 19 overs, but there was a dramatic collapse against Foster's speed and Gooch's accuracy and movement. With Kent at 182 for 7, Essex were very much on top, but 72 runs came from the last ten overs. Pringle offered a large sprinkling of no-balls, and Chris Cowdrey, shouldering all responsibility, hit hard to reach a magnificent 122 not out, his highest score for Kent in any form of cricket.

Facing a target of 275, Essex required a good start, and this they were given by Gooch and Hardie, who opened with a stand of 147. Gooch was in magnificent form, as he had been the previous Sunday when he lashed the Glamorgan attack for 176 off 117 balls in a record John Player League innings. He moved down the wicket to drive with the greatest power, and there seemed no stopping him, but, at 210, with his score on 122, Gooch drove rather too adventurously at Baptiste and was caught behind.

When Gooch was dismissed Essex needed 65 to win off 16 overs with eight wickets standing, a seemingly easy task, but the ghosts of Essex past began to assert themselves. Fletcher was bowled by Underwood in the 49th over. In the 51st, McEwan was caught off Underwood, and then Pont was lbw to Ellison without scoring. Even so, with seven overs left, only 31 runs were needed and five creditable wickets remained.

Phillip and Pringle scraped towards the target, but on 267, Phillip was caught driving at Ellison. Thirteen runs were needed from 14 balls.

Ellison bowled a maiden. When the last over began Essex needed six to win with three wickets standing. Ellison bowled David East with his third ball and Pringle, swinging desperately, with his last. In his last four overs Ellison had taken 4 for 12, and Kent had won by four runs. As so often before 1979, Essex had snatched defeat from the jaws of victory – and the week was not over.

On Saturday 23 July, at Lord's, for the first time since its inauguration, the Benson and Hedges Cup Final was contested by the current two best sides in the country. Lever passed himself fit, although whether this was wise is debatable, and replaced Phillip. Middlesex had Tomlins in for the injured Butcher.

The weather was uncertain after recent sunshine, and Fletcher asked Middlesex to bat first in dull conditions when he won the toss. Barlow crashed two fours in Lever's first two overs, but at the other end, Foster was fast, smooth and menacing. In his second over, he found the edge of Slack's bat and Gooch took a wonderful catch, right-handed, low-down at slip. Middlesex were 10 for 1. Foster also bowled Barlow with a ball that came back sharply, and Essex had taken a hold on the game. Radley and Gatting attempted to drag Middlesex back into contention, but Turner and Gooch in tandem were both economic and constantly threatening.

The medium-pacers frustrated the batsmen to such an extent that, in the 29th over, the score was 72. Gatting turned Gooch to leg and scampered for an improbable third run as Foster, having pursued the ball, stopped it inches from the Tavern boundary. The fielder picked up and turned in one movement, and his throw was fast into the hands of David East to leave Gatting groping short of the line. Tomlins was lbw first ball, and Middlesex were 79 for 4.

Radley dabbed, scurried and cajoled. An important catch was dropped, and Middlesex ended their 55 overs with 196 for 8. It was more than Essex should have allowed them to make, but it was still only a meagre target.

Hardie crashed Daniel through the covers in the opening over, and in the first over bowled by Cowans, Gooch launched a violent assault. Three times Gooch pulled Cowans to the boundary through a sparsely guarded leg-side. Sixteen runs came from the over. Williams replaced Cowans, but after ten overs Essex had scored 71 without loss, Gooch 40, Hardie 25. It was batting of the greatest majesty.

Williams, bowling from the Nursery end, was driven straight for four by Gooch with unquestioned authority, but the next ball Gooch attempted another drive and was caught low down by Downton. Essex were 79 for 1, and Gooch, out for 46, had failed to reach 50 for what proved to be the only time in five Lord's finals.

McEwan, nursing an injured wrist, failed to assert himself and Hardie had lost his touch, but at tea, Essex were 113 for 1 from 25 overs, victory looming. McEwan was caught low at mid-off, and Fletcher prodded and was caught bat-pad, yet, in spite of these lapses, Essex needed only 61 from 23 overs with seven wickets standing.

Pont was dropped by Cowans, but three overs later, he was hit on the helmet by a bouncer from Williams. The impact pressed the helmet stud into the temple and stunned Pont, who staggered and dropped his bat, which dislodged a bail. Essex were 151 for 4 in the 38th over. Two overs later, Hardie, who had become becalmed, flashed at Cowans and was caught behind, 156 for 5.

Emburey held a tight grip on the batsmen, and Gatting had bullied his side into believing that a win could still be achieved. Pringle and Turner nudged and ran and showed sound temperament, and in nine overs, they added 24.

Pringle managed two fours and Turner one, but Daniel had Pringle lbw with the first ball of the 52nd over. Essex needed 12 off 23 balls with four wickets standing.

Turner clouted Cowans high to deep mid-on, where substitute John Carr took a fine running catch. David East touched a ball down the leg-side to the boundary, and Essex needed six to win with more than two overs and three wickets to get them. The next delivery David East tried to pull over mid-wicket for four, but Gatting got a hand to the ball, knocked it up and turned to catch it as it dropped behind him.

Daniel bowled a wide and then hit Ray East on the pad. The batsman charged down the wicket in search of an impossible leg-bye as the ball squirted out on the off-side; East was run out. Lever played out the last ball of the over so that Neil Foster, who was playing his first limited-over innings of the season, faced Cowans for the last over with five needed to win. Cowans first ball was a yorker, and Foster's stumps were spread. Middlesex had won by four runs, and Essex were left contemplating four days of agony.

One cannot help feeling that, a decade earlier, the narrow defeats at the hands of Kent and Middlesex in vital matches within the space of a few days would have marked the end of the Essex season, but now the side was of sterner character and resolution. Four days after the defeat at Lord's, Essex travelled to Hove and beat Sussex by an innings. Lever, throwing off his recent injury, took 12 for 95. Gooch and Hardie opened with a stand of 133, and David East, coming in as night-watchman, hit 91. Gooch hit 16 off Pigott's opening over and gave another display of tremendous power before being out ten minutes before the close of the first day. The Essex win took them to within one point of Middlesex, who were the next visitors to Chelmsford.

Feeling the need of both middle-order stability and a left-hander, Essex brought Chris Gladwin in as Gooch's opening partner and moved Hardie to number five. On a morning of lowering cloud and threatening humidity, Fletcher asked Middlesex to bat first. The opening ball of the match went for a bye. The second was touched by Slack to the bounding David East off John Lever. Radley was lbw to Lever at 9, and once Pringle dismissed Gatting at 41, Middlesex collapsed. Barlow carried his bat for 44, but the visitors were out for 83. Pringle took a career best 7 for 32, and with Gladwin scoring an excellent 61, and David East giving late order support, Essex took a first innings lead of 206.

It is worth mentioning in the context of this match, that one Sunday newspaper chose to condemn Essex for 'doctoring' the wicket. The journalist, not having stayed late into the afternoon, failed to comment on Gladwin's fine innings in circumstances similar to those in which Middlesex had floundered. So are opinions shaped.

In their second innings, Middlesex reached 634 for 7, the highest championship score for 36 years, and, disappointingly, the game ended in farce with Fletcher, Gladwin and McEwan bowling the final overs.

Middlesex had strengthened their lead in the championship race when Essex were not playing, and Essex failed to take advantage of a Middlesex defeat at Northampton by themselves having the worst of a draw with Leicestershire at Chelmsford, and this in spite of Gooch's century and Phillip's six wickets.

Rain and a poor showing gained Middlesex only four points at Old Trafford, but Essex gained a thrilling victory at Wellingborough to narrow the gap at the top to five points. On a slow and uncertain wicket, Gooch and Gladwin put on 98 for the first wicket, but Essex failed to capitalise on this and were out for 282. Lever took five wickets and Northamptonshire declared 35 runs behind. Essex scored briskly, and Fletcher set the home side to make 272 in 200 minutes. Aided by the spectacular David East, Lever and Turner made early inroads into the Northamptonshire batting, and they were soon struggling at 58 for 4, and with Sharp absent ill, they faced defeat. It came in sensational fashion. Phillip, in the side because Pringle had broken a finger, had Steele caught at slip with the last ball of one over, Mallender caught at 'boot hill' by Hardie off the first ball of the next and bowled Griffiths off his pads to complete the first hat-trick of his career and win the match.

While Somerset were beating Middlesex at Lord's, Essex trounced Gloucestershire by an innings inside two days at Colchester. McEwan scored 181; and Lever, seven wickets, and Phillip, nine, bore the brunt of the bowling. Graveney had elected to bat when he won the toss, and Gloucs were shot out for 82.

Worcestershire fared no better in the second half of the week. Put in to bat, they were bowled out for 84, Lever taking 4 for 43 and Phillip 6 for 38. In reply, Essex made 413 for 8. Gooch hit 102 and McEwan, who became the first player in the country to reach 2000 runs, 189 not out. Once more Essex won by an innings inside two days and led Middlesex by 14 points at the top of the championship table, although Middlesex had a game in hand.

Essex were beaten at The Oval over the Bank Holiday period, but took eight points while Middlesex took one less from their draw at Hove.

At Old Trafford, Lever and Phillip each took five wickets as Lancashire were bowled out for 122. Thanks to David East, named as 'Wicket-keeper of the Season', and Lever, Essex took a lead of 123, but rain thwarted them in their victory bid. Middlesex drew at Headingley, and Essex led by 19 points.

Middlesex needed victory over Northamptonshire at Lord's to overtake Essex, but Larkins and Lamb batted magnificently on the last afternoon to win the match, so that Middlesex went to Trent Bridge and Essex

77. The crowd gathers in front of the Pavilion at Chelmsford to acknowledge another championship success, in 1983. The placard reads 'Gnome Rule 4 Essex'. (Colchester Evening Gazette)

entertained Yorkshire at Chelmsford in the last games of the season with Essex 13 points in the lead.

Essex asked Yorkshire to bat, and after Boycott and Moxon had put on 86 for the first wicket, Lever devastated the visitors, taking 7 for 78 and reaching 100 wickets in an injury-affected season. Essex stumbled in reply, but Gooch, coming in at number six because of injury, hit a broodingly violent 111, and Essex reached 288, a lead of 84. Lever and Turner each took four wickets, but the rain came, as it had done at Trent Bridge, and Essex were champions for the second time in their history by a margin of 16 points.

It was another triumph for team work and unquenchable spirit. McEwan, Player of the Year, Gooch, Pont and Hardie had all batted well, but even in moments of failure there was always somebody who would contribute runs, like David East or Norbert Phillip, who came back so splendidly with his bowling in the latter part of the season when Foster was injured.

At the end of the season, Ray East, the great humorist and entertainer, became coach and 2nd XI captain in succession to Mike Denness and effectively ended his playing career. Denness took up a business appointment.

Essex, strangled by a defeat and three abandonments in their first four matches, had finished sixth in the John Player League in 1983. In 1984, they started with defeat at home to Nottinghamshire and a tie against Middlesex at Lord's. Thereafter, they won 12 of their next 13 games and won the title on 26 August when, in fact, they had no match. The title that had eluded them for so long by the cruellest of margins had now been won twice, and the list of honours was growing every season.

There was defeat in the quarter-final of the 1984 Benson and Hedges Cup when Lancashire played with great zest at Chelmsford, and Surrey were winners in similar conditions in the second round of the NatWest Bank Trophy. The main concern, however, was whether Essex could retain the County Championship. They had been winners in the last year of Schweppes's sponsorship, and 1984 was the first year in which Britannic Assurance sponsored the competition.

The opening first-class match of the season, at Cambridge, saw Gladwin score 162, his maiden first-class century, and each of the seven Essex players who were dismissed score at least 50.

A rather limp defeat at the hands of MCC at Lord's led cricket writers to suggest that Essex would not be in contention for the championship in 1984. Three days later, several had reassessed this judgment.

Leading Essex in the absence of Fletcher, Gooch won the toss at Southampton and elected to bat. By the end of the day, Essex had made 449 for 5 declared, and Hampshire were 32 for 1. In just over five hours, Gooch

78. *One of the delights of winning the County Championship is an invitation to Buckingham Palace to receive the Lord's Taverners Trophy from their Patron and 12th Man, the Duke of Edinburgh. Keith Fletcher accepts the trophy after the Essex victory in 1983.*

79. *The 1983 team members at Buckingham Palace, from left: Ken McEwan, Alan Lilley, Stuart Turner, Keith Fletcher, Chris Gladwin, Keith Pont, Ray East, David East, Brian Hardie and David Acfield.* (Clive Tarling)

hit the second double century of his career, 220, with five sixes and 29 fours, and Essex went on to win by ten wickets. There was a reversal at Canterbury in the second match when Ellison bowled well in overcast conditions, but with Foster having match figures of 9 for 121, Hardie scoring 99 and Gladwin 94, Northamptonshire were beaten by ten wickets at Northampton.

The first championship match of the season at Chelmsford brought brave resistance from Gooch, but a ten-wicket victory to Nottinghamshire after Essex had been bowled out for 93 in the first innings early on the second day.

The first two days of the Bank Holiday match with Surrey were lost to rain, and Butcher, acting captain of the visitors, declined to entertain or to provide a competitive match as Surrey batted throughout the final day, assuring that neither side took any points.

David Acfield was to remark at the end of the season: 'Nobody gave us anything.' And barring the game at Eastbourne in August, which was ended by a thunderstorm, this was true. In all other matches, a challenging declaration was never forthcoming. Essex had to bowl out their opponents twice if they wanted to force victory. In 1979, there had been pleasure that Cinderella had at last arrived at the ball. Five years later, there was a feeling abroad that she was coming too often.

At Worcester, Paul Prichard made his first-class debut. He came to the wicket with the score at 22 for 4. He showed admirable technique and maturity and scored 86. David Acfield took 6 for 58, and Essex led by 44 on the first innings, but rain denied a result. No play on the last day at Hinckley brought the same frustration.

The inconsistency of the weather had mirrored the inconsistency of Essex's cricket, and when Ilford week began there was little indication that the County could hold on to the Championship. It is strange that since Essex ceased to be a totally nomadic club and began to play the majority of its home games at Chelmsford, the dramatic events which have excited hopes of a title have tended to occur at Ilford, Southend or Colchester. So was it to be in 1984.

On 9 July, the opening day of Ilford week, Warwickshire made 334, with Alvin Kallicharran hitting a fine century. On the Monday, under heavy cloud on an uncertain pitch, Essex were bowled out for 114 and forced to follow-on. Gooch hit 54, Gladwin 92 and McEwan 97 when Essex batted again, and eventually the County reached 374 so that Warwicks had 56 overs in which to make 155.

In his third over, Lever had Andy Lloyd caught behind and then bowled Kallicharran. Paul Smith and Dennis Amiss seemed to have set the visitors on the way to success, but they fell in successive overs to Acfield. Lever then sent back Asif Din and Old. A stand of 32 between Ferreira and

Humpage took the score to 100, but Pringle took the last four wickets to give Essex an astonishing victory by 35 runs.

The second half of the week welcomed Derbyshire, but Gladwin, Fletcher and McEwan, who made 101, savaged their attack, and Essex made 333 for 9. Derbyshire's middle order kept them in touch, and Fletcher asked them to make 336 in 82 overs on the last day. With 22 overs left, they needed 135 with seven wickets standing and looked to be heading for victory. It was Gooch who brought about a middle order collapse, and the last five wickets went down for 12 runs. When Taylor was lbw for nought without offering a shot for the second time in the match Essex had gained an exciting victory with 3.3 overs to spare.

Northamptonshire forced a draw at Chelmsford, and at Chesterfield, Gooch hit a career best 227, but Essex could not beat Derbyshire for a second time. Gooch's runs came off 224 deliveries, and he hit five sixes and 32 fours. It was John Hampshire who saved Derbyshire on the last day.

The exclusion of Gooch and Lever from the England side was, of course, a considerable boon to Essex if not to England, and the County were to win seven of their next nine matches in a thrilling run of form which took them to the top of the championship table in contention with Nottinghamshire.

Another Gooch century and 106 from Fletcher helped Essex to 524 for 7 in the innings win over Yorkshire at Leeds. This was the highest score Essex had ever made against Yorkshire. In the John Player League game in the middle of the same match, John Lever became the first bowler to reach 300 wickets in the Sunday competition, beating Derek Underwood to the target by half an hour.

A dreadful performance in the first match of Southend week when Glamorgan had the better of a draw was followed by an innings win over Lancashire, achieved amid the showers. Lever had match figures of 10 for 81, and he had an even greater personal triumph at Bristol. Gloucestershire made 327 for 6. Gladwin again just missed his century, caught for 94, and Fletcher declared at 300 for 2. On a blameless wicket, Gloucs were out for 90 in their second innings. Lever had a career best 8 for 37, and Essex won by eight wickets.

A Fletcher century and the all-round quality of the Essex attack brought a comfortable win over Worcestershire at Chelmsford, and, by now, Essex and Nottinghamshire had forged ahead of the rest of the pack.

Both sides were hampered by rain in early August, but Essex went 22 points clear a few days later when Nottinghamshire lost by 28 runs to Derbyshire at Trent Bridge while Essex won a marvellous victory at Lord's.

The first innings scores were Middlesex 329 for 9; Essex 364 for 7. Middlesex had no thought of a challenging declaration as they batted

80. *Ray East's humorous exploits are legendary in cricketing circles, and sometimes hide the fact that he was a most successful bowler for Essex, being one of only nine to have taken 1000 wickets for the County.*

Ray and humour are never too far apart, however, and he could not resist the temptation to help the maintenance staff in painting the sightscreen.

81. *A captain's lot is not always an easy one, but after beating Lancashire in two days at Old Trafford, a win which clinched the 1984 championship, Keith Fletcher is pleased to relax with a cup of tea.*

82. *Neil Foster had a dramatic 1983 season. He started in the second XI, forced his way into the first team with some outstanding performances, shared with Norbert Phillip the rout of Surrey for 14 at Chelmsford, was selected to play for England, and played his first Test match at Lord's. But by the end of July he was in hospital having a major operation which included the insertion of two metal plates to cure a damaged spine. By the end of the season, however, he had rejoined the team, and was selected to tour Pakistan with the England team.*

through the last day. When they were out for 245, 33 overs remained and Essex needed 211 to win. In the gathering dusk, most were accepting that the match was drawn, but Fletcher's philosophy towards the championship has been a simple one. If a side can win 12 or 13 of its matches, it is likely to take the title. A draw brings no extra points so victory must be sought at all times. It excites a positive approach to the game, yet it is the most uncomplicated of ideals. In the first four overs of the innings, which began at 5.10 pm, 43 runs were scored. Gooch's fifty came off 42 balls, and he flayed the Middlesex attack of Daniel, Williams, Emburey and Edmonds to all parts of the field. Wickets fell, but each man made a dashing contribution. At 7.30 pm, with seven balls to spare and Gooch 105 not out, Essex gained one of their greatest victories by four wickets.

Nottinghamshire kept in contention by winning a maximum point victory over Middlesex, as Essex won a low scoring game with Somerset.

At Colchester, Gooch became the first man to reach 2000 runs, Lever the first to reach 100 wickets in the season. McEwan scored an exquisite hundred, and Essex won by eight wickets, the winning runs coming at nearly seven an over. Nottinghamshire failed to beat Kent, and Essex were 38 points clear at the top.

This was quickly reduced to 18, however, for Nottinghamshire beat Lancashire by ten wickets while Essex were losing by the same margin to Kent at Colchester. Gladwin was awarded his county cap, but Alderman spoiled the pleasure. The home side could make only 90 and 118 as Chris Cowdrey hit a courageous 125 not out.

Stands of 156 and 208 between Gooch and McEwan at The Oval set up a win which was completed by Foster's bowling and eager fielding. The batting of Gooch and McEwan in this match was as glorious as anything that had been seen in England since the days of Compton and Edrich. There was a shudder of excitement among friend and foe when they came together, and a sigh of regret from foe at least when they were parted. Their 208 came in 145 minutes, and Gooch overtook Jack O'Connor's record number of runs in a season for Essex.

The euphoria subsided quickly, for Middlesex, scorning Fletcher's declaration after Essex had been asked to bat first, settled for a dull draw at Chelmsford. Nottinghamshire had two matches left and had only to win one to snatch the Championship. Essex went to Old Trafford for the last game.

Nottinghamshire failed to beat Sussex at Hove, but they entered the last round with a four-point lead. Nottinghamshire were at Taunton, and by the third day, they knew exactly what they had to do. At Old Trafford, Fletcher asked Lancashire to bat, and a zestful attitude in the field had the home side dismissed for 229. Essex plundered runs at an amazing rate.

McEwan reached 95 in 75 minutes, but, denied an adequate share of the bowling, just missed the fastest century of the season. His 132 came off 117 balls, with four sixes and 13 fours. Paul Prichard hit a maiden first-class century. Essex reached 446, the last 291 runs coming in just over three hours. Jack Simmons, the Lancashire off-spinner, had the remarkable figures of 7 for 176 from his 40 overs.

John Lever, though not fully fit, reduced Lancashire to 50 for 5, and Ray East, called back for this match, whittled away at the tail. Lancashire were out for the same score that they had made in the first innings, and Gooch and Prichard hit 14 runs in three overs to win the game by seven o'clock on the Monday evening.

With Nottinghamshire having picked up six bonus points, Essex now led the championship by 14 points and they could only be deprived of the title if Nottinghamshire won on the last day at Taunton.

In mid-afternoon Botham declared, setting Nottinghamshire to make 297 in what turned out to be 60 overs. Broad, in particular, batted well, but at 92 for 3, Nottinghamshire looked doomed. Rice then played an innings of outstanding quality. He hit 98 before clouting a full toss from Vic Marks into the hands of Richard Ollis, a substitute who was fielding on the square-leg boundary.

With two overs remaining, Nottinghamshire needed 27 to win with Bore and French at the wicket and only Pick to come. Bore launched a glorious assault and hit Marks for six. French was caught on the boundary where all save wicket-keeper Gard and one other were fielding, and when Booth began the last over 14 were needed with one wicket to fall.

The Essex players had returned to Chelmsford and were gathered nervously round the radio to listen to Henry Blofeld's commentary, their fate no longer in their hands.

Mike Bore savaged the first two balls of the over for four and turned the third for two, so that four runs were needed off three balls. He was forced to play defensively to the fourth delivery, but the fifth, the penultimate ball of the season, he lashed high to long-off where substitute Ollis held a fine catch just inside the boundary. Essex had retained the Championship.

The County, who for so many years had been faced with financial crises, had now become the first side to win the County Championship and the John Player League in the same season. In five years, they had become first among the counties. They had also staged a Prudential World Cup match, between India and Australia, and they had provided England's captain.

Fletcher's record in Test and county cricket places him among the first rank of batsmen in the history of the game, yet few have ever had to take so much unjustified and unthinking criticism. It did not go unnoticed that several who had clamoured for him to be replaced at the end of

83. *Celebrations at the end of a long season are always enjoyable. Here the Essex team receive the Britannic Assurance cheque as winners of the 1984 championship. Left to right, back row: David Acfield, Brian Hardie, Derek Pringle, Stuart Turner, Paul Prichard, Neil Foster, Keith Pont, Ken McEwan. Middle row: Chris Gladwin, David East. Front: Graham Gooch, Keith Fletcher, John Lever.* (Clive Tarling)

England's tour to India were urging his recall as England's captain at the end of the 1984 season. With his cap tilted and his shoulders slightly hunched, Fletcher, smilingly but firmly, marshalling his men into position, had at last inherited the respect and admiration he deserved.

On 19 February 1985, he went to Buckingham Palace to receive the Order of the British Empire from Her Majesty The Queen. It was an honour richly deserved, and one which reflected on the whole Club, but Essex, and Fletcher, still had one world left to conquer.

In the early weeks of the 1985 season, there appeared to be little likelihood that Essex would conquer anything, yet the season ended as the most momentous in the history of any club.

The staff was strengthened by the arrival of Topley, Ian Pont and Childs, all of whom, like Stephenson, were to make their first appearances for Essex during the season. Childs had taken 426 wickets in ten successful years with Gloucestershire, but there was a general feeling that he had lost confidence in his slow left-arm bowling and surprise that

84. *Reflecting Essex's new commercial image: The bus above runs on normal Eastern National routes throughout Essex. On the back are the current year's home fixtures, while inside the various advertising cards give details of membership, the cricket school, entertaining and sponsorship opportunities, etc.* (Clive Tarling)

Essex had engaged him. His five wickets for 528 runs in first-class cricket in 1985 served only to substantiate the critics' view, yet once again the guardians of Essex cricket were to be proved wise in judgment.

A poor start in both the county championship and the John Player League diverted all interest to the Benson and Hedges Cup. Gooch, twice, Foster and Lever won the Gold Awards as Essex swept to the quarter-finals with four victories in four matches. Gooch took his third Gold Award in five matches as Derbyshire were beaten in a match which rain had reduced to a 20-over thrash. The semi-final against Middlesex at Chelmsford was also hindered by rain, but produced a memorable match.

Essex reached 114 for 4 off 33 overs before rain ended play, and next morning they reached 202 for 8 due to some clean hitting by David East and Neil Foster, who added an unbeaten 35 for the ninth wicket. In much improved conditions, Middlesex faced a relatively simple task, particularly as Slack and Barlow had been in such outstanding form.

Essex needed to break the opening partnership quickly if they were to win, and they did so when Barlow, wrongly sent back by Slack, slipped and was beaten by Prichard's long, fast, accurate throw. Gatting seemed

85. *Tom Pearce celebrated his 80th birthday in November 1985, with a dinner in the Pavilion at the County Ground. It was attended by most of the current players, and others whose careers stretched back into the 1920s. Left to right, standing: Doug Insole, Frank Rist, 'Hopper' Read, David East, George Unwin, Neil Foster, Ken Preston, Paddy Phelan, Graham Saville, Jimmy Cutmore, Dickie Dodds, Harold Faragher, 'Sonny' Avery, David Acfield, Keith Fletcher, Keith Pont and Robin Hobbs. Front row: Brian Hardie, Brian Taylor, Paul Prichard, Tom Pearce, Gordon Barker and Mickey Bear.* (Clive Tarling)

in total command, but after lunch he drove square on the off-side at Turner, and Lilley held a legendary catch at cover, clasping the ball in his left hand as he was knocked backwards by the force of the shot. The Essex out-cricket was dynamic, and this breathtaking catch proved to be the turning point of the match. Pringle bowled quickly and accurately. Hardie took a stunning diving catch to get rid of Downton. Hardie also ran out Edmonds, and Turner wore down Slack, who lost his head and was bowled for 60 in the 43rd over. In Foster's ninth over, three wickets fell, and Essex had won by 62 runs. Never has a side played better in the field.

Essex's fourth appearance in a Benson and Hedges Cup final was a disappointment. Fletcher was injured and unable to play. Gooch hit 57, but the batsmen could never quite shake off the tight grip of the Leicestershire bowlers. The Essex out-cricket never reached the standard it had attained in the semi-final, and, chasing 213 for 8, Leicestershire won by five wickets with three overs to spare.

Leicestershire and Essex went to Lord's for the Benson and Hedges Cup Final on 20 July having started the month as 16th and 17th in the championship. Essex were also only two points off the bottom in the John Player League.

The first championship match of the season, against Warwickshire in cold weather at Chelmsford, was won, but not another victory was recorded until Somerset came to Southend on 10, 11 and 12 July. Gladwin had been recovering from a back injury, Prichard had suffered a broken finger and Gooch was on Test duty much of the time; the side could find no rhythm. Southend week brought renewed vigour.

Against Somerset, Hardie equalled his highest score with 162, and Lever and Acfield bowled out the visitors for 98 in their second innings to give Essex victory by 149 runs. In the second match, against Gloucestershire, who were then heading the table, Topley made his debut, David East hit a violent maiden first-class century, and the match was drawn.

Middlesex were beaten at Chelmsford and, at Taunton, Ian Pont made his debut; his elder brother Keith was also in the side. On the first day, 27 July, David East equalled Wally Grout's world record by taking eight catches in the innings. It was the Essex wicket-keeper's 26th birthday. Ian Pont took 5 for 103, and on the last afternoon Gooch hit 171 not out off 190 balls, and Essex won by seven wickets.

Derbyshire and Gloucestershire, where Pringle took nine wickets, were beaten, and Gooch and David East saved the match at Lord's with second innings centuries. Gooch hit his seventh first-class hundred of the season in the last match when Yorkshire were beaten by an innings at Chelmsford. This win took Essex to a final fourth place in the championship table.

The progress in the John Player League was even more exciting. One win, against Glamorgan, one tie, with Leicestershire, two abandonments, and three losses was the Essex record from the first seven matches. At Southend, Gloucestershire were beaten by seven wickets, and this sparked a run wherein eight of the last nine games were won and one abandoned.

The most significant win came in the penultimate match of the season, against Nottinghamshire at Trent Bridge. Gooch and Hardie set up a John Player League record opening partnership with a stand of 239 in 38 overs. Gooch with three sixes and 18 fours, hit 171 off 135 balls. This win left Essex two points ahead of Sussex at the top of the table with one game to play.

On 15 September, Sussex won quickly at Cardiff, but Yorkshire posed greater problems for Essex at Chelmsford. Put in to bat, Yorkshire suffered an early reverse when Boycott was run out by David East. Gooch bowled Moxon and Love and had Neil Hartley caught by Pringle so that, at the half-way stage, Yorkshire were 80 for 4. Kevin Sharp then played a splendid innings of 114 off 106 balls. Yorks took 90 runs from the last ten overs, and Essex faced a daunting target of 232.

Gooch and Hardie began firmly, but Gooch was taken at mid-off and Hardie was caught behind in the 15th over with the score on 53. Ken McEwan, making his last appearance in the Sunday league, was cheered all the way to the wicket by a crowd that, in truth, seemed above capacity. People were standing in rows four and five deep behind the seats such had become the attraction of Essex, who had once begged for members and support.

McEwan responded with the elegant power and graceful charm that had been a feature of Essex cricket for 11 years. From 67 deliveries, he hit 62 before being caught on the long-on boundary in attempting to repeat the hit for six he had just made. Fletcher, Lilley and East went quickly, but Pringle, now a mature all-rounder of the highest class, played an aggressive and responsible innings of 60 from 54 balls. He fell to Oldham, and with Prichard and Turner together, 30 were needed from four overs.

Prichard played a majestic innings, never deviating from the orthodox. He hit Oldham for a regal cover-drive, and in the penultimate over, bowled by Stuart Fletcher, he drove three twos and cut excitingly for four. The last ball of the over was down the leg-side and in the flurry went for four leg-byes. Essex needed three from the last over.

Turner, the old campaigner, took a single off Oldham's first ball, but Prichard, in his first lapse of temperament, gave a simple return catch next ball. Foster, nervously, twice swung wildly at Oldham and missed. Turner called him to the centre of the wicket and chatted to him. The fifth ball of the over, Foster placed through mid-wicket for two. Essex had retained the John Player League title.

It was their second title of the season. Victories over Oxfordshire, Middlesex, Kent and Hampshire had taken them to the NatWest Bank Trophy Final. Oxfordshire had been beaten comfortably, and the relentless Essex out-cricket had again accounted for Middlesex with some ease. When Kent threatened to spoil the work of Gooch and Prichard, Fletcher and Pringle had brought a decisive victory. Fletcher also played a vital part in the semi-final win at Southampton.

Hampshire were restricted to 224 for 8, Turner taking 3 for 38, but Essex lost Hardie and Prichard for 48. Gooch stayed throughout the 60 overs to hit 93 not out. McEwan made 35 and Pringle was run out for eight, but,

86. *There are many ups and downs in captaining a county cricket side but there can be few better moments than holding up one of the game's major trophies in front of a large crowd at the County Ground. It is an experience enjoyed on many occasions by Keith Fletcher, this one being after victory in the John Player Special League in 1985.* (Clive Tarling)

although he made only 19, Fletcher withstood the last furious assault of Malcolm Marshall and so thwarted Nicholas's plan.

Lilley was splendidly caught after some gigantic blows, and David East was also caught from a hit which might have gone for six over long-on. Turner defied Cowley and then hit him into the crowd. Greenidge began the last over with a wide which levelled the scores, and Turner played out the over to take Essex to Lord's.

We began our narrative with the story of that memorable NatWest Final and the one-run victory over Nottinghamshire. It brought Essex their eighth trophy in seven seasons, and Keith Fletcher became the first captain to have led a county to the game's four major honours. In 1985, Essex had won the NatWest Bank Trophy, the John Player League, had been runners-up in the Benson and Hedges Cup and finished fourth in the Britannic Assurance County Championship. It was a record unapproached by any other county. It also marked the end of an era.

87. *Essex captains do not change too often as only six captains have been used since 1945. Keith Fletcher stood down at the end of the 1985 season to enable Graham Gooch to gain experience in the job while he was still playing, able to offer advice and to take over when Gooch was away on Test Duty.*

In this picture Graham Gooch is fully entitled to be wearing Keith Fletcher's England cap, but Fletcher cannot claim any right to be wearing a Western Province sun hat.

In mid-season, when little cricket had been played and Essex were at or near the bottom of both league tables, Keith Fletcher had told Doug Insole that he was finding the job of skippering the side a burden and that he was thinking about retiring at the end of the season. Insole told him that he had quite a few years of good cricket left in him and that the obvious move would be to hand over the captaincy to Graham Gooch, play when he felt like it, and deputise for Gooch when the latter was required to play for England. In that way he could avoid the 'chores' of the captaincy – making speeches, attending meetings, dealing with the press – and have the odd match off when he felt like it, but still do his stuff as Gooch's deputy. The idea appealed, but Fletcher wondered whether Gooch would agree. As expected, Graham Gooch was very enthusiastic, and it was agreed that the new arrangement would be announced at the end of the season. The weight on Keith Fletcher's shoulders disappeared immediately and the season, as we know, ended in triumph for him and for Essex.

The Essex debt to Fletcher is immeasurable. Norbert Phillip, so important a player in the first years of success, left the staff, and Ken McEwan, after 12 seasons for which one will remain ever grateful, not just for the runs, but for their manner of making, decided to retire to his farm in South Africa.

McEwan is a man without conceit, transparently honest and unflinchingly loyal, but because of his nationality, the ultimate honours were denied to him. Why did he leave when surely there were another 10,000 runs and 16 or 17 centuries to come? His answer was sad and simple: 'I'm tired of driving up and down the motorways of England without the prospect of Test cricket at the end of it.'

After the NatWest Trophy Final, Ken McEwan stood for a moment on the steps that led up to the Essex Committee box above the Tavern Stand. He looked out over Lord's in the twilight, perhaps, like Sir Bedivere, 'revolving many memories'.

They must have been happy ones, for he had been an integral part of the greatest period of glory in Essex cricket. One of today's publicity men might well call it 'The Age of the Gnome'.

CHAPTER 18

Beginning of a New Era

To replace Ken McEwan, Essex signed the Australian captain, Allan Border. This was a break with tradition, for in the past, the County's importations had been overseas cricketers who were virtually unknown. In answer to criticism that this break with past policy was primarily a publicity move, Peter Edwards stated that the administration saw the team's batting as a potential weakness, particularly with the departure of McEwan and the absence of Gooch on international duty, and that Border had been engaged to provide necessary substance in this area. Once more, the decision of those responsible for the running of the Club was proved to be a sound one, and Border was to be a most loyal and conscientious member of the Club in his brief stay.

Hardie and Gooch began the Benson and Hedges Cup challenge with a stand of 139 in 27.3 overs at Hove, where Sussex were beaten, and the next day, 4 May, they opened with 184 in 28 overs in the John Player League match against Warwickshire.

At Taunton, put in to bat, Essex were 118 for 7, but Turner and Pringle, justly recalled to the England side, added 72 in 11 overs, and these two destroyed the bulk of the Somerset batting for Essex to win by 12 runs. Gloucestershire and Glamorgan were beaten at Chelmsford, and Essex entertained Nottinghamshire in the quarter-final. A fine all-round performance by Rice and some hard hitting from Hadlee gave Notts the edge in a close, well contested match, and the visitors won by three wickets. An early, and rather inglorious exit from the NatWest Bank Trophy focussed attention on the Championship and the Sunday league.

When Essex went to Sheffield on 25 May 1986, they had enjoyed a run of 16 consecutive wins in one-day matches. Yorkshire ended the sequence when Sidebottom hit a six off the last ball of the match to earn his side a victory which took them to the top of the John Player League. Essex won at Derby and beat Nottinghamshire at Chelmsford, but Hampshire gained a mighty victory at Ilford when, after Essex had made 256 for 5, they reached their target with nine balls to spare. An abandonment at Lord's and a loss at Old Trafford, in spite of a hundred from Paul Prichard, seemed to have put Essex out of the running in their attempt to win the John Player League for the third year in succession.

The last eight matches, however, included seven victories, form following the pattern that it had done the previous season, but the defeat by Hampshire was to prove crucial, and the south coast county took the title with 50 points to the 46 of Essex, who finished second.

At Southchurch Park, Southend, during the game with Worcestershire, Stuart Turner received a plaque from the Association of Cricket Statisticians to commemorate his achievement to become the first player to score 3000 runs and take 300 wickets in the John Player League, but Turner was to play only one more game in the League after this presentation.

The pressure was very much on Allan Border at the beginning of the season. Many expected him to score a century every time he went to the wicket, and in a damp English summer this was not an easy task. The team began hesitantly. There was a draw at Edgbaston and a loss at home to Kent in an exciting match. The game at Northampton was ruined by rain, but on the only day on which play was possible, the second, John Childs, took 5 for 97. The event, crowded out by Benson and Hedges Cup matches, went almost unnoticed at the time, but it proved to be one of the most significant of the season.

A gentle, polite and kind man, Childs had been the surprise signing of the previous season. Insole had pointed out that Acfield was the only spinner on the staff with championship experience and that neither Golding nor Field-Buss had yet proved himelf ready for first-team cricket. Childs had suffered a miserable first year at Essex, but help from Don Wilson and Fred Titmus and the encouragement of his team-mates helped him to regain confidence. The success that was to be his in 1986 was a credit not only to his own perseverance and determination, but also a testimony to the excellence of an administration which has trust in its own judgment of a player.

88. *Graham Gooch.* (Steve Lindsell)

The first championship win of the season came when Yorkshire were beaten in a match on which no play was possible on the first day. Hardie hit 110 and Prichard 82, but it was the bowling of Pringle, 7 for 46, as Yorkshire strove to make 278, that won the match.

At Derby, on 31 May, Allan Border hit his first century for Essex. To defeat the weather, Derbyshire declared quickly and Essex forfeited their second innings. Lever took 5 for 32, Childs 4 for 36, and Essex won by 116 runs.

The same players were prominent in the next match, which brought an emphatic win at Swansea very early on the last day. Border hit 150. Lever took 6 for 57, and when Glamorgan followed-on Childs took 7 for 51. Essex moved to the head of the championship table.

At Chelmsford, at the beginning of June, Paul Prichard saved the game against Nottinghamshire with a career best of 147 not out. Ilford week began with an important match against Hampshire. On a fiery wicket, Hampshire, thanks mainly to Robin Smith and Bobby Parks, recovered from 130 for 7 to score 260. Foster and Pringle shared the wickets, but the Essex wickets were shared between four bowlers. Border, 71, played splendidly in conditions totally foreign to him, and Childs hit 30 at the close to take Essex to 198. Foster again produced pace and menace, and Hampshire succumbed for 135. In search of 198, Essex lost 3 for 36, but David East and Border raised hope until East was foolishly run out. Pringle and Lilley batted sensibly, but when Border departed to a furious lifter from Malcolm Marshall, Essex were 156 for 6, and the game had tilted in favour of Hampshire. Foster hit bravely, but he skied Maru to cover, and Hampshire had won by 12 runs.

Essex remained at the top despite this loss, but Hampshire joined Yorkshire and Nottinghamshire as serious challengers. The second match in Ilford week was amazing. Essex scored 242, and Sussex were 16 for 6 by the end of the first day. They rallied to make 112, but, following a scintillating 96 not out by Border, Essex won by 69 runs with only 16 balls left.

This was one of the games in which Fletcher led Essex because Gooch was on international duty. There was some criticism when he declared with Border only four short of a century, but again Fletcher's judgment proved correct in the time that was needed to bowl Sussex out.

One is inclined to highlight centuries and big partnerships, but there are times when a quick 50 or a courageous 30 is vital to the side. Such was the case in the match with Middlesex at Lord's. Missing Gooch and Lever on Test duty, and with Hardie out of the side with a broken hand, Essex asked Middlesex to bat first on a wicket which assisted the seam bowlers. Topley and Keith Pont took four wickets each, but the home side made 208. Essex collapsed to Daniel and Cowans and trailed by 78, but Foster and Topley bowled unchanged to shoot out Middlesex for 97.

Needing 176 on a wicket which was fierce and threatening, Essex sought victory aggressively. Prichard batted thrillingly for 35, and Lilley hit well in support of Border who, with 59 not out, saw Essex to a brave five-wicket win. The cost of the victory was a broken finger to Keith Fletcher, which kept him out of the side when Essex lost badly to both Lancashire and Leicestershire.

Defeat had come in the first game of Southend week, and when Gooch, along with Foster and Pringle, returned to the side for the second match, against Worcestershire, an exciting win was achieved. Foster had the best match figures of his career, 11 for 157, and the significant contributions with the bat came from Gooch, 151, and Stephenson, 85, who was down from Durham University. They put on 214 for the first wicket on the opening day, and it is worth noting that, until this point, 19 July, Gooch had scored only 133 championship runs for the County. He was to miss 11 matches in all, a fact which underlines the importance of the contributions made by the bread-and-butter players like Hardie who, all like Fletcher, missed several matches through injury.

A Border century saved Essex from overwhelming defeat at The Oval, and another Border century, his fourth and last for Essex, almost brought a sensational win at Hove. Set to make 319 in 49 overs, Essex finished on 303 for 7.

Then came two decisive victories. Middlesex were routed at Chelmsford, Lilley and Fletcher hitting exuberantly, and Leicestershire were beaten in a rain-affected match at Leicester. Gloucestershire, the Championship leaders, had faltered at Cheltenham, and Essex were 19 points behind them with two games in hand.

The two teams were to meet in the second match of Colchester week, but in the first part of the week, Border's last game, against Northamptonshire, they suffered a big shock. Northamptonshire raced to 302, and Essex, equally quickly, scored 337. John Childs, in an immaculate display of controlled spin bowling, took 8 for 61, and Essex needed only 147 to win and to go ahead in the championship table. They were bowled out for 44.

In compensation, Essex had very much the better of the game with the leaders, Gloucestershire. David East hit 82 and 100 not out, relishing the fast bowling of Lawrence and Walsh, while Childs took 8 for 58 in the first innings against his old county. Rain interrupted and, in the end, Gloucestershire's last pair thwarted Essex and held out for a draw. Gloucestershire led the table by 11 points.

Allan Border played 18 championship matches for Essex, scored more runs, 1287, than anyone else at a better average, 51.48, than anyone else, yet to measure him solely on those statistics would be a grave error. His contribution to the team and to the Club as a whole was immense. He

89. *Caught Fletcher, bowled Childs. John Childs came to Essex at the start of the 1985 season and through a mixture of injury and lack of opportunity, not to mention the poor weather, he had little chance to show his true worth to his new County. However, in 1986 he took 89 first-class wickets, many of them thanks to some brilliant catching around the bat by Keith Fletcher, Brian Hardie, Paul Prichard and David East. In this picture, David Graveney of Gloucestershire is caught by Keith Fletcher at Colchester.* (All-Sport/Simon Bruty)

was unstinting of his time given to repaying the generosity of sponsors, never failing to support a function which he was asked to attend. Moreover, his help and advice to younger players was invaluable. Paul Prichard, in particular benefited greatly from Border's presence, on and off the field, and this aspect of his contribution to Essex cricket should not be forgotten.

The County were forced to play the last six matches of the season without him, and the second of these matches, the Bank Holiday game with Surrey, was, like all others in the country, ruined by rain.

On 27, 28 and 29 August, Essex went to Taunton, a ground which seems to feature prominently in notable Essex achievements. Gooch won the toss and chose to bat first on a wicket which was damp. He may have regretted his decision, for the County slipped to 57 for 7. David East again hit bravely and added 52 in ten overs with John Lever, but, in spite of John Childs's four wickets before the close, the Essex score of 129 looked very small as Botham and Richards, the latter in his last championship match for Somerset, began to hit freely. However, on the second day matters improved for Essex and the Somerset lead was restricted to 71. Gooch and Stephenson were out before that deficit was cleared, but Hardie became the rock on which the Essex second innings was founded. It was typical that his highest innings of the season should come when it was most needed. For six hours he held the batting together, given sound support by all who went to the wicket. Hardie finished with 113 not out, and Gooch declared on 343 for 7, made in 131 overs of tenacious cricket.

That tenacity was soon to be seen in the field. Somerset needed 273 in 68 overs. They were 110 for 4 when Richards was joined by Marks, and 88 were added in 17 overs. The West Indian captain launched a blistering attack, hitting 94 off 94 balls before being caught at mid-on, a spectacular diving effort by Brian Hardie. Botham hit 41 off 29 balls, but he was caught at long-on by Stephenson off Childs, and with 18 overs left, Somerset needed 20 runs to win with five wickets standing.

The strength of the Essex side, founded on the years of success and the confidence that they had brought, was that they never doubted that they could still win the game. Every ball was chased. Every delivery was meaningful. Every field adjustment had purpose. Gard was lbw to Pringle for nought, and then Pringle captured the prize wicket when he bowled Marks for 56. In a dreadful moment of panic and confusion, Harman was run out, and Somerset were 261 for 9.

Dredge and Taylor held out for ten minutes, and then Childs trapped Taylor lbw. In 40 minutes, five Somerset wickets had fallen for ten runs. Essex had won an improbable victory by nine runs and went to the top of the championship table with a seven points' lead.

Essex then went to Folkestone in bitterly cold and damp weather. It was not until the last morning that Essex brought the Kent first innings to an end. Stephenson and Hardie then hit quick runs, and Gooch declared, leaving Kent 47 overs in which to score 184. The sun was now shining, and the challenge was fair and positive. At tea, Kent were 47 for 0, but Fletcher dived forward to catch Taylor off Lever on the second ball after the resumption. Three overs later, Tavare was taken at backward short-leg off the bowling of Acfield.

John Childs now dominated the game. He captured seven wickets in a row, teasing and turning, ably backed by his field. Kent were always in sight of victory, but with 20 balls remaining, Marsh, who had batted admirably, went down the wicket to Acfield, was beaten and beautifully stumped on the leg side by David East, who claimed eight victims in the

90. *The County Ground, Chelmsford, was purchased in 1965 and developments commenced a year late The ground is now considered to be one of the best of the non Test match grounds, and in the picture abo the buildings shown are the Executive Suite with the entertainment boxes below, the Press Box and t Pavilion and offices.* (Clive Tarling)

91. *On the opposite side of the ground, by the river, the Britvic Picnic Area behind the River Ro Restaurant is a popular place for lunches.* (John Barker)

match. Essex had snatched another improbable victory by 23 runs. With two matches left, they needed only three points for their third Championship in four years.

At 3.49 pm on Wednesday, 10 September, at Trent Bridge, David East dived low to his right to catch Bruce French off the bowling of Graham Gooch. Nottinghamshire were 207 for 7, and Essex were Champions.

The excitement was none the less than it had been in 1979, and although there were some different players on the field, the team retained the essential characteristics of the originally successful side. As players had grown older, younger ones had been introduced to keep a balance of youth and experience, vitality and wisdom. David East, Prichard, Pringle, Foster, who took 100 championship wickets in 1986, Stephenson, Topley, Lilley and Childs had all eased their way into the side, yet the character, the abundant spirit had remained constant.

The success had been earned by a formula that was a trust and belief in self and each other. Pearce had given fun, Insole organisation and professional endeavour, Taylor had inculcated fitness and discipline and Fletcher had combined all their qualities and added the winning dimension of tactical perception. He was still the mind behind much that happened in 1986, but Gooch had embraced the philosophy that the important thing is to win a match, not to worry about losing it. Gooch had started Essex well on a new era.

Individual performances of quality abounded. John Childs took 54 wickets in August, 89 in the season, and 44 of them were taken on opponents' grounds. David East was again the leading wicket-keeper in the country and his 83 dismissals included 19 stumpings, a figure which no keeper had approached for a generation. Lever had won back a place for one Test in the England side, and he still represented all that was good in team commitment and effort. But to dwell on individuals is wrong. The Essex triumph is of a Club and of all those on and off the field.

At the end of the season, the County lost two old friends as Keith Pont, after an excellent benefit and several years of wit and good humour, announced his retirement, as did Stuart Turner. Turner had been one of the 'magnificent twelve' under Brian Taylor, and if one man can encapsulate the Essex spirit of these later years, it is he. Told originally that he was not good enough, he played the rest of his career, 20 years of it, proving that those who told him so were wrong. He bristled with endeavour every time he was given the ball or bat. He forced himself to play over and above his natural ability, and he never acknowledged that a cause was lost.

Perhaps, he, like the rest of the side, inherited something from Green and Douglas and others they never knew, for there is a spirit that has run through Essex cricket from the beginning, and it is well that we should

92. *The 1897 team. Standing, left to right: Armour (scorer), Sherwin (umpire), J W Bonner, P A Perrin, C P McGahey, T M Russell, Tichmarsh (umpire). Seated: C J Kortright, F G Bull, H Carpenter, H G Owen (captain) W Reeves, H Pickett, W Mead.*

93. *The 1979 team. Left to right, back row: Clem Driver (scorer), Keith Pont, Graham Gooch, Neil Smith, Norbert Phillip, Mike Denness, David Acfield, Peter Edwards (Secretary/General Manager). Front row: Ken McEwan, John Lever, Keith Fletcher, Tom Pearce (President), Ray East, Stuart Turner and Brian Hardie.*

remember it. In applauding the triumphs of the Club since 1979, we should never forget those whose endeavours ensured its survival in less palmy days. A nation which has no respect for its past has no hope for its future, so it is with a cricket club.

James Round, Charles Green, Johnny Douglas, Hugh Owen, Charles Kortright, 'Bunny' Lucas, and an abundance of others are part of what has happened in the past decade. Without them, none of it would have been possible, and they should be remembered, as, too, should those 11 cricketers of Pattiswick who, in 1824, were bowled out for four. They have long since been revenged.

Chronology

This chronology contains many 'firsts' and 'lasts' during the period that Essex have been a first-class county. Positions in the various competitions have in the main been excluded. So have records of Essex players selected for England and those who achieved the 'double' of 1000 runs and 100 wickets. Nor is there a record of births and deaths. Much of this information is contained in the statistical section of the book.

1894 Essex granted first-class status
Captain: A P Lucas
Secretary: O R Borradaile
First first-class match: Essex v Leicestershire, at Leyton, 14, 15 and 16 May. H G Owen scored first century in the Club's first-class status, 109 v Oxford University.

1895 First season in county championship – finished eighth.
H G Owen appointed captain following the resignation of A P Lucas. Highest total recorded – 692 v Somerset at Taunton (won by an innings and 317).
H Pickett took 10 wickets for 32 in Leicestershire's first innings at Leyton.

W Mead took 17 wickets for 119 v Hampshire at Southampton.
W Mead first Essex bowler to take 100 wickets in a first-class season.
H Carpenter first Essex batsman to score 1000 runs in a season.
Essex beat Yorkshire by 16 runs at Harrogate.

1896 Finished fifth in the County Championship.
Beat MCC by an innings and 21 runs at Lord's, dismissing them for 41 in their first innings.

1897 Finished third in the County Championship (not bettered until 1978).
Beat Yorkshire by three wickets at Leyton and by one run at Huddersfield.

1898 Beat Lancashire by four wickets after being set 336 to win in fourth innings.
Lost to Gloucestershire by one wicket at Leyton, W G Grace, in his first appearance in a county match on this ground, scored 126 and 49 and took 7 for 44 in the Essex first innings. C J Kortright took 12 for 98 in the match.
F G Bull chosen as one of *Wisden's* 'Five Cricketers of the Year'.

1899 Beat the Australians by 126 runs at Leyton, H Young taking 11 for 74 and W Mead 6 for 88, in the match.
In the Essex total of 673 against Leicestershire at Leicester, F L Fane scored the County's first double century (207).

1900 First 300 partnership by P A Perrin and C P McGahey – 323 v Kent.

1901 C P McGahey became the first Essex batsman to score two separate hundreds in a first-class match – against Gloucestershire at Leyton.
This was closely followed by a similar feat in the next match (against Kent at Leyton) by H Carpenter.
In an extraordinary match against Yorkshire at Leyton, on a rain damaged pitch, 30 wickets fell for 175 runs, Essex being dismissed for 30 (their lowest-ever score) and 41.

1902 C P McGahey chosen as one of *Wisden*'s 'Five Cricketers of the Year'.

1903 C J Kortright appointed captain.

1904 F L Fane appointed captain.
P A Perrin scored the highest individual score for the County – 343 not out against Derbyshire at Chesterfield. Essex scored 597 in their first innings, yet lost the match by nine wickets. Never before had a side been beaten in first-class cricket after scoring 500 runs in their first innings.
W Mead chosen as one of *Wisden*'s 'Five Cricketers of the Year'.

1905 Beat the Australians by 19 runs – the only county to beat the tourists. C P Buckenham and B Tremlin took all 20 wickets between them in this match.

In the match against Yorkshire at Leyton J W H T Douglas took five wickets in eight balls, including the first Essex hat-trick, without having a run hit off him.

P A Perrin chosen as one of *Wisden*'s 'Five Cricketers of the Year'.

C. E. Green elected President of MCC.

1906 Beat West Indies at Leyton by 111 runs.

First first-class match at Southend – against Leicestershire, which Essex won by 5 wickets, J W H T Douglas taking 11 for 128 in the match.

First opening partnership of 200 – 209 by F L Fane and J W H T Douglas v Middlesex.

1907 C P McGahey appointed captain.

Southend granted a full week.

1908 Financial difficulties only resolved through a second mortgage on the Leyton ground being taken up by J H Douglas, the father of J W H T Douglas.

1910 Finance a problem. It was decided to promote a shilling subscription fund in the winter.

1911 J W H T Douglas appointed captain.

Financial situation improved – the shilling fund met with a successful response.

J W H T Douglas chosen to tour Australia in 1911–12, taking over the captaincy when P F Warner fell ill. England won the series 4–1.

1912 Financial position very unfavourable. C E Green resigned as chairman, but before doing so paid off the Club's debts of £400.

1913 J W H T Douglas chosen to captain MCC team to tour South Africa in 1913–14. MCC won the series 4–0.

1914 First first-class match played at Castle Park, Colchester – against Worcestershire, Essex winning by 193 runs.

J W H T Douglas became the first Essex player to achieve 'the double', scoring 1,288 runs and taking 138 wickets.

Record second wicket partnership of 237 by C A G Russell and H Carpenter v Worcestershire.

Record seventh wicket partnership of 261 by J W H T Douglas and J R Freeman v Lancashire.

1915 J W H T Douglas one of *Wisden*'s 'Five Cricketers of the Year'.

J W H T Douglas resumed captaincy.

1919 The experiment of playing two-day matches instead of three, proved a failure. Many matches were drawn, especially those at Leyton where match after match was left unfinished.

1920 First first-class match played at the Garrison Ground, Colchester.
C A G Russell became the first Essex batsman to score 2000 runs in a season (2042 runs).
Douglas and Russell chosen to tour Australia in the winter of 1920–21, Douglas being appointed captain.

1921 Australian tour under J W H T Douglas disastrous, with all five Tests being lost. Douglas played in five Tests; Russell played in four, scoring 135 not out at Adelaide. Douglas captained England in the first two Tests against Australia at home, then being replaced as captain, although he played in the remaining three Tests.
Thirty-nine players called upon during the season.
N R E Wilkinson appointed secretary.
Leyton Ground purchased by the Army Sports Control Board, thereby relieving Essex of a £10,000 mortgage. The Club were, however, still allowed to use the ground for most of their home matches.
Record ninth wicket stand of 251 by J W H T Douglas and S N Hare v Derbyshire.

1922 For the first time since 1885 Essex played a match at Brentwood, against Dublin University.
H Ashton chosen as one of *Wisden*'s 'Five Cricketers of the Year'.

1923 Russell played in four Tests in South Africa during the 1922–23 winter, scoring 140 and 111 in the fifth Test at Durban, the first time an Englishman scored two separate hundreds in a Test match.
Record sixth wicket partnership of 206 by J W H T Douglas and J O'Connor v Gloucestershire.
First first-class match played at Ilford – against the West Indians, which Essex lost by three wickets.
At a Special General Meeting the Committee was reconstructed on a basis of direct representation of various districts with a view to increasing the interest in cricket throughout the county. C A G Russell chosen as one of *Wisden*'s 'Five Cricketers of the Year'.

1925 First first-class match played at Chelmsford, against Oxford University.
P A Perrin in his 49th year scored his 66th century.

1926 The second first-class match played at Chelmsford – against Somerset – resulted in a tie – the first recorded in the first-class history of Essex.
Douglas absent until end July, following an operation for appendicitis. Perrin, at the age of 50, acted as deputy-captain.

1927 Beat the New Zealanders by five wickets at Leyton.

1928 Russell scored 2,243 runs and J O'Connor 2,325 runs. This was the first time that two Essex batsmen reached 2000 runs in a season.
J W H T Douglas dismissed from the captaincy.

1929 H M Morris appointed captain.
Nichols became the first Essex professional to perform 'the double', with 1301 runs and 104 wickets.

1930 B K Castor appointed secretary.
P A Perrin appointed a Test selector.
J W H T Douglas and his father, J H Douglas, both drowned in a North Sea shipping accident.

1931 First first-class match played at Clacton, against Lancashire.

1932 P Holmes and H Sutcliffe established a world record for the first wicket, scoring 555 for Yorkshire against Essex at Leyton.

1933 T N Pearce and D R Wilcox appointed joint-captains.
Finished fourth in the county championship, the highest since 1897, with more wins (13) than ever before.

1934 The lease at Leyton was discontinued, thus ending a playing period of nearly 50 years. Headquarters moved to Chelmsford.
First first-class match played at Westcliff.
First first-class match played at Brentwood since 1922.
First first-class match played at Castle Park, Colchester since 1914.
Kent scored 803 for 4 at Brentwood, the highest total against the County.
M S Nichols chosen as one of *Wisden*'s 'Five Cricketers of the Year'.
Record fifth wicket partnership of 287 by C T Ashton and J O'Connor v Surrey at Brentwood.

1935 Beat the South Africans at Southend by seven wickets, J W A Stephenson took 7 for 66 in the South African first innings.
Beat Yorkshire by an innings and 204 runs at Huddersfield, bowling Yorkshire out for 31 and 99, M S Nichols taking 11 for 54 and scoring 146 runs and H D Read taking 9 for 62 in the match.

1936 Beat the Indians by seven wickets at Brentwood.

1938 Farnes, Nichols, J W A Stephenson and P Smith all played in the Gentlemen v Players match at Lord's, taking 26 wickets between them.
J O'Connor became first professional to captain the County.

1939 Three joint-captains appointed – D R Wilcox, F St G Unwin and J W A Stephenson (T N Pearce absent for business reasons).
Farnes took 16 wickets, including a hat-trick, at Clacton.
P A Perrin appointed chairman of selectors.
K Farnes chosen as one of *Wisden*'s 'Five Cricketers of the Year'.

1946 T N Pearce appointed captain.
T C Dodds and A V Avery established a record first-wicket partnership of 270 v Surrey, at The Oval, Dodds scoring 103 and Avery 210.
D R Wilcox and R M Taylor established a record eighth wicket partnership of 263 v Warwickshire at Southend, Wilcox scoring 134 and Taylor 142.

1947 Tied with Northamptonshire at Ilford, the first tie in post-war first-class cricket.
Peter Smith, batting at number 11 against Derbyshire at Chesterfield, scored 163 – a world record for the last man in. He and F Vigar put on 218 for the tenth wicket, an Essex record, and only 31 runs short of the record in this country.
Peter Smith achieved 'the double', with 1065 runs and 172 wickets. His total of 172 wickets was more than any other Essex player in history.
T P B Smith chosen as one of *Wisden*'s 'Five Cricketers of the Year'.

1948 Essex were defeated by the Australians at Southend by an innings and 451 runs, the Australians scoring 721 in one day, Bradman making 187. Essex, however, were the only county side to bowl out the Australians in one day.
R Smith scored the fastest hundred of the season – 100 in 63 minutes v Derbyshire at Colchester.
A V Avery and R Horsfall established an Essex record for the fourth wicket, with a partnership of 298 v Worcestershire at Clacton.

1949 T E Bailey took all ten wickets for 90 runs, in Lancashire's first innings at Clacton.
T N Pearce appointed a Test selector.

1950 T N Pearce and D J Insole appointed joint-captains.
First first-class match played at Romford.
The match against Warwickshire at Ilford was the first Essex match to be televised.
T E Bailey took 7 for 0 in 31 balls v Glamorgan.
T E Bailey chosen as one of *Wisden*'s 'Five Cricketers of the Year'.

1951 D J Insole appointed captain.
H G Clark appointed secretary and T E Bailey assistant-secretary.
P A Gibb and R Horsfall established a new Essex third wicket record with a partnership of 343 v Kent at Blackheath.
D J Insole scored over 2000 runs – the first Essex amateur to reach this target.
R Smith scored the fastest hundred of the season, 147 v the South Africans.

1952 Essex won the *News Chronicle* 'Brighter Cricket Table', which was based on runs per 100 balls received. Essex headed the table with 50.44 runs.

C Griffiths scored the fastest century of the season v Kent.

A V Avery and P A Gibb established a new Essex second wicket record of 294 v Northamptonshire at Northampton.

The match against Lancashire at Brentwood ended in a tie.

Membership exceeded 5000 for the first time in the Club's history.

1953 Essex won the *News Chronicle* 'Brighter Cricket Table' for the second year running.

Southchurch Park, Southend, flooded by sea water to a depth of four feet.

1954 Diamond Jubilee of Essex in first-class cricket.

G Barker, in his first match for Essex against the Canadians at Clacton, scored 107 not out.

1955 T E Bailey appointed secretary.

Ray Smith scored the fastest century of the season, in 73 minutes, against Northamptonshire at Wellingborough.

D J Insole scored 2427 runs, including nine centuries, reaching both 1000 runs and 2000 runs before any other batsman and scoring more runs than anyone else.

1956 D J Insole chosen for the 1956–57 tour of South Africa, being appointed vice-captain to Peter May. T E Bailey and B Taylor also chosen for this tour.

D J Insole chosen as one of *Wisden*'s 'Five Cricketers of the Year'.

B Taylor chosen as 'Best Young Cricketer of the Year' by the Cricket Writers' Club.

1957 A festival week was staged at Leyton, the first time the County played on this ground since 1933. Chelmsford dropped.

1958 Very wet summer with five matches abandoned and rain interfering with almost every home week.

1959 The match against Gloucestershire at Leyton ended in a tie. T E Bailey recorded another 'double', with 2011 runs and 100 wickets. This was the only time an Essex player achieved this particular 'double'.

D J Insole appointed Test selector.

1960 Sir Hubert Ashton elected president of MCC.

1961 T E Bailey appointed captain.

T N Pearce appointed manager of MCC tour to Pakistan and India.

1962 Essex beat the Pakistan tourists at Leyton by nine wickets, becoming the first English county to achieve victories against all the major touring countries.

1962 B R Knight and R A G Luckin equalled 1923 sixth wicket record, 206 v Middlesex.
1964 Beat the Australians at Southend by six wickets, K W R Fletcher scoring 125 and G Barker 123.
B R Knight won the Carling Single Wicket Competition.
1966 Major C A Brown appointed secretary.
Essex CCC purchased the Chelmsford ground at New Writtle Street, thanks to generous financial assistance from the Warwickshire Supporters' Association.
The first county match to include Sunday play was staged at Ilford in May, Essex playing Somerset before a crowd of 6000 spectators. Last festival week at Clacton.
1967 B Taylor appointed captain.
County cricket returned to Chelmsford.
A serious financial loss resulted in the introduction of a strict economy drive.
1968 Last festival week at Romford.
B L Irvine hit more sixes than any other player in first class cricket.
1969 Beat the New Zealanders by 15 runs at Westcliff, R E East taking 8 for 68 in the match and R N S Hobbs 6 for 88.
First John Player League match staged at Purfleet.
Last festival week at Brentwood.
1970 First first-class match played at Harlow.
Sir Cyril Hawker elected President of MCC.
1971 Dismissed Northamptonshire for 45 in a John Player League match at Ilford, K D Boyce taking 4 for 10.
Finished second in the John Player League.
1972 Dismissed Middlesex for 41 in the Gillette Cup tie at Westcliff, J K Lever taking 5 for 8 and K D Boyce 5 for 22.
B Taylor completed 301 consecutive county championship appearances – an Essex record.
B Taylor chosen as one of *Wisden*'s 'Five Cricketers of the Year'.
S R Cox appointed secretary.
1973 Reached the semi-final of the Benson and Hedges Cup, losing to Kent. B Taylor appointed a Test selector.
1974 K W R Fletcher appointed captain.
The county championship match against Sussex at Hove ended in a tie.
K W R Fletcher and K D Boyce both chosen for inclusion in *Wisden*'s 'Five Cricketers of the Year'.
1975 Against Leicestershire at Chelmsford K D Boyce scored 113 (100 in 58 minutes), including eight sixes and seven fours – the fastest hundred for 38 years; he also took 12 for 73 in the match.

1975 R N S Hobbs scored 100 in 44 minutes against the Australians at Chelmsford, the fastest hundred for 55 years. He hit seven sixes and 12 fours and his second fifty took only 12 minutes.

D J Insole appointed chairman of Test and County Cricket Board.

1976 Essex CCC Centenary Year.

Finished second in the John Player League.

Last festival week at Westcliff.

Centenary fund-raising resulted in the building of an indoor cricket school at the Chelmsford ground.

1977 Finished second in the John Player League.

Last festival week at Leyton.

Indoor cricket school opened.

B Sheret appointed the Club's first general manager.

1978 Finished second in the County Championship, higher than ever before.

Reached the semi-final of the Gillette Cup, losing to Somerset, the scores being level but Somerset having lost fewer wickets.

G A Gooch (129) and K S McEwan (186) broke the Essex second wicket record scoring 321 v Northamptonshire, at Ilford.

D J Insole appointed manager of England tour to Australia.

K S McEwan chosen as one of *Wisden*'s 'Five Cricketers of the Year'.

A W Lilley scored 100 not out on his debut for the County v Nottinghamshire at Trent Bridge.

1979 P J Edwards appointed secretary/general manager.

Essex won their first title by beating Surrey in the final of the Benson and Hedges Cup by 35 runs, following this by winning the county championship for the first time in their history by the decisive margin of 77 points.

G A Gooch and A W Lilley set a new Benson and Hedges first wicket record in the match against Combined Universities at Chelmsford with a partnership of 223 (Gooch 133, Lilley 119). The Essex total of 350 for 3 wickets was also a record.

G A Gooch scored the first century in a Benson and Hedges final.

J K Lever chosen as one of *Wisden*'s 'Five Cricketers of the Year'.

1980 Reached the final of the Benson and Hedges Cup, losing to Northamptonshire by six runs.

G A Gooch chosen as one of *Wisden*'s 'Five Cricketers of the Year'.

1981 Essex won the John Player League Trophy.

Reached the semi-final of the NatWest Trophy, losing to Derbyshire with the scores level but Essex having lost more wickets.

G A Gooch and B R Hardie shared in a partnership of 180 (in 30 overs) for the first wicket in a John Player match against Yorkshire.

1981 K W R Fletcher, G A Gooch and J K Lever chosen for the 1981/2 tour of India and Sri Lanka, Fletcher being appointed captain.

1982 Scored 327 for 2 in a Benson and Hedges match against Sussex. G A Gooch scored 198 not out and K W R Fletcher 101 not out.

D J Insole appointed England manager for tour to Australia and New Zealand.

1983 Won the County Championship by 16 points.

Reached the final of the Benson and Hedges Cup, losing by four runs to Middlesex.

Bowled Surrey out for 14 in a county championship match at Chelmsford. This was the lowest total against the County and was only two runs more than the all-time record low of 12. N Phillip took 6 for 4 and N A Foster 4 for 10.

Scored 310 for 5 in the John Player League match against Glamorgan at Southend, G A Gooch making 176, establishing new records for this competition.

Essex allocated a Zone B World Cup match at Chelmsford between Australia and India, won by India by 118 runs.

1984 Won the County Championship after a close finish with Nottinghamshire.

Won the John Player Special League Trophy by a clear eight points.

1985 Won the NatWest Bank Trophy, beating Nottinghamshire by one run in the final. G A Gooch (91) and B R Hardie (110) put on 202 for the first wicket – the highest partnership in any Lord's Final.

Won the John Player Special League Trophy.

Reached the final of the Benson and Hedges Trophy, losing to Leicestershire by five wickets.

D E East, in the county championship match against Somerset at Taunton, took eight catches behind the stumps in Somerset's first innings, thus equalling the world record held by Wally Grout of Australia.

In the John Player League match against Nottinghamshire at Trent Bridge G A Gooch (171) and B R Hardie (60) scored 239 for the first wicket – a new record for this competition.

1986 G A Gooch appointed captain.

Won the County Championship for the third time in four years and the fourth time in eight years.

Finished second in the John Player Special League, four points behind Hampshire.

The Australian captain, Allan Border, played for the County for most of the season, scoring 1385 runs, average 49.46, including four centuries.

Statistical Record

Sadly, Leslie Newnham died on 4th June 1987,
after completing the statistical section
of this book.

Career records in first-class matches for Essex

The records are complete to the end of the 1986 English season. * denotes not out; †denotes 8-ball over; @ 5-ball over; in all other cases overs are 6-ball.

Name	*Seasons*	*Birth*	*Death*	*M*	*I*	*NO*	*R*	*HS*
D L Acfield	1966–1986	24.7.47	—	378	353	191	1259	38
F Appleyard	1946–1947	26.9.05	11.10.71	14	19	11	55	15*
H A Arkwright	1894–1895	11.11.72	10.12.42	3	6	0	35	19
C T Ashton	1921–1938	19.2.01	31.10.42	89	146	10	3193	118
H Ashton	1921–1939	13.2.98	17.6.79	21	35	1	819	90
P Ashton	1924	27.2.95	18.9.34	1	2	0	52	31
A V Avery	1935–1954	19.12.14	—	268	453	35	14045	224
G W Ayres	1899	5.7.71	28.8.34	12	17	1	263	83
J A Bailey	1953–1958	22.6.30	—	71	88	24	295	27*
T E Bailey	1946–1967	3.12.23	—	482	774	152	21460	205
R K Baker	1972	28.4.52	—	1	1	1	14	14*
A E Banfield	1921	28.1.97	3.1.72	1	2	1	0	0*
A N Barber	1925	23.11.98	—	2	4	0	46	31
G Barker	1954–1971	6.7.31	—	444	797	46	21895	181*
J D Barnfather	1924	22.7.96	21.8.57	5	5	3	50	28*
P L Barrow	1922	22.1.93	7.5.74	1	1	0	0	0
J F Bawtree	1895–1896	26.11.73	25.3.38	5	9	1	96	47
M J Bear	1954–1968	23.2.34	—	322	562	44	12564	137
B H Belle	1935–1937	7.4.14	—	26	42	3	776	63
C E Benham	1904–1909	24.6.81	13.12.61	57	80	11	985	65*
M Berkley	1894	6.9.72	9.8.47	2	3	1	6	5
F D Billham	1924	27.9.96	16.11.80	2	3	1	12	12*
J W Bonner	1896–1898	3.4.69	26.11.36	16	27	1	339	59
A R Border	1986	27.7.55	—	20	32	4	1385	150
O R Borradaile	1894	9.5.59	11.5.35	1	2	0	7	5
N F Borrett	1937–1946	1.10.17	—	3	4	2	33	15*
C S R Boswell	1932–1936	19.1.10	15.8.85	30	46	8	406	69
K D Boyce	1966–1977	11.10.43	—	211	319	18	6848	147*
M J H Boyers	1969	16.4.48	—	1	2	0	2	2
A Bradfield	1922	5.1.92	25.12.78	5	7	3	7	4*
C Bray	1927–1937	6.4.98	—	95	154	14	3474	129
O C Bristowe	1913–1914	12.4.95	27.12.38	11	16	1	249	81
V C G Brooks	1970–1971	29.6.48	—	3	5	0	53	22
A Brown	1921	—	—	2	4	0	59	52
G R R Brown	1924–1932	8.12.05	—	23	35	10	302	38*
H J Brunwin	1937	28.4.12	—	1	1	1	2	2*
C P Buckenham	1899–1914	16.1.76	23.2.37	258	394	63	4882	124
F G Bull	1895–1900	2.4.75	16.9.10	88	125	31	1171	41*
J Burns	1894–1896	20.6.65	11.9.57	26	47	1	713	114
N D Burns	1986	19.9.65	—	2	3	0	54	29
Rev H J E Burrell	1895	15.11.66	22.5.49	2	4	0	15	10
R J Burrell	1894–1895	26.8.70	16.3.48	6	9	0	127	40
C N Calnan	1919–1929	25.12.88	30.1.74	4	8	0	49	24
P Campbell	1911–1919	26.12.87	18.3.60	13	21	2	270	35
G N Capel-Cure	1929	28.9.08	—	1	2	0	6	6
N J O Carbutt	1923	25.12.95	31.10.64	2	1	1	12	12*

Av	*100s*	*Ov*	*Mdns*	*R*	*W*	*Av*	*5wI*	*10m*	*BB*	*Ct*	*St*
7.77	0	9908.1	2790	23509	855	27.49	30	4	8–55	120	—
6.87	0	334	86	817	19	43.00	1	0	5–14	6	—
5.83	0	@ 38	9	109	4	27.25	0	0	3–25	2	—
23.47	3	888.5	149	2923	97	30.13	3	0	7–51	72	—
24.08	0									21	—
26.00	0	12	1	55	1	55.00	0	0	1–55	0	—
33.60	25	203.5	41	627	9	69.66	0	0	1–11	119	—
		† 7									
16.43	0	@ 55.4	19	139	5	27.80	0	0	1–2	12	—
4.60	0	1782.4	385	4553	198	22.99	11	0	7–32	49	—
34.50	22	14415.5	3599	35042	1593	21.99	91	10	10–90	320	—
—	0									2	0
0.00	0	17	3	62	2	31.00	0	0	2–62	0	—
11.50	0	25	4	76	1	76.00	0	0	1–42	2	—
29.15	30	73.1	19	200	5	40.00	0	0	2–34	232	—
25.00	0	110.5	18	355	13	27.30	1	0	6–32	1	—
0.00	0	12	2	43	1	43.00	0	0	1–21	0	—
12.00	0	@ 21	4	66	2	33.00	0	0	1–16	5	—
24.25	9	16.2	2	53	0	—	0	0	—	113	—
19.89	0									20	—
14.27	0	717.4	133	2176	65	33.47	4	0	7–60	31	—
3.00	0	@ 27.3	3	103	7	14.71	1	0	6–50	2	—
6.00	0	23	1	72	0	—	0	0	—	0	—
13.03	0									5	—
49.46	4	26	3	120	1	120.00	0	0	1–8	17	—
3.50	0									1	—
16.50	0	16	3	43	0	—	0	0	—	2	—
10.68	0	432.5	64	1345	36	37.36	0	0	4–22	12	—
22.75	3	5578.3	1060	15704	662	23.72	30	6	9–61	181	—
1.00	0									0	—
1.75	0									2	3
24.81	5	32.5	5	104	2	52.00	0	0	1–1	54	—
16.60	0	221.2	30	901	22	40.95	0	0	4–74	2	—
10.60	0									1	—
14.75	0	14	0	44	1	44.00	0	0	1–25	1	—
12.08	0	321.4	64	834	30	27.80	1	0	5–55	14	—
—	0	4	1	5	1	5.00	0	0	1–5	0	—
14.74	2	7224.5	1093	24629	934	26.36	72	16	8–33	143	—
		@ 59.3									
12.45	0	77	952	7923	365	21.70	29	5	9–93	41	—
		@3246.4									
15.50	1	@ 125.3	25	310	6	51.66	0	0	3–24	11	—
18.00	0									2	2
3.75	0	@ 1	1	0	0	—	0	0	—	0	—
14.11	0									1	—
6.12	0	3	0	25	0	—	0	0	—	1	—
14.21	0	3	0	26	0	—	0	0	—	6	—
3.00	0	11	1	58	2	29.00	0	0	2–58	0	—
—	0	36	1	202	2	101.00	0	0	2–23	0	—

Name	*Seasons*	*Birth*	*Death*	*M*	*I*	*NO*	*R*	*HS*
H A Carpenter	1894–1920	12.7.69	12.12.33	262	466	24	13043	199
R B Carr	1960	12.1.38	—	1	1	1	7	7*
G Carter	1921–1923	10.5.01	—	7	11	1	163	44*
G R Cass	1964–1967	23.4.40	—	45	77	11	1447	104*
B K Castor	1932	21.10.89	2.10.79	1	1	0	13	13
I Chapman	1929	12.10.06	00.2.76	1	1	0	9	9
J H Childs	1985–1986	15.8.51	—	28	27	8	231	34
H G Clark	1923	23.1.89	28.2.67	2	3	0	13	11
L S Clark	1946–1947	6.3.14	—	24	44	3	745	64
R D Clark	1912–1919	22.2.95	20.2.83	7	11	1	61	14
Dr C B Clarke	1959–1960	7.4.18	—	18	27	14	177	39
D F Cock	1939–1946	22.10.14	—	14	20	2	355	98
E C Coleman	1912	5.9.91	2.4.17	2	3	0	10	6
E J Connor	1905	00.00.72	11.1.47	2	4	0	43	26
R M O Cooke	1973–1975	3.9.43	—	40	66	5	1373	139
A V Cooper	1923	3.12.93	3.5.77	1	2	0	14	12
F J Cooper	1921–1923	00.00.88	27.6.58	8	14	1	111	32
W Cooper	1905–1910	—	—	3	6	0	32	18
F Cottam	1922	6.6.00	—	1	—	—	—	—
P Cousens	1950–1955	15.5.32	—	39	50	26	72	13
H P Crabtree	1931–1947	30.4.06	28.5.82	24	41	1	1281	146
C L Crawley	1929	1.5.08	24.7.35	1	2	0	3	3
L G Crawley	1926–1936	26.7.03	9.7.81	56	91	4	2949	222
S J Cray	1938–1950	29.5.21	—	99	172	6	4062	163
J A Cutmore	1924–1936	28.12.98	30.11.85	342	593	36	15937	238*
A G Daer	1925–1935	22.11.06	16.7.80	100	141	42	1469	59
H B Daer	1938–1939	10.12.18	19.12.80	9	12	3	60	17
G B Davies	1912–1914	26.10.92	26.9.15	32	51	8	757	118
W Davis	1920	—	—	4	6	0	26	13
M H Denness	1977–1980	1.12.40	—	83	137	9	4050	195
J N Dennis	1934–1939	4.1.13	—	22	33	3	530	53
H W de Zoete	1897	13.2.77	26.3.57	2	2	2	2	2*
W J Dines	1947–1949	14.9.16	—	20	30	7	431	69*
S C Dinsdale	1970	30.12.48	—	5	7	0	97	29
J G Dixon	1914–1922	3.9.95	19.11.54	93	148	12	2214	173
T C Dodds	1946–1959	19.5.19	—	380	663	17	18565	157
C H Douglas	1912–1919	28.6.86	30.9.54	21	27	0	326	78
J W H T Douglas	1901–1928	3.9.82	19.12.30	459	746	108	17915	210*
W D F Dow	1958–1959	27.11.33	—	2	3	2	9	9*
A W Durley	1957	30.9.33	—	5	8	0	38	16
D E East	1981–1986	27.7.59	—	141	190	27	3433	131
R E East	1965–1984	20.6.47	—	405	513	111	7103	113
G F Eastman	1926–1929	7.4.03	—	48	66	28	265	34*
L C Eastman	1920–1939	3.6.97	17.4.41	442	679	49	12965	161
B E A Edmeades	1961–1976	17.9.41	—	335	555	69	12593	163
G J Edwards	1907	11.5.81	30.9.62	2	3	0	45	21
H D E Elliott	1913	30.3.87	26.4.73	2	4	0	3	3
R E Evans	1950–1957	22.7.22	—	17	29	0	482	79
V J Evans	1932–1937	4.3.12	28.3.75	62	96	37	469	23*
S C Eve	1949–1957	18.12.25	—	32	51	4	1041	120
F L Fane	1895–1922	27.4.75	27.11.60	292	512	30	12599	217

Av	*100s*	*Ov*	*Mdns*	*R*	*W*	*Av*	*5wI*	*10m*	*BB*	*Ct*	*St*
29.50	22	411.3	122	2163	46	47.02	0	0	4–57	220	—
		@ 256.1									
—	0	16	1	62	0	—	0	0	—	0	—
16.30	0	4	0	18	0	—	0	0	—	3	—
21.92	1									27	5
13.00	0									0	—
9.00	0	7	2	18	0	—	0	0	—	0	—
12.15	0	837.1	276	1977	94	21.03	5	3	8–58	5	—
4.33	0									0	—
18.17	0	5	1	15	0	—	0	0	—	11	—
6.10	0									10	1
13.61	0	439.4	88	1353	58	23.32	3	0	7–130	6	—
19.72	0									5	—
3.33	0									1	1
10.75	0	42	9	131	2	65.50	0	0	2–21	0	—
22.50	2	34	3	149	3	49.66	0	0	2–55	24	—
7.00	0									0	—
8.53	0	95.4	9	341	7	48.71	1	0	5–71	2	—
5.33	0	19	1	69	0	—	0	0	—	1	—
—	—	10	3	25	0	—	0	0	—	0	—
3.00	0	663.2	193	1707	44	38.79	0	0	4–63	3	—
32.02	4	15	1	63	0	—	0	0	—	12	—
1.50	0									1	—
33.89	6	12	0	39	0	—	0	0	—	17	—
24.46	7	7	1	40	1	40.00	0	0	1–0	22	—
28.61	15	160.1	13	687	11	62.45	0	0	2–31	121	—
14.83	0	2311.2	495	6183	195	31.70	3	0	6–38	48	—
6.66	0	95	16	387	11	35.18	0	0	3–21	4	—
17.60	2	512.3	73	1769	68	26.01	2	0	6–51	27	—
4.33	0	14	1	69	1	69.00	0	0	1–67	2	—
31.64	6	1	1	0	0	—	0	0	—	38	—
17.66	0									13	—
—	0	@ 32	8	91	3	30.33	0	0	2–44	0	—
18.73	0	325.2	71	980	15	65.33	0	0	3–35	7	—
13.85	0									4	—
16.27	3	1870.4	257	6484	206	31.47	9	2	7–61	48	—
28.73	17	293.1	54	1053	35	30.08	0	0	4–34	176	—
12.07	0	74.1	2	350	6	58.33	0	0	3–46	4	—
28.07	18	10552.5	1800	33653	1443	23.32	93	21	9–47	265	—
9.00	0	55.2	10	171	4	42.75	0	0	4–51	0	—
4.75	0									3	—
21.06	3	3.2	0	12	0	—	0	0	—	361	43
17.66	1	10836.1	3179	25804	1010	25.54	49	10	8–30	251	—
6.97	0									29	21
20.57	7	9995	2493	26102	975	26.77	29	3	7–28	254	—
		† 131.7									
25.91	14	3793.1	829	9688	374	25.90	10	1	7–37	105	—
15.00	0									2	—
0.75	0	23	1	107	1	107.00	0	0	1–67	1	—
16.62	0									8	—
7.94	0	1304.4	277	3843	129	29.79	5	1	6–47	12	—
22.14	1									17	—
26.13	18	6.5	0	32	0	—	0	0	—	141	—

Name	*Seasons*	*Birth*	*Death*	*M*	*I*	*NO*	*R*	*HS*
H A Faragher	1949–1950	20.7.17	—	6	9	2	274	85*
K Farnes	1930–1939	8.7.11	20.10.41	79	94	31	590	97*
G G Farnfield	1921	13.7.97	22.3.74	12	20	1	252	41
W F O Faviell	1908	5.6.82	14.2.50	7	12	4	104	27
K W R Fletcher	1962–1986	20.5.44	—	538	871	116	28206	228*
M K Fosh	1976–1978	26.9.57	—	14	23	0	481	66
N A Foster	1980–1986	6.5.62	—	75	84	23	1260	63
B C Francis	1971–1973	18.2.48	—	47	84	7	2962	188*
H W F Franklin	1921–1931	30.6.01	25.8.85	73	104	14	1757	106
R C Franklin	1924	9.9.04	28.9.82	1	2	0	1	1
A J Freeman	1920	2.4.92	28.4.72	1	2	1	1	1
E C Freeman	1894–1896	7.12.60	16.10.39	5	9	0	95	35
E J Freeman	1904–1912	16.10.80	22.2.64	55	91	3	1280	84
J R Freeman	1905–1928	3.9.83	8.8.58	336	577	56	14507	286
W T Garrett	1900–1903	9.1.76	16.2.53	15	25	1	516	92
J S B Gentry	1925	4.10.99	16.4.78	1	—	—	—	—
P A Gibb	1951–1956	11.7.13	7.12.77	145	250	12	6328	141
A L Gibson	1895–1910	4.9.77	29.7.43	23	36	3	492	71
K L Gibson	1909–1912	11.5.88	14.5.67	36	55	6	795	75
F W Gilligan	1919–1929	20.9.93	4.5.60	79	108	27	1808	78*
Rev F H Gillingham	1903–1928	6.9.75	1.4.53	181	307	21	9160	201
C Gladwin	1981–1986	10.5.62	—	57	97	5	2614	162
A K Golding	1983	5.10.63	—	1	2	2	8	6*
G A Gooch	1973–1986	23.7.53	—	232	381	32	15610	227
C H Gosling	1930	22.2.10	19.5.74	2	4	0	61	33
R C Gosling	1894–1896	15.6.68	8.4.22	4	8	1	55	21*
L Graham	1926	20.8.01	21.12.62	2	3	1	14	12
D A A Gray	1947	19.6.22	—	1	1	0	6	6
W J Gray	1894	26.11.64	18.12.98	1	2	0	4	3
M A Green	1930	3.10.91	28.12.71	2	4	0	27	13
W T Greensmith	1947–1963	16.8.30	—	371	550	149	8042	138*
C Griffiths	1951–1953	9.12.30	—	27	41	3	615	105
A S Grimwood	1925	8.9.05	—	4	6	0	26	15
T G Grinter	1909–1921	12.12.85	21.4.66	8	13	1	201	49*
W C Gunary	1929	5.8.95	26.1.69	1	1	0	0	0
S Hadden	1912–1920	26.8.77	00.00.34	6	5	2	29	17*
H Hailey	1894–1895	00.00.51	24.9.32	13	22	5	301	66*
B R Hardie	1973–1986	14.1.50	—	305	494	62	14678	162
S N Hare	1921	31.3.00	30.9.77	3	5	0	117	98
J Harris	1905	—	—	2	3	1	0	0*
J G W Harrold	1923–1928	00.00.92	7.10.50	11	19	3	88	17
R C Harvey	1952	7.5.34	—	1	2	2	12	12*
F C Hawker	1937	21.7.00	—	1	2	0	26	16
A F G Hayzelden	1929–1931	10.1.04	10.4.55	2	3	1	5	4*
E W Hazelton	1919	00.00.94	13.3.58	1	2	0	8	8
A E Heatley	1894	00.00.66	1.7.41	1	2	1	20	13*
R M Heaven	1939	8.10.18	—	1	1	1	5	5*
P A Hector	1977	29.7.58	—	3	5	1	75	40
R Herbert	1976–1980	1.12.57	—	6	9	1	62	14*
J P Herringshaw	1921–1922	22.5.92	13.11.74	9	14	5	94	18
G F Higgins	1894–1895	00.00.68	16.8.51	9	17	0	306	118
H M Hills	1912–1919	28.9.86	?	14	21	4	139	26

Av	*100s*	*Ov*	*Mdns*	*R*	*W*	*Av*	*5wI*	*10m*	*BB*	*Ct*	*St*
39.14	0									4	—
9.36	0	2265.5	458	7086	367	19.30	28	5	8–38	42	—
		† 149									
13.26	0									5	—
13.00	0	5	1	13	0	—	0	0	—	4	—
37.35	44	260.5	39	1259	29	43.41	1	0	5–41	498	—
20.91	0									5	—
20.65	0	2362.2	504	7242	305	23.74	19	2	6–46	35	—
38.46	7									10	—
19.52	2	393	45	1596	36	44.33	0	0	4–40	36	—
0.50	0	11	1	41	1	41.00	0	0	1–20	1	—
1.00	0	24	1	95	0	—	0	0	—	0	—
10.55	0	@ 12	3	40	0	—	0	0	—	1	—
14.54	0	18	3	50	1	50.00	0	0	1–6	14	—
27.84	26	96.4	17	365	10	36.50	0	0	3–31	230	46
21.50	0	44	8	142	1	142.00	0	0	1–72	4	—
—	—	8	1	20	0	—	0	0	—	0	—
26.58	8	0.5	0	4	0	—	0	0	—	273	63
14.90	0	@ 6	0	16	0	—	0	0	—	6	—
16.22	0	1.5	0	9	1	9.00	0	0	1–9	53	9
22.32	0	0.2	0	6	0	—	0	0	—	87	33
32.02	19	1.2	0	13	0	—	0	0	—	91	0
28.41	1	21	1	71	0	—	0	0	—	26	—
—	0	28	3	97	2	48.50	0	0	1–44	0	—
44.72	41	1664	407	4501	150	30.00	3	0	7–14	222	—
15.25	0									2	—
7.85	0									1	—
7.00	0									2	—
6.00	0	29	5	63	1	63.00	0	0	1–34	0	—
2.00	0									0	—
6.75	0									1	—
20.05	1	7322.1	1747	20711	720	28.76	21	2	8–59	147	—
16.18	1	3	0	22	0	—	0	0	—	4	—
4.33	0	1	0	5	0	—	0	0	—	0	—
16.75	0									2	—
0.00	0	19	6	58	0	—	0	0	—	1	—
9.66	0									5	1
17.70	0									5	—
33.97	20	33	2	173	3	57.66	0	0	2–39	279	—
23.40	0									1	—
0.00	0									4	0
5.50	0	30	1	123	3	41.00	0	0	1–15	13	—
—	0	16	1	88	3	29.33	0	0	3–88	0	—
13.00	0									0	—
2.50	0	37.5	6	110	6	18.33	0	0	3–30	3	—
4.00	0	18	1	77	0	—	0	0	—	0	—
20.00	0	@ 1	0	10	0	—	0	0	—	4	—
—	0									4	—
18.75	0	56	7	190	7	27.14	0	0	3–56	0	—
7.75	0	36.4	3	148	3	49.33	0	0	3–64	5	—
10.44	0	150.2	28	498	9	55.33	0	0	2–48	7	—
18.00	1									2	—
8.17	0	191.1	9	738	15	49.20	1	0	5–63	7	—

Name	*Seasons*	*Birth*	*Death*	*M*	*I*	*NO*	*R*	*HS*
C Hilton	1964	26.9.37	—	24	23	9	128	29*
A B Hipkin	1923–1931	8.8.00	11.2.57	231	326	55	4239	108
R N S Hobbs	1961–1975	8.5.42	—	325	429	102	4069	100
G W Hockey	1928–1931	1.1.05	—	19	33	5	305	23
G W Horrex	1956–1957	27.12.32	—	7	13	0	141	41
R Horsfall	1947–1955	26.6.20	25.8.81	207	349	25	9583	206
W G Hubble	1923	20.6.98	00.00.78	1	1	0	0	0
M G Hughes	1983	23.11.61	—	1	2	0	10	10
F E Hugonin	1927–1928	16.8.97	5.3.67	6	8	3	42	17
A Hurd	1958–1960	7.9.37	—	35	34	14	115	20*
G C Hurst	1962	8.12.41	—	1	2	1	0	0*
R W J G Hyndson	1919	00.00.94	27.9.43	1	2	0	7	6
J H Inns	1898–1904	30.3.76	14.6.05	10	14	3	73	28
D J Insole	1947–1963	18.4.26	—	345	574	54	20113	219*
B L Irvine	1968–1969	9.3.44	—	54	89	12	2674	109
V E Jarvis	1925	30.9.98	30.4.75	2	4	0	44	37
C V Jenkinson	1922–1923	15.5.91	6.11.80	5	6	2	9	8
L C S Jerman	1950–1951	23.4.15	—	3	2	0	8	8
A S Johnston	1894–1896	16.3.63	8.8.29	7	12	1	235	63
A M Jorden	1966–1970	28.1.47	—	60	85	20	704	59*
R C G Joy	1922–1928	30.7.98	12.12.74	13	16	2	142	35
H D Keigwin	1906–1907	14.5.81	20.9.16	4	6	0	69	20
R P Keigwin	1903–1919	8.4.83	26.11.72	20	32	3	455	75
C J M Kenny	1950–1953	19.5.29	—	18	14	6	26	16
T Kent	1960–1962	21.10.39	—	10	10	4	74	23*
I M King	1957	10.11.31	—	28	36	21	131	33
R J S King	1928	10.5.09	—	1	1	0	3	3
B R Knight	1955–1966	18.2.38	—	239	399	42	8798	165
C J Kortright	1894–1907	9.1.71	12.12.52	160	255	18	4182	131
J C Laker	1962–1964	9.2.22	23.4.86	30	29	8	248	28
A W E Lapham	1921	00.00.79	9.2.64	3	5	0	31	16
A E Lashbrooke	1908	30.11.83	00.00.63	1	2	0	9	9
A B Lavers	1937–1953	6.9.12	—	25	44	2	695	42*
T P Lawrence	1933–1935	26.4.10	—	7	14	0	133	39
J M Leiper	1950	17.2.21	—	2	4	0	50	44
R J Leiper	1981–1982	30.8.61	—	2	4	0	53	49
J K Lever	1967–1986	24.2.49	—	406	414	165	2661	91
D C Levick	1950–1951	27.5.29	—	3	6	0	14	6
A W Lilley	1978–1986	8.5.59	—	62	100	6	2295	100*
P J Lindsey	1964	29.5.44	—	1	1	1	7	7*
Rev C G Littlehales	1896–1904	20.5.71	28.8.45	6	10	1	109	23
J Littlewood	1905	8.4.78	27.10.42	1	1	1	5	5*
G M Locks	1928	00.00.98	17.9.65	2	4	2	5	3*
G M Louden	1912–1927	6.9.85	28.12.72	82	125	33	844	74
F A Loveday	1921–1923	14.9.92	18.10.54	7	14	0	321	81
A P Lucas	1894–1907	20.2.57	12.10.23	98	153	21	3554	135
R A G Luckin	1962–1963	25.11.39	—	29	46	3	735	82
R V Lynch	1954	22.5.23	—	3	3	2	7	6*
L W Lywood	1930	23.12.06	31.10.71	2	3	0	12	7
M S A McEvoy	1976–1981	25.1.56	—	43	74	1	1371	67*
K S McEwan	1974–1985	16.7.52	—	282	458	41	18088	218

Av	*100s*	*Ov*	*Mdns*	*R*	*W*	*Av*	*5wI*	*10m*	*BB*	*Ct*	*St*
9.14	0	630.3	96	1999	58	34.46	1	0	6–86	12	—
15.64	2	5432	1267	13377	518	25.82	18	3	8–71	209	—
12.44	2	7322.3	1897	19844	763	26.00	32	5	8–63	222	—
10.89	0	5	2	20	0	—	0	0	—	4	—
10.84	0									0	—
29.59	17	12	2	41	1	41.00	0	0	1–4	85	—
0.00	0	17.4	3	60	2	30.00	0	0	2–3	0	—
5.00	0	31.2	2	162	6	27.00	0	0	4–71	0	—
8.40	0									8	1
5.75	0	818.4	225	2221	84	26.44	5	1	6–15	5	—
0.00	0									1	—
3.50	0	14	1	71	0	—	0	0	—	0	—
6.63	0	5	1	15	0	—	0	0	—	8	0
38.67	48	1284.1	259	4061	119	34.12	1	0	5–22	279	1
34.72	1	18	0	70	1	70.00	0	0	1–39	40	—
11.00	0	6	0	23	0	—	0	0	—	0	—
2.25	0									4	4
4.00	0	82	20	222	1	222.00	0	0	1–39	2	—
21.36	0									3	—
10.83	0	1140.4	170	3501	117	29.92	0	0	4–29	36	—
10.14	0	131.4	23	398	12	33.16	0	0	3–41	10	—
11.50	0	56	14	179	4	44.75	0	0	1–23	1	—
15.68	0	164.2	24	639	14	45.64	0	0	4–49	3	—
3.25	0	415.3	84	1212	39	31.07	1	0	5–80	4	—
12.33	0	211	64	561	15	37.40	0	0	4–54	5	—
8.73	0	525.5	197	1146	34	33.70	0	0	4–25	29	—
3.00	0	7	0	20	0	—	0	0	—	0	—
24.64	8	6287.5	1213	17162	761	22.55	39	8	8–69	171	—
17.64	2	886	625	9036	440	20.53	35	8	8–57	167	—
		@2145.3									
11.80	0	979.5	279	2367	111	21.32	7	2	7–73	11	—
6.20	0	29.2	0	90	5	18.00	0	0	2–25	0	—
4.50	0	17	0	61	1	61.00	0	0	1–26	0	—
16.54	0	156	29	483	13	37.15	0	0	4–68	6	—
		+ 3									
9.50	0									3	—
12.50	0	32	5	79	1	79.00	0	0	1–38	1	—
13.25	0									2	—
10.68	0	11449.5	2542	31716	1370	23.15	74	11	8–37	151	—
2.33	0									1	—
24.41	1	56.3	3	309	7	44.14	0	0	3–116	29	—
—	0	18	6	50	1	50.00	0	0	1–8	0	—
12.11	0									4	1
—	0	11	1	36	0	—	0	0	—	1	—
2.50	0	73	11	227	3	75.66	0	0	2–86	0	—
9.17	0	3040.1	552	9066	415	21.84	33	5	8–36	54	—
22.92	0									2	—
26.92	2	15	1	90	1	90.00	0	0	1–17	50	0
		@ 5									
17.09	0									8	—
7.00	0	43	15	107	4	26.75	0	0	4–64	2	—
4.00	0	26	3	83	2	41.50	0	0	1–7	0	—
18.78	0	30	8	103	3	34.33	0	0	3–20	42	—
43.37	52	46.1	3	301	4	75.25	0	0	1–0	197	0

Name	*Seasons*	*Birth*	*Death*	*M*	*I*	*NO*	*R*	*HS*
C P McGahey	1894–1921	12.12.71	10.1.35	400	685	61	19079	277
C D McIver	1902–1922	23.1.81	13.5.54	59	101	6	2544	134
M Mackinnon	1927	11.5.91	13.2.75	3	4	0	55	31
S J Malone	1975–1978	19.10.53	—	2	—	—	—	—
J W Marston	1923–1924	25.10.93	9.7.38	2	4	1	12	6
A D Martin	1920–1921	00.00.88	00.00.58	3	3	0	0	0
E G Martin	1928	4.2.07	27.1.78	2	4	0	25	13
O. Martyn	1922	00.00.87	14.9.59	1	1	0	0	0
W H J Mayes	1914	17.7.85	5.2.46	1	2	0	2	2
H Mead	1913–1914	13.6.95	00.4.21	4	8	2	19	8*
W Mead	1894–1913	1.4.68	18.3.54	332	469	125	3843	119
G C Melluish	1926	25.8.06	14.4.77	4	3	1	18	16*
C F Mercer	1929	00.00.96	00.00.65	2	4	0	26	8
A H Meston	1926–1927	1.6.98	00.00.80	12	17	4	143	41
S P Meston	1907–1908	19.11.82	9.1.60	17	29	2	476	130
J Milner	1957–1961	22.8.37	—	66	117	12	2688	135
E S Missen	1921	00.00.75	17.11.27	1	2	0	20	12
G F Mitchell	1926	00.3.97	—	1	1	0	4	4
K F Moore	1961	4.1.40	—	1	1	0	2	2
H M Morris	1919–1932	16.4.98	30.11.84	240	383	29	6974	166
P E Morris	1909–1924	26.11.77	6.7.45	28	43	5	418	55*
W B Morris	1946–1950	28.5.17	—	48	78	10	1219	68
H C Mortlock	1912–1921	13.10.92	29.3.63	4	4	0	32	26
A S Moule	1921–1924	31.7.94	5.2.73	17	31	5	317	64
W Naylor	1906	—	—	1	2	0	2	2
F W H Nicholas	1912–1929	25.7.93	20.10.62	63	101	2	2255	140
M S Nichols	1924–1939	6.10.00	26.1.61	418	664	66	15736	205
G J Nolan	1968	6.10.37	—	1	2	0	14	11
G Norman	1920	23.8.90	24.11.64	4	5	1	44	21
R O G Norman	1932	30.7.11	26.7.83	1	2	0	20	10
J O'Connor	1921–1939	6.11.97	22.2.77	516	866	76	27819	248
C E L Orman	1896	6.9.59	11.2.27	2	2	0	16	12
H G P Owen	1894–1902	19.5.59	20.10.12	133	222	17	4459	134
E J Palmer	1957	16.6.31	—	4	6	5	39	11*
H J Palmer	1924–1932	30.8.90	12.2.67	53	65	23	257	25*
L F Parslow	1946	11.11.09	6.8.63	1	2	0	9	5
C H Pascoe	1909	00.00.77	26.1.57	1	1	1	3	3*
R F T Paterson	1946	8.9.16	29.5.80	25	40	5	680	80
J H Pawle	1935–1938	18.5.15	—	6	11	0	194	68
T N Pearce	1929–1950	3.11.05	—	231	376	48	11139	211*
P A Perrin	1896–1928	26.5.76	20.11.45	525	894	88	29172	343*
P J Phelan	1958–1965	9.2.38	—	154	192	70	1505	63
N Phillip	1978–1985	12.6.48	—	144	201	22	3784	134
L J Phillips	1919–1922	20.1.99	22.4.79	4	5	1	38	19
H G Pickering	1938	18.1.17	4.3.84	3	6	0	62	17
H Pickett	1894–1897	26.3.62	3.10.07	52	80	34	387	35
S G Plumb	1975–1977	17.1.54	—	2	3	1	68	37*
I L Pont	1985–1986	28.8.61	—	9	11	5	121	43

Av	*100s*	*Ov*	*Mdns*	*R*	*W*	*Av*	*5wI*	*10m*	*BB*	*Ct*	*St*
30.57	29	2855.1	547	9481	306	30.98	12	3	7–27	140	—
		@ 148									
26.77	4	10.2	3	25	1	25.00	0	0	1–4	47	13
13.75	0									0	—
—	—	41	7	101	2	50.50	0	0	1–28	0	—
4.00	0	28	1	112	2	56.00	0	0	2–47	1	—
0.00	0	51	1	210	5	42.00	0	0	3–43	1	—
6.25	0	44	4	140	2	70.00	0	0	1–63	1	—
0.00	0									1	—
1.00	0	14	0	69	0	—	0	0	—	0	—
3.16	0	55.4	5	194	3	64.66	0	0	2–84	3	—
11.17	1	8147.2	4037	28423	1472	19.30	117	30	9–40	151	—
		@4529									
9.00	0	37	5	115	3	38.33	0	0	1–17	0	—
6.50	0									0	—
11.00	0	98	16	352	4	88.00	0	0	2–18	9	—
17.62	1	8.2	0	48	1	48.00	0	0	1–10	7	—
25.60	3	2	0	14	0	—	0	0	—	57	—
10.00	0									0	—
4.00	0	17	3	45	1	45.00	0	0	1–25	0	—
2.00	0	29	10	43	4	10.75	0	0	4–21	2	—
19.70	3	226.5	20	839	14	59.92	0	0	2–16	78	—
11.00	0	598.5	75	1848	83	22.26	6	1	8–106	13	—
17.92	0	671	156	1975	43	45.93	0	0	4–90	18	—
8.00	0	97	12	380	7	54.28	1	0	5–104	6	—
12.19	0	1	0	6	0	—	0	0	—	5	—
1.00	0									2	0
22.77	1									41	13
26.31	20	11250.5	2218	34201	1608	21.26	108	22	9–32	279	—
		† 629.5									
7.00	0									0	—
11.00	0	3	0	18	0	—	0	0	—	1	—
10.00	0									0	—
35.21	71	6330.1	1212	17523	537	32.63	17	2	7–52	215	1
		† 3.2									
8.00	0									1	—
21.75	3	@ 114.3	26	321	9	35.66	0	0	2–37	38	—
39.00	0	72	20	225	7	32.14	0	0	2–35	1	—
6.11	0	1189.4	233	3477	142	24.48	6	0	6–68	19	—
4.50	0									0	—
—	0	7	3	16	0	—	0	0	—	0	—
19.42	0	118	9	464	13	35.69	0	0	4–98	12	3
17.63	0									4	—
33.96	20	232.2	38	927	15	61.80	0	0	4–12	144	—
36.19	65	183.4	40	740	16	46.25	0	0	3–13	284	—
		@ 33									
12.33	0	2960	731	8510	300	28.36	17	2	8–109	67	—
21.13	1	3477.1	645	10638	423	25.14	18	1	6–4	45	—
9.50	0	4.2	0	31	0	—	0	0	—	0	—
10.33	0									0	—
8.41	0	@1230.4	377	2780	114	24.38	4	1	10–32	19	—
34.00	0	14	3	47	2	23.50	0	0	2–47	0	—
20.16	0	166.1	21	675	22	30.68	1	0	5–103	1	—

Name	Seasons	Birth	Death	M	I	NO	R	HS
K R Pont	1970–1986	16.1.53	—	198	305	44	6558	125*
D F Pope	1928–1934	28.10.06	8.9.34	148	248	14	6443	161
A G Powell	1932–1937	17.8.12	7.6.82	23	35	7	495	62*
H C Preece	1895	27.10.67	17.9.37	2	4	0	74	49
E R Presland	1962–1970	27.3.43	—	30	41	4	625	51
K C Preston	1948–1964	22.8.25	—	391	460	165	3024	70
E J Price	1948–1949	27.10.18	—	43	56	16	214	26*
P J Prichard	1984–1986	7.1.65	—	67	107	9	3009	147*
D R Pringle	1978–1986	18.9.58	—	101	144	25	2743	121*
G C Pritchard	1965–1966	14.1.42	—	10	11	2	19	8
S Proffitt	1937	8.10.10	—	7	14	0	170	39
S C Puddefoot	1922–1923	17.10.94	2.10.72	8	8	2	101	42
G R Pullinger	1949–1950	14.3.20	4.8.82	18	20	11	53	14*
J H Purves	1960–1961	4.12.37	—	5	7	0	36	14
A B Quick	1936–1952	10.2.15	—	19	32	1	433	57
S E V Quin	1924	3.4.96	9.4.70	1	1	0	0	0
M Raison	1928–1930	7.11.01	—	17	27	2	451	57
L H R Ralph	1953–1961	22.5.20	—	174	262	39	3763	73
A H Read	1904–1910	24.1.80	20.5.57	22	30	6	419	70
H D Read	1933–1935	28.1.10	—	32	41	15	104	17*
D Reese	1906	26.1.79	12.6.53	8	15	2	198	70
W Reeves	1897–1921	22.6.75	22.3.44	271	422	34	6451	135
R J Richards	1970	5.6.34	—	1	—	—	—	—
C S Richardson	1914	23.3.85	5.4.48	1	1	0	15	15
J V Richardson	1924–1926	16.12.03	—	14	18	3	300	82
P J Richardson	1912	2.4.91	23.3.63	2	2	0	34	21
K R Rickards	1953	22.8.23	—	1	2	0	25	13
H W Riding	1921	19.9.99	21.5.23	1	2	0	23	16
G V N Ridley	1922–1926	23.10.97	12.11.53	6	11	0	113	54
F H Rist	1934–1953	30.3.14	—	65	108	9	1496	62
D C Robinson	1908	20.4.84	30.7.63	7	12	1	148	37
R H Robinson	1912	00.00.85	23.8.17	4	7	2	25	11*
C J Round	1921	3.9.85	6.10.45	2	4	0	9	8
F E Rowe	1894–1895	30.11.64	17.5.28	3	5	0	32	19
Sir G W Rowley	1926	10.5.96	8.8.53	5	7	1	53	23
A E Russell	1898–1910	9.1.75	8.9.40	130	196	42	2025	100
C A G Russell	1908–1930	7.10.87	23.3.61	379	628	51	23610	273
T M Russell	1894–1905	6.7.68	28.2.27	162	246	45	3106	139
Sadiq Mohammad	1970	5.5.45	—	1	1	0	20	20
G E Sainsbury	1979–1980	17.1.58	—	3	2	2	2	2*
N H Saint	1920–1923	22.4.01	15.8.30	44	72	7	757	36
L A Savill	1953–1961	30.6.35	—	125	200	16	3919	115
G J Saville	1963–1974	5.2.44	—	124	214	29	4265	126*
D Sayers	1967	17.3.34	—	1	1	1	0	0*
F J Scoulding	1912–1920	00.00.87	25.8.28	22	28	11	92	21
C J Searle	1947	12.5.21	—	1	1	1	5	5*
L D Sears	1925	12.1.01	—	2	4	0	18	16
D J Semmence	1962	20.4.38	—	1	2	0	33	24
E H D Sewell	1902–1904	30.9.72	20.9.47	55	91	5	1822	107
R H Sharp	1925–1928	11.6.93	15.3.61	16	25	7	169	36*
J R Sheffield	1929–1936	19.11.06	—	177	272	40	3822	108
H R Sherman	1967–1969	15.6.43	—	13	21	3	448	66

Av	*100s*	*Ov*	*Mdns*	*R*	*W*	*Av*	*5wI*	*10m*	*BB*	*Ct*	*St*
25.12	7	1088.3	217	3189	96	33.21	2	0	5–17	92	—
27.53	7	58	3	272	4	68.00	0	0	1–11	35	—
17.67	0									30	8
18.50	0									0	—
16.89	0	295.1	61	761	13	58.53	0	0	2–19	24	—
10.25	0	11453	2482	30288	1155	26.22	37	2	7–55	344	—
5.35	0	1031.3	238	3013	92	32.75	4	0	8–125	24	—
30.70	2	1	0	5	0	—	0	0	—	44	—
23.05	2	2243.3	524	6371	239	26.65	8	0	7–32	57	—
2.11	0	129	20	406	7	58.00	0	0	4–24	3	—
12.14	0	9	0	32	0	—	0	0	—	1	—
16.83	0	33	6	105	1	105.00	0	0	1–34	2	—
5.88	0	519.3	109	1557	41	37.97	1	0	5–54	14	—
5.14	0									1	—
13.96	0	1.5	0	10	0	—	0	0	—	12	—
0.00	0	7	1	13	0	—	0	0	—	0	—
18.04	0	153.2	18	575	14	41.07	1	0	5–104	6	—
16.87	0	4071.1	903	11053	460	24.02	19	3	7–42	143	—
17.45	0	360.2	77	1192	38	31.36	1	0	7–75	7	—
4.00	0	749.5	122	2765	131	21.10	7	1	7–35	14	—
15.23	0	43	5	165	6	27.50	0	0	4–55	0	—
16.62	3	4939.1 @ 175.2	1085	16137	581	27.77	37	5	7–33	115	—
—	—									0	0
15.00	0									1	—
20.00	0	78	11	253	7	36.14	0	0	2–55	8	—
17.00	0	5	0	12	0	—	0	0	—	1	—
12.50	0									0	—
11.50	0									0	—
10.27	0									3	—
15.11	0	4.1	2	8	1	8.00	0	0	1–8	35	5
13.45	0									12	1
5.00	0									9	4
2.25	0	13	1	62	1	62.00	0	0	1–49	0	—
6.40	0									1	—
8.83	0	10	1	29	0	—	0	0	—	0	—
13.14	1									163	44
40.91	62	3210.1	741	7480	276	27.10	5	0	5–25	280	—
15.45	3									246	88
20.00	0									0	—
—	0	80	12	268	8	33.50	0	0	4–85	1	—
11.64	0	179.3	17	800	17	47.05	0	0	3–32	10	—
21.29	4	2	0	26	1	26.00	0	0	1–26	50	—
23.05	2	15	4	59	3	19.66	0	0	2–30	101	—
—	0	21	2	64	1	64.00	0	0	1–22	0	—
5.41	0	410.5	68	1252	32	39.12	0	0	4–50	6	—
—	0									1	1
4.50	0									0	—
16.50	0	8	3	31	0	—	0	0	—	0	—
21.18	2	110	19	388	7	55.42	0	0	2–79	45	—
9.38	0	179	15	696	16	43.50	1	0	5–66	16	—
16.47	1	12	2	28	0	—	0	0	—	194	54
24.88	0	7	1	23	0	—	0	0	—	4	—

Name	*Seasons*	*Birth*	*Death*	*M*	*I*	*NO*	*R*	*HS*
R N Shorter	1927–1929	26.7.06	20.1.84	23	29	11	104	21
I J Skinner	1950	1.4.28	—	13	21	7	28	7*
G J Smith	1955–1966	2.4.35	—	239	412	30	8519	148
G W O Smith	1929–1930	7.3.06	—	10	18	3	206	39*
H T O Smith	1929–1935	5.3.06	—	23	36	5	361	38
H W Smith	1912–1922	6.9.90	?	20	31	12	195	22
N Smith	1973–1981	1.4.49	—	178	226	47	3225	126
R Smith	1934–1956	10.8.14	—	419	646	81	11125	147
T P B Smith	1929–1951	30.10.08	4.8.67	434	647	115	9652	163
W G Spencer	1938–1948	2.8.12	20.7.71	3	5	1	52	25
P A Spicer	1962–1963	11.5.39	18.8.69	17	29	2	526	86
E F Spinks	1926	3.8.02	19.10.82	2	3	1	2	2
H Spurr	1923	17.6.89	21.12.62	1	2	0	13	9
E A W Stanley	1950–1952	27.9.26	—	13	21	3	226	35
A R Stanyard	1960	5.4.38	—	2	3	0	47	26
B Stead	—	21.6.39	15.4.80					
J P Stephenson	1985–1986	14.3.65	—	15	27	1	661	85
J W A Stephenson	1934–1939	1.8.07	20.5.82	61	93	21	1050	65
E A W Steward	1964–1965	27.6.41	—	15	23	2	272	47
F Street	1898–1899	31.5.70	7.7.16	9	11	0	246	76
B T Strutton	1914–1919	00.00.92	9.2.68	4	6	1	64	19
G Sutton	1912	—	—	1	1	0	0	0
C F Swann	1912	00.00.83	7.3.60	1	1	0	0	0
B J Swyer	1923	6.6.98	7.7.64	1	2	0	12	7
A G Taylor	1923	29.12.91	—	2	3	0	7	7
B Taylor	1949–1973	19.6.32	—	539	901	69	18240	135
J F Taylor	1960–1961	9.6.37	—	14	23	6	436	86
R M Taylor	1931–1946	30.11.09	00.1.84	206	349	21	6755	193
E C Tedder	1946	5.9.15	9.9.72	8	14	0	208	55
E C Thompson	1926–1929	27.2.07	18.3.82	44	61	17	696	45*
H W Thorn	1928	21.4.09	20.5.82	1	2	0	12	7
P Toone	1912–1922	00.00.83	00.00.55	29	42	13	215	24
T D Topley	1985–1986	25.2.64	—	13	14	3	122	45
G Tosetti	1898–1905	1.8.79	16.4.23	41	63	6	1054	132*
E M O'B Toulmin	1899–1912	13.8.77	7.1.45	2	2	0	1	1
A F M Townsend	1910	1.8.85	00.00.48	1	—	—	—	—
C J H Treglown	1922–1928	13.2.93	7.5.80	34	55	3	792	77
B Tremlin	1900–1919	18.9.77	12.4.36	132	193	63	1776	61
S A Trick	1905–1919	13.6.84	11.2.58	5	9	0	69	26
A J Turner	1897–1910	10.7.78	8.9.52	68	116	12	3730	124
S Turner	1965–1986	18.7.43	—	354	503	98	9264	121
W M F Turner	1899–1926	4.4.81	1.2.48	48	81	7	2004	172
P W Turrall	1927	00.6.83	17.5.41	1	1	0	45	45
E J Unwin	1932–1939	18.9.12	—	7	14	0	152	48
F St G Unwin	1932–1950	23.4.11	—	52	85	8	1125	60

Av	*100s*	*Ov*	*Mdns*	*R*	*W*	*Av*	*5wI*	*10m*	*BB*	*Ct*	*St*
5.77	0	259.4	55	695	15	46.33	0	0	3–14	12	—
2.00	0	243	37	808	21	38.47	0	0	4–56	5	—
22.30	4	367.4	112	913	33	27.66	1	0	5–39	131	—
13.73	0									2	—
11.64	0	539.1	100	1618	61	26.52	3	0	6–56	19	—
10.26	0	323.5	53	1055	35	30.14	1	0	5–59	12	—
18.01	2									381	47
19.69	6	13358.3	2964	39817	1317	30.23	73	10	8–63	179	—
		† 394.5									
18.14	8	14263.4	2935	42314	1610	26.28	117	27	9–77	330	—
		† 541.4									
13.00	0	3	0	8	1	8.00	0	0	1–8	0	—
19.48	0	11.1	0	55	2	27.50	0	0	2–1	4	—
1.00	0	20	0	81	0	—	0	0	—	1	—
6.50	0									0	—
12.55	0	0.3	0	8	0	—	0	0	—	2	—
15.66	0									0	—
Selected for one match for Essex in 1962 but failed to appear											
25.42	0	2	0	5	0	—	0	0	—	7	—
14.58	0	1023.5	236	4156	174	23.88	10	1	8–46	30	—
		† 297.3									
12.95	0									17	0
22.36	0	@ 2	0	14	0	—	0	0	—	4	—
12.80	0	49	4	197	0	—	0	0	—	1	—
0.00	0									0	—
0.00	0									0	—
6.00	0	13	1	56	0	—	0	0	—	0	—
2.33	0	19	4	77	1	77.00	0	0	1–40	0	—
21.92	9	8.3	2	21	1	21.00	0	0	1–16	1040	191
25.64	0									19	3
20.59	5	415.5	66	2933	92	31.88	3	0	7–99	185	—
		† 272.3									
14.85	0									3	—
15.81	0	291.4	45	938	17	55.17	0	0	2–12	10	—
6.00	0	10	0	42	1	42.00	0	0	1–42	0	—
7.41	0	484.3	47	1954	62	31.51	2	1	6–51	23	—
11.09	0	383.5	91	1144	47	24.34	2	0	5–52	9	—
18.49	1	256.3	60	891	16	55.68	0	0	3–67	15	—
		@ 45									
0.50	0	5	10	57	2	28.50	0	0	2–16	2	—
		@ 24									
—	—									0	—
15.23	0									11	—
13.66	0	3650.3	706	11734	452	25.96	23	4	9–126	62	—
7.66	0									1	—
35.86	11	24	25	438	12	36.50	0	0	3–47	26	2
		@ 115.3									
22.87	4	8778.1	2249	20987	810	25.90	27	1	6–26	215	—
27.08	2	21	10	180	3	60.00	0	0	2–12	58	—
		@ 30									
45.00	0									0	—
10.85	0	30	3	103	0	—	0	0	—	2	—
14.61	0	12	1	41	0	—	0	0	—	33	—

Name	*Seasons*	*Birth*	*Death*	*M*	*I*	*NO*	*R*	*HS*
J Valiant	1912	00.00.84	28.10.17	1	2	1	3	3
H H van Straubenzee	1938	7.3.14	—	1	1	1	4	4*
N Vere Hodge	1936–1939	31.10.12	—	23	38	6	713	108
F H Vigar	1938–1954	14.7.17	—	256	397	62	8660	144
J E W Waddington	1931	22.5.10	—	1	1	0	8	8
T H Wade	1929–1950	24.11.10	—	318	472	135	4972	96
H Wagstaff	1920–1921	15.10.95	2.3.70	5	6	4	19	17*
K W Wallace	1967–1972	27.8.36	—	10	16	0	219	55
B Ward	1967–1972	28.2.44	—	128	222	19	4799	164*
G H Ward	1950	22.11.26	—	1	2	0	4	2
B Warsop	1931–1932	12.1.04	—	5	10	2	128	51
A G Waterman	1937–1938	13.5.11	—	10	15	1	380	103
D Watkins	1949–1954	18.8.28	—	12	17	4	210	32
A C Watson	1913–1914	17.3.84	16.1.52	2	4	0	89	37
C J M Watts	1928	30.9.05	—	8	11	0	119	41
H P Waugh	1919–1929	24.12.98	13.12.54	8	14	0	213	128
G H S West	1949–1953	7.8.23	—	2	4	0	79	55
L H West	1928	24.1.05	12.11.82	3	5	0	33	30
H M Whitcombe	1922	15.8.00	2.4.84	3	4	2	13	7*
P S Whitcombe	1922	3.10.93	—	1	2	0	9	5
D R Wilcox	1928–1947	4.6.10	6.2.53	118	186	8	5482	142
J W T Wilcox	1964–1967	16.8.40	—	19	30	5	596	87
C C P Williams	1954–1959	9.2.33	—	40	68	3	1518	119
H R H Williams	1919–1920	7.6.00	17.7.74	10	12	2	67	23*
A D Womersley	1910	27.7.89	11.4.59	1	2	0	9	9
A E Wright	1931–1934	11.8.02	—	3	5	1	45	14
J V Wright	1962–1967	31.12.35	—	4	6	0	60	40
R W Wrightson	1965–1967	29.10.39	—	12	20	4	332	84
N G Wykes	1925–1936	19.3.06	—	30	42	3	879	162
H I Young	1898–1912	5.2.76	12.12.64	128	186	50	1413	44

Notes

1. These figures have been compiled in accordance with the 'Guide to First Class Cricket Matches Played in the British Isles' (second edition 1982) published by the Association of Cricket Statisticians, Haughton Mill, Nottinghamshire. In consequence the following three-day matches have been disregarded: Essex v Hampshire at Leyton and at Southampton, 1894; Essex v Dublin University at Dublin, 1905; Essex v Sir Julien Cahn's XI at West Bridgford, 1930; Essex v Wilfred Isaacs's XI at Basildon 1969; Essex v Scotland at Perth, 1973. This also applies to other first class records elsewhere in this book.
2. The career figures do not include appearances for Middlesex and Essex v Surrey and Kent at Kingston in 1947.
3. Only ten players appeared for Essex in the match against Oxford University at Oxford in 1962. B Stead was selected but failed to appear choosing instead to play for Nottinghamshire II v Worcestershire II at Halesowen. He subsequently joined the Nottinghamshire staff.
4. In the match against Somerset at Leyton in 1920 A D Martin was allowed to replace the injured F W Gilligan who kept wicket in the early stages of the match, J R Freeman assuming the duties of wicket-keeper. The match is counted for both players in the appropriate column of the career figures. In effect twelve players appeared for Essex in the match.
5. The argument has been advanced that the figures of A Brown should be added to those of F J Cooper. Brown is shown in the Essex scorebook and contemporary scoresheets as playing for Essex v Gloucestershire and Middlesex in July 1921 and then without explanation his figures are then merged with those of Cooper. My research in national and local newspapers has, to date, produced no valid reason for doubting the existence of 'A Brown' and until convincing evidence is produced to refute this contention I shall continue to list him separately.

Av	*100s*	*Ov*	*Mdns*	*R*	*W*	*Av*	*5wI*	*10m*	*BB*	*Ct*	*St*
3.00	0	4	0	20	0	—	0	0	—	0	—
—	0	6	1	12	0	—	0	0	—	0	—
22.28	2									11	0
25.58	11	2463.2	359	8958	236	37.95	8	0	8–128	195	—
		† 51									
8.00	0									0	—
14.75	0	452	72	1391	47	29.59	1	0	5–64	413	177
9.50	0	33	5	135	2	67.50	0	0	1–19	0	—
13.68	0									2	—
23.64	4	24.4	4	68	5	13.60	0	0	2–5	60	—
2.00	0									1	0
16.00	0	6	1	18	0	—	0	0	—	1	—
27.14	1	93	9	348	11	31.63	0	0	4–79	7	—
16.15	0	115.3	20	421	8	52.62	0	0	2–45	5	—
22.25	0									2	—
10.81	0	0.2	0	4	0	—	0	0	—	2	2
15.21	1	44	7	135	3	45.00	0	0	1–6	8	—
19.75	0									0	—
6.60	0									0	—
6.50	0	40	5	199	1	199.00	0	0	1–34	1	—
4.50	0	4	1	22	0	—	0	0	—	0	—
30.79	8	18.5	1	117	1	117.00	0	0	1–46	88	—
23.84	0									11	—
23.35	1	2.1	1	5	0	—	0	0	—	23	—
6.70	0									18	7
4.50	0									0	—
11.25	0	40	8	86	0	—	0	0	—	1	—
10.00	0									2	—
20.75	0									8	—
22.53	1	18	3	52	0	—	0	0	—	5	—
10.38	0	2435.4	883	9092	368	24.70	18	3	8–54	59	—
		@1108.1									

6. With effect from the 1985 season in the British Isles wides and no balls have been debited against the bowler's analysis, following a decision of the International Cricket Conference. It follows that the 'runs' column in the career bowling averages actually consists of runs from the bat plus wides plus no balls from which no runs were scored in matches from 1985 onwards. The new ruling also alters the definition of a maiden over from that date. Essex bowlers who have bowled since 1985 are: D L Acfield, A R Border, J H Childs, D E East, K W R Fletcher, N A Foster, C Gladwin, G A Gooch, B R Hardie, J K Lever, A W Lilley, N Phllip, I L Pont, K R Pont, D R Pringle, J P Stephenson, T D Topley and S Turner.

Note on Sources

Essex County Cricket Club is extremely fortunate in having an almost complete run of scorebooks dating back to 1879. The only missing years are 1885, 1922 and 1955 and the first three years of the club's existence, 1876, 1877 and 1878. First class status was achieved in 1894.

The statistics have been compiled direct from the scorebooks with the exception of 1922 and 1955, where the invaluable 'Wisden's Cricketers Almanacks' have been used and cross checking and consultation has been undertaken with fellow members of the Association of Cricket Statisticians, particularly Mr Philip Bailey of Orpington and Mr Philip Thorn of Colsterworth, to whom I am greatly indebted.

My greatest debt is, however, to those unsung heroes, the Essex scorers. I have worked closely with Clem Driver and the late Jack Bartlam in recent years and know them to be unequalled for neatness and accuracy. To them and their predecessors, whose names will, I hope, one day be listed in an Essex publication, I remain eternally grateful.

Record of County Championship positions and results

Year	Position	Played	Won	Lost	Drawn	Tied	Abandoned
1895	8th Joint	16	5	7	4	—	—
1896	5th	12	5	4	3	—	—
1897	3rd	16	7	2	7	—	—
1898	5th	20	10	6	4	—	—
1899	6th	20	6	6	8	—	—
1900	10th	22	4	6	12	—	—
1901	10th	21	4	5	12	—	1
1902	13th	20	2	5	13	—	—
1903	8th Joint	20	7	6	7	—	2
1904	14th	20	3	10	7	—	—
1905	12th	20	3	10	7	—	—
1906	7th	22	9	6	7	—	—
1907	7th	22	10	7	5	—	—
1908	11th	22	5	7	10	—	—
1909	14th	18	2	7	9	—	2
1910	11th	17	5	8	4	—	—
1911	6th	18	8	5	5	—	—
1912	15th	17	1	8	8	—	1
1913	15th	18	2	9	7	—	—
1914	8th	24	9	9	6	—	—
1919	14th	18	2	4	12	—	—
1920	9th	24	9	9	6	—	—
1921	15th	26	5	13	8	—	—
1922	8th	26	7	4	15	—	—
1923	13th	26	6	11	9	—	—
1924	15th	26	2	12	12	—	2
1925	7th	28	9	7	12	—	—
1926	9th	30	6	9	14	1	—
1927	8th	30	8	8	14	—	—
1928	16th	30	2	13	15	—	—
1929	12th	28	6	9	13	—	—
1930	6th	28	7	5	16	—	—
1931	10th	28	7	11	10	—	—
1932	14th	28	4	14	10	—	—
1933	4th	28	13	8	7	—	—
1934	8th	28	9	4	15	—	—
1935	9th	28	11	12	5	—	—
1936	9th	26	8	8	10	—	—
1937	6th	28	13	11	4	—	—
1938	6th	28	12	11	5	—	—
1939	4th	28	12	10	6	—	—
1946	8th	26	8	9	9	—	—
1947	11th Joint	26	6	9	10	1	—
1948	13th	26	5	8	13	—	—
1949	9th Joint	26	7	9	10	—	—
1950	17th	28	4	12	12	—	—
1951	8th	28	6	2	20	—	—
1952	10th Joint	28	8	4	15	1	—
1953	12th Joint	27	6	7	14	—	1
1954	15th	28	3	11	14	—	—
1955	14th	28	6	15	7	—	—
1956	11th	28	6	10	12	—	—
1957	5th	28	11	6	11	—	—

Year	*Position*	*Played*	*Won*	*Lost*	*Drawn*	*Tied*	*Abandoned*
1958	6th	28	9	7	12	—	—
1959	9th	28	11	7	9	1	—
1960	6th	27	9	3	15	—	1
1961	6th	28	10	8	10	—	—
1962	9th	28	8	6	14	—	—
1963	12th	28	6	4	18	—	—
1964	10th	28	7	11	10	—	—
1965	15th	28	4	7	17	—	—
1966	16th	28	4	10	14	—	—
1967	15th	28	3	9	16	—	—
1968	14th	27	5	6	16	—	1
1969	6th	24	6	6	12	—	—
1970	12th	24	4	6	14	—	—
1971	10th	24	6	5	13	—	—
1972	5th	20	6	4	10	—	—
1973	8th	20	6	5	9	—	—
1974	12th	20	4	3	12	1	—
1975	7th	20	7	6	7	—	—
1976	6th	20	7	4	9	—	—
1977	6th	21	7	5	9	—	1
1978	2nd	22	12	1	9	—	—
1979	1st	21	13	4	4	—	1
1980	8th	22	4	3	15	—	—
1981	5th	21	8	4	9	—	1
1982	7th	22	5	5	12	—	—
1983	1st	24	11	5	8	—	—
1984	1st	24	13	3	8	—	—
1985	4th	23	7	2	14	—	1
1986	1st	24	10	6	8	—	—
Total 1895–1914		385	107	133	145	—	6
Total 1919–1939		570	158	193	218	1	2
Total 1946–1986		1029	288	257	480	4	7
Total 1895–1986		1984	553	583	843	5	15

Record of Gillette Cup and National Westminster Bank Trophy results

Year	*First Round*	*Second Round*	*Quarter-finals*	*Semi-finals*	*Final*	
Gillette Cup						
1963	L					
1964	W	L				
1965	L					
1966	Bye	W	L			
1967	Bye	L				
1968	L					
1969	W	W	L			
1970	Bye	L				
1971	W	W	L			
1972	Bye	W	L			
1973	Bye	W	L			
1974	W	L				
1975	Bye	L				
1976	W	L				
1977	Bye	L				
1978	Bye	W	W	L		
1979	L					
1980	Bye	W	L			
National Westminster Bank Trophy						
1981	W	W	W	L		
1982	Bye	W	L			
1983	W	L				
1984	W	L				
1985	W	W	W	W	W	
1986	W	L				
1963–80	W5, L4, B9	W7, L7	W1, L6	L1	—	Total W13, L18, B9
1981–86	W5, B1	W3, L3	W2, L1	W1, L1	W1	Total W12, L5, B1
1963–86	W10, L4, B10	W10, L10	W3, L7	W1, L2	W1	Total W25, L23, B10

Record of John Player League positions and results

Year	*Position*	*Played*	*Won*	*Lost*	*Tied*	*No result*	*Abandoned*
1969	3rd	16	11	4	—	1	—
1970	4th	15	8	5	—	2	1
1971	2nd	16	11	5	—	—	—
1972	3rd	16	10	5	—	1	—
1973	9th Joint	15	7	8	—	—	1
1974	15th Joint	15	4	11	—	—	1
1975	4th	16	10	6	—	—	—
1976	2nd Joint	16	10	6	—	—	—
1977	2nd	15	12	2	—	1	1
1978	6th	13	7	6	—	—	3
1979	6th Joint	15	8	6	—	1	1
1980	14th Joint	16	6	10	—	—	—
1981	1st	16	12	3	—	1	—
1982	5th Joint	16	9	7	—	—	—
1983	6th Joint	12	7	5	—	—	4
1984	1st	16	12	3	1	—	—
1985	1st	15	9	3	1	2	1
1986	2nd	16	11	4	—	1	—
Total 1969–1986		275	164	99	2	10	13

Record of Benson & Hedges Cup results

Year	*Zonal Group Position*	*Competition Won*	*Competition Lost*	*Quarter-finals*	*Semi-finals*	*Final*	
1972	5th	—	4				
1973	2nd	2	2	W	L		
1974	3rd	2	2				
1975	1st	4	—	L			
1976	2nd	3	1	L			
1977	4th	1	3				
1978	5th	1	3				
1979	1st Joint	3	1	W	W	W	
1980	1st Joint	3	1	W	W	L	
1981	3rd	2	2				
1982	3rd	2	2				
1983	1st	3	1	W	W	L	
1984	1st	4	—	L			
1985	1st	4	—	W	W	L	
1986	1st	4	—	L			
1972–1986		38	22	W5, L4	W4, L1	W1, L3	Total W48, L30

Record of Fenner Trophy and Asda Challenge Trophy results

Year	*Semi-finals*	*Final*	
Fenner Trophy			
1977	W	L	
1981	W	L	
Asda Challenge Trophy			
1983	L		
1986	W by toss	L	
1977–1981	W2	L2	
1983–1986	L1	L1	
1977–1986	W2, L1	L3	Total W2, L4

Record wicket partnerships

First Wicket		
270	A V Avery & T C Dodds	v Surrey at Kennington Oval, 1946
263	G A Gooch & B R Hardie	v Cambridge University at Cambridge, 1983
Second Wicket		
321	G A Gooch & K S McEwan	v Northamptonshire at Ilford, 1978
294	A V Avery & P A Gibb	v Northamptonshire at Northampton, 1952
Third Wicket		
343	P A Gibb & R Horsfall	v Kent at Blackheath, 1951
333	R M Taylor & J O'Connor	v Northamptonshire at Castle Park, Colchester, 1937
Fourth Wicket		
298	A V Avery & R Horsfall	v Worcestershire at Clacton, 1948
271	J O'Connor & T N Pearce	v Lancashire at Clacton, 1931
Fifth Wicket		
287	J O'Connor & C T Ashton	v Surrey at Brentwood, 1934
216	D J Insole & T E Bailey	v Hampshire at Bournemouth, 1959
Sixth Wicket		
206	J W H T Douglas & J O'Connor	v Gloucestershire at Cheltenham College, 1923
206	B R Knight & R A G Luckin	v Middlesex at Brentwood, 1962
205	P A Perrin & C P McGahey	v Kent at Tunbridge Wells, 1906
Seventh Wicket		
261	J W H T Douglas & J R Freeman	v Lancashire at Leyton, 1914
171	T E Bailey & B R Knight	v Worcestershire at Leyton, 1959
Eighth Wicket		
263	D R Wilcox & R M Taylor	v Warwickshire at Southend, 1946
214	J A Cutmore & T P B Smith	v Indians at Brentwood, 1936
Ninth Wicket		
251	J W H T Douglas & S N Hare	v Derbyshire at Leyton, 1921
184	C A G Russell & L C Eastman	v Middlesex at Lord's, 1920
Tenth Wicket		
218	F H Vigar & T P B Smith	v Derbyshire at Chesterfield, 1947
157	C A G Russell & A B Hipkin	v Somerset at Taunton, 1926

Essex are the only county with wicket partnerships of over 200 for each wicket.

Most catches by a fielder in an innings

Five	
Rev F H Gillingham	v Surrey at Kennington Oval, 1919
M S Nichols	v Sussex at Hove, 1926
F H Vigar	v Middlesex at Westcliff, 1946
F H Vigar	v Northamptonshire at Brentwood, 1946
F H Vigar	v Surrey at Kennington Oval, 1951
D J Insole	v Lancashire at Blackpool, 1958
G A Gooch	v Gloucestershire at Cheltenham College, 1982

Most catches by a fielder in a match

Six	
W M F Turner	v Leicestershire at Aylestone Road, Leicester, 1914
M S Nichols	v Sussex at Hove, 1926
F H Vigar	v Nottinghamshire at Ilford, 1950
K D Boyce	v Hampshire at Bournemouth, 1967
K W R Fletcher	v Glamorgan at Brentwood, 1967
R E East	v Northamptonshire at Westcliff, 1973
K W R Fletcher	v Worcestershire at Worcester, 1977
K W R Fletcher	v Derbyshire at Southend, 1978
G A Gooch	v Gloucestershire at Cheltenham College, 1982
G A Gooch	v Middlesex at Lord's, 1985

Most dismissals by a wicket-keeper in an innings

Eight			
All caught		D E East	v Somerset at Taunton, 1985
Six			
Ct.	*St.*		
3	3	T M Russell	v Lancashire at Old Trafford, 1898
2	4	T M Russell	v Kent at Canterbury, 1901
5	1	K L Gibson	v Derbyshire at Leyton, 1911
2	4	F W Gilligan	v Gloucestershire at Cheltenham College, 1928
4	2	T H Wade	v Lancashire at Clacton, 1947
6	—	D E East	v Sussex at Hove, 1983

Most dismissals by a wicket-keeper in a match

Ct.	St.		
Nine			
7	2	K L Gibson	v Derbyshire at Leyton, 1911
9	—	D E East	v Sussex at Hove, 1983
Eight			
8	—	T M Russell	v Kent at Leyton, 1899
7	1	P A Gibb	v Kent at Tunbridge Wells, 1952
5	3	B Taylor	v Leicestershire at Grace Road, Leicester, 1970
8	—	D E East	v Derbyshire at Southend, 1982
8	—	D E East	v Lancashire at Ilford, 1985
8	—	D E East	v Somerset at Taunton, 1985
3	5	D E East	v Kent at Folkestone, 1986
Seven			
4	3	T M Russell	v Leicestershire at Grace Road, Leicester, 1898
6	1	J R Sheffield	v Leicestershire at Chelmsford, 1932
3	4	J R Sheffield	v Middlesex at Leyton, 1933
5	2	T H Wade	v Surrey at Westcliff, 1938
7	—	B Taylor	v Kent at Castle Park, Colchester, 1961
7	—	B Taylor	v Gloucestershire at Clacton, 1962
7	—	B Taylor	v Gloucestershire at Castle Park, Colchester, 1964
7	—	B Taylor	v Middlesex at Westcliff, 1964
7	—	B Taylor	v Somerset at Leyton, 1971
7	—	N Smith	v Cambridge University at Cambridge, 1976
4	3	N Smith	v Middlesex at Chelmsford, 1978
7	—	D E East	v Derbyshire at Derby, 1983
7	—	D E East	v Lancashire at Southend, 1984
7	—	D E East	v Nottinghamshire at Trent Bridge, 1986

Highest and lowest innings totals for Essex

Opponents	*Highest*	*Year*	*Ground*	*Lowest*	*Year*	*Ground*
Derbyshire	609–4*	1912	Leyton	58	1949	Burton-on-Trent (Ind Coope)
Glamorgan	499–8*	1928	Swansea	74	1966	Leyton
Gloucestershire	578–6*	1927	Bristol	63	1925	Gloucester (Wagon Wks)
Hampshire	584–9*	1927	Southampton	69	1931	Colchester (Garrison)
Kent	551	1900	Leyton	34	1969	Brentwood
Lancashire	559–9	1904	Leyton	59	1931	Liverpool
Leicestershire	673	1899	Leicester (Grace Rd)	53	1977	Leicester (Grace Rd)
Middlesex	477	1929	Leyton	64	1902	Lord's
Northamptonshire	604–7*	1921	Northampton	44	1986	Colchester (Castle Pk)
Nottinghamshire	593–7	1951	Clacton	44	1910	Trent Bridge
Somerset	692	1895	Taunton	69	1924	Ilford
Surrey	616–5*	1904	Kennington Oval	37	1899	Leyton
Sussex	560–9*	1933	Leyton	71	1902	Hove
Warwickshire	522–8*	1930	Leyton	47	1968	Leyton
Worcestershire	560–5*	1921	Leyton	65	1947	Chelmsford and
				65	1973	Chelmsford
Yorkshire	524–7*	1984	Leeds	30	1901	Leyton
Australians	425–6*	1964	Southend	67	1930	Leyton
Australian Imp. Fces.	169	1919	Leyton	117	1919	Southend
Cambridge University	463–4*	1984	Cambridge	157	1935	Westcliff
Canadians	272–2*	1954	Clacton	242	1954	Clacton
Combined Services	295	1922	Leyton	244	1950	Chelmsford
Commonwealth XI	267–9*	1953	Romford	235	1953	Romford
Dublin University	267–6*	1922	Brentwood	—		
Indians	410	1952	Ilford	169	1932	Leyton
Jamaica	107–6*	1970	Leyton	—		
MCC	356	1949	Lord's	78	1951	Lord's
New Zealanders	373	1927	Leyton	113	1931	Leyton
Oxford University	414	1927	Chelmsford	151	1925	Chelmsford
Pakistanis	303	1962	Leyton	116	1967	Colchester (Castle Pk)
T N Pearce's XI	205	1952	Chelmsford	159	1952	Chelmsford
South Africans	380	1947	Southend	89	1907	Leyton
S African Fezela	292	1961	Chelmsford (RHP)	144	1961	Chelmsford (RHP)
West Indians	395	1906	Leyton	56	1963	Southend

Essex are the only county who have never been dismissed for an innings total of less than 30.

* Denotes innings declared closed

Highest and lowest innings totals against Essex

Opponents	*Highest*	*Year*	*Ground*	*Lowest*	*Year*	*Ground*
Derbyshire	552	1928	Chesterfield	31	1914	Derby
Glamorgan	586–5*	1948	Brentwood	43	1935	Neath
Gloucestershire	523	1928	Chelmsford	67	1908	Leyton
Hampshire	534–7*	1913	Leyton	54	1931	Southampton
Kent	803–4*	1934	Brentwood	43	1925	Southend
Lancashire	510	1947	Clacton	70	1978	Southport
Leicestershire	521	1914	Leyton	45	1957	Brentwood
Middlesex	634–7*	1983	Chelmsford	61	1925	Lord's
Northamptonshire	539	1933	Kettering	45	1923	Southend
Nottinghamshire	662–8*	1947	Trent Bridge	58	1931	Southend
Somerset	488	1949	Clacton	48	1951	Bath and
				48	1961	Westcliff
Surrey	528–6*	1947	Kennington Oval	14	1983	Chelmsford
Sussex	611	1905	Leyton	47	1914	Southend
Warwickshire	614–8*	1904	Birmingham	53	1957	Birmingham
Worcestershire	515	1934	Chelmsford	49	1922	Leyton
Yorkshire	555–1*	1932	Leyton	31	1935	Huddersfield
Australians	721	1948	Southend	73	1899	Leyton
Australian Imp. Fces.	447–8*	1919	Southend	130	1919	Southend
Cambridge University	464–8*	1929	Cambridge	37	1965	Cambridge
Canadians	141	1954	Clacton	—		
Combined Services	313	1950	Chelmsford	215	1922	Leyton
Commonwealth XI	310	1953	Romford	84	1953	Romford
Dublin University	256	1922	Brentwood	143	1922	Brentwood
Indians	370–9	1946	Southend	138	1946	Southend
Jamaica	116–3	1970	Leyton	—		
MCC	378–8*	1949	Lord's	41	1896	Lord's
New Zealanders	425	1931	Leyton	140	1958	Ilford
Oxford University	344	1925	Chelmsford	89	1972	Oxford (University Parks)
Pakistanis	251–8*	1967	Colchester (Castle Pk)	80	1978	Chelmsford
T N Pearce's XI	389–9*	1952	Chelmsford	—		
South Africans	503–4*	1955	Colchester (Castle Pk)	155	1907	Leyton
S African Fezela	227	1961	Chelmsford (RHP)	—		
West Indians	379	1906	Leyton	115	1957	Ilford

Other Totals of over 600

621–6* Kent at Tonbridge, 1922

609–6* Australians at Leyton, 1909

* Denotes innings declared closed

Individual innings of 200 or more for Essex

343*	P A Perrin	v Derbyshire at Chesterfield, 1904
286	J R Freeman	v Northamptonshire at Northampton, 1921
277	C P McGahey	v Derbyshire at Leyton, 1905
273	C A G Russell	v Northamptonshire at Leyton, 1921
248	J O'Connor	v Surrey at Brentwood, 1934
245	P A Perrin	v Derbyshire at Leyton, 1912
238*	J A Cutmore	v Gloucestershire at Bristol, 1927
237	J O'Connor	v Somerset at Leyton, 1933
230	C P McGahey	v Northamptonshire at Northampton, 1908
228*	K W R Fletcher	v Sussex at Hastings, 1968
227	G A Gooch	v Derbyshire at Chesterfield, 1984
225	C P McGahey	v Nottinghamshire at Leyton, 1904
224	A V Avery	v Northamptonshire at Northampton, 1952
222	L G Crawley	v Glamorgan at Swansea, 1928
220	G A Gooch	v Hampshire at Southampton, 1984
219*	D J Insole	v Yorkshire at Castle Park, Colchester, 1949
218	K S McEwan	v Sussex at Chelmsford, 1977
217	F L Fane	v Surrey at Kennington Oval, 1911
214*	A V Avery	v Worcestershire at Clacton, 1948
211*	T N Pearce	v Leicestershire at Westcliff, 1948
210*	J W H T Douglas	v Derbyshire at Leyton, 1921
210	A V Avery	v Surrey at Kennington Oval, 1946
208*	A V Avery	v Glamorgan at Westcliff, 1953
208*	K S McEwan	v Warwickshire at Edgbaston, Birmingham, 1979
207	F L Fane	v Leicestershire at Grace Road, Leicester, 1899
206	R Horsfall	v Kent at Blackheath, 1951
205	P A Perrin	v Kent at Leyton, 1900
205	M S Nichols	v Hampshire at Southend, 1936
205	T E Bailey	v Sussex at Eastbourne, 1947
205	G A Gooch	v Cambridge University at Cambridge, 1980
202	G A Gooch	v Nottinghamshire at Trent Bridge, 1985
201	Rev F H Gillingham	v Middlesex at Lord's, 1904

Fifteen or more wickets in a match for Essex

17–119	W Mead	v Hampshire at Southampton, 1895
16–215	T P B Smith	v Middlesex at Castle Park, Colchester, 1947
15–113	K Farnes	v Glamorgan at Clacton, 1938
15–115	W Mead	v Leicestershire at Leyton, 1903
15–115	R E East	v Warwickshire at Leyton, 1968
15–154	H I Young	v Warwickshire at Edgbaston, Birmingham, 1899
15–165	M S Nichols	v Gloucestershire at Wagon Works Ground, Gloucester, 1938

N.B. W Mead also took 17–205 for Essex v Australians at Leyton in 1893 but at that time Essex were not a first class county and the match does not rank as first class.

Nine or more wickets in an innings for Essex

10–32	H Pickett	v Leicestershire at Leyton, 1895
10–90	T E Bailey	v Lancashire at Clacton, 1949
9–32	M S Nichols	v Nottinghamshire at Trent Bridge, 1936
9–37	M S Nichols	v Gloucestershire at Wagon Works Ground, Gloucester, 1938
9–40	W Mead	v Hampshire at Southampton, 1900
9–47	J W H T Douglas	v Derbyshire at Leyton, 1921
9–52	W Mead	v Hampshire at Southampton, 1895
9–59	M S Nichols	v Hampshire at Chelmsford, 1927
9–61	K D Boyce	v Cambridge University at Brentwood, 1966 (Essex debut)
9–75	W Mead	v Leicestershire at Leyton, 1896
9–77	T P B Smith	v Middlesex at Castle Park, Colchester, 1947
9–93	F G Bull	v Surrey at Kennington Oval, 1897
9–108	T P B Smith	v Kent at Maidstone, 1948
9–116	M S Nichols	v Middlesex at Leyton, 1930
9–117	T P B Smith	v Nottinghamshire at Southend, 1948
9–126	B Tremlin	v Derbyshire at Leyton, 1905

Century in each innings of a match

C P McGahey (1)	114	145*	v Gloucestershire at Leyton, 1901
H A Carpenter (1)	127	104	v Kent at Leyton, 1901
P A Perrin (4)	170	102*	v Nottinghamshire at Trent Bridge, 1903
	140	103*	v Middlesex at Lord's, 1905
	112	100*	v Nottinghamshire at Trent Bridge, 1911
	126	101*	v Kent at Leyton, 1919
C A G Russell (2)	115	118	v Surrey at Kennington Oval, 1922
	131	104	v Lancashire at Liverpool, 1928
J O'Connor (1)	138	120*	v Gloucestershire at Bristol, 1930
D R Wilcox (1)	104	129	v Kent at Westcliff, 1937
A V Avery (1)	117	100	v Glamorgan at Ebbw Vale, 1949
D J Insole (1)	111	118	v Kent at Gillingham, 1955
K W R Fletcher (1)	111	102*	v Nottinghamshire at Trent Bridge, 1976
K S McEwan (1)	102	116	v Warwickshire at Edgbaston, Birmingham, 1977

C A G Russell also scored 140 and 111 for England v South Africa at Kingsmead, Durban, in 1922–23, becoming the first batsman to perform this feat for England in a Test match.

A R Border, in scoring 150* and 153 for Australia v Pakistan at Lahore, in 1979–80, became the first batsman to score 150 in each innings of a Test match.

One thousand or more runs in a season for Essex

Batsman	*Times*					*Seasons*					
K W R Fletcher	19	1963	1964	1965	1966	1967	1968	1969	1970	1971	1972
		1976	1977	1978	1979	1980	1981	1982	1983	1984	
P A Perrin	17	1898	1899	1900	1901	1902	1903	1904	1905	1906	1907
		1908	1911	1914	1921	1922	1923	1925			
J O'Connor	16	1923	1925	1926	1927	1928	1929	1930	1931	1932	1933
		1934	1935	1936	1937	1938	1939				
G Barker	15	1955	1956	1957	1958	1959	1960	1961	1962	1963	1964
		1965	1966	1967	1969	1970					
C A G Russell	13	1913	1914	1919	1920	1921	1922	1923	1924	1925	1926
		1927	1928	1930							
T C Dodds	13	1946	1947	1948	1949	1950	1951	1952	1953	1954	1955
		1956	1957	1958							
K S McEwan	12	1974	1975	1976	1977	1978	1979	1980	1981	1982	1983
		1984	1985								
J A Cutmore	11	1925	1926	1927	1928	1929	1930	1931	1932	1933	1934
		1935									
D J Insole	11	1950	1951	1952	1953	1954	1955	1956	1957	1958	1959
		1960									
T E Bailey	10	1949	1952	1954	1955	1957	1959	1960	1961	1962	1963
B R Hardie	10	1974	1975	1978	1979	1980	1981	1982	1983	1984	1985
C P McGahey	9	1898	1900	1901	1902	1903	1904	1905	1906	1907	
M S Nichols	9	1929	1932	1933	1934	1935	1936	1937	1938	1939	
J W H T Douglas	8	1908	1911	1912	1914	1920	1921	1923	1927		
B Taylor	8	1956	1957	1959	1960	1964	1966	1967	1970		
J R Freeman	7	1919	1921	1922	1923	1924	1925	1926			
A V Avery	7	1939	1946	1948	1950	1951	1952	1953			
G A Gooch	7	1976	1980	1981	1982	1983	1984	1985			
H A Carpenter	6	1898	1900	1901	1904	1905	1906				
L C Eastman	5	1929	1933	1937	1938	1939					
B R Knight	5	1961	1962	1963	1964	1965					
B E A Edmeades	5	1967	1969	1970	1972	1975					
D F Pope	4	1930	1932	1933	1934						
T N Pearce	4	1935	1946	1947	1948						
R Horsfall	4	1948	1951	1952	1953						
P A Gibb	4	1951	1952	1953	1955						
M J Bear	4	1962	1963	1964	1966						
F H Vigar	3	1947	1949	1950							
R Smith	3	1947	1950	1951							
G J Smith, Junr	3	1960	1961	1962							
R M Taylor	2	1933	1938								
D R Wilcox	2	1937	1938								
S J Cray	2	1947	1949								
B L Irvine	2	1968	1969								
B C Francis	2	1971	1973								
M H Denness	2	1977	1979								

Batsman	*Times*	*Seasons*
F L Fane	1	1902
W Reeves	1	1905
T P B Smith	1	1947
L A Savill	1	1959
J Milner	1	1961
G J Saville	1	1970
C Gladwin	1	1984
A R Border	1	1986
P J Prichard	1	1986
	273	

Two thousand or more runs in a season for Essex

Batsman	*Runs*	*Average*	*Season*
G A Gooch	2559	67.34	1984
J O'Connor	2308	56.29	1934
J O'Connor	2256	48.00	1928
C A G Russell	2243	53.40	1922
J O'Connor	2224	48.34	1929
K S McEwan	2176	64.00	1983
D J Insole	2142	47.60	1955
J O'Connor	2077	44.19	1933
C A G Russell	2062	66.51	1928
C A G Russell	2042	45.37	1920

One hundred or more wickets in a season for Essex

Bowler	*Times*	*Seasons*									
M S Nichols	11	1926	1927	1929	1930	1932	1933	1935	1936	1937	1938
		1939									
R Smith	7	1946	1947	1948	1949	1950	1952	1953			
T P B Smith	6	1933	1937	1938	1946	1947	1950				
W Mead	5	1895	1899	1900	1903	1907					
J W H T Douglas	5	1914	1920	1921	1922	1923					
T E Bailey	4	1958	1960	1961	1962						
J K Lever	4	1978	1979	1983	1984						
B R Knight	3	1959	1963	1965							
F G Bull	2	1897	1898								
H I Young	1	1899									
W Reeves	1	1904									
C P Buckenham	1	1906									
B Tremlin	1	1914									
A B Hipkin	1	1924									
K C Preston	1	1957									
L H R Ralph	1	1957									
B E A Edmeades	1	1966									
N A Foster	1	1986									
	56										

Four or more centuries in a season

1899	P A Perrin 6
1900	H A Carpenter 4; P A Perrin 4; C P McGahey 4
1901	H A Carpenter 6; P A Perrin 5; C P McGahey 4
1903	P A Perrin 4
1904	P A Perrin 5
1906	P A Perrin 5
1908	Rev F H Gillingham 4
1911	P A Perrin 6
1919	C A G Russell 4
1921	C A G Russell 6
1922	C A G Russell 7; P A Perrin 4
1924	J R Freeman 4
1925	C A G Russell 7
1926	C A G Russell 6; J R Freeman 6
1927	C A G Russell 5; J O'Connor 4
1928	C A G Russell 8; J O'Connor 6
1929	J O'Connor 9
1930	J O'Connor 5; C A G Russell 4
1931	J O'Connor 6
1932	J O'Connor 4
1933	J O'Connor 6
1934	J O'Connor 9; D F Pope 4
1937	D R Wilcox 4
1938	J O'Connor 6
1939	J O'Connor 4
1946	T N Pearce 5
1947	F H Vigar 4
1948	A V Avery 6
1950	D J Insole 4
1951	A V Avery 4; P A Gibb 4
1953	R Horsfall 5
1954	D J Insole 4
1955	D J Insole 9
1956	D J Insole 4
1957	D J Insole 4
1959	T E Bailey 6; D J Insole 5
1970	K W R Fletcher 4; B E A Edmeades 4
1971	B C Francis 4
1972	K W R Fletcher 5
1976	K S McEwan 6; K W R Fletcher 4
1977	K S McEwan 8
1978	K S McEwan 5
1980	G A Gooch 5
1981	K S McEwan 6; G A Gooch 5; K W R Fletcher 4
1983	K S McEwan 8; G A Gooch 4
1984	G A Gooch 8; K S McEwan 4
1985	G A Gooch 6; B R Hardie 4
1986	A R Border 4

The five batsmen to score most runs in career for Essex

Batsman	*Runs*	*Average*	*Seasons*
P A Perrin	29172	36.19	1896–1928
K W R Fletcher	28206	37.35	1962–1986
J O'Connor	27819	35.21	1921–1939
C A G Russell	23610	40.91	1908–1930
G Barker	21895	29.15	1954–1971

The five bowlers to take most wickets in career for Essex

Bowler	*Wickets*	*Average*	*Seasons*
T P B Smith	1610	26.28	1929–1951
M S Nichols	1608	21.26	1924–1939
T E Bailey	1593	21.99	1946–1967
W Mead	1472	19.30	1894–1913
J W H T Douglas	1443	23.32	1901–1928

The six wicket-keepers with most dismissals in career for Essex

Wicket-keeper	*Total*	*Ct.*	*St.*	*Seasons*
B Taylor	1205	1014	191	1949–1973
T H Wade	573	396	177	1929–1950
N Smith	428	381	47	1973–1981
D E East	404	361	43	1981–1986
T M Russell	334	246	88	1894–1905
P A Gibb	334	271	63	1951–1956

N.B. These figures do not include catches taken in the field when not keeping wicket.

The five fielders with most catches in career for Essex

Player	*Catches*	*Seasons*
K W R Fletcher	498	1962–1986
K C Preston	344	1948–1964
T P B Smith	330	1929–1951
T E Bailey	320	1946–1967
P A Perrin	284	1896–1928

Hat tricks for Essex

Year	*Bowler*	*Opponents*	*Players dismissed*
1905	J W H T Douglas	Yorkshire at Leyton	W Rhodes, S Haigh, H Myers
1907	H I Young	Leicestershire at Leyton	A E Knight, S Coe, V F S Crawford
1914	B Tremlin	Derbyshire at Derby	A G Slater, R R Baggallay, T Forester
1920	P Toone	Kent at Leyton	G C Collins, James Seymour, F E Woolley
1921	G M Louden	Somerset at Southend	R C Robertson-Glasgow, J J Bridges, S L Amor
1923	J W H T Douglas	Sussex at Leyton	M W Tate, E H Bowley, T E R Cook
1924	A B Hipkin	Lancashire at Blackpool	J L Hopwood, R K Tyldesley, G Duckworth
1925	J O'Connor	Worcestershire at Worcester	H K Foster, M K Foster, G Ashton
1931	M S Nichols	Yorkshire at Leeds	W Barber, E Robinson, A Wood
1935	H D Read	Gloucestershire at Bristol	W L Neale, T W J Goddard, H Smith
1939	K Farnes	Nottinghamshire at Clacton	G F H Heane, J Hardstaff Junr, G V Gunn
1950	P Cousens	Combined Services at Chelmsford	A C Shirreff, L N Devereux, D B Close
1950	T E Bailey	Glamorgan at Newport	J E Pleass, N G Hever, D J Shepherd
1971	S Turner	Surrey at Kennington Oval	S J Storey, A Long, R D Jackman
1974	K D Boyce	Warwickshire at Chelmsford	R N Abberley, M J K Smith, D L Murray
1983	N Phillip	Northamptonshire at Wellingborough School	D S Steele, N A Mallender, B J Griffiths

Players scoring one thousand or more runs and taking one hundred or more wickets in a season for Essex

Player	*Times*	*Year*	*Runs*	*Average*	*Wickets*	*Average*
M S Nichols	8	1929	1281	29.11	100	25.56
		1932	1381	32.11	106	25.52
		1933	1311	29.13	120	21.55
		1935	1171	24.39	138	15.70
		1936	1224	29.85	108	18.47
		1937	1159	25.19	136	18.56
		1938	1310	35.40	160	18.31
		1939	1363	35.86	119	17.84
J W H T Douglas	4	1914	1151	39.68	118	18.88
		1920	1200	35.29	124	20.98
		1921	1211	46.57	110	18.10
		1923	1043	30.67	139	22.01
T E Bailey	3	1960	1597	40.94	113	20.26
		1961	1179	29.47	120	20.25
		1962	1420	36.41	111	21.00
R Smith	2	1947	1201	27.93	118	36.74
		1950	1109	23.59	101	34.57
B R Knight	2	1963	1412	30.04	125	21.94
		1965	1001	21.76	121	18.52
T P B Smith	1	1947	1065	23.66	172	27.13
	20					

Twenty or more dismissals by a wicket-keeper in a season for Essex

Wicket-keeper	*Times*	*Seasons*										
B Taylor	18	1956	1957	1958	1959	1960	1961	1962	1963	1964	1965	1966
		1967	1968	1969	1970	1971	1972	1973				
T H Wade	11	1934	1935	1936	1937	1938	1939	1946	1947	1948	1949	1950
T M Russell	9	1895	1896	1897	1898	1899	1900	1901	1902	1903		
N Smith	9	1973	1974	1975	1976	1977	1978	1979	1980	1981		
D E East	6	1981	1982	1983	1984	1985	1986					
J R Sheffield	5	1929	1930	1931	1932	1933						
P A Gibb	5	1951	1952	1953	1954	1955						
A E Russell	4	1905	1906	1907	1908							
J R Freeman	4	1921	1924	1925	1926							
K L Gibson	2	1910	1911									
C D McIver	1	1914										
F W Gilligan	1	1919										
H R H Williams	1	1919										
G F Eastman	1	1927										
F H Rist	1	1948										
	78											

These figures exclude catches made when not keeping wicket.

Most dismissals by a wicket-keeper in a season for Essex

Total	*Ct.*	*St.*	*Wicket-keeper*	*Season*
89	79	10	B Taylor	1962
83	66	17	P A Gibb	1952
	64	19	D E East	1986
79	64	15	P A Gibb	1953
	70	9	B Taylor	1961
78	62	16	T H Wade	1938
77	76	1	D E East	1984
76	38	38	T H Wade	1947
	71	5	B Taylor	1963
	66	10	B Taylor	1964
	72	4	D E East	1985
74	65	9	D E East	1982
73	59	14	B Taylor	1957
70	58	12	B Taylor	1956
	58	12	B Taylor	1959
	51	19	B Taylor	1970

These figures exclude catches made when not keeping wicket.

Twenty or more catches by a fielder in a season for Essex

Player	*Times*	*Seasons*
K W R Fletcher	13	1963 1964 1965 1966 1967 1968 1969 1971 1977 1978 1980 1984 1986
K C Preston	10	1951 1952 1953 1955 1956 1957 1958 1961 1962 1963
T P B Smith	9	1930 1931 1933 1934 1936 1937 1938 1947 1950
D J Insole	8	1951 1952 1954 1955 1956 1957 1958 1959
C A G Russell	7	1914 1920 1922 1924 1925 1926 1930
F H Vigar	7	1946 1947 1948 1949 1950 1952 1953
B R Hardie	7	1976 1978 1979 1980 1983 1984 1985
A B Hipkin	6	1923 1925 1926 1927 1928 1929
M S Nichols	6	1926 1927 1929 1930 1932 1933
R M Taylor	6	1932 1933 1937 1938 1939 1946
T E Bailey	5	1958 1959 1960 1961 1965
R N S Hobbs	5	1965 1966 1968 1969 1970
K D Boyce	5	1967 1969 1970 1971 1972
G A Gooch	5	1979 1982 1983 1984 1985
L C Eastman	4	1927 1931 1933 1935
B R Knight	4	1961 1962 1963 1965
C J Kortright	3	1897 1900 1902
H A Carpenter	3	1905 1906 1911
R E East	3	1967 1973 1982
K S McEwan	3	1976 1978 1984
L H R Ralph	2	1957 1959
G Barker	2	1959 1962
G J Smith, Jnr	2	1963 1965
S Turner	2	1970 1975
G J Saville	2	1970 1971
W M F Turner	1	1906
C P Buckenham	1	1910
J W H T Douglas	1	1921
J O'Connor	1	1929
T N Pearce	1	1947
A V Avery	1	1950
T C Dodds	1	1951
W T Greensmith	1	1952
I M King	1	1957
J Milner	1	1961
B L Irvine	1	1969
P J Prichard	1	1986
	141	

Most catches by a fielder in a season for Essex

Total	*Player*	*Season*
40	K W R Fletcher	1966
39	K W R Fletcher	1965
38	K C Preston	1958
36	T P B Smith	1933
35	K C Preston	1957
	G A Gooch	1983
34	A B Hipkin	1927
	A B Hipkin	1929
	R M Taylor	1938
33	K D Boyce	1967
32	L C Eastman	1933
	T E Bailey	1959
	K C Preston	1962
30	H A Carpenter	1906
	W M F Turner	1906
	A B Hipkin	1926
	R N S Hobbs	1966
	K W R Fletcher	1967
	G J Saville	1971
	B R Hardie	1979
	B R Hardie	1983

Highest and lowest innings totals for Essex in Gillette Cup and National Westminster Bank Trophy

Opponents	*Highest*	*Year*	*Ground*	*Lowest*	*Year*	*Ground*
Bedfordshire	301–9*	1971	Chelmsford	—		
Cambridgeshire	182–8*	1964	Sawston	—		
Derbyshire	200–8	1966	Chesterfield	100	1965	Brentwood
Dorset	117–3	1983	Bournemouth	—		
Durham	137–3	1973	Chester-le-Street	—		
Glamorgan	201	1964	Neath	180	1971	Ilford
Gloucestershire	207	1981	Bristol	206	1973	Chelmsford
Hampshire	224–7*	1985	Southampton	—		
Hertfordshire	306–8*	1981	Hitchin	120	1976	Hitchin
Kent	270–9*	1983	Chelmsford	127	1972	Leyton
Lancashire	191	1971	Chelmsford	132	1963	Old Trafford
Leicestershire	310–7*	1980	Leicester	138	1977	Southend
Middlesex	214	1985	Chelmsford	155	1968	Lord's
Northumberland	298–9*	1986	Newcastle	—		
Nottinghamshire	280–2*	1985	Lord's	180–9*	1969	Trent Bridge
Oxfordshire	307–6*	1985	Chelmsford	—		
Scotland	327–6*	1984	Chelmsford	—		
Shropshire	180	1974	Wellington	—		
Somerset	287	1978	Taunton	216	1974	Westcliff
Staffordshire	316–6*	1976	Stone	—		
Surrey	268–9*	1978	Colchester (Castle Pk)	121	1984	Chelmsford
Sussex	195–9*	1981	Hove	174–9*	1970	Chelmsford
Warwickshire	191	1986	Birmingham	—		
Wiltshire	272–6*	1969	Chelmsford	—		
Worcestershire	149	1975	Worcester	129	1966	Worcester
Yorkshire	132	1982	Leeds	—		

N.B. The scores in the match v Leicestershire at Leicester in 1978 which was reduced to 10 overs a side have been ignored for the purposes of these tables.

Essex have not yet played Northamptonshire in this competition.

* Denotes innings closed after 60 overs

Highest and lowest innings totals against Essex in Gillette Cup and National Westminster Bank Trophy

Opponents	*Highest*	*Year*	*Ground*	*Lowest*	*Year*	*Ground*
Bedfordshire	204–8*	1971	Chelmsford	—		
Cambridgeshire	151	1964	Sawston	—		
Derbyshire	199	1966	Chesterfield	149–8*	1981	Derby
Dorset	111	1983	Bournemouth	—		
Durham	134	1973	Chester-le-Street	—		
Glamorgan	208–9*	1964	Neath	82	1971	Ilford
Gloucestershire	236–9*	1973	Chelmsford	85	1981	Bristol
Hampshire	224–8*	1985	Southampton	—		
Hertfordshire	153	1976	Hitchin	115	1981	Hitchin
Kent	274–8*	1983	Chelmsford	137	1972	Leyton
Lancashire	247–5*	1979	Old Trafford	203–9*	1971	Chelmsford
Leicestershire	225–7*	1977	Southend	197	1980	Leicester
Middlesex	161	1968	Lord's	41	1972	Westcliff
Northumberland	219–5*	1986	Newcastle	—		
Nottinghamshire	279–5*	1985	Lord's	—		
Oxfordshire	81	1985	Chelmsford	—		
Scotland	137	1984	Chelmsford	—		
Shropshire	41	1974	Wellington	—		
Somerset	287–6*	1978	Taunton	—		
Staffordshire	207–7*	1976	Stone	—		
Surrey	196	1978	Colchester (Castle Pk)	195–7*	1980	Chelmsford
Sussex	175–6	1970	Chelmsford	170	1981	Hove
Warwickshire	255	1986	Birmingham	146	1969	Birmingham
Wiltshire	147	1969	Chelmsford	—		
Worcestershire	261–7*	1975	Worcester	211	1966	Worcester
Yorkshire	133–1	1982	Leeds	—		

N.B. The scores in the match v Leicestershire at Leicester in 1978 which was reduced to 10 overs a side have been ignored for the purposes of these tables.

* Denotes innings closed after 60 overs

Highest and lowest innings totals for Essex in the John Player League

Opponents	*Highest*	*Year*	*Ground*	*Lowest*	*Year*	*Ground*
Derbyshire	220–9	1984	Derby	69	1974	Chesterfield
Glamorgan	310–5*	1983	Southend	109	1974	Harlow
Gloucestershire	283–6*	1975	Cheltenham	118	1980	Gloucester
Hampshire	256–5*	1986	Ilford	125	1971	Leyton
Kent	250–6*	1983	Chelmsford	96	1970	Blackheath
Lancashire	269–3*	1982	Old Trafford	75	1984	Old Trafford
Leicestershire	232–5*	1976	Westcliff	125–7*	1971	Leicester
Middlesex	255–5@	1980	Lord's	93	1972	Lord's
Northamptonshire	240–7*	1980	Chelmsford	150	1976	Chelmsford
Nottinghamshire	306–2*	1983	Trent Bridge	137	1980	Chelmsford
Somerset	253–4*	1986	Chelmsford	92	1982	Chelmsford
Surrey	234–4*	1975	Kennington Oval	94	1969	Leyton
Sussex	259–8†	1980	Hastings	102	1970	Eastbourne
Warwickshire	299–4*	1982	Colchester (Castle Pk)	96	1969	Birmingham
Worcestershire	273–6*	1986	Southend	99	1973	Chelmsford
Yorkshire	250–3*	1981	Chelmsford	120	1973	Hull

N.B. Scores in matches which were reduced to 30 overs a side or less have been ignored in the table showing lowest innings totals.

* Denotes innings closed after 40 overs † Closed after 39 overs @ After 38 overs

Highest and lowest innings totals against Essex in the John Player League

Opponents	*Highest*	*Year*	*Ground*	*Lowest*	*Year*	*Ground*
Derbyshire	219–6*	1970	Leyton	110	1981	Chelmsford
Glamorgan	254–4*	1983	Southend	128–8*	1976	Colchester (Castle Pk)
Gloucestershire	229–7*	1974	Chelmsford	94	1984	Bristol
Hampshire	257–4	1986	Ilford	43	1972	Basingstoke
Kent	243–7†	1973	Chelmsford	117	1977	Chelmsford and
				117	1979	Chelmsford
Lancashire	214–2*	1986	Old Trafford	87	1971	Old Trafford
Leicestershire	201–6*	1975	Leicester	104	1979	Leicester
Middlesex	245–5§	1982	Lord's	90	1979	Chelmsford
Northamptonshire	217–4	1985	Luton	45	1971	Ilford
Nottinghamshire	217–9*	1983	Trent Bridge	106–9*	1975	Trent Bridge
Somerset	218	1986	Chelmsford	58	1977	Chelmsford
Surrey	207–9*	1971	Kennington Oval	88	1979	Kennington Oval
Sussex	267–5†	1980	Hastings	102–7*	1972	Chelmsford
Warwickshire	301–6	1982	Colchester (Castle Pk)	100	1974	Chelmsford
Worcestershire	230	1986	Southend	134	1977	Chelmsford
Yorkshire	231–7*	1985	Chelmsford	88	1969	Hull

N.B. Scores in matches which were reduced to 30 overs a side or less have been ignored in the table showing lowest innings totals.

* Denotes innings closed after 40 overs † Closed after 39 overs § After 37 Overs

Highest and lowest innings totals for Essex in the Benson & Hedges Cup

Opponents	*Highest*	*Year*	*Ground*	*Lowest*	*Year*	*Ground*
Cambridge University	101–1	1974	Cambridge	—		
Derbyshire	150–4†	1985	Chelmsford	—		
Glamorgan	206–4	1986	Chelmsford	124	1981	Swansea
Gloucestershire	271–7*	1986	Chelmsford	222–8*	1984	Chelmsford
Hampshire	260–6*	1983	Southampton	254–4*	1984	Southampton
Kent	222–6*	1978	Dartford	123	1973	Canterbury (Semi-final)
Lancashire	157	1984	Chelmsford	—		
Leicestershire	213–8*	1985	Lord's	—		
Middlesex	202–8*	1985	Chelmsford	181–7*	1972	Lord's
Minor Counties	158–1	1980	Watford (Town)	—		
Minor Counties (E)	294–4*	1976	Norwich	212–7*	1977	Chelmsford
Minor Counties (S)	261	1975	Bedford (Goldington Bury)	—		
Northamptonshire	230–5*	1979	Northampton	187	1977	Chelmsford
Nottinghamshire	254–7*	1978	Chelmsford	195–9*	1986	Chelmsford
Oxford and Cambridge Universities	350–3*	1979	Chelmsford	333–4*	1985	Chelmsford
Somerset	278–5*	1981	Chelmsford	206	1986	Taunton
Surrey	290–6*	1979	Lord's	157–8*	1972	Kennington Oval
Sussex	327–2*	1982	Hove	144–8*	1972	Chelmsford
Warwickshire	271–5*	1979	Chelmsford	153	1975	Birmingham
Worcestershire	240–2	1980	Worcester	—		
Yorkshire	174–7	1979	Chelmsford	143	1977	Barnsley

N.B. Scores in matches which were reduced to 10 overs a side have been ignored.

* Denotes innings lost after 55 overs † Closed after 20 overs

Highest and lowest innings totals against Essex in the Benson & Hedges Cup

Opponents	*Highest*	*Year*	*Ground*	*Lowest*	*Year*	*Ground*
Cambridge University	100	1974	Cambridge	—		
Derbyshire	132–6†	1985	Chelmsford	—		
Glamorgan	206–9*	1981	Swansea	147	1980	Chelmsford
Gloucestershire	254–9*	1986	Chelmsford	217–9*	1984	Chelmsford
Hampshire	227–8*	1984	Southampton	130	1982	Chelmsford
Kent	226–4	1978	Dartford	118	1975	Chelmsford
Lancashire	158–6	1984	Chelmsford	—		
Leicestershire	215–5	1985	Lord's	177–8*	1973	Ilford
Middlesex	232–6*	1972	Lord's	73	1985	Lord's
Minor Counties	157	1980	Watford (Town)	140–9*	1983	Slough
Minor Counties (E)	156	1977	Chelmsford	154	1976	Norwich
Minor Counties (S)	83	1975	Bedford (Goldington Bury)	—		
Northamptonshire	227–7*	1979	Northampton	168–9*	1976	Horton
Nottinghamshire	245–7	1976	Ilford	201–6*	1978	Chelmsford
Oxford and Cambridge Universities	203–6*	1985	Chelmsford	120	1981	Chelmsford
Somerset	240	1981	Chelmsford	172	1983	Chelmsford
Surrey	276–6*	1982	Kennington Oval	139	1985	Kennington Oval
Sussex	259–6*	1986	Hove	87	1973	Hove
Warwickshire	227	1979	Chelmsford	168	1983	Chelmsford
Worcestershire	236–9*	1980	Worcester	—		
Yorkshire	173–9*	1979	Chelmsford	—		

N.B. Scores in matches which were reduced to 10 overs a side have been ignored.

* Denotes innings closed after 55 overs † Closed after 20 overs

Highest and lowest innings totals for Essex in Fenner Trophy and Asda Challenge Trophy at Scarborough

Opponents	*Highest*	*Year*	*Lowest*	*Year*
Hampshire	195	1983	124	1977
Northamptonshire	262–8*	1981	—	
Yorkshire	262–8*	1981	187–7*	1977

* Denotes innings closed after 50 overs

Highest and lowest innings totals against Essex in Fenner Trophy and Asda Challenge Trophy at Scarborough

Opponents	*Highest*	*Year*	*Lowest*	*Year*
Hampshire	250–9*	1986	168	1977
Northamptonshire	252–7*	1981	—	
Yorkshire	264–5*	1981	175	1977

* Denotes innings closed after 50 overs

Record wicket partnership in Gillette Cup and National Westminster Bank Trophy

First Wicket
202 G A Gooch and B R Hardie — v Nottinghamshire at Lord's, 1985

Second Wicket
87 G A Gooch and P J Prichard — v Kent at Chelmsford, 1985

Third Wicket
179 G A Gooch and K S McEwan — v Scotland at Chelmsford, 1984

Fourth Wicket
120 K S McEwan and B R Hardie — v Leicestershire at Leicester, 1980

Fifth Wicket
80 K W R Fletcher and K R Pont — v Somerset at Taunton, 1978

Sixth Wicket
62 K D Boyce and S Turner — v Wiltshire at Chelmsford, 1969

Seventh Wicket
77 B R Hardie and N Phillip — v Surrey at Chelmsford, 1980

Eighth Wicket
60 A W Lilley and D E East — v Northumberland at Newcastle, 1986

Ninth Wicket
67 S Turner and R E East — v Gloucestershire at Chelmsford, 1973

Tenth Wicket
81 S Turner and R E East — v Yorkshire at Leeds, 1982

Record wicket partnership in the John Player League

First Wicket
239 G A Gooch and B R Hardie — v Nottinghamshire at Trent Bridge, 1985

Second Wicket
273 G A Gooch and K S McEwan — v Nottinghamshire at Trent Bridge, 1983

Third Wicket
190 K S McEwan and D R Pringle — v Warwickshire at Edgbaston, Birmingham, 1985

Fourth Wicket
123 K S McEwan and N Phillip — v Glamorgan at Cardiff, 1982

Fifth Wicket
128 G Barker and K D Boyce — v Surrey at Kennington Oval, 1971

Sixth Wicket
83* K R Pont and S Turner — v Leicestershire at Westcliff, 1976

Seventh Wicket
92 B E A Edmeades and S Turner — v Nottinghamshire at Chelmsford, 1969

Eighth Wicket
59 K W R Fletcher and D E East — v Middlesex at Chelmsford, 1983

Ninth Wicket
65 D E East and J K Lever — v Derbyshire at Derby, 1982

Tenth Wicket
25* R E East and J K Lever — v Glamorgan at Ebbw Vale, 1973

Record wicket partnership in the Benson & Hedges Cup

First Wicket		
223	G A Gooch and A W Lilley	v Oxford and Cambridge Universities at Chelmsford, 1979
Second Wicket		
172	B E A Edmeades and K S McEwan	v Minor Counties (East) at Norwich, 1976
Third Wicket		
268*	G A Gooch and K W R Fletcher	v Sussex at Hove, 1982
Fourth Wicket		
107	K S McEwan and D R Pringle	v Oxford and Cambridge Universities at Cambridge, 1984
Fifth Wicket		
108*	K W R Fletcher and D R Pringle	v Glamorgan at Chelmsford, 1986
Sixth Wicket		
99*	S Turner and K R Pont	v Nottinghamshire at Ilford, 1976
Seventh Wicket		
91	G J Saville and R N S Hobbs	v Middlesex at Lord's, 1972
Eighth Wicket		
109	R E East and N Smith	v Northamptonshire at Chelmsford, 1977
Ninth Wicket		
46	G A Gooch and R E East	v Surrey at Kennington Oval, 1976
Tenth Wicket		
51	B E A Edmeades and J K Lever	v Warwickshire at Edgbaston, Birmingham, 1975

Individual innings of 100 or more for Essex in the Gillete Cup and National Westminster Bank Trophy

G A Gooch (3)	133	v Scotland at Chelmsford, 1984
	122	v Kent at Chelmsford, 1983
	101	v Hertfordshire at Hitchin, 1981
K S McEwan (1)	119	v Leicestershire at Leicester, 1980
A W Lilley (1)	113	v Northumberland at Jesmond, Newcastle, 1986
B R Hardie (1)	110	v Nottinghamshire at Lord's, 1985
B Ward (1)	101	v Bedfordshire at Chelmsford, 1971

Individual innings of 100 or more for Essex in the Benson & Hedges Cup

G A Gooch (5)	198*	v Sussex at Hove, 1982
	138	v Warwickshire at Chelmsford, 1979
	138	v Somerset at Chelmsford, 1981
	133	v Oxford and Cambridge Universities at Chelmsford, 1979
	120	v Surrey at Lord's, 1979
K S McEwan (3)	133	v Nottinghamshire at Chelmsford, 1978
	116	v Minor Counties (East) at Norwich, 1976
	100*	v Oxford and Cambridge Universities at Chelmsford, 1985
B R Hardie (2)	119*	v Sussex at Hove, 1986
	113	v Oxford and Cambridge Universities at Chelmsford, 1985
B E A Edmeades (1)	125*	v Minor Counties (East) at Norwich, 1976
K D Boyce (1)	123	v Minor Counties (South) at Goldington Bury, Bedford, 1975
A W Lilley (1)	119	v Oxford and Cambridge Universities at Chelmsford, 1979
K W R Fletcher (1)	101*	v Sussex at Hove, 1982

Individual innings of 100 or more for Essex in the Asda Challenge Trophy

C Gladwin (1)	100	v Hampshire at Scarborough, 1983

Individual innings of 100 or more for Essex in the John Player League

K S McEwan (9)	162*	v Nottinghamshire at Trent Bridge, 1983
	156*	v Warwickshire at Castle Park, Colchester, 1982
	136	v Sussex at Hastings, 1980
	129*	v Worcestershire at Castle Park, Colchester, 1980
	123	v Warwickshire at Ilford, 1976
	118	v Warwickshire at Edgbaston, Birmingham, 1985
	109	v Middlesex at Chelmsford, 1981
	105*	v Worcestershire at Ilford, 1982
	104	v Warwickshire at Edgbaston, Birmingham, 1977
G A Gooch (7)	176	v Glamorgan at Southend, 1983
	171	v Nottinghamshire at Trent Bridge, 1985
	125*	v Hampshire at Castle Park, Colchester, 1984
	122	v Lancashire at Old Trafford, 1982
	116	v Nottinghamshire at Trent Bridge, 1983
	100	v Yorkshire at Chelmsford, 1981
	100	v Warwickshire at Chelmsford, 1986
B R Hardie (2)	109	v Northamptonshire at Castle Park, Colchester, 1986
	108*	v Yorkshire at Chelmsford, 1981
B C Francis (2)	107	v Lancashire at Old Trafford, 1971
	106	v Lancashire at Leyton, 1973
P J Prichard (1)	103*	v Lancashire at Old Trafford, 1986
M H Denness (1)	102	v Warwickshire at Castle Park, Colchester, 1978
B Taylor (1)	100	v Derbyshire at Buxton, 1971

Twenty or more sixes in career for Essex in the John Player League

Batsman	*Sixes*	*Seasons*
G A Gooch	75	1973–1986
K S McEwan	73	1974–1985
K D Boyce	53	1969–1977
K R Pont	47	1972–1986
S Turner	39	1969–1986
N Phillip	32	1978–1985
K W R Fletcher	31	1969–1986
B Taylor	22	1969–1973
A W Lilley	21	1978–1986

Five or more wickets in an innings for Essex in the Gillette Cup and National Westminster Bank Trophy

D R Pringle (2)	5 for 12	v Oxfordshire at Chelmsford, 1985
	5 for 23	v Middlesex at Chelmsford, 1985
J K Lever (1)	5 for 8	v Middlesex at Westcliff, 1972
K D Boyce (1)	5 for 22	v Middlesex at Westcliff, 1972
B R Knight (1)	5 for 41	v Derbyshire at Brentwood, 1965

Five or more wickets in an innings for Essex in the Benson & Hedges Cup

J K Lever (2)	5 for 13	v Middlesex at Lord's, 1985
	5 for 16	v Middlesex at Chelmsford, 1976
B E A Edmeades (1)	5 for 22	v Leicestershire at Ilford, 1973
N A Foster (1)	5 for 32	v Surrey at Kennington Oval, 1985
R E East (1)	5 for 33	v Kent at Chelmsford, 1975
D R Pringle (1)	5 for 35	v Lancashire at Chelmsford, 1984

Five or more wickets in an innings for Essex in the John Player League

R E East (4)	6 for 18	v Yorkshire at Hull, 1969
	5 for 18	v Worcestershire at Harlow, 1969
	5 for 20	v Yorkshire at Castle Park, Colchester, 1979
	5 for 30	v Middlesex at Lord's, 1971
J K Lever (4)	5 for 13	v Glamorgan at Ebbw Vale, 1975
	5 for 18	v Warwickshire at Edgbaston, Birmingham, 1972
	5 for 21	v Somerset at Chelmsford, 1986
	5 for 36	v Lancashire at Old Trafford, 1978
K D Boyce (2)	8 for 26	v Lancashire at Old Trafford, 1971
	5 for 19	v Somerset at Chelmsford, 1977
D L Acfield (2)	5 for 14	v Northamptonshire at Northampton, 1970
	5 for 28	v Worcestershire at Dudley, 1976
N Phillip (1)	6 for 13	v Lancashire at Old Trafford, 1982
R N S Hobbs (1)	6 for 22	v Hampshire at Harlow, 1973
N A Foster (1)	5 for 17	v Derbyshire at Derby, 1986
S Turner (1)	5 for 35	v Hampshire at Chelmsford, 1978
D R Pringle (1)	5 for 41	v Gloucestershire at Southend, 1985

Five or more wickets in an innings for Essex in the Fenner Trophy

K R Pont (1)	5 for 36	v Yorkshire at Scarborough, 1977

Gillette Cup and National Westminster Bank Trophy

The five batsmen to score most runs in career for Essex

Batsman	*Runs*	*Average*	*Seasons*
G A Gooch	1226	42.17	1973–1986
K W R Fletcher	957	25.86	1963–1985
B R Hardie	928	34.37	1973–1985
K S McEwan	842	35.08	1974–1985
S Turner	449	17.96	1968–1985

The five bowlers to take most wickets in career for Essex

Bowler	*Wickets*	*Average*	*Seasons*
J K Lever	62	17.53	1968–1986
S Turner	50	20.54	1968–1985
K D Boyce	26	12.15	1967–1974
B E A Edmeades	26	21.30	1964–1976
R E East	26	25.26	1966–1983

The three wicket-keepers with most dismissals in career for Essex

Wicket-keeper	*Total*	*Ct.*	*St.*	*Seasons*
D E East	24	21	3	1981–1986
B Taylor	23	20	3	1963–1973
N Smith	8	6	2	1974–1980

The five fielders with most catches in career for Essex

Player	*Catches*	*Seasons*
K W R Fletcher	16	1963–1985
R E East	13	1966–1983
G A Gooch	12	1973–1986
B R Hardie	11	1973–1985
K S McEwan	11	1974–1985

Hat tricks for Essex

Year	*Bowler*	*Opponents*	*Players dismissed*
1968	R N S Hobbs	Middlesex at Lord's	R W Hooker, J S E Price, R S Herman

Man of the Match Awards

Essex players have gained 26 awards. The most have been by G A Gooch 5 and J K Lever 4.

Benson & Hedges Cup

The five batsmen to score most runs in career for Essex

Batsman	*Runs*	*Average*	*Seasons*
G A Gooch	2938	48.16	1973–1986
K W R Fletcher	1953	34.26	1972–1986
K S McEwan	1925	35.64	1974–1985
B R Hardie	1331	29.57	1974–1986
B E A Edmeades	708	35.40	1972–1976

The five bowlers to take most wickets in a career for Essex

Bowler	*Wickets*	*Average*	*Seasons*
J K Lever	132	17.34	1972–1986
S Turner	107	20.76	1972–1986
R E East	49	25.75	1972–1983
N Phillip	44	25.29	1978–1985
D R Pringle	42	20.19	1978–1986

(In all Benson & Hedges Cup matches Pringle has taken 52 wickets (average 24.57))

The three wicket-keepers with most dismissals in career for Essex

Wicket-keeper	*Total*	*Ct.*	*St.*	*Seasons*
D E East	38	38	—	1982–1986
N Smith	37	34	3	1974–1982
B Taylor	11	11	—	1972–1973

The seven fielders with most catches in career for Essex

Player	*Catches*	*Seasons*
G A Gooch	41	1973–1986
K W R Fletcher	21	1972–1986
K S McEwan	21	1974–1985
B R Hardie	18	1974–1986
R E East	16	1972–1983
J K Lever	16	1972–1986
S Turner	16	1972–1986

Gold Awards

Essex players have gained a total of 49 awards. The most have been by G A Gooch 12, K W R Fletcher 8, K S McEwan 6 and S Turner 4.

John Player League

The five batsmen to score most runs in career for Essex

Batsman	*Runs*	*Average*	*Seasons*
K S McEwan	5531	34.78	1974–1985
K W R Fletcher	5524	30.25	1969–1986
G A Gooch	4805	31.82	1973–1986
B R Hardie	3960	26.05	1973–1986
S Turner	3165	19.65	1969–1986

The five bowlers to take most wickets in career for Essex

Bowler	*Wickets*	*Average*	*Seasons*
J K Lever	344	18.69	1969–1986
S Turner	303	23.86	1969–1986
R E East	187	24.08	1969–1984
K D Boyce	179	15.19	1969–1977
N Phillip	134	21.48	1978–1985

The three wicket-keepers with most dismissals in career for Essex

Wicket-keeper	*Total*	*Ct.*	*St.*	*Seasons*
N Smith	93	76	17	1974–1982
D E East	85	73	12	1981–1986
B Taylor	81	62	19	1969–1973

The five fielders with most catches in career for Essex

Player	*Catches*	*Seasons*
R E East	85	1969–1984
K W R Fletcher	82	1969–1986
S Turner	82	1969–1986
J K Lever	60	1969–1986
G A Gooch	58	1973–1986

Hat tricks for Essex (1)

Year	*Bowler*	*Opponents*	*Players dismissed*
1971	K D Boyce	Somerset at Westcliff	P J Robinson, H R Moseley, D J S Taylor

Internationals

T E Bailey
A R Border (Australia)
K D Boyce (West Indies)
C P Buckenham
C B Clarke (West Indies)
*M H Denness
J W H T Douglas
F L Fane
K Farnes
K W R Fletcher
N A Foster
B C Francis (Australia)
*P A Gibb
G A Gooch
R N S Hobbs
D J Insole
B L. Irvine (South Africa)
H I Young
B R Knight
*J C Laker
J K Lever
*A P Lucas
C P McGahey
W Mead
†K S McEwan (South Africa)
M S Nichols
J O'Connor
N Phillip (West Indies)
D R Pringle
H D Read
K R Rickards (West Indies)
C A G Russell
Sadiq Mohammad (Pakistan)
T P B Smith
H M Taberer (South Africa)

* Gained International honours when playing for another County, prior to joining Essex
† Not Test player

Captains of England

*M H Denness
J W H T Douglas
F L Fane
K W R Fletcher

* Appointed when playing for another County, prior to joining Essex

Presidents of MCC

C E Green
H Ashton
Sir Cyril Hawker

England Selectors

P A Perrin
J W H T Douglas
T N Pearce
D J Insole
B Taylor

'Wisden's five cricketers of the year'

F G Bull
C P McGahey
W Mead
P A Perrin
J W H T Douglas
H Ashton
C A G Russell
M S Nichols
K Farnes
T P B Smith
T E Bailey
D J Insole
B Taylor
K W R Fletcher
K D Boyce
K S McEwan
J K Lever
G A Gooch
J H Childs

Essex County Cricket Club: Officers, Past and Present

The following is a list of Presidents, Chairmen, Secretaries and Captains of the Club since 1876.

Presidents

1886–1895	Lord Carlingford
1896–1910	Lord Rayleigh
1911	Lord O'Hagan
1912	Col Mark Lockwood
1913	Mr C E Green
1914	Col Mark Lockwood
1915–1918	Mr R C Gosling
1919	Mr James Tabor
1920	Mr E J Whythes
1921	Mr W J Courtauld
1922	Mr C E Ridley
1923	Lt-Col F H D C Whitmore
1924–1926	Sir F Carne Rasch, Bart.
1927	Sir H Curtis Bennett
1928	Mr J H Douglas
1929–1930	Mr J D Cassels
1931–1935	Brig Gen Sir R B Colvin
1936–1943	Mr H S Ashton
1944–1946	Vacant
1947–1948	Mr C Stewart Richardson
1949–1970	Mr Hubert Ashton (from 1959 Sir Hubert Ashton)
1970–	Mr T N Pearce

Patrons

1921–1933	H R H The Duke of York

Patronesses

1927–1930	Mrs C E Green

Chairmen

1876–1882	J Round
1886–1912	C E Green
1915–1925	H D Swan
1927	R B Robinson
1928–1945	C Stewart Richardson
1946–1951	Hubert Ashton
1952–1972	T N Pearce
1972–1976	A B Quick
1976–1978	D J Insole
1978–1984	A G Waterman
1984–	D J Insole

Captains

1876–1882	J Round
1883–1888	C E Green
1889–1891	C D Buxton
1892–1894	A P Lucas
1895–1902	H G P Owen
1903	C J Kortright
1904–1906	F L Fane
1907–1910	C P McGahey
1911–1928	J W H T Douglas (P A Perrin acted as deputy captain in the absence of Douglas in 1926)
1929–1932	H M Morris
1933–1938	T N Pearce and D R Wilcox
1939	J W A Stephenson, F St G Unwin and D R Wilcox
1946–1949	T N Pearce
1950	T N Pearce and D J Insole
1951–1960	D J Insole
1961–1966	T E Bailey
1967–1973	B Taylor
1974–1985	K W R Fletcher
1986–	G A Gooch

Secretaries

1876	J F Lescher (honorary secretary)
1884–1885	J J Read
1886–1887	T Ratcliff (first paid secretary)
1888–1890	M P Betts
1891–1921	O R Borradaile (Mr Palmer acting-secretary 1920–21)
1921–1925	N R E Wilkinson (L C Eastman acting-secretary 1925)
1926–1928	G H Thompson
1929	F W Milton
1930–1946	B K Castor (A J Spelling acting-secretary 1940–45, Wing-Cdr L L Bray temporary secretary 1945)
1947–1950	R F T Paterson
1951–1954	H G Clark
1955–1965	T E Bailey
1966–1972	Major C A Brown
1972–1978	S R Cox
1979–	P J Edwards

General Managers

1977–1978	W B Sheret
1979–	P J Edwards

Further Activities

Supporters' Club

The Supporters' Club was formed with the blessing of the Essex County Cricket Club Executive Committee in November 1955 and Ken Preston was appointed secretary.

Most of the County Cricket Clubs were already receiving donations from their Supporters' Clubs through the operation of 'football goals' tickets and Ken's brief was to obtain voluntary agents to sell 5d tickets in factories, clubs, offices, etc.

Arthur Sedgwick was elected chairman in 1956 and with the help of Eric Gray as assistant secretary, ticket sales soon became widespread throughout Essex. By the time Ken Preston retired from County Cricket and as the Supporters secretary at the end of 1964, donations to the County Club had reached £8000 per year. Eric Gray succeeded Ken Preston as secretary.

After the resignation of Eric Gray in 1969 Alf Brown of Upminster was elected as honorary secretary in 1970 and since then the Supporters' Club has been run entirely on a voluntary basis. Upon the retirement of Alf Brown in 1974 Graham Saville was appointed honorary secretary until 1979 when Clem Driver continued in this position until 1982. Peter Butler is the present secretary.

Arthur Sedgwick retired as chairman in 1962 and was succeeded in turn by George Hurd, Rob Gibbons, Alf Brind, Alan Viney, Peter Keith and Geoff Lucock. The present chairman, 'Jerry' Jerman, has occupied this position since 1981.

A founder comittee member, Dickie Bird, was elected president in 1962 and continued in this office until his death at the beginning of 1981. His complete involvement in the running of the Romford office, the tent on the County Grounds during the summer months, the Christmas and Derby Draws, ensured the continuation of the fund-raising activities.

Development Association

The Development Association was formed in June 1978 to organise the sale of 25p lottery tickets throughout the County of Essex under the chairmanship of LCS ('Jerry') Jerman, with Geoff Greaves of Wishbone Print (Birmingham) Ltd, as consultant and Preston Keeling appointed secretary/executive on the 1 September 1978.

By the middle of October 1978 over 300 sales outlets had been obtained and a fortnightly lottery was operated for several years with continuous donations to the Essex County Cricket Club, the Benefit Association, cricket and other sports clubs throughout Essex.

During the years of 1980 and 1981 Mike Denness was also active in the running of this Association.

Junior Cricket

Essex County Cricket Club considers itself to be the focal point of all cricket within the County and has maintained strong links with junior cricket.

Until 1966 the Club ran a Club & Ground Eleven which had a full fixture list of matches with clubs and schools within the county, and this team was made up mainly of young professionals and of amateurs competing for places in the County's second eleven.

With the formation of the Essex Cricket Association, the link with club cricket has continued, and the Association's secretary M L Chapman, as well as its president and chairman, are members of the Club's Executive Committee. The ECA is involved with all the clubs within the County and has coaching and advisory committees to assist its members.

At the more junior level, the County has been fortunate to have such stalwarts as Jim Carter, Bertie Gough, Don Smith and Reg Hilliard to look after the Essex Young Amateurs, renamed Young Essex in the post-war years. These people looked after the Club's Under 19 XI, which was composed of the most promising young players in Essex, several of whom graduated to the County's first eleven.

Since the retirement of Reg Hilliard, the Club has itself taken over the role with, briefly, Harold Faragher and now Graham Saville chairing the Under 19 Committee, with Ray East responsible for coaching and organisation.

Even further down the age ladder, Roger Bayes and Rod Greig now run the Under 16s and the efforts of the Essex Schools Cricket Association, which runs teams at under 11, 12, 13, 14 and 15 makes a major contribution towards the establishment of the 'pyramid' of cricket in Essex, which has the County side as the pinnacle.

Select Bibliography

C W Alcock, F S Ashley-Cooper et al (eds) *Cricket: A Weekly Record of the Game*, W R Wright, 1882–1913
H S Altham *The History of Cricket, Volume 1*, Allen & Unwin, 1947
R L Arrowsmith & B J W Hill *I Zingari*, Stanley Paul, 1982
Association of Cricket Statisticians *First-Class Cricket Matches, 1864–1895*, 22 Vols, 1982–86
Philip Bailey, Philip Thorne & Peter Wynne-Thomas *Who's Who of Cricketers*, Newnes Books, 1984
Trevor Bailey *Championship Cricket*, Frederick Muller, 1961
Trevor Bailey *Wickets, Catches and the Odd Run*, Willow Books, 1986
Charles Bray *Essex County Cricket*, Convoy Publications, 1950
G B Buckley (ed) *Fresh Light on Eighteenth Century Cricket*, Cotterell, 1935
G B Buckley (ed) *Fresh Light on Pre-Victorian Cricket*, Cotterell, 1937
Kenneth Farnes *Tours and Tests*, R T S Lutterworth Press, 1940
Keith Fletcher *Captain's Innings*, Stanley Paul 1983
Bill Frindall *The Wisden Book of Test Cricket*, Macdonald and Janes, 1979
Bill Frindall *The Wisden Book of Cricket Records*, Queen Anne Press, 1981
C B Fry *The Book of Cricket*, Newnes, 1899
Sir Home Gordon, Bart *Background to Cricket*, Arthur Barker, 1939
Benny Green *The Wisden Book of Obituaries*, Queen Anne Press 1986
Arthur Haygarth, F S Ashley-Cooper (eds) *Cricket Scores and Biographies*, 15 Vols, Longmans, 1925
G D Martineau *They Made Cricket*, Museum Press, 1956

Christopher Martin-Jenkins *The Wisden Book of County Cricket*, Queen Anne Press, 1981
A R Hope Moncrieff *Essex*, A & C Black, 1909
Leslie Newnham *Essex County Cricket, 1876–1975*, privately published, 1976
M S Nichols *Bowling*, Blackie & Son, 1937
Charles Sale *Korty*, Ian Henry, 1986
E H D Sewell *Cricket Up-To-Date*, John Murray, 1931
Roy Sheffield *Bolivian Spy?*, Marchand Press, 1935
E W Swanton, George Plumptre & John Woodcock, *Barclays World of Cricket 1986*, Newnes Books, 1984
Frank Thorogood (ed) *The Daily News Cricket and Tennis Annual, 1921–26*, The Daily News Ltd
Frank Thorogood (ed) *The Daily News Cricket Annual, 1927–30*, The Daily News Ltd
Leslie Thompson *Cricketing in Essex*, privately published, 1963
H T Waghorn (ed) *Cricket Scores and Notes, 1730–1773*, Blackwood, 1899
H T Waghorn (ed) *The Dawn of Cricket*, M.C.C., 1906

The Cricketer 1921–1986
Essex County Cricket Handbooks, 1927–1986
Wisden Cricketers' Almanack, 1864–1986
Wisden Cricket Monthly, 1977–1986

Index

Numbers in *italics* refer to photographs